HANDBOOK OF RESEARCH METHODS AND
APPLICATIONS IN HETERODOX ECONOMICS

# HANDBOOKS OF RESEARCH METHODS AND APPLICATIONS

**Series Editor:** Mark Casson, *University of Reading, UK*

The objective of this series is to provide definitive overviews of research methods in important fields of social science, including economics, business, finance and policy studies. The aim is to produce prestigious high quality works of lasting significance. Each *Handbook* consists of original contributions by leading authorities, selected by an editor who is a recognized leader in the field. The emphasis is on the practical application of research methods to both quantitative and qualitative evidence. The *Handbooks* will assist practising researchers in generating robust research findings that policy-makers can use with confidence.

While the *Handbooks* will engage with general issues of research methodology, their primary focus will be on the practical issues concerned with identifying and using suitable sources of data or evidence, and interpreting source material using best-practice techniques. They will review the main theories that have been used in applied research, or could be used for such research. While reference may be made to conceptual issues and to abstract theories in the course of such reviews, the emphasis will be firmly on real-world applications.

Titles in the series include:

# Handbook of Research Methods and Applications in Heterodox Economics

*Edited by*

Frederic S. Lee

*University of Missouri–Kansas City, USA*

Bruce Cronin

*University of Greenwich, UK*

HANDBOOKS OF RESEARCH METHODS AND APPLICATIONS

**EE** Edward Elgar
PUBLISHING

Cheltenham, UK • Northampton, MA, USA

Published by
Edward Elgar Publishing Limited
The Lypiatts
15 Lansdown Road
Cheltenham
Glos GL50 2JA
UK

Edward Elgar Publishing, Inc.
William Pratt House
9 Dewey Court
Northampton
Massachusetts 01060
USA


A catalogue record for this book
is available from the British Library

Library of Congress Control Number: 2015952676


This book is available electronically in the **Elgar**online
Economics subject collection
DOI 10.4337/9781782548461

FSC
www.fsc.org
MIX
Paper from
responsible sources
FSC® C013056

ISBN 978 1 78254 845 4 (cased)
ISBN 978 1 78254 846 1 (eBook)

Typeset by Servis Filmsetting Ltd, Stockport, Cheshire

Printed and bound in Great Britain by
TJ International Ltd, Padstow, Cornwall

# Contents

# Contributors

**Valerie Adams** is a Research Associate with the Hawke Institute at the University of South Australia. Her research interests are centered on empirical investigations of care work, the undervaluation of care work, the care economy, gender equity issues, and feminist economics theorizing on caring labor.

**Siobhan Austen** is Associate Professor and Head of the Department of Economics and Property at Curtin University in Perth, Western Australia. Siobhan is currently engaged on a range of research projects relating to feminist and institutional economics.

**Amit Basole** is Assistant Professor of Economics at the University of Massachusetts, Boston, USA, where he teaches development economics and political economy. He holds a PhD in economics from the University of Massachusetts Amherst, USA. His research addresses poverty and inequality, political economy of the informal sector, and the economics of informal knowledge. His work has been published in several edited volumes and in journals such as *Economic and Political Weekly*, *World Development*, *Development and Change*, *Rethinking Marxism*, and *International Review of Applied Economics*. He also writes for general audiences at ideasforindia.in, populareconomics.org, sanhati.org, and other online fora, and has recently edited a book titled *Lokavidya Perspectives: A Philosophy of Political Imagination for the Knowledge Age* published by Aakar Books, New Delhi. Prior to switching to economics, he completed a PhD in Neuroscience from Duke University where his research on the neurophysiology of the mammalian visual system was published in journals such as *Nature* and *Progress in Brain Research*.

**Michael Bewley** is President and Chief Executive Officer of Enalysis, a firm he founded in 2005. Enalysis, based in Louisville, Kentucky, USA, provides survey research and economic analysis for a wide range of clients, including associations, non-profit organizations, national unions; various federal, state, county and city agencies; and educational institutions, from universities to community college districts and school districts. Dr Bewley specializes in economic impact research, strategic planning, and survey design. He has a PhD in Economics from the University of Kentucky and a MA in Higher Education from the University of Louisville. He is an Adjunct Professor of Economics at McKendree University and Spalding University, USA and is a board member of the Kentucky Economics Association.

**Natalia Bracarense** is an Assistant Professor of Economics at North Central College, USA. Her research interests are the history of economic thought, heterodox economic theory, development economics, and the history of US–Latin American relations. She has in recent years published articles in the *Review of Political Economy*, *Journal of Economic Issues*, and *Review of Radical Political Economy*, as well as in various Brazilian heterodox journals. She has earned several grants and awards, of which the most recent include the Center for the History of Political Economy at Duke University

Summer Institute Participant Award, History of Economics Society's Warren J. and Sylvia J. Samuels Young Scholar Program Travel Grant, and European Society for the History of Economic Thought Travel Grant.

**Tiago Cardão-Pito** is an Assistant Professor at the University of Lisbon, Portugal. He has recently obtained a PhD from the University of Strathclyde in Glasgow, UK. He develops and studies multidisciplinary research conducted in the fields of economic sociology, management and organizational studies, and heterodox economics.

**Zachary B. Catanzarite** is an interdisciplinary social scientist with a Master's degree in Psychology from New York University, USA and a Master's degree in Sociology from the University of Florida, USA. Throughout his career he has focused on advanced analytic methods, study designs, and statistical analyses. Since 2011 he has been a research associate with the Gender Asset Gap project at the Center for Latin American Studies, University of Florida.

**Lynne Chester** is Senior Lecturer in Political Economy at the University of Sydney, Australia. Her research is grounded in using the theoretical to develop methodological frameworks for empirical analysis of contemporary issues such as the economic–energy–ecological relation, energy impoverishment, the restructuring of production from financialization, the structure and operation of markets, and Australian capitalism's institutional architecture. She is the author of *Neoliberal Structural Change and the Electricity Sector: A Régulationist Analysis* (Routledge, 2016), and co-editor of *Challenging the Orthodoxy: Reflections on Frank Stilwell's Contribution to Political Economy* (Springer, 2014), the *Review of Political Economy*, the *Proceedings of the Annual Conference for the Australian Society of Heterodox Economists (Refereed Papers)*, and a special issue on heterodox economics for *On the Horizon* (2012). She has contributed chapters to *Advancing the Frontiers of Heterodox Economics: Essays in Honor of Frederic S. Lee* (Routledge, 2015), *Neoliberalism: Beyond the Free Market* (Edward Elgar Publishing, 2012) and *Readings in Political Economy* (Tilde, 2011). Her research has also been published in the *American Journal of Economics and Sociology*, *Australian Journal of Social Issues*, *Economic and Labour Relations Review*, *Economic Papers*, *Energy Policy*, *European Journal of Economics and Economic Policies*, *International Journal of Green Economics*, *Journal of Australian Political Economy*, *Journal of Economic Issues*, and *Review of Radical Political Economics*.

**Jonathan F. Cogliano** is Assistant Professor of Economics at Dickinson College in Carlisle, Pennsylvania, USA. He received his PhD in Economics from the New School for Social Research, USA in 2013 and holds a BA in Economics from the University of Massachusetts Amherst, USA. His research interests are as follows: classical/Marxian political economy, value theory, agent-based computational modeling, history of economic thought, and macroeconomics with a focus on growth, distribution, and climate change.

**Bruce Cronin** is Professor of Economic Sociology at the University of Greenwich in London, UK. He is Director of Research for the Faculty of Business and Director of the Centre for Business Network Analysis, having previously been Head of the Department of International Business and Economics (2006–14). He researches the ways in which social networks contribute to the formation and reproduction of epistemic communities within and among businesses and social elites. With Frederic Lee he was co-author of the influential

'Research quality rankings of heterodox economic journals in a contested discipline' (*American Journal of Economics and Sociology*, **69** (5), 1409–52). His work has appeared in the *Review of Political Economy, Critical Perspectives on Accounting, On the Horizon, American Journal of Economics and Sociology, International Journal of Knowledge, Culture and Change Management, Emergence: Complexity and Organization, International Journal of Decision Sciences, Risk and Management.* He serves as Treasurer of the Association of Heterodox Economics and as a Director of the World Economics Association.

**Bob Davidson** is a researcher and private consultant who has had extensive experience in the government, community, and corporate sectors in Australia across a range of economic, social, and environmental fields. He has held senior positions with national and state government agencies, government business enterprises, and as an adviser to ministers. He couples the management of his company that specializes in policy, program and organizational development and review, with conducting academic research. His current research at the Social Policy Research Centre (University of New South Wales), Australia, is concerned with the economics of human services and organizational theory and practice.

**Carmen Diana Deere** is Distinguished Professor Emerita of Latin American Studies and Food and Resource Economics at the University of Florida, USA and Honorary Professor Emerita at the Latin American Faculty of Social Sciences (FLACSO) in Quito, Ecuador. She holds a PhD in Agricultural Economics from the University of California, Berkeley, USA. Deere was Director of the UF Center for Latin American Studies (2004–09), and previously was Professor of Economics at the University of Massachusetts Amherst, USA. She is co-author of *Empowering Women: Land and Property Rights in Latin America* (2001), among other books and articles, and an associate editor of *Feminist Economics.* Her current research is on the factors that shape women's ability to accumulate assets, including property regimes and the role of remittances, savings, and access to credit.

**Paul Downward** is Reader in Sport Economics in the School of Sport, Exercise and Health Sciences, Loughborough University, UK. Previously he was Professor of Economics at Staffordshire University, UK. He has a strong interest in the research philosophy, methods, and ethics of economics and has published widely in these areas in both academic journals and books. He currently applies these interests in the analysis and evaluation of sport in society, also publishing widely in this area in journals and books. He has worked with and consulted for many policy agencies including UK Sport, Sport England, and the Department for Culture, Media and Sport.

**Armağan Gezici** is an Associate Professor of Economics at the Keene State College in New Hampshire, USA, where she has been a faculty member since 2007. She holds a MSc degree in Science and Technology Policy Studies from Middle East Technical University in Turkey, and a PhD in Economics from University of Massachusetts in Amherst, USA. Her research interests lie in the broad areas of development and international economics, whereas methodologically her work can be considered as 'macro-founded microeconomics'.

**Gyun Cheol Gu** is a Fellow at the Korea Institute of Local Finance, Korea's leading think-tank for local public finance and public policy. Dr Gu obtained his PhD degree in Economics from University of Missouri–Kansas City, USA under the direction of Professor Frederic S. Lee with a dissertation entitled 'Pricing, price stability, and post Keynesian price theory'.

**Therese Jefferson** is an Associate Professor at the Curtin Graduate School of Business in Perth, Western Australia. Her research interests focus on issues related to feminist economics and economic research methods.

**Xiao Jiang** is Assistant Professor of Economics at Denison University in Granville, Ohio, USA. He received his PhD in Economics from the New School for Social Research, USA, in 2013 and holds a BA in Economics and Philosophy from Bucknell University, USA. His research interests are as follows: classical political economy, nonlinear dynamics, input–output analysis, history of economic thought, and international trade with a focus on development, employment, and global value chains.

**A. Reeves Johnson** is Clinical Professor at Loyola University, Chicago and a PhD candidate at the University of Missouri–Kansas City, USA. His research interests include economic theory, business cycles, mathematical economics, and the history of economic thought. He has recently received the Young Scholars Award from the History of Economics Society and published in the *Journal of Post Keynesian Economics*.

**Thomas E. Lambert** is Assistant Professor of Public Administration at Northern Kentucky University, USA. He has done and continues to perform research in the areas of public policy analysis, program evaluation, urban economics, and urban planning as well as the applications of heterodox theory and concepts to these issues. His publications have appeared in *Benchmarking: An International Journal*, *Economic Development Quarterly*, *International Journal of Housing Markets and Analysis*, *International Journal of Services and Operations Management*, *Journal of Economics Issues*, *Journal of Public Management and Social Policy*, *Journal of Transportation Management*, *Population Research and Policy Review*, *Review of Radial Political Economics*, *Social Science Quarterly*, *State and Local Government Review*, *Transportation Journal*, and *World Review of Political Economy*.

**Frederic S. Lee** died from lung cancer while completing this edited volume, holding the post of Professor of Economics at the University of Missouri–Kansas City, USA. A major figure in the foundation of heterodox economics, his research interests were heterodox microeconomic theory, heterodox production and price models, and the history of heterodox economics. He was the author of *Post Keynesian Price Theory* (Cambridge University Press, 1998), *A History of Heterodox Economics* (Routledge, 2009), and in recent years published articles in the *Cambridge Journal of Economics*, *Journal of Post Keynesian Economics*, *Review of Political Economy*, *Journal of Economic Issues*, *Review of Social Economy*, *Review of Radical Political Economy*, *American Journal of Economics and Sociology*, *Bulletin of Political Economy*, and other heterodox journals. Finally, he was the founder and editor of the *Heterodox Economics Newsletter* and the editor of the *American Journal of Economics and Sociology*.

**Gill Lewin** has been involved in research on ageing and aged care provision since she joined Silver Chain as the Research Manager in 1993. Since 2008 she has combined her role as Research Director at the Silver Chain Group with that of Professor of Ageing at the Centre for Research on Ageing, Curtin University, Australia.

**Nuno Ornelas Martins** is Lecturer in Economics at the Católica Porto Business School and a researcher at CEGE, Universidade Católica Portuguesa, Portugal. He is also a member of the Cambridge Social Ontology Group, UK. His research interests are critical realism in economics, the Cambridge economic tradition, the capability approach to human development, and the social surplus approach. He is the author of *The Cambridge Revival of Political Economy* (Routledge, 2013), and in recent years has published articles in the *Cambridge Journal of Economics, Journal of Critical Realism, Journal of Post Keynesian Economics, Review of Political Economy, Journal of Economic Methodology, Review of Social Economy, American Journal of Economics and Sociology, Ecological Economics, Economic Thought, Evolutionary and Institutional Economics Review, New Political Economy, Journal for the Theory of Social Behaviour, Journal of Applied Mathematics and Physics*, and other journals.

**Andrew Mearman** is Director of Student Education at Leeds University Business School, having previously been a research centre director and Head of Subject at the University of the West of England, Bristol, UK. He has published extensively on economic methodology, teaching in economics, sport and arts and economics, and on economics and ecology, in journals including the *Cambridge Journal of Economics, Oxford Economic Papers, Journal of Economic Methodology, Capital and Class*, and the *Review of Social Economy*. He is a member of the editorial board for the *International Journal of Pluralism and Economics Education* and is a Trustee of the Association for Social Economics. He is an Associate of the Economics Network and is a former Co-ordinator of the Association for Heterodox Economics, for which he has organized a number of postgraduate training events in research methods. He was a member of a UK Government Advisory Panel and is working with the UK Office for National Statistics.

**Mieke Meurs** is Associate Dean of Graduate Studies, College of Arts and Sciences and Professor of Economics, American University, USA. She has published extensively on household behavior, including gender issues, and with particular focus on rural households. She holds a PhD from University of Massachusetts Amherst, USA and a BSc in political science from the University of Wisconsin–Madison, USA.

**Jamie Morgan** works at Leeds Beckett University, UK. He is Coordinator of the Association for Heterodox Economics (2013–15) and co-edits the *Real World Economics Review* with Edward Fullbrook. He has published widely in economics, philosophy, sociology, and area studies, including in the *Cambridge Journal of Economics, Economy & Society, Sociology*, and *Philosophy of Social Sciences*.

**Jamee K. Moudud** is Professor of Economics at Sarah Lawrence College, USA. His current research work focuses on the study of the ways in which political, legal, and institutional factors in capitalist societies shape and are shaped by state–business relations, business competitiveness, and the phases of economic cycles. He is investigating these issues in connection with taxation, social, and labor market policies in comparative international and historical contexts. He is the author of *Strategic Competition, Dynamics, and the Role of the State* (Edward Elgar Publishing, 2010) and co-editor of *Alternative Theories of Competition: Challenges to the Orthodoxy* (Routledge, 2012). He is an associate editor of the *Review of Keynesian Economics* and a member of the coordinating committee and editorial board of *Research on Money and Finance* (School of Oriental and

African Studies, University of London, UK). He has also published in the *International Journal of Political Economy*, *Review of Keynesian Economics*, *African and Asian Studies*, *Challenge* and has contributed an article for the United Nations Research Institute for Social Development's (UNRISD) project on the Politics of Domestic Resource Mobilization for Social Development.

**Jesús Muñoz** is Professor of Economics and Finance at the University of the Incarnate Word, Mexico City. His personal research interests are heterodox macroeconomic theory, history of economic thought (mainly Keynes, Minsky, Marx, and Friedman), methodology of economics, economics philosophy, international finance, and migration. He is author of *Colapsos Financieros: Mexico tras la Crisis de 1994* (ININEE, 2004), and in recent years has published articles in *World Review of Political Economy*, *World Development*, *Journal of Development Economics*, Levy Economics Institute Working Papers, and book chapters in heterodox books.

**Michael J. Murray** is an Associate Professor of Economics at Bemidji State University, Minnesota, USA. He is co-editor of *The Job Guarantee: Toward True Full Employment* and *Employment Guarantee Schemes*. His current research includes heterodox production theory and employment stabilization programs.

**Rachel Ong** is Deputy Director of the Bankwest Curtin Economics Centre at Curtin University, Perth, Western Australia. Her main research interests are in housing, ageing and labor economics. Her principal areas of research include housing decisions in later life, housing assets and retirement outcomes, intergenerational wealth transfers, impacts of the tax-transfer system on work incentives, and labour force participation by mature age persons.

**Lynda Pickbourn** is Assistant Professor of Economics at Hampshire College, USA, where she teaches courses on gender and economic development, feminist economics, labor economics, and the history of economic thought. Her primary areas of research are in economic development, political economy, and feminist economics, with a focus on sub-Saharan Africa. Her research interests include labor migration, informal employment, and the role of foreign aid in achieving human development and gender equality in the region. She received her BA in Economics and History from the University of Ghana and her MA and PhD in Economics from the University of Massachusetts, Amherst, USA.

**Smita Ramnarain** is Assistant Professor of Economics at Siena College, USA. She received her PhD from the University of Massachusetts Amherst, USA in 2012 and her BA from Madras Christian College, India. Her research interests lie at the intersection of political economy, development, and feminist economics. Her work focuses on the gendered political economy of development in the global South, particularly in South Asia, with a specific focus on post-conflict reconstruction. Her work has been published in diverse and interdisciplinary fora such as *Feminist Economics*, *Gender Place & Culture*, and the *Community Development Journal*, and in edited volumes. Since carrying out fieldwork in Nepal for her PhD dissertation, Smita has also been interested in research methodologies within economics, using both qualitative and quantitative methods in her work.

**Susan K. Schroeder** is a lecturer in the Department of Political Economy at the University of Sydney, Australia. Her research analyzes the interface between business cycle analysis and the detection of financial fragility, tracing the implications for policies that attenuate country risk for economic and financial crises. Her publications have appeared in the *Journal of Economic Issues, Journal of Economic Surveys, Australian Economic History Review, International Journal of Social Economics, Review of Political Economy,* and *World Economic Association Newsletter*. She is the author of *Public Credit Rating Agencies* (Palgrave Macmillan, 2015), *Business Cycles, Financial Fragility and Country Risk* (Edward Elgar Publishing, 2016) and co-editor of *Challenging the Orthodoxy: Reflections on Frank Stilwell's Contribution to Political Economy* (Springer, 2014).

**Rhonda Sharp** is Adjunct Professor at the Hawke Research Institute at the University of South Australia where she was formerly a Research Chair and Professor of Economics. She has served as President of the International Association for Feminist Economics (IAFFE) and as a member of the editorial board of *Feminist Economics*. Her research interests in feminist economics include research methods and gender-responsive budgeting.

**Rick Szostak** has been Professor of Economics at the University of Alberta, Canada since 1985. He served as Associate Dean in the Faculty of Arts from 2002 to 2005 and Associate Chair (Undergraduate) in Economics 2012 to 2015. His BA is from McGill University, Canada and his PhD from Northwestern University, USA. Szostak's research interests span the fields of economic history, methodology, history of technology, ethics, study of science, information science, world history, and the theory and practice of interdisciplinarity. He has served on the board of the Association for Interdisciplinary Studies for most of the last decade, and was President in 2011–14. He has taught courses in economic history, economic growth and development, microeconomics, interdisciplinarity, and science technology and society. He is the author of a dozen books, almost 50 journal articles, and 20 book chapters.

**Gennaro Zezza** is Associate Professor in Economics at Dipartimento di Economia e Giurisprudenza, Università di Cassino e del Lazio meridionale, Italy, and a Senior Research Scholar at the Levy Economics Institute of Bard College, USA. His main area of research is in post-Keynesian stock-flow-consistent modeling; he helped to develop this approach working with the late Wynne Godley in the United Kingdom, Denmark, as well as at the Levy Institute. He contributed to several Levy Institute Strategic Analysis papers on the US economy and Greece. His most recent publication is 'Reforming the international monetary system: a stock-flow-consistent approach' (jointly with S. Valdecantos), in the *Journal of Post-Keynesian Economics* (2015). He holds a degree in Economics from the University of Naples, Italy.

# Dedication

The first editor of this *Handbook*, Professor Frederick S. Lee, died during the final stages of its preparation, following the rapid onset of lung cancer. The *Handbook* represents the culmination of a tenacious academic career engaging thousands of economists in a project to construct a heterodox alternative to the aggressive monolithism of orthodox economics.

Fred had an infectious enthusiasm and doggedness in his heterodox mission; he is remembered by colleagues for his firm opinions solidly grounded in a broad interdisciplinarity yet thorough scholarship; by his students for his generous, inspirational teaching and mentoring; and by his opponents for his tenaciousness. He was not content to be an armchair academic but built institutions to carry heterodox research and teaching forward independently of any individuals. He established the Association of Heterodox Economics, originally conceived as a fringe event at the Royal Economic Association, in 1999; the *Heterodox Economics Newsletter* in 2004; he served on the boards of numerous heterodox organizations and journals; and documented the growth of the movement in his *History of Heterodox Economics* (Lee, 2009). In his last weeks, he fondly recalled lines from the ballad of 'Joe Hill': 'Says Joe, "What they forgot to kill/Went on to organize . . ."' (Hayes and Robinson 1936).

Fred saw the future of heterodox economics in the emerging generations of graduate students and always went out of his way to welcome new faces at the various heterodox conferences worldwide. There are numerous accounts of conference newbies being approached by Fred with the question, 'What have you brought here?' On hearing of his cancer diagnosis, Fred's reaction was not to wallow in regret but to immediately establish a Heterodox Economics Scholarship Fund, to support graduate student studies in heterodox economics: http://heterodoxnews.com/leefs/fsl-scholarship.

*The Handbook of Research Methods and Applications in Heterodox Economics* was a vitally important project for Fred in this context; graduate student access to mixed methods training was critical to challenging the monolithic hand of orthodox econometric modeling. A *Handbook* with a solid introduction to a wide range of methods would provide tools for emergent heterodox economists to find their own way in the absence of formal training programs, and to spur the development of mixed methods training in existing programs.

I am greatly honored to have worked with Fred in the past and on this final project.

Bruce Cronin

## REFERENCES

Hayes, Alfred and Earl Robinson (1936), 'Joe Hill.'
Lee, Frederick S. (2009), *A History of Heterodox Economics: Challenging the Mainstream in the Twentieth Century*, London: Routledge.

# Introduction
*Frederic S. Lee and Bruce Cronin*

The origin of the *Handbook of Research Methods and Applications in Heterodox Economics* is found in developments in methodology that occurred in the 1960s and 1970s which rejected deductive and non-causal forms of theorizing and questioned the sole use of quantitative statistical methods for evaluating theories that dominated much of the social sciences at the time. One outcome of the developments was the emergence of critical realism, which constitutes the philosophical foundation of this *Handbook*. Specifically, critical realism has its roots in the 1970s philosophical developments which argued that, for cause-and-effect events to occur in the world, there must be underlying causal mechanisms combined with structures to make them happen. By the late 1980s, critical realism had emerged as the philosophical foundation for a causal analysis in the social sciences; and by the early 1990s, it had entered heterodox economics through Tony Lawson (1997, 2003), his colleagues and students (Fleetwood 1999), and the critical realism workshop at Cambridge that has been ongoing since 1989/90. A second outcome was the development of the research strategy for theory development and evaluation known as the 'method of grounded theory'. Initially developed in 1967 by Barney Glaser and Anselm Strauss, it was first used in sociology and nursing; but over time it spread to other disciplines where qualitative research on social relations, social networks, and intentional actions through acting persons are important. In particular, it has become an accepted research strategy in management and organizational studies, business, marketing, and leadership research (Locke 2001; Goulding 2002), but not in economics to any great extent.[1]

With hindsight, it is clear that critical realism (CR) and the method of grounded theory (GTM) are compatible, with the former providing the philosophical foundations for the latter, and the latter as a specific research strategy that establishes through empirical evidence the structures and causal mechanisms required by the former for theoretical-analytical explanation. However, this awareness was and is slow in coming because of some perceived limitations on the part of GTM. That is, from a critical realist perspective, it appeared to have an inductivist, empiricist, and/or a constructivist (with multiple realities) bias, to underestimate the value of general abstract theories, and to reject engagement with any previous theories (Layder 1990; Danermark et al. 2002). In any case, there are only a few efforts to show the compatibility between CR and GTM, with the earliest being by Yeung (1997), with subsequent contributions by Kempster and Parry (2011) and Oliver (2012).

As critical realism became more broadly accepted by heterodox economists, it became evident that its application to heterodox economic theorizing was not proceeding at the same pace. In fact, Tony Lawson and others repeatedly stated that critical realism is only the starting point and others will have to do the work of figuring out how to apply it to heterodox economics, to creating new heterodox theories and new ways to evaluate them. In the late 1990s and subsequent years, those critical realists who were interested in filling in the gap turned to the pragmatist research strategy of abduction for theory creation and implicitly for theory evaluation.[2] Coincidently at this same time, the first editor of this *Handbook*, Frederic Lee, was looking for a research strategy that gave form and articulation to the way he engaged in developing theoretical arguments and analytical, historical narratives. Following a hint by Warren Young regarding the method of grounded theory, he started reading articles and books on GTM which appeared to be precisely the research strategy he was looking for; and through a discussion with Steve Fleetwood about methodology, he became convinced that his research strategy needed a philosophical foundation, specifically CR. Frederic Lee first presented his integration of CR and GTM at the Critical Realist Workshop Seminar in Cambridge on May 11, 1998; and then presented a more developed version of the paper in 2000 at the Cambridge Realist Workshop Conference, Critical Realism in Economics: What Difference Does It Make?

The introduction of GMT into critical realism discussion occurred at the same time that Lawson's negative critique of econometrics (which was an important component of the critical realist discussion at the time) was being questioned to some degree by young heterodox economists such as Wendy Olsen, Paul Downward, and Andrew Mearman through presentations at the Critical Realist Workshop and the 2000 Conference and in publications over the next few years; see Downward (2003). They could not see why critical realism necessarily rejected the use of econometrics and other analytical statistical tools. In fact they did not see any necessary conflict between quantitative and qualitative research methods, if properly used; rather, they thought that the distinction between the two was rather fuzzy. This set them on a collision course with both critical realism and the dominant view that econometrics was the only valid research method for economics (heterodox or mainstream); and at the same time provided an opening for GTM (through its traditional emphasis on qualitative research methods) to enter the discussion. The upshot of this was the establishment of an advanced training workshop for postgraduate students on heterodox research methodologies under the auspices of the Association of Heterodox Economics (AHE).

The first AHE workshop was organized by Wendy Olsen in 2001. It featured presentations by Tony Lawson on causal explanation (philosophical foundation CR), Frederic Lee on the GTM (research strategy), and Wendy Olsen on statistical analysis and the use of various statistical (research methods) approaches and software packages to analyze qualitative data. The subsequent workshops in 2002, 2004, 2005, 2007, 2009, 2012, 2014, 2015 and 2016 were organized by Downward, Mearman, and Olsen, followed the same format but with greater emphasis given to research methods (and the kind of data associated with them) and their integrated use in the examination of a research topic.[3] So over time, workshop research methods topics have included modeling strategies for analyzing complexity, triangulating quantitative and qualitative data, multilevel modeling, factor analysis, cluster analysis, regression analysis as econometrics, large data set analysis, fuzzy set analysis, qualitative comparative analysis, and social network analysis (Bruce Cronin). This increasing emphasis on research methods was fueled by two concerns: the first being the need to reorient economics so to match research methods with the diverse social material needed to be analysed, and the second to explain that any research topic that economists (especially heterodox economists) are engaged with requires the use of mixed research methods to deal with the mixed data.[4]

The outcome of the first two workshops was the first book that engaged critical realism and doing empirical economic research: *Applied Economics and the Critical Realist Critique* (Downward 2003). It followed the format of the workshops: the first part dealt with critical realism, the second with conceptual issues between critical realism and empirical work which included research strategies and research methods, and the last part applied critical realism to empirical analysis. However, the book did not have the hoped-for impact on heterodox economists. For it is painfully obvious that heterodox economics (and economics in general) remains dominated by a single research method – econometrics – with mathematical modeling being in second place. Currently, no core heterodox economics journal explicitly encourages that submitted papers should use more than one research method (and one kind of data). If, for example, you look at the *Journal of Post Keynesian Economics*, you come away with the opinion that econometrics is the only (and hence only legitimate) research method to be used by post-Keynesian heterodox economists.

The dominance of econometrics and mathematical modeling research methods courses taught in heterodox doctoral programs is also shockingly obvious.[5] For example, in the USA the recognized heterodox doctoral programs at the University of Utah, University of Massachusetts Amherst, and New School for Social Research have for the past 30 years or so only provided a single research methods course: econometrics.[6] This is in contrast to having their students take a course on methodology and/or learning different heterodox theoretical approaches, such as Marxist epistemology and theory.[7] Consequently, when the time comes to write their dissertations, some students discover a disjuncture between the only research method they know, and what they actually want to research and write upon. Whether their dissertation advisors suggested alternative research methods or the students discovered them on their own, the end result was that they had to learn about them on their own, reading other people's research and imitating what they did, or to take classes outside of economics, such as in an undergraduate major in geography or history, or an MA in regional planning. In all cases there was no department support.[8] Heterodox economists who received their training in other American doctoral programs had the same kind of experiences, such as taking an outside minor field in women's studies and learning about oral interviewing, learning ethnographic methods by doing independent reading, or going to different departments to learn about the research methods they use.[9]

This rather dismal state of affairs became strikingly obvious when former University of Massachusetts Amherst students formed a Union for Radical Political Economics (URPE) panel at the 2012 Allied Social Sciences Association (ASSA) to present papers on the importance of fieldwork for economics.[10] This was driven by the fact (as noted above) that their doctoral program did not introduce them to any research method other than econometrics and hence they were unprepared to carry out the kind of research they wanted to do for their dissertation. Of course, without exposure in graduate school to alternative research methods that more accurately match the social data relevant to a research project, heterodox economists have to flounder around to find such approaches and then spend a great deal of time learning about them. This *Handbook of Research Methods and Applications in Heterodox Economics* is designed to overcome this omission of heterodox doctoral programs and the possible locked-in effects that result, and provide doctoral students and searching heterodox economists with an introductory overview of alternative possible research methods for their research.

## I.1   THEMATIC OUTLINE OF THE BOOK

For any factual field of inquiry or scientific research field to exist, its object of study must be real (as opposed to fictitious or non-existent) and relate to the problems and issues that are the focus of the research community. Moreover, the methods used by the researchers to study the objects and address the problems and issues need to be grounded in the real world. Heterodox economics is concerned with explaining and advocating changes in the real historical process of producing the social surplus that provides the flow of goods and services required by society to meet its recurring needs and to promote the well-being of those who participate in its activities. In other words, heterodox economics is a historical science of the social provisioning process, and this is the general research agenda of heterodox economists. Drawing from all heterodox approaches, its explanation involves both human agency embedded in a transmutable, hence uncertain, world with fallible knowledge and expectations and in a cultural context, and social processes situated in historical time which affect resources, consumption patterns, production, and reproduction, and the meaning (or ideology) of market, state, and non-market, non-state activities engaged in social provisioning. This implies that agency can only take place in an interdependent social context which emphasizes the social and de-emphasizes the isolated nature of individual decision-making; and that the organization of social provisioning is determined outside of markets, although the provisioning process itself does, in part, currently take place through capitalist markets. Thus heterodox economic theory is a theoretical explanation of the historical process of social provisioning, currently within the context of a capitalist economy; and hence it is also a historically contextual explanation. Therefore, it is concerned with explaining those factors that are part of the process of social provisioning, including the structure and use of resources, the structure and change of social wants, structure of production, and the reproduction of the business enterprise, family, state, and other relevant institutions and organizations, and distribution. In addition, heterodox economists extend their theory to examining issues associated with the process of social provisioning, such as racism, gender, and ideologies and myths.

Heterodox economic theory is not a pre-existing doctrine to be applied to an invariant economic reality. Rather, there are many heterodox theoretical arguments which appear to contribute to its construction, but there is no reason why they should command blind acceptance; and, in any case, they fall short of making a comprehensive theory. Consequently, new theories are needed to fill the gaps and omissions. In either case, there needs to be a basis for accepting the theories as reasonable scientific theoretical contributions to explaining the social provisioning process. This suggests that the development of heterodox theory requires theory creation and theory evaluation. Scientific theory creation requires a philosophical foundation on which a research strategy for theory creation and evaluation is based. Moreover, and relevant to this *Handbook*, graduate students (and even seasoned researchers) need to be familiar with a greater range of research methods on which theories are developed and evaluated.

The objective of this *Handbook* is to introduce heterodox economists to a range of research methods that might prove useful in their research and the construction and evaluation of their economic analysis. Consequently, the *Handbook* is arranged into three parts: 'Philosophical foundation and research strategy', 'Research methods and data collection', and 'Applications'. Part I consists of three chapters that set out the basis for the rest of the book's emphasis on research methods and their application. Jamie Morgan deals with the philosophical foundation in Chapter 1 on 'Critical realism as a social ontology for economics'. He argues that the nature of social reality determines how it should be studied and what kind of knowledge claims about it can be made. Critical realism is a particular ontological argument that has social reality consisting of agency, structure, and ongoing historical transformational process. Consequently, social qua economic events are not the result of correlative, but otherwise unconnected, outcomes of two variables; rather, all economic events are causally constituted. With critical realism providing the social ontological foundation for economic analysis, the next step is to adopt a research strategy (which is a way of constructing explanations of economic events) that is consistent with it. Jamie makes a number of suggestions: abduction, retroduction and retrodiction, contrast explanation, and the method of grounded theory. Frederic Lee follows on in Chapter 2 on 'Critical realism, method of grounded theory, and theory construction' by dealing with research strategy of the method of grounded theory, and connecting it to critical realism on the one hand and to research methods and data collection on the other hand, which comprises Part II of the *Handbook*. The heart of the chapter is the delineation of the critical realist–grounded theory (CR–GT) approach to theory creation and evaluation which illuminates their historical character and directly engages with mixed research methods (such as historical method, survey methods, participation observation method, analytical statistics, social network analysis, modeling, and cases), data triangulation, and historical theorization. Because critical realism is concerned with the social ontology of the domain of economics, and the method of grounded theory promotes the use of mixed research methods and data triangulation, heterodox economics does not have a preference for a particular method or data. This, Rick Szostak argues in Chapter 3, 'An interdisciplinary perspective on heterodoxy', makes heterodox economics predisposed to interdisciplinarity rather than towards a narrow disciplinary perspective. He then discusses the implications interdisciplinarity has for the practice of heterodox economics.

Part II of the *Handbook* consists of 12 chapters dealing with different research methods (although it is not inclusive of all research methods that may be useful to heterodox economists). It starts off with Lynda Pickbourn and Smita Ramnarain in Chapter 4 examining the widely held belief that quantitative, qualitative, and historical research methods are clearly distinct, with a great distance between them. They argue that the distinction is much less clear than most economists want to believe, and that since social reality is complex, the choice of methods is better determined by the research question being pursued than by disciplinary norms. Chapters 5, 6 and 7 examine more closely historical and qualitative research methods, while Chapter 8 is more quantitative in orientation. What is common to these four methods is that they create information which can be used as data (see Chapter 2 for the distinction), as opposed to relying on given data to be analyzed. Natalia Bracarense and A. Reeves Johnson start Chapter 5 by reiterating the inherent role of historical material in the CG-GT approach. They then present different historical methods and show how they can be used in heterodox economics in both their traditional and nontraditional forms. What is interesting about the latter forms, such as oral history, is that they 'create' historical data where it was presumed none existed. In Chapter 6, Tiago Cardão-Pito covers the use of survey methods for the creation of data for heterodox economic research. While often seen as a qualitative research method, Tiago shows that it can also be seen as a quantitative research method. Amit Basole and Smita Ramnarain in Chapter 7 show the usefulness of qualitative and ethnographic methods for the creation of non-numerical data regarding social relationships and motivation. Andrew Mearman in Chapter 8 shows that experimental methods, which fall somewhere between quantitative and qualitative methods, can be used to create data that can be used to answer certain theoretical questions.

Chapters 9 to 14 deal with a broad range of quantitative methods. Common to these methods is that they utilize pre-existing data as opposed to creating their own data and that they analyze the data systematically. Chapters 9, 10, and 11 by Michael Murray, Paul Downward, and Nuno Martins, respectively, deal with the use of various statistical methods to examine quantitative data. What is evident in the three chapters is that the use of statistical methods, especially econometrics, is not incompatible with critical realism if done carefully. Consequently the methods can provide an understanding of the quantitative data. In Chapter 9, Michael Murray argues that factor analysis and cluster analysis are highly compatible with critical realist–grounded theory approaches as they help to clearly delineate causal mechanisms and structures. Paul Downward and Nuno Martins argue in Chapters 10 and 11, respectively, that econometric techniques are not the exclusive preserve of orthodox economics but can be effectively utilized as components in mixed methods approaches.

The next three chapters, Chapters 12, 13, 14, by Bruce Cronin, Jonathan Cogliano and Xiao Jiang, and Frederic Lee, respectively, deal with social network analysis, agent-based computational analysis, and modeling, which are research methods based on non-statistical mathematical techniques. Social network analysis explores relational data using graph theoretic techniques. Computational economics is used to explore theoretical issues using hypothetical economies, helping the heterodox economist come to a better understanding of various theoretical arguments. In Chapter 12, Bruce Cronin introduces the techniques of social network analysis, arguing that with their focus on social relationships, these are particularly useful in evidencing questions of interest to heterodox economics. Jonathan Cogliano and Xiao Jiang introduce agent-based modeling approaches in Chapter 13; their flexibility in incorporating highly heterogeneous agents with high degrees of freedom also makes this a useful tool for issues of heterodox interest. Contrary to the use of modeling by mainstream economists, Frederic Lee argues in Chapter 14 that modeling is a research method that contributes to theory construction and development. Moreover, he argues that mathematical modeling is consistent with critical realism and the method of grounded theory when the structures and causal mechanisms in the real world are constituents of the world in the model. As a result the working of the world in the model helps develop the CR–GT narrative of how the real world works.

The last chapter in Part II, Chapter 15, on multiple and mixed research methods, essentially brings together all the above research methods and their data. Bruce Cronin demonstrates how multiple and mixed methods contribute to a heterodox approach to economics and provides a 'how to' guide. Good research, and good theory development, involve at least two different research methods and data types; and so the monolithic econometric approach of mainstream economics is necessarily limited.

Part III consists of 14 applications of research methods to different economic topics.

What is central to most of these chapters is that mixed research methods and data triangulation are used, and the reasons why they are being used. Thus the reader is provided with an in-depth introduction to how to use different research methods, and what they bring individually and together to understanding the research topic at hand.

In Chapter 18, Lynne Chester supplements quantitative analysis of secondary data with interviews, focus groups, and surveys to provide otherwise unobtainable policy insight into the effects of energy price changes on low-income households. The chapter relays valuable field experience of recruiting and working with 'economically marginalized' populations in research projects. In Chapter 19, Bob Davidson builds a case study of the marketization of the home care industry in New South Wales from a historical analysis of documents, quantitative analysis of secondary data, interviews with participants, focus groups, and participant observation. In Chapter 23, Therese Jefferson, Siobhan Austen, Rhonda Sharp, Rachel Ong, Valerie Adams and Gill Lewin use mixed methods to examine employment decisions of aged care workers in Australia. Quantitative analysis of secondary and survey data was used to identify 'demi-regularities' that were then interpreted with richer insights drawn from participant interviews, highlighting the role of 'recognition' and 'signals' in employment decisions. In Chapter 24, Lynda Pickbourn uses mixed methods to enrich economic analyses of migration and remittance behavior. She contrasts the use of unstructured interviews, participant observation, and focus groups to generate data in qualitative research with standard approaches that use surveys to collect data to test hypotheses; with qualitative approaches broadening understanding, such as the role of gender in migration and remittance behavior. In Chapter 29, Lynne Chester presents an analysis of changes to the Australian electricity sector within a *Régulationist* framework, employing an historical interpretation of an extensive range of quantitative and qualitative data. She provides a systematic framework for the selection and evaluation of data sources.

A number of chapters highlight the value of supplementary methods when there are weaknesses in available quantitative data. In Chapter 16, Armağan Gezici uses interviews and quantitative analysis of secondary data as supplementary methods to compensate for deficiencies in data needed for a conventional analysis of investment behavior in Turkey. These highlight risk-aversion, shorter time horizons, and export propensity as important factors not considered by standard approaches. Jesús Muñoz combines documentary analysis with interviews within an historical perspective in Chapter 20, to develop a case study of the operation of the Mexican stock market, where volatile and emerging market characteristics make conventional quantitative analysis difficult, which in any case is prone to superficiality. He finds participants cling to a certainty paradigm in the face of market turbulence. In Chapter 25, Mieke Meurs supplements statistical analysis of economic data with interviews, providing opportunities for smallholders to explain their motivations for behavior, opening up alternative explanations to standard models, prompting alternative policy proposals. Carmen Deere and Zachary Catanzarite employ a mixed methods approach in Chapter 26, to examine intra-household distribution of wealth, using focus groups, interviews, and participant observation to supplement quantitative analysis of secondary data. This allows questions to be asked about wealth distribution by gender that are not accessible from the statistical analysis of standard data sets.

Finally, a set of applications highlight the use of a specialized single methodological approach to tackle questions of heterodox interest. In Chapter 17, Gyun Cheol Gu uses a grounded theory approach, drawing on empirical studies of price formation, to refine the post-Keynesian price stability and cyclicality framework and models. Jamee Moudud employs econometric time series techniques in Chapter 21, to demonstrate persistent differences in policy regimes, indicating policy-making as a contested process. In Chapter 22, Gennaro Zezza provides an application of modeling – stock-flow-consistent models – demonstrating how modeling whole economies can address post-Keynesian questions ignored by conventional economic models. Thomas Lambert and Michael Bewley present an application of experimental methods in Chapter 27, to evaluate the effectiveness of enterprise zones in Kentucky. And in Chapter 28, Susan Schroeder demonstrates how econometric time series techniques can be used to distinguish different types of business cycles, a long-standing heterodox theoretical concern.

## I.2   REFERENTIAL STRUCTURE

Beyond this thematic introduction, the structure of the *Handbook* can also be considered in terms of its referential structure, the citation pattern of its chapters. Figure I.1 presents a visualization of the links among the authors cited in each chapter, the squares representing chapters, the circles authors cited, and the arrows contributions to the chapter. In most part, the first two parts of the *Handbook* engage with a core of common references, broadly within a triangle of Chapters 1–3, constituting Part I. Part II, Chapters 4–15, fills this triangle, with the exception of Chapter 6 on formal survey methods and Chapter 12 on social network analysis; these concern specialist methodologies, somewhat novel in their application to heterodox economics. The application chapters, Chapters 16–29, ring this core, with some connections to the core-cited authors and many links to specialized sources.

Figure I.2 presents the core author citations in the *Handbook*, what is known as the '3-core', as detailed in Chapter 12. Chapters are represented as squares and authors represented as circles and an arrow representing an input to the chapter; larger squares and circles represent more citations and cites respectively. Chapters 15 (Cronin), 4 (Pickbourn and Ramnarain), 2 (Lee), 1 (Morgan), and 11 (Martins) make the greatest number of citations to authors within this core. Perhaps not surprisingly, as lead editor of the *Handbook*, Frederick S. Lee is the most cited and most central author in the citation network, followed by Tony Lawson, Paul Downward, and Andrew Mearman. The proximity of the last three reflects the close collaboration of Downward and Mearman, with Lawson's critical realism as a major reference point. Also of particular note in structuring the centre of the citation network are Shelia Dow and Andrew Sayer, and the paradigmatic figures of Karl Marx and John Maynard Keynes, either side of Chapter 16 (Gezici), and Milton Friedman between Chapter 1 (Morgan) and Chapter 2 (Lee). To the left, Barney Glaser and Anselm Strauss, Alan Bryman, and Yvonna Lincoln (but interestingly, not frequent co-author Norman Denzin), pioneers of grounded theory and mixed method methodologies, and around the edge of the core, important contributors to the critique of methodological individualism and post-Keynesian perspectives.

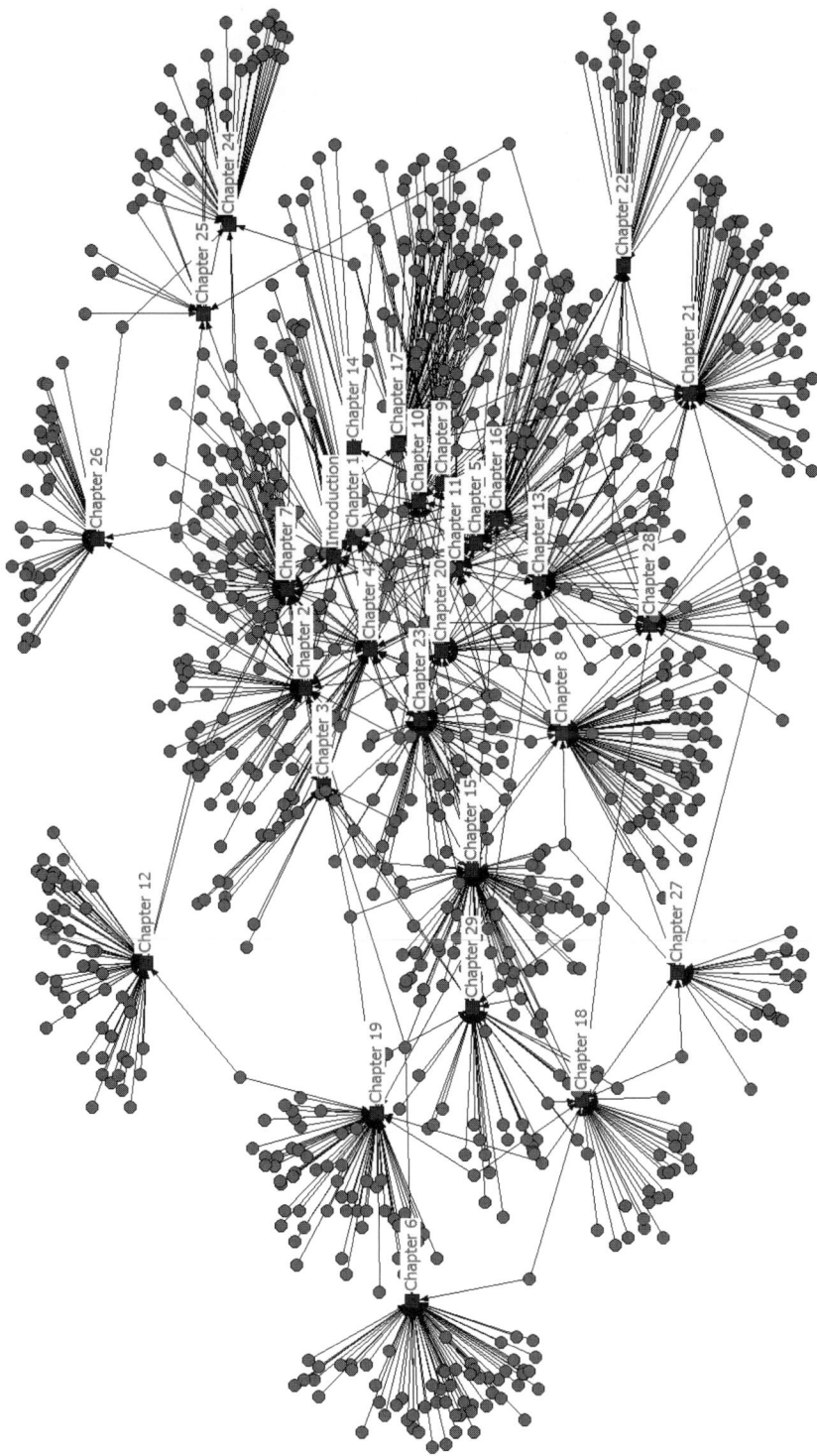

*Figure I.1  Citation structure of the* Handbook

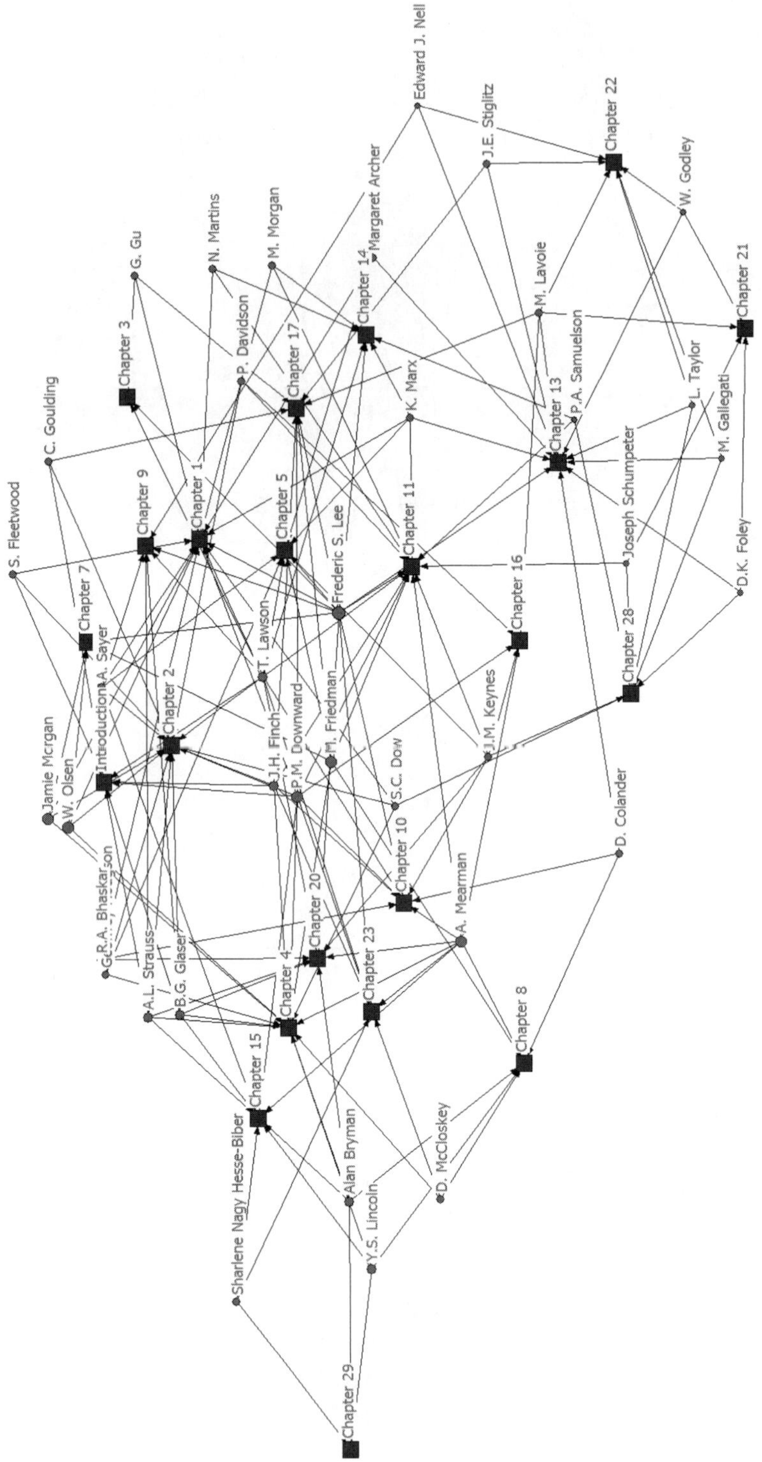

*Figure I.2   Core citations in the* Handbook

## I.3   CONCLUSION

This introduction has provided both thematic and referential pathways to help readers locate related material in both the exposition of methods and application examples. We are confident that the chapters in this *Handbook* will provide a solid scaffolding for those wishing to rise from a broad critical realist–grounded theory understanding to more rigorous concrete enquiry. We are hopeful that new generations of heterodox economists will find the means here to take their investigations forward with confidence, and that established academics will find tools here to explore or refine new approaches and perhaps help generate broader research methods programs in our graduate schools.

## NOTES

1. For the few who have used GTM in economics, see Reid (1993), Reid et al. (1993), Finch (2002), and Scheibl and Wood (2005).
2. Abduction (or sometimes called retroduction) is a form of theory construction that goes from the surface event to the structures and causal mechanisms that produce it by inferring causes from the effects. The first step in this process is a 'hypothetical' theoretical-abstract redescription of the events based on existing theoretical arguments and qualitative and quantitative material. The next step is to postulate and identify the structures and causal mechanisms underpinning the theoretical redescription, thereby producing a theoretical explanation (hence theory) of the event. The final step is to check whether the theory is empirically valid. Although, advocated by critical realists, abduction is in fact weak on realism. That is, there is no requirement that the theoretical redescription be empirically grounded; and nor is there any requirement that the postulated structures and causal mechanisms be real and empirically grounded. Hence, it is argued by some critical realists that abduction permits the use of analogies, similes, and metaphors as useful ways to identify causal mechanisms and structures. But since the latter are by their nature not real, they cannot contribute in any manner to the construction of a realist theory and in any case may direct the attention of the researcher towards fictitious, hence empirically ungroundable, causal mechanisms and structures and thus to non-factual theories. Finally, abduction does not indicate how the causal processes should be delineated and articulated; that is, the analytical and literary form the theory should take. In short, abduction is insufficient as a research strategy for the creation of a critical realist grounded theory (Lawson 1996, 1998, 1999, 2003; Sarre 1987; Sayer 1992; Pratt 1995; Boylan and O'Gorman 1995; Yeung 1997; Runde 1998; Downward 1999; Oliver 2012).
3. The workshop initially obtained its funding from the Economic and Social Research Council (UK). But in 2006 the composition of the panel evaluating the applications for funding changed so that it was dominated by mainstream economists. The outcome was that the AHE's application for funding was rejected largely on the grounds that it did not involve mainstream economics. The subsequent workshops were funded by the Cambridge Political Economy Society Trust and/or the AHE. For further information about the AHE and its workshop, see http://www.hetecon.net.
4. The lecturers and postgraduate students at the workshops include many who are contributing chapters in this *Handbook*: Jamie Morgan (Chapter 1), Frederic Lee (Chapters 2 and 14), Andrew Mearman (Chapter 8), Paul Downward (Chapter 10), Bruce Cronin (Chapter 12), and Therese Jefferson (Chapter 23).
5. Mathematical economic modeling as a recognized, independent research method has emerged over the past 25 years. Its differentiation from mathematics as a way to do economics as opposed to just representing economic theory and arguments emerged when economists started considering that it was the world in the economic model that was the subject of their research interests rather than the model of the actual world; see Chapter 14 for further discussion.
6. This was also the experience of heterodox economists who attended mainstream programs at the US universities of Stanford, MIT, Harvard, Yale, and Rutgers from the 1960s to early 1980s.
7. In the case of Notre Dame, when it still had a heterodox graduate program, students were introduced to the Institutionalist's research strategy of pattern modeling.
8. Doctoral students at the University of Missouri–Kansas City also only take econometrics as their research methods course. But the department makes it quite clear that they need to be familiar with more

than a single research method and encourages the students to take research methods courses in other departments.

9. Heterodox postgraduate students in Australia, the United Kingdom, Germany, and elsewhere face similar issues. In short, if a student is associated with an economic department then learning about alternative research methods is quite difficult to come by (unless you are at the University of Leeds, Greenwich, Kingston or the West of England, UK; or the University of Bremen, Germany). But if a student is located in, say, a business school and is doing an economics research topic, then they are faced with an abundance of research methods to choose from; yet this richness of methods isolates them from most economists who cannot handle such diversity.

10. The presenters included many who are contributing chapters in this *Handbook*: Smita Ramnarain (Chapters 4 and 7), Amit Basole (Chapter 7), Lynda Pickbourn (Chapters 4 and 24), and Armağan Gezici (Chapter 16).

# REFERENCES

Boylan, T. and P. O'Gorman (1995), *Beyond Rhetoric and Realism in Economics: Towards a Reformulation of Economic Methodology*, London: Routledge.

Danermark, B., M. Ekstrom, L. Jakobsen, and J. Karlsson (2002), *Explaining Society: Critical Realism in the Social Sciences*, London: Routledge.

Downward, P. (1999), *Pricing Theory in Post Keynesian Economics: A Realist Approach*, Cheltenham, UK and Northampton, MA, USA: Edward Elgar.

Downward, P. (ed.) (2003), *Applied Economics and the Critical Realist Critique*, London: Routledge.

Finch, J.H. (2002), 'The role of grounded theory in developing economic theory', *Journal of Economic Methodology*, **9** (2), 213–34.

Fleetwood, S. (ed.) (1999), *Critical Realism in Economics: Development and Debate*, London: Routledge.

Glaser, B.G. and A.L. Strauss (1967), *The Discovery of Grounded Theory: Strategies for Qualitative Research*, New York: Aldine Publishing Company.

Goulding, C. (2002), *Grounded Theory: A Practical Guide for Management, Business and Market Researchers*, London: Sage.

Kempster, S. and K.W. Parry (2011), 'Grounded theory and leadership: a critical realist perspective', *Leadership Quarterly*, **22** (1), 106–20.

Lawson, T. (1996), 'Developments in economics as realist social theory', *Review of Social Economy*, **54** (4), 405–22.

Lawson, T. (1997), *Economics and Reality*, London, Routledge.

Lawson, T. (1998), 'Social relations, social reproduction and stylized facts', in P. Arestis (ed.), *Method, Theory and Policy in Keynes: Essays in Honour of Paul Davidson*, Vol. 3, Cheltenham, UK and Northampton, MA, USA: Edward Elgar, pp. 17–43.

Lawson, T. (1999), 'Critical issues in economics as realist social theory', in S. Fleetwood (ed.), *Critical Realism in Economics: Development and Debate*, London: Routledge, pp. 209–57.

Lawson, T. (2003), *Reorienting Economics*, London: Routledge.

Layder, D. (1990), *The Realist Image in Social Science*, Basingstoke: Macmillan.

Locke, K. (2001), *Grounded Theory in Management Research*, London: Sage.

Oliver, C. (2012), 'Critical realist grounded theory: a new approach for social work research', *British Journal of Social Work*, **42** (2), 371–87.

Pratt, A. (1995), 'Putting critical realism to work: the practical implications for geographical research', *Progress in Human Geography*, **19** (1), 61–74.

Reid, G.C. (1993), *Small Business Enterprise: An Economic Analysis*, London: Routledge.

Reid, G.C., L.R. Jacabsen, and M.E. Anderson (1993), *Profiles in Small Business: A Competitive Strategy Approach*, London: Routledge.

Runde, J. (1998), 'Assessing causal economic explanations', *Oxford Economic Papers*, **50** (1), 151–72.

Sarre, P. (1987), 'Realism in practice', *Area*, **19** (1), 3–10.

Sayer, A. (1992), *Method in Social Science: A Realist Approach*, 2nd edn, London: Routledge.

Scheibl, Fiona and Andrew Wood (2005), 'Investment sequencing in the brick industry: an application of grounded theory', *Cambridge Journal of Economics*, **29** (2), 223–47.

Yeung, H. (1997), 'Critical realism and realist research in human geography: a method or a philosophy in search of a method?', *Progress in Human Geography*, **21** (1), 51–74.

# PART I

# PHILOSOPHICAL FOUNDATION AND RESEARCH STRATEGY

# 1 Critical realism as a social ontology for economics
*Jamie Morgan\**

## 1.1 INTRODUCTION

In the editor's introduction to *Ontology and Economics* (2009, pp. 1–3) Edward Fullbrook makes the point that Tony Lawson (1997, 2003) has changed the nature of the 'conversation' regarding economic methodology. Specifically he has made the issue of social ontology a central one. Lawson's work along with that of a number of other proponents of critical realism has important implications for economics (Fleetwood 1999; Lewis 2004). The focus on social ontology in critical realism puts forward a position based on causal powers inhering in entities (such as structures and agents), complex interactions between causal powers in terms of arising events, and a consequent account of systems as 'open'. According to its proponents, this social ontology is implicit within heterodox economic positions but is antithetical to mainstream economics. This is because mainstream economics pursues theorizations and applications that reduce to closed systems and typically assume and/or explore event regularities, often based on uses of mathematical models that are expressed in a deductive form. Critical realism's great strength is that it provides a more plausibly realistic account of the economy as an intrinsic aspect of society; in so doing it 'under-labours' for heterodox approaches. However, insofar as it only under-labours, critical realism can also be developed in a variety of ways that are consistent with its approach to social ontology. This extends also to issues of method and methodology (e.g., Downward 2003; Carter and New 2004). This chapter provides an introductory account of the core elements of a generic critical realist social ontology for economics based on the development of critical realism within the philosophy of science and of social theory originating with Roy Bhaskar and a number of others (Bhaskar 1975, 1979; Harré and Madden 1976).

## 1.2 WHY SOCIAL ONTOLOGY SHOULD MATTER

Taken in isolation the following can seem a ridiculous statement; ridiculous in the sense that it is so obvious it ought not to require such statement: Any science, including a social science such as economics, ought to be about reality, the nature of reality ought to make a difference to how we study it and what we then claim about it as a form of knowledge.

However, when one considers that knowledge is a social product then the need to be reminded of the significance of the obvious becomes considerably less ridiculous. Knowledge is a set of claims based on particular theories, and particular investigations, using particular methods. These develop over time. They become a set of resources to draw upon, but are more than this. They are components in knowledge organizations, such as disciplinary departments in universities. One learns how to do things in recognized ways and these provide accepted practice. One realizes that some ways of doing things have attractive characteristics, and these may be of many kinds. There may be puzzles to solve and lacunae to investigate; an approach might carry a certain difficulty or apparent complexity within it that creates status through mastery; an approach might carry an external status significance – it seems analogous to what is done in other disciplines that already have status, such as physics, and it might have the attractiveness of simplicity as a tool for policy advice or for policy 'evidence'. It may attract funding. Careers are created and ways of doing things can be reproduced and augmented, becoming dominant. Those who reproduce them come to accept them and can do so non-reflexively as simply how things are done, the best we have, or more cynically, as profoundly flawed but part of the game we play to get on. The process of reproduction can then also create prejudice and foster exclusions and marginalizations that serve to simply eliminate whole frames of reference, and with them possibilities of viewing the world differently (a 'that's not what we do' that prevents things from being seen or understood). A status quo can be reinforced because power (benign or otherwise) is intrinsic to the processes of knowledge as a social product.

The point, then, is that it is not inexplicable that a discipline develops in ways that lose touch with the basic statement of the obvious given above. Ways of doing things become 'locked-in', seemingly 'better' arguments in terms of recognized reality need not win out, and a discipline can become focused in terms of developing characteristics (technical skills, the puzzles of a theory or a model form) that are not all directed in any primary sense towards investigating reality. At the same time, a discipline can be developing whilst still notionally adhering to the idea that it does investigate reality, or contribute to our understanding of it at some level, but can fail to actually exhibit that commitment. It can fail to maintain a critical check on how knowledge is produced: the significance of the use of assumptions, the value of ways of theorizing, and of given theories and models; that is, it can fail to place a critical check on the common trajectory of the field. And it can fail to address persistent failures: the failure to produce consistent and coherent types of knowledge, able to fulfil the goals set by its own adherents for how knowledge is to be adjudicated (such as the derivation of significant laws or predictive power); and, more profoundly, the failure to provide widely accepted meaningful insight into reality (recognizable explanatory success in regard of the key phenomena of the field).

It is not, of course, just explicable that a discipline can lose touch with the basic statement of the obvious above. In the case of economics it is a widely acknowledged issue. The issue is not new but the role of economics in the global financial crisis has brought the issue to the fore. There is a widespread dissatisfaction with the state of economics, and not least amongst its students. If you recognize the general problems above as specific to economics then you are by inclination, if not yet self-identification, a heterodox economist. If you see only minor cause for concern, the chances are you are a mainstream economist.

Now, consider the significance of what I have said so far. Knowledge is a social product, and can for various reasons lose sight of or become deformed in terms of its primary concern: the investigation of reality. This creates a warrant for some form of check or critical framework of analysis of knowledge as a social product. In order to keep a discipline honest it would benefit from a domain of argument that challenges that discipline in terms of its commitments or goals (such as seeking laws or formulating predictions) as well as its ongoing explanatory success in relation to its ways of theorizing, and its use of methods. This critique needs a general domain within which it can engage the identified issues, and traditionally this is the realm of philosophy in the form of meta-physics. However, the revival since the 1970s of a concern with this general domain in relation to the social sciences has used the term 'ontology' or 'social ontology'. An ontology is a theory of being. It starts from the question, 'What must be the case for x?' in order to build up, using varieties of evidence and argument, a general set of claimed characteristics of reality in some context. Note, however, that the initial justification for the importance of ontology is not a specific ontology, it is the value of explicitly addressing key issues of general critique of a discipline, such as economics, in terms of their realism because these can easily be neglected by that discipline.

Social ontology then is an invitation to consider general aspects of knowledge in terms of critique. However, for that critique to be meaningful, one assumption and a further claim are required. The assumption (though one might state this more assertively as a warranted insight) is that all theories and ways of investigating the world involve at least an implicit ontology; that is, what the world must be like for the approach to be appropriate, fruitful, successful and so forth. The further claim is that for critique within social ontology to be feasible and constructive (rather than merely disruptive and destructive) the critique requires an explicit ontology as a point of comparison with any theory and way of investigating the world.

Here, the transition to a substantive ontology as a resource has sometimes caused unease amongst economists. It can appear as though a fixed prior or 'foundational' body of theory, smuggled in as a 'here is reality', is simply being imposed upon the field as a standard to which all else must conform. The impression can be given that this is imperialism for economics, as problematic in its own way as economics imperialism. There are two relevant responses here. First, as an invitation to consider general aspects of knowledge in terms of critique, social ontology is intended as a dialogue within a domain of argument. In this sense, proponents of social ontology are merely claiming that it is important not to neglect this domain of argument, since it provides one (not the only) appropriate arena for dialogue. There is no assumption in modern philosophy that foundationalism is tenable. Second, a substantive ontology need not be 'news from nowhere'. For example, the one that is set out in the next section, commonly termed critical realism (though various other terms have been applied),[1] derives from engagement with recognized problems of fields of study. It is not a form of rationalism, where an isolated philosopher explores the content of their own mind in search of indisputable truths. It is a response to tensions in knowledge claims and pre-existing disciplinary and philosophical positions that seek to justify or shape those knowledge claims. As such, it is a collection of general claims regarding reality – an ontology – derived from the analysis of problem sets (conceptual and/or evidential). The general question form, 'What must be the case for x?' is a conditional one where the 'must' arises from argument and can be disputed. It follows then that a substantive social ontology is no more fixed or immune to critique or change than any other body of theory. In practice, to a large degree the process of critique is the source of a social ontology. So it further follows that, based on the ontological implications of problems and failures, the development of a given social ontology can provide more than critique only.

Ultimately, social ontology should matter because the combination of critique in a domain of argument and of a substantive ontology, derived from recognized problems, provides a multifaceted 'under-labouring' service for any particular field of study. In so doing it can provide a ready response to two forms of scepticism regarding ontology. First, the often-heard comment that this is just philosophy and I have actual economics to get on with. This position is no more tenable than the modern neglect of the history of economic thought or of pluralism in economics. It leads directly to practitioners falling short in terms of the statement of the obvious that this section began with. Second, the sometimes-heard comment that an economist's approach already has a fully formed philosophical position or perspective or worldview, and does not require another one. An explicit social ontology is not necessarily some alien artefact. Substantive social ontology derives from problem sets and can provide a constructive generalization of commonalities between disciplinary approaches or schools of thought, as well as a focus on differences and potential problems. Here, various issues can be reconsidered from new perspectives. Social ontology challenges us to consider our commitments and provides constructive yet contingent insights for theory and practice.[2] With this in mind I now set out the key concepts for a critical realist social ontology. I say 'for' because the best way to set out the line of reasoning by which the social ontology is constructed is to briefly begin from issues arising in terms of natural science. This provides clarity and prevents misunderstanding.

## 1.3    KEY CONCEPTS FOR A CRITICAL REALIST SOCIAL ONTOLOGY

### Philosophy and the Epistemic Fallacy

Critical realism emerged in response to a core problem in the philosophy of science.[3] Empiricism, the claim that all knowledge is derived from sense experience, and then positivism, the claim that knowledge can be developed or refined according to particular strict criteria, had resulted in an approach to science that focuses on the product of scientific practice (the statement of laws) and on forms of testing for the validity of laws (in general, verification and confirmation, subject to the hypothetico-deductive model or the inductive-probabilistic model). Popper's falsification reversed the significance of testing but maintained the same focus on the product (the statement of laws). A number of philosophers, most notably Rom Harré and Roy Bhaskar, began to question this focus in the 1970s. A stated law remains always contingent because knowledge is fallible. Testing criteria seek to express the certainty of that law and thus cannot fulfil the function for which they are devised. Moreover, it requires particular conditions to observe or express the law, and these are often artificial, constructed by the scientist. This led Bhaskar to ask: what is it that makes science, including the work that leads to the statement of laws, manifestly fruitful and yet also incomplete? More specifically, what is it about the nature of reality that makes laboratory experiment necessary in order to express some forms of law-like activity? The scientist is not simply producing arbitrary activity, they are isolating aspects of a more complex reality to observe particularized relations and effects.

For Harré and for Bhaskar, positivism had misunderstood the practice of science and the significance of this practice, and in so doing it had produced a false understanding, affecting how we think about the significance of knowledge in terms of reality. The emphasis had been placed on the statement of the laws, and the test of the laws, focused around their repeated expression as outcomes. Laws were thus expressed as 'constant conjunctions' of the form 'whenever x then y', observed in events. But any observation of reality tells us that one rarely encounters this kind of regularity in events. It typically requires intervention in order to produce the conditions for regularity. Positivism, therefore, had set up an impossible measure of knowledge for science. It had done so by seeking something that would not typically be found in reality, even though the underlying activity being investigated, properly conceived, remained insightful and important (we are capable of manipulating the world based on the understanding of principles). According to Bhaskar, positivism had committed an 'epistemic fallacy'; it had confused an issue of ontology or the nature of reality with an issue of epistemology or the nature of how we can know something about reality. Bhaskar essentially argued that by investigating the failure of the epistemology in the light of scientific practice one could infer something about the nature of reality in terms of which the failure had occurred. Harré made the case that what science was investigating was the powers of entities that are then expressed in complex ways, and Bhaskar developed this focus to make the ontological case that reality has 'depth'.

**Depth Realism**

One can make sense of Table 1.1 in the following way.[4] Time does not stop and we live in a continual flow of events. However, we can pause to consider that flow of events. The first thing to note is that not everything that occurs is experienced. As such, experience is a subset of events that occur. The flow of events, moreover, is a series of expressions of what could have occurred. Until they occur, events are merely potential outcomes. For them to be potential there must be something that can give rise to the event, and this is the powers or capacities of entities and structuring processes. The multiplicity of powers or capacities of entities, and of a mix of different entities, can be conceptualized as generative mechanisms or structuring processes that cause things to occur as events. One can, therefore, make sense of a reality that we experience as relatively stable much of the time, and in which we are able to knowingly intervene to attempt to manifest given outcomes. Events may rarely be regular (in the 'whenever x then y' sense of a constant conjunction) but they are not thereby, when properly understood, uncaused or simply arbitrary.

Consider this in terms of laboratory experiment. Laboratory experiment creates controlled situations in which given entities are deliberately isolated in order to express particular powers as events to be observed (often with the aid of technological

*Table 1.1   Depth realism*

| Domains ⇒<br>Related distinctions<br>⇓ | Real | Actual | Empirical |
|---|---|---|---|
| Mechanism | • | | |
| Event | • | • | |
| Experience | • | • | • |

augmentation). Laboratory experiment is a deliberate bringing together of experience, event, and generative mechanism. That the three can be brought together is a strong indication that there are structured entities and structuring processes with powers. Moreover, the necessity of intervention to align the three and express an isolated relation of causation is also a strong indication that there is more to reality than the isolation might imply. It is then also a strong indication that it is an error to conflate experience, event and generative mechanism, as an always experienced and definite outcome, as though that is a sufficient conception of reality – a constant conjunction – merely because the three can be brought together.[5] In order to avoid this conflation, critical realism then distinguishes three domains of reality. There is an empirical domain of what is experienced, and this is a subset of the actual or what occurs as events, and this is an expression of what could occur based on the powers or capacities of relevant entities operating as generative mechanisms in complex ways. Note here that the empirical and the actual are also real. The distinction is between domains of reality. The distinction is to prevent a conflation and to allow further consideration of the ways in which each may be real. For example, experience may be real in the sense that it occurs for people and has consequences for their conduct thereafter, but it is not necessarily a true or complete account of given events. This brings us to a further distinction.

**The Stratification of Reality and Emergence**

The example of laboratory science has been used to make the initial ontological distinction between experience, events and generative mechanisms. Clearly, there are many kinds of scientific practice and many subject domains of natural science, such as physics, chemistry, and biology, as well as of social science. This creates the further issue of in what sense each refers to a different aspect of reality. According to critical realism, reality has both depth and strata. Strata refer to the possible order of aspects of reality, and stratification is a claim that is contingent on the findings of science. Physics investigates the basic principles of relation of energy and particles, chemistry investigates the properties of combinations of particular atoms and molecules, biology investigates aspects of organic life and so on. A biological entity cannot exist without atoms or molecules, and atoms or molecules are constituted on the basis of relations of energy and particles. Each then would seem to refer to a more basic aspect of reality. However, it does not thereby follow that any given aspect can be reduced to another. A biological entity does not break principles of chemistry since it is chemically constituted, and nor does it break laws of physics. However, one cannot explore all significant aspects of biology in terms of chemistry or physics without doing violence to our understanding of biological entities. For example, the behaviour of a cow is not solely describable as a process of digestion of grass, nor of the energy exchange of mitochondria within processes rooted in the laws of thermodynamics. This insight then leads to the concept of emergence.

Emergence is the concept that there are powers, capacities, or identifiable features of given specifiable entities that cannot be reduced to the powers and capacities of their parts. Rather, the arrangement of the parts creates further emergent properties that only exist insofar as the arrangement continues. Clearly, there is a great deal of scope here for debate concerning what is a specifiable emergent entity, since any given emergent entity could also then be considered a part of a greater whole. However, insofar as emergence is a defensible concept, then the issue is one of empirical dispute (the identification of non-reducible powers and so forth). The key point remains that in order to prevent what seems an empirically untenable reduction of all entities to some primary unit that fully accounts for all aspects of properties and causal processes, a genuine whole must be more than simply an epiphenomena of the parts.

It should also be clear here that the concept of strata and that of emergence provide further conceptual insight when thinking about the significance of depth reality. Insofar as events occur, then aspects of many generative mechanisms of different emergent entities may be involved, and, concomitantly, powers may be exercised or expressed that can be investigated in terms of different strata. The concepts of strata and of emergence can be used to focus on different aspects of events because they allow us to consider different generative mechanisms and to do so in different ways. This returns us to the point that emergent entities are not 'breaking' laws identifiable in terms of different strata, they are acting according to particular powers and capacities that may also be conditioned by different strata. The multiplicity and complexity here would seem to be an important reason why the reality we experience is not regular in a constant conjunction sense, and this brings us to the concept of an open system. This is a concept best introduced via the problem of closed systems.

**Closed and Open Systems**

From a critical realist perspective, the major identified error in positivism is that it tacitly assumes an automatic and continued coincidence of a given individual generative mechanism, events expressing that mechanism, and our experience of them. In so doing it commits an epistemic fallacy. By seeking constant conjunctions in events, which can be stated as significant laws, it makes constant conjunctions the necessary measure of adequate knowledge. This focus then becomes the core of an implicit ontology and the question can then be asked: what kind of reality would make this approach to knowledge appropriate or successful? This brings us back to the coincidence of isolated mechanisms and events that can then be observed. For such a situation to pertain then a system must be 'closed'. It must exhibit an 'intrinsic' closure, that is, the given event y must always follow from the mechanism x; and it must exhibit an 'extrinsic' closure, that is, the system must be separated from external influences that would affect the intrinsic closure, and that would create irregularity.

To be clear, the point being made here is that reality would have to be intrinsically and extrinsically closed for a constant conjunction focus to be adequate (sufficient to fully explore the nature of reality). A reality of this kind would be one where there could be neither irregularity in events or the possibility of genuine change. It would be 'atomistic': that is, involving the repetitive association of x and y in isolation. If one tried to imagine such a reality, it would be one of individualized systems reduced to hermetically sealed permanently cycling sets of separated x and y relations. It would be a multiplicity of non-interactive monads. Clearly, no one would attempt to defend such a position regarding reality, and as such one might think a straw man was being constructed here. This, however, is not the case. The ontological implications are an unintended consequence of the epistemological focus. Recall that the original warrant for a focus on ontology was the argument that approaches to knowledge can lose sight of the core issue of realism in various ways.

A discipline, for example, can develop whilst still notionally adhering to the idea that it does investigate reality in some sense, and yet fail to do so adequately because it does not recognize or address its basic problems of realism, and this may be precisely because the discipline continues to be shaped by a problematic philosophy of science. A discipline strongly influenced by positivism, for example, might attempt to adapt its knowledge claims and practices to the experienced irregularity of events, but do so whilst preserving the focus on constant conjunctions, and might consider this to be 'good science'. So, models might be constructed as closed systems that can express an isolated repeating constant conjunction. The model might require ideal assumptions (of a kind that do not just hold other effects at bay but are actually impossible or false) that separate out the conjunction. Caveats may be applied to the model – it is a partial or limited expression that may or may not have real-world significance as it is – whilst the model is still used as the basis of understanding and further insight.

One might also develop more or less sophisticated approaches to constant conjunctions. Exogeneity may be allowed for, and the constant conjunction may be between several xs and a y or a range of possible ys, and this may be expressed stochastically. But consider what is being done here. Allowing for exogeneity is to model distortions and deviations for the constant conjunction, whilst preserving the central and perpetual significance of the constant conjunction. Stochastics meanwhile produce patterned variation rather than genuine irregularity or novelty; that is, stochastics are typically limited to prior definable separated causal links and to changes of state rather than open-ended transformations of relations and things.[6]

Again, one is preserving the focus on the 'whenever x then y' and so one is perpetuating the fundamental problem of the epistemic fallacy, which distorts everything else. Moreover, in neither case is closure genuinely put aside, it is merely adjusted. The important underlying and general point is that a process of preservation of the approach to knowledge claims can dominate the development of a field because one does not stop to reconsider the original problem, and it is here that ontology is useful or insightful. From the perspective of ontology, rather than seeking to preserve the nature of a knowledge claim as a primary (if sometimes tacit) goal, one ought first to ask: what seems to be an appropriate conceptualization of reality about which knowledge claims can then be made? It is from the ontological focus that the concept of an open system then follows.

Reality does not seem to typically be one of strict regularity expressed in events; rather, it seems to be one in which we experience relatively stable but also irregular events. The failures of a constant conjunction approach based on closed systems then allow us to infer that reality may be more adequately represented by an ontology of open systems. An open system is one in which there are many generative mechanisms and thus the continual possibility that similar events are brought about through different mixes, and where there is also the converse possibility that variations in events may occur because of different mixes. An open system is one that allows for the possibility of both relative stability in events but also degrees of irregularity; it allows for the possibility of complex causation; it recognizes the possibility of basic uncertainty of outcomes; and the possibility that there can be qualitative changes to aspects of the system that then result in transformations of that system, so there can be change within and change from a given system to something else. An open system is thus potentially 'dynamic', and it may then also be emergent and a source of further emergence.[7] It is, as such, radically different in conception from a closed system concept expressed through a constant conjunction focus.

A constant conjunction focus cannot allow for irregularity and thus can only approximate or track relative stability in a highly conditioned way, and then breaks down, must be reconceived, or adjusted, or becomes irrelevant under circumstances of irregularity. An open system approach, meanwhile, can accommodate the situations in which a constant conjunction approach may be relevant, but goes beyond this. An open system is still recognizably a 'system' because it exhibits organization whose characteristics and complex mixes (including in terms of stratification) can be explored. For the concept of an open system to be meaningful as a 'system' there must be something substantively connected and at least relatively enduring to explore and thus to use as the focus for explanatory endeavour; openness does not simply mean absence of explicable aspects – there may be degrees of openness, but a fully open system would be conceptually incoherent since by definition it would not be a system.[8] Thereafter, what makes a particular system 'open' depends on the nature of the significant powers of its aspects; that is, what are the sources of its generative mechanisms and how do these arise and how do they manifest in events? This brings us more specifically to social ontology and the issue of social science.

**Agency, Structure, and Historical Process (the Transformational Model of Social Activity, and Morphogenesis)**

Starting from issues arising in terms of natural science may give the impression that critical realism simply transposes natural science issues into the context of society and for social science in some unadulterated fashion. This is not the case. Rather, it was in response to problems created by such a transposition that critical realism (and others with a family resemblance) developed a social ontology. More specifically, a critique in terms of problems of realism was manifestly relevant for the social sciences because of the transmission of characteristics of positivism to the social sciences and because of some of the response to this. The adoption by the social sciences of a positivist approach to knowledge created a focus on identifying constant conjunctions in different aspects of society and a concomitant and overwhelming focus on methods that identified, expressed, or tested constant conjunctions. Positivism led to a particular focus on quantity and measurement, subject to forms of hypothesis testing, as the gold standard of social science research.[9] Positivism in the social sciences thus arrogated status and prestige from the natural sciences, but did so based on positivism's already existing errors in representing the natural sciences: an epistemic fallacy leading to a focus on atomistic relations as isolated constant conjunctions in events and indicative of a closed system. This was not the application of science to society to create social science, but rather scientism. Some responses to this approach, however, emphasized that society was not explicable in terms of the positivist project. Humans, unlike electrons, think and change their mind; they have an interior world that affects their exterior activity and one must understand this interior world to appreciate and explore social significance. This then led to the counterposing of forms of phenomenology, hermeneutics, and social construction to positivism.[10]

From a critical realist position, and considering the social sciences in general, the rejection of positivism by hermeneutics and similar positions had created a false split between natural science and the exploration of society. The hermeneutic critique conflated positivism and natural science, as though positivism was an adequate account of nature but inappropriate for society; in so doing it failed to consider what was both ontologically similar and different about the rest of reality and the human being and their situation. From a critical realist position this is about the nature of generative mechanisms and powers of entities; that is, the emergent and stratified elements of social reality, which make it a distinct area of study. Here, the core ontological concepts were developed in terms of recognized problems of methodological individualism and structuralism, voluntarism and determinism, freedom and necessity, or what is typically termed the agent–structure problem, rooted in Marx's well-known statement in the 'Eighteenth Brumaire' that 'Men make their own history, but they do not make it just as they please; they do not make it under circumstances chosen by themselves; but under circumstances directly encountered, given and transmitted from the past' (Marx 1852 [1950], p. 225).

According to critical realism, agents and structures are analytically distinct. Structure consists in developed forms (expressed materially, technologically, organizationally, and so forth) infused with primarily concept-dependent social relations, which provide material (in the broadly Aristotelian sense of contextual) causation that serves to influence what seems possible, what is done, how it is done, and under what general institutional rubrics. Agents occupy roles or positions in social relations and draw upon them to engage in particular activity, creating effective causation. Agents are intelligent interpretive beings, and have reasons for acting as they do, of which they may in any particular instance be more or less conscious, depending on how they are socialized and the degree to which reflexivity is applied to any given situation. Agents act under multiple influences and may have a wide range of reasons for acting. As such, events are not typically a result of a constant conjunction situation, and outcomes can be highly variable. At the same time, there can often be a general stability to contexts and outcomes, social structure often develops to achieve particular goals and ensure some security in terms of those goals, so generalized reproduction of structure through the activity of agents is not untypical (moreover, choice can be constrained and sometimes highly limited because social relations are also power relations: in capitalism one typically works for wages to survive and cannot refuse all employment). However, structural reproduction is not typically the reason for the activity of the agent (one does not work in order to reproduce the corporation or use money in order to reproduce the medium of exchange or the banking system, but one must have a concept of money as an institutional form for both). Reproduction, then, can be an everyday unintended consequence of activity, but equally changes brought about by activity (including the reflexivity of the human) can transform structure, and this could be gradual or rapid. Bhaskar (1979), for example, originally refers to the social ontology as the transformational model of social activity (TMSA), in which the individual is socialized but then also acts back to reproduce or transform the conditions of that socialization (see Figure 1.1).

The sociologist Margaret Archer (1995, 2000, 2003) then provides an important additional point of emphasis for this social ontology.[11] Archer emphasizes the significance of time (see also Patomaki 2011). The process is one of interaction, and this happens in time and in recognizable phases. When agents do (or fail to do) something they do so in the context of the products of previous cycles of activity, which provide a context of

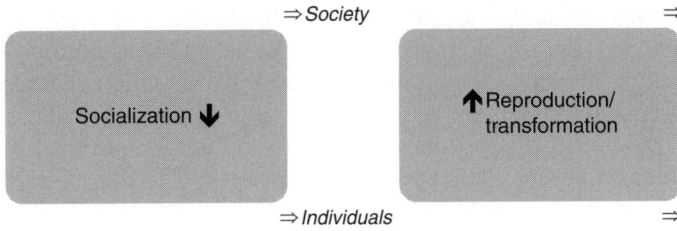

*Figure 1.1   Transformational model of social activity*

structural conditioning in terms of which the activity occurs ($T^1$). Structure is deemed to be real because it has distinct emergent properties: it is a means by which things are conceived and done, and thus both constrains and enables agency in specific ways.[12] These conditions remain relevant through interactions engaged by agents ($T^2$ to $T^3$) and the agent is deemed to be distinct from structure insofar as they also have emergent properties (moving, doing, thinking, deliberating, believing, intending, loving, cooperating, and so forth) that are applied to the conditions of structure. The product over the time of interaction may then be relative reproduction of structure (and also, by degree, of the agent's sense of self in different contexts), that is, 'morphostatis'; or some more fundamental transformation, that is, 'morphogenesis' (in either case there is a $T^4$ that can then become the source of another cycle) (Figure 1.2). What Archer brings to the fore here is that the separation of agency and structure is a necessary conceptualization because each has different emergent properties, and because if the separation is not acknowledged,

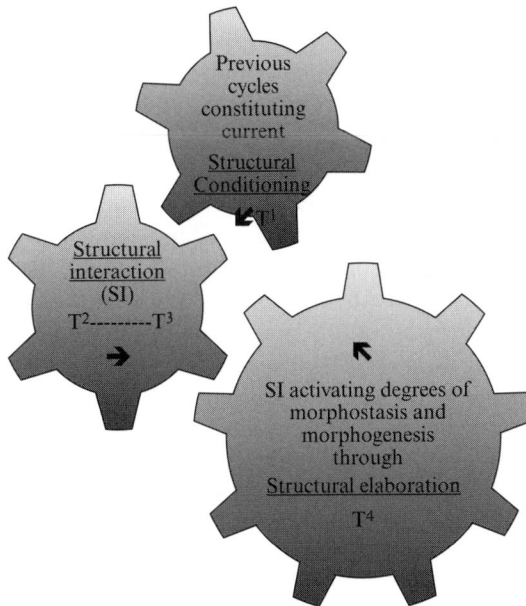

*Figure 1.2   Archer's temporal cycles: morphostasis/morphogenesis*

then it becomes difficult to explore interactions as occurrences or events in time (that is, as subject to process). The ontology also emphasizes the relative duration of the grounds of events and emphasizes that the grounds are historical (extending backwards in a significant sense) as well as ongoing.

The specific generative mechanisms of structure and agency can then be explored, in terms of different geographies and over different periods. This follows from the historical nature of processes: they need not be universal or uniform in space and time. Open systems can be explored at different scales in terms of different aspects.[13] It is thus possible to have many different varieties of investigation of given social reality. An economist, therefore, is one who studies the economy as an aspect of a broader social reality and can do so by investigating different aspects of the economy in a variety of ways, based on different motivating questions and foci.

**Critical Realist Social Ontology and Economics**

It is important to emphasize at this point that critical realism is a general social ontology and not a school of thought in economics. It is not intended to be a replacement for groups of substantive theorizations that seek to explain and explore aspects of an economy. There is no critical realist economics in this sense. Critical realism remains an under-labouring approach in the sense set out in section 1.1 regarding social ontology. It has a variety of proponents with diverse interests in theory (see Fleetwood 1999; Lewis 2004). Its most well-known long-standing proponent is Tony Lawson (see 1997, 2003), a founding member of the Cambridge Social Ontology Group, which has served as a place for the discussion and dissemination of social ontology in economics for many years.[14] Nuno Martins (2014) has subsequently made the case that the work in social ontology is part of a broader 'Cambridge tradition', encompassing Keynes, Sraffa, Robinson, Sen, and others. The core of the social ontology articulated by Lawson and others is that an economy is an aspect of a social reality that exhibits emergence and is characteristically a dynamic open system of a historical-process form in which change is cumulative through social interaction. Whilst this is not a substantive theory of an economy for economists it does have implications for economic theorization.

One of the under-labouring claims made by Lawson is that heterodox economists (see Lee 2009) are united by a common, and sometimes only implicit, open systems ontology (Lawson 2006). According to Lawson it is this, expressed in different ways, which differentiates heterodoxy from mainstream economics. Mainstream economics is dominated by approaches whose underlying ontology is based on deductivism in which constant conjunctions (including through stochastics) are the focus. Theory and practice are thus built around closed systems and use ideal assumptions and ahistorical categories (that deform real-world investigations, including any subsequent approach to structure in terms of history and institutions) to facilitate closure. It is because of this basic mismatch with social reality that the mainstream exhibits persistent explanatory failure, a failure that becomes more noticeable and controversial during periods of significant change.[15]

Heterodox approaches, by contrast, focus on different aspects of open systems.[16] So, classical political economists focus on the conditions of reproduction of the economic surplus, including the significance of its distribution; old institutionalists might focus on the constraining and enabling dynamics of institution formation and their consequences;

feminist economists might focus on patriarchy; Marxists on class relations in the reproduction and development of capitalism; Keynesians and post-Keynesians on the vulnerabilities in relations of production, consumption, investment, and employment; finance system economists on the creation of money in a fiat system dominated by the credit–debt powers of private banking and subject to a complex institutional web of financialization; eco-economists might focus on the complex relations between the economy and the sustaining environment in which it is embedded; and so forth.

Here, the claim is that underlying aspects of social ontology unite heterodox diversity, just as they differentiate heterodoxy from the mainstream. This then implies a form of relativism for heterodox knowledge claims, in the sense that there are many ways to adequately investigate an economy. This, however, is subject to a constructive pluralism (for issues see, for example, Dow 2000, 2008). Any theory or approach may be improved based on continued research and based on the primary tenet that the world can be more or less adequately investigated. It may also be that any given theory or approach is superseded because more adequate ways of investigating its key issues are developed or because the world simply changes in its significant aspects (for example, new forms of emergence). For improvement or supersession of theory to occur effectively then diversity within economics needs to be more than simply tolerance of different positions: it ought also to be critically engaged across positions. So, there is a curious tension in the development of economics as knowledge, from a heterodox point of view. Social ontology provides a domain for dialogue and critique, diversity within heterodoxy provides many potentially adequate ways of investigating an economy, all approaches may become more adequate in terms of investigating some aspect of an economy as social reality (and may also be superseded), and one way in which each might develop is through evidence, critique, and dialogue provided by other branches of heterodoxy. This process involves also further conceptual development and critique of issues in social ontology, including of critical realism, since ontology is theory and not reality (see, e.g., Boylan and O'Gorman 1995; Brown 2007; Chick and Dow 2005; Dow 2004; Fullbrook 2009; Milonakis and Fine 2009; Mohun and Veneziani 2012; J. Morgan 2012; Nielsen and Morgan 2006).

Constructive pluralism is then also a basis by which a problem of judgemental relativism, a simple 'anything goes', is rejected. Instead, there is a loose normative commitment to a form of 'judgemental rationality': the active pursuit of the possibility that competing knowledge claims can be reasoned out in terms of their justifications, and can then perhaps also be moved beyond. In practice such judgemental rationality is an open-ended process, rather than something that can be considered complete. It requires a community of scholars who do more than pay lip service to the possibility that others may identify errors in their work and that the world may simply confound their previous best efforts. The commitment is simple to state but it would be simplistic to suggest that the commitment is easily realized. One of the important insights that social ontology also brings to economics is that economics is knowledge as a social product and the economics discipline is also a system of sorts.

A closed system ontology is not just expressed in the theory and practice of mainstream economics; it is reproduced through the activity of mainstream economists. This has had consequences for the marginalization of heterodox economics (e.g., Lee et al. 2013). It has also meant that one can explore the way in which the mainstream has historically developed. There are many ways to do this and not all of them are about ontology (see Mohun and Veneziani 2012), but one can note the way that the initial recognition that economics was a subject with great potential in terms of a focus on definable quantities and measurements (trade, prices, outputs, costs, employment, and so forth) made it highly conducive to translation into a mathematically oriented subject (see Lawson 2003, Ch. 10). One might consider this important because the mainstream has translated the use of quantities into the dominance of quantification. This is exhibited in terms of methods (an overwhelming focus on econometrics), the expression of theory (typically stated in symbolic form, and developed as mathematical proofs of theorems), and also the presumption that model building, testing, and application are core to the economist's skill set (so attempts to incorporate structures, institutions, processes, differentials, and so on must be made compatible with this core).

The key point here is that the reproduction of this dominance of quantification serves to reproduce a closed system ontology and so one might also note that the mainstream, though it may exhibit some changes, is also conformist. It cannot easily be constructively pluralist in a way that is also genuinely committed to judgemental rationality, and this is not an additional point to the argument for ontology in economics, it is one that can be made through thinking in terms of ontology – if one considers economics as a knowledge product. This brings us to the issue of methodology and methods, following from matters of social ontology.

**Economics, Methodology, and Methods**

Heterodox economics is not simply an attempt to defend and advocate long-standing schools of thought and theorizations. It is a living body of inquiry that draws critically on existing schools and theorizations, but also develops others. Social reality is only relatively enduring in its forms and so new problems and issues arise and old ones wane. One way that mainstream economics has dealt with this problem is by emptying itself of substantive content, becoming a set of idealized ahistorical universals, reductively applicable everywhere but genuinely relevant nowhere: the rational actor, the game player, the utility maximizer under conditions of constraint, and so forth. This, and the transferability of model building, has provided an important basis for economics imperialism (see M. Morgan 2012; Fine and Milonakis 2009). The heterodox approach is quite different: rather than the ontology undermining any attempt to be continually relevant, the ontology recognizes that relevance is about engaging with a changing and multifaceted world and requires both that theory encompasses change and that theory can also be restructured around a changing world. This is extremely difficult to do if one starts from a closed system ontology. An open system ontology provides a more consistent point of departure for methodology and for methods (see Danermark et al. 2002; Carter and New 2004).

Methodology is often, but should not be, confused or conflated with research methods (see Frauley and Pearce 2007, p. 9; Olsen and Morgan 2005; Sayer 1992). Methodology is an overall research strategy. It is imbued with a research perspective that shapes how the research process is understood and how different methods are used, and the sense that is made of their use. A research method is a given technique of data collection and processing. Methods may be qualitative or quantitative, or involve stages such as quantitative processing of qualitative data (Olsen 2012). Methodologies in practice may involve the use of only one method or selection from only one type of method (a restricted mix) or may involve different types of methods (a broad mix). In standard research method texts methodology is familiarly stated in inductive or deductive terms and typically subject to broadly positivist understandings of how knowledge is acquired and processed (such as hypothesis testing of large data sets) or as subject to phenomenological understandings of how knowledge is acquired and processed (such as detailed interpretive explorations of case studies and interviews, or significant forms of participant observation).

Heterodoxy, as an empirically oriented endeavour, is not restricted to standard methodology and selection of methods (see Downward 2003). It is possible that one simply absorbs the general ontology and uses it intuitively as the basis of research, producing work rooted in open systems (e.g., Morgan 2009). Equally, one might develop an explicit methodology and justification of methods. A heterodox approach to research methods is diverse, different methods can be used and multiple methods can be used. This, however, is not arbitrary or random – the throwing of methods at data and the compiling and processing of data through any available method (see, e.g., Byrne 2013). It is a structured process of iterative engagement, partly reliant on the growing competency and insight of the researcher and a community of researchers. This can involve exploratory and experimental use of methods in particular circumstances that can then be refined or abandoned. The point of departure, in the broadest sense, is the nature of the empirical problem, conceived in terms of an open systems ontology. This is not empiricism in disguise but rather recognition that there are real-world problems to be addressed by theory and through investigation. The ultimate guide is the explanatory success provided by the use of methods and based on some given methodology. As a matter of consistency, from an open systems point of view, there can be no a priori exclusion of methods, though there can be the gradual development of reliance upon particular methods in given circumstances based on the insights they provide. This, however, is a phased a posteriori process.

The main restriction on methodology is whether in practice it provides for explanatory success. Tentatively, this involves the anticipation that the methodology is appropriate as a means of investigating and building theory in regard of an open systems social reality with emergent features, relatively enduring structures, and ways of proceeding by conscious agents, and which exhibits historical and geographical diversity. Research must be in a sense historical, involve an understanding of agents, and of persons, of the institutions in which they are immersed, and of the facilitating and constraining role of structures of social relations and structures of such structures. It must be sensitive to the complexity of causation; that relative stability may disguise some quantitative and qualitative changes that are cumulatively changing the way in which events are currently unfolding and relative reproduction is occurring (the dynamics of depth realism in the context of social reality).

Any or all of the above could become a focus or emphasis for research, and do so at different scales. One might, for example, focus on types of individual within the household, the household, the consumer, the firm, the supply chain, a market, markets, the state in its various roles, the employee, labour, trade, the economic sector, the economy, or capitalism. One might be exploring dynamics or focusing on a particular phenomenon (some -ism or concept dependency such as money) or narrowing down to a particular kind of agent or form of agency, or of significant identity, but always with a sense of the broader context. Given the issue of potential complexity in open systems, an important general point here is the need to identify some cut-off point to delineate the research without damaging the potential insights of the research. This implies a need to justify the limits of the focus and also implies the potential use of abstraction, carefully distinguished from idealization (see Sayer 1992).

The basic point here is that one adapts and develops research to the nature of the problem under investigation and to the type of research question one is asking in terms of that investigation. As a general point this hardly seems controversial. It seems no more a matter of common sense than the statement in section 1.1 that any science, including a social science such as economics, ought to be about reality, the nature of reality ought to make a difference to how we study it and what we then claim about it as a form of knowledge.

Essentially, the basic point is simply a methodological specification of this statement. It may, therefore, seem uncontroversial, but considered in the context of economics it is extremely significant. Mainstream economics is heavily reliant on a narrow range of methods, and many economics departments do not teach philosophy and methodology as part of research training or introduce the postgraduate to a range of possible methods – particularly qualitative methods and more innovative ways of processing data (NVivo, QCA, network analysis, and so on).[17] As such, they simply reproduce a focus on a narrow range of technical skills that then become the basis by which research is typically done, because researchers are unaware of the alternatives or lack the competency in them. They become by default methods a priori and thus irrespective of other possibilities, rather than arise and are renewed a posteriori. So one might note that many economists are simply incapable of approaching the basic point above in an open and creative way.

Heterodoxy, by contrast, is receptive to methodological range and to mixed methods because of, and insofar as it takes seriously, an open systems ontology. Various approaches to methodology have been suggested that go beyond the inductive–deductive and positivist–phenomenological splits. These have included abduction, retroduction and retrodiction, contrast explanation and grounded theory.

Abduction, following Peirce, is a form of inference, usually distinguished from deduction and induction. As a form of reasoning with a logical structure the key difference is that deduction is based on premises from which the conclusions then necessarily follow, while induction is based on premises that are then exceeded by the conclusions, but where the conclusions are not stated as an explanation from the premises, and abduction is a form in which the conclusions also exceed the premises, but where an inference is also made to the best explanation of the situation under scrutiny. In terms of research the difference is usually stated in terms of the context of theory: deduction starts from theory, induction builds theory (but does so based on frequencies), and abduction focuses on a range of explanations included as theory, and considers them in some context of justification for elimination. Abduction is less 'rigorous' in the formal sense of a logical construct and in the range of possible ways one might distinguish between explanations. It is, however, a closer fit with the complexity of an open system, since it embraces the possibility of irregularity and of many forms of potential evidence, and thus also the use of many different methods, as deemed appropriate.

Retroduction and retrodiction are often discussed in the same terms as abduction, but starting from an explicit open systems ontology. They involve the identification of some generative mechanism and an attempt to account for the form of that generative mechanism, drawing on a range of possible formulations that extend to a role for metaphor and analogy (the abstract phase of retroduction), but which also then involve empirical investigation subject to some devised tests of the plausibility of the account; an iterative process of investigation (or retrodiction) from which some ways of viewing the problem are eliminated (see Bhaskar 1979, p. 15).

Contrast explanation provides another alternative strategy that starts explicitly from an open systems perspective (Lawson 2003, pp. 86–109). Contrast explanation starts from how a research focus arises or is motivated: the economist observes an unexpected or unusual event or series of events, and that may mean an unexpected degree of continuity or stability, or some degree of change. The capacity to make such an observation implies a competent economist immersed in real-world problems, a degree of acquired and oriented expertise, and the observation invites the question 'Why x rather than y?', where the contrast is to the possibilities that did not arise or were not realized in some given time and place. This can then be rooted in terms of contrasts with what has occurred under apparently similar circumstances in the past or some comparable location, providing some degree of specification for understanding and explaining the basis of events as they have occurred, and could have occurred, and also, tentatively, for what may occur (since one may be identifying underlying changes to the reproduction of what appears to currently be expressed as relative stability; for example, Morgan 2013). Again, this is an approach with a wide degree of latitude.

Grounded theory is an attempt to provide a more programmatic or specified form of open systems investigation and is set out in Chapter 2 of this *Handbook* (see also Lee 2012). The key point to take forward here is that all the stated forms of approaches to methodology are compatible with or are located within an open systems ontology and allow for a more creative use of mixed methods. Insofar as they are oriented towards realism (in the philosophical-empirical sense) they also allow for the possibility of triangulation (Olsen 2004).

## 1.4   CONCLUSION

Social ontology provides important under-labouring functions for economics. It provides a relevant domain of argument in terms of which continued critique of the realism of economics can occur. It provides a domain in which substantive ontologies can be constructed in terms of problem sets arising in social science and in economics specifically. One might argue that heterodoxy is united by a common open systems ontology and is also distinguished from mainstream economics by this ontology. However, one needs to be careful in regard of what is claimed for and from ontology. Ontology is still, in a general sense, theory, and so must also be treated with some degree of scepticism and critique. It is also not a replacement for substantive theory in economics; it is not itself a school of thought in economics. It does have implications for methodology and for methods. Those implications, however, are positive – an opening up – rather than negative, since the basic point is that economics can legitimately be more creative in its methodology and broader based in its use of methods. This is illustrated throughout this book. As a final point I would also note that the claim regarding methodology and methods leaves a major point of controversy untouched. Mainstream economics is often, as it is here, criticized for its formalism and for its overwhelming reliance on quantitative methods, and especially the use of econometrics. This raises the issue of whether quantitative methods are still relevant if one rejects the mainstream approach. There is a tendency to assume that critical realists in particular reject quantitative methods, but this is not the case. There is some degree of disagreement regarding the relative use of them, rather than a rejection of them (see, e.g., Lawson 2003; Downward 2003; Fullbrook 2009). As a matter of ontological consistency one cannot reject them a priori. Lawson, who is most closely associated with scepticism regarding formalism and econometrics, states:

> I hope by now the highly conditional nature of my criticism is apparent. It is not, and has never been, my intention to oppose the use of formalistic methods in themselves. My primary opposition, rather, is to the manner in which they are everywhere imposed, to the insistence on their being almost universally wielded, irrespective of, and prior to, considerations of explanatory relevance, and in the face of repeated failures. (Lawson 2003, p. xix)

There are two underlying issues here. First, whether the way in which quantitative methods are used and understood allows methods that are based on closed systems to be insightful in terms of a dynamic open system. Put another way: does recognition in terms of an ontological critique facilitate the continued use of methods – are they then contributions to an explanatory investigation? Second, whether all quantitative methods assume or rely on or identify, express, and test some form of constant conjunction as a closed system. If not, are they subject to the ontological critique? Again, different contributors to this text have different opinions on this. I would just suggest here that the very fact that debate is occurring in regard of this is a major advance for economics, since it is, as Lawson suggests, the non-reflexive default to given quantitative methods that provides one of the major grounds for critique of economics. Much of the rest of this book is taken up with related issues and demonstrations.

## NOTES

\*   Thanks to Fred Lee and Tony Lawson for comments on this chapter.
1.   For example, Roy Bhaskar uses the term 'transcendental realism' in *A Realist Theory of Science* (1975), which addresses issues surrounding the philosophy of science; the term 'critical naturalism' in *The Possibility of Naturalism* (1979), which addresses issues in the social sciences; and the catch-all term 'critical realism' in the later collection of essays *Reclaiming Reality* (1989). Bhaskar also has his own taxonomy of phases of critical realism, though that need not concern us here. In general, many proponents of similar positions use the term 'scientific realism' (though there is of course also a degree of differentiation and critical dialogue between specific positions).
2.   One does not need to be a follower of Nietzsche to acknowledge that often 'Convictions are more dangerous enemies of truth than are lies' (Nietzsche 1995, Ch. 9,#483, p. 264).
3.   The following material is condensed and does not follow the order of argument in the texts from which it is drawn (Archer 1995; Bhaskar 1975, 1979, 1989; Collier 1994; Lawson 1997, 2003; Morgan 2007; Sayer 1984, 2000). It is constructed for simplicity. Note also that much of the development of similar insight regarding social science began around the same time: Russel Keat, John Urry, Ted Benton, William Outhwaite, Tony Lawson, and others, all were responding to a general problem set created by contemporary developments.

4. Note, the table has heuristic value if one is unfamiliar with this subject but it is also an oversimplification. One might argue that typically mechanisms are actualized potentials; so they are as much actual as real, and in this sense so are the powers or potentials themselves.

5. The opposed error would be to ascribe the powers or potentials solely to the humans who induced the events in the laboratory; a strong form of social construction associated with the work of Woolgar and Latour.

6. Though complexity models, fuzzy set approaches and other methods involve further issues.

7. Concomitantly systems might be conceived also as nested, overlapping, and/or interactive.

8. The more difficult conceptual and empirical issue is: what is the boundary of a system?

9. The original meaning of positivism according to Comte was the gradual movement in knowledge acquisition from the natural sciences to the social, as scientific principles of investigation took root, and superstition and mysticism were banished by the application of reason and evidence. The process turned out somewhat differently.

10. And later also post-structuralism and postmodernism (see Sayer 2000), and more latterly, actor network theory (ANT).

11. Archer also adds an additional significant emphasis. There is more to the agent than simply a role or position since the agent is also a person, so the range of activity engaged through the role can be complex, based on how the agent fulfils their role but also based on further aspects of the person (personal psychology, projects, and so on). If one fails to recognize this then the human tacitly reduces to an oversocialized product of a series of positions in society.

12. Archer distinguishes structural and cultural emergent properties but there is insufficient space here for a full discussion.

13. So one might, for example, differentiate the internal social relations; that is, those that are 'necessary' to an identified form in the sense that the relation could not be what it is without them – wage labourer and capital ownership – from those that are external or not necessary to the form; and then explore how the form develops historically.

14. The course of critique and debate in economics has been somewhat different than in other areas such as sociology. Significant recognition and debate has been mainly in terms of philosophical theories (including ontologies). An immanent critique of various conceptions has led to growing support for critical realism, but also some misunderstanding. There is then also the question of moving from philosophical to scientific ontology (see Lawson 2014).

15. The ontology also acknowledges that open systems when viewed in the aggregate can be more or less integrated or cohesive in their structural aspects. This is a point also explored by regulation school political economists, such as Bob Jessop, based on a 'strategic-relational' approach influenced by critical realism, and also Poulantzas. In economics it is a matter of current concern in regard of the global financial crisis.

16. The following are not intended as discrete or complete categories.

17. NVivo is computer software for qualitative data analysis. QCA refers to qualitative data analysis, a series of systems for combining variables in data sets to support logical inference regarding the data. Network analysis refers to a set of software packages that allow the research to build up a visual representation of the direction, strength, and breaks in key relations within and between phenomena, often organizations. For use of these three see subsequent chapters in this volume.

# REFERENCES

Archer, Margaret (1995), *Realist Social Theory: The Morphogenetic Approach*, Cambridge: Cambridge University Press.

Archer, Margaret (2000), *Being Human: The Problem of Agency*, Cambridge: Cambridge University Press.

Archer, Margaret (2003), *Structure, Agency and the Internal Conversation*, Cambridge: Cambridge University Press.

Bhaskar, R.A. (1975), *A Realist Theory of Science*, London: Verso.

Bhaskar, R.A. (1979), *The Possibility of Naturalism*, Brighton: Harvester.

Bhaskar, R.A. (1989), *Reclaiming Reality: A Critical Introduction to Contemporary Philosophy*, London: Verso.

Boylan, T. and P. O'Gorman (1995), *Beyond Rhetoric and Realism in Economics: Towards a Reformulation of Economic Methodology*, London: Routledge.

Brown, A. (2007), 'Reorienting critical realism: a system-wide perspective on the capitalist economy', *Journal of Economic Methodology*, **14** (4), 499–519.

Byrne, D. (2013), 'Evaluating complex social interventions in a complex world', *Evaluation*, **19** (3), 217–28.

Carter, B. and C. New (eds) (2004), *Making Realism Work: Realist Social Theory and Empirical Research*, London: Routledge.

Chick, V. and S. Dow (2005), 'The meaning of open systems', *Journal of Economic Methodology*, **12** (3), 363–81.

Collier, A. (1994), *Critical Realism: An Introduction to Roy Bhaskar's Philosophy*, London: Verso.

Danermark, B., M. Ekstrom, L. Jakobsen, and J. Karlsson (2002), *Explaining Society: Critical Realism in the Social Sciences*, London: Routledge.

Dow, S. (2000), 'Prospects for progress in heterodox economics', *Journal of the History of Economic Thought*, **22** (2), 157–70.

Dow, S. (2004), 'Reorienting economics: some epistemological issues', *Journal of Economic Methodology*, **11** (3), 307–12.

Dow, S. (2008), 'Plurality in orthodox and heterodox economics', *Journal of Philosophical Economics*, **1** (2), 73–96.

Downward, P. (ed.) (2003), *Applied Economics and the Critical Realist Critique*, London: Routledge.

Fine, B. and D. Milonakis (2009), *From Economics Imperialism to Freakonomics*, London: Routledge.

Fleetwood, S. (ed.) (1999), *Critical Realism in Economics: Development and Debate*, London: Routledge.

Frauley, J. and F. Pearce (eds) (2007), *Critical Realism and the Social Sciences: Heterodox Elaborations*, Toronto: University of Toronto Press.

Fullbrook, E. (ed.) (2009), *Ontology and Economics: Tony Lawson and His Critics*, London, UK and New York, USA: Routledge.

Harré, R. and E. Madden (1976), *Causal Powers*, Oxford: Blackwell.

Lawson, T. (1997), *Economics and Reality*, London: Routledge.

Lawson, T. (2003), *Reorienting Economics*, London: Routledge.

Lawson, T. (2006), 'The nature of heterodox economics', *Cambridge Journal of Economics*, **30** (4), 483–505.

Lawson, T. (2014), 'A conception of social ontology', in Stephen Pratten (ed.), *Social Ontology and Modern Economics*, London: Routledge, pp. 19–52.

Lee, Frederic S. (2009), *A History of Heterodox Economics: Challenging the Mainstream in the Twentieth Century*, London: Routledge.

Lee, Frederic S. (2012), 'Critical realism, grounded theory and theory construction in heterodox economics', MPRA Paper: 40341.

Lee, Frederic S., X. Pham, and G. Gu (2013), 'The UK Research Assessment Exercise and the narrowing of UK economics', *Cambridge Journal of Economics*, **37** (4), 693–717.

Lewis, P. (ed.) (2004), *Transforming Economics: Perspectives on the Critical Realist Project*, London: Routledge.

Martins, N. (2014), *The Cambridge Revival of Political Economy*, London: Routledge.

Marx, K. (1852 [1950]), 'The eighteenth Brumaire of Louis Bonaparte', in K. Marx and F. Engels (1950), *Selected Works Volume 1*, London: Lawrence & Wishart.

Milonakis, D. and B. Fine (2009), *From Political Economy to Economics*, London: Routledge.

Mohun, S. and R. Veneziani (2012), 'Reorienting economics', *Philosophy of the Social Sciences*, **42** (1), 126–45.

Morgan, J. (2007), 'Critical realism', in G. Ritzer (ed.), *The Blackwell Encyclopaedia of Sociology: Vol II*, Oxford: Blackwell, pp. 870–73.

Morgan, J. (2009), *Private Equity Finance: Rise and Repercussions*, Basingstoke: Palgrave Macmillan.

Morgan, J. (2012), 'Economics critique: framing procedures and Lawson's realism in economics', *Journal of Critical Realism*, **11** (1), 94–125.

Morgan, J. (2013), 'Forward-looking contrast explanation illustrated using the Great Moderation', *Cambridge Journal of Economics*, **37** (4), 737–58.

Morgan, M. (2012), *The World in the Model*, Cambridge: Cambridge University Press.

Neilsen, P. and J. Morgan (2006), 'From mainstream economics to the boundaries of Marxism', *Capital and Class*, **89** (1), 91–120.

Nietszche, F. (1995), *Human All Too Human*, Stanford: Stanford University Press.

Olsen, W. (2004), 'Triangulation in social science research: qualitative and quantitative methods can really be mixed', in M. Holborn (ed.), *Developments in Sociology*, Ormskirk, UK: Causeway Press, pp. 103–21.

Olsen, W. (2012), *Data Collection: Key Debates and Methods in Social Research*, London: Sage.

Olsen, W. and J. Morgan (2005), 'A critical epistemology of analytical statistics: addressing the skeptical realist', *Journal for the Theory of Social Behavior*, **35** (3), 255–84.

Patomaki, H. (2011), 'On the complexities of time and temporality: implications for world history and global futures', *Australian Journal of Politics and History*, **57** (3), 339–52.

Sayer, A. (1984), *Method in Social Science*, London: Routledge.

Sayer, A. (1992), *Method in Social Science: A Realist Approach*, 2nd edn, London, UK and New York, USA: Routledge.

Sayer, A. (2000), *Realism and Social Science*, London: Sage.

# 2 Critical realism, method of grounded theory, and theory construction
*Frederic S. Lee*

This chapter has two roles. The first is to delineate the research strategy of grounded theory method (GTM) and secondly to connect it, on the one hand, to critical realism, and on the other hand, to research methods and their applications. Therefore, the chapter is organized in the following manner. Section 2.1 deals with the philosophical foundation relevant for GTM, which consists of realism, critical realism, and epistemological relativism. Section 2.2 constitutes the major part of the chapter and delineates GTM as the research strategy for heterodox economics for theory creation and evaluation, and discusses the historical character of critical realist–grounded theory and its implication for heterodox economic theories. Once the critical realist–grounded theory approach is articulated, it is connected, in section 2.3, to research methods and hence the rest of the *Handbook*; and this is followed by a conclusion in section 2.4.

## 2.1 THIS PHILOSOPHICAL FOUNDATION

Being both participants in and observers of the social and economic activity around them, heterodox economists approach their study of economics with a common sense understanding of the world. By 'common sense' is meant a complex set of beliefs and propositions (many of which are historically grounded) about fundamental features of the world that individuals assume in whatever they do in ordinary life. Thus, they take particular features, characteristics, institutions, and human actors of economic activity as real, obvious, and practical initial starting points for further research. To be real, obvious, and practical means that various features, institutions, and actors as acting persons[1] exist, are ingrained in everyday properties of the world of economic activity, and are encountered when observing or participating in ongoing economic activity. In particular, heterodox economists can, as observers, see them in action in the economy; or they can directly experience them as participants in economic activity. In short, they interact with what they study. By being a participant-observer, they are able to be close to the real, concrete form of the economy. Consequently their common sense beliefs and propositions provide the background against which they carry out their research. Hence, this common sense understanding of economic activity informs the methods which heterodox economists actually use to examine economic activity, particularly with regard to the way it is explained; it is impossible for any heterodox economists, or indeed any researcher, to approach the study of economics with a 'blank mind' (Coates 1996; Maki 1989, 1996, 1998a, 1998b; Dow 1990, 2001).

Heterodox economists characterize their common sense propositions by stating that the real (actual) economy is a non-ergodic, independent system with human agency and economic-social-political structures and institutions embedded in an historical process located in historical time. Other propositions accepted and articulated that support and clarify the above include: the actual economy and the society in which it is embedded is real and exists independently of the heterodox economist; the economy is transmutable, hence its future is uncertain and unknowable; ends are not entirely knowable nor independent of the means to achieve them; economic outcomes and change come about through acting persons interacting with social, political, and economic structures, and hence are ethical and political outcomes as well; and a capitalist society is a class society and the economy is permeated with hierarchical power derived in part from it. The final common sense proposition is that the study of particular economic activity cannot be done independently of the whole economy or the social system in which it is embedded. Mutually shared among heterodox economists, these common sense propositions provide the basis for its ontological realism foundation (Wilber and Harrison 1978; Gruchy 1987; Lawson 1994, 1999; Arestis 1996; Davidson 1996; Dow 1999, 2001; Downward 1999; Rotheim 1999)

From the common sense propositions, heterodox economists conclude that the economy works in terms of causal-historical processes. Moreover, because they accept the ontological constraint implicit in this, a specific form of realism, critical realism (CR), is the ontological basis of heterodox economics. Not only do they posit that economic phenomena are real, but heterodox economists also argue that their explanations or theories only have real components, refer to real things, represent real entities, are judged good or bad, true or false by virtue of the way the economy works, and are causal explanations.[2] As a causal explanation, theory provides an account of the process as a sequence of economic events and depicts the causes that propel one event to another in a sequence. In addition, while accepting that theories are evaluated on the accuracy of their explanations, heterodox economists also accept epistemological relativism, which is that explanations of economic events are historically contingent, and integrate the two. Finally, to ensure that their theories are causal explanations of real things, it is necessary to adopt the method of grounded theory as the research strategy to create and evaluate economic theories (Maki 1989, 1992, 1996, 1998a, 1998b, 2001; Ellis 1985).

**Critical Realism[3]**

Critical realism starts with an account of what the economic world must be like before it is investigated by economists and for economic analysis to be possible. Thus its fundamental claim is that the economic world is causally structured, which means that economic theories are historical and narratively structured. CR begins with four propositions, the first being that the economic world consists not only of events and our experiences, but also of underlying structures and causal mechanisms that are in principle observable and knowable. Second, it is argued that economic events, structures, and causal mechanisms exist independently of their identification. Third is the argument that all economic events are produced by an underlying set of causal mechanisms and structures. Finally, as an a posteriori observation, it is commonly noted that the social world is open in that economic events are typically produced as a result of interactions of numerous, unanticipated, often counteracting structures and contingently related causal mechanisms. Consequently, there is a three-tier view of economic reality. The first two tiers are the empirical events of experience and impression and the actual events underlying them. Understanding the former depends on the explanation of the actual events, and that is derived from causal mechanism(s) and economic structures, which constitute the third tier of economic reality. The causal mechanisms and structures together are the ontological core of heterodox economics in that when they are identified and understood, the empirical and actual events are jointly understood. Moreover, because causal historical processes are knowable and observable, so are the causal mechanisms and structures. This implies that agency qua decision-making by the acting person is an objective activity as opposed to a purely subjective one and hence as objective as 'objective structures'. Thus for the heterodox economist, identifying structures and causal mechanisms and describing their way of influencing or acting on specific events in the open economic world is their scientific undertaking; putting critical realism into practice thereby making the unknown knowable and the unseen observable, although it will not be perfect.

A causal mechanism in the context of heterodox economics is irreducible, has a relatively constant internal organization whose components are intentionally not mechanistically related, is real, observable, and underlies – hence governs or produces – actual events, and acts transfactually (that is, acts and has effects even when it does not generate discernable actual events). Being irreducible means the form and organization cannot be disaggregated into its constituent components and still function as a causal mechanism. In this sense, a causal mechanism is an emergent entity in that its properties and powers cannot be completely traced to its individual components. To have a constant form and organization means that the mechanism can be empirically identified by stable patterns of behavior and organizational format and hence empirically observed and delineated. Furthermore, the ability to act means that the mechanism has the power to generate qualitative and/or quantitative outcomes; and the triggering of the mechanism comes from agency, human intentionality via the acting person, which is embedded in, yet distinct from, the form and organization that constitutes the mechanism. This means that the causal mechanism cannot be thought of as a machine or 'mechanistic': that is, not completely structurally determined. Thus economic actors – that is, acting persons – have independent power to initiated actions (and so making the system open), thereby setting in motion causal mechanisms which generate outcomes that underlie, hence govern, actual economic events. Because the causal mechanism utilizes the same processes when producing results, the same results are repeatedly produced; and conversely, a causal mechanism does not produce accidental, random, transitory results.[4] To say that a causal mechanism acts transfactually, producing the same results, is also to say that its form, internal organization, and agency are constant, thereby making it a relatively enduring entity. Hence, if the same causal mechanism operates in different situations, it will produce the same, or transfactual, results each time it is in operation; but the empirical and actual events need not be regular or repeatable, as other contingently related causal mechanisms may be affecting them. So, in an open system, a causal mechanism only has the tendency to produce regular, repeatable qualitative or quantitative actual economic events denoted as 'demi-regularities'.

Structure is different from causal mechanism in that it does not include agency;

hence it can only help to shape or govern the actual event. Otherwise it is similar to a causal mechanism in that it is real, observable, relatively enduring in form and organization, irreducible, and governs transfactually. The structures of an economy have two additional properties: (1) being sustained, reproduced, and slowly trans- formed by economic and social events that are caused by acting persons through their causal mechanisms; and (2) their form and organization have a historical character. Moreover, all economic structures are social structures in that they represent and delineate recurrent and pattern interactions between acting persons, or between acting persons and technology and resources. Economic structures include economic and social norms, practices, and conventions; social networks such as associational net- works or interlocking directorates; technological networks such as the production and cost structures of a business enterprise or the input–output structure of an economy; and economic, political, and social institutions such as markets or the legal system. As distinct entities, neither causal mechanisms nor structures can separately cause and govern actual economic events. Rather, they must work jointly where the structures provide the medium or the conditions through which causal mechanisms act. So, as long as they remain enduring, there will be a tendency for regular and repeatable actual economic events to occur. In fact, in a transmutable world where the future is not completely knowable, acting persons are only possible if causal mechanisms and structures are relatively enduring so that they can connect their acts to outcomes; for if acting persons could not see themselves producing transfactual results, they would not act.[5]

**Epistemological Relativism**

Epistemological relativism is the view that knowledge of economic events is historically contingent. That is, because the social and economic activities of interest to heterodox economists change over time, knowledge and understanding of them is historically contingent; hence there are no eternal 'truths' and knowledge is always in the process of being created, even for past events. Consequently, what is known about actual economic events of the past need not be knowledge about current or future economic events. As a result, heterodox economists are continually engaged in creating new knowledge, new explanations to take the place of those that cease to refer to real things, represent real entities, and explain actual economic events. Thus CR explanations or theories are his- torically conditioned, hence historically contingent, which implies that, for heterodox economists, there are no ahistorical economic laws or regularities. Moreover, it is not possible to make ahistorical, general statements with absolute certainty beyond the historical data and context in which the statements are embedded. Another implica- tion is that theories must be, in some sense, grounded in historical data in order to tell historical stories explaining historical economic events. A third implication is that the difference between good and not-so-good, between true and simply plain wrong theories is how well their explanations correspond to if not 'embody' the historically contingent economic events being explained. Finally, epistemological relativism implies that the continual creation of knowledge is a social act carried out by informed actors – that is, by heterodox economists – in a socially, historically contingent context (Sayer 1992; Lawson 1997).

## 2.2   RESEARCH STRATEGY: METHOD OF GROUNDED THEORY

To develop a critical realist empirically grounded theory that analytically explains causally related, historically contingent economic events, the critical realist heterodox economist needs to identify and delineate the structures, causal mechanisms, and causal processes producing them. The research strategy for creating causally explanatory theories that is also consistent with realism, critical realism, and epistemological relativism is the method of grounded theory (GTM). First delineated by Barry Glaser and Anselm Strauss (1967), it was subsequently developed by them, their students, and others to become a widely used research strategy, especially when qualitative research methods are used to deal with issues of agency (Strauss 1987; Strauss and Corbin 1990, 1994; Dey 1999; Locke 2001; Goulding 2002; Bryant and Charmaz 2007; Morse et al. 2009). At roughly the same time, similar (but not as fully developed) guidelines for theory creation and evaluation going by the names of holism, pattern model, method of structured-focused comparison, and participant-observer approach using case study method were also proposed and developed (Diesing 1971; Wilber and Harrison 1978; George 1979; Fusfeld 1980).

The method of grounded theory is a process by which researchers create their theory 'directly' from data (which is defined below); and in which data collection, theoretical analysis, and theory building proceed simultaneously; see Figure 2.1. The use of the method begins with the economist becoming familiar with, but not dogmatically committed to, the relevant theoretical, empirical, and historical literature that might assist them in approaching, understanding, and evaluating the data relevant to their research interest. Then, they engage in 'fieldwork' by collecting comparable data from economic events from which a number of specific categories or analytical-theoretical concepts and their associated properties are isolated and the relationships between them identified. With the theoretical concepts and relationships empirically grounded in detail and hence empirically justified, the economist then develops a theory in the form of a complex analytical explanation based on the data's core concepts. The essential property of the theory is that it explains why and how the sequence of economic events represented in the data took place. Hence, the economist does not attempt to construct a simplified or realistically deformed empirically grounded theory by ignoring or rejecting particular data. Rather, the economist endeavors to capture the complexity of the data by establishing many different secondary concepts and relationships, and weaving them together with the core concepts into structures and causal mechanisms. This ensures that the resulting theory is conceptually dense as well as having causal explanatory power. The process of selecting the central theoretical concepts and developing the theory brings to light secondary concepts and relationships that also need further empirical grounding, as well as suggesting purely analytical concepts and relationships which need empirical grounding if they are to be integrated into the theory. After the theory is developed, the economist will evaluate it by seeing how it explains actual economic events. Let us now consider aspects of the grounded theory method in more detail.

```
┌─────────────────────────────────────┐
│    Becoming familiar with pre-existing │
│    ideas, concepts, arguments, and    │
│              evidence                 │
└─────────────────────────────────────┘
                   ↓
┌─────────────────────────────────────┐
│      Data collected with constant     │
│              comparisons              │
└─────────────────────────────────────┘
                   ↓
┌─────────────────────────────────────┐
│    Emerging theoretical categories with │
│      subcategories and properties     │
└─────────────────────────────────────┘
                   ↓
┌─────────────────────────────────────┐
│          Theoretical sampling          │
│                   ↓                    │
│   Additional data collected with constant │
│              comparison               │
│                   ↓                    │
│       Core theoretical categories      │
│  (identified, developed, densified, saturated) │
└─────────────────────────────────────┘
                   ↓
┌─────────────────────────────────────┐
│   Substantive theory/basic social process │
└─────────────────────────────────────┘
                   ↓
┌─────────────────────────────────────┐
│        Many substantive theories       │
│                   ↓                    │
│   Additional data collected with constant │
│              comparison               │
│                   ↓                    │
│             Formal theory             │
└─────────────────────────────────────┘
```

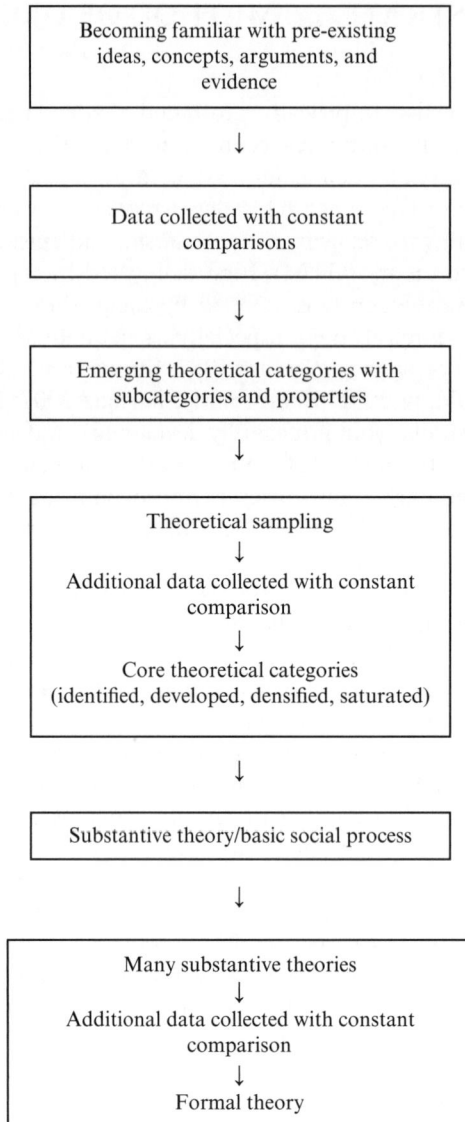

*Figure 2.1   Schema of the grounded theory method*

**Pre-Existing Ideas and Concepts**

Any researcher undertaking a project of economic theory creation is already aware, to one degree or another, of various 'competing' economic theories. So the question is: how aware should they be of the 'local' research frontier of the project as well as what lies behind it? To use the GTM fruitfully, the heterodox economist must be familiar with the contemporary heterodox and mainstream theoretical and non-theoretical literature, the controversies between economists, and the relevant literature from the history of economic thought. In particular, they need to make a detailed and critical investigation of the pre-existing heterodox ideas and concepts to see which might lend themselves to empirical grounding. The economist also needs to be familiar with some of the empirical literature as well as with the relevant literature from economic history. By acquiring a critical awareness of the pre-existing economic theories and empirical findings, they acquire a theoretical sensitivity regarding the data and theoretical concepts they will be examining, comparing, and empirically grounding. As a result, the economist will have the ability to recognize what might be important in the data and to give it meaning, as well as recognizing when the data do not support a pre-existing theoretical concept or category, require a large or small transformation of the pre-existing concept or category, or 'produce' a new category. Thus, the GTM not only recognizes that observations, data, and descriptions are conceptually theory-laden; it also reinforces the latter by demanding that all economists enter into theory creation as theoretically knowledgeable and aware individuals, as well as with the conviction that the creation of a new substantive economic theory will most likely require them to set aside forever some of that acquired knowledge. Consequently, the economist can still pursue the GTM even though they may favor particular non-grounded concepts and theories. Hence the grounded theory economist is not a neutral observer sifting through given 'facts' that present them, through some sort of immaculate conception, with a theory without a moment of forethought; rather, the economist is actively and reflectively engaged with it and is aware of the possibility of 'observer bias' (Olsen 2012: 65–71). By acknowledging the issue of conceptually laden observations while at the same time demanding that the economist be skeptical of all pre-existing theory, the grounded theory method is a highly self-conscious, engaging, and open-minded approach to economic research, data creation and collection, and theory building and evaluation.

## Data, Constant Comparisons, and Theoretical Categories

The development of theoretical categories is a complex task that starts by using various or mixed research methods to collect analytically and theoretically unembedded, different kinds of quantitative, qualitative, and historical information that is believed to be relevant for the task at hand. Information is obtained from interviews, surveys, oral histories, historical and current documents, videos, images, questionnaires, ethnographic investigations, observations, experiments, and site visits. Through comparing, analyzing, and interpreting the information while simultaneously organizing it into generalized categories as theoretical concepts, information is transformed into data. This has three implications, the first being that data are created rather than pre-existing, which means that the economist has a direct and reflective relation to them. Secondly, not all information gets transformed into data. Through critical evaluation of data, some may be deemed not relevant, while other information may be found as inaccurately reflecting reality relevant to the task at hand. The third implication is that data are not restricted to just sense experience. For example, historical documents or field reports contain data that cannot be verified by the reader's sense experience. The same can also be said for oral histories that deal with past events. On the other hand, non-written data, such as informal rules, hierarchical power, and expectations inside the business enterprise, are not unobservable in that they can be verbally articulated and hence written down, filmed and then identified at a later point in time, or observed as institutions, that is, as observable patterns of behavior hence capable of being recorded. Thus all data are observable, although the sources and media in which they exist vary; to be unobservable in this sense is not to be real and hence to be no data at all. Hence, the theoretical categories that emerge come from the information as data, not after they are all collected, but in the process of collecting them. Consequently each category is tied to or empirically grounded in its data; and since the data are real, observable, measurable, so is the theoretical category. Moreover, since the data lie in time and history, each theoretical category is anchored in a particular historical setting. In short, a grounded theory category is theoretical and actual, grounded in real time, and historically specific (Olsen and Morgan 2005; Olsen 2012).

The purpose of constant comparison of the data is to see whether they support and continue to support emerging categories.[6] Thus, each theoretical category that becomes established is repeatedly present in very many comparable pieces of data derived from multi-sources; in other words, a category represents a 'pattern' that the researcher recognizes in the data generated by replicatory or comparative studies. Consequently, categories are created by the researcher rather than 'discovered' in the data; hence categories are one conceptual outcome that arises from the researcher's immersion in the data. It is in this sense that categories emerge from the data (Dey 2007). In this way data, that would not be significant on their own, obtain a collective, emergent significance. The categories that emerge are of two types: one that is derived directly from the data and the other that is formulated by the economist. The former tend to denote data self-description and actual processes and behavior, while the latter tend to denote explanations. In either case, the language used to describe the categories may be quite different from the existing theoretical language. As a result, the building of a grounded theory may require the creation of a new language, and discarding old words and their meanings. On the other hand, the language used may come directly from the data collected and/or from commonly used language (which is generally not theoretical language) (Konecki 1989; Coates 1996). Finally, each category has properties also derived from data in the same manner, that is, by using constant comparisons. The more properties a category has, the denser and hence the more realistic it is. A grounded theory category does not ignore the complexity of reality; rather, it embraces it.

**Theoretical Sampling and Saturation**

In the process of collecting data, the economist may feel that what is being collected is not revealing additional properties of a specific kind that they believe might exist, owing to their familiarity with the relevant theoretical, empirical, and historical literature. As a result, they engage in theoretical sampling. This involves sampling or collecting data that are expected to increase the density of a specific category by producing more properties, as well as increasing the number of pieces of data supporting each of the properties, hence making it more definitive and analytically useful.[7] Theoretical sampling and collection of data for a single category, as well as for a range of categories, continues until theoretical saturation is reached, that is, when no new data regarding a category and the relationships between the categories continue to emerge. A saturated category is not a function of the number of pieces of data, as it may become saturated after only a small portion of the available data has been analyzed. The significance of this empirical grounding process is that the theoretical categories cannot be unrealistic, hence false, since they are derived from the data. If the data collection and theoretical sampling is incomplete then the categories are not adequately dense, as relevant properties are missing; thus such categories are incompletely realistic. On the other hand, if future data emerge which the empirical grounding process shows do not fall into a previously existing category, then that category is not relevant, but it is not empirically false.

### Structures, Causal Mechanisms, Demi-Regularities, and Grounded Theories

Once the real, observable theoretical categories are delineated and grounded, the economist, perceiving a pattern of relationships among them, puts critical realism into practice by classifying some directly as economic and social structures and others as components of them. Continuing the practice, other categories that center on acting persons' motivation and action and a set of outcomes are woven together into a causal mechanism; and finally, some categories are identified as demi-regularities. The resulting structures, causal mechanisms, and demi-regularities are real and observable as opposed to unreal, metaphoric, and hidden. So, to observe a structure or causal mechanism is to observe the working together of its observed concrete components. Hence structures, causal mechanisms, and demi-regularities are real and observable precisely because their categories are real and observable.

Given their research interest, the economist selects, from the causal mechanisms identified, one as the central causal mechanism around which the structures and secondary causal mechanisms and their outcomes are arranged. Criteria for selecting the central causal mechanism from among a number of possible causal mechanisms include its frequency in the data as a cause of the outcomes, its implications for a more general theory, and its allowance for increasing the number of interrelationships between the structures and causal mechanisms. Thus the causal mechanism is central to the narrative being analytically developed in conjunction with the economic structures and secondary causal mechanisms. More specifically, the narrative is not a description of present or a recounting of past unique and/or demi-regular economic events, although both techniques of presenting empirical and actual economic events are included in the narrative. Rather, it is a complex analytical explanation of those described or recounted events. Even when the basic narrative is decided upon, its development will involve further theoretical sampling and collecting of data as new properties for and interrelationships between the existing structures and causal mechanisms emerge. Consequently, the narrative evolves into an economic theory while at the same time becoming increasingly denser (in terms of increasing number of interrelationships between the structures and causal mechanisms).

The critical realist–grounded theory (CR–GT) that eventually emerges is an intrinsically complete or closed (but 'externally' open via its causal mechanism) analytical explanation (which is inclusive of but not reduced to schemas, models, graphs, and other forms of representations of the data) or interpretation of the actual economic events represented in the data. Thus the theory is not a generalization from the data, but of the data; that is, a grounded theory does not go beyond the data on which it is based – it does not claim universality or the status of an empirical-theoretical law. This means that the GTM is not the same as induction. That is, the GTM establishes, that is, creates, structures and causal mechanisms (which CR says must exist for scientific research to be possible) from the data, with the point of arguing that the relevant economic events, assuming that the structures and causal mechanisms remain relatively enduring, remain relatively ongoing as well. In this manner, the CR–GT approach is not an inductivist research strategy leading to empirical-theoretical laws, with the implication that it cannot be evaluated or judged in terms of logical coherence of a deductivist kind. Rather, the coherence of the CR–GT is evaluated and judged on how rigorously, that is, strictly exactly or accurately, its explanation corresponds to the actual historically contingent economic events (Sarre 1987; Sayer 1992).

Since the theory is a clear theoretical account of empirical and actual events that occur in historical time, the critical realist three-tier view of economic reality collapses into a single integrated tier for the CR–GT heterodox economist. In other words, reality is built into the theory (as opposed to having a non-grounded theory representing reality). With the grounded theory in hand, the heterodox economist can directly 'see' the causal mechanisms and structures and 'hear' the acting persons determining the empirical and actual events; the mystery, randomness, and unintelligibility is replaced by clear explanation. Moreover, being a weave of a central causal mechanism, secondary causal mechanisms, and economic structures designed to explain actual economic events in historical time, the theory also consists of realistic (as opposed to stylized, fictionalized, or idealized) descriptions of economic events and accurate narratives of sequences of economic events. As a result, the grounded economic theory is an emergent entity, a concatenated theory that cannot be disassembled into separate parts which compose it.

Economic theory centered on a single central causal mechanism is classified as a substantive economic theory since it is an explanation of a single basic economic process that occurs widely in the economy. From a number of substantive theories, a more holistic or macroeconomic theory is developed in a concatenated manner where the relationship or pattern among the substantive theories is its analytical explanation. That is, the holistic theory is built up from substantive theories; it has no prior existence. As in the process of grounding the substantive economic theory, the holistic theory also has to be grounded. In particular, the relationships between the substantive theories that constitute the macro theory need to be grounded in data assisted and directed by theoretical sampling. Consequently, the macroeconomic theory is grounded, historically contingent, and its analytical explanations are not empirical extrapolations. Moreover, it is no more (or less) abstract than a substantive grounded theory. Because a grounded theory must at all times be grounded, it cannot be an abstract theory where the modifier denotes some degree of non-groundness, such as the use of fictional categories or the elimination of data. Hence grounded theories cannot be differentiated according to the levels of abstraction.

**Evaluating Grounded Theories**

Since the categories and their relationships that constitute the theory are intimately linked with the data, the grounded theory itself cannot be falsified. More specifically, because a grounded theory is developed with the data rather than prior to it, it does not stand independently of the data. Thus, it is not possible to test for the truth or falsity of a grounded theory by checking it against the data from which it is constructed. But a grounded theory is evaluated by how well it explains actual economic events: that is, how well it identifies empirically and weaves together the causal mechanisms, structures, and descriptions into a narrative of the economic events being explained. In short, a grounded theory refers to real things, represents real entities, and is evaluated on how well it rigorously accounts for the causal manner in which the economy actually operates. The evaluation process takes place within a community of scholars where delineating tentative drafts of the theory are presented to colleagues at conferences and seminars for critical comments; and more refined presentations of the theory are published where colleagues have the opportunity to point out inadequacies. Through this cooperative process of economic writing, economic reading, and critical commentary, the community of heterodox economists arrives at, hopefully but not necessarily, adequate theories (which illustrates the social nature of knowledge construction). Consequently, a grounded theory as socially constructed knowledge is, in the first instance, only as good as its theoretical categories. If the data selected do not cover all aspects of the economic event(s) under investigation; if the economist compiles categories and properties from only part of the data collected or forces data into predetermined categories; if the density of the categories is small or the relationships between categories are not identified or under-grounded due to incomplete data collected; if the economist choose the 'wrong' central causal mechanism; and/or if the narrative is static, terse, unable to fully integrate structures and central and secondary causal mechanisms, and relatively uncomplex, then the commentary of critics will make it clear that the economic theory is poor, ill-developed, and hence to a greater or lesser extent less realistic, and unable to provide a comprehensive and convincing explanation of actual economic events. That is to say, all grounded theories are realistic in that they are grounded in every detail in data. A grounded theory may be relatively complete or a much incomplete explanation of an economic event, but in either case it is entirely realistic. To be unrealistic from a grounded theory perspective is to include non-grounded concepts in the theory, but then it would not be grounded.

A second way to evaluate a grounded economic theory is to see how well it deals with new data: data are taken seriously and the continued validity of previously developed knowledge is always questioned. The relatively enduring structures, causal mechanisms, and their outcomes of a grounded theory are based on data collected in a specific time period. So it is possible to evaluate whether they have remain enduring outside the time period by confronting them with 'new' data derived from replicating studies, especially data from actual events that at first glance appear to fall outside existing categories and not to support demi-regularities and expected transfactual results. If the new data fall within the existing categories and conform to the transfactual results – that is, the pattern of data and narrative of the new data match that of the existing theory – then the structures and causal mechanisms have been relatively enduring (Wilber and Harrison 1978; Yin 1981a, 1981b). On the other hand, if the new data fall outside the existing categories and do not support the transfactual results – that is, the pattern of the data and narrative does not match the existing theory – then at least some of the structures and causal mechanisms have changed. Consequently, the existing grounded economic theory needs to be modified or replaced by a completely new one. Therefore, theory evaluation is designed to check the continual correspondence of the theory with the real causes of ongoing unique and demi-regular economic events. Hence, it is essentially a positive way of promoting theory development and reconstruction as well as new theory creation when the correspondence between theory and events breaks down.

The fact that good or poor research practices lead to better or worse grounded economic theories indicates that choices made by economists do affect the final outcome. Therefore, within the GTM it is possible, although not likely, to have good but different substantive and macroeconomic theories for the same economic events. Given the same theoretical categories, a different choice of a central causal mechanism produces a different theory; or if the same central causal mechanism is used but integrated with different structures and secondary causal mechanisms, a different theory will also be produced. However, since heterodox economists are critical realists, and their theories concern causal historical events, they do not accept the possibility that there are multiple valid grounded theories explaining the same economic events; and hence they reject the possibility that there is no empirical evidence that could distinguish between two incompatible grounded theories. Thus, following the same procedures as above, the way forward for the grounded theorist is to collect new data to see which of the two theories they support, supplemented by critical commentary from colleagues. Hence, although the procedures used are the same and the data collected are, in principle, the same, checking the continual explanatory adequacy of a grounded theory is a different activity from choosing between two different grounded theories, for the former produces a historically linked sequence of grounded theories, while the latter concludes that one of the two theories is not an explanation after all.[8]

**Historical Character of CR–GT Economic Theories**

The common sense propositions combined with critical realism exclude, as part of heterodox theorizing, ahistorical, atemporal entities and theoretical concepts, atemporal diagrams, given known ends independent of means or processes to attain them, models and other forms of analysis unaccompanied by temporal-historical analysis, and the utilization of ahistorical first principles or primary causes. Being outside of history, historical time, and an unknowable transmutable future, these ahistorical entities and concepts are also rejected by the GTM as fictitious since they do not emerge as categories in the historical data. Consequently, ahistorical theories with their ahistorical concepts are not connected to the range of economic events they intend to explain, and hence are not capable of explaining them. In contrast, the concatenated integration of the common sense propositions and critical realism with the grounded theory method – that is, the CR–GT approach – prescribes that heterodox theorizing include the delineation of historically grounded structures of the economy, and the development of historically grounded emergent causal mechanisms. Consequently, they are historical theories in that they are historical narratives that explain the present or past internal workings of historical economic processes and events connected to the social provisioning process in the context of relatively stable causal mechanisms (whose actions and outcomes can be temporally different) and structures. That is, the simultaneous operation of primary and secondary causal mechanisms with different time dimensions ensures the existence of historical economic processes that are being explained. But even when the primary causal mechanism concludes its activity, the historical processes do not come to an end, for the secondary and other causal mechanisms can also have an impact on the structures so that the slowly transforming structures (and their impact on causal mechanisms) maintain the processes.

Historical processes are organized and directed by structures and causal mechanisms and are what constitutes historical time. Since those same structures and causal mechanisms also change slowly, historical processes change as well, implying that there are no end points, 'constants' to which the processes tend or lock-in, evolutionary pathways that must be followed irrespective of agency, or cyclical 'movements'. In short, historical change is non-teleological, non-historicist, non-cyclical, and hence can only be change. With historical process and historical change as intrinsic properties of historical theories, such outside-of-history concepts and methods as equilibrium, optimization–maximization–minimization short-period/long-period positions, centers of gravitation, market clearing, states of rest, or comparative statics cannot be utilized to organize and direct economic inquiry and to narrate economic events. These concepts are sometimes theoretically justified in the context of a layered view of reality and economic events, since it allows some structures and mechanisms to exist essentially outside of time and historical process. At other times, they are justified in terms of slow-moving variables (structures and causal mechanisms) and fast-moving variables (outcomes) where the latter do not have an impact upon the former. However, the interplay and linkages between structures, causal mechanisms, and outcomes mean that the distinction between the two kinds of variables is not sustainable and that, consequently, historical outcomes are not based on accidental, random, or autonomous factors; hence no structures, causal mechanisms, and outcomes can be independent of historical processes. In short, it is not possible to start with a static theory and dynamize it into a theory that explains historical processes; no amendments to an outside-of-history theory can transform it into a historical theory.

Historical economic theories are possible because, as noted under critical realism, all historical events are, due to the existence of structures and causal mechanisms, narratively structured: there are no accidental or uncaused events, that is, events without a narrative. Hence, heterodox economists do not impose narratives on actual economic events to make sense of them, but derive them from the events via the GTM. Moreover, as long as historical events are narratively structured, subjectivity, uncertainty, and expectations do not introduce indeterminacy into heterodox theories. In addition, being a narrative, theories have a plot with a beginning, middle, and end centered on a central causal mechanism and set within structures and other causal mechanisms. Therefore, antedated events prompt the causal mechanisms to initiate activity to generate particular results and hence start the narrative; and it comes to an end when the causal mechanisms conclude their activity. Finally, the storyteller of the narrative is the heterodox economist whose objective is to help the audience – which includes fellow economists, students, politicians, and the general public – understand theoretically how and why the actual economic events transpired[9] (Carr 1986; Norman 1991; McCullagh 1984; Pentland 1999; Dey 1999; Appleby et al. 1994, Ch. 7, 8).

As narratives linked with critical realism and centered on causal mechanisms and structures, CR–GTs as historical heterodox theories are not completely aggregated or disaggregated; and nor are they devoid of explicit human intentionality and activity. That is, because causal mechanisms embody data from many case studies, they aggregate economic reality or, put differently, compact the scale of reality and therefore the degree of detail and specificity required of the narrative. However, the degree of aggregation is limited because of the existence of structures and causal mechanisms that cannot be aggregated or disaggregated and human intentionality and activity that are both differentiated and specific. As a result, for the CG–GT approach, heterodox economic theories are neither an aggregate theory where the differentiation among the causal mechanisms with its agency and structures disappear, nor such a disaggregated theory that causal mechanisms with agency and structures are individual-event-specific and hence of little interest.[10] The impossibility of aggregating emergent entities to produce representational aggregate entities – that is, aggregate entities with the same properties and behavior as the individual entities – means that heterodox economic theory must consist of linked causal mechanisms and structures. Thus, heterodox theories tell quasi-aggregated narratives explaining the many and overlapping actual economic events occurring in a differentiated economy.[11] The fact that the narrative is embedded in the events as opposed to mimicking them (as is the nature of non-CR–GTs) is perhaps the most compelling reason to use the CR–GT approach for theory creation and evaluation.

## 2.3   RESEARCH METHODS

Because a critical realist–grounded heterodox economic theory consists of a heterogeneous array of structures and primary and secondary causal mechanisms, various research methods are needed to collect the various kinds of data as information needed for their empirical grounding. Since some structures are based on statistical data while others are based on social-relational data, and causal mechanisms require some data that clearly reveal intentionality, that is, decision-making, the development of CR–GT involves multiple research methods and their data. Such use of mixed research methods and data triangulation (see Chapter 15 in this *Handbook*) creates a different and quite distinct research environment with regard to theory development and evaluation relative to that which characterizes economics. As an illustration, to construct a critical realist–grounded explanation of a particular set of past and present economic events, such as pricing and price stability (see Chapter 17 in this *Handbook*), the use of historical and quantitative-statistical methods to examine existing written, recorded, physical, and quantitative records and artifacts is warranted. Since these methods and data sources might very well prove insufficient for the task at hand, it is necessary to use other research methods – such as surveys, interviews and oral histories, industrial archaeology investigations, questionnaires, mapping, direct observation, participation in activities, fieldwork, and various types of statistical analysis – to create new data (see Chapters 4–12 in this *Handbook*). In this context, subjective evaluations and interpretations of future possibilities constitute a particular kind of data that require particular research methods to observe and record. When it is important to explain how and why particular pricing decisions are made and who made them, the economist needs to create narrative accounts of relevant lived-historical experiences embedded within the cultural milieu of particular business enterprises. Thus the economist needs to examine letters and other written documents, undertake interviews and other oral documentation, and possibly engage in participant observation, in which they may directly engage with, for example, the enterprise in the process of collecting data that is used in the pricing decision. Finally, when constructing the overall narrative explanation of pricing and price stability, recourse might be made to the use of a single pricing equation, a system of pricing equations as a pricing model of the economy, and/or agent-based computational analysis (see Chapters 13 and 14 in this *Handbook*). So what constitutes appropriate research methods and data depends on the object of inquiry. Consequently, real, observable, and measurable theoretical categories, and hence real, observable, and measurable economic structures and causal mechanisms that constitute the CR–GT, are grounded in the data via different research methods obtained from various sources.

Research methods vary depending upon the 'data-task' at hand, but because the boundaries between quantitative, qualitative, and historical data are fuzzy, it is at times not very useful to solely characterize a research method and its data in such a manner. Some research methods, such as historical, surveys, interviews, ethnography, participant observation, and experimental directly generate data; while other methods, such as econometrics as regression analysis, factor analysis, cluster analysis, nonparametric methods, and social network analysis examine already existing data generated by the aforementioned research methods. In particular, these latter methods are used to examine various types of quantitative and qualitative data for the purpose of assisting in delineating structures, causal mechanisms, transfactual outcomes, and demi-regularities; in evaluating CR–GTs for their accuracy in explaining past and present economic events; and in evaluating claims in the historical literature regarding causal mechanisms and transfactural outcomes and demi-regularities.

Other research methods, such as agent-based computational simulations, schemas, and (mathematical) modeling represent the empirically grounded structures and causal mechanisms and then interrogate them in a manner that contributes to further development of the structures and mechanisms as well as to developing and evaluating the analytical narrative of the critical realist–grounded heterodox economic theory. Finally, there are research methods, such as case studies, that are instrumental in establishing theoretical categories and that contribute to building the analytical narrative. A case study is defined as an in-depth, multifaceted investigation of a particular object or theme where the object or theme is ontologically real and gives it its unity. Thus, the case study approach is an exemplary method of data collection and comparison used to develop categories, structures, and causal mechanisms. Moreover, providing information from a number of different data sources over a period of time permits a more holistic study of structures and causal mechanisms.

## 2.4   CONCLUSION

The GTM of theory creation effectively dismisses not only the traditional issue of the realism of assumptions, but also the role of assumptions in theory creation and development. The reason is that assumptions are by definition not grounded in the real world, so their use for theory creation cannot be part of the GTM. Consequently, the degree of their realism or their adequacy as a logical axiomatic foundation for theory is not a concern. This implies that logical coherence is irrelevant for evaluating grounded theories. Moreover, because the role of theoretical isolation in traditional theory building and theorizing is dependent on assumptions, their absence in the GTM means that grounded theories are not isolated theories that exclude possible influencing factors. The combination of CR – with its structures, causal mechanisms, and epistemological relativism – and the GTM produces theories that include all the relevant factors and influences, are historically contingent, and exist in 'real' space and time. To deliberately exclude some factors would leave the mechanisms, structures, and theories insufficiently grounded; and to claim to establish laws and certain (timeless) knowledge would remove the mechanisms, structures, and theories from the real-world economic events they are to explain. Thus, the integration of critical realism and grounded theory results in theories and theorizing fundamentally different from the traditional mode: it is not an axiomatic-based approach to theory creation, does not use deductivist methods to create theory, and rejects every research strategy of theory creation that is not empirically grounded.

The CR–GT approach to theory creation and evaluation overcomes the perceived shortcomings of CR and the GTM: the former has little to say about theory, while the latter lacks the ontological foundation and so appears to be little more than an inductive research strategy. However, CR provides the ontological realist foundation for GTM and identifies its objects for empirical grounding – structures and causal mechanisms – while the GTM provides the research strategy by which they are empirically grounded. The theory resulting from the CR–GT approach is a conceptually dense analytical explanation of the actual events represented in the data; and its relatively enduring capability in this regard can be evaluated by confronting it with new data. Hence the CR–GT approach is not based on deductive or inductive logic, but on a reflective form of scientific knowledge creation data that is interactively fused with the creation of theory. So the theory is of the mixed data obtained from using mixed research methods, not separate from it; if new data support the theory, they becomes part of it; while if the new data do not support it, then those data become part of a new theory with different structures, causal mechanisms, and perhaps demi-regularities. One significant outcome of the use of mixed methods and data triangulation for theory creation is that the CR–GT approach is inherently interdisciplinary. This has numerous implications for how heterodox economics is actually practiced; see Chapter 3 in this *Handbook*.

## NOTES

1. The acting person is a theoretical conceptualization and representation of decision-making and implementation by a going concern organization, such as a business enterprise, or institution, such as a household. It has an ongoing, repeated pattern of culturally particular, ethically informed social relationships. Moreover, the acting person is reflexive in terms of its decisions and thus visualizes the possible impact of its actions. Finally, it can determine the extent to which its decisions qua actions achieve the desired outcomes.
2. The contrast to a factual theory is a theory which is concerned exclusively with conceptual objects (scarcity) that have no connection to the real world or with theoretical objects (utility functions) that are explicitly divorced from the real world.
3. See Chapter 1 in this volume for a more in-depth discussion of critical realism.
4. This property of causal mechanisms obviates the need for an inductivist approach for theory creation (Sayer 1992).
5. Maki (1989, 1998b), Sayer (1992), Lloyd (1993), Lawson (1994, 1997, 1998a, 1998b, 1998c), Lawson et al. (1996), Wellman and Berkowitz (1997), Fleetwood (2001a, 2001b), Hodgson (1998, 2000), Joseph (1998), Downward (1999), Lewis (2004).
6. Constant comparison can also involve exactly replicating previous studies to see how robust they are.
7. The point of theoretical sampling is specifically to find data to make categories denser, more complex. Since the aim of the grounded theory method is to build theories based on data collected, the issue of generalizing in a statistical sense is not relevant (Glaser and Strauss 1967; Corbin and Strauss 1990).

8.  Glaser and Strauss (1967), Charmaz (1983), Strauss (1987), Konecki (1989), Strauss and Corbin (1990, 1994), Corbin and Strauss (1990), Glaser (1992, 2007), Dey (1999, 2007), Finch (2002), Tsang and Kwan (1999), Bigus et al. (1994), Tosh (1991), Boylan and O'Gorman (1995), Runde (1998), Sayer (1992), Megill (1989), McCullagh (2000), Hunt (1994), Pentland (1999), Ellis (1985).
9.  The historical character of heterodox economic theories is closely aligned with the view of economic theories espoused by the German historical school (Betz 1988; Spiethoff 1952, 1953).
10. The outcome of a grounded theory approach to constructing causal mechanisms is a rejection of methodological individualism. While acting persons make decisions based on subjective and objective evaluations of a somewhat uncertain future and generate outcomes, for theoretical purposes, their decisions and outcomes are aggregated and embedded in a causal mechanism. Hence, the empirically grounded role of the subjective and the uncertainty in the causal mechanism is observable, persistent, and systematic.
11. See Dopfer and Potts (2008, pp. 21–26) for a similar argument regarding meso and macro.

# REFERENCES

Appleby, J., L. Hunt, and M. Jacob (1994), *Telling the Truth About History*, New York: W.W. Norton & Company.
Arestis, P. (1996), 'Post-Keynesian economics: towards coherence', *Cambridge Journal of Economics*, **20** (1), 111–35.
Betz, H.K. (1988), 'How does the German historical school fit?', *History of Political Economy*, **20** (3), 409–30.
Bigus, O.E., S.C. Hadden, and B.G. Glaser (1994), 'The study of basic social processes', in B.G. Glaser (ed.), *More Grounded Theory Methodology: A Reader*, Mill Valley, CA: Sociology Press, pp. 38–64.
Boylan, T. and P. O'Gorman (1995), *Beyond Rhetoric and Realism in Economics: Towards a Reformulation of Economic Methodology*, London: Routledge.
Bryant, A. and K. Charmaz (eds) (2007), *The SAGE Handbook of Grounded Theory*, Los Angeles, CA: Sage.
Carr, D. (1986), 'Narrative and the real world: an argument for continuity', *History and Theory: Studies in the Philosophy of History*, **25** (2), 117–31.
Charmaz, K. (1983), 'The grounded theory method: an explication and interpretation', in R.M. Emerson (ed.), *Contemporary Field Research: A Collection of Readings*, Boston, MA: Little, Brown & Company, pp. 109–26.
Coates, J. (1996), *The Claims of Common Sense: Moore, Wittgenstein, Keynes and the Social Sciences*, Cambridge: Cambridge University Press.
Corbin, J. and A. Strauss (1990), 'Grounded theory research: procedures, canons, and evaluative criteria', *Qualitative Sociology*, **13** (1), 3–21.
Davidson, P. (1996), 'Reality and economic theory', *Journal of Post Keynesian Economics*, **18** (4), 479–508.
Dey, Ian (1999), *Grounding Grounded Theory: Guidelines for Qualitative Inquiry*, San Diego, CA: Academic Press.
Dey, Ian (2007), 'Grounding categories', in Antony Bryant and Kathy Charmaz (eds), *The Sage Handbook of Grounded Theory*, Beverley Hills, CA: Sage, pp. 167–90.
Diesing, P. (1971), *Patterns of Discovery in the Social Sciences*, New York: Aldine.
Dopfer, K. and J. Potts (2008), *The General Theory of Economic Evolution*, London: Routledge.
Dow, S.C. (1990), 'Post-Keynesianism as political economy: a methodological discussion', *Review of Political Economy*, **2** (3), 345–58.
Dow, S. (1999), 'Post Keynesianism and critical realism: what is the connection?', *Journal of Post Keynesian Economics*, **22** (1), 15–33.
Dow, S.C. (2001), 'Post Keynesian methodology', in R.F. Holt and S. Pressman (eds), *A New Guide to Post Keynesian Economics*, London: Routledge, pp. 11–20.
Downward, P. (1999), *Pricing Theory in Post Keynesian Economics: A Realist Approach*, Cheltenham, UK and Northampton, MA, USA: Edward Elgar.
Ellis, B. (1985), 'What science aims to do', in P.M. Churchland and C.A. Hooker (eds), *Images of Science*, Chicago, IL: University of Chicago Press, pp. 48–74.
Finch, J.H. (2002), 'The role of grounded theory in developing economic theory', *Journal of Economic Methodology*, **9** (2), 213–34.
Fleetwood, S. (2001a), 'Causal laws, functional relations and tendencies', *Review of Political Economy*, **13** (2), 201–20.
Fleetwood, S. (2001b), 'Conceptualizing unemployment in a period of atypical employment: a critical realist perspective', *Review of Social Economy*, **59** (1), 45–69.
Fusfeld, D.R. (1980), 'The conceptual framework of modern economics', *Journal of Economic Issues*, **14** (1), 1–52.

George, A.L. (1979), 'Case studies and theory development: the method of structured, focused comparison', in P.G. Lauren (ed.), *Diplomacy: New Approaches in History, Theory, and Policy*, New York: Free Press, pp. 43–68.

Glaser, B.G. (1992), *Emergence vs Forcing: Basics of Grounded Theory Analysis*, Mill Valley, CA: Sociology Press.

Glaser, B.G. (2007), 'Doing formal theory', in A. Bryant and K. Charmaz (eds), *The SAGE Handbook of Grounded Theory*, Los Angeles, CA: Sage, pp. 97–113.

Glaser, B.G. and A.L. Strauss (1967), *The Discovery of Grounded Theory: Strategies for Qualitative Research*, New York: Aldine Publishing Company.

Goulding, C. (2002), *Grounded Theory: A Practical Guide for Management, Business and Market Researchers*, London: Sage.

Gruchy, A.G. (1987), *The Reconstruction of Economics: An Analysis of the Fundamentals of Institutional Economics*, New York: Greenwood Press.

Hodgson, G.M. (1998), 'Emergence', in J.B. Davis, D.W. Hands, and U. Maki (eds), *The Handbook of Economic Methodology*, Cheltenham, UK and Northampton, MA, USA: Edward Elgar, pp. 156–60.

Hodgson, G.M. (2000), 'From micro to macro: the concept of emergence and the role of institutions', in L. Burlamaquiun, A.C. Castro, and H.-J. Chang (eds), *Institutions and the Role of the State*, Cheltenham, UK and Northampton, MA, USA: Edward Elgar, pp. 103–26.

Hunt, S.D. (1994), 'A realist theory of empirical testing: resolving the theory-ladenness/objectivity debate', *Philosophy of the Social Sciences*, **24** (2), 133–58.

Joseph, J. (1998), 'In defense of critical realism', *Capital and Class*, **65** (1), 73–106.

Konecki, K. (1989), 'The methodology of grounded theory in the research of the situation of work', *Polish Sociological Bulletin*, **2** (1), 59–74.

Lawson, T. (1994), 'The nature of post Keynesianism and its links to other traditions: a realist perspective', *Journal of Post Keynesian Economics*, **16** (4), 503–38.

Lawson, T. (1997), *Economics and Reality*, London: Routledge.

Lawson, T. (1998a), 'Tendencies', in J.B. Davis, D.W. Hands, and U. Maki (eds), *The Handbook of Economic Methodology*, Cheltenham, UK and Northampton, MA, USA: Edward Elgar, pp. 493–98.

Lawson, T. (1998b), 'Transcendental realism', in J.B. Davis, D.W. Hands, and U. Maki (eds), *The Handbook of Economic Methodology*, Cheltenham, UK and Northampton, MA, USA: Edward Elgar, pp. 504–10.

Lawson, T. (1998c), 'Social relations, social reproduction and stylized facts', in P. Arestis (ed.), *Method, Theory and Policy in Keynes: Essays in Honour of Paul Davidson*, Vol. 3, Cheltenham, UK and Northampton, MA, USA: Edward Elgar, pp. 17–43.

Lawson, T. (1999), 'Connections and distinctions: post Keynesianism and critical realism', *Journal of Post Keynesian Economics*, **22** (1), 3–14.

Lawson, C., M. Peacock and S. Pratten (1996), 'Realism, under-labouring and institutions', *Cambridge Journal of Economics*, **20** (1), 137–51.

Lewis, P. (2004), 'Transforming economics? On heterodox economics and the ontological turn in economic methodology', in P. Lewis (ed.), *Transforming Economics: Perspectives on the Critical Realist Project*, London: Routledge, pp. 1–32.

Lloyd, C. (1993), *The Structures of History*, Oxford: Basil Blackwell.

Locke, K. (2001), *Grounded Theory in Management Research*, London: Sage.

Maki, U. (1989), 'On the problem of realism in economics', *Ricerche Economiche*, **43** (1–2), 176–98.

Maki, U. (1992), 'The market as an isolated causal process: a metaphysical ground for realism', in B.J. Caldwell and S. Boehm (eds), *Austrian Economics: Tensions and New Directions*, Boston, MA: Kluwer Academic Publishers, pp. 35–59.

Maki, U. (1996), 'Scientific realism and some pecularities of economics', in R.S. Cohen, R. Hilpinen, and Q. Renzong (eds), *Realism and Anti-Realism in the Philosophy of Science*, Dordrecht: Kluwer Academic Publishers, pp. 427–47.

Maki, U. (1998a), 'Realism', in J.B. Davis, D.W. Hand, and U. Maki (eds), *The Handbook of Economic Methodology*, Cheltenham, UK and Northampton, MA, USA: Edward Elgar, pp. 404–9.

Maki, U. (1998b), 'Aspects of realism about economics', *Theoria*, **13** (2), 310–19.

Maki, U. (2001), 'The way the world works (www): towards an ontology of theory choice,' in U. Maki (ed.), *The Economic World View: Studies in the Ontology of Economics*, Cambridge: Cambridge University Press, pp. 369–89.

McCullagh, C.B. (1984), *Justifying Historical Descriptions*, Cambridge: Cambridge University Press.

McCullagh, C.B. (2000), 'Bias in historical description, interpretation, and explanation', *History and Theory: Studies in the Philosophy of History*, **39** (1), 39–66.

Megill, A. (1989), 'Recounting the past: "description," explanation, and narrative in historiography', *American Historical Review*, **94** (3), 627–53.

Morse, J.M., P.N. Stern, J. Corbin, B. Bowers, K. Charmaz, and A.E. Clarke (2009), *Developing Grounded Theory: The Second Generation*, Walnut Creek, CA: Left Coast Press.

Norman, A.P. (1991), 'Telling it like it was: historical narratives on their own terms', *History and Theory: Studies in the Philosophy of History*, **30** (2), 119–35.

Olsen, W. (2012), *Data Collection: Key Debates and Methods in Social Research*, Los Angeles, CA: Sage.

Olsen, W. and J. Morgan (2005), 'A critical epistemology of analytical statistics: addressing the skeptical realist', *Journal for the Theory of Social Behavior*, **35** (3), 255–84.

Pentland, B.T. (1999), 'Building process theory with narrative: from description to explanation', *Academy of Management Review*, **24** (4), 711–24.

Rotheim, R.J. (1999), 'Post Keynesian economics and realist philosophy', *Journal of Post Keynesian Economics*, **22** (1), 71–104.

Runde, J. (1998), 'Assessing causal economic explanations', *Oxford Economic Papers*, **50** (1), 151–72.

Sarre, P. (1987), 'Realism in Practice', *Area*, **19** (1), 3–10.

Sayer, A. (1992), *Method in Social Science: A Realist Approach*, 2nd edn, London: Routledge.

Spiethoff, A. (1952), 'The "historical" character of economic theories', *Journal of Economic History*, **12** (2), 131–9.

Spiethoff, A. (1953), 'Pure theory and economic gestalt theory: ideal types and real types', in F.C. Lane and J.C. Riemersma (eds), *Enterprise and Secular Change: Readings in Economic History*, Homewood, IL: Richard D. Irwin, pp. 444–63.

Strauss, A.L. (1987), *Qualitative Analysis for Social Scientists*, Cambridge: Cambridge University Press.

Strauss, A.L. and J. Corbin (1990), *Basics of Qualitative Research: Grounded Theory Procedures and Techniques*, Newbury Park, CA: Sage.

Strauss, A.L. and J. Corbin (1994), 'Grounded theory methodology: an overview', in N.K. Denzin and Y.S. Lincoln (eds), *Handbook of Qualitative Research*, Thousand Oaks, CA: Sage, pp. 273–85.

Tosh, J. (1991), *The Pursuit of History*, 2nd edn, London: Longman.

Tsang, E. and K.-M. Kwan (1999), 'Replication and theory development in organization science: a critical realist perspective', *Academy of Management Review*, **24** (4), 759–80.

Wellman, B. and S.D. Berkowitz (eds) (1997), *Social Structures: A Network Approach*, Greenwich, CT: JAI Press.

Wilber, C.K. and R.S. Harrison (1978), 'The methodological basis of institutional economics: pattern model, storytelling, and holism', *Journal of Economic Issues*, **12** (3), 61–89.

Yin, R.K. (1981a), 'The case study crisis: some answers', *Administrative Science Quarterly*, **26** (1), 58–65.

Yin, R.K. (1981b), 'The case study as a serious research strategy', *Knowledge: Creation, Diffusion, Utilization*, **3** (1), 97–114.

# 3 An interdisciplinary perspective on heterodoxy
## Rick Szostak

The literature on interdisciplinary research has come of age. There is now a fair degree of consensus around a definition of interdisciplinarity and a set of strategies that work well in the performance of interdisciplinary research. These definitions and strategies are outlined in Repko (2012) and Bergmann et al. (2012), and applied in Repko et al. (2012).[1] The emerging consensus reflects and is reflected in the efforts of several scholarly organizations, including the Association for Interdisciplinary Studies (based in North America but with an international membership), Transdisciplinarity-Net (a network of mostly European scholars funded by the Swiss Academy), and Integration and Implementation Sciences (based in Australia but with international involvement); these and others are loosely affiliated through the International Network for Interdisciplinarity and Transdisciplinarity.

This chapter will draw lessons for heterodox economics from the literature on interdisciplinarity. Heterodox economics is in many ways an interdisciplinary endeavor.[2] As many chapters in this *Handbook* illustrate, heterodox economists often utilize methods and/or study phenomena that are most often addressed by disciplines other than economics. And they draw upon political, cultural, social, and psychological variables in seeking to explain economic outcomes such as income distribution, poverty, price determination, and firm behavior. Yet there is an even more central link between interdisciplinarity and heterodoxy. The methodological critique of the discipline inherent in heterodoxy is characteristic of the interdisciplinary critique of disciplines in general.[3] Scholars of interdisciplinarity emphasize the fact that all disciplines necessarily exclude valuable types of research from their purview; heterodox economists critique economics in particular for doing so. Though economics may well be the most constrained discipline in the social sciences, it is nevertheless true that the discipline's preferences for particular methods, theories, and research questions are characteristic of disciplines in general.

Section 3.1 introduces the concept of 'disciplinary perspective'. Disciplines do not randomly choose favored methods, theories, and subjects. Rather, they choose methods that are particularly amenable to investigating favored theories (and vice versa), and then apply these theories and methods to appropriate variables. This coherent set of methods, theories, and subject matter is then justified philosophically, instantiated in conceptual definitions, and institutionalized in career progress (including publication) decisions. There is thus an important synergy between the heterodox methods outlined in Part II of this *Handbook*, and the heterodox subjects addressed in Part III. These will often be a poor fit for the methods, subjects, and theories pursued by mainstream economists. The brief section 3.2 of this chapter addresses Lawson's analysis of 'open systems' in the light of this discussion of disciplinary perspective.

Section 3.3 surveys the strengths and weaknesses of the dozen methods used within the scholarly enterprise. Though all disciplines favor some subset of these, no method is perfect, and all methods have some value for any research enterprise. Scholarship in general, and interdisciplinarity and heterodoxy in particular, will benefit from an appreciation of the value of all methods. Section 3.4 then shows that disciplines tend to choose methods that justify their favored theories. Alternative methods will often prove less supportive of these theories, but the results of such methods are generally disdained by the discipline in question. Heterodox economists can readily identify with this sort of outcome, and perhaps take some solace in the fact that it is a general characteristic of disciplinarity.

Section 3.5 relates choice of method to choice of subject matter. Though all methods have something to contribute to all research questions, particular methods will be particularly good at investigating certain variables. The arguments of this section support the logic of this *Handbook*, which treats methods and subjects together. Section 3.6 nevertheless reminds us that no method is perfect, and that multiple methods have a place in any research enterprise.

Sections 3.7 and 3.8 then address the two other critical elements of disciplinary perspective. Section 3.7 looks at peer review: disciplines will develop criteria that will favor those who employ preferred methods, theories, and research questions. Section 3.8 then examines philosophy: what sort of philosophical justifications are employed by disciplines, and what should be advocated by those pursuing the interdisciplinary, heterodox project? A brief concluding section, section 3.9, follows.

## 3.1   DISCIPLINARY PERSPECTIVE

Scholars of interdisciplinarity stress the importance of 'disciplinary perspective', a mutually supportive set of theories, methods, subject matter, philosophical attitudes, concepts, and assessment guidelines that guide research in each discipline.[4] That is, disciplines choose methods that are well suited to investigating (and thus biased in favor of) their theories, investigate variables that their theories and methods can handle well, define concepts in accord with their theories and methods, develop epistemological and metaphysical attitudes that support this research enterprise, and develop standards for evaluating publications and career progress that reflect these interconnected preferences. In the field of interdisciplinary studies, the concept of disciplinary perspective is crucially important: it means that disciplinary research reflects a largely unconscious set of preferences that enhance intra-discipline communication but necessarily guide researchers to omit important aspects of complex problems (unless they carefully reflect on the nature of the disciplinary perspective in which they operate). In evaluating disciplinary research a useful starting point is to ask to what extent it reflects these hidden assumptions.

Recognizing the importance and power of disciplinary perspective within the academy is also critical for heterodox economics. The rational choice theories at the heart of economics lend themselves very well to mathematical modeling and statistical analysis (as will be seen below). The discipline has thus tended to stress a small number of easily quantified variables. The theories favored by heterodox economists may at times also be well suited to modeling, statistical analysis, and the same set of variables, but often will not. Most heterodox economists will thus have recourse not only to non-mainstream theories but also to non-mainstream methods and variables. Mainstream economists may well be baffled by research that offends their sensibilities in three different ways: they will object simultaneously to unfamiliar theory, method, and variables. They will likely be blissfully unaware that mainstream economics has itself chosen a mutually supportive set of neoclassical theories, mathematical modeling, and statistical analysis, and a small number of quantifiable variables.

The concept of disciplinary perspective thus provides a powerful motivation for the present *Handbook*. Since heterodox economists will often be guided by the nature of their theories to employ a much wider range of methods and variables than is common within mainstream economics, it is a valuable exercise for heterodoxy to gather in one place an overview of the methods and variables that they might employ. Scholars using novel methods or variables for their field are often forced to justify these choices, and are thus at a disadvantage relative to scholars pursuing more common methods and variables. This *Handbook* serves as both a survey and a justification, and can hopefully lessen the disadvantage faced by those pursuing novelty.

This chapter will discuss in some detail why particular methods and variables are well suited to the investigation of some theories, but less suited to others. This discussion can hopefully guide heterodox economists in their choice of method and variables. It can then also aid them in justifying the choices they make.

A similar argument can be made in the other direction. Economists interested in applying heterodox methods or in studying variables usually ignored by economists will often be guided to heterodox theories. Theory choice can then be justified in terms of methods and/or variables investigated.

But the discussion of disciplinary perspective should not simply encourage the emergence of multiple sets of theory, method, and variables within economics. While certain methods are better suited to investigating some theories than others, no method is perfect at any task. And indeed it can (and will) be argued that all methods are generally biased. Models and statistical analysis make rational choice theories look better than do experiments and observation. And thus interdisciplinary scholars urge the use of multiple methods in the investigation of any question or theory. Heterodox economists in particular should thus be aware of the compensating strengths and weaknesses (and thus biases) of different methods.

A final point should be made here. It is good scholarly practice to test one theory against another. This practice is often ignored in economics, where it is common to test one theory against no theory. Any insight provided by that theory can then be celebrated, even if an alternative theory, or a combination of alternative theories, would yield even greater insight. Once we recognize that different methods are better suited to certain theories we must appreciate that there may be no (unbiased) method with which to test a particular pair of theories against each other. Rather, the relative merits of competing theories can only be gauged through careful evaluation of evidence from multiple methods (and likely variables). Such an evaluation is unlikely if each group clings stubbornly to its favored method. Mainstream economists have often been dismissive of evidence from alternative methods. Heterodox economists should not mimic this attitude.

## 3.2   OPEN SYSTEMS

Tony Lawson has argued in many places (e.g., Lawson 2003) that the systems studied by economists are open systems: the variables we study interact causally with variables studied in other disciplines. By ignoring these external influences we can easily imagine that economic processes are simpler, more regular, and more easily understood than is actually the case. Chapter 1 in this *Handbook* addressed the closed versus open system distinction at length, and noted in particular the implication that multiple methods should be employed. Interdisciplinary scholarship likewise urges the study of linkages between the variables studied in different disciplines. Complex social problems are widely appreciated to reflect the interaction of economic, political, cultural, and other variables. One major failing of disciplinary scholarship in general involves ignoring the potential influences of variables studied by others. Economics in particular is diminished in its ability to understand the world if it arbitrarily excludes variables from analysis even though these clearly interact with those being studied. Interdisciplinary analysis steps in largely because each discipline refuses to extend its gaze to related variables.

Disciplinary preferences are not arbitrary, as we have seen. Economists ignore culture in large part because it is hard to measure. They have until recently ignored psychology because it made models of behavior unmanageable. Embracing the openness of systems often necessitates the use of multiple methods. Lawson has critiqued the conceit of mathematical models that they can cordon off a certain area of inquiry. The lesson from interdisciplinarity is that different causal relationships may require different methods of investigation. The dream of one tidy mathematical model must give way to the careful accretion of evidence from different methods (which may include models) for different parts of a complex whole.

Interdisciplinary scholarship encourages the visual mapping of complex systems.[5] It recognizes that it is sometimes necessary in practice to abstract away from causal relationships of limited importance. Nevertheless the goal should be to strive to understand all relevant relationships, as well as any emergent properties that can only be comprehended at the level of the system as a whole.

## 3.3   APPRECIATING MULTIPLE METHODS

It is argued above that different methods are best suited to different theories and different variables. This simple argument must confront a key belief of every discipline: that one or two (occasionally more) methods are always and everywhere superior. This section outlines a simple classification system that will show that each method has different strengths and weaknesses, and that these correlate with different theories and variables.

Journalists are advised to consider each of the five 'W' questions when investigating any event: who, what, where, when, and why? These same five questions can be asked of any causal process that a scholarly method (or theory) might investigate. In each case, a subsidiary question that can be asked of any method suggests itself.

1.   Who is the causal agent investigated? There are two important distinctions here: non-intentional (including volcanoes or institutions) versus intentional agency (of

beings that can act on purpose), each of which can take the form of individual, group, or relationship agency.

2.  How many agents can a method investigate?
3.  What does the agent do? There are three broad answers, which map imperfectly onto the six types of agency: both intentional and non-intentional agents can passively react to external stimuli, whereas intentional agents can also engage in active action or changes in attitude.
4.  Does the method identify any or all of the criteria for specifying a causal relationship? These are: that the cause and effect are correlated, that the cause occurs before the effect (at least, this is the general case), that intermediate causal factors be identified, and that alternative explanations of correlation be excluded (Singleton and Strait 1999).
5.  Why does the agent do what it does? With non-intentional agents, action can only be understood in terms of their inherent nature. With intentional agents, scholars can explore the five distinct types of decision-making that can be employed: rational, intuitive, process (virtue)-oriented, rule-based, and tradition-based. For groups and relationships, scholars can also ask how individual preferences are aggregated.
6.  Does the method allow scope for induction (or is it entirely deductive)? Philosophers appreciate that scientific understanding advances best through a mix of induction and deduction. All methods lend themselves to empirical evaluation – though in different ways and to different degrees, as evidenced by their evaluation below in terms of the other nine questions – and thus serve some deductive purpose. Methods differ markedly in terms of their inductive potential. One might worry that a discipline reliant on methods with limited inductive potential will not generate or accept many new ideas.
7.  Where does the causal process occur? This question can be interpreted as addressing how generalizable the results of the investigation will be. Two broad answers are possible (though they might be seen as representing two ends of a continuum of generalizability): nomothetic analyses are highly generalizable, while idiographic analyses are not.
8.  Does the method allow movements through space to be tracked?
9.  When does the causal process occur? There are five broad time-paths that a causal process might follow: the system of variables investigated might return to the original equilibrium, move to a new equilibrium, exhibit change in a particular direction, exhibit cyclicality, or move in a stochastic or uncertain fashion.
10. Does the method allow movements through time to be tracked?

These questions, and the possible answers to each, will be fleshed out in the context of economics below. But it is first useful to identify the scholarly methods that might be classified according to these questions. How many scholarly methods are there? There is no obvious way to answer this question deductively by identifying some logical typology of 'types of method'. It is possible, however, to inductively – by investigating what scholars do across disciplines – identify some dozen methods used in the scholarly enterprise. Several of these methods are accorded individual chapters in this *Handbook*. Others are captured through exploration of case study and historical approaches.[6]

Economics has tended for the last several decades to stress just two of these dozen methods: mathematical modeling (including simulations and game theoretic models) and statistical analysis (often, though not always, associated with models). Heterodox economists have suggested not just that these need to be supplemented, but that they can be applied in ways that reduce their bias toward rational choice theory. Lee, Chapter 14 in this *Handbook*, argues that models should reflect agents and causal processes observed to exist in the world. Downward, in Chapter 10, suggests changes in how regressions are used and interpreted. Martins, in Chapter 11, suggests limited applications of basic econometrics with careful attention to data plots.

Experiments have long been disdained (despite being viewed as 'the' scientific method in the natural sciences that economists often seek to emulate), but have recently received some grudging acceptance.[7] Lambert and Bewley, Chapter 27 in this *Handbook*, discuss the advantages of quasi-experiments, in which only imperfect control is possible. Surveys have also been viewed with suspicion but have now become accepted, at least when there is no other measure available (as in using surveys to measure institutional quality). Cardão-Pito, Chapter 6 in this *Handbook*, provides detailed advice on the several stages in survey analysis, and notes that surveys allow us to investigate populations rather than assume that we know how they behave.

Several other methods have generally been even less common in economics. Interviews may have been eschewed in large part due to a belief among mainstream economists that theory already tells us what people (should) think. Several chapters in this *Handbook* advocate interviews (and often surveys too), noting variously that these give us unique insights into decision-making processes and hidden economic activities, suggest new theoretical hypotheses, allow us to investigate complex causal interactions, and often suggest policy responses. They also provide much practical advice on how to perform interviews and avoid common difficulties.

Ethnographic and observational analysis ('participant observation', in which the investigator interacts with those under observation, is most common in other disciplines, but discreet observation is also possible) has likewise been downplayed. Basole and Ramnarain, Chapter 7 in this *Handbook*, identify 27 works that have employed ethnographic methods in economics (though perhaps stressing interviews over observation); these have tended to focus on a handful of key issues: trust, power, motivations, identity, labor relations, and management.

Experience or intuition (some would treat this as an important subset of observational analysis, since we are in effect 'observing' ourselves here) is likely important in the background, but is rarely officially referenced. Textual (content, discourse) analysis, classification (including evolutionary analysis), mapmaking (both representational and conceptual), hermeneutics and semiotics (the study of symbols and their meaning), and physical traces (as in archaeology) have all seen relatively little use in economics.[8] Bracarense and Johnson, Chapter 5 in this *Handbook*, advocate historical methods, with a particular stress on consulting a wide array of different texts.

Table 3.1 shows how ten of the above methods answer the ten questions outlined above. Table 3.1 establishes that there is no 'one' scientific method, but rather a dozen such methods with different strengths and weaknesses. In trying to comprehend the full complexity of human life we can usefully have recourse to each (while remaining cognizant of each method's limitations). Table 3.1 can guide scholars as to which methods to employ in a particular inquiry. In all cases, there are multiple methods than can potentially shed

*Table 3.1   Typology of strengths and limitations of method*

| Criteria | Classification | Experiment | Interview | Intuition/ experience | Mathematical modeling |
|---|---|---|---|---|---|
| Type of Agent | All agents | All; but group agency only in natural experiment | Intentional individuals; relationships only indirectly | Intentional individuals; others indirectly | All agents |
| Number of Agents Investigated | Few or many, but generally many | Few | Few | One | Few or many |
| Type of Causation | Action (evolutionary) | Passive reaction, Action | Attitudes; acts indirectly | Attitudes | All |
| Criteria for identifying a causal relationship | Aids each, but limited | Potentially all four | Might provide insight on each | Some insight on correlation, temporality | All; but limited with respect to intermediate, alternatives |
| Decisionmaking Process | Indirect insight | No | Some insight; but biased | Yes; may mislead | Some insight |
| Inductive Potential? | Little | Some | If open in style | Yes; bias | Little |
| Generalizability | Both | Both | Idiographic | Idiographic | Both |
| Spatiality | Some potential | Constrained | From memory | From memory | Difficult to model |
| Time Path | No insight | Little insight | Little insight | Little insight | Emphasizes equilibrium |
| Temporality | Some potential | Constrained | From memory | From memory | Simplifies |

| Criteria | Participant observation | Physical traces | Statistical analysis | Survey | Textual analysis |
|---|---|---|---|---|---|
| Type of Agent | Intentional individual; Relationships groups? | All; groups and relationship indirect | All; groups and relationship indirect | Intentional individuals; groups indirect | Intentional individuals; others indirect |
| Number of Agents Investigated | Few individuals or one group | Few | Many/all | Many | One/few |
| Type of Causation | Action; some insight into attitudes | Passive reaction; Action | Action; Attitudes indirectly | Attitudes; Actions indirectly | Attitudes; Action |
| Criteria for identifying a causal relationship | All, but rarely done | Some insight to all four | Correlation and temporality well; others maybe | Some insight on correlation | Some insight on all |
| Decisionmaking Process | All | No | No | Little | Some insight; Biased |
| Inductive Potential? | Much | Much | Some | Very little | Much |
| Generalizability | Idiographic; nomothetic from many studies | Idiographic; nomothetic from many studies | Both | Both | Idiographic; nomothetic. from many studies |

*Table 3.1*   (continued)

| Criteria | Participant observation | Physical traces | Statistical analysis | Survey | Textual analysis |
|---|---|---|---|---|---|
| Spatiality | Very good; Some limits | Possibly infer | Limited | Rarely | Possible |
| Time Path | Some insight | Some insight | Emphasizes equilibrium | Little insight | Some insight |
| Temporality | Very good up to months | Possibly infer | Static, often frequent | Somewhat if longitudinal | Possible |

*Note:*   The 'criteria' reflect the ten questions listed in the text.

*Source:*   Szostak (2004, pp. 138–9).

light on a particular question. A proposition that is supported by investigation using multiple methods should be trusted more than a proposition supported by only one.

Philosophers have long debated whether there is a 'best' scholarly method. For much of the last two centuries, experimentation was viewed as at least the best and perhaps the only scientific method. Biologists, though, only rarely have recourse to experiments, and thus have instead urged careful observation of the world (and the physical traces left by past life forms) and careful attempts at classification. Economists in recent decades have pursued mathematical modeling and statistical analysis to the exclusion of almost all other types of analysis. Historians have stressed the careful evaluation of particular 'cases' employing a variety of methods to this end, but particularly textual analysis. Humanists have emphasized textual analysis and/or the application of intuition. Given these differing perspectives on appropriate method, it should hardly be surprising if it turned out that multiple methods should be applied within the scholarly enterprise.

## 3.4   COMPARING METHOD AND THEORY

It was noted above that the five 'W' questions could also be asked of scholarly theories. It is thus possible to empirically establish that disciplines do indeed choose mutually compatible sets of theory and method. Economics has tended to employ variants of rational choice theory. These stress individual intentional agency, active action, rational decision-making, and equilibrium outcomes, and results are assumed to be highly generalizable. Mathematical modeling and statistical analysis, as we can see from Table 3.1, are also best suited to investigating individuals, actions, and equilibrium processes. Though neither method is good at investigating the process of decision-making, one key advantage of assuming rationality is that one need not do so: if one knows (or assumes) an individual's preferences and decision set, one can predict or explain their decisions without needing to observe those decisions. They will optimize their utility given their preferences (and if we assume they wish only to maximize income, explanation is straightforward). Both methods lend themselves to generalization.

If one wants to relax the rationality assumption, then it becomes much more valuable to observe the actual decision-making process. How exactly do agents employ intuition or follow their values, traditions, or explicit rules? Behavioral economists have often turned to experiments as a method. Their results have often been derided by mainstream economists.[9] Though it is beyond the scope of this chapter, it could be argued that behavioral economics has made inroads in the discipline in part because some non-rational decision-making rules lend themselves to modeling and/or statistical analysis.

Heterodox economists often wish to relax the rationality assumption. They wish to theorize a more complex psychological reality. They wish to theorize about cultural or political influences on decision-making. As with behavioral economists, they may well find uses for mathematical modeling and statistical analysis. But they may often wish to observe people making decisions (using experiments or observation), or interview or survey people about how and why they make particular decisions.

The rationality assumption frees mainstream economists from worrying about what people think. But heterodox economists will often wish to investigate attitude formation. Statistical analysis and mathematical modeling can be employed here. But other methods are designed to investigate attitudes more than actions. Interviews and surveys are particularly useful here, but textual analysis, and intuition or experience, are also important.

Most methods are better at investigating individual rather than group or relationship processes. Information about groups or relationships often comes indirectly from the study of individuals. Network analysis (treated here as a form of mapmaking) is an exception, for its essence is the analysis of relationships. Mainstream economics has been willing over the last decades to embrace one (competitive) form of relationship agency in game theory models, but models of games often yield no or multiple equilibria. Observation, interviews, or perhaps surveys might establish how such relationships unfold over time (likely through the use of non-individually rational strategies). For collaborative relationships, which tend to focus on the sharing of information (and emotional bonds), network analysis may prove invaluable. It is noteworthy here that network analysis can take many forms. In its most mathematical form it resembles modeling. But for many situations a visual approach to network analysis may prove analytically superior, if perhaps less convincing to those accustomed to only mathematical models.

Heterodox economists may also wish to emphasize the causal role of at least one type of non-intentional agent: institutions. Though institutions are created by intentional agents, they then exert influences that their creators may never have intended. The method best suited to non-intentional agents, the experiment, is only occasionally feasible (history does perhaps provide some natural experiments here). Governments do occasionally experiment with institutions. Several other methods can provide some insight.

It is possible but much more difficult to model non-equilibrium processes. Though no method excels at studying non-equilibrium processes, several methods can provide some insight into these. The best method will depend on the theorized source of non-equilibrium outcomes. Many theories, for example, attribute cyclicality in output to non-rational decision-making. Such theories will best be investigated in the manner suggested above for non-rational decision-making.

Last but not least, we should address generalizability. Economists generally pursue highly generalizable theories. Heterodox economists may believe that there is an important degree of uniqueness to a particular country's growth processes, or particular business cycles, or particular markets (see the discussion of epistemological relativism in

Chapter 2 and historical uniqueness in Chapter 5). They might, for example, wish not to study China's development with the exact same theory used to analyze modern Europe. They may then wish to have recourse to the set of methods commonly employed by the historian: textual analysis, interviews, and in some cases examination of physical traces. Observation, and intuition or experience, may at times prove useful.

The analysis in this section has highlighted a handful of ways in which heterodox theory might differ from mainstream theory: assuming some sort of non-rationality; examining groups, relationships, or non-intentional agents; studying attitudes rather than just actions; exploring non-equilibrium processes; and exploring idiographic processes. In each case, a handful of methods best suited to this sort of investigation has been identified. This conclusion is similar to that reached in Chapter 2: that investigating different causal mechanisms will require different methods.

These methods, and the types of theory that they are best suited to investigating, are all employed in other social science disciplines. Only a sinister belief that these other social sciences are completely wasting their time could rationalize a refusal to recognize the evidence for these theories produced by these methods. Each of these methods is practiced by some group(s) of scholars that have identified criteria by which the application of these methods can be judged. A discipline as large as economics can certainly aspire to have expertise in a dozen methods rather than just two. This *Handbook* serves a valuable purpose here in identifying how diverse methods are best pursued.

This section has argued that particular theories suggest particular methods. It should be stressed in closing that the same argument can be made in reverse: choosing a particular method will encourage the pursuit of a particular kind of theory. Interviewing individuals as to why they made the choices that they did will guide one away from assuming simple rationality. Case study analysis will guide one away from assuming that people always behave in a simple predictable manner. Observation will alert one to the importance of spatial and temporal variables. Heterodox economists need to be consciously aware that their methodological choices have theoretical implications.

## 3.5   LINKING METHOD AND SUBJECT MATTER

It was argued at the start of this chapter that disciplines each choose a compatible set of theories, methods, and subject matter. The previous section discussed at some length how particular methods are better suited to some theories than others. It is straightforward to appreciate that these theory–method pairs will be associated with certain variables. People's beliefs as identified in surveys or interviews will be associated with theories that do not assume rationality. Cultural attitudes may also be identified by surveys and applied in theories of group behavior. Individual idiosyncrasies may be established through interviews and employed in idiographic analysis.

As the later chapters in this *Handbook* indicate, heterodox economists will often bring novel theories and methods to bear on the variables studied by mainstream economists: prices, investment, or employment. Yet they will often include novel variables in their analysis. They will worry about the nature of policy processes. They will investigate the details of decisions about job-seeking behaviors. They will investigate temporal and spatial processes. They will study the cultural and political and social context in which markets operate. They will find that diverse methods are called for in these varied investigations.

Economic processes are arguably affected by virtually every phenomenon studied by scholars.[10] Basic human abilities, motivations, and goals are clearly important, as are various aspects of individual personalities and beliefs and relationships. Social divisions along gender, ethnic, class, occupational, and other lines have been appreciated mainly in the economic development literature, but undoubtedly have effects in developed countries as well. The same can be said of family and kinship structures. Political, economic, and social ideologies likely influence the goals that individuals pursue as well as the means they employ. Political and economic institutions affect both incentives and capabilities. Crime rates influence a host of decisions, including investment decisions. Technology and science determine what is possible in many spheres of activity. Nutrition, disease incidence, age distribution, population growth rates, and migration have myriad effects on what both individuals and groups can accomplish. Languages, religions, rituals, and a host of cultural values (and also public opinion regarding issues of the day) influence human behavior, as do art and literature. Transport infrastructure and other elements of the built environment facilitate economic activity. Various elements of the natural environment, notably resource availability, climate, and natural disasters, also facilitate or constrain activity. These various phenomena interact with each other and are influenced in turn by economic processes. Heterodox economists may thus look very widely in their research on economic processes.

It is worth reiterating here the insight of Lawson (2003) regarding open systems. Since the variables studied by economists are causally related to a host of phenomena that economists tend to ignore, our understanding of complex processes is severely limited. One key task of heterodoxy, then, is to identify and investigate the cultural, political, social, environmental, and psychological influences on economic outcomes.

There is a further link between method and variables investigated. It was noted in section 3.3 that some methods have more inductive potential than others. Philosophers of science commonly recognize that scientific understanding advances best when both induction and deduction are employed: induction suggests new hypotheses that can then be evaluated deductively. A purely deductive enterprise can easily become untethered from reality, while a purely inductive enterprise can too easily miss the connections between diverse observations (Gower 1997, p. 254). In general, the methods favoured by neoclassical economists have limited inductive potential. Observation, interviews, and textual analysis are much more likely to suggest novel lines of inquiry to a researcher. And they are thus likely to encourage the exploration of novel variables (or indeed phenomena that are hard to quantify).

## 3.6   USING MULTIPLE METHODS

It has been argued above that different methods are best suited to different theories and variables. But this does not mean that any sort of investigation is best served by exclusive reliance on any one method. The community of heterodox economists should not escape the methodological narrowness of other economists only to embrace a different methodological orthodoxy. Each theory and each variable can be investigated using multiple methods. These will each have strengths and weaknesses.

Sometimes different methods are useful in investigating different aspects of a complex problem. Experiments can identify how likely it is that a particular decision is made in a particular circumstance. But interviews may be necessary to comprehend why certain agents made certain decisions. Likewise surveys can identify common attitudes but interviews can find out why these attitudes are held and observation can explore how these are applied in practice. Statistical analysis may establish some central tendency but historical methods[11] are necessary to appreciate deviations from this.

More generally, methods that investigate many agents can often be usefully combined with methods that investigate a few in detail (a point stressed by Ragin 2000). Likewise methods that identify a particular decision can be combined with methods that investigate why it was made. Methods that test a theory can be combined with inductive methods that suggest new hypotheses. Methods that identify the results of a process can be combined with methods that follow agents through time and space. And methods that generalize can be combined with methods that study individual cases.

Even when investigating one thing it is still advisable to use multiple methods. People may lie on surveys. They may pretend if they know that they are being observed. Each method has its biases and imperfections. If multiple methods point in the same direction we can have much greater confidence in our results. If they suggest different answers, we can aspire to 'triangulate' across these (triangulation is discussed in detail in later chapters).

The use of multiple methods is especially important when different theory types are compared. Scholarly understanding advances by comparing theoretical explanations, and seeing which is most important along a particular causal link (but not necessarily dismissing the losing theory as completely unimportant). If only one method is used in such a test, the results will generally be biased toward whichever theory that method is particularly suited to investigating. Mainstream economics habitually 'cheats' in two important ways in this regard. First, it tends to test its favored theory not against alternatives but against no alternative. That is, it casually assumes away the possibility of alternative theoretical explanations. Any explanatory power whatsoever of the favored theory can thus be celebrated. Second, it insists on the use of its favored methods. It thus casually assumes away the validity of other methods. If it does ever entertain alternative theories, these will generally be unfairly evaluated through recourse to methods less suited to their investigation.

Above, heterodox economics has been urged to embrace methodological flexibility. Flexibility with respect to method will both encourage and reflect flexibility with respect to theory as well. Multiple methods will almost certainly establish the value of multiple theories.

## 3.7   PEER REVIEW

Heterodox economists seeking to publish in mainstream journals will often face the difficult task of simultaneously justifying non-mainstream choices of theory, method, and variables. It is hoped that this chapter (and *Handbook*) will facilitate this unfortunate and unfair task. Authors can cite this chapter to show that it is no coincidence that they are deviating from common practice in each of these three ways. Journal editors and referees can be guided likewise to appreciate the synergies between theory, method, and variables. They can likewise be guided to appreciate that different methods have compensating strengths and weaknesses.

Referees are asked to provide an expert opinion. It should come as no surprise if they then tend to prefer works that employ methods (and variables) with which they are very familiar. Editors of heterodox journals may thus wish to identify referees with expertise in different methods. But researchers will often employ multiple methods in a single work. And editors themselves will need to engage with a wide variety of methods. An openness to multiple methods, and an appreciation of the potential strengths of all methods, are thus to be encouraged among both referees and editors.

Ignorance breeds contempt. Scholars are naturally more familiar with the standards employed to judge research employing 'their' theories and (especially) methods. It is easy to assume that alternative theories or methods lack any – or at least similar – standards by which their application can be judged. Yet there are good and bad ways of applying any theory or method. From the point of view of a journal editor, misguided standards are preferable to (even the perception of) no standards. One potential value of a *Handbook* such as this is that it can aid in the evaluation of works applying diverse methods, and thus in editorial appreciation that this is possible. This chapter in particular can aid in the important decision as to whether a particular method(s) is well suited to a particular research question.

## 3.8   PHILOSOPHY OF HETERODOXY

It was noted at the outset of this chapter that disciplines choose philosophical attitudes that accord well with their choices of theories, methods, and variables. Heterodox economists have long appreciated that there are problems with the logical positivism that (subconsciously at least) is associated with the pursuit of rational choice theory, mathematical modeling, and statistical analysis in economics. Critical realism is often recommended as a philosophical guide to heterodoxy (see Chapters 1 and 2 in this *Handbook*).

Scholars of interdisciplinarity and scholars of mixed methods research have also sought to identify guiding philosophical principles. Johnson et al. (2007) wonder if pragmatism can and should serve as the guiding philosophy of mixed methods research. They worry that any guiding philosophy must be flexible enough that all mixed methods scholars feel comfortable with it. They note that quantitative researchers are often guided by a post-positivist philosophy and that qualitative researchers are often guided by a post-structuralist philosophy. A mixed methods philosophy would likely lie somewhere in between these.

Szostak (2007) investigated how interdisciplinarity relied on a set of (generally implicit) philosophical attitudes that generally lay between what were termed 'modernist' and 'postmodernist' approaches. Indeed, these 'interdisciplinary' attitudes could generally be seen as Aristotelian 'Golden Means'. Notably many of these might be embraced by affirmative postmodernists – who accept various postmodern concerns, but still believe it is possible to enhance human understanding (Rosenau 1992) – as well as many who might be thought to be modernist in outlook. Moreover, these various interdisciplinarity attitudes were shown to be complementary to (parts of) diverse intellectual traditions, including complexity, critical theory, critical thinking, discourse analysis, feminism, pragmatism, rhetoric, and social constructionism.

Several attitudes that can be identified as interdisciplinary might also well serve the community of heterodox economists. The first attitude seeks a middle ground between a positive belief in the possibility of disproof and a nihilist skepticism regarding the possibility of enhanced understanding: proof and disproof are impossible, but we can increase our confidence in any statement by compiling arguments and evidence in favor. Such an attitude – in line, it might be noted, with recent thinking in the philosophy of science – works against the idea, commonly held in economics, that one method holds the key to truth, but rather supports the value of compiling different types of argument and evidence. The value of methodological plurality is likewise supported by a middle-ground attitude toward reality: there is an external reality, though humans are limited in their abilities to accurately and precisely perceive this. If we instead think that reality is entirely subjective, we are again guided to doubt the possibility of increased understanding. But if we ignore perceptual and cognitive limitations we may instead be guided to imagine that we are capable of flawless understandings. Recognition of the interconnectedness of all phenomena is also important here: if empirical regularities must be carefully contextualized, then it is particularly unlikely that one method will tell us all that we need to know.

Scholars of interdisciplinarity generally hold that it is possible to integrate across perspectives associated with different disciplines or social divisions. If instead we were to imagine that disciplines were incommensurate, then there would be little hope that mainstream economists would ever comprehend, much less heed, the advice of heterodox economists. If we accept the possibility of integration, then heterodox economists might be guided to show how heterodox and mainstream perspectives can be integrated.

Interdisciplinarians, as we have seen, are inevitably sensitive to the biases inherent in disciplinarity. This sensitivity leads to a belief that all scholars should reflect on their own biases, and those of their scholarly communities. It is possible that any scholar or community will be more willing to interrogate their own biases if it is appreciated that biases infuse the entire scholarly enterprise.

These attitudes are complementary. Improved understanding and integration are possible because we can imperfectly perceive, identify contextual regularities, and converse. Special note might be made here of reflection. While interdisciplinarians back away from extreme arguments that scholarly biases and errors are so profound as to prohibit enhanced understanding, they are guided by an appreciation that specialized scholarly research is necessarily biased. Only by constantly reflecting on such biases can we hope to transcend these. (Self-reflection is also stressed in Chapter 2's discussion of grounded theory.)[12]

Most of these attitudes have been discussed in this or the preceding chapters. Integration deserves some further discussion. Most scholars of interdisciplinarity stress the importance of integration – the synthesis of contrasting insights into a more holistic understanding – as critical to interdisciplinary research. Several strategies for achieving integration have been identified (see Repko 2012). Interdisciplinary scholars would thus urge heterodox economists to see their theories or methods not as substitutes but rather as complements – to other heterodox theories and methods, and to mainstream theories and methods. Interdisciplinary scholarship recognizes, that is, both the strengths and limitations of disciplinary scholarship. It encourages the application of all relevant theories and methods to complex problems, and the appreciation of all relevant variables. It aspires to integrate across the insights generated from all types of research. Heterodox economists should be encouraged to apply new theories, methods, and data, but then (not necessarily in the same publication) to synthesize across multiple research methodologies.

Last but not least, communication issues should be briefly addressed. One key barrier to interdisciplinary communication and thus integration is ambiguous terminology. Different research communities over time come to attach different meanings to concepts. Those skeptical of the possibility of cross-group understanding often ground their skepticism in observations of different meanings and terminology employed in different disciplines or social groups. Heterodox economists should be wary of the possibility of miscommunicating with each other and with non-heterodox economists by employing concepts in unusual but unspecified ways. Heterodox economists should not be constrained to define concepts the way others do but should be strongly encouraged to carefully define deviations from wider usage.[13]

## 3.9   CONCLUDING REMARKS

If interdisciplinarity were more firmly entrenched in the academy, then the plea for integrating across theories and methods and variables in the study of the economy would appear obvious rather than revolutionary. The pretence of mainstream economists that one theory and two methods should suffice would be laughable in such an environment. The project for a heterodox economics can thus benefit greatly from looking beyond economics to ask how the scholarly enterprise as a whole should be organized.

This chapter has drawn upon the literature on interdisciplinarity, and particularly its stress on the idea of disciplinary perspectives. It has shown that choices regarding theories, methods, and phenomena of study are inextricably linked. It has also explored in detail the strengths and weaknesses of the different methods that might be employed. It is hoped that the chapter will both encourage and support the exploration of the full range of relevant methods and subject matter.

## NOTES

1. See also the 'About interdisciplinarity' section of the website of the Association for Interdisciplinary Studies (2013) at http://www.oakland.edu.ais which provides an overview of the literature, especially on interdisciplinary best practices.
2. The author began his career as an economic historian, published a book and a few articles of a methodological and heterodox nature, and then, frustrated by the difficulty in finding relevant material in related disciplines, increasingly became a scholar of interdisciplinary practice.
3. Economists, it might be noted, have been much more suspicious of interdisciplinarity than have other social scientists. Confident in the superiority of their favored theory and method, they have doubted that they have much to learn from the theories and methods of others. Heterodox economists are regularly punished by this suspicion of alternative theories and methods, and thus the insights of interdisciplinary scholarship should be of particular interest.
4. Lee et al. (2013, p. 700) appreciate that, 'All academic disciplines and professions, such as economics, have a multi-element set (or structure) of values and perceptions that help define what it is to its members and

to others, such as external evaluators.' They discuss in detail how economics departments and granting agencies institutionally enforce preferences regarding theory, method, and subject matter.

5. Such as the conceptual model of economics departments in Lee et al. (2013). Lee again addresses the role of conceptual models in Chapter 14 of this *Handbook*. The literature on interdisciplinary mapping is surveyed in https://sites.google.com/a/ualberta.ca/rick-szostak/research/about-interdisciplinarity/best-practices/interdisciplinary-research/mapping-interdisciplinary-connections.

6. Other chapters explore particular kinds of modeling or statistical analysis. Still others discuss how methods can be combined.

7. Natural or quasi-experiments are often referred to by economists as subsidiary evidence in articles focused on models and/or statistical analysis.

8. Some would treat 'evaluation' of programs as distinct, though it can be seen as a combination of some of the above methods. Similar arguments can be made with respect to demography, case study, feminism, historical method, and perhaps also hermeneutics.

9. Experiments are particularly well suited to the investigation of the actions or reactions of non-intentional agents. With intentional agents, legitimate questions arise as to whether these behave the same in the real world as in experimental circumstances. Still, since experiments are understandably valued in most natural sciences, economists should have been less hasty in dismissing these.

10. Szostak (2009, Ch. 3) reviewed the plausible impacts of diverse phenomena on economic growth. He drew in turn on a classification of the phenomena studied in human science from Szostak (2004).

11. Ironically econometrics is the preferred method even in economic history, though arguably the field's main insights come from the careful comparison of historical cases.

12. Repko (2012) urges reflection throughout the interdisciplinary research process.

13. Szostak (2014) proposes a set of guidelines for coping with ambiguity.

# REFERENCES

Association for Interdisciplinary Studies (2013), 'About interdisciplinarity', accessed 15 August 2015 at http://www.oakland.edu/ais/.

Bergmann, Matthias, Thomas Jahn, Tobias Knobloch, Wolfgang Krohn, Christian Pohl, and Engelbert Schramm (2012), *Methods for Transdisciplinary Research: A Primer for Practice*, Berlin, Germany: Campus.

Gower, B. (1997), *Scientific Method: An Historical and Philosophical Introduction*, London: Routledge.

Johnson, R.B., A.J. Onmegbuzie, and L.A. Turner (2007), 'Toward a definition of mixed methods research', *Journal of Mixed Methods Research*, 1 (2), 112–33.

Lawson, T. (2003), *Reorienting Economics*, London: Routledge.

Lee, Frederic S., X. Pham, and G. Gu (2013), 'The UK Research Assessment Exercise and the narrowing of UK economics', *Cambridge Journal of Economics*, 37 (4), 693–717.

Ragin, Charles F. (2000), *Fuzzy-Set Social Science*, Chicago, IL: University of Chicago Press.

Repko, Allen F. (2012), *Interdisciplinary Research: Process and Theory*, 2nd edn, Thousand Oaks, CA: Sage.

Repko, Allen F., William H. Newell, and Rick Szostak (eds) (2012), *Case Studies in Interdisciplinary Research*, Thousand Oaks, CA: Sage.

Rosenau, Pauline Marie (1992), *Post-modernism and the Social Sciences*, Princeton, NJ: Princeton University Press.

Singleton, R.A. and B.C. Strait (1999), *Approaches to Social Research*, 3rd edn, New York: Oxford University Press.

Szostak, Rick (2004), *Classifying Science: Phenomena, Data, Theory, Method, Practice*, Dordrecht: Kluwer Academic Publishers.

Szostak, Rick (2007), 'Modernism, postmodernism, and interdisciplinarity', *Issues in Integrative Studies*, 26 (1), 32–83.

Szostak, Rick (2009), *The Causes of Economic Growth: Interdisciplinary Perspectives*, Berlin: Springer.

Szostak, Rick (2014), 'Communicating complex concepts', in Michael O'Rourke, Stephen Crowley, Sanford D. Eigenbrode, and J.D. Wulfhorst (eds), *Enhancing Communication and Collaboration in Interdisciplinary Research*, Thousand Oaks, CA: Sage, pp. 34–55.

# PART II

# RESEARCH METHODS AND DATA COLLECTION

# 4 Separate or symbiotic? Quantitative and qualitative methods in (heterodox) economics research
## *Lynda Pickbourn and Smita Ramnarain*

## 4.1 INTRODUCTION

The qualitative–quantitative debate that flourished in the 1980s and 1990s within the social sciences hinged on the philosophical oppositions between the ontological and epistemological approaches to research that motivate a researcher's choice of research method (see Sale et al. 2002; Smith 1983). Discussion focused on how the epistemological and ontological foundations of quantitative and qualitative methods are directly in opposition to one another. More recently, however, there has been a greater effort to integrate techniques from both traditions to formulate a better understanding of social phenomena, under the umbrella of 'mixed methods'. The development of critical realism and grounded theory as lenses of social analysis, as well as a growing commitment to methodological pluralism, especially among the heterodoxy, has spearheaded this effort.

In this chapter, we look into the differences – philosophical and technical – between qualitative and quantitative methods of research, identify perspectives regarding their integration (both for and against), and advance our own reasoning for why, as social scientists, economists need to take this question of methodological pluralism seriously. While we do not discuss historical methods separately, it is worth noting here that similar dilemmas underlie economic history: indeed, social and economic historians have sometimes found themselves on the front lines of the qualitative and quantitative debate, caught between economists with their skepticism of qualitative evidence, on the one hand, and historians with their suspicion of quantitative research on the other (Carus and Ogilvie 2009). We point readers to Chapter 5 of this *Handbook* for a detailed discussion of qualitative and quantitative methodologies in historical research.

In this chapter, we begin by defining what quantitative and qualitative approaches are, taking care to draw a distinction between method, methodology, and epistemology in section 4.2. In section 4.3, we compare the technical aspects of both methodological traditions, looking into the typical objections quantitative researchers in economics have against qualitative methods, and the responses qualitative researchers have to these objections. We argue that these misunderstandings arise from a fundamental misapprehension of the nature of qualitative research, as well as from the fundamentally disparate epistemological and ontological stances of the two traditions. Section 4.3 thus sets the stage for exploring the possibility integrating the two traditions. We take up this issue in greater detail in section 4.4, presenting different perspectives on the compatibility of methodologies and methods, as well as practical barriers to their greater integration within economics. Section 4.5 concludes the chapter.

## 4.2    DESCRIBING QUANTITATIVE AND QUALITATIVE METHODOLOGIES

At the outset it is important to clarify what we mean by the term 'methodology' and how it differs from 'methods'. Following Bryman (1984) we use the term 'methodology' – be it quantitative or qualitative – to refer to the ontological base and epistemological assumptions guiding the preference for a particular set of methods. As we will see later in this chapter, a methodology carries particular significance in terms of representing a view about the nature of knowledge and the nature of reality and being. 'Methods' on the other hand refer to the set of techniques used for the collection and analysis of data. Quantitative and qualitative methodologies reflect respectively, therefore, the choice of a particular ontological and epistemological base (Bryman 1984). Thus we can think of methodology as providing justification for the choice of different research methods, so that 'quantitative methodology' in this chapter refers to the epistemological and ontological justification for quantitative methods, while 'qualitative methodology' refers to the epistemological and ontological justification for qualitative methods.[1]

**What is Quantitative Methodology?**

The term 'quantitative', when applied to empirical analysis in economics, has been used variously to describe the method of data collection, the type of data collected, and the ways in which data is analyzed and interpreted. According to the typology proposed by Kanbur (2003), a quantitative approach to data collection is generally understood to be general in population coverage, and to require only the passive involvement of the population being researched. The data collected is usually quantifiable – either numerical data, or non-numerical data that can be condensed into a numerical value – and as such, can be analyzed and interpreted through the use of statistical techniques. For the purpose of this chapter, we could begin by adopting an understanding of quantitative research as involving the analysis of numerical data that has been collected through the use of methods that include, but are not limited to, random sample surveys and structured interviews. Blaikie (2003) argues, for instance, that quantitative data is characterized by the transformation of information received from the respondent into numbers, either immediately or prior to analysis (p. 20). Such data may then be subject to univariate, bivariate, explanatory or inferential analyses (see Blaikie for detailed descriptions of each). However, this definition raises more questions than it answers: for example, does the use of open-ended interviews with a randomly selected sample to generate information about attitudes and motivations that can then be quantified using a simple ranking or scoring exercise count as qualitative or quantitative research (see, for example, Ragin 2000)? Indeed, notwithstanding the schematic Blaikie (2003) lays out to identify and distinguish quantitative from qualitative, he also states that 'all primary data start out as words' (p. 20). Perhaps a better approach would be to explore the implicit assumptions that quantitative methods make about the nature of reality, and the best way to gain access to knowledge about that reality.

**Epistemological Underpinnings of Quantitative Research**

Quantitative researchers are seen as committed (whether consciously or unconsciously) to a realist ontology and empiricist epistemology in which reality is single, external, observable, and measurable and in which the knower and the known are separate and independent, so that the truth is not defined by the research context, or by the values of the researcher or the researched (Horsewood 2011; Christiaensen 2003; Downward and Mearman 2007). According to this epistemology, the purpose of the researcher is to determine the truth of alternative theoretical claims by determining their correspondence to data obtained by observation; only data that is intersubjectively observable and subject-invariant (that is, not based on the perceptions of participants) is valid for this purpose (Kanbur and Shaffer 2007). In other words, knowledge produced within this framework must be objective (that is, true regardless of the subject's individual biases), verifiable through empirical evidence, and replicable.

In this methodology, objectivity is ensured by maintaining a distance between the researcher and the researched – the researcher is perpetually an outsider looking upon the researched – and through the possibility of external reviews of any instruments used in qualitative research (such as questionnaires) (Bryman 1984). Verifiability emerges from empirical evidence collected purely through observation, and presumably free of the values, purposes, and ideals of individuals involved (Howe 1988). Replicability is ensured through the possibility of implementing the same research instrument in other contexts (Bryman 1984). Thus, at the level of data collection, it is the job of the researcher to ensure that the data collected has these properties by making use of statistical principles in the study design, for example, through the use of representative sampling and standardization of questions and responses to minimize the occurrence of reporting biases, variability in the interviewer–interviewee interaction, and other sources of error in the data. For instance, survey questionnaires that can be analyzed through quantitative techniques lend themselves easily to this mode of inquiry by affording precisely these checks and balances. Theory validation also takes place at the level of data analysis, as for example when the researcher undertakes formal testing of alternative hypotheses using econometric techniques.[2] Only knowledge that meets these standards is regarded as valid and authentic.

Proponents of quantitative methodology often focus on the potential generalizability and replicability of the results of quantitative research, traits that are seen as desirable by adherents of a realist ontology and epistemology. Other strengths of quantitative methods that have been mentioned include the ability to identify trends over time and make cross-sectional comparisons; the potential for identifying correlations that may identify associations among critical variables and that raise questions of causality and covariant changes; the potential for estimating prevalence and distributions within population areas; and the credibility of numbers in influencing policy-makers (Chambers 2003).

Critics point to the potential for sampling and non-sampling errors in quantitative methods, to the inability of these methods to capture phenomena that are not easily quantifiable, and to the fact that numbers may be imprecise and even subjective (Uphoff 2003; Kanbur 2003). For instance, Rao (2003, p. 104) points to a number of shortcomings of traditional econometric analyses of secondary quantitative data, including the tendency to neglect ground-level realities in favor of abstract hypotheses and 'stagnant conceptualizations of human behavior', the inability of researchers to respond when their preconceptions are confronted by different realities, and the resulting reproduction of existing stereotypes.

**What is Qualitative Research?**

Qualitative research methodology emerged in opposition to positivism in the social sciences and has flourished across disciplines such as anthropology, sociology, and nursing. Qualitative research seeks to provide complex textual descriptions of how a given population might experience a particular phenomenon. By providing an in-depth analysis of how complex, often intangible human and family systems, social norms, belief systems, and cultural experiences impact the topic being studied, qualitative research brings to light information that would otherwise not be readily apparent, and which might not be captured by any measurement scale or multivariate methods. Rather than generalizability, or breadth, qualitative explorations emphasize depth of analysis, that is, richness of detail and description pertaining to the phenomenon being researched, tailored to a specific time and place. In economics, the term 'qualitative' is understood to encompass analyses based on non-numerical information, which are specific and targeted in their population coverage, which in their design require active involvement from the population covered, which use inductive (rather than deductive) logics of inference, and which operate in the broad framework of social sciences other than economics (Kanbur 2003, p. 9).

Chapter 7 of this *Handbook* describes particular methods within qualitative research in greater detail. Here, it suffices to mention that three qualitative methods have been used most commonly in economics, namely in-depth interviews, focus groups, and case studies. In addition, site visits, participant observation, and document analysis have also appeared in interdisciplinary work carried out by economists in recent decades (see Chapter 7 of this *Handbook*).

An important characteristic of qualitative research that is often used to distinguish it from quantitative research is that the development of the hypothesis is part of the research process. Qualitative research frequently leads to the evolution of an adequate theory based on first-hand observations and worldviews collected from a small number of key participants, rather than testing a pre-existing hypothesis on a large scale (Horsewood 2011). This emerges from the unique epistemological and ontological stance taken by qualitative research, discussed below.

**Epistemological Underpinnings of Qualitative Research**

The epistemology underlying qualitative research, in diametric opposition to the positivist paradigm in quantitative research, most often holds that objectivity within the research process is: (1) not possible – that is, human beliefs, values and intentions can never be fully eliminated and true objectivity can never be achieved due to the inextricable link between the knower and the known (Horsewood 2011; Christiaensen 2003); and (2) not desirable since empathic understanding between the researcher and the researched is key to discovering knowledge from the perspective of the latter. Proponents of qualitative methodology thus 'share the goal of understanding the complex world of lived experience from the point of view of those who live it', their *Verstehen* (Schwandt 1998, p. 118).

The role of the qualitative researcher is to provide an interpretive understanding of the experiences, perspectives, beliefs, and values that give meaning to social phenomena; what Kanbur and Shaffer describe as 'intersubjective meanings' become the privileged unit of information in this approach (Kanbur and Shaffer 2007; see also Schwandt 1998).

The hermeneutic and interpretivist paradigms underlying qualitative methodology posit that social reality is constructed intersubjectively, that is, through social and experiential learning (Kinsella 2006). Therefore, knowledge emerges from a negotiation of meaning between the parties participating in the research process and is grounded in context, space, and time. As Schwandt (1998, p. 191) points out, the context of human action is what imparts meaning to it: 'Because human action is understood in this way, one can determine that a wink is not a wink, or that a smile can be interpreted as wry or loving . . . depending upon the context and the intentions of an actor.'

Further, since knowledge creation is itself a contested process based on a specific moment, valid knowledge is constantly open to reinterpretation, and indeed, multiple social realities can coexist (Lincoln and Guba 1985). A researcher's decision to use qualitative methodology is thus thought to reflect a commitment to an ontology of reality as a multiple and socially constructed phenomenon (Horsewood 2011). To fully understand the topic of interest within its context, inquiry methods seek to involve multiple stakeholders and to obtain multiple perspectives on the subject of research through semi-structured or unstructured, and exploratory data collection methods.

The constructivist stance within this ontology is based on the premise that knowledge 'is not disinterested, apolitical, and exclusive of affective and embodied aspects of human experience, but is in some sense permeated with values' (Schwandt 1998, p. 198; cf. Rouse 1996). Exploring what values these are is a central mandate of qualitative research. This critical application of qualitative methodology may also seek to bring about change and empowerment of the stakeholders in the process (Christiaensen 2003). Qualitative methodology thus frequently embraces activism within and through research as an explicit goal.

Proponents of qualitative methodology argue that it allows for the development and formulation of hypotheses from the lived experiences of actors (Barrett 2003; Rao 2003; Moser 2003), provides greater insight into causal processes (Carvalho and White 1997; Mahoney and Goertz 2006), and depth of information. Chambers (2003), on the other hand, perhaps represents most economists' views with respect to qualitative research when he points to its weaknesses, such as limits of qualitative data when it comes to representativeness, difficulties in verifying information provided by participants, and 'vulnerability' of the analysis to distortion and misrepresentation.

These points of comparison between quantitative and qualitative research are taken up in greater detail in the following sections, where we explore the nature and source of each faction's views of the other, as well as the multiplicity of perspectives on the compatibility of qualitative and quantitative research. At this point, however, we point out that critiques of each tradition frequently tend to conflate particular research techniques with the overall philosophical bent of each tradition. We attempt, therefore, to clarify the differences between the two lines of criticism before taking on perspectives on the compatibility of quantitative and qualitative research.

## 4.3   A TALE OF TWO TRADITIONS: COMPARING TECHNIQUES OF QUALITATIVE AND QUANTITATIVE RESEARCH

Until the emergence of mixed methods research – through work on triangulation spear-headed by Campbell and Fiske (1959), who argued for the use of more than one method to validate a result to ensure that the variation observed was not an outcome of the method – quantitative and qualitative methodologies tended to occupy fairly distinct terrains in social science research. In economics the systematic mathematization of the economist's toolkit has meant a short shift to formalizing the use of qualitative methods in the discipline although, as argued in Chapter 7 of this *Handbook*, qualitative descriptions have long constituted an integral part of the works of political economists such as Adam Smith and Ronald Coase. The debate continues in other disciplines such as political science and sociology as to the relative merits of one method over another; indeed, Mahoney and Goertz (2006, p. 227) argue that the two traditions are akin to 'alternative cultures', each with its set of values, beliefs, and norms: 'Each is sometimes privately suspicious or skeptical of the other though usually more publicly polite . . . When members of one tradition offer their insights to members of the other community, the advice is likely to be viewed (rightly or wrongly) as unhelpful and even belittling.'

Having taken up the philosophical differences in the previous section, here we recapitulate some of the purely technical distinctions between quantitative and qualitative methods that appear to thwart an easy integration of the two.[3]

**Purpose of Inquiry**

Qualitative methodology focuses on an understanding of the processes – that is, causal mechanisms – by which two or more aspects of social reality may be connected. Researchers seek to identify these processes through deep documentation and observation, usually over an extended period of time, using narrative techniques. In contrast, quantitative methodology seeks to offer general explanations of causal relationships between variables using quantifiable indicators, measurement, and statistical analysis. Quantitative scholars are concerned with refining techniques of measurement since better techniques may mean that key causal relationships are better able to be isolated. As such, quantitative research tends to be product oriented (for example, what is the impact of a policy or intervention?), while qualitative methodology is suitable for 'process tracing rather than quasi-statistical generalization' (for example, why did the policy or intervention work or not work?) (Shively 2006; cf. Mahoney and Goertz 2006, p. 231; Heyink and Tymstra 1993).

**Consideration of Causality**

Qualitative researchers are concerned with necessary and/or sufficient causes. Three features of causality within qualitative research may be identified:

1.   To be of interest to qualitative scholars, the cause need neither be individually necessary nor individually sufficient.

2.  Instead, scholars focus on one cause within a combination of causes that are jointly sufficient for an outcome.
3.  Distinct combinations of causes may each be sufficient, implying that there may be multiple causal paths to the same outcome (this is known also as equifinality).

Qualitative research focuses on the impacts of combinations of variables and only rarely on the effects of individual variables. Therefore, there is typically no effort to estimate the net effect of a particular variable.

Quantitative researchers, in contrast, are concerned with causes that produce, on average, certain outcomes across a large population. This approach to causation may be characterized for an individual case as the difference between the treatment ($T$) and control ($C$) for the same unit, $i$. For multiple cases, the causal effect is obtained through a comparison of the control and treatment groups, each group consisting of many units $i = 1, \ldots , N$. In other words, quantitative researchers compare the mean or average causal effect of a variable between two groups. The net effect of each variable $X$ is estimated using a statistical model of the type:

$$Y = \beta_0 + \beta_1 X_1 + \beta_2 X_2 + \ldots + \beta_N X_N + \varepsilon \qquad (4.1)$$

where the $\beta$s represent these average net effects, and can be estimated using statistical analysis.

The upshot: both quantitative and qualitative methodology may deal with causality, but approach it in different ways. A useful example of this contrast is provided by Mahoney and Goertz (2006, p. 231) in the following words:

> scholars from either tradition may start their research with a general question such as 'What causes democracy?' To address this question, however, researchers will typically translate it into a new question according to the norms of their culture. Thus, qualitative researchers will rephrase the research question as 'What causes democracy in one or more particular cases?' Quantitative researchers will translate it differently: 'What is the average causal effect of one or more independent variables on democracy?'

**Scope and Sample Selection**

Qualitative scholars' emphasis on explaining the processes behind particular outcomes means that their starting point is selecting cases where the said outcome of interest has indeed occurred (that is, positive cases). While qualitative scholars sometimes choose to discuss negative cases to compare and contrast them with positive ones, it is not always necessary to do so. Such in-depth descriptive analysis is possible with a smaller number of cases which are typically chosen purposefully or theoretically. Purposeful sampling is done by the researcher after several observational site visits, such that they know whom to include in sampling, as per the aims of the research (Schatzman and Strauss 1973). Theoretical sampling arises in grounded theory research where new elements or categories discovered during research may require further sampling along particular lines (Glaser 1978). Qualitative researchers deliberately restrict their analysis to a limited number of cases since this methodology assumes 'causal heterogeneity' for large populations; that is, that the larger the population, the more likely it becomes for key variables to be missing or misspecified in the theory (Mahoney and Goertz 2006, p. 238).

Because quantitative scholars are concerned with generalizable outcomes, researchers must have a larger number of cases or observations (N) in order to use statistical techniques effectively. Quantitative researchers must also select individual cases without any regard for their impact on the dependent variable so that 'unbiased' results of the average net effects of the independent variables on the dependent variable may be obtained from statistical analysis. A significant implication of this requirement is that researchers choose populations of cases through random selection or sampling.

**Weighting Observations and Treatment of Outliers**

The emphasis on detailed fact-gathering and on looking into 'positive' cases in qualitative research means that certain pieces of information or some cases may be weighted more in the construction or confirmation of a theory, contributing more significantly to the researcher's view that the theory is valid. Certain cases may be considered more important or interesting, given the researcher's prior theoretical knowledge. At the same instance, the norms around qualitative methodology dictate that even a single case that does not adhere to the general patterns described by the researcher must be explained, rather than dismissed as an aberration. Indeed, a single piece of new information can lead qualitative researchers to conclude that a conclusion might not be correct even if other evidence points in that direction; that is, 'a theory is usually only one critical observation away from being falsified' (Mahoney and Goertz 2006, p. 241).

In the use of quantitative methods, however, it is assumed that more often than not, there can be no *ex ante* determination of 'important' cases. Each observation carries equal weight. Since quantitative methods deal with large Ns, the failure of a theoretical model to explain individual cases is not a problem as long as the parameter estimates obtained from the model for the population as a whole are reasonably good. Idiosyncratic and anomalous factors that are relevant to only a few cases – what King et al. (1994) refer to as 'non-systematic factors' – are of little interest as long as unbiased parameter estimates can be obtained using the large sample. Quantitative researchers are typically content to have these factors be captured by an error term. This error term might indeed contain a number of variables that qualitative researchers regard as significant for individual cases.

**Validity Considerations[4]**

Perhaps the most contentious aspect of the qualitative–quantitative debate is the issue of rigor and validity. The hegemony of positivism in the social sciences, and in economics in particular, has meant the equation of 'rigor' with mathematical and statistical presentation of evidence, and therefore the privileging of one methodology (quantitative) over the other. Quantitative researchers in economics are skeptical about the value of qualitative research on several counts. The most common objections, and responses to these, are addressed below.

**'The standards for evaluating quality in qualitative research methods are contested, unlike for quantitative methods where the standards of evaluation (identification, specification, or aggregation) are clearer'**

For quantitative researchers, the yardsticks for measuring the quality of quantitative research seem to be more clearly represented, whereas qualitative research is relegated to the realm of storytelling since the methods seem nebulous. Further, since the ability to generalize from the research sample to the population is crucial for quantitative research, external validity is a primary concern.

Qualitative researchers point out in response that the issue is with how validity is defined and understood in the two traditions. In quantitative research, validity refers to the degree to which an instrument measures what it is designed to measure; in qualitative research, validity means gaining knowledge and understanding of the phenomenon under study (Leininger 1985). Since the nature and purpose of quantitative and qualitative research traditions are different, it would be a mistake to apply the quantitative definition of validity to qualitative research.

At the same time, the above caution does not mean that qualitative research cannot be held to standards of rigor, organization, and meticulousness. This is ensured through a variety of ways, all entailing close attention to and documentation of the research process, which may include: (1) providing thorough descriptions of the methodology used and its evolution; (2) keeping detailed records of procedures used to select cases and samples under study; (3) considering all available alternative explanations and theories while outlining findings; and (4) care in writing up results, including providing detailed examples and narratives when appropriate. Indeed, Helper (2000, p. 230) argues that not providing these details while presenting findings from field research is akin to 'asking readers to believe a summary of econometric results without tables of regression coefficients'. A second way of ensuring the soundness of findings from qualitative research is through 'triangulation', that is, cross-checking findings with information from other sources (journals, magazines, archives, other existing research, or data collected through another method). Greater faith may be had in findings that are cross-checked rather than those that are not. Ultimately, good qualitative and quantitative research should seek to represent the object of study in as faithful a manner as possible, so that any 'decisions, programs or interventions based on the representation would permit better outcomes than would have been possible had the research not been done' (Starr 2012, p. 19).

**'There is too much scope for the researcher's personal biases to creep in, that is, concerns emerge regarding objectivity of the researcher'**

The emphasis on objectivity in economics arises from the efforts of economists to emulate the physical sciences, especially physics, an agenda that dates back to the nineteenth century (Mirowski 1989; Drakopoulos 1991). To be trustworthy, findings from research must be unbiased (that is, must not depend upon the researcher's personal views), value-free, and reproducible (that is, must not depend on the specific measurement instruments used) (Starr 2012; McCloskey 1983). As mentioned earlier, quantitative methods depend on respondent information typically (but not only) gathered through closed-ended questions that can be transmuted into numerical form through coding into conceptual categories that are also numerical (that is, variables) (Blaikie 2003). Arguably, the data collected in this way is independent of the person collecting it or the place in which it is collected. Economists used to this mode of inquiry are therefore suspicious when confronted with qualitative data collected through detailed, open-ended personal interactions with respondents, and through observations and notes maintained by the researcher in the course of study. To these economists, there is too much scope for the researcher's personal opinions and biases to creep in, in the latter framework.

This criticism against qualitative methods has been addressed in different ways. Critical social science scholars (feminist researchers, for instance) point out that true objectivity is unachievable in both quantitative and qualitative traditions (for instance, the options provided in closed-ended survey questions may reflect particular understandings of the world). Other economists propose ways by which objectivity may be afforded by qualitative methods, again through detailed documentation of methods and strategies (Starr 2012; Helper 2000), and clear acknowledgments of the researcher's own positionality, power, state of knowledge, and perspectives on the issue under study (Esim 1997). Besides attenuating sources of potential bias, presenting this information helps the researcher to specify unique aspects of the research design or the researcher's circumstances that might make the results different from what another study on the same issue might find (Starr 2012).

**'The quality of self-reported information is dubious'**
The gathering of qualitative information through interviews and focus groups frequently entails open-ended questions that stimulate detailed responses from interviewees. A concern arises that data obtained in this way might be of suspect quality, because:

> a). Respondents may actively be untruthful about their behaviors and motivation (for instance, underreport behaviors that are considered less socially desirable, even if they have personal preferences for that behavior), or b). Respondents may themselves be unaware of why they do certain things or not be able to articulate explanations in a manner useful to the researcher. [An oft-cited case is Friedman's famous example of a billiard player in *The Methodology of Positive Economics*, 1953 [1970], where a billiard player might not know or be able to explain what laws of physics he is using to make expert shots: 'The billiard player, if asked how he decides where to hit the ball, may say that he "just figures it out" but then also rubs a rabbit's foot just to make sure' (p. 158)]. (Starr 2012)[5]

The concern with the quality of data obtained through qualitative methods reveals a double standard in the world of positivist economics where the quantitative is privileged over the qualitative. Note that the issue of response quality may also arise in quantitative research that uses secondary data collected through survey research; however, economists are able to elide these concerns by virtue of their preoccupation with data analysis rather than collection, and the separation that frequently occurs between the person collecting the data and the one analyzing it in quantitative economic research. Curiously, the issue of response quality emerges as a serious criticism leveled by economists against qualitative researchers who frequently both collect and analyze their own data.

This double standard aside, the issue of response quality in both qualitative and survey research has occupied social scientists for some time, and has elicited a vast amount of research focused on creating the circumstances necessary for ensuring high-quality responses. These emphasize the appropriate framing of research queries and prompts, choosing a suitable mode of research, ethical ways of approaching respondents for answers to sensitive questions, and ways of building trust between the researcher and the researched (through ensuring anonymity and confidentiality, emphasizing the value of the research, processes of informed consent, and so on) before the questionnaire or interview is administered (Singer 1978; Tourangeau and Smith 1996; Schaeffer and Presser 2003).

In response to the second criticism above, that respondents may themselves be ignorant of their motivations or be unable to explain their behaviors, Helper (2000, p. 229) notes that the value of qualitative research frequently lies in discovering something previously unknown through interactions with respondents, 'even when they seem to be getting off the subject. You are likely to learn something you would not have thought to ask about.'

While qualitative research emphasizes understanding the world from the perspective of the researched, letting respondents tell their story does not necessarily mean taking everything they say at face value. As Starr (2012, p. 20) emphasizes, even before research commences, initial interviews should be focused on establishing 'which respondents have the knowledge, information, perspectives, experiences and interest in the topic that will enable them to serve as good "key informants" with respect to the issues of interest'. Qualitative methods such as interviews allow interviewers to ask for clarifications, extra details, and examples from their interviewees there and then, to reduce response problems and ensure data quality. Furthermore, it falls upon the researcher to cross-check different pieces of information through different data sources to piece together an accurate picture of social reality. Such triangulation allows the researcher to gain more knowledge than their respondents and to realize when someone is lying or does not have access to important or relevant information. This allows the researcher to ask further questions in order to understand why respondents may either be unaware of or may wish to hide information.

### 'Qualitative findings do not answer any questions definitively/are non-generalizable/unstable'

The positivist epistemological bent of conventional economic methodology emphasizes the existence of a social 'truth' that research aims to uncover. One implication of this emphasis is a focus on research that seeks to settle all debate and provide an ultimate explanation for an observed social behavior or phenomenon. Qualitative methodology – with its context-specificity, constant reinterpretation of social reality, and causal heterogeneity – is seen to fall short when held to this positivist standard in economics. The lack of generalizability of findings obtained via qualitative research renders them unusable and unstable in the eyes of quantitative proponents of economic research.

Such criticism, however, misses the fact that the nature and scope of qualitative research is entirely different from that of quantitative research. The objective of qualitative research is to provide causal process information; therefore, qualitative scholars limit the scope of their arguments in recognition of causal heterogeneity. It might also be pointed out here that quantitative analysis, in turn, cannot be relied upon for providing causal process description and has corresponding limitations. With regard to the stability of findings, Mahoney and Goertz's (2006, p. 238) take on the issue may be reproduced here:

Whereas findings from qualitative research tend to be more stable than findings from quantitative research when one moves from a superset to particular subsets, quantitative findings tend to be more stable than qualitative findings when one moves from a subset to a superset. These differences are important, but they should not form the basis for criticism of either tradition; they are simply logical implications of the kinds of explanation pursued in the two traditions.

Ultimately, the suitability of each method depends upon the goal of research in each case: if the goal is to estimate average causal effects for large populations, quantitative methods are suitable; however, if the goal is to explain particular outcomes, qualitative methods should be chosen.

## 4.4   QUANTITATIVE AND QUALITATIVE METHODS IN ECONOMICS: CAN THE TWAIN MEET?

The divergent goals and scope of these two traditions raises the question: can qualitative and quantitative methods be combined meaningfully at all? Four lines of argument may be identified in answer to this all-important query: that the methodologies cannot be reconciled since they are rooted in distinct and irreconcilable ontological and epistemological traditions; that the qualitative and quantitative divide is in reality quite arbitrary, and there can be, in fact, substantial overlap; that despite distinct epistemological foundations, there may be practical grounds for mixing methods, and for allowing the research question, rather than the author's epistemological commitments, to drive the choice of methodology; and that there may indeed be epistemological grounding for the mixing of methods. In addition to exploring these arguments in the following section, we also examine practical impediments to the integration of techniques within the discipline, including the lack of a platform for economists to adopt pluralism in their methods, and the absence of tangible support to scholars wishing to use qualitative or 'mixed methods' techniques.

### Integrating Qualitative and Quantitative Methods

Much has been written regarding the incompatibility of quantitative and qualitative paradigms (see Guba 1987; Smith and Heshusius 1986; Sayer 1992; Silverman 1993). The traditional perspective is that the epistemological differences underlying the two sets of techniques – with their attendant 'dichotomies of objectivity versus subjectivity, fixed versus emergent categories, outsider versus insider perspectives, facts versus values, explanation versus understanding, and singular versus multiple realities' (Christiaensen 2003, p. 115) – are irreconcilable, so there is no legitimate basis for integrating the two methods. However, this argument flies in the face of actual research practice: as Fiorito and Samuels (2000, p. 163) have noted, 'ostensibly antinomian epistemological positions, each ostensibly meaningful on its own terms, are in practice inexorably combined in one way or another'.

   A second line of argument holds that the quantitative–qualitative divide is a false and arbitrary dichotomy. Along these lines, Hentschel (2003) observes that the qualitative–quantitative debate tends to conflate methods of data collection with the type of data collected. But, as he notes, methods that are generally thought of as 'quantitative', for example large-scale household surveys, often produce 'qualitative' data, while 'qualitative' methods produce 'quantitative' data. Others have commented on the similarity between qualitative and quantitative methods in terms of the potential pitfalls of both. Along these lines, Herring (2003) observes that all data are products of social interactions; regardless of the method by which data is collected, relations of power, interests, and values condition the production of data, and determine the correspondence between reality and its condensation and representation as values of a variable. The failure to recognize this renders any data collection method less reliable and less valid. Neither qualitative nor quantitative techniques are inherently free from this potential weakness. For Herring, then, what is crucial is for the researcher to understand the society that produces the data; thus there is a need for grounded contextual expertise in survey design, the selection of focus groups, pretesting of interview and survey questions, and the interpretation of results.

Likewise, White (2002) argues that regardless of choice of methods, quality of application matters, that is: 'Badly or misleadingly applied, both quantitative and qualitative techniques give bad or misleading conclusions' (p. 512). Moreover, both have the potential to be misused. He sees qualitative and quantitative techniques as complementary, and argues that there is a productive synergy to be gained from combining the two types of methods. For example, insights from qualitative work can be used to inform economic theory and data analysis, while quantitative data can be useful in raising questions that would be addressed by qualitative approaches.

Closely related to the argument that the two traditions of research are 'not all that different' is the argument for pragmatism in choice of methods. Proponents of mixed methods in disciplines such as sociology, nursing, and political science have furthered the integration of the two methodologies. This integration is based on a pragmatic view of research that emphasizes the research question as a prime determinant of research method, as opposed to philosophical foundations, and traces complementarities in techniques from both traditions (Bryman 1984; Lin 1998). Allowing research questions to determine the choice of methods also recognizes that no technique is inherently superior to others, but simply that a particular 'technique is likely to be more useful in some contexts than others' (Bryman 1984, p. 80). Therefore, a sample survey may be appropriate when the goal is to obtain specific quantitative information from the respondents, and when the researcher has fairly complete a priori information on the range of responses likely to emerge. On the other hand, participant observation may be employed where it is necessary to document patterns of social relationships or interaction, or latent and non-verbal belief systems that can only be revealed through observations of behavior (Warwick and Lininger 1975; cf. Bryman 1984, p. 81).

Along similar lines, Carus and Ogilvie (2009) argue that qualitative and quantitative evidence are mutually indispensable to economic and social historians. Qualitative documents from the past can only be understood within the social context that produced these documents. Because the basic categories of any social context lack cross-cultural, inherent, or universal meanings, their meanings must be teased out by comparing the society under study to other relevant societies, a comparison which they argue is inherently statistical, since it refers to the distribution of the variable of interest over a range of possible values (p. 894).

The problem with pragmatism as an argument for combining qualitative and quantitative research methods is that it does not by itself provide an epistemological or ontological basis for combining methods, nor does it resolve the epistemological and ontological tensions previously discussed.[6] The path towards this resolution, however, may be found if we begin by acknowledging that while, or perhaps because, our concern as economists is with the real world, our theories about the economy are fallible, and as such, no single economic paradigm can lay an absolute claim to truth (Caldwell 1982; Salanti and Screpanti 1997). What we can hope for, at best, is to build knowledge about the economy, while at the same time being aware that the knowledge so generated cannot be the same as reality. This perspective lends itself to arguments for the use of a range of methods in economic research, on the grounds that no single method can generate certain knowledge about the real world. In fact, because, any single method can generate only partial knowledge about the world we are trying to explain, pluralism requires that a variety of methods be used in combination with each other (Dow 1997, 2002).[7]

The open system ontology of critical realism provides one argument for combining qualitative and quantitative methods (Downward and Mearman 2007). Unlike the closed system ontology of positivist economics, in which all relevant variables of the economy are known and can be classified as exogenous or endogenous, and in which relationships between variables are predetermined and transcend space and time, an open system ontology sees the economy as a complex system in which relevant variables may be unknown, whose boundaries cannot be specified, and in which interrelationships are constantly changing. Empirical observations are thus the outcome of multiple potential causal mechanisms at work within an enabling framework of social conventions and institutions (Hodgson 1988; cf. Dow 2002). For critical realists, therefore, the exclusive reliance on empirical data as the basis for evaluating the validity of economic theory is flawed, because such data may not reveal the multiplicity of causal mechanisms that could potentially be at work over the period of observation. Instead, the role of empirical observation is to generate hypotheses about underlying causal mechanisms by a process of retroduction (Dow 2002).

Downward and Mearman, in a series of papers, argue that combining methods, or what they refer to as mixed methods triangulation (MMT), is central to retroductive activity (Downward et al. 2002; Downward and Mearman 2003; Downward and Mearman 2007). This is because different research methods do not have to be 'wedded' to different, ontological presumptions; they are 'redescriptive devices' that reveal different aspects of the object of analysis (Downward and Mearman 2007, p. 15). In fact, because human actions occur within particular institutional and structural contexts, the economist must elaborate not only on motivational dimensions of human agency, but also on the context of this agency. The use of different methods of analysis is necessary for the economist to carry out this task. Furthermore, combining methods allows for the construction of 'a nexus of mutually supportive propositions', thus resulting in the derivation of a fuller explanation of economic phenomena. As they argue, 'the logic of retroduction makes some form of MMT . . . necessary to reveal different features of the same layered reality without the presumption of being exhaustive' (p. 16).

Having explored the different lines of argument for and against the integration of qualitative and quantitative methods in social science research, we now proceed to examine the obstacles that seem to have impeded their integration in economic research.

**Practical Impediments to Integrating Methods within Economics**

In addition to the ongoing philosophical debates regarding the mixing of methods, more immediate practical concerns emerge that may present a conundrum even for economists who are willing to incorporate qualitative and mixed methods into their research toolkits. In their preliminary survey of articles published in the top mainstream and heterodox journals, Basole et al. (2012) argue that qualitative and mixed methods research continue to occupy a marginal position in economics. In addition, the authors observe that economists, even when publishing in interdisciplinary journals, tend primarily to use primary or secondary survey data, leaving mixed methods research to their counterparts in development studies, geography or political science. In addition to the technical obstacles discussed above, obstacles driven by the status quo within the discipline also help to inhibit the use of qualitative methods or the mixing of qualitative and quantitative methods in economics:

1.  Specialization within the status quo. Graduate training in economics currently comprises of coursework in statistics, econometrics, and occasionally in behavioral experiments. Primary data collection – be it quantitative (that is, survey design) or qualitative – is typically not part of the curriculum. It is therefore entirely up to the would-be researcher to acquire additional training in any of these other methods, usually by taking methods courses in other departments. Thus, a very small proportion of economists actually end up getting training in, and ultimately using, methods other than those prescribed by graduate education in economics.
2.  Legitimacy concerns leading to 'dropping out'. Basole et al. (2012) speculate that concerns around qualitative and mixed methods not being 'real' economics might dissuade economists from using alternative methods. For instance, graduate students may perceive that the use of mixed methods will disqualify them from being hired by economics departments. An unfriendly stance towards qualitative or mixed methods as 'not legitimately economics' may also lead those interested in pursuing these methods in their research to seek homes in other, methodologically pluralistic, interdisciplinary departments; that is, 'dropping out' of economics. The marginalization of alternative methods within economics thus becomes self-perpetuating as the small minority of scholars interested in these methods migrate to other disciplines.
3.  Publication issues. The invisibility of these other methods in economic research is compounded by the lack of platforms where such research might be showcased. Indeed, Basole et al. (2012) point out that even when indications are present that a multi-method approach was used and that qualitative data was also collected, only quantitative results are typically presented in economic journals (p. 13). The perception prevails – arguably reinforced by what we see gets published in economics journals (see Basole et al. 2012) – that quantitative and qualitative research have different audiences respectively. Articles based on qualitative or mixed methods research are therefore shunted to 'more appropriate' (read: interdisciplinary) journals.

Despite these roadblocks, efforts to incorporate qualitative and mixed methods within economics have gained some momentum within both mainstream and heterodox economics in the last few years (see, e.g., Starr 2012; Basole and Ramnarain, Chapter 7 in this *Handbook*; Cronin, Chapter 15 in this *Handbook*). In mainstream economics, quali-tative and mixed methods have gained the most ground in poverty research; a notable example is the Q-squared studies of poverty in developing countries that combine survey research with ethnographic techniques such as focus groups, life histories, and in-depth interviews of participants' lived experiences (see, e.g., Kanbur 2003). Mixed methods research in mainstream economics has also found its way into policy and contingent evaluation research (see Starr 2012 for several examples). Heterodox economics, which aims to highlight social factors – norms and institutions – and the role of power and privilege in driving economic outcomes, has adopted qualitative and mixed methods in analyzing labor processes, the motivations of economic actors placed in social networks, and power relations (see Basole and Ramnarain, Chapter 7 in this *Handbook*, for details).

## 4.5   CONCLUSION

This chapter has examined the question of whether or not it is possible, and indeed even desirable, to integrate qualitative and quantitative methods in economic research. As economists who use both methods in our work, the answer seems obvious to us. Despite the apparent differences in the epistemological and ontological underpinnings of these research methods, and the technical differences that arise from these philosophical dif-ferences, there is much value to be gained from permitting the research question to drive the choice of method. As researchers attempting to explain the social world, we must acknowledge that social reality is complex and multifaceted. We live in societies in which economic outcomes are driven by the interaction of multiple factors: individual agency, social norms, cultural values, and economic institutions. If we accept that our expla-nations of this reality are at best only partial, then we must also accept that no single method can lead us to discovering 'the truth' about the real world. The most we can hope for is to advance knowledge about the real world.

Different methods can tell us different parts of the story; together, they may contrib-ute to a more complete picture than we might otherwise achieve. Ultimately, we would argue, the choice of research method should not be constrained by epistemological and philosophical divides or by the norms of our profession. The choice of method should be driven by the research question, and by the desire to tell a story that reflects the complex-ity of the world that we are attempting to explain.

Nevertheless, the reality is that as economists, our choice of methods is constrained by many factors, not least of which are the norms of the discipline, which shape the expectations of our peers and colleagues regarding what counts as 'real' economics; the pressure to 'publish or perish'; as well as our own training, or rather the lack thereof, in methods other than quantitative techniques. This is perhaps as true of heterodox economists as it is of mainstream economists. Even if we agree on the desirability of mixing methods in economic research, and accept that there are epistemological and ontological justifications for doing so, these disciplinary boundaries may prove difficult to breach in practice. Perhaps the question we need to address is not so much whether it is desirable to integrate methods in economics research, but rather, what changes need to occur within the discipline in order for such integration to become feasible, and indeed acceptable.

# NOTES

1. Olsen and Morgan (2005) make a similar distinction: they argue that methods are techniques of collecting and transforming data, while methodologies comprise methods, the practices involved in implementing them, and the interpretation placed on this act by the researcher.
2. It is worth noting here that econometrics may also be used to simply find the best empirical specification that fits a theory that is already assumed to be true, as in the hypothetico-deductive approach associated with the US Cowles Commission, or to help narrow down the range of possible theoretical explanations, as in the approach associated with the London School of Economics (see Dow 2002, for a more detailed explication of empirical testing of theories in economics).
3. The discussion here is largely based on Mahoney and Goertz (2006).
4. The discussion here focuses specifically on economists' perceptions of qualitative data, their objections, and counterarguments to these perceptions. We base the discussion on Starr (2012), McCloskey (1983), Helper (2000), and other economists who have dealt with this issue in their writings.
5. As Martin Ravallion has pointed out, there is a certain inconsistency in this argument: 'Economists have traditionally eschewed subjective questions: oddly, while economists generally think that people are the best judges of their own welfare, they resist asking people how they feel' (Ravallion 2003, p. 62).
6. Downward and Mearman (2007), in particular, note that pragmatism can be viewed as an instrumentalist position and suggest we still need to explore the legitimacy of integrating methods on methodological grounds, that is: what is the epistemological justification for integrating methods?
7. Critical realism provides the ontological basis for this plurality. As Dow (2002) argues, if we understand the real world to be an open system, requiring open system knowledge, then we are accepting that one method will generate certain knowledge about the real world (p. 157).

# REFERENCES

Barrett, Chris (2003), 'Integrating qualitative and quantitative approaches, lessons from the pastoral risk management project', in Ravi Kanbur (ed.), *Q-Squared: Combining Qualitative and Quantitative Methods in Poverty Appraisal*, Delhi: Permanent Black, pp. 90–96.

Basole, Amit, Jennifer Cohen, and Smita Ramnarain (2012), 'The crucial contribution of fieldwork to (heterodox) economics: evidence from research in Nepal, India, and South Africa', paper presented at the Allied Social Sciences Association Conference, Chicago, IL, January.

Blaikie, Norman (2003), *Analyzing Quantitative Data: From Description to Explanation*, Thousand Oaks, CA: Sage Publications.

Bryman, Alan (1984), 'The debate about quantitative and qualitative research: a question of method or epistemology?', *British Journal of Sociology*, **35** (1), 75–92.

Caldwell, B. (1982), *Beyond Positivism: Economic Methodology in the Twentieth Century*, London: Allen & Unwin.

Campbell, Donald T. and D.W. Fiske (1959), 'Convergent and discriminant validation by the multi-trait-multi-method matrix', *Psychological Bulletin*, **56**, 81–105.

Carus, A.W. and Sheilagh Ogilvie (2009), 'Turning qualitative into quantitative evidence: a well-used method made explicit', *Economic History Review*, **62** (4), 893–925.

Carvalho, Soniya and Howard White (1997), 'Combining the quantitative and qualitative approaches to poverty measurement and analysis: the practice and the potential', World Bank Technical Paper no. WTP 366, Washington, DC: World Bank.

Chambers, Robert (2003), 'Qualitative approaches: self-criticism and what can be gained from quantitative approaches', in Ravi Kanbur (ed.), *Q-Squared: Combining Qualitative and Quantitative Methods in Poverty Appraisal*, Delhi: Permanent Black, pp. 28–34.

Christiaensen, Luc (2003), 'The qual-quant debate within its epistemological context: some practical implications', in Ravi Kanbur (ed.), *Q-Squared: Combining Qualitative and Quantitative Methods in Poverty Appraisal*, Delhi: Permanent Black, pp. 114–19.

Dow, Sheila C. (1997), 'Methodological pluralism and pluralism of method', in A. Salanti and E. Screpanti (eds), *Pluralism in Economics: New Perspectives in History and Methodology*, Cheltenham, UK and Northampton, MA, USA: Edward Elgar, pp. 89–99.

Dow, Sheila C. (2002), *Economic Methodology: An Inquiry*, Oxford: Oxford University Press.

Downward, P.M., J. Finch, and J. Ramsay (2002), 'Critical realism, empirical methods and inference: a critical discussion', *Cambridge Journal of Economics*, **26** (4), 481–500.

Downward, Paul and Andrew Mearman (2003), 'Presenting demi-regularities: the case of post-Keynesian pricing', in Paul Downward (ed.), *Applied Economics and the Critical Realist Critique*, London: Routledge, pp. 247–65.

Downward, P.M. and A. Mearman (2007), 'Retroduction as mixed-methods triangulation in economic research: reorienting economics into social science', *Cambridge Journal of Economics*, **31** (1), 77–99.

Drakopoulos, Stavros (1991), *Values in Economic Theory*, Aldershot, UK: Avebury.

Esim, Simel (1997), 'Can feminist methodology reduce power hierarchies in research settings?', *Feminist Economics*, **3** (2), 137–9.

Fiorito, Luca and Warren J. Samuels (2000), 'The quantitative method in economics: its promise, strength and limits: Wesley Clair Mitchell, Henry Schultz and Arthur F. Burns: Introduction', in Warren S. Samuels (ed.), *Twentieth-Century Economics (Research in the History of Economic Thought and Methodology*, Vol. 18, Part 3, Bingley: Emerald Group Publishing, pp. 263–6.

Friedman, Milton (1953 [1970]), 'The methodology of positive economics', in Milton Friedman (1970), *Essays in Positive Economics*, Chicago, IL: University of Chicago Press, pp. 3–43.

Glaser, Barney G. (1978), *Theoretical Sensitivity: Advances in the Methodology of Grounded Theory*, Vol. 2, Mill Valley, CA: Sociology Press.

Guba, E.G. (1987), 'Naturalistic evaluation', *New Directions for Program Evaluation*, **1987** (34), 23–43.

Helper, Susan (2000), 'Economists and field research: you can observe a lot just by watching', *American Economic Review*, **90** (2), 228–32.

Hentschel, Jesko (2003), 'Integrating the qual and the quant: when and why?', in Ravi Kanbur (ed.), *Q-Squared Combining Qualitative and Quantitative Methods in Poverty Appraisal*, Delhi: Permanent Black, pp. 120–25.

Herring, Ronald (2003), 'Data as social product', in Ravi Kanbur (ed.), *Q-Squared: Combining Qualitative and Quantitative Methods in Poverty Appraisal*, Delhi: Permanent Black, pp. 141–51.

Heyink, J.W. and T.J. Tymstra (1993), 'The function of qualitative research', *Social Indicators Research*, **29** (3), 291–305.

Hodgson, Geoffrey M. (1988), *Economics and Institutions*, Cambridge: Polity Press.

Horsewood, Nick (2011), 'Demystifying quantitative methods in comparative housing research: dispelling the myth of black magic', *International Journal of Housing Policy*, **11** (4), 375–93.

Howe, Kenneth R. (1988), 'Against the quantitative–qualitative incompatibility thesis or dogmas die hard', *Educational Researcher*, **17** (8), 10–16.

Kanbur, Ravi (ed.) (2003), *Q-Squared Combining Qualitative and Quantitative Methods in Poverty Appraisal*, Delhi: Permanent Black.

Kanbur, Ravi and Paul Shaffer (2007), 'Epistemology, normative theory and poverty analysis: implications for Q-squared in practice', *World Development*, **35** (2), 183–96.

King, Gary, Robert O. Keohane, and Sidney Verba (1994), *Designing Social Inquiry: Scientific Inference in Qualitative Research*, Princeton, NJ: Princeton University Press.

Kinsella, Elizabeth Anne (2006), 'Hermeneutics and critical hermeneutics: exploring possibilities within the art of interpretation', *Forum Qualitative Sozialforschung/Forum: Qualitative Social Research* [S.l.], **7** (3), accessed 29 November 2015 at http://www.qualitative-research.net/index.php/fqs/article/view/145/319.

Leininger, Madeleine M. (1985), 'Nature, rationale and importance of qualitative research methods in nursing', in Madeleine M. Leininger (ed.), *Qualitative Research Methods in Nursing*, New York: Grune & Stratton, pp. 1–28.

Lin, Ann Chih (1998), 'Bridging positivist and interpretivist approaches to qualitative methods', *Policy Studies Journal*, **26** (1), 162–80.

Lincoln, Yvonna S. and Egon G. Guba (1985), *Naturalistic Inquiry*, London: Sage.

Mahoney, James and Gary Goertz (2006), 'A tale of two cultures: contrasting quantitative and qualitative research', *Political Analysis*, **14** (3), 227–49.

McCloskey, Donald N. (1983), 'The rhetoric of economics', *Journal of Economic Literature*, **21** (2), 481–517.

Mirowski, Philip (1989), *More Heat than Light: Economics as Social Physics. Physics as Nature's Economics*, Cambridge: Cambridge University Press.

Moser, Caroline (2003), '"Apt illustration" or "anecdotal information": can qualitative data be representative or robust?', in Ravi Kanbur (ed.), *Q-Squared: Combining Qualitative and Quantitative Methods in Poverty Appraisal*, Delhi: Permanent Black, pp. 79–89.

Olsen, W. and J. Morgan (2005), 'A critical epistemology of analytical statistics: addressing the skeptical realist', *Journal for the Theory of Social Behavior*, **35** (3), 255–84.

Ragin, C.C. (2000), *Fuzzy-Set Social Science*, Chicago: University of Chicago Press.

Rao, Vijayendra (2003), 'Experiments with "participatory econometrics" in India: can conversation take the con out of econometrics?', in Ravi Kanbur (ed.), *Q-Squared: Combining Qualitative and Quantitative Methods in Poverty Appraisal*, Delhi: Permanent Black, pp. 58–67.

Ravallion, Martin (2003), 'Can qualitative methods help quantitative poverty measurement', in Ravi Kanbur (ed.), *Q-Squared: Combining Qualitative and Quantitative Methods in Poverty Appraisal*, Delhi: Permanent Black, pp. 103–13.

Rouse, Joseph (1996), *Feminism and the Social Construction of Scientific Knowledge*, Dordrecht: Springer.

Salanti, Andrea and Ernesto Screpanti (eds) (1997), *Pluralism in Economics: New Perspectives in History and Methodology*, Cheltenham, UK and Lyme, NH, USA: Edward Elgar Publishing.

Sale, Joanna E.M., Lynne Lohfield, and Kevin Brazil (2002), 'Revisiting the quantitative-qualitative debate: implications for mixed methods research', *Quality and Quantity*, **36**, 43–53.

Sayer, A. (1992), *Method in Social Science: A Realist Approach*, 2nd edn, London: Routledge.

Schaeffer, N.C. and S. Presser (2003), 'The science of asking questions', *Annual Review of Sociology*, **29** (1), 65–88.

Schatzman, Leonard and Anselm L. Strauss (1973), *Field Research: Strategies for a Natural Sociology*, Englewood Cliffs, NJ: Prentice-Hall.

Schwandt, Thomas A. (1998), 'Constructivist, interpretivist approaches to human inquiry', in N.K. Denzin and Y.S. Lincoln (eds), *The Landscape of Qualitative Research: Theories and Issues*, London: Sage, pp. 221–59.

Shively, W. Phillips (2006), 'Case selection: insights from rethinking social inquiry', *Political Analysis*, **14** (3), 344–7.

Silverman, D. (1993), *Interpreting Qualitative Data: Methods for Analyzing Talk, Text and Interaction*, London: Sage.

Singer, E. (1978), 'Informed consent: consequences for response rate and response quality in social surveys', *American Sociological Review*, **43** (1), 144–62.

Smith, J.K. (1983), 'Quantitative versus qualitative research: an attempt to clarify the issue', *Educational Researcher*, **12**, 6–13.

Smith, J. and L. Heshusius (1986), 'Closing down the conversation: the end of the quantitative–qualitative debate among educational enquirers', *Educational Researcher*, **15** (1), 4–12.

Starr, Martha A. (2012), 'Qualitative and mixed-methods research in economics: surprising growth, promising future', *Journal of Economic Surveys*, **28** (2), 238–64.

Tourangeau, R. and T.W. Smith (1996), 'Asking sensitive questions: the impact of data collection mode, question format, and question context', *Public Opinion Quarterly*, **60** (2), 275–304.

Uphoff, Norman (2003), 'Bridging qualitative–quantitative differences in poverty appraisal: self-critical thoughts on qualitative approaches', in Ravi Kanbur (ed.), *Q-Squared: Combining Qualitative and Quantitative Methods in Poverty Appraisal*, Delhi: Permanent Black, pp. 50–57.

Warwick, Donald P. and Charles A. Lininger (1975), *The Sample Survey: Theory and Practice*, New York: McGraw-Hill.

White, Howard (2002), 'Combining quantitative and qualitative approaches in poverty analysis', *World Development*, **30** (3), 511–22.

# 5 Historical method and data
*Natalia Bracarense and A. Reeves Johnson*

## 5.1 INTRODUCTION

According to Frederic Lee (2012), heterodox economics studies the social provisioning process. As a process implies movement through time, an understanding of history and of historical change is necessary to study social provisioning. Living up to this claim, however, has proven to be difficult in practice. The ahistorical nature of most economics can be traced back to the late-nineteenth-century *Methodenstreit*, the outcome of which was to methodologically ordain economics a nomothetic science, while designating history an idiographic science.[1] The rigid separation established between these two social sciences poses a set of challenges for heterodox economists who have struggled to incorporate historical methods into their work (Bracarense 2013). As a step towards overcoming these challenges, the present chapter argues that a critical realist–grounded theory approach to economics, as outlined in Chapter 2 in this *Handbook*, is consistent with the use of genuinely historical methods and data. We further highlight the linkages between this methodological framework and contemporary historiography. By revealing these linkages we show how historians have attempted to overcome the separation between history and other social sciences over the last century. To support these arguments, this chapter evaluates research methods suitable to an economics that is informed by history and understands social change as the interaction between agents and social structures.

Since part of our objective in this chapter is to demonstrate the history-friendly nature of the critical realist–grounded theory approach to economics, a few summary remarks on the latter seem in order. Our focus will be on those aspects of critical realism and grounded theory that are relevant to the purposes of the chapter. More specifically, we consider how a methodological approach whose basic categories consist of agents, structures, and contexts of action can be used to understand and explain social reality, its reproduction and transformation.

First of all, what justifies the use of such a framework for social inquiry? One possible answer is the general consensus that both methodological individualism and methodological holism have proven to be incapable of explaining social reality. The agency–structure framework then is a kind of middle-of-the-road answer to the insufficiencies of both these methodological positions. A more reflective answer to the question could be excerpted from the following quote by the influential sociologist Anthony Giddens: 'Every research investigation in the social sciences or history is involved in relating action [synonymous with agency] to structure . . . there is no sense in which structure "determines" action or vice versa' (Giddens 1984, p. 219).[2] What is acknowledged in both answers to the question, implicitly in the first and explicitly by Giddens, is that agents and social structures are conceptually distinct, each irreducible to the other. We now elaborate further on this aspect of the framework.

While it is true that human behavior derives in part from a historical context characterized by some set of social as well as material structures, behavior cannot be reduced to these structures. As expressed in Chapter 2, heterodox economists are in agreement that social structures impose limits on what agents can do; social structures, moreover, tend to routinize behavior. Still, as long as agents are presumed to be capable of making choices – and alternative courses of action must be available to agents if they are even to be considered agents – it follows that they can choose whether to conform or not to social rules and relations as well as to the roles they occupy in society. Otherwise, an agent would not be worthy of their name, their behavior over time unfolding with neither intention nor purpose, this 'agent' being merely a subject to society's rules and relations. Thus, agents have the capacity to reproduce social structures with which they interact, but need not, and hence the actions on behalf of both conformers and non-conformers presuppose that agents are not reducible to social structures (Lawson 1997, p. 162).

Conversely, social structures are not reducible to agents. Although the latter's very existence is required to reproduce them, social structures transcend agents in historical time. Language, for example, is necessary if social reality is to exist, but it also must logically precede the existence of any particular individual (Hodgson 2001, p. 21). In a well-known quote that represents his clear denial of methodological individualism, Karl Marx writes, 'individuals make their own history, but they do not make it just as they please; they do not make it under circumstances chosen by themselves, but under circumstances directly encountered, given, and transmitted from the past' (Marx 1852 [1977], p. 30).

The content of the last two paragraphs is concisely summarized by Tony Lawson when he writes that social reality is 'conceived as intrinsically dynamic and complexly structured, consisting in human agency, structures and contexts of action, none of which are given or fixed, and where each presupposes each other without being reducible to, identifiable with, or explicable completely in terms of, any other' (Lawson 1997, p. 159).

In what follows, we present different historical methods and show how they can be used in economics in both their traditional and nontraditional forms.[3] What will appear as a common theme throughout these sampled texts is the implicit understanding by the authors of the distinction between the agents involved, the social structures present, and the context of action within which the causal powers of agents and structures intersect.

With that in mind, the chapter is divided into five sections. Following this introduction, section 5.2 considers the origins and salient features of traditional historical methods as well as their shortcomings, while section 5.3 examines the use of juridical and social documents in economics. Section 5.4 looks at other nontraditional historical methods and their use in heterodox economics. Section 5.5 concludes. We also include an Appendix that presents a basic introduction to the practical aspects of archival research. Some sections include brief discussions into historiography because they reveal how historians have responded to the constraints imposed by the *Methodenstreit*. These digressions may therefore serve as a signpost to economists who aim to overcome similar problems.

## 5.2   TRADITIONAL HISTORICAL METHODS

Historians typically divide the written sources of their research into three broad categories: narrative sources, social documents, and juridical sources. This categorization is not without its problems, as there is considerable overlap among the three categories, and some sources, deemed essential by many historians, do not easily fall under any one of these categories. While these objections should not go unnoticed, what is of greater importance is the fact that written sources have generic properties such that any given source should be examined based on its formal properties in addition to its content (Howell and Prevenier 2001, p. 21). The next few paragraphs introduce these three types of historical sources.[4]

Some examples of narrative sources include novels and poetry, memoirs, newspaper articles, and scholastic tracts. In each of these examples, the source has been written in order to impart to the reader a particular message. While these messages differ from one narrative source to another – for example, the message encapsulated in a poem is of a qualitatively different nature to that of a journal article – what remains constant is the need of the writer to convey information to the reader. It is not uncommon for heterodox economists to use narrative sources in their work, for example by consulting newspaper articles or the academic work of economists.[5]

Social documents are the result of bureaucratic recordkeeping often documented by state ministries, charitable organizations, foundations, churches, and schools (Howell and Prevenier 2001, p. 22). They are also the most pervasively used source for the researching economist, who may need numerical data for statistical work provided by one of the various economic ministries of the state and other organizations. But numerical data when culled and put in tabular form is not the only social document of interest to economists. Reports on monetary and fiscal policy, the minutes of policy meetings, among others, are also widely used in economic research.

The last type of source, juridical sources, has held a prestigious place in historiography and, as is discussed below, was originally thought to be the only genuine source for the professional historian. A juridical source registers new or existing legal situations, and is typically authenticated by a seal as proof of a legal fact or in order to serve as evidence in a judicial proceeding (Howell and Prevenier 2001, p. 22). These documents are sometimes subcategorized depending on whether the document under consideration is issued by the state (such as the Declaration of Independence) or by a private party (such as labor contracts or a mortgage agreement). The use of juridical sources can be found in economics mainly in the areas of economic history, industrial organization, and labor economics, which often rely on the legal documents of business enterprises, cartels, and trade unions. These legal documents can be used to contextualize the economic conditions of a country in a specific period of time or to investigate the structural breaks that may occur following the implementation of new laws. In contrast to narrative sources and social documents, the history capable of being expressed through juridical sources is constrained due to its strictly legal aspect.

Nevertheless, historical research has traditionally relied on juridical documents – and more specifically the written documents of governmental entities – as its principal source of information. Early historians identified juridical documents with historical reliability. Hence the prevalence of juridical documents-based history. In fact, the juridical documents approach was part of an effort to remove history from philosophy and literature in the nineteenth century to a realm of its own. At the same time, professional historians increasingly distinguished their work from that of amateurs by emphasizing the scientific nature of their work, due, in their estimation, to the objectivity implicit in the juridical documents approach (Hoefferle 2011, p. 69). It was, in part, by this process of professionalization that history and economics were placed at opposite ends in the nomothetic–idiographic spectrum.[6]

One of the most important figures in the professionalization of history was Leopold von Ranke, a German scholar who maintained the belief that historians could reveal the truth about the past and see it *'wie es eigentlich gewesen'* ('as it essentially was'). For Ranke, the truth about the past was only accessible through empirical methods, which he identified with meticulous and exhaustive research on juridical sources. He emphasized the importance of objective interpretations and well-trained intuition to glean the essentials of historical events. Due to Ranke's influence, professional historians in Europe and the United States were trained to perform archival research and interpret sources with complete neutrality. It was generally believed that by using Ranke's method on historical data, professional historians could uncover the whole truth about the past and thus accomplish Ranke's original objective.

Ranke's approach was a particular form of historicism, a term that in its broadest sense means that the past must be understood on its own terms. In contrast to most of his colleagues who focused on universal truths and recurrent patterns of the past, Ranke emphasized specific events and their singular properties. His historical methods eventually gained widespread adoption due, in large part, to the purported objectivity inherent in his approach. But the concentration on the singular made it all too easy for the pigeon-holers who, following the nomothetic–idiographic rubric, had no trouble labeling history as idiographic following the *Methodenstreit*.

Ranke's method still remains the most widely used in historical work today. Yet due to the restrictive nature of the sources Ranke considered reliable, his method is not without its shortcomings. The two most significant shortcomings for the purpose of this chapter relate to Ranke's commitment to scientific rigor, which encouraged the view that 'if it is not in the documents, it did not happen'. First of all, since most of the documents available during his time concerned newly formed nation-states, what did happen was the propagation of historical work that proclaimed the legitimacy of these nation-states. History, thus, became the subject matter of great men and great events.

Moreover, despite Ranke's claim to objectivity, the interpretation of juridical or diplomatic documents is always the responsibility of a historian, a socialized being with their own set of interests. That is, similar to economists vis-à-vis the economy, historians are also participant-observers of their field. But what was perhaps most detrimental to Ranke's conviction in the objectivity of his approach was that historians of the day were wont to conclude their manuscript with wider meaning, or with some moral of the story they told (Hoefferle 2011, p. 67). To put it differently, historians of the period were bad deconstructivists, infusing extra-textual content into their work. By propagating a glorious past with romantic heroes, 'history played a crucial political role in uniting diverse ethnic groups in each nation-state and gaining loyalty to newly formed republican and democratic governments' which were 'typically narratives about national heroes who rallied the troops, destroyed the enemy, and illustrated idealized traits for all citizens to emulate' (Hoefferle 2011, p. 69).

Such a bias was further reinforced by Ranke's romanticized view of nation-states, which he perceived as 'spiritual entities with the purpose of civilizing mankind', which consequently meant that they should 'be the central concern of the historian' (Breisach 1994, p. 234). The nation-state was a unique configuration of law, politics, and customs, with each newly formed nation-state representing a stepping-stone along a march of progress. Ranke himself emphasized in each of his works that 'the modern European states were different manifestations of the divine will, mediated through the universal idea of the state' (Breisach 1994, p. 234).

As is evident from the previous paragraph, the emancipation of history from philosophy did not mean the extrication of Enlightenment ideas. The latter, for example the idea of 'progress', were part of the undisclosed background assumptions of traditional history, these ideas being a common thread running through both Enlightenment and post-Enlightenment history. In fact, the only substantive difference in historical work following the arrival of professional historians was that this progressive view was founded upon empirical research and data. As a result, traditional historians viewed progress towards nineteenth-century Europe as a result of universal and natural laws.

In the next section, we consider a few case studies of economic research based on both juridical and social documents. Our objective is to distinguish appropriate uses of historical sources from inappropriate uses by examining how historical documents have been applied in economics.

## 5.3   ECONOMICS AND THE LIMITATIONS OF TRADITIONAL METHODS

As discussed above, Ranke's method was important to consolidate history as a respected field of inquiry primarily due to its systematic use of juridical sources, which were thought to be the most reliable sources. As was also mentioned, the use of juridical sources can be found in economics, primarily in works of economic history, industrial organization, and labor economics, which often rely on the legal documents of business enterprises, cartels, and trade unions.

One juridical document that frequently appears in the industrial organization literature is the patent law. Patent law studies are closely related with traditional historical methods as they typically examine the economic impacts of newly introduced legislation. According to Petra Moser (2013, p. 24), '[h]istorical events, such as the creation of the first patent pool in 1856 and the compulsory licensing of enemy-owned US patents as a result of World War I, create opportunities to examine the effects of policies that strengthen or weaken the monopoly power of patents', and may guide patent policies today. Scholars have tried to understand, for instance, the role of patent laws in promoting innovation and growth, as well as to explain how these laws affect workers, consumers, and other economic agents (Khan and Sokoloff 1993; Khan 2005).[7] More specifically, there is a literature that concentrates on how innovations are affected by patent laws, the explanations typically using the number of patents issued as a proxy for innovation (Schmookler 1962; Sokoloff 1988). It should be noted that by choosing the number of patents issued as a proxy, the study can easily be translated into statistical analysis.

In response to these studies, several authors have argued that additional sources are necessary to arrive at a more accurate account of innovations and their numbers. These economists have pointed out that since innovators frequently resort to tactics like secrecy and lead-time to protect their property rights, the number of patents issued does not tell the whole story of innovation (Levin et al. 1987). A more complete story of innovation and its relation to economic variables would require additional sources beyond data on patents issued. Some of these additional sources, which have been used in other studies, are not traditional sources, and include surveys (Cohen et al. 2000), business archives such as personal records of key individuals (Bieri 2011; Pozzi 2014), documentation of private companies (Hills 2007; Arnold 2011), and archives of industry associations (Moser 2013).

Just as Ranke's juridical document-based history became in large part a fragmented account of noteworthy events, so economic research based on a single type of document often gives an incomplete account of the subject under investigation. In the case just considered, the number of patents issued neglects, for example, innovations that went undocumented by juridical sources. This same problem drove some nontraditional historians in the 1930s toward the adoption of sociological methods, which had the consequence of expanding the definition of a reliable source. Reliable sources started to include the two other types of written documents listed above, namely, narrative and social sources. These documents (as well as oral histories which were later reincorporated) were widely available, much more so than juridical documents which were usually kept classified for 30 to 60 years. Furthermore, with the arrival of new reliable sources came the idea of contemporary history, which meant that historical methods could now be applied to near-current events. Economists could then use historical methods in a much larger capacity.

As mentioned above, economic ministries are repositories for social documents. For example, the United States Federal Reserve publishes its *Bulletin*. The *Bulletin* was introduced in 1914 as a way to report on policy issues of the Federal Reserve (Fed), and also to provide data on the public to the public (Federal Reserve 2014). It is widely used and referenced in research as an important source of information.

To make things concrete, we consider the Survey of Consumer Finance (SCF), a triennial survey reported in the *Bulletin* on the financial situation of consumers. The survey tracks changes in household income and net worth in the US over three-year periods. To conduct such a study 6500 families are randomly selected to answer a questionnaire that includes questions regarding their assets and liabilities, from holdings of corporate stocks and their credit card balance to any holdings of nonfinancial assets. The SCF classifies households by a number of demographic dimensions, including race and ethnicity, age, and maximum education attainment.

The 2012 edition of the SCF captured the effects of the 2008 Great Recession on household finances with the first interviews being conducted in 2007 and then again in 2010 using the same sample. The *Bulletin* shows that mean and median income decreased by 7.7 percent and 11.1 percent, respectively, while mean net worth declined by 14.7 percent and median net worth decreased by 38.8 percent. After a detailed analysis of different types of assets and the variation of its value across different groups, the report concludes that, 'data from the 2007 and 2010 SCF show that median income fell substantially and that mean income fell somewhat faster, an indication that income losses, at least in terms of levels, were larger for families in the uppermost part of the distribution' (Federal Reserve 2012, p. 74). Similar conclusions were derived with respect to wealth, these declines being largely the result of depressed housing and stock markets. How helpful, though, would the SCF be for economists inquiring into the financial situation of families?

The Fed's report, though based on a social rather than a juridical document, again exhibits the limitations of studies based on a single type of historical source. By comparing mean and median income the report concludes that families within the highest income brackets were more affected by the recession. It does not say, however, anything about the everyday life experience of the families interviewed. Can one really draw the conclusion that families in the uppermost part of the distribution were the most affected, based on a comparison of means and medians? To actually capture the social impacts of the crisis, different questions would have to be posed. For example, how did your life change in the past three years? What were the adjustments necessary to deal with a decline in income and wealth? Did anyone in the household have to enter the labor market or work at more than one job? What kind of expenses did you have to cut to service your debt commitments? The list of unraised questions is long, and casts doubt on how well the report alone can accurately capture the financial situation of the families interviewed.

Based on the results from the SCF, the wealthiest households were the most affected by the crisis. Yet the *Bulletin* does not specify whether the wealthiest households were the most affected in absolute or relative terms, giving the reader the impression that the crisis decreased inequality. A study based on this same SCF, however, clarifies that although the wealthiest families were the most affected in absolute terms, 'the declines in percentage terms were greater for less advantaged groups as measured by minority status, education, and prerecession income and wealth, leading to a substantial rise in wealth inequality in just a few years' (Pfeffer et al. 2014, p. 98).

Independently of the conclusions of both studies, neither gives the reader a clear picture of how declines in income and wealth affect the everyday life of the families interviewed in the survey. The everyday life, as defined by Fernand Braudel, is constituted by the customs, habits, and mentality of a people and links common people to their geographical and environmental space. To capture a clearer image of the dialectical relationship of the everyday life against political and economic interests more information or additional sources – such as narrative sources and oral histories – are needed.[8]

Recall that it was for this precise reason – the narrow focus on a particular type of document – that reliable sources were redefined in the 1930s. Thirty years later a second redefinition occurred. The redefinition of the 1960s occurred because nontraditional historians began to impugn the presumed scientific objectivity that empirical data was believed to contain. According to nontraditional historians, data collection is not unbiased, since it incorporates theory into the definition of its categories and into the methods by which data is treated. In other words, data collection presupposes, and what it presupposes is not trivial.

The redefinition of what was considered a reliable source and the subsequent introduction of new methods marked a movement away from Rankean history. Nontraditional historians repudiated traditional methods along with the nomothetic–idiographic dualism, which had received support from Ranke's approach since the *Methodenstreit*. For nontraditional historians, history is not coextensive with singularities, but neither are they unrelated. This meant that in history, as in the other social sciences, '[t]he nomothetic/idiographic dichotomy is untenable because all sciences are nomothetic as well as idiographic' (Bunge 1998, p. 23). What precipitated claims such as these, it is important to reiterate, was the questioning of Ranke's traditional documents-based history, which led to the introduction of new methods and data. The next few paragraphs present a case study where a social document is used to illuminate how the Federal Reserve conducts policy.

Studies on how the Federal Reserve determines the targeted federal funds rate (also called the neutral federal funds rate) normally centers on the social documents of government bureaus that collate and publish the time-series data of macroeconomic variables. Different economists, of course, think different variables are more significant than others in the Fed's decision, but there is a consensus that the time-series data is what is relevant to the Fed's decision. But, as the following example shows, by considering other documents – in this case the minutes of the Fed's policy meetings – the Fed's decision is not always so straightforward.

In a paper on Greenspan's Fed and the so-called 'New Monetary Consensus', L. Randall Wray uses the official minutes of the Federal Open Market Committee's (FOMC) meetings during 1994 (Wray 2004). The FOMC meets eight times per year to discuss the interbank Federal funds rate target, among other things. The minutes from these meetings are released with a five-year lag and provide the reader closed-door access to how the Fed decides upon its chief policy tool.

Two things are immediately apparent from the FOMC meetings in 1994 that Wray considers: (1) the significant degree of clout Chairman Greenspan has over the rest of the Committee; and (2) the complexity involved in the policy decision. Before discussing the intricacies of the Committee's policy decision, we first take a look at the high-ranking personages of these meetings.

As the Chairman of the Board of Governors and thus the superintendent of these meetings, Greenspan is naturally positioned atop the hierarchical structure of the Fed. But these documents reveal Greenspan exercising something more than mere bureaucratic obligation, and in fact, during the February 1994 meeting his behavior at times is decidedly coercive. For example, when some members of the Committee want a 50-basis-point increase of the target rate, in opposition to Greenspan's proposal for a 25-basis-point hike, he pleads with the Committee, saying, 'I rarely ask this, as you know. This is one of the times when we really are together and I'd hate to have our vote somehow imply something other than the agreement for a tightening move that in fact exists in this Committee' (Wray 2004, p. 57).[9] Later on, after the Committee has unanimously voted for the 25-basis-point increase, Greenspan is full of gratitude, saying, 'I thank you for that. I think it's the right move. I think in retrospect when we're looking back at what we're doing over the next year we'll find that it was the right decision' (Wray 2004, p. 58).

It is worth mentioning that within this context of action – the February 1994 FOMC meeting – Greenspan cannot unilaterally determine the outcome due to the one member, one vote rule of these meetings. But at the same time he does not yield in the face of opposition. The Committee members and Greenspan are internally related[10] but, as is clear from the outcome, the distribution of power is not uniform: the position occupied by Greenspan, along with the special rights it affords its holder, enables him to establish a consensus among the Committee members. Causation in this context is intentional, as Greenspan is able to align his intent with the outcome.

Returning to the February meeting, why was consensus over raising the rate so important for Greenspan? Prior to 1994, the Fed did not publicly announce its interbank target rate, leaving it to the markets to figure out what rate it had decided on. But for the first time ever, after the February meeting the Fed funds target rate was announced through a press release. In the meeting Greenspan insists that the vote to raise the target rate be unanimous, affirming that he, 'would be concerned if this Committee were not in concert because at this stage we as a Committee are going to have to do things which the rest of the world is not going to like. We have to do them because that's our job' (Wray 2004, p. 55).

The February meeting was no doubt a momentous one for the FOMC since the way monetary policy had been conducted was about to change. The minutes of the FOMC's meeting seem to corroborate the view that monetary policy is not undertaken in a mechanical fashion. The Committee, for example, does not simply plug data into a Taylor equation to settle upon its interest rate target. The willful disposition of the Chairman along with the complexity of historical circumstance, the latter including a break with past policy and a new focus on public-relations considerations, also entered the equation. Furthermore, as the minutes attest, these were not merely second-order influences on the interest rate target that was ultimately decided upon. Indeed, Greenspan's push for consensus in anticipation of the new precedent[11] had a decisive influence on the Committee's vote and consequently the decision ultimately reached.

This is not to say that the usual economic indicators used in deciding the target rate (for example, current rates of growth, inflation, and estimates of the non-accelerating inflation rate of unemployment, the NAIRU) are inconsequential in the decision-making process. The minutes clearly demonstrate that they are not. In the February meeting, for example, Greenspan's justification for a smaller increase in the interest rate is his concern with how financial markets will respond to it. Indeed, the FOMC minutes as well as the Chairman's congressional testimony designate those indicators the Committee regards as consequential to their decision, while implicitly revealing those the Committee finds of less consequence. From testimony given before Congress in 2004, Greenspan voices the Committee's passive stance toward profits-led inflation despite its openly aggressive attitude towards inflation in general (Wray 2004, pp. 22–3). On the other hand, when wage growth was expected to outstrip productivity, the Fed took pre-emptive action by raising the targeted rate. Summarizing the apparent double standard on distribution-led inflation, Wray notes, 'It's hard to avoid the conclusion that the Fed is biased against labor' (Wray 2004, p. 23).

By utilizing this social document, one not normally used in economics, what comes to light is that the enactment of monetary policy does not conform to a 'rules versus discretion' typology. As mentioned above, there is no Taylor rule that would ultimately make monetary policy an exercise in number-crunching. And, as we have seen, even the discretion of the Chairman is not entirely discretionary. Nevertheless, the role of agency to sway policy is manifested. Wray's work suggests that agents are not constrained to behave in one particular way, as rational choice theory would have it. On the contrary, in an environment of uncertainty, economic decisions can often be influenced by 'whim or sentiment or chance', as opposed to rational calculation. A historically grounded account of agents and the social spaces they inhabit can therefore illuminate the complexities involved in actual contexts of action.

As exposited in Chapter 2 in this *Handbook*, what this means is that a grounded theory approach implies that historical specificity must enter the core of economic theory, rather than being a mere *ex post* addition to already existing theory. Though most economists continue to accept the traditional separation between nomothetic and idiographic sciences, historians have gradually moved away from this centenarian dualism. As discussed above, historians in the 1930s and 1960s started to call into question traditional methods, at first assailing the narrow focus of traditional historians, and then later disclosing the previously undisclosed background assumptions made when collecting and interpreting primary sources. One important consequence of these interventions for subsequent historical work was the novel focus on marginalized groups who, in traditional history, were simply 'people with no history'. To give a voice to those who never had one required new source documents and therefore new methods. In the next section we discuss some of these new sources and methods, and show how they can be incorporated into economics.

## 5.4  SOURCE DIVERSITY IN ECONOMICS

After revealing the background assumptions of the juridical documents approach to history and the biases they betrayed, contemporary historians started to advance novel methods in order to articulate a more comprehensive history. As a result of their interventions, contemporary historians gave new life to unwritten sources, which are often used to accentuate the multifaceted and layered nature of history. In this section we show how economists use unwritten sources. Our primary focus will be on oral histories and narrative sources.[12]

The use of oral histories, for example, questionnaires and interviews, as a research method tends to come in and out of fashion in economics. Researchers doing work in industrial organization, however, have frequently found a use for these types of documents, fluctuations in fashion notwithstanding. The pioneering work in this regard came from the University of Oxford in the midst of the Great Depression. In 1936 a group of economists at Oxford, known as the Oxford Economists' Research Group, was organized to design questionnaires and arrange interviews as a way to investigate the real-world practices of businessmen. In a seminal paper, Robert Hall and Charles Hitch (1939) reported the results of the Research Group's interviews, which they conducted with 38 managers. No doubt the most substantial finding that arose out of the interviews was that businessmen tended to administer their prices to the market based on full-cost pricing procedures. In its most simple formulation, a full-cost pricing scheme means the firm sets its price by adding its average costs of materials and labor to its indirect costs (based on some expected rate of output), and to the terms of this summation multiplies a predetermined profit margin. The firm's price is then equal to the summation of costs plus these costs multiplied by a profit margin. Although the Research Group did not immediately recognize the full implications of their findings, they were aware that they departed from orthodox theory (Lee 1998, pp. 90–91). That is, the results summarized in Hall and Hitch's paper seemed to offer decisive evidence that firms do not adopt marginalist pricing procedures when deciding their price. Nontraditional data collection, in this case the use of questionnaires and interviews, again seems to emphasize the role agents have in making economic decisions. That is, the interviews did not support the orthodox view that firms follow the maxim 'marginal revenue equals marginal cost' when determining their prices. Rather, the interviews indicated that businesses had veritable choices to make with regard to their estimates of expected demand and their profit margins.

The paper had an immediate impact on the discipline, eventually prompting the so-called 'marginalist controversy' that graced the pages of the *American Economic Review* from 1947 until 1953.[13] But the paper's immediate impact was precisely that, as the marginalist controversy prompted what has become the most well-known paper on method in economics, namely Milton Friedman's (1970 [1953]) 'Essay on the methodology of positive economics'. Friedman does not try to hide his intention to dissolve these controversies:

> The articles [in the *American Economic Review*] on both sides of the controversy largely neglect what seems to me clearly the main issue – the conformity to experience of the implications of the marginal analysis – and concentrate on the largely irrelevant question whether businessmen do or do not in fact reach their decisions by consulting schedules, or curves, or multivariable functions showing marginal cost and marginal revenue. (Friedman 1970 [1953], p. 15)

Given the influence of Friedman's methodological project on the discipline, it is little wonder that Alan Blinder, in a study similar in spirit to the work of Hall and Hitch, remarks that the latter's inquiry 'was the first and last interview study of pricing to have a major impact on the thinking of economists' (Blinder et al. 1998, p. 40).

The influence of Friedman's essay on the discipline cannot be understated. That its legacy continues is attested by nearly every mainstream principles textbook, academic journal, and, what is most relevant to this chapter, the work of mainstream defectors from Friedman's brand of positivism. Some of these defectors, including Blinder himself and Truman Bewley, have adopted similar methods to the ones pioneered by the Research Group. To evaluate different theories on price rigidity, Blinder and his colleagues gave questionnaires to businesspeople. Bewley conducted interviews with businesspeople, labor representatives, and labor market intermediaries in search of a better explanation of wage rigidity. Due to their unorthodox approach, these orthodox economists naturally felt obligated to justify their 'controversial' methods. In fact, Bewley's (1999) book, *Why Wages Don't Fall During a Recession*, devotes a considerable part of his introduction to addressing Friedman's 1953 essay.[14] But the significance of his book regards his research methods, not his meta-discussion on Friedman. We therefore provide a brief account of the research methods used in his book.

Unsatisfied with the existing theories on wage and employment determination, Bewley decided to use the interview method as a way to construct novel explanations. To that end, he felt the need to 'understand the context in which businesspeople and labor leaders make personnel and compensation decisions' (Bewley 1999, p. 29). Despite being unfamiliar with critical realism and the method of grounded theory, Bewley's approach to the problem, as he set out to explain it, indicates that he understands social reality as the composition of agents, structures, and contexts of action. As the quote above reveals, Bewley expresses the need to understand the specific context of action in which wages and employment decisions are undertaken. He then demonstrates awareness to different social positions and their associated roles by interviewing three different agents involved in the process: businesspeople, labor representatives, and labor market intermediaries. As each of these agents occupies a distinct position, each also possesses distinct, and therefore differential, causal powers with regard to the determination of the price labor receives, the number of workers hired, and the number of hours worked.

One of Bewley's objectives was to understand the context in which negotiations take place and decisions are made. In other words, he wanted to understand the context of action existing between employers and those they employ. These interactive spaces are also of interest to historians, although their 'contact zones' are typically drawn on a bigger canvas, depicting the interactions among entire cultures or nations. Mary Louise Pratt, the originator of the term 'contact zone', used the latter to describe 'social spaces where cultures meet, clash, and grapple with each other, often in contexts of highly asymmetrical relations of power, such as colonialism, slavery, or their aftermaths as they are lived out in many parts of the world today' (Pratt 1991, p. 575). In undertaking her work, Pratt relied on narrative sources, such as travelers' journals and personal letters, to argue that cultural interactions between European travelers and their Latin American and African hosts prompted daily negotiations between these different groups. Her analysis of these negotiations reveals the power realities of the everyday life and those associated with geopolitical and economic structures. She shows how the intersection of the everyday-life power reality and the power realities of geopolitical and economic structures work to shape the history of the communities in question.

Aside from interviews, questionnaires, and travel journals, other documents may be used to conduct this type of research, such as correspondence (for example, personal letters or documented conversations), and unpublished notes. Countless journal articles and books take shape from or are directly written on the correspondences and unpublished notes of a departed thinker, with some examining those still living. The use of these types of narrative documents is most conspicuous in the work of historians of economic thought who have forged for themselves new research tools, namely contextual analysis and historical narratives. Contextual analysis seeks to uncover the historical circumstances in which a body of knowledge was created to then make sense of it, while historical narratives focus not only on the work of 'intellectual giants', but also on the work of lesser economists, their connections, intellectual circles, and so on (Marcuzzo 2008, pp. 111–12).

Narrative documents are also instrumental in fields outside the history of thought. As an example, to construct an empirically grounded model of pricing, Frederic Lee (1998) relies in part on published and unpublished letters and notes.[15] This raises a question: why use such material to develop a theory of how modern corporations decide their prices? For one thing, by providing additional context these sources can expose a writer's 'struggle of escape from habitual modes of thought and expression' as well as signal an author's inability to express themselves due perhaps to a lack or the nonexistence of terms and concepts that would capture their intended meaning. This is especially important if the work under examination is pioneering work, as it is in Lee's book where the key developers of post-Keynesian price theory – Gardiner Means, Michał Kalecki, and Philip Andrews and the Oxford Economists' Research Group – are studied in detail.

Lee's theoretical framework was also built upon an analysis of unknown or obscure writings.[16] Since the ideas disseminated in published form are not always representative of the author's original views or are sometimes truncated accounts of their views, these sources provide additional context of the broader setting in which the writer and their text are situated. For example, in its final, published form the work may omit any justification of the questions it seeks to answer or for the assumptions it makes. If the text is dated, what is answered and the assumptions made may strike the reader as outlandish or empirically ungrounded. In some cases, only the historical context can provide those justifications.

But apart from interpretive problems with what is actually contained in published work, there are also issues with what is omitted from it. An editor or the author themself may decide to eliminate or not even include certain ideas in the text because they are deemed superfluous. What is relevant to understand, say, price determination, the author may see as extraneous to their work. But to a researcher of the text, such omissions may provide a crucial link in the author's theoretical project. In this regard, unknown or unpublished notes and personal correspondence can prove beneficial to fill some of the gaps of a text.

As mentioned above, a pluralistic approach to source types, like Lee's, has much to recommend it, for it permits a more comprehensive account of the social structures, agents, and the contexts of action that pertain to the historical subject under investigation. But, of course, what sources should be consulted depends on the questions to be answered, which in some cases may require only a single type of source.

## 5.5   CONCLUSION

Historical methods and data are essential if economic research is to be relevant. This is just to say that 'history matters' when it comes to many problems that interest economists, and should not be taken as an injunction decreeing the use of historical documents in all economic work. That would be silly. To say 'history matters' is also to say that history must be part of the core of all economic research that self-identifies as historical. History does not matter when it is introduced after the theory has been constructed.

But simply applying the historical methods we have discussed does not, of course, guarantee that history has been integrated in a satisfactory manner. This is largely a question of the source documents used. Studies based solely on a particular type of document will typically offer a selective account of the topic under investigation. This need not be a problem, provided the topic itself is narrow. In any case, as discussed earlier, the reason historians sought new types of sources, and therefore new methods, was related to the restrictive nature of traditional history and its sole use of juridical documents. This narrow perspective precluded an understanding of history as both complex and multilayered. Indeed, as Braudel contended, what mattered – what shapes history – is the everyday life, which implies that human behavior is to a large extent 'structured', consisting of routinized forms of conduct that tend to allay radical disruptions. Like critical realists, but unlike Ranke, nontraditional historians recognize that human behavior exhibits a significant degree of continuity, stability, and sameness in daily affairs.[17] As this concerns method, nontraditional historians affirm that these characteristics of human behavior cannot be neglected in historical accounts of culture and society that also purport to be comprehensive. If heterodox economists are going to incorporate this aspect of behavior into their theoretical frameworks, they will have to consult nontraditional sources.

Moreover, nontraditional sources clarify the roles of agents and structures in particular contexts, perhaps most evident in Wray's use of the FOMC minutes to analyze the Fed's decision on its interest rate target. Interviews and questionnaires also shed light on routinized behavior, as well as offering a deeper understanding of disruptive effects on individuals or groups. They also provide insight into the decision-making processes of businesses, which was discussed with respect to Blinder, Bewley, and Hall and Hitch's studies on price rigidity.

But although work on price rigidity is perhaps the most well-known area that has used interviews and questionnaires, the latter methods are by no means limited to questions of price. What determines, for instance, the decision to invest by business enterprises, and what are the relevant structures in making investment decisions, are no doubt important questions, and ones that could be studied by means of interviews and questionnaires. Yet, with very few exceptions these questions are answered in a department office at some university by an economist, not by directly speaking with those who answer the questions by their very actions. Needless to say, there are many possible applications of these methods in areas of economics that hitherto have been dominated by theories based on a priori arguments.

As one of many research methods at the disposal of heterodox economists, historical methods have a substantive part to play in our research program. A core principle of heterodox economics is that history matters in the sense that an understanding of the economy and its workings requires an understanding of its history as well. Staying true to this principle means adopting historical methods to study the social provisioning process and, thereby, aligning our actions with our principles.

## NOTES

1. The *Methodenstreit* was a controversial debate in the late nineteenth century concerning the appropriate methods to be used in social science. The upshot of the debate was the following dualism: a social science was nomothetic if it dealt with absolute or universal statements, and idiographic if it dealt with the concrete or unique.
2. It should be noted that Giddens's way of handling the interrelationship between agents and structures – elaborated in his 'theory of structuration' (Giddens 1984) – is different from how critical realists handle the problem. See Archer (1995, Ch. 4).
3. The difference between traditional and nontraditional historical methods comes down to the written sources believed to be reliable. Traditional history only uses juridical and diplomatic documents, while nontraditional historians, in addition to those documents, accept social and narrative documents as well as oral histories. Each type of source just mentioned is explained in the following pages.
4. The following discussion on source typologies relies on Howell and Prevenier's (2001) account of written sources.
5. For example, in John Kenneth Galbraith's (1954) *The Great Crash 1929*, the author consulted contemporary newspapers to describe the days leading up to the Great Depression; while the interpretation of scientific tracts – an example of textual exegesis – is the technique *par excellence* of historians of economic thought (Marcuzzo 2008, p. 108).
6. Economists, of course, played no small part in this process. But due to the extensive literature on the subject, we omit any discussion on this topic.
7. Similar to patent law studies, there is much work on antitrust laws. See, for example, Dennis Mueller (1996) who analyzes how changes in antitrust laws have impacted microeconomic theory.
8. The present section is largely concerned with social documents. Narrative and oral sources are discussed in the next section.
9. All quotes in the next few paragraphs are taken from Wray (2004).
10. An internal or necessary relation is defined as a relation in which the existence of one of the relation's components is dependent on the other (Sayer 1992, p. 89). The canonical example of an internal relation is the relation between master and slave.
11. Although in retrospect the announcement did set a (non-binding) precedent, Greenspan was adamant about finding a way to make it appear as though no precedent had been or would be set (Wray 2004, p. 29).

12.   Although oral histories are considered to be a nontraditional, they were actually the first historical method to be used. Proto-professional historians used folk songs and popular rituals to transmit past experiences to current generations. Since these oral histories were part history and part myth, it is little wonder they had no role to play in Rankean history.
13.   For details on this controversy see Phillipe Mongin (1998).
14.   See Bewley (1999, pp. 8–12). In their first chapter, Blinder et al. (1998, pp. 6–7) also confront orthodox methods, but defend their approach from that other influential brand of positivism in economics, Paul Samuelson's operationalism.
15.   While Lee (1998) does research on the history of thought in the first sections of his book, for the purpose of this chapter we focus on the final part, which aims to construct an empirically grounded model of pricing.
16.   It should be noted that the historical sources in Lee's book are not limited to letters and correspondences. As the author states in his introduction, 'in addition to published works, recourse will be made to biographical data, to unpublished personal letters, lectures, and papers, to oral histories and interviews, and to notes, memoranda, and letters located in the files of private and public institutions' (Lee 1998, p. 6).
17.   For more details on critical realists in this matter, see Lawson (1997, p. 180).

# REFERENCES

Archer, Margaret (1995), *Realist Social Theory: The Morphogenetic Approach*, Cambridge: Cambridge University Press.
Arnold, A.J. (2011), '"Out of light a little profit?" returns to capital at Bryant and May, 1884–1927', *Business History*, **53** (4), 617–40.
Bewley, Truman (1999), *Why Wages Don't Fall During a Recession*, Cambridge, MA: Harvard University Press.
Bieri, Alexander (2011), 'Roche: a Swiss pharmaceutical company in the United Kingdom', *Business Archives Journal*, **103** (1), 25–39.
Blinder, Alan, Elie Canetti, David Lebow, and Jeremy Rudd (1998), *Asking About Prices: A New Approach to Understanding Price Stickiness*, New York: Russell Sage Foundation.
Bracarense, Natália (2013), 'Development economics in Latin America and the *Methodenstreit*: Lessons from history of thought', *Journal of Economic Issues*, **47** (1), 113–34.
Breisach, Ernst (1994), *Historiography: Ancient, Medieval, and Modern*, Chicago, IL: Chicago University Press.
Bunge, Mario (1998), *Social Science under Debate: A Philosophical Perspective*, Toronto: University of Toronto Press.
Cohen, Wesley, Richard Nelson, and John Walsh (2000), 'Protecting their intellectual assets: appropriability conditions and why US manufacturing firms patent (or not)', NBER Working Paper 755.
Federal Reserve (2012), 'Changes in US family finances from 2007 to 2010: evidence from the survey of consumer finances', *Federal Reserve Bulletin*, **98** (2), A1–A80.
Federal Reserve (2014), 'Changes in US family finances from 2010 to 2013: evidence from the survey of consumer finances', *Reserve Bulletin*, **100** (4), A1–A40.
Friedman, M. (1970 [1953]), 'The methodology of positive economics', in Milton Friedman, *Essays in Positive Economics*, Chicago, IL: University of Chicago Press, pp. 3–43.
Galbraith, John Kenneth (1954), *The Great Crash 1929*, Boston, MA: Houghton Mifflin Company.
Giddens, Anthony (1984), *The Constitution of Society: Outline of the Theory of Structuration*, Cambridge: Blackwell.
Hills, Jill (2007), 'Regulation, innovation and market structure in international telecommunications: the case of the 1956 TAT1 submarine cable', *Business History*, **49** (6), 868–85.
Hodgson, Geoffrey (2001), *How Economics Forgot History: The Problem of Historical Specificity in Social Science*, London: Routledge.
Hoefferle, Carolina (2011), *The Essential Historiography Reader*, Boston, MA: Prentice Hall.
Howell, Martha and Walter Prevenier (2001), *From Reliable Sources: An Introduction to Historical Methods*, Ithaca, NY: Cornell University Press.
Khan, Zorina (2005), *The Democratization of Invention: Patents and Copyrights in American Economic Development, 1790–1920*, Cambridge: Cambridge University Press.
Khan, Zorina and Kenneth Sokoloff (1993), 'Schemes of practical utility: entrepreneurship and innovation among "great inventors" in the United States, 1790–1865', *Journal of Economic History*, **53** (2), 289–307.
Lawson, T. (1997), *Economics and Reality*, London: Routledge.
Lee, Frederic S. (1998), *Post-Keynesian Price Theory*, Cambridge: Cambridge University Press.

Lee, Frederic S. (2012), 'Heterodox economics and its critics', in Marc Lavoie and Frederic Lee (eds), *In Defense of Post-Keynesian and Heterodox Economics: Responses to Their Critics*, New York: Routledge, pp. 104–32.

Levin, Richard, Alvin Klevorick, Richard Nelson, and Sidney G. Winter (1987), 'Appropriating the returns from industrial research and development', *Brookings Papers on Economic Activity*, **3** (Special Issue on Microeconomics), 783–832.

Marcuzzo, Maria Cristina (2008), 'Is history of economic thought a "serious" subject?', *Erasmus Journal for Philosophy and Economics*, **1** (1), 107–23.

Marx, Karl (1977 [1852]), 'The eighteenth Brumaire of Louis Bonaparte', reprinted in David Maclellan (ed.), *Karl Marx: Selected Writings*, Oxford: Oxford University Press, pp. 329–55.

Mongin, Philippe (1998), 'The marginalist controversy', in John Davis, D. Wade Hands, and Uskali Mäki (eds), *The Handbook of Economic Methodology*, Cheltenham, UK and Lyme, NH, USA: Edward Elgar Publishing, pp. 558–62.

Moser, Petra (2013), 'Patents and innovation: evidence from economic history', *Journal of Economic Perspectives*, **27** (1), 23–44.

Mueller, Denis (1996), 'Lessons from the United States' anti-trust history', *International Journal of Industrial Organization*, **14** (6), 415–45.

Pfeffer, Fabian, Sheldon Danziger, and Robert Schoeni (2014), 'Wealth disparity after and before the Great Recession', *Annals of the American Academy of Political and Social Sciences*, **650** (1), 98–123.

Pozzi, Daniele (2014), 'An elastic managerial revolution: family, managers and multidivisional organization at Pirelli 1943–1956', *Business History*, **56** (5), 765–88.

Pratt, Mary Louise (1991), 'Arts of contact zones', *Profession*, **91**, 33–40.

Sayer, A. (1992), *Method in Social Science: A Realist Approach*, 2nd edn, London: Routledge.

Schmookler, Jacob (1962), 'Economic sources of inventive activity', *Journal of Economic History*, **22** (1), 1–20.

Sokoloff, Kenneth (1988), 'Inventive activity in early industrial America: evidence from patent records, 1790–1846', *Journal of Economic History*, **48** (4), 813–15.

Wray, L. Randall (2004), 'The Fed and the new monetary consensus: the case for rate hikes, part two', Public Policy Brief, 80, New York: Levy Economics Institute of Bard College.

# APPENDIX 5A.1   THE BASICS OF ARCHIVAL RESEARCH

In this Appendix we provide a brief and practical introduction to archival research. Though researching historical archives may appear straightforward, any Masters student in history has no doubt to take a course on historical methods, which includes an extensive and usually hands-on section on archival research. Economists, on the other hand, including heterodox ones, are more likely to take a course in say, topology, than one related to archival research. And so, appearances aside, it is worthwhile to outline some of the basics of researching historical archives, in addition to providing some practical suggestions for those economists either uninitiated in or inexperienced with archives and who wish to incorporate their contents in their research.

Archival research, it cannot be overemphasized, requires special attention not only during the examination of documents but also, more importantly, prior to the trip to an archival library. Before beginning your research you must become familiar with existing archives and the type of sources that are contained therein. This should be the first step taken in preparation for your trip to the archive.

After ascertaining the location of your targeted documents,[1] the second step is to contact the archivist associated with these documents. In your correspondence, it is important to provide a description of your research and what you are specifically looking for. The archivist can then direct you to online resources, construct a list of materials pertaining to your research, and instruct you on how to access the archives. It is worth mentioning in passing that policies vary by library. Most libraries have online resources, so a third step, and one that will make the trip more productive, is to study these resources and become as familiar as possible with them before your trip. This will save you time, which, as most archival researchers can attest, is in shorter supply than anticipated. Once you have an idea of which collections and boxes pertain to your research, you are ready for the trip.

Well, almost ready. Aside from these tactical steps, there are also some details that will make your visit more profitable. First and foremost, once in the archives befriend, or at least be polite to, the archivist(s), lest you create unnecessary obstacles to your research. Archivists are Sherpa guides in whose absence you will tend to wander around the library while your research freezes. Also, bring a camera with you since most archives charge for photocopies. Because your time and finances are limited, it is also of the utmost importance to stay organized. You will thank yourself later. In that regard, make sure you know which picture or photocopy corresponds to which collection and box of the archive because you will need to cite your findings later.[2] As a final suggestion, take time to read documents carefully and become familiar with the collection. This is especially important in the first few days and will give you a better idea of which photos or photocopies to take and the order of boxes you should research.

**Notes**

1.   One of the most important archival resources in the United States is the United States National Archives, which includes several presidential libraries as well as personal archives of some economists. For research in the history of economic thought, the McMaster University Archive for the History of Economic Thought is a good place to start. It has documents of more than 200 economists from all schools of thought.

Another useful source is the Library of Congress which houses collections on a variety of topics, including records of US enterprises in addition to other juridical documents. It also has one of the most extensive newspaper collections in the world.

2.  My own method of organization is to make a spreadsheet with each photo or photocopy corresponding to each row and consisting of the following information: an identification of the collection and box that photo or photocopy belongs, a brief description of the photo or photocopy, and finally the import of the photo or photocopy to the project. This method has proven beneficial to me, but it is by no means the only way to organize archival research.

# 6 Using survey methods in heterodox economic research
*Tiago Cardão-Pito*

## 6.1 INTRODUCTION

By asking a few questions of some economists affiliated with the American Economic Association (AEA), Klein and Stern (2007) managed to exhibit a fundamental contradiction in contemporary economics. Although mainstream publications and departments advocate 'free market' ideologies, only 8 percent of those AEA members who answered the survey could be considered as supporting those 'free market' ideologies. Even the average Republican AEA member was found to be a 'middle-of-the-road' free market supporter. Therefore, Klein and Stern's survey study suggests that the persons controlling the dominant agenda in economics do not represent the views of the majority of economists.

Despite its relevance to the social sciences, survey studies are rarely featured in mainstream economic journals. Nonetheless, mainstream publications claim to describe or predict human and organizational behavior through their 'economic-man' sandcastle constructions. Survey methods can test the scientific validity of those constructions with real people. Thus, offering the capacity to engage with people in the real world, survey methods provide powerful instruments for heterodox economics. Yet, the potential of survey methodologies is much wider than that of merely questioning the mainstream economic theory of man (and woman). Survey methodologies can be used to make new discoveries, formulate new concepts and theories, and test existing theories in heterodox economics.

## 6.2 WHAT IS SURVEY RESEARCH?

One can understand surveys as means of making inferences about populations. A relevant characteristic of the methodologies described in this chapter is that they aim to learn something about human populations. Thus, they always involve a group of people. The methods described here are used to portray and quantify characteristics and features of the population under study. These methodologies must not be confused with structured interviews or ethnographic research where one may also pose questions and interact with people without making inferences about the population. Furthermore, surveys can also be used to study population groups of non-human beings, such as objects, houses, plants, institutions, events, and papers (Hibberts et al. 2012).

In surveys of human populations, inferences are made using a relatively large sample of individuals who are believed to be part of or related to that population (Sapsford 2007; Scheuren 2004). Distinct from censuses, which study all members of a population, surveys gather information from only a portion of the population of interest. The size of the sample normally depends on the study's purpose. Nonetheless, samples that are too small generally fail to provide statistically significant results (Scheuren 2004). Methodologies are quite relevant in survey research. Some handbooks describe surveys directly through their major components and potential survey errors, instead of providing a concrete definition of survey research (Leeuw et al. 2008).

As noted by Czaja and Blair (2005), survey research is inherently interdisciplinary. Sampling and estimation procedures require an understanding of probability theory and statistics. Data collection requires that researchers convince persons to respond to questions, and in some cases involves social interaction between interviewers and interviewees. The collection of information via interviews and questionnaires depends upon respondents' cognition, memory, language comprehension, and discourse. Programing skills in a variety of software are quite useful for the implementation of digital and internet questionnaires, as well as data analysis. Management skills are also necessary in conducting survey projects with different stages distributed over weeks, months, or in some cases, years. Although survey practitioners may not be experts in statistical theory, linguistics, sociology, psychology, or management, each of these disciplines is related to one area of survey research.

Survey studies are often conducted in contemporary societies not only by academics, but also, for instance, by media organizations, governmental agencies, and corporations. Such studies, however, can fall far short of producing useful, reliable, and valid results because of failing to employ adequate methodologies (Czaja and Blair 2005). Surveys should be perceived as complex endeavors. Generally, no two surveys are identical (Stoop and Harrison 2012). This chapter cannot provide readers with an advanced acquaintance with all areas of survey research, but it introduces the key principles, decisions, and practical guidelines guiding such research.

The first step in a survey study is not statistical, but conceptual. It consists of defining and specifying the concepts under study. As described in Figure 6.1, four cornerstones are required to support conceptualization: (1) coverage (identifying the target population and percentage of the population included in the study frame); (2) sampling (drawn from the population); (3) response (and how to deal with non-response); and (4) measurement (of data obtained). These cornerstones must be solid (Leeuw et al. 2008; Salant and Dillman 1994; Groves 1989).

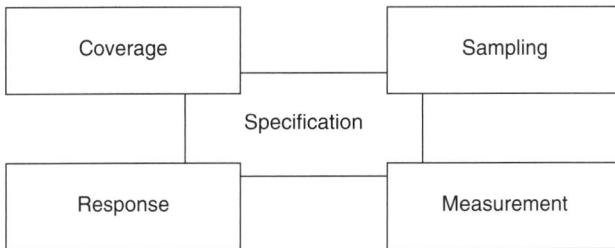

*Source:*   Adapted from Leeuw et al. (2008), Salant and Dilman (1984), and Grooves (1989).

*Figure 6.1   The cornerstones of survey research*

As noted above, researchers conducting survey studies use specific methods to make inferences about a population without questioning the entire population. A crucial issue is thus the potential for error associated with these inferences, which is unavoidable in survey research (Bautista 2012). Several authors (e.g., Zikmund 2000; Groves et al. 2004; Weisberg 2005; Lohr 2008; Gideon 2012a; Bautista 2012) have argued that errors must not be seen in isolation, but characterized through an estimation of total survey error. According to Gideon (2012a), Bautista (2012), and Weisberg (2005), survey errors can be classified as sampling and non-sampling errors. Sampling errors arise from the sampling methods used. The category of non-sampling errors encompasses all other possible errors, which can be very complex and influential. Although attention to errors tends to focus on issues associated with the population–sample relationship, survey research is much more complex than pure sampling. For instance, errors may arise from administration issues, insufficient interviewer training, or questions about the accuracy of data obtained. Similarly, Groves et al. (2004) and Lohr (2008) have recommended the identification of total survey error based on the framework illustrated in Figure 6.1, using four corresponding components: (1) coverage error; (2) sampling error; (3) non-response error; and (4) measurement error. The robustness and usefulness of survey research are related directly to the ways in which researchers handle possible errors in data collection, inferences, and findings.

## 6.3   EXAMPLES OF SURVEY RESEARCH IN HETERODOX ECONOMICS

Table 6.1 presents a summary of five survey studies in heterodox economic research. As explained above, survey studies can be used to: (1) make direct confrontations with mainstream economic theory; and/or (2) make new discoveries, formulate new concepts and theories, and test existing heterodox theories.

For the first group, one can find for instance Klein and Stern's (2007) study mentioned in the introduction, where a sample of AEA's members were asked about their views about 'free market' ideologies. One can also mention Gahan's (2002) work, where survey methods were used to demonstrate that mainstream economic models of union behavior are not consistent with several union leaders' positions. Mainstream economic models advocate that most goals pursued by unions can be reduced to wage (or wage equivalent) and employment trade-offs. Gahan distributed his questionnaires at Australian union leaders' meetings. His results seem to show that standard mainstream models of union activity do not adequately capture union bargaining behavior or union goals and preferences. For instance, union leaders seem to be quite concerned with productivity, quality, and training.

On the other hand, Table 6.1 shows that survey methodologies can also be used to study phenomena with undeniable bearing on economics and sociology that, however, are rarely investigated by mainstream economic publications. For instance, the relation between sleep and work–life balance (Chatzitheochari and Arber 2009), socio-economic uncertainty (Mau et al. 2012), or workers' observations about their bosses' gender (Elsesser and Lever 2011).

Sleep is functional for individual and societal well-being. Partial sleep deprivation can

Table 6.1  Examples of survey research in heterodox economics

| Authors | Journal | Population studied | Data collection method | Final sample size | Response rate | Major findings |
|---|---|---|---|---|---|---|
| Chatzitheochari and Arber (2009) | *Work, Employment and Society* | UK workers aged 20–60 years. | Data are analyzed from the 2000 UK Time Use Survey (UKTUS), a large household survey conducted by the Office for National Statistics (ONS). The UKTUS used a multi-stage sampling design | n = 2882 | 45% | Sleep is functional for individual and societal well-being, with partial sleep deprivation associated with adverse health and safety consequences. Surprisingly, sleep is absent from work–life balance debates and has remained largely under-researched. This article examines the relationship of insufficient sleep duration with occupational circumstances and family responsibilities. It identifies the segments of the working population getting a short sleep duration that if sustained may have negative health outcomes. An inverse relationship between working hours and sleep duration is found, which is stronger for men than women. Shift work and social class are also significant predictors of short sleep for men. |
| Elsesser and Lever (2011) | *Human Relations* | Employed American population who have a boss. | Internet survey through the site of MSNBC.com | n = 60470 | Not available | The gender of the boss is not irrelevant. A cross-sex bias emerged in the ratings of one's current boss, where men judged their female bosses more favorably and women judged male bosses more favorably. Moreover, the majority (54%) of participants claimed to have no preference for the gender of their boss, but the remaining participants reported preferring male over female bosses by more than a 2:1 ratio. Results are discussed. |

*Table 6.1* (continued)

| Authors | Journal | Population studied | Data collection method | Final sample size | Response rate | Major findings |
|---|---|---|---|---|---|---|
| Gahan (2002) | *Cambridge Journal of Economics* | Australian Union Leaders | Questionaires handed at meetings | n = 284 | Not available | Mainstream economic models of union behavior claim that most goals pursued by unions can be reduced to wage (or wage equivalent)–employment trade-offs. However this survey to union leaders finds that standard mainstream models do not adequately capture union bargaining behavior, or union goals and preferences. |
| Klein and Stern (2007) | *American Journal of Economics and Sociology* | Members of the American Economic Association | Questionnaires sent by mail to a randomly generated list of 1000 AEA members | n = 264 | 26.40% | Although mainstream publications and departments advocate 'free market' ideologies, only 8% of those AEA members who answered the survey could be considered as supporting 'free market' ideologies. Even the average Republican AEA member was found to be 'middle-of-the-road' free market supporter. |
| Mau et al. (2012) | *Socio-Economic Review* | Population of 19 European countries | The data were obtained from the European Social Survey, which uses mixed methods of data collection (face-to-face, telephone, internet, and paper self-completion) for a standardized questionnaire | n = 18412 | Ranging from 48% in Germany to 76% in Portugal | This study tries to understand more about the phenomenon of socio-economic insecurity. It finds that socio-economic (GDP) and institutional (welfare state effort) factors are relevant to subjective socio-economic insecurity, whereas the degree of internationalization (economic globalization, share of foreign-born population) plays a surprisingly negligible role. Moreover, significant cross-level interactions among social class and income inequality, unemployment, labor market regulation, and economic globalization indicate that these country-level factors have a class-specific impact. |

be associated with adverse health and safety consequences. Nonetheless, sleep is commonly absent from work–life balance debates. It is quite under-researched. In a survey of 2882 households involving workers aged 20–69 years, Chatzitheochari and Arber (2009) observe that sleep may be associated with occupational circumstances and family responsibilities. They found a negative relationship between working hours and sleep duration. Moreover, they found that shift work and social class are predictors of short sleep, which when sustained may have negative health outcomes.

Another study using survey methods in heterodox economics is Mau et al.'s (2012) paper. They used data from the European Social Survey (n = 18 412) to learn more about socio-economic uncertainty, that is, the uncertainty that individuals may have about the eventual deterioration of their socio-economic conditions such as employment, income, or access to goods and services. Mau et al. found that socio-economic (gross domestic product, GDP) and institutional (as the effort of welfare spending by states) factors are relevant to subjective socio-economic insecurity, whereas the degree of internationalization (economic globalization, share of foreign-born population) plays a surprisingly negligible role. Moreover, significant cross-level interactions among social class and income inequality, unemployment, labor market regulation, and economic globalization indicate that these country-level factors have a class-specific impact.

Elsesser and Lever (2011) have demonstrated that the gender of the boss is not irrelevant to workers. They implemented a survey through the news site of MSNBC.com, which attracted the attention of 60 470 respondents. The findings identified a cross-sex bias in the ratings of one's current boss, where men judged their female bosses more favorably and women judged male bosses more favorably. Moreover, the majority (54 percent) of participants claimed to have no preference for the gender of their boss, but the remaining participants reported preferring male over female bosses by more than a 2:1 ratio. These examples are just a few illustrations. Quite interesting survey studies are currently being conducted in heterodox economic research. Thus, many other papers could be cited in here.

## 6.4   DESIGNING AND PLANNING A SURVEY STUDY

### Key Elements

Survey research is founded on the underlying specifications established by the researchers. Stoop and Harrison (2012) linked survey research requirements to Rudyard Kipling's poem: 'I keep six honest serving-men/(they told me all I knew)./Their names are What and Why and When/and How and Where and Who.' Accordingly, the researcher must answer the following questions: (1) What is the target population? (2) Why is the study being conducted (that is, what are the topics of study)? (3) When will the study be conducted (that is, what is the study time frame)? (4) How will the survey mode be chosen and implemented? (5) Where will the study be conducted (that is, is the survey design regional, national, cross-national, or international)? and (6) Who will conduct and sponsor the study?

The specific methodological approach chosen for a survey must be linked to two key issues: testing and controlling. A survey study is rarely a one-step process. Before data gathering commences, the researcher should construct prototypes of the research models to be implemented, and pretest and improve them (Figure 6.2). Likewise, one must implement control procedures throughout the research process to monitor how the work is going. As in management, survey research involves three major types of control: (1) preventive control, which takes place before the performance of activities to establish standards and prevent problems; (2) concurrent control, which involves the monitoring of activities while they are performed; and (3) feedback control, in which activities are evaluated after they are performed (Dubrin 2012).

The availability of resources to conduct a study is also highly relevant. A talented and skilled team of researchers can be more productive than a researcher working alone, with no one with whom to discuss the findings. The availability of financial resources is also almost always of great importance. Besides the researchers' remuneration, supplementary costs may be related to travel, lodging, hiring of team members, and communication, among other elements. Time can also be considered a constraint. A very short deadline may have negative consequences for the quality of findings. Modern survey research also requires skills in the utilization of sophisticated software for data processing. Other vital inputs include the knowledge provided by an understanding of the literature in the field of study and the research methods to be employed.

**Stages**

According to Czaja and Blair's (2005) model, a survey can be divided into the five stages described in Figure 6.2, namely: (1) survey design and preliminary planning; (2) pretesting; (3) final survey design and planning; (4) data collection; and (5) data coding, data file construction, analysis, and final reporting.

In the first stage, which comprises the initial design and planning of a survey, researchers must provide robust specification for the study to be conducted; in particular, they must define the research questions and problems being addressed. Researchers should also produce a preliminary survey design, including plans for the sample, questionnaire, data collection methods, and operations. Eminently practical questions, such as the availability of time and money, must also be addressed. The development of a preliminary plan for analysis and reporting is also beneficial in this stage.

Before beginning data collection, researchers are strongly advised to conduct two additional preliminary phases of the survey. In many cases, researchers will have only one chance to collect information from the persons being studied. Thus, they must be extremely well prepared for data collection. A second stage, in which the design and plans produced in the first stage are pretested, should be performed. Researchers should draft the questionnaire and sampling frame to be used, and train potential interviewers to conduct data collection. Pretesting of the data collection process by conducting a simulation with real persons is also recommended, as it enables evaluation of the process and improvement of details.

In the third stage, researchers are advised to apply what they have learned by pretesting to improve the design and planning developed in the first stage, thereby finalizing the survey sample, questionnaire, and operations (as well as related administrative issues) before systematic data collection. Researchers should also anticipate how possible findings from data collection could impact the final report outline.

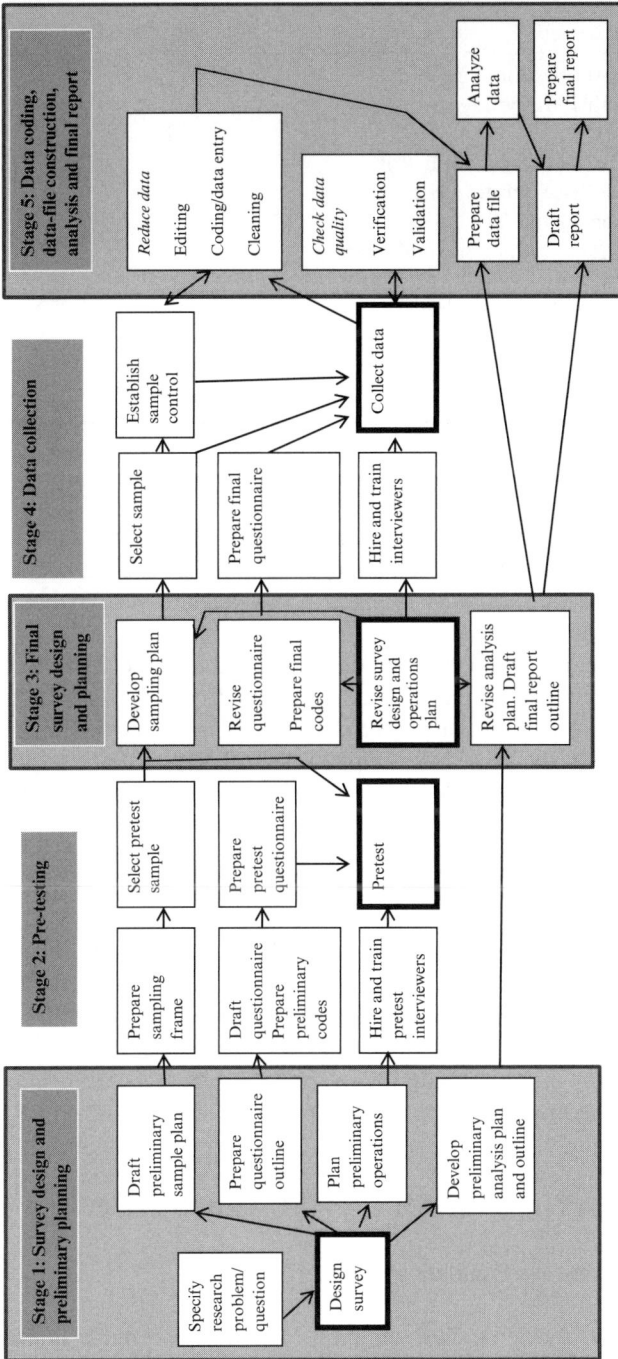

*Source:* Adapted from Czaja and Blair (2005).

*Figure 6.2   Stages of a survey*

*Table 6.2   Time schedule for a study involving 1000 random-digit-dialed interviews*

| Activity | Number of weeks | Week number |
| --- | --- | --- |
| Review literature and draft questionnaire | 8 | 1–8 |
| Assemble think aloud with 10 respondents | 1–2 | 8–9 |
| Revise questionaire | 2 | 10–11 |
| Conduct pretest 1 (number between 25 and 40) | 1 | 12 |
| Debrief interviewers and revise questionnaire | 3 | 13–15 |
| Pretest 2 (number between 20 and 30) | 1 | 16 |
| Debrief interviewers, revise questionnaire and develop training materials | 4 | 17–20 |
| Select sample (for pretests and main study) | 12 | 8–19 |
| Conduct main data collection | 8 | 21–28 |
| Code data and prepare data files | 12 | 21–32 |
| Analyze data and write report | Open | Open |

*Source:*   Adapted from Czaja and Blair (2005).

Data collection should commence only in the fourth stage, after the researchers have defined the sample, finalized the questionnaire, and hired and trained interviewers. Robust control mechanisms should be in place in this stage to verify whether activities are proceeding according to the plan.

In the fifth stage, researchers analyze the data obtained and produce the final report. The data must be verified and validated. Modern data processing is performed with the assistance of software prepared for survey studies, which facilitates data editing, coding, entering, and cleaning for analysis (for example, SAS,[1] STATA,[2] SPSS,[3] or R[4]). The final report is utterly dependent upon the specifications produced for the survey. Control mechanisms should also be associated with the final report. The discussion of draft versions of the final report with colleagues before ending the survey study may also be of great benefit.

### Illustration of a Survey Study Schedule

As noted above, time is an important prerequisite in survey research. To demonstrate their five-stage model, Czaja and Blair (2005) provided an example of the schedule for a planned telephone survey of 1000 randomly selected households, with respondents aged 18 years or older. This example appears at Table 6.2.

## 6.5   THE POPULATION–SAMPLE RELATIONSHIP

### Obtaining the Sample from the Population

As explained above, in survey studies, samples are utilized to make inferences about populations. The choice of a sample and its relationship to the population under study are thus of great importance. Lohr (2008) recalled the case of a survey amply reported in the US media (for example, *USA Today*, *CBS News*, *Time*, and *Forbes*). The newsmakers reported that after surveying 1.1 million people, researchers concluded that sleeping longer – eight or more hours per night – could be detrimental to one's health, as people who slept less seemed to live longer. However, the journalists failed to notice how the study sample had been selected; all data were obtained from friends and relatives of American Cancer Society volunteers. Hence, although this study may provide findings relevant for the identification of factors associated with the development of cancer, it could not be used to describe a general relationship between sleeping and mortality, as reported in the media.

A good understanding of several concepts within survey research, in particular the population–sample relationship, is thus highly important (for more details, see Czaja and Blair 2005; Sapsford 2007; Lohr 2008; Levy and Lemeshow 2008; Bethlehem 2009; Hibberts et al. 2012). As mentioned previously, a population comprises the entire group of persons whom researchers intend to describe and understand. For this purpose, researchers use samples, that is, a group of elements selected from a larger group, in the expectation that studying this smaller group (the sample) will reveal important information about the larger group (the population). The element or basic unit of a population is an individual who is understood to be a part thereof. In common survey research notation, an uppercase N is generally used to denote the population size (that is, the total number of elements in a population) and a lowercase n is used to denote the sample size (that is, the number of elements in a sample). For example, if one selects a sample of 1500 individuals from a population of 52000 persons, these sizes would be denoted as n = 1500 and N = 52000.

The goal of sample selection is to obtain a representative sample, which stands in opposition to a biased sample. A representative sample is similar to the population from which it was drawn. A parameter is a numeric characteristic of a total population (for instance, the average height of a country's population), whereas a statistic is a numeric characteristic of a sample. Systematic dissimilarity of a parameter to the statistics obtained by a researcher may indicate the presence of sampling error related to the use of a biased sample. The sampling distribution exhibits the variability of a statistic reflected by repeated sampling of a specific population. It is obtained by plotting all averages from all samples drawn from the population. For instance, the statistics (for example, average weight) describing ten samples of 1000 individuals each selected from a population of 40000 will probably differ. Nonetheless, most statistics should closely approximate to the population's parameter. Sampling distributions are relevant because they allow researchers to make probability statements.

The central theorem limit applies to many situations in the social sciences. This useful theorem posits that, regardless of the shape of the population, the sampling distributions of many statistics (for instance, means, sums, and linear combinations thereof, such as differences between two means or two proportions, regression coefficients) will be normally distributed around the true population parameter (with a known standard error) if the sample is sufficiently large (Hibberts et al. 2012).

There are two major types of sample: (1) probability samples, also called random samples; and (2) non-random samples. In probability or random samples, each type of element of a population has an identified probability of being selected for the survey. In simple probability samples, each element of the population has an equal probability of being selected. Researchers can also adopt systematic, stratified, or clustered sampling methods to examine subgroups of a population (for example, percentages of men and women, age groups, occupations, geographic locations). In contrast, non-random samples comprise subjects who are not randomly selected from the population. Although non-random samples may be convenient, they are rarely adequate for survey research because they can lead to biased findings and conclusions about the populations under study (Czaja and Blair 2005; Sapsford 2007; Lohr 2008; Levy and Lemeshow 2008; Bethlehem 2009; Hibberts et al. 2012).

### Why Would Someone Answer a Survey? The Problem of Non-Response in Survey Research

Non-response to surveys is a crucial problem affecting the population–sample relationship. Some individuals in every planned sample will not respond to the survey, which can affect the findings in many cases. Thus, the problem of non-response must be handled with great care. For example, surveys conducted using certain methods, such as mail- or internet-based surveys, may obtain a larger proportion of responses from more educated people, who might feel more comfortable with writing or internet use than do those with less education. Thus, findings might be biased toward the positions of more educated people in the sample. Lynn (2008) provided a hypothetical example of the population of a city with 14000 adults of which 8000 are arbitrarily classified as high ability and 6000 as low ability (this classification may be itself subjective, but we will not address this issue here for the purpose of the example). The sample design calls for the selection of one participant for every 200 adults. Thus, responses are expected from 400 high-ability and 300 low-ability individuals. However, if the probabilities that low-ability and high-ability individuals will respond to the survey are 60 percent and 80 percent, respectively, the researcher would obtain 180 responses from low-ability adults and 320 responses from high-ability adults. Thus, low-ability persons comprise only 36 percent of the sample, whereas they comprise 43 percent of the population (6000/14000 individuals). Hence, measurement error could arise from non-response. The use of a larger sample is quite helpful when the population is known to be highly heterogeneous (Hibberts et al. 2012).

Respondents' cooperation is thus an important issue. To increase response rates, researchers must understand why someone would care to answer a survey. For instance, theoretical propositions stressing the importance of trust, reciprocity, and reputation for cooperation in social exchange relationships are deeply rooted in classical sociological thought (you may see, for instance, Diekmann et al. 2014), and these factors can all be very significant in survey implementation. The question of why respondents answer surveys has in itself developed into a research field. Han et al. (2009) and Albaum and Smith (2012) summarized the major theoretical explanations of why individuals respond to surveys. These explanations involve: (1) social exchange; (2) cognitive dissonance (for example, avoidance or reduction of unpleasant feelings associated with non-response as the motive for survey response); (3) self-perception; (4) commitment or involvement; (5) reciprocity (that is, responding to a positive action with a positive action, and a negative action with a negative action); (6) leverage salience (that is, response according to one's interest in the topic); (7) trust; and (8) costs and rewards (tangible or intangible). Besides direct sample member–interviewer interaction, the possibility of response can also be influenced by the social environment, research design, and characteristics of the sample member (Groves and Couper 1998; Lynn 2008).

### Other Possible Sources of Sample Bias

In addition to non-response bias, three other major forms of sample bias may occur: coverage bias, sample selection bias, and sample attrition bias (Hibberts et al. 2012). Coverage bias occurs when some groups are systematically excluded from the sampling frame. For example, persons who have no permanent address, telephone, or internet presence will be underrepresented in several types of survey.

Sample selection bias can occur when individuals do not participate because of the researcher's behavior, rather than choosing not to respond to the survey (non-response bias). This form of bias can be generated by a researcher's tendency to prefer or avoid certain subjects or communities in the sample selection process. Non-probabilistic samples have a high risk of selection bias. For example, surveys or surveyors that avoid very poor or very wealthy neighborhoods because they are not perceived as accessible or safe are likely to produce biased results for most items related to socio-economic status.

Sample attrition bias may arise when researchers conduct panel studies requiring multiple interviews with the same individuals at different timepoints. Not all participants in the initial interview will participate in subsequent interviews. Thus, panels tend to shrink with each successive 'wave' or interview. Attrition bias can occur for many reasons. Keeping track of many respondents over months or years is very difficult. Respondents may move, get married or divorced, change their names, or even die. Some populations are also more prone than others to attrition bias. First-interview participants who have international careers or lack permanent addresses may be very difficult to locate at a later time.[5]

## 6.6   THE ART OF CRAFTING QUESTIONS

### Question Framing and Question Making

In survey research, questions are the major means of obtaining findings. Hence, the formulation of questions should also be deeply connected to the survey specification. Underdeveloped specifications and poorly constructed questions may jeopardize the entire research project. Before the formulation of questions, a review of relevant literature and tools tested in previous studies is strongly advised (Johnson and Christensen 2010; Gideon 2012a). The researcher must have a good command of theories, conceptions, and findings in the field of research encompassing the planned survey.

The notions of construct and framing are important for questionnaire production. Construct is an operational concept used for the survey. For example, to conduct a study of social support, the researcher must define social support and identify an empirical manner by which it can be measured (Gideon 2012a). Saris and Gallho (2007) and Blalock (1990) distinguish concepts developed by postulation from those developed by intuition. The former gain meaning from the deductive theory in which they are embedded, whereas the latter can be more or less immediately perceived by our sensory organs.

Although one should not ignore intuition, a literature review can aid the formulation of more fully developed concepts by postulation.

As defined by Stalans (2012), the frame is the essence of the story, the central guiding theme or salient strategy that suggests how a decision should be made. Frames can be part of the survey introduction, a phrase in a question, a salient media story, or habitual internal ways of approaching a particular issue or question. As an example, consider the framing of news about the economy or income inequality in the media. Framing can take various forms, such as issue frames, decision frames, value frames, visual frames, and emotional frames. A framing effect may occur when the framing of a message might cause individuals to assign greater importance to the considerations highlighted in the message in forming their opinions about an issue (Druckman 2001; Stalans 2012).

**The Psychology of Answering Questions**

Good question formulation is not sufficient in survey research. The psychology of question answering is an area of research in its own merit (for more details, see Dillman 2008; Schwartz et al. 2008; Gideon 2012b; Stalans 2012). Survey implementation is impacted by factors such as whether respondents understand the questions, the vocabulary employed, the order of questions, questionnaire introductions, the survey environment, data collection methods, human interaction, and other factors with concrete psychological influences.

Stalans (2012) and Groves et al. (1992) highlighted findings from psychological research that may enhance response rates and respondents' cooperation. These include discoveries about:

1. The reciprocity principle. People generally believe that they are obligated to return favors, gifts, and concessions. Researchers have taken advantage of this principle by, for example, providing small incentives (for instance, money, prizes), asking an individual to answer just a few questions when they decline to complete the entire survey, and providing favorable information (see also Toepoel 2012). However, the evidence that incentives necessarily increase the response rate is not entirely conclusive (Baruch and Holton 2008).
2. Sensitivity to negative consequences. For goals or personally relevant actions, information about the negative consequences of failing to take action is more effective than information about the benefits of taking action. For instance, the approval rate for the testing of a new cure for a fatal disease may differ according to whether the expected cure rate of 60 percent or the expected mortality rate of 40 percent is mentioned (see also Kahneman and Tversky 1984).
3. The civic duty principle. Good citizens try to help for the larger good. Most people may believe that participation in survey research is part of their civic duty, if asked to participate by a legitimate research authority.
4. The scarcity principle. Individuals may attribute higher value to a survey if it is associated with limited opportunities. Thus, statements that the survey is sent to a selective group or will only be available for a short time may increase participation (see also Porter and Whitcomb 2003).
5. The consistency principle. Individuals prefer to be consistent in their beliefs and

behaviors. Thus, if individuals agree to a similar request or express a view that supports participation, they are more likely to participate.
6.   The legitimate authority principle. Individuals judge the credibility and legitimacy of the requestor, and are more likely to comply if the source is a legitimate, credible authority. For example, response rates to research on health or social security issues may be greater when interviewers mention that the study is sponsored by a well-known university or the government than when no sponsor or a less legitimate source, such as a newspaper, is mentioned.

The concept of survey cooperation must not be confused with the response rate. In a narrow sense, Glaser (2012) defines survey cooperation as the level and comprehensiveness of participation achieved on a particular survey data collection effort, which is related to potential respondents accepting the research invitation participating in the research study. An individual who answers to a survey might do so in a limited capacity where they may participate in the research project as a whole, but refuse (or even sabotage) their participation with respect to particular questions, portions, or activities within the research.

In their model of survey cooperation, Groves and Couper (1998) explain that survey cooperation is not only affected by the survey's design. Other factors are highly relevant such as the social environment (for example, the respondent might be afraid that their answers will be known by their boss, and respond strategically), the sample member themself (for instance, their sense of civic duty, their willingness to cooperate), and the researchers involved. Furthermore, the cooperation results from concrete interactions between potential respondents and the researcher or research team.

Glaser (2012) and Roose (2002) summarize previous findings about how sociodemographic characteristics may associate to respondent cooperation. In regard to gender, most studies achieve either no influence from gender on participation, or a small amount of impact leading to slightly higher participation by women. As to age, older individuals tend to have higher non-cooperation rates, but also tend to be easier to contact, due to their reduced mobility. When it comes to the issue of education, lower education levels tend to result in reduced levels of cooperation. However, some highly educated groups may be more difficult to reach. For example, surveys to members of the corporate elite may face relatively lower response rates (Bednar and Westphal 2006).

**Question Pretesting**

Closed questions – for example: 'How do you classify the new government's policy? (awful, poor, medium, good, very good, excellent)' – may produce more quantifiable answers than open questions. On the other hand, responses to open questions – for instance: 'What is happiness to you?' – may provide interesting and useful information. Czaja and Blair (2005) propose key decision guidelines for the inclusion of questions in a survey, which they note should be connected to the usefulness of each question in relation to the research questions being investigated by the survey (Box 6.1).

Furthermore, several statistical issues related to variable definition and their measurement, such as their validity, scale, and factor analysis, or regression analysis, require addressing. Murray (Chapter 9 in this *Handbook*) and Downward (Chapter 10 in

---

**BOX 6.1    KEY DECISION GUIDE: THE USEFULNESS OF QUESTIONS**

A.  Does the survey question measure some aspect of one of the research questions?
B.  Does the question provide information needed in conjunction with some other variable?
    *[If no, to both A. and B., drop the question. If yes to one, or both, proceed.]*
C.  Will most respondents have the information to answer it?
    *[If no, revise or drop. If yes, proceed.]*
D.  Will most respondents be willing to answer it?
    *[If no, drop. If yes proceed.]*
E.  Is other information needed to analyze this question?
    *[If no, proceed. If yes, proceed if the other information is available or can be gotten from the survey.]*
F.  Should this question be asked of all respondents or of a subset?
    *[If all, proceed. If a subset, proceed only if the subset is identifiable beforehand or through questions in the interview.]*

*Source:*   Czaja and Blair (2005).

---

this *Handbook*), Bethlehem (2009), Levy and Lemeshow (2008), and Groves (1989) provide an introduction to these topics. The appraisal of questions to be included in the survey comprises three stages: development, testing, and dress rehearsal (Campanelli 2008).

**A Methodology for Questionnaire Construction**

As described in detail in Box 6.2, Johnson and Christensen (2010) and Gideon (2012a) have proposed a five-step method of questionnaire construction. The first step consists in making a review of relevant literature and previously tested tools. One needs to carefully investigate what previous studies have produced in relation to the theme addressed by the intended survey. Previous texts may have already communicated relevant findings, and devised useful variables that can be applied in the new study.

The second step involves writing the items to be included in the questionnaire. At this stage one needs to clearly identify the concepts and constructs that provide the foundation for the study. Concepts and constructs must also cover the scope of issues intended. In this second stage, one has a first attempt at delineating the survey's questions.

The layout and overall questionnaire design is built at the third step. One needs to define the structure and logic connection of the survey questions. Furthermore, a title, introduction and section directions also need to be developed. The layout and design must enhance respondents' participation in the survey.

The empirical examination and pilot testing of the survey is conducted at the fourth stage. Quite importantly, one should learn how the simulation goes, and if necessary enhance and improve the questionnaire. For example, did the simulated respondents have difficulty in answering some questions? Did they take too much time to complete the survey? Were there some questions unanswered? Do the answers seem valid? In the extreme, if the examination and testing of the survey study seriously fail at the fourth stage, the survey study ought to be abandoned before the fifth stage, where the questionnaire is finalized and administered.

## BOX 6.2    FIVE-STEPS MODEL FOR QUESTIONNAIRE CONSTRUCTION

**Step 1: Review Relevant Literature and Previously Tested Tools**
If a questionnaire that fits your needs already exists and is tested for reliability, then there is no point in reinventing the wheel. If you proceed with writing your own survey, ask yourself the following questions:

- Who is your target population?
- Do you fully understand the issues and concepts to be examined?
- What are the main variables of interest?
- What do you want to learn about the above variables from your target population?
- How will the questionnaire be administered?

Keep in mind that certain questions will not be appropriate for self-administered modes, while others are not appropriate for face-to-face and phone interviews.

**Step 2: Write the Items to be Included in your Questionnaire**
Think about the following:

- Have you clearly identified the concept and construct of the variables of interest?
- Have you examined other relevant and related questionnaires?
- Have you consulted others to make sure your items are clear?
- Are the questions simply presented?
- Do the questions cover the scope of issues intended?
- Are items too complex and convoluted and potentially confusing to potential participants?
- Do any items use double negatives?
- Are any questions leading or loaded?

**Step 3: Design the Layout and Overall Questionnaire**

- Does the questionnaire have a title, clear introduction, and section directions?
- Do the title and introduction promote interest in the research?
- Do the title and introduction promote participation and completion?
- Are items logically arranged?
- Are directions in each section clear and easy to follow?

**Step 4: Empirical Examination and Pilot Testing**
Try the questionnaire on a sample from the target population. In the process, note:

- How long does it take participants to complete the questionnaire?
- What items are difficult for them to answer?
- Are there items that were not clear to the participants?
- What items are left unanswered?
- Is there any information that pilot group participants added?
- Are items reliable and valid?
- Do the reliability and validity of the data provide evidence that the questionnaire examines the trait intended by the research question and variables?

**Step 5: Finalize and Administer the Questionnaire**
- Take a final look at your creation to make sure it is suitable for dissemination in the population of interest.
- Make sure there are no typos, grammar, or items out of place, and that instructions are clear.

*Sources:*   Johnson and Christensen (2010) and Gideon (2012a).

**Training of Team Members Who Will Ask the Questions**

For survey methods that require direct human interaction with respondents, such as telephone or face-to-face interviews conducted by a team of interviewers, training of the interviewers is required. The interviewers need a good understanding of what is expected from them. Poorly trained members of staff can affect findings, for instance by not following instructions, or conditioning the respondents' answers with their own opinions about the questions under research. The training can better prepare the survey team for approaching the sample's members, and obtaining the required information for the study.

## 6.7   METHODS OF DATA COLLECTION: ADVANTAGES AND DISADVANTAGES

The most frequently used methods for data collection in surveys are questionnaires distributed by mail, internet, and telephone surveys, and face-to-face interviews. This section presents the key advantages and disadvantages of these methods, which are described in Table 6.3 (Zikmund 2000; Czaja and Blair 2005; Leeuw 2008; Bethlehem et al. 2011). Due to space considerations, other relevant but less commonly used survey methods, such as observation and other methods that do not employ questions (see, e.g., Bethlehem 2008), are not described in this chapter.

**Mail-Based Surveys**

Mail-based surveys require that target subjects receive the questionnaire proposal by mail and are sufficiently diligent to respond. These processes necessarily take time and depend on a certain level of respondents' good will. Mail-based surveys involve some costs, such as postage and office materials, but these costs are lower than those incurred by hiring and supervising an interview team. Letters and questionnaires can be sent to eligible individuals in different postal codes, regions, or countries.

To increase the likelihood that respondents will reply, researchers must produce relatively short questionnaires with little complexity of the overall structure and of specific questions. The use of personal records, inclusion of delicate questions, exploration of sensitive topics, and maintenance of a high level of anonymity are possible because the research team can be kept relatively small. This method also has the advantage of allowing call-back or follow-up of respondents, which of course takes additional time.

Mail-based surveys are highly dependent on the cooperation of persons who receive the letter containing the questionnaire. In addition to the risk of a low response rate to the full questionnaire or particular sections, this form of survey may be affected by bias toward more educated people. The reasons for non-response may not always be clearly perceptible. On the other hand, responses are not affected by the influence and characteristics of interviewers, who are not involved in this method.

*Table 6.3   Comparison of advantages and disadvantages of the most used survey methods*

| Aspect of survey | Mailed questionnaires | Internet surveys | Telephone surveys | Face-to-face interviews |
|---|---|---|---|---|
| **Administrative, resource factors** | | | | |
| Cost | Low | Very low | Low/medium | High |
| Length of data collection period | Long | Very short/short | Short | Medium long |
| Geographical distribution | May be wide | May be wide | May be wide | Must be clustered |
| Supervision of interviewers | Not applicable | Not applicable | High | Moderate/high |
| **Questionnaire issues** | | | | |
| Length of questionnaire | Short/medium (4–12 pages) | short (<15 minutes) | Medium/long (15–35 minutes) | Long (30–60 minutes) |
| Complexity of questionnaire | Must be simple | May be complex | May be complex | May be complex |
| Complexity of questions | Simple/moderate | Simple/moderate | Must be short and simple | May be complex |
| Control of question order | Poor | Poor/fair | Very good | Very good |
| Use of open-ended questions | Poor | Fair/good | Fair | Good |
| Use of visual aids | Good | Very good | Usually not possible | Very good |
| Use of household/personal records | Very good | Very good | Fair | Good |
| Sensitive topics | Good | Poor/fair | Fair/good | Fair |
| Anonymity of respondents | High or open to choice | High or open to choice | Moderate | Low |
| Nonthreatening questions | Good | Good | Good | Good |
| Ease of call back or follow-up | Easy, but takes time | Difficult | Easy | Difficult |
| **Data quality issues** | | | | |
| Sampling frame bias | Usually low | Low/high | Low | Low |
| Response rate | Poor/good | Poor/good | Fair/good | Good/very good |
| Item nonresponse | High | High, but software can help. | Medium | Low |
| Response bias | Medium/high | Medium/high | Low | Low |
| Respondent cooperation | Moderate/fair | Moderate/fair | Fair/good | Good when interview is accepted |
| Knowledge about refusals and noncontact | Fair | Fair | Poor | Fair |
| Control of response situations | Poor | Poor | Fair/good | Good |
| Quality of recorded response | Fair/good | Fair/good | Very good | Very good |
| Degree of interviewer's influence on answers | None | None | Moderate | High |

*Source:*   Adapted from Zikmund (2000), Czaja and Blair (2005), Leeuw (2008), and Bethlehem et al. (2011).

**Internet-Based Surveys**

The internet survey is perhaps the least expensive and least time-consuming method of data collection. Nevertheless, some internet survey services will ask you for a fee to implement more sophisticated surveys or access more developed analytical tools. The most well-known web surveys services are perhaps the following: SurveyMonkey (www.survey-monkey.com), Zoomerang (www.zoomerang.com), SurveyGizmo (www.surveygizmo.com), and Google Forms (www.google.com/google-d-s/createforms.html).

Internet surveys can be applied throughout a vast geographic area, provided that information about potential respondents in that area is available. This method also does not require the training and supervision of interviewers. Moreover, software can assist in the calculation of response rates and identification of persons who have not yet responded.

Anonymity can be maintained in an internet survey, according to its specification. However, although the concepts explored by the questionnaire may be complex and related to personal records, the questions must be simple and the entire process must be relatively short (no more than 15 minutes according to Czaja and Blair 2005) to avoid the risk of unduly generating lack of cooperation by members of the potential sample. Follow-up and re-contact of potential respondents are also difficult, especially when respondents have displayed a lack of cooperation from the start.

Response rates for the full questionnaire or specific items included in an internet survey can be low or good, depending on the specification of the survey, persons contacted, and software used. However, the manner in which an internet survey is specified may lead to bias in the responses. In contrast to personal interviews, such surveys are characterized by poor control over response situations or the order in which questions are answered. As in mail-based surveys, the findings of internet surveys may be biased toward persons who are more educated and trained in internet use.

**Telephone Surveys**

The work of contacting potential respondents by telephone is generally conducted by teams of interviewers, who must be hired, trained, and supervised. Thus, the costs of telephone surveys are inherently higher than those of the two previous described methods. However, the data collection period is generally shorter than that of mail-based surveys.

In telephone surveys, interviewers face the issue of potential respondents' failure to answer calls or hanging up almost immediately. Hence, although the interview can be relatively long (15–35 minutes) and the questionnaire relatively complex, the questions must be fairly short and simple. In this type of survey, the anonymity of interviewees is highly dependent on the team of interviewers. The interviewer can control the order of questions, but they are communicating mainly by voice, without physical proximity. Nonetheless, re-contacting of respondents, if necessary, is relatively straightforward.

Depending on the interviewers' skills, response rates to the full questionnaire and specific sections can be fair or good. The same applies to respondents' cooperation. However, the interviewers' potential influence on the responses obtained must be considered. The recording of interviews allows their review and provides high-quality records to support the study's findings.

Several technological developments, such as video conferencing and other advances in communication technology, offer the potential to develop enhanced forms of surveying in the future (see, e.g., Conrad and Schober 2008).

**Face-to-Face Surveys**

Face-to-face interviews require an on-site research team to contact potential respondents. This data collection method is perhaps the most expensive and time-consuming. It must also be confined to a relatively small geographic area, which implies that the sample will be small.

On the other hand, face-to-face interviewing is the method of choice for long surveys involving complex questions. In such interviews, interviewers use a full range of verbal and non-verbal communication modes, and they may detect clues in the non-verbal behavior of respondents. Good control over the order of questions can be maintained, and visual documents can be used. However, the presence of a large research team may render the assurance of discretion difficult, and the ability to conduct subsequent interviews with the same respondents may be limited.

This method is associated with a high level of respondent cooperation, and thus high response rates. Furthermore, it offers the ability to record responses, control response situations, and protect against sampling frame bias. However, the interviewer can profoundly influence the quality of data obtained. Thus, the research team must be very carefully selected, trained, and monitored.

**Use of Mixed Methods**

A survey methodology must be crafted according to the characteristics of the study being implemented. Researchers can use more than one method. For example, they may conduct face-to-face interviews with respondents who have previously been contacted by mail, or ask to telephone potential respondents who take too much time to respond to an internet questionnaire.

**Response Rates in Survey Data Collection Methods**

It is possible to present statistics about response rate in the different survey data collection methods. However, they are intended for reference, not as definitive benchmarks. Each survey study must do a careful assessment of the population under study and can take concrete measures to increase response rates. Those initiatives may include to pre-notify participants, publicize the survey, carefully design the survey, manage survey length, provide ample response opportunities, monitor survey response, establish survey importance, foster survey commitment, and provide feedback (Rogelberg and Stanton 2007).

Baruch and Holton (2008) identified 490 different studies on the subject of organizational research that utilized survey methods, published in the years 2000 and 2005 in 17 refereed academic journals. They covered more than 100 000 organizations and 400 000 individual respondents. The reported average response rate for studies that used data collected from individuals was 52.7 percent (standard deviation, SD, of 20.4), while the

*Table 6.4   Response rate by survey method*

| Method | n | Minimum | Maximum | Mean | Std dev. |
|---|---|---|---|---|---|
| Mail | 309 | 19.7 | 94.0 | 44.7 | 21.8 |
| Internal mail | 79 | 3.0 | 92.2 | 55.5 | 18.3 |
| Face-to-face | 31 | 30.0 | 83.0 | 62.4 | 16.9 |
| Email | 11 | 23.7 | 89.0 | 54.7 | 23.9 |
| Phone | 10 | 10.0 | 86.2 | 49.1 | 24.1 |
| Web | 6 | 10.6 | 69.5 | 38.9 | 15.1 |

*Source:* This table was obtained from Baruch and Holton's (2008) study, where 490 different studies that utilized survey methods are investigated. Those studies were published in the years 2000 and 2005 in 17 refereed academic journals, which address the subject of organizational research.

reported average response rate for studies that utilized data collected from organizations was lower at 35.7 percent (SD = 18.8).

Baruch and Holton (2008) could identify that 446 studies had used a single survey method, and discriminated the respective response rate. The results are described in Table 6.4. The majority of studies conducted surveys by regular mail (n = 309; 69 percent) or internal organizational mail (n = 79; 18 percent). Curiously, the survey by mail studies had the lowest average response rate, namely, 44.7 percent (standard deviation 21.8 percent). The average response rate was higher in surveys by internal organizational mail (55.5 percent; SD = 18.3 percent).

Baruch and Holton's sample contains also some studies conducting surveys by phone (n = 10; 2.4 percent) and email (n = 11; 2.5 percent). Their average response rates were 49.1 percent (SD = 24.1 percent) and 54.7 percent (SD = 23.9 percent). The highest average response rate was obtained by the 31 (6.9 percent) studies conducting face-to-face surveys. These studies had an average response of 62.4 percent (SD = 16.9 percent). The lowest response rate was obtained in the six (1.3 percent) studies involving internet surveys. They had an average response of 38.9 percent (SD = 15.1 percent). However, the sample in Baruch and Holton (2008) covered a period where the internet was not as developed as it is today.

Moreover, one cannot ignore the issue of costs. Internet-based surveys are likely to involve fewer costs than, for instance, face-to-face surveys, or paper-based surveys. However, educated populations might be more willing to answer online surveys. Greenlaw and Brown-Welty (2009) tested three types of survey methods with members of the American Evaluation Association. The 3842 members were randomly divided into three groups. A survey method was administered to each group; namely, a paper-based survey, a web-based survey, or a mixed methods survey (potential respondents were contacted both by paper and the internet). The results are partially displayed in Table 6.5. By and large, the web-based survey was the cheapest and fastest to conduct. It also had a higher response rate than the paper survey. However, Greenlaw and Brown-Welty's results might not be replicated to other populations because their research involved highly educated persons (who might be familiar with research methods), and was institutionally supported by the American Evaluation Association. As explained above, these statistics are intended solely for reference.

*Table 6.5    Response rate by survey method*

| Method | N | Number of responses | Response rate (%) | Hours | Total cost | Cost per response |
|---|---|---|---|---|---|---|
| Paper-based | 1280 | 538 | 42.03 | 57 | US$2573 | US$4.78 |
| Web-based | 1281 | 672 | 52.46 | 2 | US$429 | US$0.64 |
| Mixed methods | 1281 | 772 | 60.27 | 44 | US$2785 | US$3.61 |
| Total | 3842 | | | | | |

*Note:*   Greenlaw and Brown-Welty (2009) randomly divided the 3842 members of the American Evaluation Association into three groups. To each group they applied the same questionnaire through a different data-collection method, namely, paper-based, web-based, and mixed method. The members of the mixed methods group were contacted both by the web and paper.

*Source:*   Greenlaw and Brown-Welty (2009).

**Use of Surveys Produced by Other Sources**

Researchers can also obtain data using a myriad of very noteworthy sources that administer large-scale surveys and publish the raw data online for scientific use (for more details, see Stoop and Harrison 2012). Evidently, the data must be provided by credible and reliable sources. These may include surveys about:

- Attitudes, values, beliefs and opinions. For example: European Social Survey (ESS, www.europeansocialsurvey.org), Eurobarometer (http://ec.europa.eu/public_opinion/index_en.htm www.gesis.org/en/eurobarometer-data-service);, Latinobarómetro (www.latinobarometro.org), or World Values Survey (WVS, www.worldvaluessurvey.org).
- Living conditions. For instance, European Foundation for the Improvement of Living and Working Conditions (EUROFOUND, www.eurofound.europa.eu/surveys), EU Labour Force Survey (EU LFS, http://epp.eurostat.ec.europa.eu/portal/page/portal/microdata/lfs), or Eurostat microdata (http://epp.eurostat.ec.europa.eu/portal/page/portal/microdata/introduction).
- Literacy and skills. Such as the Adult Literacy and Lifeskills Survey (ALL, http://nces.ed.gov/surveys/all/), Programme for the International Assessment of Adult Competencies (PIAAC, www.oecd.org/piaac), Trends in International Mathematics and Science Study (TIMSS), or Progress in International Reading Literacy (PIRLS, http://timss.bc.edu/).
- Information on elections. For instance, the comparative Study of Electoral Systems (CSES, www.cses.org), or Infrastructure for Research on Electoral Democracy (PIREDEU, www.gesis.org/en/institute/competence-centers/rdc-international-survey-programmes/piredeu).

These sources can be used to practice research skills, as well as to produce and test new research concepts, theories, and hypotheses.

## 6.8   ANALYSIS AND REPORTING OF FINDINGS

**Data Analysis**

The analysis of survey data requires both qualitative and quantitative skills. The quality of surveys has been traditionally addressed through sophisticated statistical approaches. Limited attention has been paid to the qualitative issues of comprehension and meaning (Hardy and Ford 2014). However, these issues are quite pertinent for interpreting the data. There are at least three forms of miscomprehension in survey studies, namely: instructional miscomprehension (where instructions are not followed), sentential miscomprehension (where the syntax of a sentence is enriched or depleted as it is interpreted), and lexical miscomprehension (where different meanings of words are deployed). These differences in comprehension might not be noticeable using conventional statistical analyses. Yet, they can produce significantly different results and cause respondents to tap into dissimilar concepts (Hardy and Ford 2014).

On the other hand, the analysis of survey data requires adequate quantitative skills to enable the understanding of findings and analytical statistics, and to avoid measurement error. In survey research there is a statistical relation between the sample and population, which needs to be addressed with quantitative tools. This chapter is an introduction to the use of survey methods; sources for further reading on this important subject include Downward (Chapter 10 in this *Handbook*), Murray (Chapter 9 in this *Handbook*), Bethlehem (2009), Levy and Lemeshow (2008), and Groves (1989).

Modern data analysis is assisted by software designed specifically for survey work. However, it must be emphasized that the use of software is not an alternative to the possession of adequate quantitative skills. Heeringa et al. (2010, Appendix A) described procedures for survey research employing some of the most commonly used software for data analysis, including SAS, STATA, SPSS, and R.[6] Heeringa et al. provide actual codes for these software programs that may aid analysis. Data may need to be reduced to avoid redundancies or errors. Researchers must also verify and validate the data before proceeding to analysis.

**Reporting of Findings**

Researchers must take time to think about what they have found, and implications for previous knowledge on the subject. They should write multiple drafts of the final report, and seek advice on those drafts from peers. Questions that should be considered include: Are the findings interesting and exciting? Were these results expected? Have sampling and non-sampling errors been avoided in the analysis?

## 6.9   FINAL WORDS

This chapter presents an introduction to the use of survey methodologies. It describes key issues, themes, difficulties, and problems in implementing survey studies. However, as this book describes several different research frameworks with promise to heterodox economics, it can only attribute a limited space to each one. Nonetheless, some of this chapter's references are quite helpful should you wish to investigate more about survey methodologies. Since economics is a social science, concerned about how people and their institutions act, think, feel, and behave, there is undeniable potential for a research agenda focused on interacting with real people.

## NOTES

1. www.sas.com.
2. www.stata.com.
3. http://www-01.ibm.com/software/analytics/spss/.
4. http://www.r-project.org/.
5. To learn more: Levy and Lemeshow (2008), Bethlehem (2009), Bethlehem et al. (2011), and other references cited above describe tools and techniques used to address the risk of sample bias in greater detail.
6. The web addresses for these four software programs appear in the notes above.

## REFERENCES

Albaum, G. and S. Smith (2012), 'Why people agree to participate in surveys', in L. Gideon (ed.), *Handbook of Survey Methodology for the Social Sciences*, Heidelberg: Springer, pp. 179–93.

Baruch, Y. and B. Holton (2008), 'Survey response rate levels and trends in organizational research', *Human Relations*, **61** (8), 1139–60.

Bautista, R. (2012), 'An overlooked approach in survey research: total survey error', in L. Gideon (ed.), *Handbook of Survey Methodology for the Social Sciences*, Heidelberg: Springer, pp. 37–49.

Bednar, M.K. and J. Westphal (2006), 'Surveying the corporate elite: Theoretical and practical guidance on improving response rates and response quality in top management survey questionnaires', in David J. Ketchen and Donald D. Bergh (eds), *Research Methodology in Strategy and Management (Research Methodology in Strategy and Management, Volume 3*, Bingley, UK: Emerald, pp. 37–55.

Bethlehem, J. (2009), *Applied Survey Methods: A Statistical Perspective*, Hoboken, NJ: Wiley.

Bethlehem, J., F. Cobben, and B. Schouten (2011), *Handbook of Nonresponse in Household Surveys*, Hoboken, NJ: Wiley.

Blalock H.M., Jr (1990), 'Auxiliary measurement theories revisited', in J.J. Hox and J. de Jong-Gierveld (eds), *Operationalization and Research Strategy*, Amsterdam: Swets & Zeitlinger, pp. 33–49.

Campanelli, P. (2008), 'Testing survey questions', in E. Leeuw, J. Hox, and D. Dillman (eds), *International Handbook of Survey Methodology*, New York: European Association of Methodology/Erlbaum, pp. 176–200.

Chatzitheochari, S. and S. Arber (2009), 'Lack of sleep, work and the long hours culture: evidence from the UK Time Use Survey', *Work, Employment and Society*, **23** (1), 30–48.

Conrad, F. and M.F. Schober (2008), *Envisioning the Survey Interview of the Future*, Hoboken, NJ: Wiley.

Czaja, R. and J. Blair (2005), *Designing Surveys: A Guide to Decisions and Procedures*, London: Pine Forge Press.

Diekmann, A., B. Jann, W. Przepiorka, and S. Wehrli (2014), 'Reputation formation and the evolution of cooperation in anonymous online markets', *American Sociological Review*, **79** (1), 65–85.

Dillman, D. (2008), 'The logic and psychology of constructing questionnaires', in E. Leeuw, J. Hox and D. Dillman (eds), *International Handbook of Survey Methodology*, New York: European Association of Methodology/Erlbaum, pp. 161–75.

Druckman, J.N. (2001), 'On the limits of framing effects: who can frame?', *Journal of Politics*, **63** (4), 1041–66.

Dubrin, A. (2012), *Management Essentials*, New York: South-Western-Cengage Learning.

Elsesser, K. and J. Lever (2011), 'Does gender bias against female leaders persist? Quantitative and qualitative data from a large-scale survey', *Human Relations*, **64** (12), 1555–78.

Gahan, P. (2002), '(What) do unions maximize? Evidence from survey data', *Cambridge Journal of Economics*, **26** (3), 279–98.

Gideon, L. (2012a), 'The art of question phrasing', in L. Gideon (ed.), *Handbook of Survey Methodology for the Social Sciences*, Heidelberg: Springer, pp. 91–107.

Gideon, L. (ed.) (2012b), *Handbook of Survey Methodology for the Social Sciences*, Heidelberg: Springer.

Glaser, P. (2012), 'Respondents cooperation: demographic profile of survey respondents and its implication', in L. Gideon (ed.), *Handbook of Survey Methodology for the Social Sciences*, Heidelberg: Springer, pp. 195–207.

Greenlaw, C. and S. Brown-Welty (2009), 'A comparison of web-based and paper-based survey methods: testing assumptions of survey mode and response cost', *Evaluation Review*, 33 (5), 464–80.

Groves, R. (1989), *Survey Errors and Survey Costs: An Introduction to Survey Errors*, Hoboken, NJ: Wiley.

Groves, R., R. Cialdini, and M. Couper (1992), 'Understanding the decision to participate in a survey', *Public Opinion Quarterly*, 56 (4), 475–95.

Groves, R. and M. Couper (1998), *Non-response in Households Interview Surveys*, Hoboken, NJ: Wiley.

Groves, R., F. Fowler, M. Couper, J. Lepkowski, E. Singer, and R. Tourangeau (2004), *Survey Methodology*, Hoboken, NJ: Wiley.

Han, V., G. Albaum, J.B. Wiley, and P. Thirkell (2009), 'Applying theory to structure respondents' stated motivation for participating in web surveys', *Qualitative Market Research*, 12 (4), 428–42.

Hardy, B. and L. Ford (2014), 'It's not me, it's you: miscomprehension in surveys', *Organizational Research Methods*, 17 (2), 138–62.

Heeringa, S., B. West, and P. Berglund (2010), *Applied Survey Data Analysis*, London: Chapman & Hall.

Hibberts, M., R.B. Johnson, and K. Hudson (2012), 'Common survey sampling techniques', in L. Gideon (ed.), *Handbook of Survey Methodology for the Social Sciences*, Heidelberg: Springer, pp. 53–74.

Johnson, L.B. and L.B. Christensen (2010), *Educational Research: Quantitative, Qualitative, and Mixed Approaches*, Thousand Oaks, CA: Sage Publishing.

Kahneman, D. and A. Tversky (1984), 'Choices, values, and frames', *American Psychologist*, 39 (4), 341–50.

Klein, D. and C. Stern (2007), 'Is there a free-market economist in the house? The policy views of American Economic Association members', *American Journal of Economics and Sociology*, 66 (2), 309–34.

Leeuw, E. (2008), 'Choosing the method of data collection', in E. Leeuw, J. Hox, and D. Dillman (eds), *International Handbook of Survey Methodology*, New York: European Association of Methodology/Erlbaum, pp. 113–35.

Leeuw, E., J. Hox, and D. Dillman (2008), 'The cornerstones of survey research', in E. Leeuw, J. Hox, and D. Dillman (eds), *International Handbook of Survey Methodology*, New York: European Association of Methodology/Erlbaum, pp. 1–17.

Levy, P. and S. Lemeshow (2008), *Sampling of Populations: Methods and Applications*, Hoboken, NJ: Wiley.

Lohr, S. (2008), 'Coverage and sampling', in E. Leeuw, J. Hox and D. Dillman (eds), *International Handbook of Survey Methodology*, New York: European Association of Methodology/Erlbaum, pp. 97–112.

Lynn, P. (2008), 'The problem of non-response', in Leeuw, E., J. Hox, and D. Dillman (eds), *International Handbook of Survey Methodology*, New York: European Association of Methodology/Erlbaum, pp. 35–55.

Mau, S., J. Mewes, and N. Schoneck (2012), 'What determines subjective socio-economic insecurity? Context and class in comparative perspective', *Socio-Economic Review*, 10 (4), 655–82.

Porter, S. and M. Whitcomb (2003), 'The impact of contact type on web survey participation: description and illustration', *Public Opinion Quarterly*, 64 (3), 299–308.

Rogelberg, S. and J. Stanton (2007), 'Understanding and dealing with organizational survey nonresponse', *Organizational Research Methods*, 10 (2), 195–209.

Roose, H.W. (2002), 'Response behavior in audience research: a two-stage design for the explanation of non-response', accessed September 12, 2014 at http://mrvar.fdv.uni-lj.si/pub/mz/mz18/roose.pdf.

Salant, P. and D. Dillman (1984), *How to Conduct Your Own Survey*, Hoboken, NJ: Wiley.

Sapsford, R. (2007), *Survey Research*, 2nd edn, London: Sage.

Saris, W. and I. Gallho (2007), *Design, Evaluation, and Analysis of Questionnaires for Survey Research*, Hoboken, NJ: Wiley.

Scheuren, F. (2004), *What is a Survey?*, Alexandria, VA: American Statistical Association.

Schwartz, N., B. Knauper, D. Oyserman, and C. Stich (2008), 'The psychology of asking questions', in E. Leeuw, J. Hox, and D. Dillman (eds), *International Handbook of Survey Methodology*, New York: European Association of Methodology/Erlbaum, pp. 18–34.

Stalans, Loretta J. (2012), 'Frames, framing effects, and survey responses', in L. Gideon (ed.), *Handbook of Survey Methodology for the Social Sciences*, Heidelberg: Springer, pp. 75–90.

Stoop, I. and E. Harrison (2012), 'Classification of surveys', in L. Gideon (ed.), *Handbook of Survey Methodology for the Social Sciences*, Heidelberg: Springer, pp. 7–21.

Toepoel, V. (2012), 'Effects of incentives in surveys', in L. Gideon (ed.), *Handbook of Survey Methodology for the Social Sciences*, Heidelberg: Springer, pp. 209–23.

Weisberg, H. (2005), *The Total Survey Error Approach: A Guide to the New Science of Survey Research*, Chicago, IL: University of Chicago Press.

Zikmund, W. (2000), *Business Research Methods*, Orlando, FL: Dryden.

# 7 Qualitative and ethnographic methods in economics

## Amit Basole and Smita Ramnarain

## 7.1 INTRODUCTION

'Modern economics' begins with a factory visit (Smith 1776 [1937]). Alfred Marshall's industry visits are equally well known. Arthur Pigou points out that what Marshall wanted was to get a 'direct feel of the economic world', something 'more intimate than can be obtained from merely reading descriptions'. Such direct contact with economic actors would, Pigou argued, 'enable one, with sure instinct, to set things in their true scale of importance, and not to put in the forefront something that is really secondary merely because it presents a curious problem for analysis' (quoted in Reisman 1990, p. 96).

In this chapter we outline some arguments in favor of encouraging this tradition in economic research through the use of 'ethnographic techniques', alongside more commonly used quantitative primary and secondary data-based methods. We also acquaint the reader with what such techniques entail and how economists have used them in the recent past.

In the context of the natural sciences it is more or less non-controversial to assert that diverse approaches reveal more about a phenomenon than a single approach. 'Mixed method approaches' are the norm in biology, for example, though not referred to as such, and any modern neuroscience department houses researchers using molecular, cellular, cognitive, psychological, and computational techniques to understand brain function. On the other hand, the social sciences continue to be defined not only by their subject matter but also by the particular methods they use to study their subject. Anthropology is as closely identified with qualitative, ethnographic approaches, as economics is with quantitative, statistical ones.

Further, it is commonly observed that, unlike most scientists, empirical economists are data analysts rather than data gatherers working with data generated by someone else, in many instances an international or governmental agency, or a national or international non-governmental organization (NGO) (see Jacobsen and Newman 1997 for an analysis of data sources used in labor economics and industrial relations).[1] There has been a resurgence in empirical economics (development economics in particular; see Udry 2003) of researchers conducting their own field studies; however, these are still mostly quantitative exercises (increasingly in the form of randomized trials). In most of these cases, researchers outsource the actual work of data collection to data collecting agencies or NGOs. We may join Bewley (1999, p. 15) in asking: 'should economics differ from other sciences, where researchers spend much of their time collecting data?'

Even though from Adam Smith's division of labor, to Coase's transaction costs, to Piore's flexible specialization, economists have often relied on personal observations of a qualitative nature to create new and influential theoretical concepts, a researcher using qualitative data is still very much an outsider in the profession. Out of 498 articles published between 2009 and 2011 in the *American Economic Review*, the *Journal of Political Economy*, and the *Quarterly Journal of Economics*, 82 (16.4 percent) used primary data collection either through lab experiments (42), field experiments (25), surveys (4), interviews (1), case studies (1), or some combination thereof (9). In five heterodox journals – *Review of Radical Political Economics* (RRPE, 2005–2011), *Cambridge Journal of Economics* (CJE, 2009–2011), *Feminist Economics* (FE, 2009–2011), *Capital and Class* (CC, 2008–2011) and *International Review of Applied Economics* (IRAE, 2009-2011)[2] – only 39 (7.6 percent) out of a total of 509 articles surveyed used primary data. As might be expected, lab or field experiments constituted only a small fraction (2/39) and most studies used some form of survey, interview, or case study analysis (Basole et al. 2012).

We argue that heterodox economists have much to gain by embracing qualitative methods in their work, given the nature of their interests. Participatory ethnographic methods can help in figuring out what the relevant questions should be, rather than having the research agenda predetermined by available data. These methods involve people in a way that is minimally structured and less hierarchical. Finally, data can be collected on those aspects of economic reality that are missed in official surveys but are central to the concerns of feminist, Marxist, institutional, and other heterodox economists. Ethnography can also be a building block for quantitative and survey-based techniques. However, we would like to emphasize that mainstream economics has as much, if not more, to gain from these methods. Ultimately, to paraphrase Duke Ellington, there are only two kinds of economics: good economics, and the other kind. We believe that qualitative research is important for good economics.

The remainder of this chapter is organized as follows. In section 7.2 we discuss the principal reasons why heterodox economists should be employing ethnographic techniques. In section 7.3 we enter into the specifics of various types of techniques and point readers to resources on how to do such work. In section 7.4 we discuss some recent studies in economics that have employed ethnographic methods. We do not attempt to evaluate the strengths and weaknesses of the research itself; rather we focus on how interviews, field observations, or other types of qualitative data lent insights that would not have been obtainable easily through other means. Section 7.5 outlines some proposals for encouraging more such work in economics, and concludes.

## 7.2   WHY QUALITATIVE AND ETHNOGRAPHIC METHODS?

The terms 'qualitative research', 'ethnography', and 'fieldwork' are sometimes used interchangeably. In the next section we distinguish between these terms and provide more details on the methods themselves. At this stage, it is sufficient to say that interviews, focus groups, participant and non-participant observation, oral histories, diaries, and document analysis form the core of ethnographic work. Interviews are the most commonly used technique in economics and themselves can be of several types, such as structured, semi-structured, unstructured, in-depth, and so on.

As noted earlier, such techniques are usually identified with anthropology. One may say that economic anthropologists already do work on class, race, gender relations, labor process, informal sector working conditions, and so on. So what distinguishes an economic anthropologist doing ethnography, from an economist doing the same? In the following pages we hope to convince the reader that such techniques can play a crucial role in economic research as well. Of course, we are not advocating a renunciation of the usual tools of empirical economic analysis. Rather, we make a case for the inclusion of ethnographic techniques such as interviews, focus groups, field observations, and participant diaries in addition to quantitative statistical analysis. We show that such data can play a crucial role in providing information that is missing from surveys, in building an intuition for economic phenomena, in creating an awareness of the larger social context in which economic decisions are taken, and in helping to generate better models. Further, the process of generating our own data can help us do research that is relevant to the needs of the participants and involves them in its planning.

**Recent Interest in Ethnographic Methods**

Bergmann (2007) complains that two bottlenose dolphin groups recently studied by biologists for hunting behavior have 'probably received more close attention in this single study than any of the human groups known as business establishments had received from professional economists in the last 200 years' (p. 1). She goes on to argue: 'economists would do best if they adopted the strategy of anthropologists, who go to live with the tribe they are studying and become participant-observers'. Bergman's is just one among a growing chorus of voices advocating the use of qualitative and ethnographic data in economics (Bewley 2002; Helper 2000; Piore 2006; Starr 2014).

Susan Helper, in a 2000 article in the *American Economic Review*, argues for the inclusion of interview-based data, based on the experience of the Sloan Foundation-funded National Bureau of Economic Research (NBER) project on Industry Studies. The program invokes a time-honored tradition in economics of observing firms at work:

> The intellectual roots of industry studies can be traced to the economists Adam Smith (1723–1790) and Alfred Marshall (1842–1924), who demonstrated that the scientific foundation of economics and its social effects are enhanced by grounding analysis in the practical experience of industry and in the direct observation of production processes . . . In his preface to *Industry and Trade* (1919), Alfred Marshall explains that he had a career-long practice of visiting manufacturing plants so that he might be better informed by the experience.[3]

A 1998 special issue of the *Journal of Industrial Economics* was dedicated to papers emerging out of this program. In their introduction to the special issue, Borenstein et al. (1998, p. 123) note:

> We believe that these papers demonstrate the value of such a combined interview/observation/ analysis approach. All of these papers present traditional economic evidence (primarily statistical analysis) for the propositions they advance, but they also have benefited by supplementing this evidence with qualitative information that can only be gathered by direct observation and discussion.

Articles advocating the use of mixed methods research have also appeared in a variety of other field journals (Berik 1997; White 2002; Burton 2007; Starr 2014). Noteworthy is the 2001 special issue of the *Journal of Financial Economics*, the field's premier journal, on 'Contemporary research methodologies: the interplay of theoretical, empirical and field-based research in finance', which according to Burton (2007) has been responsible for a renaissance of qualitative methods in the field. Starr (2014) is a particularly useful review of mixed methods research in areas of interest to heterodox economists. The article surveys the 'small explosion' of qualitative research in the past decade and half in areas such as:

> studies designing or gauging the effects of social programs, especially among lower income groups; studies of willingness to pay for environmental interventions; studies related to poverty and capabilities sponsored by the World Bank; case-study research into innovation, R&D [research and development], and technological diffusion; and feminist-economics research into the 'lived experiences' of women's economic lives. (Starr 2014, p. 1)

The author calls the growth of qualitative research 'surprising' and foresees a 'promising future' for it.

### Objections to Ethnographic Data

We do not deal with commonly encountered objections such as lack of rigor or 'softness' of qualitative data since other economists advocating these methods address these critiques elsewhere (Bewley 1999, 2002; Helper 2000; White 2002; Starr 2014; see also Pickbourn and Ramnarain, Chapter 4 in this *Handbook*). Many advocates note that even economists who do not dismiss qualitative methods for lack of rigor resist attempts to introduce them into the profession on the ground that this is 'not economics'. The resistance is particularly strong among mainstream economists. That these economists are not shy of encompassing other areas' subject matter is clear. In the past few decades many subjects such as family, marriage, and religion, which were traditionally studied by other disciplines, have become legitimate subjects of economic analysis. Even as economics expands its domain of analysis, it refuses to accept methodological pluralism. In fact, an argument can be made that mainstream economics is open to a very wide range of topics (including 'heterodox' concerns such as altruism, co-operatives, irrational behavior, distribution of property rights, and so on), but a very narrow range of methods. But we expect non-mainstream paradigms to be, a priori, more welcoming on this score, if only because an important heterodox critique of mainstream economics is its excessive reliance on mathematical formalism and statistical analysis (econometrics).

Since many of the examples of qualitative research we cite here have to do with uncovering motivations and decision-making processes of economic actors, we deal with one common criticism of ethnographic approaches, noted by Bewley (2002): that people do not always know their motives, and so their comments in this respect should not be taken seriously. A related concern mentioned by Brav et al. (2005) is that market participants do not have to understand why they do what they do (just as Friedman's famous billiards player does not know the physics necessary to plan his stroke). The authors point out that the exclusive focus on the predictive value of a model, as advocated by Friedman (1953 [1970]), makes it impossible to provide explanations for economic phenomena. If we seek to understand the motivations behind actions of economic actors, we have to investigate the realism of assumptions.

Objections arising out of such methodological positivism have been considered and refuted in detail by Bewley (1999, 2002). He remarks that this attitude places too much power in the hands of the economists. Noting that economists often privilege introspection over talking to economic actors as a source of assumptions needed to make theory, Bewley points out that workers and their employers take economic decisions under complex and stressful work conditions that may be unfamiliar to academic economists. Bewley (2002, p. 350) asks: 'Why should an investigator's prejudices take precedence over those of the people studied? If you give yourself the right to ignore evidence, such as what decision makers say, there is little limit to what you can assert.' To take the author's example, it may be true that a baseball player can catch a ball without knowing the mathematics of its trajectory (behaving 'as if' he does), and by extension that economic actors act unconsciously in accordance with a complicated model they know nothing about. But if you want to learn how to play baseball (or even just learn something about how baseball is played), you are better off talking to a baseball player than a mathematician (Bewley 1999).

### Reasons for Undertaking Qualitative and Ethnographic Work

Everyone acknowledges that ethnographic work is time-consuming, expensive, and difficult. Is it worth it? Alongside many others whose work is cited here, we answer 'yes' to this question. In this section we outline some reasons for saying so.

Ritchie and Lewis (2003) outline some kinds of questions that require detailed information, warranting qualitative techniques, and contextual analysis of the information thus gathered. These include:

- Mapping the nature, features and dimensions of a phenomenon. For example, manifestations of racism, concepts around standard of living or a living wage, what 'good behavior' entails.
- Descriptions of meanings people may attach to an event, experience or circumstance. For example, homelessness or incarceration.
- Identification of typologies. For example, models of organizing 'self-help' groups, systems of managing household accounts, or approaches to including women in development interventions.
- The contexts in which certain phenomena, actions, or decisions might occur. For example, the shaping of beliefs around racism, welfare, or environmental protection; factors leading to racism, domestic violence or childlessness.

While many more justifications may be given for undertaking ethnographic work, we focus here on five broad categories: going beyond official and existing categories of data collection; understanding the larger context in which economic decisions are taken and relations built, and building intuition for economic processes as well as better models for them; developing inclusive research processes; achieving reflexivity; and triangulating results from a variety of approaches.[4]

### Going beyond existing data

By far the most common reason economists undertake field research or employ ethnographic techniques in their work is because survey data (either pre-existing or author-generated) fail to provide the required type of information. Data gathered from such methods are used either as a supplement to quantitative analysis or as the principal form of empirics.

A classic example of this is the 'informal economy,' which encompasses economic activity that is outside the regulatory reach of the state. In developing countries the informal sector is the dominant sector of the economy, and it encompasses sophisticated and intricate economic institutions and relationships that have evolved over centuries. Official data sources usually do a poor job of capturing these relations, when they do so at all. The study of the informal economy has thus benefitted hugely from fieldwork and qualitative research by anthropologists as well as economists. Barbara Harriss-White has been advocating (and practicing) qualitative field-based research in economics for decades. Regarding the functioning of small-town informal markets in India, she notes: '[since] official statistics for local trade are extremely poor there is no alternative to field research to find out how it works' (Harriss-White 2003, p.9). Similarly, income and expenditure surveys as well as labor force participation surveys in developing countries are often poorly tailored to the local context. White (2002) advances the example of the Zambia Living Conditions Monitoring Survey that, in rural areas, asks questions about paid annual leave but not about payment in kind for hired labor. In a context where the former is rare and the latter abundant, such a survey would give a distorted picture of the rural labor market.

Berik (1997) similarly cautions against relying solely on other-generated survey data, for feminist economics. She argues, 'survey-generated data bear the imprint of values and ideological beliefs in survey design and implementation, and often produce male-biased accounts' (p. 121). Excessive reliance on secondary data isolates the economist from the economic life of their research subjects and they '[lose] the opportunity to understand the subtleties of economic life' (p.122). And most importantly, empirical questions being circumscribed by available data, the method chosen prevents the asking of certain questions, especially when they are of marginal concern to data collecting agencies. For instance, Varley (1996), in her assessment of household headship data, remarks on the inadequacy of the category of 'head of household' since a patriarchal bias in data collection often means that the role is automatically ascribed to the oldest male in the family. Similarly, other feminist scholars have pointed to conflicting agendas and unequal power relations within the household, displacing the prevalent notion of the household as a unified (and non-controversial) economic unit (see, e.g., Katz 1997).

A third well-known example is Bewley (1999) on wage rigidity during the recession. Labor force surveys generally do not contain the information necessary to understand why firms prefer lay-offs to wage cuts during an economic downturn. Rather than treating these variables as 'unobservables', Bewley interviews managers, headhunters, advisers of the unemployed, labor leaders and lawyers, and management consultants (336 interviews in total, mostly managers) in the US Northeast to find out reasons for wage rigidity. He encourages the economic actors to produce their own understandings and explanations rather than only test pre-existing theories.

### Building intuition, insight, and better models

Hammersley and Atkinson (1995, p.1) argue that researchers using ethnographic methods are better able to understand the issue they are researching. Further, over a period of time, such engagement develops economic intuition and builds a 'bullshit detector'. That is, the researcher begins to develop a sense of what types of information are plausible and what are anomalous or unreliable, what mechanisms are reasonable to pursue, and so on. Good instincts can be developed by contact with the phenomenon studied. In a recent interview given to the *Financial Times*, Angus Deaton, Nobel Laureate in Economics for 2015, mentions the following in regards to the work of his long-time collaborator, Jean Dreze:

> ... he and I have done a lot of empirical work together looking at calories and nutrition and poverty rates and so on in India, and for me he's invaluable because he wanders around the country in sandals all the time talking to poor people and trying to do things with them. He sharecrops with people for years on end – he really knows what's going on on the ground – and you can't get that by just looking at the data. (http://ftalphaville.ft.com/files/2015/11/AngusDeatonTranscript.pdf)

Colorful language about 'sandals' aside, Deaton makes a crucial point that both Alfred Marshall and Ronald Coase have also singled out. Helper (2000, p. 229) quotes Coase (pers. comm.): 'It's important to go out and discover the facts for yourself.' Indeed, Coase's description of the data collection process for his article 'The nature of the firm' reads very much like a mixed methods strategy (Coase 1988, p. 9):

> During my time in the United States I attended very few classes and although I visited a number of universities, most of my time was spent in visiting businesses and industrial plants ... I read the reports of the Federal Trade Commission and books describing the organization of different industries, such as Copeland's study of the cotton textile industry. I also read trade periodicals and used more unusual sources (for an economist), such as the yellow pages of the telephone directory, where I was fascinated to find so many specialist firms operating within what we thought of as a single industry as well as such interesting combinations of activities as those represented by coal and ice companies.

Burton (2007, p. 5), introducing a special qualitative research issue of *Studies in Economics and Finance*, reviews the 'pedigree and renaissance' of qualitative research in finance and financial economics. Burton argues that this body of work, using mostly key informant interviews with market actors, has offered new empirical insights into intangible assets such as inside information as well as provided a basis for the development of theoretical models of asset pricing. The author also avers that 'conventional quantitative analysis' by itself could not have arrived at such insightful conclusions regarding information flows. Brav et al. (2005, p. 487), in a study of financial pay-out behavior by firms, conclude:

> Scrutiny of stated assumptions should be important to theorists for two reasons. First, following Friedman, our results can provide for an even wider range of assumptions than have been used previously, some of which might lead to improved predictability. Second, for those who favor more realistic assumptions, our ability to distill which assumptions are deemed important by managers, and thus relevant to their decisions, has the potential to lead to better explanatory models.

Similarly, Bewley (1999, p. 7) notes:

> The economics literature contains a great many tests of models of wage rigidity and unemployment, but most of these rely on indirect evidence, for economists usually obtain information only from introspection and from surveys made by public institutions that produce data on easily quantifiable variables.

Engaging directly with economic agents forces the investigator to acknowledge the complexities of human motivations, thinking, and behavior; that is, the context-based nature of decisions. This can lead to a nuanced understanding of survey and experimental data as well. To put it another way, to consider official surveys and censuses as objective may at times simply mean confusing ignorance with objectivity. Ignorance of the data generation process should not form the basis for believing in its 'objectivity'. Even brief fieldwork stints, a few months long, can help in understanding the social context, leading to better interpretation of research findings. An example of how qualitative and ethnographic research methods have led to nuanced findings is Koopman's (1991) work in Africa that debunked the prevailing notion that households pooled incomes. Similarly, Agarwal's (1994) work on gender and land tenure in South Asia presents a detailed analysis of use rights as different from rights of ownership.

**Developing inclusive research processes**
Berik (1997, p. 121) points out that even when economists occasionally undertake fieldwork, the fieldwork most often takes the form of administering one's own survey questionnaire. Such scripted surveys and interview schedules – which also seek to minimize contact with respondents – ostensibly serve to minimize possible sources of bias in the data. It is the researcher who subsequently analyses the data thus collected, and formulates categories and definitions from the data to explain economic phenomena. The researcher therefore presents as the 'expert', untouched and above both the research process as well as the respondent population who are the objects of study.

In contrast, qualitative methods strive to describe economic phenomena as experienced by the study population (Ritchie and Lewis 2003). Feminist researchers, in particular, have argued that the point of view of unrepresented and marginalized participants, as presented in their own terms, is likely to reveal new knowledge about socio-economic phenomena, grounded in the lived experiences of participants (Hartsock 2004).

The use of qualitative and ethnographic research methods is especially salient where respondents' views of their own situations are of interest, and where it is desirable to challenge the conventional hierarchy of the research process through an inclusion of the voices and participation of the studied. Esim (1997) remarks that in her study of gender-based constraints faced by women entrepreneurs in Turkey, respondents felt power hierarchies were strongest during survey research when respondents were forced to give specific answers. In contrast, during qualitative interviews and focus groups, women could express their voice on matters most important to them. Kim (1997) finds that allowing a freer participation of interviewees in setting the agenda improved the quality of research by reducing interviewer bias, improving response rates, and facilitating trust in answering questions that may have been sensitive in nature.

Further, because of its time-consuming nature, qualitative research methods can force a higher level of commitment to the study and the subject. Scholars also argue that the affective experience of ethnographic research provides a motivation to researchers to invest in the community they are studying (see, e.g., Smith and Kleinman 2010). Qualitative methods also provide significant opportunities to reduce distance between the researcher and the researched, and build a less instrumental and more empathic relation between the two. Participatory and action research frameworks have emerged from these very antecedents. A sense of responsibility develops on the part of the researcher towards the group being studied, in turn reducing power hierarchies between the researcher and the researched (Esim 1997).

## Achieving reflexivity[5]

A defining feature of sound ethnographic research is reflexivity (Banister et al. 1994). The value of reflexivity in qualitative and ethnographic research has become the subject of much scholarly discussion in the social sciences over the past decade. While economics lags behind due to an emphasis on objective, dispassionate approach to uncover social 'truth', sociologists, anthropologists, and geographers committed to ethnographic research underscore reflexive practice – critical, ongoing self-reflection of 'the ways in which researchers' social background, assumptions, positioning and behavior impact on the research process' (Finlay and Gough 2003, p. ix) – as a way of placing the researcher within the social context being researched. Feminist researchers, in particular, have espoused reflexivity as a means of identifying relationships of power in social research, and the impact of these relationships on the findings of research. Rather than treat the researcher as an impartial, impersonal, and neutral observer of events in the field,[6] reflexivity encourages acknowledgment of the values, opinions, freedoms, and preconceived notions of the researcher and a deeper reflection into how they may impact both the process and the outcomes of research.

A researcher using ethnographic methods that entail direct confrontation of those being researched and a degree of immersion into the social setting of the researched over a significant period of time is not only able to better understand the issue being researched, but also able to examine their motivations in reaching specific conclusions from the research. Given that researchers spend significant time reading about the context and the people they wish to carry out research amongst before even venturing into the field, it is likely that certain preconceived notions are formed regarding the group being studied. These notions may color the interpretation of any data – interviews, observations, or documents – collected during the course of research. Further, personal characteristics of the researcher (age, gender, race, ethnicity, nationality, academic credentials, sexuality, among others) and geopolitical power disparities between the researcher and the researched can also mediate how data is collected in the field, or which data are collected. Through an awareness of these aspects and documentation of them, ethnographic and qualitative researchers acknowledge their integral role in the research process. Finlay and Gough (2003) argue that researchers using ethnographic methods increase the validity of their findings through reflexivity that transforms personal experience into public – and therefore accountable – knowledge (p. 4).

Fonow and Cook (1991, pp. 2–5) outline the value of reflexivity in raising consciousness, forming collaborations and alliances, and examining hitherto unexamined stages of the research process. In addition to these noteworthy aims, we argue that the reflexivity afforded by ethnographic research methods is of especial value to heterodox economics, which embraces the notion of the 'socially embedded individual' and is 'built upon the institutions-history-social structures nexus' (Davis 2008, p. 58). Further, much heterodox economics research is inspired by considerations on the part of the researcher of contributing to positive social change (in the spirit of Marx's '11th Thesis on Feuerbach').

Rather than technical fads or 'coolness', the heterodox researcher is typically driven by the human and social significance of the subject. Branches such as feminist economics or Marxian economics are explicitly concerned with understanding how gender or class positions affect economic outcomes. Ethnographic research methods allow much more easily for acknowledgment of the researcher's own class, race, or gender position, and reflection on how it affects the data generation process. Further, the social structures of inequality or privilege that make possible primary data collection can also be rendered visible. Finally, the research agenda itself can be brought under scrutiny. Talking to participants in open-ended sessions may disabuse the researcher of preconceived notions and contribute to the creation of a research agenda more in tune with the heterodox aims of the study.

**Triangulation of quantitative results**
Findings from qualitative data also help to corroborate results obtained through the use of quantitative techniques, or vice versa. This technique, known as triangulation, is discussed in greater detail in Chapter 15 in this *Handbook*. Here, we will simply mention that qualitative and quantitative methods can be used in conjunction with one another, as mixed methods, to validate research findings. Mixed methods have become increasingly popular within development economics in particular, including poverty research – for instance, in the Q-squared research by Kanbur and Shaffer (2007) – and in assessing the impacts of development and welfare programs (microfinance, health, education, infrastructure, and social services) (see, e.g., Goetz and Sen Gupta 1996; Olmsted 1996; Rao and Woolcock 2003; Bird et al. 2010).

## 7.3   ETHNOGRAPHIC TECHNIQUES

Harding (1986) distinguishes methodology from methods in that the former pertains to the broad principles of research being carried out, while the latter refers to specific tools, procedures, and techniques used in research practice. As such, a range of tools is available to the qualitative researcher, depending upon the aims of the research and the kinds of questions it seeks to answer. These different methods, and the specific kinds of data they yield, are discussed in the following sections.

**Interviews**

Personal interviews tend to be the most common ethnographic technique employed by economists. Categorized by degree of structure, interviews may be structured, semi-structured, or unstructured and open-ended. Structured interviews are usually carried out when the number of respondents is large, to ensure standardization and comparability across interviews (Starr 2014). Structured interviews follow a predetermined sequence of questions with little to no variation in phrasing of questions or the order in which questions may be posed. As such, structured interviews are typically used in survey research and produce quantitative data, rather than data suitable for qualitative analysis. Piore (1979, p. 561) remarks on the unsuitability of highly scripted, close-ended interviews to elicit respondents' stories:

If I took the latter approach (i.e. forcing respondents to give a codable response to each item), the respondents soon lost interest in the project and began to concentrate on getting through the questionnaire and on to their next appointment. In this process, they often provided misinformation in order to avoid an anticipated follow-up question.

Semi-structured interviews are typically organized around a set of predetermined questions (an interview guide); however, the questions are open-ended, with other follow-up questions emerging organically from the conversation between the interviewer and the respondent. Semi-structured interviews are a scheduled activity (Bernard 2011, p. 210). Unstructured interviews are more like guided conversations on a set of topics, with minimum control over responses. Questions can emerge over time, based on the researcher's observations of a set of practices or behaviors. As a result, unstructured interviews usually take place hand-in-hand with participant observation (DiCicco-Bloom and Crabtree 2006). Unstructured and semi-structured interviews are usually aimed at gathering respondents' perceptions on the issue(s) discussed in their own words; that is, they aim to recover largely 'unfiltered' responses from participants based on their lived experiences (Starr 2014; Bernard 2011).

Deep inquiries into lived socio-economic or cultural experience may also warrant personal in-depth interviews. While not very common in economics, in-depth interviews are especially useful in contextualizing lives in conflict or economic transition, and reconstructing perceptions of events and experiences relating to the topic (see, e.g., Olmsted 1997; Ruwanpura 2004). In-depth interviews are versatile in that the questions may be organically included to incorporate participants' interests, and can inform a wide range of research issues. Life histories are examples of a kind of in-depth interview focused on obtaining biographical information regarding important phases in a person's life. Starr (2014) notes that life histories, while not a commonly used method in economic research, can nevertheless facilitate inquiry into 'longitudinal processes that shape life outcomes' (p. 5), as for instance in Buckland et al.'s (2010) study on persistent poverty in Canada. Life histories are more common in interdisciplinary fields of research such as development. Davis (2006) collected life histories in nine locations in western Bangladesh in order to identify episodes of crisis in people's lives and the way in which these crises were dealt with. The aim of the research was to obtain a better understanding of informal forms of social protection.

Interviews typically require a careful record of data, either through detailed notes maintained by the researcher, or through recordings and transcriptions that may then be coded for analysis. The choice of interview techniques depends upon the topic of study, the circumstances in which interviews are carried out (time or location), and the preferences of the researcher. For instance, Bewley (2002, p. 347) mentions that he took detailed notes in a labor study because he believed that participants might be inhibited in their responses if a recording device was used, while the extensive information and data he received during a pricing study necessitated the use of a recorder, with the permission of participants.

## Key-Informant Interviews

Emerging from participant observation, key-informant interviews are a valuable interview methodology. Originally developed in cultural anthropology, key-informant interviews have been used within economics in studies on pricing, firm behavior, and the labor market (see, e.g., Bewley 1999; Brav et al. 2005). Bewley (2002) emphasizes the importance of finding key informants, 'people in critical institutions [or] that are very knowledgeable about the topics studied' (p. 345). A significant advantage of key-informant interviews is that good-quality data may be collected within a short period of time, which may then be useful in further developing research questions.

**Focus Groups**

Focus groups are loosely structured group discussions with multiple participants sharing their perspectives on a given issue, mediated by a facilitator-researcher. The focus group methodology emerged from marketing research (Bernard 2011) and is usually used in economic research in conjunction with other qualitative and quantitative methods. The data generated through focus groups typically includes not only what was said, but also observations regarding group dynamics, thought processes of respondents, and points of agreement or conflict. DiCicco-Bloom and Crabtree (2006) warn that each focus group represents a single entity within a sample of groups and therefore, these are not shortcut methods for collecting data from several respondents at the same time.

For van Staveren (1997, p. 132), the value of focus group research lies in the fact that it is able to bridge the dichotomy between theory and empirics in important ways:

> First, the researcher steps down from the position of objective and detached scientist, confident that she always asks the right questions . . . Second, a focus group makes it possible to include active participation and diverse representation from the start by opening up the first phase of the research to empirical input from its context.

As such, focus groups are invaluable tools that ground research in the context in which it is carried out, as well as contribute to the reflexive process of the researcher in terms drawing awareness to held beliefs and values. For instance, van Staveren's research in Nairobi with African women allowed her to re-examine her own assumptions about the value of economic independence for women:

> I was accustomed to regard economic independence as a basic right, or a goal in itself. The African women who participated in the group, however, indicated that economic independence or empowerment can also be viewed as a necessary but insufficient means for human flourishing . . . economic independence was regarded as a group issue for women, not as an individual matter. (Van Staveren 1997, p. 133)

Focus groups are also useful tools to explore the reasoning behind decision-making processes. For instance, Albelda and Shea (2010) use data collected through focus groups to understand the ways in which the employment focus of anti-poverty programs and corresponding reductions in levels of public support for poor families have impacted the decisions parents make about whether or not to work more.

Besides development and feminist economics, focus groups have also been used in environmental economics as a method of valuating natural resources (Kaplowitz and Hoehn 2001), in contingent evaluation (Johnston et al. 1995), and ecological preservation programs (Kline and Wichelns 1996).

**Ethnography and Participant Observation**

While various types of interviews and focus groups can all be considered 'ethnographic methods', we use the term 'ethnography' to specifically describe a prolonged stint of fieldwork including participant observation.[7] Starr (2014) considers 1–3 years as the required amount of fieldwork for ethnography. Such work is even more rare in economics than research based on qualitative data collected via interviews or non-participant observation (discussed next).

Participant observation is a mode of ethnographic research that entails spending time with, observing, and listening to respondents over a period of time, outside of interviews or structured interaction situations, 'without any pretension of detachment' (Berik 1997, p. 124). The researcher, rather than relying on direct inquiries into the motivations and behaviors of the study population, carefully documents everyday interactions and occurrences with the aim of understanding the nuances of complex and interconnected socio-economic processes within the community under study. Participant observation is therefore an active research process – indeed, a 'mode of being-in-the-world for researchers' (Hammersley and Atkinson 1996, p. 249) – that enables the researcher to confront their assumptions, preconceptions, and initial conceptual framework, and to carry out revisions to the framework to reflect social reality better.

While economists have not typically used ethnography and participant observation, sociology, geography, anthropology, and interdisciplinary areas of study (such as development studies) have used these methods to examine topics of economic significance. Some select examples include Keith Hart's (1973; see also 1987) seminal work on the informal economy in Ghana; Venkatesh's (2006) exploration of the underground economy of a poor, black community in Chicago's Southside; David Mosse's (2005) ethnography of development aid policy; Carla Freeman's work on the impacts of globalization in the Caribbean; and Elizabeth Chin's (2001) study of consumption. Economists have also co-authored works with scholars from disciplines that use ethnographic methods. A popular and oft-cited example is the collaborative exploration undertaken by economist Steven Levitt and anthropologist Sudhir Venkatesh on drug gangs and urban youth (Levitt and Venkatesh 2000, 2001). James Boyce, an economist, and Betsy Hartmann, a development studies scholar, undertook ethnographic work in rural Bangladesh (Hartmann and Boyce 1983) to understand the nature of poverty and the political economy of development, reporting their findings in *A Quiet Violence* (see also Starr 2014 for other examples).

**Non-Participant Observation (Site Visits)**

A distinction is sometimes drawn between the participant observer, that is, the researcher who plays an established participant role in the research, and the non-participant researcher who simply observes but does not actively participate or play a designated role. Non-positivist scholars who observe that researchers cannot study the social world without participating in it have criticized this dichotomy (Hammersley and Atkinson 1995). At the same time, however, within economic studies, there are examples of non-participant observation (pure observation). Examples include studies that rely on site visits to workshop and factory floors where the researcher has simply recorded observations regarding the production process. Adam Smith's notes on the pin factory and the

18 stages of producing a pin – resulting in the development of theories on the division of labor and productivity – are a notable example here. Site visits may take place in conjunction with other ethnographic methods such as interviews, or quantitative methods such as surveys, being used to gather data.

**Document Analysis**

Document analysis is a qualitative method used to systematically examine and evaluate documents to order to elicit meaning, gain understanding, and develop empirical knowledge (Bowen 2009; Corbin and Strauss 2008). The documents could include reports produced by institutions and organizations, memos, background papers, evaluation studies, diary entries, newspaper and magazine articles, books, meeting minutes, maps and charts, letters and other communication, or various public records available in libraries, archives, and through organizational record-keeping. Analysis of these documents may include obtaining and synthesizing data, information, figures, or excerpts that can then be used to provide support for the researcher's arguments when organized into major themes or case examples (Bowen 2009, p. 28).

While economists do analyze documents as part of their research, document analysis rarely occupies the center stage. Most frequently, the analysis of documents appears as a part of the literature review, serving as the background for quantitative or qualitative data analysis, as a source of research questions, and as context for the interpretation of results. Documents and reports produced by international agencies often serve as the starting point for a scholarly investigation: for instance, Brück and Schindler (2009), in their analysis of widow-headed households in the aftermath of conflict, point to the large number of policy-oriented empirical case studies produced by development organizations, such as the United Nations, that address the role of women during wartime and the reconstruction period, in comparison to the relatively sparse scholarly work on this issue (Brück and Schindler 2009, p. 6). Document analysis has also been used on rare occasions for an analysis of the discourses prevailing in economics, and for self-reflection into the discipline's direction; Fine's (1999) critique of social capital based on previous studies and World Bank reports is a notable example here.

## 7.4   RECENT STUDIES EMPLOYING ETHNOGRAPHIC TECHNIQUES

As the foregoing discussion makes clear, qualitative research methods have been recently employed in a wide variety of areas: development economics, poverty and inequality, industrial organization, environment, social and institutional economics, labor economics, feminist economics, and financial economics.

In this section we discuss some recent studies in economics that have made use of ethnographic methods. In considering a study to be 'in economics' we employed the following criteria: one of the authors should be in an economics department or have a PhD degree in economics, or the study should have been published in an economics journal. Another recent review of such studies is Starr (2014), who also offers a schematic look at the value added by qualitative approaches. While our typology differs from Starr's, we would like to direct the reader to her paper for more examples.

Instead of evaluating a study's merits, we focus on the author's aims and how qualitative data is used to achieve this aim. In the process we create five broad categories that emerge from these studies as particularly amenable to a qualitative approach:

1.  Trust, social networks, institutions (family, kinship, community), and norms: studies that investigate the role of trust in market transactions, or identify the role played by social networks of economic actors, as well as informal institutions and norms in economic outcomes.
2.  Power relations between actors in institutions: qualitative approaches have been particularly useful in understanding how gender, race, or ethnic hierarchies constrain participation of oppressed groups in economic decision-making.
3.  Motivation, decision-making processes: interview techniques have frequently been employed in economics to describe the motivations of economic actors or to understand their decision-making processes.
4.  Identity and perceptions: techniques such as interviews and observation have also helped economists investigate how people perceive effects of macroeconomic events (such as recessions) or outcomes of policy measures.
5.  Labor process and managerial strategies: a classic concern of Marxist economists, qualitative methods have been employed to investigate working conditions, challenges to unionization, and deskilling.

In Table 7.1 we present 23 studies that fall within one of these categories.

## 7.5   EMERGING HORIZONS, NEW FRONTIERS: ENCOURAGING MORE ETHNOGRAPHIC AND QUALITATIVE WORK

In this chapter, we have examined the relevance of ethnographic and qualitative methods for the discipline of economics. We have presented evidence that qualitative observations have always been an important part of economic theory, from Smith, Marshall, and Coase to contemporary researchers. In recent times, there has been increasing interest in qualitative and mixed methods research in economics that utilizes data collected through ethnographic techniques; interviews, focus group discussions, participant observations, site visits, and document analyses have been applied to varying degrees in mainstream and heterodox research in development, applied microeconomics, feminist economics, institutional economics, and labor economics.

Despite these developments, qualitative and ethnographic methods remain on the sidelines within the discipline. Even as more studies have emerged in recent times that attempt to bridge methodological (and disciplinary) divides, several structural constraints remain in place that discourage scholars and students from methodological pluralism. The most substantial barrier in economics remains lack of training and the methodological imperialism of econometrics and models. Indeed, a primary reason that heterodox economists and graduate students do not take on projects requiring

*Table 7.1   Recent studies employing ethnographic techniques*

| Theme | Study | Abstract | Method and Sample |
|---|---|---|---|
| Trust, social networks, informal norms, and kinship relations | Adato et al. (2006) | This is an article on post-apartheid South Africa. The authors argue that an apartheid pattern continues, leaving few avenues for upward social mobility and trapping poor blacks in a cycle of poverty; failure of the Washington Consensus suggests a very persistent poverty. Qualitative research shows that social connections are important in helping households look for work, get by in times of need, or cope with shocks. Yet, they are not connections that provide pathways out of poverty. Thus, social capital becomes more narrowly constructed and increasingly ineffective as a mechanism of capital access for poor people in a country facing a legacy of horizontal inequality and social exclusion. | The study uses the 1993–1998 KIDS (KwaZulu Natal Income Dynamics Study) panel data set, collected from a random selection of households in KwaZulu Natal selected in 1993 and then interviewed again in 1998. It also uses in-depth interviews gathered from a subset of 50 KIDS households in 2001. |
| | Lyon and Porter (2009) | This study explores market institutions and trust in Nigeria. Although the authors are not economists, the article deals with a central question in economics: the role of trust and moral norms in complex market transactions without formal systems of contracts. The authors focus on the vegetable market in the Jos region of Nigeria. They are also interested in asking whether trust is a result of a power relation between non-equals. | The database consists of 80 interviews with farmers and traders in rural, semi-urban, and urban markets. The sampling is purposive, as is usually the case in interview-based research, and attempts to cover a cross-section of different economic activities, gender, and wealth status. While analyzing data the authors draw on grounded theory. |
| | Sanghera and Satybaldieva (2009) | This study contributes to an understanding of how economies are socially instituted and embedded. The case is Kyrgyzstan's transition to a market economy. It examines how | The data come from semi-structured interviews with 33 interviewees from a broad spectrum of occupations, who possessed some experience of the Soviet planned economy, |

economic pressures, unregulated markets, and economic and social inequalities can affect moral sentiments and emotions, and can override ethical considerations: morality is typically ignored in orthodox economics, or assumed to be value and judgment neutral. The study includes narratives and oral interview quotations on the transition to a market economy: examples of increased freedom and better planning, how corruption has also increased (experience of payment of bribery), experiences and observations of how market systems care little for poor and vulnerable groups, and anger about inequality. Respondents also talk about how the public sector has changed in terms of cost-cutting, and lack of commitment of officials, and how grades in schools can be bought ('tariffs for different grades').

and were asked questions on their views of the transition to a market economy. The interviewees were chosen to cover different professions, age groups, ethnicities, and genders. Furthermore, one of the authors worked in universities in Novosibirsk in Russia and Bishkek in Kyrgyzstan for four years, and both authors have had several years of opportunity to observe social life in the region.

Wolf (1990)

This study examines the role of kinship in determining the decision of daughters to work outside the house in factory employment in two contexts: Java and Taiwan. While Javanese daughters have relative autonomy in seeking factory employment, sometimes against their parents' wishes, Taiwanese daughters are obliged to work for years to contribute to household income. Javanese daughters are able to do so due to a greater acceptance of women as economic agents, while Taiwanese daughters are more constrained due to the patriarchal view of daughters as 'temporary' family members who must repay their debt to their parents.

The author uses ethnographic and qualitative data collected through fieldwork in both Java and Taiwan to contrast the two cases, and to complicate the conventional economic understanding of the household as a unified entity. She argues that kinship structures matter in how daughters are able to exercise their agency.

*Table 7.1* (continued)

| Theme | Study | Abstract | Method and Sample |
|---|---|---|---|
| Trust, social networks, informal norms, and kinship relations | Colin (2008) | This study looks at access to land in African households. Categories of private versus communal property, or modern versus customary systems, do not provide an adequate framework for the understanding of the variety of property rights encountered in the African context. Further, intra-family land relationships usually remain as a black box, even if kinship relations constitute a major institution governing access to land and land management. Finally, the concept of household as the main analytic unit regarding resource access may be questioned in a number of situations in Africa, where men and women separately conduct productive enterprises within households and where the family relationships regarding access to productive resources and transfers of wealth are far from circumscribed within the limits of the conjugal and residential unit. | This study addresses the weaknesses listed alongside through ethnographic study grounded in institutional economics as well as legal and economic anthropology. The author has performed long-term ethnography among matrilineal Baoules settled in the village of Djimini-Koffikro, in Lower Ivory Coast. |
| Power relations between various actors within an institution | Akbulut and Soylu (2012) | This study investigates how local power imbalances can subvert participatory resource management systems implemented by the Turkish state. The authors use their case study data to argue that even as resource management programs are participatory on paper, local power structures neglected at the policy formation stage do not allow for the opinions of all stakeholders to be included. For example, almost no women knew about the meetings being held in the community to solicit opinions | The authors use a case-study approach based on surveys, focus groups, and interviews (including key informant interviews with state officials in charge of implementing polices). |

| | | of the local population. In interviews, women confessed to thinking that their opinions were probably considered irrelevant. |
|---|---|---|
| Harriss-White (2003) | Capital accumulation at the local level, class formation in villages and smaller towns, are all mostly missing from large-scale surveys and require the researcher to do field research. The author constructs a narrative account of evolving gender relations, capital accumulation at the local level, caste-based market institutions, and how access to the state is shaped by religion, ethnicity, and gender. Long-term ethnography creates a rich description of commerce in small-town India. | Harriss-White has been visiting the southern Indian town of Arni (population around 100 000) for more than three decades. But she rarely uses direct quotes from interviews, preferring to construct a narrative based on qualitative and quantitative information gathered from repeated visits. |
| Sangameswaran (2008) | The author investigates the construction of an 'ideal village' community in the context of a watershed development project in western India. The study looks at how diverse interests within a village are reconciled to produce a 'community'. Villagers' visions of justice and development are explored, as are the roles of volunteer labor and self-help groups in the implementation of the watershed development project. The study challenges narratives that depict 'the community' as homogenous (conflict-free) or 'ideal' on the one hand, and backward and divided on the other. | Based on a three-month stay in the village the study employs a combination of semi-structured interviews, participation in village-level activities, open-ended discussions, and observation. These are combined with secondary data collected from village officials and organizations implementing the watershed development program. |
| Koopman (1991) | This is a classic study that challenges the characterization of rural African households as 'unified production/consumption units' having one objective function ('benevolent dictator' or identical preferences). It shows that men and women conduct separate enterprises and manage separate budgets. It measures differences in women's and men's labor times, incomes, and investment capacities. | Five years of fieldwork doing qualitative and quantitative work in rural Cameroon. |

153

*Table 7.1* (continued)

| Theme | Study | Abstract | Method and Sample |
|---|---|---|---|
| Power relations between various actors within an institution | Rao (2008) | The study takes the case of the Indian state of Andhra Pradesh to investigate the operation of a women's empowerment program. The content of the empowerment policy is investigated and the author shows that the state lowered shares of expenditure devoted to social reproduction, while women's empowerment was equated with micro-credit programs. Determinants of participation in these programs are investigated. Qualitative data show that programs: (1) lack administrative support; and (2) tend to rely upon the expenditure of time and resources by participants, which eventually undermines the broader project of empowerment. | The study uses a combination of econometric estimation and qualitative interview data. Data collected from two villages over nine months include participant observation as well as surveys and interviews. |
| | Dema-Moreno (2009) | The study focuses on financial decision-making among dual-income heterosexual couples in Spain. The author provides evidence that, despite claims of equality, there are decisions about income pooling and income use that are not negotiated or made by consensus. Established social norms and gender relations are important and, frequently, there are issues that couples exclude from negotiation. In-depth interviews were employed because they give insights into the internal dynamics and negotiation strategies of each member through the observation of real negotiations. | Qualitative, in-depth interviews were undertaken with couples, with each couple being interviewed together and separately. This allowed researchers to study financial decision-making processes and to detect gender inequalities that may appear during negotiations. The author notes that surveys are frequently used tools in this kind of study, but do not provide much information on the financial decision-making process, and about the role each family member plays. |
| Motivations and decision-making processes of economic actors | Bewley (1999) | The principal finding of the study is that managers are reluctant to lower wages during a recession for fear of destroying employee morale, a result that the author says he would | Adopting an ethnographic approach Bewley interviewed 246 managers in small and large manufacturing and service sector firms in the Northeast of the US. |

| | | |
|---|---|---|
| | not have taken seriously prior to undertaking the study. The study presents extensive interview data in the form of direct quotations. The author was motivated to undertake the study because the usual survey variables such as wages, salaries, employment status, firm size, age, sex, and race of workers are not sufficient to distinguish between theories of wage rigidity. | |
| Brav et al. (2005) | This study investigates factors that drive dividend payment and stock-repurchase decisions. The authors believe that the 'field interviews provide a benchmark describing where academic research and real-world dividend policy are consistent and where they differ' (p. 484), and note that interviews allow for open-ended questions so that answers can guide further questions (unlike preset survey questions). | Based on a survey of 384 financial executives and 23 in-depth interviews. The authors combine regression analysis with analysis of interview data. |
| Cobb et al. (2009) | This study explores the gray area between formality and informality in the US labor market. The subject of the study lends itself to an ethnographic analysis since official data sources and other secondary data are likely to underreport undocumented migrants and their economic activity. The study reports some counter-intuitive findings based on worker interviews. For example, some workers report preferring wages below the legal minimum wage. This is because being paid at the legal rate would reduce take-home pay due to taxes. | Based on 12 in-depth (hour-long) and 80 shorter interviews with Mexican migrant workers in Oregon. |
| Goldstein and Hillard (2008) | The study documents increased rate of exploitation of wood harvesters in the North Maine Woods and a transition from a 'high-road' to 'low-road' labor relations over a | Uses a mark-up pricing model alongside quantitative survey data from the Maine Department of Labor and qualitative interview data. |

*Table 7.1* (continued)

| Theme | Study | Abstract | Method and Sample |
|---|---|---|---|
| Motivations and decision-making processes of economic actors | | 20-year period. The qualitative portion of the study attempts to 'uncover the motivations, strategies, and responses of the interacting classes that led to a high-road policy and its later reversal through extensive interviews/oral histories of industry experts, industry decision makers, labor movement leaders, and independent logging contractors'. The authors do not use extensive quotes (a companion paper does this) but instead use the data to create a narrative of changing corporate strategies in the paper industry. The focus is on managing supply chain uncertainty and the diffusion of mechanical harvesting technology. | |
| | Scheibl and Wood (2005) | The investment behavior of firms in the British brick industry is studied. The authors ask how investments are coordinated between firms to avoid excess capacity in the industry. They adopted an exploratory approach to theory building, using inductive methodology to draw insights from qualitative and quantitative data. Qualitative data are used to 'get inside the black box of the market adjustment process'. | The authors address the question using interview data. Methods and instruments were adapted as the study progressed. Interviews were conducted via site visits and by telephone (senior managers of larger firms). Authors report not using a tape recorder due to the sensitivity of the information. |
| | Morgan and Olsen (2011) | The authors study micro-credit programs in the form of women's self-help groups (SHGs) in two villages in the state of Andhra Pradesh, in south India. Looking specifically at loans taken for cow ownership, the authors explore escalating debt and aspirational components of borrowing by the poor. They also look at the | Authors have been conducting research in the area since 1985. Data are collected via questionnaires completed by a representative sample from each village followed by semi-structured interviews. Interestingly, the authors have also made interview transcripts as well as field notes available with the ESRC |

| | | |
|---|---|---|
| | 'fallacy of composition' effect, that is, falling incomes in petty production due to increased competition resulting from proliferating micro-businesses. | QualiData Archive (http://www.esds.ac.uk/qualidata/). |
| Gezici (Chapter 16 in this *Handbook*) | The author uses mixed methods: interview data from semi-structured discussions with the managers of 33 manufacturing companies in Turkey. The variables that are salient in the interviews are then used in the investment specification, which is then tested econometrically with panel data. | 33 interviews with managers of firms in Turkey to identify the factors impacting investment of manufacturing firms. |
| Clark et al. (2000) | This is a study of contingent valuation (CV) and willingness to pay (WTP). Authors note that in the debates about the validity and legitimacy of CV, researchers do not engage directly with respondents to explore what survey-generated the WTP figure means. The study uses qualitative methods coupled with a CV survey performed to appraise conservation policy in the UK. The results show that respondents have problems in contextualizing the worth of a scheme in both monetary and non-monetary terms, and express feelings that values for nature are not commensurable with monetary valuation. Participants also challenge claims that the CV process democratically incorporates public values in policy decisions. Instead they argue for a decision-making institution where local people can contribute to environmental policy decisions. | The qualitative research was conducted with respondents after they had completed the CV questionnaire. The principal technique employed is in-depth group discussions with lay people to explore values, meanings, knowledge, and practices. |

*Table 7.1* (continued)

| Theme | Study | Abstract | Method and Sample |
|---|---|---|---|
| Motivations and decision-making processes of economic actors | Albelda and Shea (2010) | The authors explore factors taken into account by low-income parents when deciding about how much to work. Parents make decisions based not only on immediate needs, but also taking into account future opportunities. They also weigh long-term risks that accompany more work and less time with children. The study reveals that mothers are forced to choose between the families' immediate financial and care needs and investing in the labor market for (uncertain) long-term pay-offs. | Data were collected from 22 focus groups with 166 parents whose incomes ranged from 75 per cent to 325 per cent of the federal poverty line. Conversations lasted 1.5 hours during which participants were asked to comment on specific scenarios such as: 'a low-income single mother, receiving housing assistance and health insurance, finds herself being offered more hours of work, and with it more pay but likely less government support'. Participants were asked what they would do in such (and other) situations. Participants were paid $25 and food was provided. Childcare was available on-site. |
| Identity and perceptions | Erbaş and Turan (2009) | This study investigates the social impact of the 2001 Turkish economic crisis through fieldwork conducted among workers and small employers. The impact of the crisis is analyzed in terms of both the changes in household expenditures and people's perception of neoliberal policies. The authors use qualitative data to understand how the participants evaluate the crisis. | The survey was then carried out in textile, food, and furniture sectors from February to April 2002. The questionnaire was administered to 240 people: 120 workers and 120 small employers. Sampling was purposive. Questionnaire included open- and close-ended questions. Each interview took about 35–40 minutes. |

| | | | |
|---|---|---|---|
| | Olmsted (1997) | This study is a brief account of education and employment patterns among Palestinian women. The author motivates the qualitative approach by noting that she could not separate lived (or qualitative) experience from quantitative data. Neoclassical models obscured the complexity and interrelatedness of observed processes and outcomes. Through the stories of three Palestinian women, the author identifies questions such as how we gather evidence, and what is considered acceptable evidence within economics. | Life histories of three women. |
| Labor process and managerial strategies | Mutari and Figart (2008) | This study is an account of a successful unionization campaign among casino dealers, based on an ethnographic study of workers in Atlantic City, New Jersey's 11 casinos. Objective is to look into whether economic development strategies are creating jobs that provide workers with the resources they need to build fulfilling lives, and what constitutes a 'good' job. Casino gaming has become more competitive, with cost-cutting strategies in place: temporary dealers and fewer full-time dealers hired as part of cost cutting, benefits reduced or taken away, penalties for sick days increased, work intensity increased (serving more tables), and more electronic games. The smoking ban in public places is not applicable for casino floors. These factors emerge from the interviews with employees that authors report on: context and factors are made explicit here. | Based on interviews with nonrandom sample of employees. |

159

ethnographic techniques and qualitative data collection is that they lack methodological preparation. Coursework in economic methodology generally consists of mathematics and econometrics. Students seeking to incorporate any alternative methods into their research must, as a result, either educate themselves by reading materials on these techniques on their own, or seek such training in other departments such as sociology, anthropology, or education. The difficulty here is the relative isolation that economics graduate student researchers interested in alternative methodologies find themselves in. The isolation is compounded by the fact that since these techniques have not been used, advising on them may be inadequate.

There are a myriad other challenges for scholars who transgress traditional methodological boundaries. Qualitative research is frequently expensive, time-consuming, and requires a local professional support network. In cases of ethnographic research or participant observation, it may also take the researcher to unfamiliar (and occasionally unsafe) locales where they may confront linguistic barriers or new social positioning based on their class, ethnicity, gender, and/or race. These challenges are not insurmountable, however. Some departments in other disciplines require fieldwork as a dissertation component. Special funding opportunities could be set up to encourage methodological pluralism. Most crucially, a refereed outlet for the publication of methodologically diverse research would be a valuable addition to further the discussion on methods within the discipline.

In heterodox economics, in particular, ethnographic and qualitative research methods broaden the scope of economic inquiry afforded by existing data sets and allow us to map some of the power dimensions of the research questions we pursue; an essential contribution to transforming the discipline. Indeed, the examples cited above illustrate the value of ethnographic methods in capturing social reality more accurately, be it mapping the role of social institutions, cultural norms, and social networks in determining economic outcomes, developing a better understanding of the economic decision-making process, tracing the role of social hierarchies and cultural norms in decision-making, or exposing power relations between actors in social and economic institutions. Further, since heterodox economics aims to be self-aware of the hierarchies prevalent in data collection and knowledge construction, it is hoped that an inclusion of ethnographic methods will allow for more inclusive and accountable research processes, greater involvement of the researcher in and accountability to the groups that have participated in the research, and greater self-reflection on the part of the researcher towards the goals of the research. As we economists venture out into the world more and more, we will undoubtedly discover, in the words of Truman Bewley (1999, p. 39), that 'it is better to face economic reality than to invent it'.

## NOTES

1. 'Economists rely heavily on a few data sources, particularly on those collected by the federal government, and are much more likely to use survey data collected by another party. Papers with at least one non-economist author are much more likely to use self-collected data (for example, interviews, author-designed surveys, experiments)' (Jacobsen and Newman 1997, p. 129).
2. The journals were chosen such that their overall rank in the world of heterodox journals (Lee et al. 2010) was in the top 25, and the research they published covered a broad range of paradigms and approaches.

3. 'What is industry studies?', http://www.sloan.org/major-program-areas/recently-completed-programs/indus try-studies/what-is-industry-studies/.
4. Helper's (2000) reasons include the following: 'researchers can ask people directly about their objectives and constraints, fieldwork allows exploration of areas with little preexisting data or theory, fieldwork facili- tates use of the right data, fieldwork provides vivid images that promote intuition'.
5. Note that we use 'reflexivity' to mean critical self-reflection here; it is not used in the sense used by George Soros (2008, 2013) in his theory of economic agents.
6. England (1994) attributes this idea of the researcher to the prevalence of 'positivist-inspired training' emerging from the 'methodological hegemony of neopositivist empiricism' (p. 242). The emphasis on objec- tivity within neopositivist empiricism entails a strict dichotomy between the subject and object of study in this framework.
7. Hammersley and Atkinson (1995) draw attention to the controversy around the term 'ethnography', which has been difficult to define. They state: 'For some it refers to a philosophical paradigm to which one makes a total commitment, for others it designates a method that one uses as and when appropriate. And, of course, there are positions between these extremes' (p. 248).

# REFERENCES

Adato, Michelle, Michael Carter, and Julian Ma (2006), 'Exploring poverty traps and social exclusion in South Africa using qualitative and quantitative data', *Journal of Development Studies*, **42** (2), 226–47.
Agarwal, Bina (1994), *A Field of One's Own: Gender and Land Rights in South Asia*, Cambridge: Cambridge University Press.
Akbulut, Bengi and Ceren Soylu (2012), 'An inquiry into power and participatory natural resource manage- ment', *Cambridge Journal of Economics*, **36** (5), 1143–62.
Albelda, Randy and Jennifer Shea (2010), 'To work more or not to work more: difficult choices, complex decisions for low-wage parents', *Journal of Poverty*, **14** (3), 245–65.
Banister, Peter, Erica Burman, Ian Parker, Maye Taylor, and Carol Tindall (1994), *Qualitative Methods in Psychology: A Research Guide*, Buckingham: Open University Press.
Basole, Amit, Jennifer Cohen, and Smita Ramnarain (2012), 'The crucial contribution of fieldwork to (hetero- dox) economics: evidence from research in Nepal, India, and South Africa', paper presented at the Allied Social Sciences Association Conference, Chicago, IL, January.
Bergmann, Barbara (2007), 'Needed: a new empiricism', *Economists' Voice*, **4** (2), 1–4.
Berik, Günseli (1997), 'The need for crossing the method boundaries in economics research', *Feminist Economics*, **3** (2), 121–5.
Bernard, Harvey Russell (2011), *Research Methods in Anthropology: Qualitative and Quantitave Approaches*, 5th edn, Lanham, MD: Rowman Altamira.
Bewley, Truman F. (1999), *Why Wages Don't Fall During a Recession*, Cambridge, MA: Harvard University Press.
Bewley, Truman (2002), 'Interviews as a valid empirical tool in economics', *Journal of Socio-Economics*, **31** (4), 343–53.
Bird, Kate, Kate Higgins, and Andy McKay (2010), 'Conflict, education and the intergenerational transmission of poverty in Northern Uganda', *Journal of International Development*, **22** (8), 1183–96.
Borenstein, Severin, Joseph Farrell, and Adam B. Jaffe (1998), 'Inside the pin-factory: empirical studies aug- mented by manager interviews', *Journal of Industrial Economics*, **46** (2), 123–4.
Bowen, Glenn A. (2009), 'Document analysis as a qualitative research method', *Qualitative Research Journal*, **9** (2), 27–40.
Brav, Alon, John R. Graham, Campbell Harvey, and Roni Michaely (2005), 'Payout policy in the 21st century', *Journal of Financial Economics*, **77** (3), 483–527.
Brück, Tilman and Kati Schindler (2009), 'The impact of violent conflicts on households: what do we know and what should we know about war widows?', *Oxford Development Studies*, **37** (3), 289–309.
Buckland, Jerry, Antonia Fikkert, and Rick Eagan (2010), 'Barriers to improved capability for low-income Canadians', *Journal of Interdisciplinary Economics*, **22** (4), 357–89.
Burton, Bruce (2007), 'Qualitative research in finance: pedigree and renaissance', *Studies in Economics and Finance*, **24** (1), 5–12.
Chin, Elizabeth (2001), *Purchasing Power: Black Kids and American Consumer Culture*, Minneapolis, MN: University of Minnesota Press.
Clark, Judy, Jacqueline Burgess, and Carolyn M. Harrison (2000), 'I struggled with this money business: respondents' perspectives on contingent valuation', *Ecological Economics*, **33** (1), 45–62.

Coase, Ronald H. (1988), 'The new institutional economics', *American Economic Review*, **88** (2), 72–4.

Cobb, Carrie L., Mary C. King, and Leopoldo Rodriguez (2009), 'Betwixt and between: the spectrum of formality revealed in the labor market experiences of Mexican migrant workers in the United States', *Review of Radical Political Economics*, **41** (3), 365–71.

Colin, Jean-Philippe (2008), 'Disentangling intra-kinship property rights in land: a contribution of economic ethnography to land economics in Africa', *Journal of Institutional Economics*, **4** (2), 231–54.

Corbin, Juliet and Anselm Strauss (2008), *Basics of Qualitative Research: Techniques and Procedures for Developing Grounded Theory*, 3rd edn, Los Angeles, CA: Sage.

Davis, Peter (2006), 'Poverty in time: exploring poverty dynamics from life history interviews in Bangladesh', CPRC Working Paper 69, Manchester: Chronic Poverty Research Centre/Institute of Development Policy and Management, University of Manchester.

Davis, Peter (2008), 'Poverty dynamics and life trajectories in rural Bangladesh', *International Journal of Multiple Research Approaches*, **2** (2), 176–90.

Dema-Moreno, Sandra (2009), 'Behind the negotiations: financial decision-making processes in Spanish dual-income couples', *Feminist Economics*, **15** (1), 27–56.

DiCicco-Bloom, Barbara and Benjamin F. Crabtree (2006), 'The qualitative research interview', *Medical Education*, **40** (4), 314–21.

England, Kim V.L. (1994), 'Getting personal: reflexivity, positionality, and feminist research', *Professional Geographer*, **46** (1), 80–89.

Erbaş, Hayriye and Feryal Turan (2009), 'The 2001 economic crisis, its impacts and evaluations: the case of workers and small employers in Ankara', *Review of Radical Political Economics*, **41** (1), 79–107.

Esim, Simel (1997), 'Can feminist methodology reduce power hierarchies in research settings?', *Feminist Economics*, **3** (2), 137–9.

Fine, Ben (1999), 'The developmental state is dead – long live social capital?', *Development and Change*, **30** (1), 1–19.

Finlay, Linda and Brendan Gough (eds) (2003), *Reflexivity: A Practical Guide for Researchers in Health and Social Sciences*, Oxford: Blackwell.

Fonow, Mary Margaret and Judith Cook (1991), 'Back to the future: a look at the second wave of feminist epistemology and methodology', in Mary Margaret Fonow, and Judith Cook (eds), *Beyond Methodology: Feminist Scholarship as Lived Research*, Bloomington, IN: Indiana University Press, pp. 1–15.

Friedman, Milton (1953 [1970]), 'The methodology of positive economics', in Milton Friedman (1970), *Essays in Positive Economics*, Chicago, IL: University of Chicago Press, pp. 3–43.

Goetz, Anne Marie and Rina Sen Gupta (1996), 'Who takes the credit? gender, power, and control over loan use in rural credit programs in Bangladesh', *World Development*, **24** (1), 45–63.

Goldstein, Jonathan P. and Michael G. Hillard (2008), 'Taking the high road only to arrive at the low road: the creation of a reserve army of petty capitalists in the North Maine woods', *Review of Radical Political Economics*, **40** (4), 479–509.

Hammersley, Martyn and Paul Atkinson (1995), *Ethnography: Principles in Practice*, 2nd edn, London, UK and New York, USA: Routledge, pp. 171–87.

Harding, Sandra (1986), *The Science Question in Feminism*, Ithaca, NY: Cornell University Press.

Harriss-White, Barbara (2003), *India Working: Essays on Society and Economy*, Vol. 8, Cambridge: Cambridge University Press.

Hart, Keith (1973), 'Informal income opportunities and urban employment in Ghana', *Journal of Modern African Studies*, **11** (1), 61–89.

Hart, Keith (1987), 'Informal economy', *The New Palgrave: a Dictionary of Economics*, London: Macmillan.

Hartmann, Betsy and James K. Boyce (1983), *A Quiet Violence: View from a Bangladesh Village*, London: Zed Books.

Hartsock, Nancy (2004), 'The feminist standpoint: developing the ground for a specifically feminist historical materialism', in Sandra Harding and Merrill B. Hintikka (eds), *Discovering Reality: Feminist Perspectives on Epistemology, Metaphysics, Methodology, and Philosophy of Science*, Amsterdam: Springer, pp. 283–310.

Helper, Susan (2000), 'Economists and field research: you can observe a lot just by watching', *American Economic Review*, **90** (2), 228–32.

Jacobsen, Joyce, and Andrew E. Newman (1997), 'What data do economists use? The case of labor economics and industrial relations', *Feminist Economics*, **3** (2), 127–30.

Johnston, Robert J., T.F. Weaver, L.A. Smith, and S.K. Swallow (1995), 'Contingent valuation focus groups: insights from ethnographic interview techniques', *Agricultural and Resource Economics Review*, **24** (1), 56–69.

Kanbur, Ravi and Paul Shaffer (2007), 'Epistemology, normative theory and poverty analysis: implications for Q-squared in practice', *World Development*, **35** (2), 183–96.

Kaplowitz, Michael D. and John P. Hoehn (2001), 'Do focus groups and individual interviews reveal the same information for natural resource valuation?', *Ecological Economics*, **36** (2), 237–47.

Katz, Elizabeth (1997), 'The intrahousehold economics of voice and exit', *Feminist Economics*, **3** (3), 25–46.

Kim, Marlene (1997), 'Poor women survey poor women: feminist perspectives in survey research', *Feminist Economics*, **3** (2), 99–117.

Kline, Jeffrey and Dennis Wichelns (1996), 'Public preferences regarding the goals of farmland preservation programs', *Land Economics*, **72** (4), 538–49.

Koopman, Jeanne (1991), 'Neoclassical household models and modes of household production: problems in the analysis of African agricultural households', *Review of Radical Political Economics*, **23** (3–4), 148–73.

Lee, Frederic S., Bruce Cronin, Scott McConnell, and Eric Dean (2010), 'Research quality rankings of heterodox economic journals in a contested discipline', *American Journal of Economics and Sociology*, **69** (5), 1409–52.

Levitt, Steven D. and Sudhir A. Venkatesh (2000), 'An economic analysis of a drug-selling gang's finances', *Quarterly Journal of Economics*, **115** (3), 755–89.

Levitt, Steven D. and Sudhir A. Venkatesh (2001), 'Growing up in the projects: the economic lives of a cohort of men who came of age in Chicago public housing', *American Economic Review*, **91** (2), 79–84.

Lyon, Fergus and Gina Porter (2009), 'Market institutions, trust and norms: exploring moral economies in Nigerian food systems', *Cambridge Journal of Economics*, **33** (5), 903–20.

Marshall, Alfred (1919), *Industry and Trade: A Study of Industrial Technique and Business Organization; and of their Influences on the Condition of Various Classes and Nations*, New York: Cosimo.

Morgan, Jamie and Wendy Olsen (2011), 'Aspiration problems for the Indian rural poor: research on self-help groups and micro-finance', *Capital and Class*, **35** (2), 189–212.

Mosse, David (2005), *Cultivating Development: An Ethnography of Aid Policy and Practice*, London: Pluto Press.

Mutari, Ellen and Deborah M. Figart (2008), 'Transformations in casino gaming and the unionization of Atlantic City's dealers', *Review of Radical Political Economics*, **40** (3), 258–65.

Olmsted, Jennifer (1996), 'Women "manufacture" economic spaces in Bethlehem', *World Development*, **24** (12), 1829–40.

Olmsted, Jennifer (1997), 'Telling Palestinian women's economic stories', *Feminist Economics*, **3** (2), 141–51.

Piore, Michael J. (1979), 'Qualitative research techniques in economics', *Administrative Science Quarterly*, **24** (4), 560–69.

Piore, Michael J. (2006), 'Qualitative research: does it fit in economics?', *European Management Review*, **3** (1), 17–23.

Rao, Smriti (2008), 'Reforms with a female face: gender, liberalization, and economic policy in Andhra Pradesh, India', *World Development*, **36** (7), 1213–32.

Rao, Vijayendra and Michael Woolcock (2003), 'Integrating qualitative and quantitative approaches in program evaluation', in Francois Bourguignon and Luiz A. Pereira da Silva (eds), *The Impact of Economic Policies on Poverty and Income Distribution: Evaluation Techniques and Tools*, Washington DC: World Bank, pp. 165–90.

Reisman, David (1990), *Alfred Marshall's Mission*, London: Routledge.

Ritchie, Jane and Jane Lewis (eds) (2003), *Qualitative Research Practice: A Guide for Social Science Students and Researchers*, London: Sage.

Ruwanpura, Kanchana N. (2004), 'Female-headship among Muslims in eastern Sri Lanka: a case of changing household structures?', *Nivedini: A Journal of Gender Studies*, **11** (1), 1–22.

Sangameswaran, Priya (2008), 'Community formation, "ideal" villages and watershed development in western India', *Journal of Development Studies*, **44** (3), 384–408.

Sanghera, Balihar and Elmira Satybaldieva (2009), 'Moral sentiments and economic practices in Kyrgyzstan: the internal embeddedness of a moral economy', *Cambridge Journal of Economics*, **33** (5), 921–35.

Scheibl, Fiona and Andrew Wood (2005), 'Investment sequencing in the brick industry: an application of grounded theory', *Cambridge Journal of Economics*, **29** (2), 223–47.

Smith, Adam (1776 [1937]), *An Inquiry into the Nature and Causes of the Wealth of Nations*, reprinted as Adam Smith (1937), *The Wealth of Nations*, New York: Modern Library.

Smith, Lindsay and Arthur Kleinman (2010), 'Emotional engagements: acknowledgment, advocacy and direct action', in James Davies and Dimitrina Spencer (eds), *Emotions in the Field: The Psychology and Anthropology of Fieldwork Experience*, Stanford, CA: University of California Press.

Soros, George (2008), *The New Paradigm for Financial Markets: The Credit Crisis of 2008 and What it Means*, New York: Public Affairs Books.

Soros, George (2013), 'Fallibility, reflexivity, and the human uncertainty principle', *Journal of Economic Methodology*, **20** (4), 309–29.

Starr, Martha A. (2014), 'Qualitative and mixed-methods research in economics: surprising growth, promising future', *Journal of Economic Surveys*, **28** (2), 238–64.

Staveren, Irene van (1997), 'Focus groups: contributing to a gender-aware methodology', *Feminist Economics*, **3** (2), 131–5.

Udry, Christopher (2003), 'Fieldwork, economic theory, and research on institutions in developing countries', *American Economic Review*, **93** (2), 107–11.

Varley, Ann (1996), 'Women heading households: some more equal than others?', *World Development*, **24** (3), 505–20.
Venkatesh, Sudhir A. (2006), *Off the Books*, Cambridge, MA: Harvard University Press.
White, Howard (2002), 'Combining quantitative and qualitative approaches in poverty analysis', *World Development*, **30** (3), 511–22.
Wolf, Diane L. (1990), 'Daughters, decisions and domination: an empirical and conceptual critique of household strategies', *Development and Change*, **21** (1), 43–74.

# 8 Experimental methods and data
### Andrew Mearman

## 8.1 INTRODUCTION

Arguably experimental methods are the *sine qua non* of science. Laboratory experiments have a long, rich, and successful history. Common images of scientists often involve them in the laboratory, adorned in a white coat with a mandatory clipboard (or, now, laptop or tablet computer). The symbols of experiment – *inter alia* the laboratory, white coat, test tube – confer on their bearers automatic authority. It is little wonder then that economists wish to ape these methods. However, at least since John Stuart Mill, it has been felt that the nature of the social world robs economists of the conditions in which to conduct *experimentum cruces*. Friedman (1953 [1970], p. 10), in his famous methodological essay, argues that at best we might use 'evidence cast up by the "experiments" that happen to occur'. More recently, Rosenzweig and Wolpin (2000, p. 827) declare: 'The costliness of and limitations on experiments involving human subjects have long been identified as major constraints on the progress of economic science'.

Nonetheless, some experiments were done; Roth (1993) cites the Bernoullis' work on the St Petersburg paradox (the reluctance to enter a game with an infinitely large payout) as the earliest example. Roth's history is of slow growth from the 1930s, culminating in an explosion of activity in the 1980s, principally in the areas of consumer choice, game theory, and industrial organization. In the recent past, under the influence of social psychologists, economists have begun to deploy laboratory methods, to test economic theories, collect novel data on which to develop new theories, model behavior, evaluate policy, enrich economics teaching, and simply 'reach new audiences' (Barankay et al. 2013, p. 1). This work has led to some potentially important insights. Some of these have had practical importance, for instance in designing mobile phone auctions (Guala 2001). Experimental economics is viewed as a key frontier in economics, as indicated by the award of Swedish Bank prizes to Vernon Smith and Daniel Kahneman for pioneering work in the area.

Experimental work and various strands of behavioral economics have asked fundamental questions about the rationality assumption, a core element of mainstream economics (see Loewenstein 1999 and accompanying articles). However, aside from that, there is little openly heterodox work which has considered experimental methods. Much of that which has, is largely critical (see, e.g., Siakantaris 2000; Mearman 2013). There are few heterodox applications of experimental data. There may be many reasons for this, one being that, like *inter alia* mathematics, econometrics, and game theory, experiments are associated with mainstream thought and de facto controversial. Further, these methods are regarded as unrealistic 'closed systems' methods imposed on 'open systems' reality. Experiments in many ways embody critiques of current methods; and indeed import criticism via their use of econometric methods. However, in other ways they are very different from econometrics. Like econometrics, also, there are a variety of experimental methods, and it is not trivial to make a general claim about their validity.

This chapter attempts to address some of the above controversies. However, it also seeks to offer practical guidance to researchers on the different types of experiments one might do. Allied to this is a discussion of the analysis of experimental data. What the chapter cannot offer is a comprehensive and thorough description of the history of experimentation, or detailed practical guidance on every aspect of experiments in economics. Nor does it offer a 'cookbook'.

The chapter takes a rather critical methodological perspective, because: (1) experimental methods are held in such esteem and need to be examined thoroughly; (2) experimenters are well aware of weaknesses and assumptions made; and (3) other texts on experiments also take a critical perspective. However, these criticisms are motivated not by the desire to dissuade researchers from using experiments; rather, they present conceptual and practical challenges which must be borne in mind. It is essential that heterodox economists are methodologically aware as well as technically sound.

The chapter proceeds as follows. Section 8.2 discusses the potential for heterodox economists to use experimental methods. Then section 8.3 moves on to the most basic form of experiment and some of its pros and cons. Section 8.4 addresses some key practical challenges of experimentation. Section 8.5 partly addresses these by examining alternative experimental designs. Section 8.6 considers some of the techniques of data analysis employed in experimental work. Section 8.7 draws conclusions.

## 8.2  'HETERODOX ECONOMICS' AND EXPERIMENTS

Given the nature of this *Handbook*, it is inevitable to ask whether or not experimental methods are, or could be, made use of by 'heterodox economics'. The definition of 'heterodox' is controversial, and I define it as multidimensional, including methodology (including ontology and epistemology), theory, and areas of interest and application. Overall, economists who could be regarded as 'heterodox' have typically not engaged in experimental work. However, it is easy to see how experimental methods could be, and indeed have been, applied to areas of actual or potential interest to heterodox economists. Indeed, Chapter 27 of this *Handbook* provides one example from urban and regional economics.

Herbert Gintis is another exception, with his work on rationality, cooperation, and evolutionary game theory, and through his editorship of the *Journal of Economic Behavior and Organisation* (JEBO). However, this very line of work has led some to question whether Gintis is indeed still heterodox. On a related theme, the experimental work of behavioral economists could be considered heterodox, given that it often raises serious questions about fundamental tenets of mainstream theory, such as individualism, rationality, and expected utility theory (Loewenstein 1999). Recent experimental work suggests consumer choice is based on networks and not on product attributes (see Salganik et al. 2006). Nonetheless, heterodox authors have criticized modern behavioral economics as too conservative and ceding too much ground to mainstream theory (Sent 2004). Similarly, while studies of labor such as those discussed by Bandiera et al. (2011) did reach the conclusion that social connections can drive behavior in the workplace, they were also framed in terms of incentives, preferences, and optimization, and did not discuss work conditions.

Heterodox economists have a long tradition in development studies, albeit recently an increasingly mainstream area. There is strong evidence of experimental work being done in this subdiscipline. Feminist economists could easily deploy experimental methods to explore the role of gender in various contexts, and in particular to explore the effects on gender relations from possible interventions in real situations. Barr (2003; also Barr et al. 2013) has applied experimental methods to development and gender issues in her work: she conducted field experiments to investigate sources of cooperation in game playing in Zimbabwean villages.

On a different theme, there is a considerable literature in human resource management and other business disciplines applying experimental methods to workplaces. Bertrand and Mullainathan (2004) conducted experimental studies on labor market discrimination. One can imagine how a heterodox labor economist might deploy experimental methods to examine workplace relations, and explore the impacts of workplace design on productivity, job quality, and the like. Mayo's famous (1933) studies at Hawthorne examined the role of non-monetary rewards to workers. Experimental designs can be set up to explore concrete power relations: indeed the classic social psychological work of Milgram (1963) explored power, authority, and responsibility.

As a final example, there is an emerging strand of 'political economy' experiments (see Morton 2014). This work deploys both laboratory and field experiments to investigate issues such as voting, cooperation, and political persuasion, including corruption. The term 'political economy' must come with a warning for heterodox economists, since the term has taken on a range of meanings recently, many of which deviate from the heterodox definition of an economics that is inherently political. Nonetheless, political behavior is an area of interest to heterodox economists and may be a place of potential contribution for them.

## 8.3 EXPERIMENTS: THE BASICS

Perhaps the first psychological experiment was conducted by an Ancient Egyptian ruler, who tested the theory that children who grew up without exposure to language would naturally speak Egyptian (Hunt 1993). Although apparently esoteric, this example demonstrates several established principles of experiment: a deliberate attempt to manipulate a 'natural' situation in order to assess its effects, with a deliberate contrast being in place. Arguably a considerable degree of scientific work deploys the same 'logic of comparison' (Bryman and Bell 2007, p. 54). Indeed, Harrison and List (2004, p. 1009) argue that '[e]very empirical researcher who behaves as if an exogenous variable varies independently of an error term effectively views their data as coming from an experiment'. They add that experiments are attractive because they allow the scientist to construct a counterfactual, which then allows them to conduct causal analysis.

It is now appropriate to start sketching out the essence of experimental design, via the pure experimental design; then address some of the issues with that, and some of the responses offered by experimenters.

**The Pure Experiment**

First it is essential to examine the 'pure' experiment. It is worth doing so because the influence of its governing logic is very clear in later variants of experiments, and because it is 'often used as a yardstick against which non-experimental research is judged' (Bryman and Bell 2007, p. 44).

The key elements of the pure experiment are: control, intervention, measure effects, attempt to generalize. The first three of these steps are represented well via the simple OXO formula (see Figure 8.1). Here two groups are created (preferably engaged in nominally the same activity): an experimental group and a control group. Ideally, the two groups are identical in terms of key characteristics: their members are 'matched pairs'. In a pure experiment, the scientist selects members randomly. The scientist then places these groups in a controlled environment amenable to intervention. Hence, these are known as randomized controlled trials (RCTs).

An intervention $(X_1)$ is then only applied to an experimental group (Campbell and Stanley 1963). Experiments can take many forms, including laboratory tests of various types. The classic example of this is to give the experimental group a treatment and the control a placebo. In some cases the size of the intervention may also be varied across the experimental group (Morrison 2009). So, a group of people may take different strength variants of a medicine, to check how much is needed to cure the particular illness. In economic research, these experiments often take the form of a game played. The standard players of the game tend to be university students.

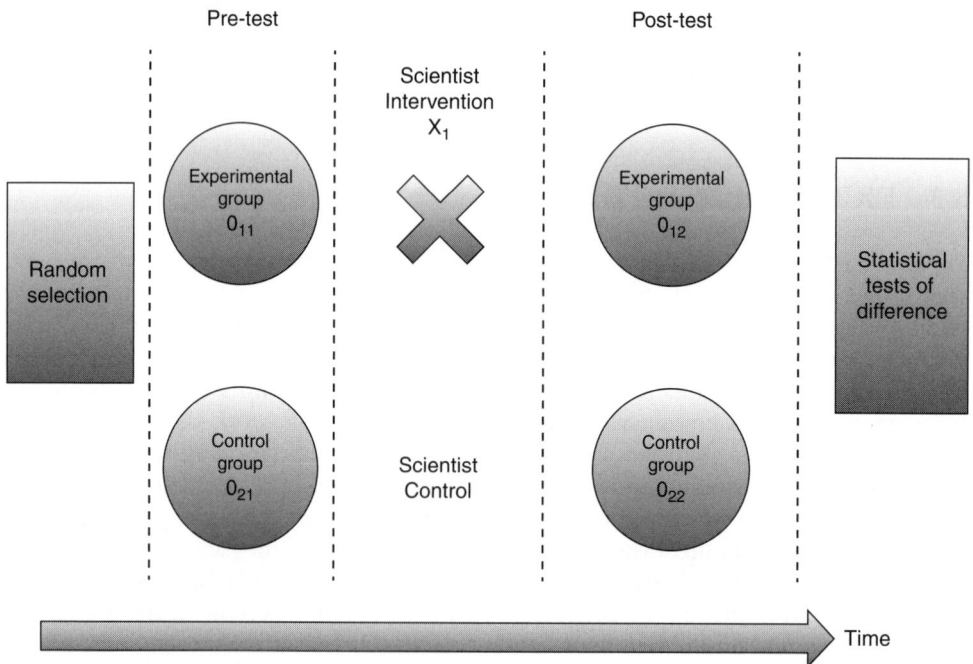

*Figure 8.1   The experimental scenario*

The groups are measured before ($0_{i1}$) and after ($0_{i2}$) the intervention ($X_1$). The measurement tool chosen varies with the goals of researchers and their predispositions to particular data types. In clinical research, typically health outcomes are measured. In economics research, various outcome measures have been used, including labor market, firm, and educational performance. In theory, measurement could mean assessment or evaluation that would admit qualitative data. However, typically, measurement is quantitative, which is claimed to afford greater accuracy and precision. Further, it renders the measurement of the effects of the intervention amenable to statistical analysis. Whatever measure is used, statistical tests are often employed to assess difference. These issues are discussed in greater detail later; however typically t-tests assess simple difference between $0_{12}$ and $0_{22}$. Assuming no systematic differences between the groups beforehand, then $0_{11} = 0_{21}$. Or if this is not the case, then the test measures whether $(0_{12} - 0_{11}) = (0_{22} - 0_{21})$. If not, the groups are different. In other cases, regression analysis is used in which test scores are the dependent variable and the intervention (or absence of) is an independent variable. Researchers might infer causality from these tests.

Pure experiments usually take place in a 'laboratory' environment. A laboratory is not necessarily a clinical or sealed environment as it would be in, say, medical research; however it might be an austere or simple setting, to minimize distractions for participants. Because the scientist has created a controlled environment, any such difference between the two groups (post-intervention) is directly attributable to the intervention. If random sampling has taken place, this causal inference is often extended to the population. Such claims are stronger when supported by meta-analysis, and by replication (Pawson and Tilley 1997).

**Benefits of Pure Experiments**

Pure experiments have several claimed benefits. Given the current emphasis on RCTs in various areas of policy, often under the flag of evidence-based policy, experimental work is likely to gain influence over decision-makers and therefore affect policy. Oakley (2007) claims that, in comparison to qualitative and ethnographic methods based on personal judgment and judgment of the researcher, experimental methods are unbiased, and transparent: those affected by the research (principally students and parents) can observe its processes.

Furthermore, experiments are appealing because they are familiar. They embody the pervasive logic of contrast. Crucially, experiments also reflect prevailing characteristics in economics. Proponents of statistical analysis advocate experiments because they appear to provide robust quantitative data amenable to analysis by sophisticated statistical techniques. Also, regression equations are compared to experiments: the effect of each cause is measured assuming others are constant; and the equation error term is held to be analogous to closing the laboratory door.

Principally, experiments represent the 'scientific method'. Experiments are claimed to be replicable (and thus verifiable), systematic, and by their nature, likely to generate reliability and validity. Reliability is where the results are repeatable and measures and concepts are consistent. As Bryman and Bell (2007, p. 43) note, these concepts of validity are challenged by qualitative researchers. However, they also note that Lincoln and Guba (1985) outline concepts such as credibility that echo the validity concepts.

There are three commonly held types of validity: internal, external, and ecological. Internal validity is when the posited causal relation makes sense or holds such that the researcher is sure they are connecting the correct things. External validity is the case in which results can be generalized, if we are aiming to achieve that (see Chapter 2 in this *Handbook* for a counter-argument). The key to achieving this is to get representative samples from the population. Ecological validity is when scientific findings are applicable to everyday situations: thus it can be problematic if the experiment is or feels unnatural to the participant (see 'Artificiality' in section 8.4, below). These three criteria are useful in the assessment of experiments.

The three types of validity can interact and, in many cases, trade off against each other. For example, the pure experiment is excellent at achieving internal validity because in it, the scientist creates a controlled environment in which nothing but their intervention changes and therefore any changes in outcome are due to that. Further, if the experiment involves effective randomization, the results ought not be sample-specific and hence are generalizable to the population (external validity). However, in creating a controlled environment, it might be that the results apply only to those conditions, and not elsewhere: ecological validity is reduced. This fact is clear in clinical research, in which laboratory work is merely one stage in the process and field tests are crucial. On the other hand, if in order to increase ecological validity the experiment is designed to reflect more closely the real world, it might be that control is lost, thereby reducing internal validity.

This brief discussion illustrates very well some of the challenges faced by experimenters, most of which they know. It is appropriate now to examine some of the challenges presented by pure experiments. This is useful partly because it helps to explain the variety in experimental design.

**Some Key Heterodox Objections to Experiments**

So far I have stressed the positives of experimental design. However, this is a handbook of heterodox research methods: part of that is to examine extant methods from heterodox perspectives. The objective is not to dissuade a potential experimenter from taking the plunge; rather it is to increase awareness of some of the limitations on the design and use of experiments. It is up to the researcher to decide whether these identified flaws are fatal. It is in this spirit that I note some fundamental heterodox objections to experiments. Space deters a lengthier account. Readers may consult Siakantaris (2000) and Mearman (2013) for fuller treatments. Within this *Handbook*, parallel arguments are made in Chapter 2 (grounded theory) and about econometrics (Chapters 9–11).

**Do not place all eggs in the experimental basket**
It is an obvious point, but often forgotten, that no method can ever hope to explain all, and that other methods and data will be necessary. As is evident, experimental methods may only be suitable to analyze certain types of situation, at specific times and places, and to ask specific types of questions. This point is particularly relevant to experimental data analysis (see section 8.6, below). Mixing data types and methods is therefore advisable. Overall, the injunction to all researchers is: do not claim too much.

Unfortunately, as some critics point out, there is a tendency, for example within evidence-based policy approaches, to regard experiments as inherently superior and their results as universally applicable. This may also lead to theories which are explanatorily empty. For Pawson and Tilley (1997, p. xv), 'experimentalists have pursued too single-mindedly the question of whether a program works at the expense of knowing why it works'.

### Reality bites

Experiments make ontological presuppositions that limit their epistemological purchase (see above point). Some contexts may simply be too complex in which to design a robust experiment: interventions take too long, or variably long, to have discernible effects, if at all. Experiments may try to deal with this complexity, but as discussed below ('Artificiality' in section 8.4), may have to resort to highly artificial designs, which may not generate knowledge applicable outside the experiment. For example, experiments often need to design out some of the most important determinants of the success of an intervention (Pawson and Tilley 1997, p. 36; Morrison 2009, pp. 154–5). If experiments are conducted in these circumstances, it may be that their findings have little weight. The researcher must be aware of these limitations.

## 8.4   KEY PRACTICAL CHALLENGES OF EXPERIMENTAL DESIGN

This section discusses three sets of specific common, practical challenges to effective experimentation. It is essential that researchers consider these and take a coherent position on them within their study.

### Logistical Challenges

#### Creating groups

Assume we do wish to carry out a pure experiment as described above. There are many logistical challenges to doing so. For example, setting up a control group may be difficult, for a number of reasons. For example, ethically, a firm may not permit two groups of its workers being treated differently. The firm's objection would rule out a typical control group study. In this case, it is necessary to carry out an experiment of a different type, perhaps one as simple as a single-group study where the effect of $X_1$ is considered, and perhaps $(0_{12} - 0_{11})$ is measured, but without being able to calculate whether $(0_{12} - 0_{11}) = (0_{22} - 0_{21})$. In a key way, then, this would be no longer an experiment at all. However, it may be all that is possible, and would generate useful data.

Let us now assume that we attempt to set up a matched-pairs pure experiment. Recall that to ensure that any post-test difference is attributable to the intervention $X_1$, ideally the control and experimental groups would be identical. Hence the subjects within them should be matched. For a pair to be matched does not mean they are identical in every way; this is not even possible for monozygotic twins. Instead we say the pairs are the same in terms of relevant background factors that affect the individuals' response to the intervention. In educational research, this might include a measure of ability, but also past performance, environment, and family attributes. These data could be used to estimate 'control' variables in statistical analysis. Sometimes this can only be done after selection is done. In either case, it would require lengthy survey work (see Chapter 6 in this *Handbook*).

### Preventing contamination

Experiments in economics almost invariably involve humans, which in itself generates logistical challenges. Recall that in the pure experiment, the two groups are strictly sepa-rate, as would be two plants in separate bell jars. Separation requires that members of the control and experimental groups do not communicate. If they did, there could be several consequences. For example, those in the experimental group could learn more about what the experiment is about. This could compromise the research. If the experimental group is being offered an advantageous treatment, members of the control group, even if allocated there randomly, could object and start to complain, change their behavior, or undermine the experiment in other ways.

Unfortunately, as Bandiera et al. (2011) note, it is more or less impossible to prevent communication between groups, even when the rules of the experiment preclude it. This is even clearer as social media increases our ability to communicate across physical boundaries. Thus it would seem that contamination is almost inevitable, undermining the notions that: (1) the control is not affected by the intervention; and (2) changes in the experimental group are only caused by the intervention. In this circumstance the researcher must take reasonable steps to minimize communication, for example by making experimental rules clear and persuading participants (perhaps with monetary incentives) that they should follow them.

### Reactive effects

The human element also enters in the ways participants respond to the experiment itself. There are two related effects here: experimenter effects and reactive effects. The first is that subjects respond highly specifically to the experimenter. This again undermines the validity of the experimental results. It is possible that the presence of a control group who also deal with the experimenter means that we can still assess differences between the groups; however, the size of response may depend greatly on that individual, render-ing the results unique. It is well established that experimenter effects may vary between men and women: for instance through social desirability bias, or fear, or perceived power relations, or disrespect towards a researcher according to gender; or one gender may react differently to the other in specific contexts (Eagly and Crowley 1986). Deploying a varied team of researchers can help to reduce or at least spread the risks of experimenter effects.

Reactive effects are well known in research methods thanks principally to the Hawthorne effect: that is, people may change their behavior in response to being observed. While there is dispute as to whether the Hawthorne effect occurs, it is some-thing of which experimenters are aware. It raises the question of whether the researcher declares the true purpose of the experiment, or even makes plain that an experiment is occurring at all. This can result in a form of deception. Milgram's (1974) portrayal of an experiment about authority and responsibility as being about feedback and learning is a classic example of deception. However, it generates ethical concerns about informed consent. An alternative is to make it unavoidable for participants to be involved, by simply experimenting on them in their normal lives, perhaps by changing governmental practices (what Harrison and List 2004 call social experiments). Again, though, this raises the ethical concern that experimental subjects are compelled to be so.

**Making the experiment 'doable'**

A final logistical difficulty regards the simple mechanics of the experiment itself. If the task, game, or scenario set is too simple or too complex, if it makes little sense to participants, if it is communicated in a way which makes it hard to follow, or dissuades participation, then either there will be flaws in the data, or none will be collected. These problems will generate further problems of what Bryman and Bell (2007) call measurement validity. This would threaten the internal validity of the experiment. However, there are other problems that affect external and ecological validity of experiments. One regards selection and another is the problem of artificiality.

**Selection**

Selection issues have already been mentioned. The pure experiment assumes that group memberships are random and therefore that any differences between groups are random, and this is crucial in allowing inferences from the experimental results to the population. If the selection process does not conform to the ideal, however, this weakens the power of the results. As we have already seen, it may be that it is not possible to set up a control group, or matched pairs. Further, it may be impossible to conduct randomization. This opens up the possibility of bias. Although statistical analysis can attempt to take account of such biases, it would be better to avoid them and it is certainly important to know their sources. There are several reasons why the experimental groups may not have the right properties to allow external validity. This is a critical problem if one's intention to generalize beyond the experiment.

**Volunteer effects**

A common feature of experiments is that participants are usually volunteers. This is desirable ethically. Nonetheless, this voluntarism has implications. For instance, certain types of people will opt in to the experimental group. For example, a researcher may wish to test an educational innovation; however, some volunteers might inherently favor innovative curricula and opt to volunteer, hence the observed outcomes from those courses reflect the pre-existing dispositions of volunteers rather than any effect of the innovation. Furthermore, as Bohm (1972) argues, if the participants do not care about the experimental task and do not engage with it, the experimental results will mean little. To counteract these 'volunteer effects', the experimenter may split up the volunteers into an experimental and a control group (Pawson and Tilley 1997). However, people who had signed up for a particular type of action may recognize they were not experiencing it, and the experiment would break down.

**Standard subjects**

Another issue with selection is the use of what Harrison and List (2004) call standard subjects. These are typically university students. This is a cheap and convenient way to conduct experiments. However, as Harrison and List (2004, p. 1018) note, university students may exhibit little socio-demographic variety, and this reduces the external (or ecological) validity. In other words, the results may only apply to university students. Harrison and List argue that this lack of variety may not matter: rather, the crucial question is whether their behavioral responses are representative. But then the question to them is: how would one know? The solution would be to engage in extensive survey work.

There are reasons to doubt that these standard subjects respond in a representative way. For example, in economics experiments, a typical subject is an economics student. Are these students, or their behavioral responses, typical? Tomer (2001) estimates that while some people behave like *Homo economicus*, they are relatively few and only at a specific point in their lives. Incidentally that point would coincide with being a university student. Further, there is evidence to suggest that economics majors are inculcated with notions of rational behavior and act untypically even for university students. The recommended solution here is simply to vary the sample, but that increases the complexity and risk of the experiment in other dimensions.

**Artificiality**

The point immediately above suggests problems in translating experimental results to the outside world. These concerns hint at the broad issue of artificiality. Aronson and Carlsmith (1968) argue that though experiments lack 'mundane realism', they do or can have 'experimental realism', in which the subject is engaged in the experiment and takes it seriously. This is a crucial area (see Bardsley 2005) because it suggests a trade-off between internal and external (and ecological) validity that may be difficult to avoid. It is also significant for heterodox economists who are typically concerned with realisticness. These are important issues: if either the subject is not engaged with the experiment, or it is unrealistic, the results lose meaning.

**Sterile environments**

Recall that the pure experiment is based on the premise that the scientist conducts the experiment in a controlled environment whereby only one factor is varied and any changes in the subject are attributable to that subject. In clinical trials there is a genuine fear of contamination, that is, the intrusion of unwanted matter, which could materially affect the experimental process. For example, the effect of heat on water is distorted by the presence of salt. Early experiments on humans, for instance in social psychology, sometimes took this analogy as far as possible, constructing strictly controlled neutral experimental environments, such as empty white rooms. This was to ensure that factors such as light levels, other visual stimuli, heat, moisture, and the like did not affect the subject. These considerations are still relevant in laboratory tests using bio-sensory equipment, for example. It could be that the experimental results reflect the impact of these other factors, rather than, or as well as, the experimental intervention.

**Interaction of treatment and setting**

However, gradually, it was felt that these unnatural environments might well generate unnatural results. We have seen a variant of this in the earlier discussion of experimenter and reactive effects. So, although the sterile lab can produce results that appear high in internal validity, Cook and Campbell (1979) recognized the interaction of setting and treatment as a threat to external validity. One response to this concern has been to shift experiments into the 'field'. That is to say, to conduct experiments in more natural settings (field experiments), or to study events which are happening anyway (natural experiments).

Both field and natural experiments are discussed below. However, a few points are worth making about them now. Bryman and Bell (2007) hold that these have greater ecological validity than sterile lab experiments. However, they may not be immune to artificiality: sometimes they ask participants to engage in tasks that are not normal to them. For instance, it would be standard practice in some experiments to conduct 'double-blind' trials. However, such a practice might make little sense in a small community. Or at least researchers need to be careful to justify the nature of the task set in the experiments as having verisimilitude (see Bryman and Bell 2007, p. 46). Barr (2003) and Barr et al. (2013), for example, extensively argue that their constructed games have sufficient verisimilitude.

### Getting stakes right

One final issue of artificiality concerns stakes. It is quite common for laboratory experiments in economics to involve university students playing games, with small cash amounts as prizes. The vast literature on dictator and ultimatum games contains many such studies. Often the games demand no entry fee, and the money being played for is supplied by the 'house'. This is clearly problematic. Relatively rich people playing games for small stakes may say little about general behavior (see Camerer and Hogarth 1999 for literature on stakes). Consequently, Slonim and Roth (1998) conducted games in Slovakia in order to make the stakes higher and the games more realistic. There has also been a move towards carrying out field experiments in developing countries. Bandiera et al. (2011) also argue that field experiments with firms work better in Latin America or South Asia, as it is easier to make large differences to their inputs (which is the favored intervention).

## 8.5   ALTERNATIVE EXPERIMENTAL DESIGNS

It is possible to read the previous section as a devastating critique of experimentalism. However, to reiterate: good experimenters know the challenges to doing (even anything approaching) gold standard pure experiments. An indicator that the above problems are recognized is in the development of alternative experimental designs, some of which have already been discussed. Below is a brief list of these alternatives. Field experiments and natural experiments will be discussed in more depth shortly.

### A Taxonomy of Alternative Designs

As shorthand, I shall use the term 'quasi-experiments' to cover the group of alternative experimental designs. These have some but not all of the characteristics of pure experiments. A taxonomy of these designs is shown in Table 8.1.

This list is not intended to be exhaustive, nor are the categories exclusive. However, it ought to give the reader a sense of the range of possible designs. The table also shows possible effects on types of validity.

It is reasonable to group the first four together, because they could all still essentially

*Table 8.1*   *Alternative experimental designs and effects on internal ( $V_1$ ), external ( $V_2$ ), and ecological ( $V_3$ ) validity*

| Experimental design | Description | Effects on validity |
| --- | --- | --- |
| (1) Laboratory experiments with non-standard subjects | Pure experiments not conducted on students (Harrison and List 2004 call these 'artefactual field experiments') | $V_2$ and $V_3$ may increase: greater variety; $V_1$ may fall: subjects not enculturated |
| (2) Non-matched or non-equivalent pairs design | Experiments in which there is a control group with pairs in it, but where these are not strictly matched | $V_2$ may fall, because bias more likely |
| (3) Non-randomized design | Pure experiments but without random selection of participants | $V_2$ may fall, because bias more likely |
| (4) Single-group design | In which no control group is set up, perhaps for logistical reasons | $V_1$ falls without a control group; $V_2$ falls, because of bias |
| (5) Field experiments | Experiments which can involve controls and randomization but occur in natural (that is, already existing) settings | $V_1$ falls because of reduced control; $V_2$ and $V_3$ may increase with realistic setting |
| (6) Natural experiments (including social experiments: Harrison and List) | Experiments in natural settings, in which the change is not generated by the scientist, but instead simply occurs, or is part of a policy or implementation change | $V_1$ neutral: no control, but responses may be more authentic; $V_2$ and $V_3$ may increase with realistic setting |
| (7) Natural natural experiments | Natural experiments in which the control variables are themselves 'natural', such as in monozygotic twin studies | $V_1$ neutral: no control, but responses may be more authentic; $V_2$ and $V_3$ may increase with realistic setting |

be laboratory designs. However, it is clear that they are different. For instance, (1) could be a pure experiment, and indeed have greater external and ecological validity than those, because of the wider variety in the sample. However, one advantage of using students is that they are most likely more familiar than non-standard subjects with the academic environment; and may have been enculturated in experimental method, and understand the rules. So internal validity may fall.

Whereas (1) may emerge as an attempt to improve on the pure experiment, (2)–(4) are probably responses to the practical impossibility of either setting up randomization, matching, or even a control group. As already mentioned, in experiments in firms, the host organization may be unwilling to allow the creation of control groups. Another barrier is the logistical difficulty discussed earlier of collecting extensive data on all experimental and control group members, which would preclude even *ex post* matching. An extra concern with *ex post* matching is that these studies often rely on extensive survey data (see Mel et al. 2008; Bandiera et al. 2011, p. 72), which have flaws in terms of response rates and biases. In all of these instances, clearly there may be selection bias in the data. In these cases the researcher would fall more heavily back on econometric techniques.

Non-equivalent pairs designs, (2), are quite common in educational studies, and in some literature on development (see, for example, Barr 2003 and papers cited within).

In the case of (4), single-group designs, it may be simply impossible to create parallel sets of subjects. For instance, in economics education research, a tutor may wish to assess the effectiveness of an innovation but only has access to one group at any one time. They might run studies on consecutive groups, perhaps with one group receiving the teaching innovation and the other not. This type of study is often all that is possible and can be instructive. However, it is undermined by temporal complication – that is, teaching the groups at different time admits a large set of historically specific contextual factors – and also ethical considerations of relatively (dis)advantaging one group (Sikes 2004, p. 25). Experimenters are aware of these problems, without clear resolution.

## Field Experiments

Field experiments are scientific experimental methods used to identify 'causal treatment effects in the field or with field subjects' (Barankay et al. 2013, p. 1). Harrison and List (2004) provide a thorough overview of field experiments (see also Barankay et al. 2013). Bandiera et al. (2011) survey field experiments on firms. There is some variety within this category, and again, distinctions between types ought not be drawn too strictly. Field experiments can be laboratory experiments run in the field (Barr et al. 2013). Or they can be 'natural field experiments', in which the participants do not know an experiment is occurring (Shearer 2004). Carpenter et al. (2008) claim to run a 'natural field experiment' because they construct a field experiment as part of the cycle of fundraising in subject hospitals.

Field experiments have been applied to a variety of research areas. Many of these appear mainstream, for example, firms' choices and constraints (Bandiera et al. 2011), consumer choice (Levitt and List 2009), and auctions (Carpenter et al. 2008). However, they have heterodox potential: for example, Bandiera et al. (2011) report a literature on monetary incentives and the social organization of the workplace. In a thoroughly heterodox work, paired-audit (matched pairs) experiments explore labor market discrimination (Riach and Rich 2002).

### Benefits and costs of field experiments

Proponents of field experiments claim a number of significant benefits for them. Some regard field experiments as superior to those held in laboratories. Their greater realism (Barr 2003) may increase external validity, perhaps without reducing internal validity (Harrison and List 2004, p. 1033), and overall better results (Carpenter et al. 2008). This occurs because, authors claim, things that happen in the field would not have happened in the lab. This supports the view that the physical environment in which the experiment takes place does matter, and that people change their environment as well as being constrained by it. Moreover, field experiments address other problems of laboratory design: the subject may not know it is an experiment, and yet there is no deception involved. Thus reactive effects are reduced, perhaps removed, and some of the ethical issues are resolved. Typically field experiments involve non-standard subjects (that is, not students). They also work best when they use physical commodities or other real goods rather than abstract ones.

Despite these advantages, as field experimenters know, there are also several challenges to running them successfully. One issue for economists is that they are not typically trained in experimental methods. This presents problems in the laboratory: a person trained in econometrics usually does not need to deal with live humans in their data collection or analysis. However, field experiments necessarily involve the soft skills that, evidence suggests, economists often lack (O'Doherty et al. 2007). To run field experiments, researchers need to be able to negotiate, often between groups. Again, these are skills not typically taught or even inculcated in economics training programs.

**Internal validity in field experiments**
There are also significant challenges in achieving internal validity in field experiments. Field experiments do not claim that they have as much control over the experimental process as in laboratories; but they assume or seek to 'achieve *sufficient* control to make the basic causal inference secure' (Pawson and Tilley 1997, p. 6). However, as discussed above ('Contamination'), in community settings potential contamination between subject and control people is high, despite rules laid out by experimenters.

There are also considerable difficulties in matching pairs in field experiments, although some researchers have tried to do this. Often this involves the reliance on *ex post* econometric analysis aimed at reducing selection bias. However, this work is itself hampered by difficulties in achieving high enough sample sizes. Field experiments may struggle to get enough participants to satisfy the demands of statistical methods. Barr (2003) used 24 Zimbabwean villages, but this only generated 141 pairs. This is more than enough to run a simple statistical test; however, as more control variables and more experimental categories are drawn up, the required sample size increases. This effect either reduces the power of statistical tests done, or may dissuade the researcher from doing some sorts of analysis. These are problems the researcher may simply have to live with; and complement their experimental findings with others.

**Ecological validity in field experiments**
Overall, field experiments have apparent clear advantages over laboratory settings in terms of reducing artificiality and increasing realisticness. However, also there are inevitable trade-offs, such as a loss of control, and the inability to construct a controlled environment. Selection issues may also be greater, generating considerable challenges for researchers in the process of recruiting participants. There are several reasons therefore to be cautious with the results from field experiments.

Once again there is a temptation to simply avoid or reject the possibility of field experiments. An alternative strategy is to adopt mixed methods. Indeed, field experimenters often do this. Barankay et al. (2013) identify this as a clear trend in field trials. Several experiments use accompanying surveys. Barr et al. (2013) did 'post-play' interviews with participants. Bandiera et al. (2011) advocate mixing evidence types, specifically to increase validity (Bandiera et al. 2011, p. 73). A common strategy is to mix field and laboratory data (Harrison and List 2004). This has some resonance with clinical research, in which field testing of medicines will sometimes confirm, and at other times inform, laboratory work.

## Natural Experiments

Natural experiments 'recognize that some event that naturally occurs in the field happens to have some of the characteristics of a field experiment' (Harrison and List 2004, p. 1011). That definition applies well to what they call 'social experiments', which are effectively large-scale field experiments often carried out by government agencies. Some of these experiments are actually intended as such: the government agency is testing its practices, trying out reforms. Natural experiments can look at a temporal contrast (specifically, before and after the policy change); but they work best when there is a change made in one area or applied to one group of people, which does not apply to a similar area or group elsewhere (Ferber and Hirsch 1982). Card and Krueger's (1994) study of minimum wages acts as a good example here: they compared the effect of the minimum wage in New Jersey with outcomes in neighboring (and in many ways similar) Pennsylvania.

In other cases, researchers are able to enter into a natural setting and introduce a change themselves, and evaluate the effects. Camerer (1998) influenced betting markets by making large-scale bets (or not) and observing their effects. In this case the intervention is artificial, in that it was done for an experimental purpose; but the experiment was otherwise natural. The participants in the experiment did not know what was going on, but arguably this is ethical because it mimicked behavior in betting markets. Harrison and List (2004, p. 1041, n. 65) offer numerous examples of natural experiments in economics. These include those occurring in labor markets (Roth 1991), with some focus on returns to schooling (Behrman et al. 1994), and time use (Deacon and Sonstelie 1985). Metrick (1995) is one of several studies of behavior on TV game shows (in this case, the US show *Jeopardy!*). There are several other studies of this type (see Harrison and List 2004, n. 66). Recently there has been some interest in the UK show *Deal or No Deal*, a game based around expected value theory and attitudes to risk. These shows involve an experimental set-up but the scientist is either involved in game design or is merely another observer.

### Benefits of natural experiments
These natural experiments have several advantages over most other field experiments. As they are natural, often everyday situations, one is more likely to witness genuine responses without worrying about the effect of the setting. Obviously this is truer for some cases – interventions by governments in their normal processes are utterly realistic – whereas there are of course elements of strangeness and artificiality about game show settings. Again, though, we can be fairly confident of experimental realism in these shows. Another advantage of natural experiments is that they should reduce selection effects because there is no initial selection moment (Harrison and List 2004, p. 1038). In a traditional experiment on a specific product market, for example, participants might be selected from those who had already selected to be in that market. In a natural experiment, the scientist's selection is removed.

### Natural natural experiments
Another frequent feature of natural experiments is that they deploy naturally occurring features of the environment or subjects to mimic a control group or act as control variables. In some cases, so-called 'natural natural experiments' (see Rosenzweig and Wolpin

2000), these naturally occurring features are indeed natural – drawn from nature. A classic example is the use of monozygotic twins to assess the effects of schooling. In this sense we have merely traveled back to our Ancient Egyptian ruler. However, such studies are seen as offering several advantages. Rosenzweig and Wolpin focus on the potential role of these natural factors as robust instrumental variables (IVs) in estimations of the effect of interventions.

Overall, as with field experiments, natural experiments of the three types discussed here have pros and cons. They clearly seem to have a greater degree of realisticness than other designs: both in terms of having engaged subjects (as they are already engaged) and in mimicking reality (as they occur in 'the wild'). They also tend to occur on a large scale and/ or have large data sets that allow their analysis (for example, data on internet usage). They also would appear to have ethical advantages, in that they tend to be less invasive than laboratory or field experiments. Twins, for example, will act in the world whether or not they are unwittingly being observed. Also, given that the data used are often gathered anyway, there is no extra data collection to consider. However, it should be noted that, particularly compared with the pure experiment, natural experiments typically afford the researcher less control. Thus, though ecological validity is greatly increased, internal validity may fall.

Overall, some clear guidelines are available to researchers aiming to deploy experimental method, but informed by heterodox methodology. Box 8.1 shows a checklist

---

BOX 8.1   TOP TIPS FOR EXPERIMENTERS

**Goals of the experiment**
The researcher has a clear rationale for using experiments
The object is suitable for experimental analysis
The question being asked is clear
The researcher has a plausible causal model
The researcher is not claiming too much

**Design of the experiment**
A control group can be established
Selection procedures are robust
The experiment has clear start and end points
The experimental task is easy enough to understand
The experiment is realistic enough to engage
Any stakes are high enough to have effects
Ethical approval has been granted: consent, withdrawal clear, harm avoided
Potential contamination been minimized
Experimenter effects are minimized
The setting is realistic

**Data collection and analysis**
Pre-test data is collected
Post-test data analysis is clearly planned
The experiment is being observed, to aid qualitative assessment
The researcher will be able to explain why the experiment might not have worked
Detailed information on the membership of the groups is available or can be collected
Data intended for statistical analysis has the correct properties, and is extensive enough for the type of analysis planned

for researchers. Ideally the researcher would say 'yes' to all of these points. Where they cannot, this is not decisive; rather it is an opportunity for the researcher to reflect and perhaps amend their research design.

## 8.6   EXPERIMENTAL DATA ANALYSIS

I have already hinted at some of the data analysis techniques favored in experimental research. This section deals briefly with some of the principal ones. As we can see, experimental data analysis relies mainly on standard techniques, such as ordinary least squares (OLS) regression. As many of these are discussed elsewhere in this book (Chapters 9–11), I shall not examine them in detail.

Note also that because of the nature of experiments, it is important to observe carefully what happens in the experiment, collect qualitative data on that, and then subject that to qualitative analysis. This is crucial if the experiment goes 'wrong', that is, does not produce clear results: the researcher needs to be able to explain this, often in a way which provides insight into the situation under study. Even if the experiment 'works', we must bear in mind the criticism that it might generate a 'black box' outcome, lacking a real explanation. Space precludes a discussion of qualitative data analysis here. Readers should consult Chapters 4, 5, 7, 12, and 15 of this *Handbook*, as well as dedicated texts such as Flick (2006).

### Descriptive Statistics

Given the way experiments work, most of the analysis techniques employed there concern tests of difference between experimental and control groups. However, it is important to note the potentially powerful role of descriptive statistics in experimental research. As has been noted several times, a crucial question in experiments is the actual composition of the groups. It is assumed that random selection of participants will generate good, usable groups. However, of course, randomization is mainly designed to remove inherent selection bias, and it is possible that the selected groups will exhibit odd traits. So it is always important to examine the groups carefully, as they are manifest.

Related to this, although experimental method seems to focus on average differences, or differences between group averages, it is also the case that an intervention may affect some group members differently to others. This is another reason to conduct thorough descriptive analysis of the group after the intervention. Thus, simple measures of location and dispersion can be highly valuable, as can various forms of associational analysis such as cross-tabulations, to examine relationships between variables within groups (and between them).

Relationships between group members, including the formation of subgroups within groups, can be assessed via cluster analysis (see Chapter 9 in this *Handbook*). By clustering of key biographical variables such as age, socio-economic status, organizational status, or other aspects of prior experience, it may be that groups emerge that illuminate why an intervention seems effective or not. This type of analysis is useful in itself, but particularly so when one considers criticisms of experimental work that it downplays heterogeneity or seeks universal findings.

**Simple Tests of Difference**

If we return to the presentation of pure experiment (see section 8.3, above), we can see several clear hints at data analysis. At the basic level, the pure experiment takes two groups, which are ideally identical, and introduces an intervention to one but not the other, and then afterwards measures the groups, according to some dimension(s). Any difference between the groups could be ascribed to the intervention. This was described above as a simple difference between $0_{12}$ and $0_{22}$. Here $0_{12}$ and $0_{22}$ are group means. Assuming no systematic differences between the groups beforehand, then $0_{11} = 0_{21}$. Or if this is not the case, then we are interested in whether $(0_{11} - 0_{12}) = (0_{21} - 0_{22})$.

**The t-test**
So, the mere existence of a difference could be evidence enough. However, with all tests of difference, the researcher must ensure that the difference is not simply due to random variation. Hence some test of statistical significance is typically used. There is some controversy about the emphasis on statistical significance (as opposed to substantive significance) and about the precise critical value used (Ziliak and McCloskey 2008). It is conventional to use the 95 percent level (or p-value of 0.05) as the critical value. Hence a test statistic with p-value $< 0.05$ is deemed to show a statistically significant (non-random) difference between groups. Typically this is done via t-tests. The simplest version of this is where:

$$t = \frac{(0_{12} - 0_{22})}{se_{(012, 022)}} \tag{8.1}$$

where $0_{12}$ and $0_{22}$ are the group means and $se(0_{12}, 0_{22})$ is the standard error of the difference in group means. Where we are not confident that $0_{11} = 0_{21}$, we would adjust the t-test accordingly.

**ANOVA and related tests**
Table 8.2 shows other options, depending on the nature of the experimental design. These options operate on the same basic logic of contrast as does the t-test, and indeed as does the experimental design. The other techniques allow us to extend analysis beyond two groups and to assess more than one dependent variable at a time, neither of which the

*Table 8.2   Statistical tests for experimental data*

|  | Number of dependent variables | |
| --- | --- | --- |
| Number of groups in independent variable | One (univariate) | Two or more (multivariate) |
| Two groups (specialized case) | t-test | Hotelling's $T^2$ |
| Two or more groups (generalized case) | Analysis of variance or covariance (ANOVA or ANCOVA) | M(ultivariate) ANOVA or ANCOVA |

*Source:*   Adapted from Hair et al. (2006, p. 388).

t-test can do. Analysis of variance (ANOVA) and t-tests are often seen in OLS and other regression results, and indeed they can be employed on survey data, for instance; but they have power in themselves. These tests are available in most common packages for data analysis, such as SPSS, Stata, Minitab, and many versions of Excel, some of which are freely available, or as part of standard software packages.

A feature perhaps striking to those most familiar with multiple regression analysis (see Chapter 10 in this *Handbook*) is that the right-hand column deals with multiple dependent variables. It is common to see regression studies that report a set of regressions each of which have different dependent variables. However, these analyses deal with the multiple dependent variables sequentially. The tests above address multiple dependent variables simultaneously.

Since ANCOVA, MANOVA, and MANCOVA are developments of ANOVA, it is sensible to explain the principles of ANOVA (see also Hair et al. 2006, Ch. 6; Field 2000, Ch. 7). As is suggested above, ANOVA tests whether or not three or more group means are the same. Thus, it might be that a multi-site firm introduces a new monitoring system. The firm might introduce it in an informal way at one site, and in a formal way at another site. These would then represent different levels of treatment. Alternatively, they might introduce a monitoring system at one site, but at the other, introduce a new work enrichment program. These would be different treatment types. At a third site, there was no change. Hence in both cases, there are three groups.

ANOVA generates an F-statistic that evaluates overall experimental effect. The F-test is very similar to the t-test in that it calculates the ratio of between-groups variance to within-group variance, the latter being similar to the standard error of the difference in group means in the equation above. Again if the F-statistic exceeds the predetermined critical value, we can say that the experimental intervention has generated differences between groups.

However, even with one control group and two experimental groups, this produces a set of possible differences: for example, there might be no difference between the experimental groups. The F-statistic in ANOVA does not provide information on this. At this point the researcher must undertake planned comparisons or post-hoc tests. The essential difference between these is that the former has clear prior hypotheses to test, whereas the latter does not. Field (2000, Ch. 7) discusses a range of planned contrasts available. It is somewhat doubtful whether post-hoc tests bear enough of the typical intentionality of experimental design. However, post-hoc tests can be thought of as: (1) checking for surprises; and (2) checking for violations of assumptions. Both of these are important rationales for extra tests.

MANOVA (see Hair et al. 2006, Ch. 6; Field 2000, Ch. 10) extends the principles of ANOVA to multiple metric dependent variables. It therefore helps to defend experimental design from the criticism that too often a single composite outcome variable is deployed (for example, the use of a single job satisfaction score to assess all effects of a change in working practices). It is also therefore very useful in quasi-experimental or survey designs. MANOVA is also superior to ANOVA in that it addresses experiment-wide error rate, in the same way as ANOVA supersedes t-tests. Its main advantage is its ability to capture interdependence of different types. This is particularly useful in complex experiments. One example is the repeated measures design (see Field 2000, Ch. 9) in which a respondent provides several measures. For instance, rather than just test a student once, they might be tested a number of times, to assess longer-term effects. Again this is useful as a response to critics of experiments in education. It also allows the researcher to capture diversity within the sample more clearly.

ANOVA and MANOVA do have criticisms, many being associated with their assumptions. In particular, they assume independence among observations. Clearly independence may be problematic over time, partly because of contamination (see above). More fundamentally it might be that group interactions may be crucial in generating the outcome of the intervention. Also, in ANOVA and MANOVA, sample size is not simply a case of overall number of observations, but of the number within each group. So, while 35 observations with one control variable might be sufficient, to add in a second control variable, at least another 20 members of that specific group are necessary for the tests to be powerful. As a general rule, the minimum cell size should be 20 (Hair et al. 2006).

### Regression-Based Analysis

ANOVA has strengths, but is poor at distinguishing between specific differences. Further it merely shows if the variation in the dependent variable(s) can be explained by variation in the independent variable(s). It says little about the source of the unexplained variable(s) or indeed about the nature of the controls being placed on the experiment.

#### Simple linear model

Partly for these reasons, experimental data analysis often involves regression analysis. The regression equation mimics experimental logic: the coefficients represent the effect of the intervention variable on the dependent, independent of other variables. This is in fact an *ex post* imposition of experimental logic on non-experimental data. Nonetheless, the logic of regression is familiar to economists and therefore attractive. It is therefore unsurprising to see regression analysis often in the literature.

As Field (2000) shows, the independent t-test (shown above) can be represented via a general linear model (GLM), thus:

$$Y_i = \beta_0 + \beta_1 Group_i + \varepsilon_i \qquad (8.2)$$

where the variable $Group_i$ is a dummy indicating membership or not of the experimental group $i$. In turn, by adding in another dummy for each additional experimental group (for instance at different levels of treatment) one can represent ANOVA. The GLM combines a variate (linear combination of variables), random component, and a link function, the latter providing 'a theoretical connection between the variate and the random component' (Hair et al. 2006, p. 411). This GLM connects together ANOVA and MANOVA with the regression techniques most often utilized by economists. See Table 8.3 for a summary.

As Table 8.3 suggests, regression analysis may be in a simple linear multiple regression framework (often OLS), or if the dependent variable is limited, via a logistic or logit regression, or some variant of that, such as probit (Carpenter et al. 2008) or tobit. These techniques are common and familiar so they will not be discussed here. However, it is worth mentioning a couple of variants of OLS. For instance Barr et al. (2013, p. 2066) use dyadic regression, in which 'pairs of individuals rather than individuals or households are

*Table 8.3   The GLM and multivariate models*

| Multivariate technique | Dependent variable | Independent variable | Link function | Probability distribution |
|---|---|---|---|---|
| Multiple regression | Metric | Metric | Identity | Normal |
| Logistic regression | Nonmetric | Metric | Logit | Binomial |
| AN(C)OVA/MAN(C)OVA | Metric | Nonmetric | Identity | Normal |

*Source:*   Adapted from Hair et al. (2006, Table 6.2, p. 413).

the unit of analysis'. Thus their dependent variable $m_{ij}$ captures whether or not individual $i$ joins a group with individual $j$.

**Interaction and control**
Another noteworthy aspect of Barr et al.'s (2013) model is the inclusion of interaction effects. These are increasingly common in regression analysis for their claimed property to capture some of the complexity of the relation between determinants. Interaction terms are clearly highly applicable to experimental design as they potentially allow the interaction of treatments, or between treatments and controls, to be captured. In Barr et al. (2013), an interaction term captured the effect of a treatment combined with other relevant characteristics of individuals. These terms are deployed normally within an OLS regression. Simply multiplying the two variables creates an interaction term; the term is then included in the regression as would a typical variable.

This use also highlights the role of control variables in the analysis: these are included as independent variables and are designed to compensate for the fact that there may be imperfections in the sample selection, and that we can identify controls which affect both experimental and control group members. Control variables are essential to the logic of comparison. Overall, then, a typical regression equation might look something like the following:

$$Y_i = \beta_0 + \beta_1 X_1 + \beta_2 X_2 + \beta_3 Z_1 + \beta_4 Z_2 + \varepsilon_i \tag{8.3}$$

where $X_i$ are the treatment variables and $Z_i$ are control variables. Interaction terms might also be included.

**Selection models**
One of the specific issues with experimental designs is selection effects. Hence, there is considerable interest in selection models. The seminal work in this sphere is the Heckman (1979) model (see Puhani 2000). Carpenter et al. (2008) use it in their study of charity auctions, because they recognize that there may be systematic differences between people who submit bids and those who do not. The Heckman model is a two-step approach. In the first stage the researcher models the probability of being a member of a group, for example a worker. Typically this is a probit estimate for each individual. In the second stage, the researcher transforms these predicted individual probabilities and incorporates them as an additional explanatory variable in a new estimation. This is designed to correct for self-selection by incorporating the selection effect directly.

Heckman took this approach as he thought of selection bias as being omitted variable bias.

**Difference-in-difference models**
A final aspect of regression analysis to be discussed briefly is difference-in-differences (DID) models. These are an application of regression techniques to experiments, commonly natural experiments (see Ashenfelter and Card 1985; Card and Krueger 1994; Bandiera et al. 2011, p. 69). This approach is once again rooted in the logic of contrast found in experimental design. The method tries to capture simultaneously, and separate out, differences within subjects (pre- and post-intervention) and differences between subjects (experimental and control group members). Thus, returning to Figure 8.1, the DID estimation attempts to capture the overall effect of the intervention, viz.:

$$\text{Treatment effect} = (0_{12} - 0_{11}) - (0_{22} - 0_{21}) \tag{8.4}$$

where the $0_{ij}$ correspond to Figure 8.1. The two terms on the right-hand side capture the within-groups differences, and the difference between them captures the between-groups differences. The method acknowledges that the overall change in the members associated with $0_{12}$ is a combination of the effect of the intervention and changes that are common to both experimental and control groups. This is necessary because of the inevitability of some influences common to both groups. So in the example from Card and Krueger (1994), some of the differences in employment observed in New Jersey would have been caused by factors that also affected Pennsylvania, which they used as the control, a place where the minimum wage did not rise.

As with all of the empirical methods discussed in this chapter (or indeed this *Handbook*), they are only as good as their assumptions. There has been criticism of DID estimations. For instance, they seem to rely on the presence of a linear common trend. Where this trend is different, or shifts, this may generate errors in the DID estimators. Several critics have made a related criticism that DID estimators perform poorly in the presence of serial correlation (Bertrand et al. 2004). As a result of these criticisms, variants of the DID method have been developed. Difference-in-difference-in-differences (DDD) methods allow for multiple dimensions of controls; for example, as if Card and Krueger (1994) had also been able to construct a control group within New Jersey. Athey and Imbens (2006) have also developed panel data and semi- and non-parametric versions of DID.

This section has briefly considered some of the main specific variants of empirical methods applied to experimental data. It cannot be comprehensive, but it should provide a flavor. In addition, it might also have discussed panel data estimation of experimental data, including fixed and random effects variants (Harrison and List 2004, p. 1020), instrumental variables estimation (Rosenzweig and Wolpin 2000), propensity score matching (Harrison and List 2004, p. 1015), and structural modeling, including DSGE analysis. However, there is no space to do this. Also, given the known issues surrounding the latter two, it is not clear it that would be appropriate.

## 8.7   CONCLUSIONS

This chapter has attempted to provide a flavor, some practical guidance, and some warnings about experimental methods. Colander (2000) identified experimental methods as one of the potential routes down which economics could travel.

To sum up, the main points from this chapter are:

- Experimental methods may have potential for heterodox economists.
- It is important to understand the pure experiment, even if it may be impossible and perhaps undesirable to conduct.
- A range of experimental designs is possible, each with its own pros and cons.
- The researcher must consider their experimental design very carefully.
- All experimental data and analysis should be treated with caution, preferably in combination with other data and analyses.

There is clear scope for heterodox economists to use these methods. Take for instance the role of class. Within that species, particular questions will require different methods. A heterodox economist interested in which decisions are taken, and why, in consumer contexts, might attempt to deploy a pure experiment, or something approaching that. For instance, they might investigate how different modes of selling of financial products generated diverse effects. However, if they are interested in class variances, one way to assess an intervention is to select group memberships based on prior notions of class. A field experiment on a possible change to working practices could be undertaken in two communities of different classes, to assess dissimilarities in outcomes. Finally, a 'natural' experiment – albeit one that is clearly social – might be to assess the divergent effects of an actual policy on different classes. In each case, the question being asked drives the specific method chosen, as does the context itself. Heterodox economists might be expected to be at least as aware as other economists about this final, crucial point.

## REFERENCES

Aronson, E. and J. Carlsmith (1968), 'Experimentation in social psychology', in G. Lindzey and E. Aronson (eds), *The Handbook of Social Psychology*, Reading, MA: Addison-Wesley, pp. 1–79.

Ashenfelter, O. and D. Card (1985), 'Using the longitudinal structure of earnings to estimate the effect of training programs', *Review of Economics and Statistics*, **67** (4), 648–60.

Athey, S. and G. Imbens (2006), 'Identification and inference in nonlinear difference-in-differences models', *Econometrica*, **74** (2), 431–97.

Bandiera, O., I. Barankay, and I. Rasul (2011), 'Field experiments with firms', *Journal of Economic Perspectives*, **25** (3), 63–82.

Barankay, I., M. Johannesson, J. List, R. Friberg, M. Liski, and K. Storesletten (2013), 'Guest editors' preface to the special symposium on field experiments', *Scandinavian Journal of Economics*, **115** (1), 1–2.

Bardsley, N. (2005), 'Experimental economics and the artificiality of alteration', *Journal of Economic Methodology*, **12** (2), 239–51.

Barr, A. (2003), 'Trust and expected trustworthiness: experimental evidence from Zimbabwean villages', *Economic Journal*, **113** (489), 614–30.

Barr, A., M. Dekker, and M. Fafchamps (2013), 'Bridging the gender divide: an experimental analysis of group formation in African villages', *World Development*, **40** (10), 2063–77.

Behrman, J., M. Rosenzweig, and P. Taubman (1994), 'Endowments and the allocation of schooling in the family and the marriage market: the twins experiment', *Journal of Political Economy*, **102** (6), 1131–74.

Bertrand, M., E. Duflo, and S. Mullainathan (2004), 'How much should we trust difference-in-difference estimates?', National Bureau of Economic Research, Working Paper No. 8841.

Bertrand, M. and S. Mullainathan (2004), 'Are Emily and Greg more employable than Lakisha and Jamal? A field experiment in labor market discrimination', *American Economic Review*, **94** (4), 991–1013.

Bohm, P. (1972), 'Estimating the demand for public goods: an experiment', *European Economic Review*, **3** (2), 111–30.

Bryman, A. and E. Bell (2007), *Business Research Methods*, Oxford: Oxford University Press.

Camerer, C. (1998), 'Can asset markets be manipulated? A field experiment with racetrack betting', *Journal of Political Economy*, **106** (3), 457–82.

Camerer, C. and R. Hogarth (1999), 'The effects of financial incentives in experiments: a review and capital–labor framework', *Journal of Risk and Uncertainty*, **19** (1), 7–42.

Campbell, D. and J. Stanley (1963), *Experimental and Quasi-experimental Evaluations in Social Research*, Chicago, IL: Rand-McNally.

Card, D. and A. Krueger (1994), 'Minimum wages and employment: a case study of the fast-food industry in New Jersey and Pennsylvania', *American Economic Review*, **84** (4), 772–93.

Carpenter, J., J. Holmes, and P. Matthews (2008), 'Charity auctions: a field experiment', *Economic Journal*, **118** (525), 92–113.

Colander, D. (2000), 'The death of neoclassical economics', *Journal of the History of Economic Thought*, **22** (2), 127–43.

Cook, T. and D. Campbell (1979), *Quasi-experimentation: Design and Analysis for Field Settings*, Boston, MA: Houghton-Mifflin.

Deacon, R. and J. Sonstelie (1985), 'Rationing by waiting and the value of time: results from a natural experiment', *Journal of Political Economy*, **93** (4), 627–47.

Eagly, A. and M. Crowley (1986), 'Gender and helping behavior: a meta-analytic review of the social psychological literature', *Psychological Bulletin*, **100** (3), 283–308.

Ferber, R. and W. Hirsch (1982), *Social Experimentation and Economic Policy*, New York: Cambridge University Press.

Field, A. (2000), *Discovering Statistics using SPSS for Windows*, London: Sage.

Flick, U. (2006), *An Introduction to Qualitative Research*, London: Sage.

Friedman, M. (1953 [1970]), 'The methodology of positive economics', in Milton Friedman (1970), *Essays in Positive Economics*, Chicago, IL: University of Chicago Press, pp. 3–43.

Guala, F. (2001), 'Building economic machines: the FCC auctions', *Studies in History and Philosophy of Science Part A*, **32** (3), 453–77.

Hair, J., W. Black, B. Babin, R. Anderson, and R. Tatham (2006), *Multivariate Data Analysis*, Upper Saddle River, NJ: Pearson.

Harrison, G. and J. List (2004), 'Field experiments', *Journal of Economic Literature*, **42** (4), 1009–55.

Heckman, J. (1979), 'Sample selection bias as a specification error', *Econometrica*, **47** (l), 153–61.

Hunt, M. (1993), *The Story of Psychology*, New York: Anchor Books.

Levitt, S. and J. List (2009), 'Field experiments in economics: the past, the present, and the future', *European Economic Review*, **53** (1), 1–18.

Lincoln, Yvonna S. and Egon G. Guba (1985), *Naturalistic Inquiry*, London: Sage.

Loewenstein, G. (1999), 'Experimental economics from the vantage-point of behavioral economics', *Economic Journal*, **109** (453), F25–F35.

Mayo, E. (1933), *The Human Problems of an Industrial Civilisation*, New York: Macmillan.

Mearman, A. (2013), 'How should we evaluate economics curricula?', *International Review of Economics Education*, accessed August 13, 2014 at http://www.sciencedirect.com/science/article/pii/S1477388013000406

Mel, S. de, D. McKenzie, and C. Woodruff (2008), 'Returns to capital in microenterprises: evidence from a field experiment', *Quarterly Journal of Economics*, **123** (4), 1329–72.

Metrick, A. (1995), 'A natural experiment in Jeopardy!', *American Economic Review*, **85** (3), 322–40.

Milgram, S. (1963), 'Behavioral study of obedience', *Journal of Abnormal and Social Psychology*, **67** (4), 371–8.

Milgram, S. (1974), *Obedience to Authority: An Experimental View*, London: Tavistock Publications.

Morrison, K. (2009), *Causation in Educational Research*, London: Routledge.

Morton, R. (2014), 'Political economy experiments: introduction', *Economic Journal*, **124** (574), F129–F130.

Oakley, A. (2007), 'Evidence-informed policy and practice: challenges for social science', in M. Hammersley (ed.), *Educational Research and Evidence-based Practice*, London: Sage, pp. 91–105.

O'Doherty, R., D. Street, and C. Webber (2007), *The Skills and Knowledge of the Graduate Economist*, Bristol: Economics Network.

Pawson, R. and N. Tilley (1997), *Realistic Evaluation*, London: Sage.

Puhani, P. (2000), 'The Heckman correction for sample selection and its critique', *Journal of Economic Surveys*, **14** (1), 53–68.

Riach, P. and J. Rich (2002), 'Field experiments of discrimination in the market place', *Economic Journal*, **112** (483), F480–F518.

Rosenzweig, M. and K. Wolpin (2000), 'Natural "natural experiments" in economics', *Journal of Economic Literature*, **38** (4), 827–74.

Roth, A. (1991), 'A natural experiment in the organization of entry-level labor markets: regional markets for new physicians and surgeons in the United Kingdom', *American Economic Review*, **81** (3), 415–40.

Roth, A. (1993), 'On the early history of experimental economics', *Journal of the History of Economic Thought*, **15** (2), 184–209.

Salganik, M.J., P.S. Dodds, and D.J. Watts (2006), 'Experimental study of inequality and unpredictability in an artificial cultural market', *Science*, **311**, 854–6.

Sent, E-M. (2004), 'Behavioral economics: how psychology made its (limited) way back into economics', *History of Political Economy*, **36** (4), 735–60.

Shearer, B. (2004), 'Piece rates, fixed wages and incentives: evidence from a field experiment', *Review of Economic Studies*, **71** (2), 513–34.

Siakantaris, N. (2000), 'Experimental economics under the microscope', *Cambridge Journal of Economics*, **24** (2), 267–81.

Sikes, P. (2004), 'Methodology, procedures and ethical concerns', in C. Opie (ed.), *Doing Educational Research: A Guide for First-time Researchers*, London: Sage, pp. 15–33.

Slonim, R. and A. Roth (1998), 'Learning in high stakes ultimatum games: an experiment in the Slovak Republic', *Econometrica*, **66** (3), 569–96.

Tomer, J. (2001), 'Economic man versus heterodox men: the concepts of human nature in schools of economic thought', *Journal of Socio-Economics*, **30** (4), 281–93.

Ziliak, S. and D. McCloskey (2008), *The Cult of Statistical Significance: How the Standard Error Costs us Jobs, Justice, and Lives*, Ann Arbor, MI: University of Michigan Press.

# 9 Factor analysis, cluster analysis, and nonparametric research methods for heterodox economic analysis
## Michael J. Murray

> To build up a causal model, we must start not from equilibrium relations but from rules and motives governing human behavior. We therefore have to specify to what kind of economy the model applies, for various kinds of economies have different sets of rules . . . The independent elements in the model must correspond with the features of reality which are given independently of each other, either by the brute facts of nature or by the freedom of individuals within the economy to decide how they will behave. (Robinson 1962, p. 34)

## 9.1 INTRODUCTION

The goal of this chapter is to delineate quantitative methods for the critical realist–grounded theory approach in heterodox economics. Critical realism, as articulated by Andrew Sayer (1992) and Tony Lawson (1997), begins with a core set of assumptions: that the world is differentiated and stratified consisting of structures and causal mechanisms which generate economic events. Causal mechanisms are real and identifiable whereas structures are real but may not be directly measurable (that is, socialism, capitalism, social class, and social networks). Because causal mechanisms and their structures generate actual events, it is imperative that the social scientist gets them right. They cannot be mis-described, nor can they be assumed (Nell 2004). Identification of causal mechanisms are dependent on a specific set of social relations within a predefined historical context. Likewise, the underlying structures are also socially determined and in the same way they are within time, meaning they are valid only for the period of historical time for which they are specified. The identification of causal mechanisms and structures gives rise to grounded theory as an application for critical realist research (Lee 2013). In this chapter, it is demonstrated that factor analysis and cluster analysis are powerful tools for conducting grounded theory research by delineating causal mechanisms and their underlying structures.

Factor analysis can be subdivided into exploratory factor analysis (EFA), and confirmatory factor analysis (CFA). Whether to utilize EFA or CFA methods depends on whether structures and causal mechanisms can be hypothesized a priori or not. EFA methods are appropriate when the relationships between the observed causal mechanisms and latent structures are unknown and cannot be formulated based upon previous research, previous theories, or previous knowledge of their relationships. For a given research question, the EFA approach sets out to identify latent structures and underpin to what extent observed causal mechanisms have an effect on latent structures. This is in contrast to a CFA model, which is used when it is possible to hypothesize about the underlying relationships between latent social structures and causal mechanisms. The model is laid out a priori and it is based upon previous theoretical work or a common knowledge of those relationships based upon everyday experiences.

Factor analysis deals with categorizing observable data into various groupings based upon common characteristics of the data, whereas cluster analysis deals with aggregating observations, or defining clusters, based upon characteristic similarities of the cases. Cluster analysis, for example, may be used to stratify the data into parcels where each parcel exhibits similar traits. The object of cluster analysis is to define groupings, whereas the object of factor analysis is to identify latent constructs.

The chapter will focus on the need for factor analysis and cluster analysis as a research method for conducting grounded theory and thereby practicing critical realism. Specifically, the focus is on the research methods required for heterodox analysis, emphasis is placed on the necessity to collect primary data, and the chapter describes the statistical techniques appropriate to conduct factor analysis and cluster analysis.

## 9.2   FOUNDATIONS OF ECONOMIC ANALYSIS

Why are the aforementioned methods outlined above appropriate for heterodox research methods? Why do heterodox economists not utilize traditional econometric methods employed by mainstream economists? The answer lies within the assumptions that guide the two theories. Heterodox economics differentiates itself from standard mainstream approaches because heterodox analysis seeks to understand actual economic reality, whereas mainstream economic theory bases itself on a very specific set of maximizing behavior abstracting from culture, time, and space. The maximizing assumptions of mainstream theories allow for traditional calculus and parametric statistical techniques to be implemented. This is in contrast to heterodox theory, which makes no such assumptions and therefore must abandon the traditional techniques and rely on research methods more geared towards qualitative analysis.

That said, there are commonalities between the contemporary branches of mainstream theory and heterodox theory. Any economic theory must consist of three elements: (1) a taxonomy that describes categories of data to construct the theory; (2) a set of assumptions relative to that theory; and (3) propositions or a set of hypotheses that may legitimately be derived from the assumptions. These common elements, perhaps paradoxically, also illuminate the fundamental differences between the two methods and therefore the need for heterodox research methods.

These tenets are now briefly examined, one by one, for mainstream economic theory and heterodox economic theory. Contemporary mainstream approaches are centered on trade. Trade itself is a static concept that is associated with a plurality of economic systems. This allows economic data to be classified into three homogenous groupings: producers, consumers, and government. It is assumed that all agents within these groups set out to maximize their own self-interest, producers maximize profits, consumers maximize utility, and government's self-interest is to stay out of the way. Or at most, government's interest is to set conditions and regulations that allow for private market efficiencies, thereby allowing consumers and businesses to maximize their individual interests. The requirements for mainstream economic analysis is to assume that all market participants are endowed with resources, knowledge, foresight, and know-how to utilize and distribute resources for their own economic gain. When these assumptions hold, an unregulated price system guarantees that full and efficient resource utilization and distribution will be efficient, ensuring the maximization of profits and utility. As such the preoccupation of mainstream theory centers on the optimal allocation of scarce resources among competing ends.

A final point is that the behavioral and motivational assumptions of mainstream theory allow the results to be applied universally across all cultures and societies. Mainstream economic theory is timeless and boundless in that it abstracts from culture, time, and space. The upshot of mainstream theory is that such an approach lends itself nicely to traditional mathematical and statistical techniques of optimization; yet the cost is that these behavioral assumptions are not descriptive of reality (see, e.g., Lowe 1951).

Fortunately, there is an alternative to mainstream economics theory. The pre-analytic vision of heterodox economic analysis centers on production rather than trade. The production paradigm considers actual formal and informal institutions that society exhibits. Formal institutions include laws, regulations, standards, and legal establishments such as governments, central banks, corporations, schools and universities, and other lawful entities. Informal institutions cannot be directly observed but are nonetheless real and impact economic decisions and social relations. These latent features of society include the habits and behaviors of households, governments, and businesses. Habits and behaviors are impacted by cultural trends and affected by social norms and the customs of individuals, households, and organizations within society (see also Baranzini and Scazzieri 1986, p. 33). The vast amount of institutional data required for heterodox economic analysis needs to be categorized into what critical realists term causal mechanisms and their underlying social structures. Further, such categorization is defined for, and constrained by, a specific geographical region for a predefined time period.

In terms of the assumptions necessary to carry out heterodox economic analysis, it is more complex than the mainstream counterpart. This complexity is because the natural environment does not produce resources in the necessary quantities that society needs to survive and thrive. Thus, heterodox economists start from the reality that, at its very basic level, all societies must organize a system of production and distribution in order to assure their survival (Heilbroner and Milberg 2012, p. 4). Thus, heterodox economic analysis is the analysis of social institutions. In this vein, economics is redefined as a study of social organization, where the central problems faced by society are the production and distribution of economic output. The redefinition of economics as a process of social organizations puts focus on the social relationships required for social reproduction. It turns focus away from scarcity and constrained optimization and toward: (1) how societies carry out production and ultimately distribution of the social product for their own members and with other societies; (2) the behaviors and motivations of individual members and organizations within particular societies and between societies; and (3) the role of governments and other public controls. It concerns itself with the objective requirements of the economic system; these requirements are partly determined by the physical requirements for the reproduction of society and partly determined by society's institutional fabric. The institutional arrangements guiding societal organization are to be studied through empirical observation; hence the need for heterodox research methods for qualitative analysis, to which I now turn.

## 9.3   ANALYTICAL DESCRIPTIONS OF QUALITATIVE DATA

As was just described, heterodox economic analysis involves the investigation of the actual institutions that make up everyday life, or what Adolph Lowe has termed 'middle principles' (Lowe 2003), and what sociologists commonly refer to as the 'theory of the middle range'. Middle principles (or the middle range) are the sociological raw materials that shape actual economic events. The task of the social scientist is to select middle principles, determine their importance, their connectedness, and arrange their order. The social scientist does not start this process from scratch. During theory construction, social scientists are guided and influenced by the analytical representations of earlier theorists (Scazzieri 1997, p. 149). A systematic analytical representation of the economic process is the result of a cumulative research effort over generations. It becomes a system of propositions that culminates in the construction of a coherent economic theory that is widely accepted by a community of scholars.

Researchers advance a pre-existing set of knowledge. All theoretical analysis must begin with a pre-analytic vision of the economy (Schumpeter 1954, p. 41): 'analytical effort is of necessity preceded by a pre-analytic cognitive act that supplies the raw material for the analytic effort'. The pre-analytic vision of the heterodox economist is that the economic process is a class-based process of circular production. The motivations, tastes, and preferences that influence consumption and production decisions are variables to be directly investigated. The economic process is a series of interdependent economic events that are both forged by, and constrained by, social order. Socio-economic conditions bring into being some economic processes while making other events more likely and other events less likely (Scazzieri 1997, p. 149). The social fabric is an interdependent mix of physical, social, political, and economic institutions that set the parameters for social and economic processes. For example, these processes are influenced by the existing structure of capital equipment, existing knowledge base, existing governments and their formal laws and regulations, and informal codes of conduct on societal behavior. Each of these influence the evolution of economic and social structure (see Scazzieri 1997).

### Social Structures as a Dynamic Concept

The institutions, motivations, and behaviors that make up the economic process must be investigated, identified, qualified, and ordered in such a way as to describe the actual happenings of the economic system. These types of institutions may be directly observable or may be underlying latent phenomena. Observable metrics are termed 'causal mechanisms'. Latent factors that underlie these metrics and explain why the observable factors exist in the first place are termed 'structures'. The identification and ordering of causal mechanisms and their underlying structures are central to the heterodox economist because they provide the contextual backbone for the explanation of actual economic processes. In this vein, the heterodox economic researcher also recognizes that causal mechanisms and their underlying structures can only be defined within a set period of historical time and geographical space. Over time and space, underlying social structures and the causal mechanisms that are created become variable as culture evolves, discoveries are made, knowledge is gained, and as people and ideas migrate.

Edward J. Nell has taken this one step further by suggesting that even within time and space social structures have the potential to change (Nell 2004). The dynamic nature of causal mechanisms and structures is also accepted by critical realists. It follows from this transformation conception of social activity that if change, or at least the potential to change, is always present, the analysis of change per se is of no greater (or lesser) significance to social explanation than the understanding of continuity and reproduction (Lawson 1997, p. 170).

However, while paying lip-service to the potential variability of social structures (and therefore variability of causal mechanisms) critical realists put most of their energy and focus on the continuity and reproduction of existing social structures rather than discussing their potential to change. Bringing in the potential for structures to change creates a new set of questions in discussing the critical realist method. Specifically: what causes social structures to come into existence in the first place? What causes them to disappear? What causes them to change? The answer to these questions are central for the critical realist because for critical realism their investigations are context dependent. In other words they are dependent upon the research question being studied and the time period being considered. Essentially, this boils down to identifying an appropriate period of time for which the social structures and causal mechanisms can be assumed invariant.

The heterodox researcher must decide at the outset what is the appropriate period of time and the geographical region in which social structures and causal mechanisms can be assumed to be invariant. The period of time and space analyzed must be predicated upon the research that is being investigated. The researcher must decide what causes observable institutions (termed 'causal mechanisms') and their underlying social structures to come into and out of existence. Nell (2004) identifies different life cycles that inform the discussion of how latent social structures and observable causal mechanisms come into and out of existence. The two life cycles that Nell defines, and are of interest to those doing heterodox research within a critical realist–grounded theory method, are the transformative life cycle and the evolutionary life cycle.

The transformative life cycle is most associated with Edward J. Nell and the theory of transformational growth. Transformational growth highlights the existence and specifically the processes of innovation and transformation of social structures and mechanisms within stages of historical time. Stages are defined by the method of production and the configuration of social structures and causal mechanisms that make the social provisioning process possible (Nell 1998, p. 21). Each stage of economic development is qualitatively different from earlier stages. Nell identifies three stages of economic and social transformation: the craft economy, the mass production economy (Nell 1998, Ch. 2) and the knowledge economy (Nell and Gualerzi 2010).

The craft economy was a period of early industrial formation. Businesses were small and typically were owned and managed by families. Agriculture was practiced on a small scale and on family farms. Both social and economic reproduction centered on the role of households and their interaction with family firms and family farms. Craft methods of production required traditional skills that were passed from generation to generation. The place of production was typically also the place of sale. Economies were local; transportation and communication were slow; and human activities were embedded within their natural environment (Nell 1998, p. 23). Business investment relied on the savings from households.

The industrial revolution transformed production methods from small-scale handicraft to large-scale mechanized methods. Over time production, communication, and transportation sped up. Craft production transformed into mass production. Mass production technology de-emphasizes traditional blue-collar skills and requires new-white collar skills. Cities tended to grow around large-scale operations. This transformation changed the way society lived, worked, and played. Mass production divorced owners from managers and created a two-class social structure: the managerial class and the laboring class. The two-class system created competing interests which are present to this day. The household was relegated to the periphery and the business enterprise became of central importance.

Now in the present day, society is undergoing a new stage of economic and social transformation toward the knowledge economy, mostly due to the invention of the internet and the innovations surrounding information processing and communication. Information and communication technology has a pivotal role within the twenty-first century production process. Technology is once again changing the way lives are lived, business is conducted, knowledge is learned, and social relationships are formed. New formal and informal institutions are continually being erected, debated, and modified. Such a social economic transformation requires re-examining the existence and relevance of social structures that were once steadfast.

The transformative life cycle allows researchers to understand how social structures transform from one stage of development to another. However, within each stage of development is the evolutionary life cycle. The evolutionary life cycle is most associated with the work of Nelson and Winter (1982). It analyzes the reasons for structural invariance and structural evolution over a particular stage of development. Some social structures remain invariant over decades, others evolve more quickly. For a defined time interval, structural invariance is maintained through a predictable pattern of routines by firms, households, and governments. For the business enterprise, there are customary patterns of research and development, training practices, customary hiring and firing practices. There is also standardization for weights and measurements among and across industries which allows for a smooth process of production.

What Nelson and Winter identify as routines, critical realists denote as demi-regularities (see Lawson 1997, pp. 204–21; Lawson 2003, p. 105). Without getting caught up in semantics, Nelson and Winter, Tony Lawson, as well as other critical realists accept the existence of socio-economic regularities, but acknowledge that these regularities are also partially unstable, meaning that they evolve over time. The goal then for critical realists is to identify an event regularity, form a causal hypothesis as to what makes these events regularly occur, and then to account for and discriminate against competing hypotheses (Lawson 2003, pp. 105–7). It may be gleaned that the critical elements for transformative and evolutionary life cycles are to appropriately define the period of time and geographical space in which structures and causal mechanisms remain intact.

Following the appropriate specification of time and space for a given research question, for social structures and causal mechanisms to be germane to what actually exists, the researcher must empirically build up structures and mechanisms from existing data. Building a theory from the ground up requires first defining the relevant time and space for the research question. Then the researcher must do fieldwork and collect data, categorize and group data, extrapolate and make inferences from the data, identify latent structures and causal mechanisms, and then finally construct the theory. The process is messy, but by doing so, the researcher will ensure that the constructed theory is pertinent to economic and social reality.

**Fieldwork**

The process of constructing a theory must start with fieldwork. There are two types of fieldwork: tangible fieldwork and intangible fieldwork. Tangible fieldwork is investigating what people actually do. It is discovering how people actually think and behave, and ascertaining the motivations that cause them to think and behave in the manner they do. Tangible fieldwork uncovers observable causal mechanisms that make up everyday life. Intangible fieldwork is more difficult. It is the process of deducing the unobservable, but very real, social structures that lie beneath the surface and that create observable phenomena. Fieldwork itself does not result in scientific theory nor universal laws and explanations. Fieldwork produces valid and reliable information (Nell 1998, pp. 101–5). The conclusions of fieldwork should be verifiable and reproducible given that the parameters in which the investigations were constructed have not changed.

## 9.4   CRITICAL REALISM AND GROUNDED THEORY

Frederic S. Lee (2003; see also Chapter 2 of this *Handbook*) advocates the integration of critical realism with grounded theory. Grounded theory is a formalized method for conducting fieldwork, and it certainly follows with the prescribed methods of critical realism. Here a quick overview shall be provided so that focus may be placed on grounded theory itself and the quantitative methods to conduct grounded theory in practice. The interested reader is advised to consult the works referenced above for more on integrating grounded theory with critical realism.

### Integrating Critical Realism with Grounded Theory

I begin with a very brief overview of the integration of the two methods. Critical realism begins with the following propositions. Firstly, critical realists accept that social reality consists of underlying, unobservable, yet very real social structures. Secondly, structures create causal mechanisms and causal mechanisms produce economic events. These events are independent of their identification (Lee 2003, p. 192). An example of a latent structure is anomie. Anomie is associated with the sociologist Robert Merton who suggests that anomie is an underlying explanation for deviant behavior. Deviant behavior is an observable causal mechanism that can partially explain chronic unemployment (Murray 2013). Here, chronic unemployment is an actual economic event. The economic world is open, meaning that it is the result of interacting and counteracting social structures and causal mechanisms.

Social structures are not directly observable, but they do exhibit reliable properties. Economic and social events and human action sustain, reproduce, and gradually transform the properties of social structures. Grounded theory is a method to collect and organize empirical data into specified categories. The categories come from the data itself so the categories are empirically grounded. The formulation and organization of categories aids in identifying similarities and differences in the data. Further, categorization allows for pieces of data to become significant within the context of a category, whereas those pieces of data by themselves may otherwise not be significant. The process of data collection and categorization continues until identified categories become saturated. The emerging theory can be evaluated by how well the theory explains actual economic events. The theory is only as good as the data and categories that make it up. The robustness of the theory may be evaluated by how well it handles new data. In other words, whether a theory is robust depends upon the scope and degree to which the causal mechanisms have changed (Lee 2003, p. 78). Thus, grounded theory provides a methodological approach toward realism for critical realists. This is a brief synopsis of grounded theory as a methodological foundation for critical realism, but the actual process of doing grounded theory, meaning the actual process of data collection and the identification and construction of categories, requires further explanation.

**Grounded Theory**

Grounded theory is the discovery of theory from data (Glaser and Strauss 1967 [2012], p. 12). During the process of this discovery, the social science researcher categorizes real-world data. The grouping and categorization of data illuminates significance when individualized data are viewed in the context of a larger group. The categories themselves are not directly observable; but since they are used to establish broader meaning to a grouping of data, latent categories themselves have real meaning. Categories are meant to be conceptual: they delineate a theoretical abstraction of an area being studied. Categories also exhibit properties. Whereas a category 'stands by itself as a conceptual element to the theory . . . properties are elements of categories' (Glaser and Strauss 2012 [1967], p. 47). The development of conceptual categories and their properties generate from empirical evidence; evidence from a category illustrates a concept; and the concept is a theoretical abstraction of the area under study. Theoretical concepts germinate from latent categories constructed from empirical evidence. Therefore this process grounds social science theory in social and economic reality. The generation of theory also establishes the boundaries for the applicability of the theory. Rather than starting from a priori assumptions, the process of generating theory is a way of arriving at a theory suitable for the stated uses (Glaser and Strauss 1967 [2012], p. 17).

Once the social scientist has mapped empirical data into categories and then used those categories to delineate a theoretical concept, next the researcher must test and verify the categories and determine the scope to which the categories and the emerging theory apply. To do this the researcher identifies groups to be sampled and then collects data for each group. Comparative groups are used to check whether, and to what extent, the initial model and the categories apply. Comparative analysis across sampling groups allows the researcher to understand the robustness of the emerging theory, establish the level of generality of the theory, and establish the boundaries of the theory. Can the theoretical model be replicated across all groups? The researcher must categorize the data, then test the conditions for which the categories exist, and then 'highlight the widest possible coverage on ranges, continua, degrees, and uniformity' (Glaser and Strauss 1967 [2012], p. 160) by testing the model across comparative groups. The identification of unique sampling groups is predicated upon the research undergone. But that said, there are some general rules of thumb. The basic criteria for selecting comparative groups are whether the potential sampling group is of theoretical relevance and whether it furthers the development of conceptual categories (Glaser and Strauss 1967 [2012], p. 160).

Comparative analysis between groups has statistical importance as it deepens the sampling. The depth of theoretical sampling is in reference to the amount of data that are collected on any one category for a given group (Glaser and Strauss 1967 [2012], p. 80). As will be further discussed below, the depth of the data becomes important when utilizing structural equation modeling techniques for grounded theory research. Deepening the data ensures that the theoretical model has sufficient degrees of freedom to conduct meaningful analysis (this is called the identification criterion).

The two general rules of thumb when selecting sampling groups are, first, to minimize differences between the groups, and then to maximize group differences. Minimizing differences among sampling groups allows the researcher to test for the parameters under which latent categories exist. This allows the researcher to build a model and construct a theory and to establish narrow boundaries for which the theory holds. That said, following the establishment of conditions for which the categories (and therefore the theory) hold, the researcher must next investigate the scope to which the categories and the theory apply. This investigation is accomplished by maximizing differences among comparative groups.

The method of comparative analysis allows social researchers to collect data on categories until they become saturated, meaning no more data on a specific category can be collected. In this process, sometimes new categories may emerge, some categories appear robust, and other categories appear relevant for only a particular group. Nevertheless, comparative analysis allows for the researcher to generalize the theory for particular groups, in a particular time period, in a particular geographical space. (Certainly, one would not expect the current conditions of social provisioning to be identical in Western Europe and in East Asia; or the social provisioning process of contemporary society in the United States to be the same as it was at the turn of the twentieth century.) The emerging theory has relevance only for the sampled populations and should not be applied universally.

## 9.5   STRUCTURAL EQUATION MODELING

Proper techniques to conduct grounded theory research involve identifying unique populations from which to draw data upon given a specific research question. The groupings may be aggregated by nationality, race, gender, age, income quintiles, or any other identifiable difference. For example, in an earlier paper, Murray (2013) analyzes the social and psychological effects of unemployment after the financial crisis. Murray identifies two distinct population groups – mid-career workers and early-career workers – in an attempt to address similarities or differences in the non-economic consequences of unemployment between the two groups. In this case study, as in many case studies that employ a grounded theory method, the author first collected data based on the research question addressed. Next, categories were developed as data were collected. The categories became saturated. A causal model of both observable and latent variables was developed which illustrated a concept. The scope of the concept was analyzed for the two population groups (mid-career workers and early-career workers) to understand whether the concept that was derived from one group applied more generally to the next group.

In another, albeit very different, study, Song et al. (2008) examined the relationship between the strategic type of firm and the firm's marketing, technical, and information technology (IT) capabilities across three countries: Japan, China, and United States. In this study the attempt was made to first construct a theory relating the type of business (industry leaders, imitators, defenders) to latent capabilities by collecting observable data on capabilities, then organizing the data into distinct categories. Next, the authors attempted to describe the causal relationships between the observable categories and the latent constructs of marketing, technical, and IT capabilities. The completed model illustrated a concept. Finally, the authors tested the robustness of the concept by seeing how well the theoretical model fit sample data from all the three groups (the countries of Japan, the USA, and China). In the final analysis they found that Japanese firms have greater technology and IT capabilities than do US firms of the same strategic type. This means that the theoretical model relating strategic type to technology and IT capabilities is constrained by geographical location. In other words, the conceptual model is not robust and a model linking strategic type to capabilities that is developed for US firms should not be applied to firms outside the US.

Limiting the bounds to which a model, concept, or theory shall be applied rests at the foundation of critical realism and grounded theory. Both the above case studies utilize a method known as factor analysis to conduct grounded theory. Factor analysis itself is a subcomponent of the broader field of structural equation modeling (often abbreviated as SEM). The family of structural equation modeling includes factor analysis, path analysis, and regression. Barbara Byrne (2009) defines structural equation methodology as:

> a series of causal processes that can be represented by structural, meaning regression, equations. Once the causal model is mapped out, the researcher examines the hypothesized model against a given grouping of data and across cross-sectional data. There are several advantages of structural equation modeling over traditional ordinary least squares regression, but probably the biggest advantage is the ability for structural equation models to incorporate both observable and latent, or unobservable variables into the model. (Byrne 2009, p. 21)

This feature becomes especially handy for social scientists, and critical realists in particular, who attempt to address the underlying and unobservable social structures when developing a theory.

There are limitations to developing causal models: particularly, that they are difficult to develop, they require historical data on all variables (independent and dependent), and the ability to predict the dependent variable is predicated upon the forecaster being able to predict future values of the independent variables accurately (Bowerman and O'Connell 1990, p. 21). That said, the traditional limitations of causal modeling are more problematic for mainstream economic theory and make causal models more conducive to heterodox theory, particularly with critical realists who utilize grounded theory. All researchers in both the critical realist and grounded theory camps would accept that causal models are difficult to develop. Both of these groups are built around the fact that actually constructing theories that explain the actual going-ons of the economy must be messy. They both accept the fact that in order to develop a theoretical concept that is reasonable about the societies in which we actually live, then it must be grounded in historical data. And lastly, whereas mainstream economic theory preoccupies itself with matters of predication, critical realists have no such concern. For critical realists, the objective is to construct a theory which identifies the relationships between observable causal mechanisms and latent social structures, a task that is quite appropriate for factor analysis, and makes factor analysis a desirable alternative for critical realists. In the social and behavioral sciences, researchers are interested in studying the theoretical constructs of observable and latent variables. Since latent variables cannot be directly observed, researchers define latent variables in terms of the behaviors that they represent. Latent variables are linked to one or more observable variables. The latent variables are indicators of underlying structure (Byrne 2009, p. 21).

A distinction can be made between two types of factor analysis: confirmatory factor analysis and exploratory factor analysis. Confirmatory factor analysis begins with a hypothesized theory of the specified relationships between observable causal mechanisms and latent structures, and then examines how well the theoretical map applies to new groups of data. CFA models are the most widely used because typically social scientists are guided by earlier theories and analytical representations of the social and economic process. Thus CFA models are appropriate for most types of critical realist–grounded theory research. However, when the underlying relationships between causal mechanisms and social structures are completely unknown, then exploratory factor analysis is appropriate. Exploratory factor analysis comes into play when the social scientist is attempting to formulate theory following (or in the midst of) a transformational change to the fabric of society. As exposited above, societies undergo long periods of social evolution, with only minor changes to social organization from year to year. However, societies do not just evolve: they also transform following a radical innovation. Societies transform from craft production, to mass production, to the knowledge economy. The institutions and social organization at each stage are vastly different from the earlier stage. In these cases, where the researcher does not have an earlier theory to begin from, the researcher must seek out under general assumptions a latent structure and then determine what observable variables should be linked to the latent constructs (Byrne 2009, p. 17).

How are CFA and EFA models constructed? How can they be utilized to conduct grounded theory and serve as a means to describing actual economic reality? The following section describes the methods for building CFA and EFA models and links these models to the methods of grounded theory and the foundations of critical realism.

## 9.6   FACTOR ANALYSIS

Factor analysis, whether confirmatory or exploratory, attempts to relate observable phenomena by some underlying factor or factors. For example, say that we have data on four socio-economic variables:

- Long-term unemployed ($LTU$).
- Drink five days a week or more ($ALC$).
- Attend regular social, community, family events ($SOC$).
- Depressed, as measured by the CESD score[1] ($DEP$).

Intercorrelations of the four variables were calculated, giving rise to the following correlation coefficients:

$$r_{12} = 0.70; r_{13} = 0.75; r_{14} = 0.65; r_{23} = 0.72; r_{24} = 0.60; r_{34} = 0.68$$

Inspection of the correlation coefficients shows immediately that these four observable variables are highly correlated, and that possibly the variation in the data may be explained by an underlying latent factor. For example, since all these observable characteristics relate to social withdrawal, an underlying latent factor such as anomie may account for their correlations. That said, it is important to be aware that factors are constructs, meaning that they are postulated in order to reasonably explain the correlations that exhibit in observable variables (Cureton and D'Agostino 1993, p. 5). They are never uniquely determined and must be supported by theory or backed by knowledge that is commonplace. To take another example, Cureton and D'Agostino (1993) cite an early study by Thurstone and Thurstone (1941) who gave 710 eighth-grade children in 15 Chicago schools the following tests:

- sentence reading;
- paragraph reading;
- multiplication;
- addition.

The following correlation coefficients were reported:

$$r_{12} = 0.68; r_{13} = 0.17; r_{14} = 0.18; r_{23} = 0.16; r_{24} = 0.19; r_{34} = 0.50$$

Paraphrasing Cureton and D'Agostino (1993, p. 5), the authors present four alternative conclusions that account for these four correlations: (1) reading ability and mathematical ability are correlated; (2) performance on the four tests display an underlying ability called intelligence; (3) the latent factor 'intelligence' is verbal in character so it may be used to explain the correlation between sentence reading and paragraph reading and not multiplication; (4) 'intelligence' is quantitative in character, so that it may be linked to the observable scores on multiplication and addition because both draw heavily on intelligence, leaving the two reading factors uncorrelated (Cureton and D'Agostino 1993). The point of the exercise is to show that there are four alternative conclusions that may conceivably account for the correlations in test scores. The factor 'intelligence' may, or may not, be an underlying factor to account for the correlation. If it is, it may account for reading test scores or quantitative test scores. The point is, however, that when the researcher links underlying factors to observable variables, those links must be based upon the correlation among observable variables within a category and based upon the pre-analytical vision of the concept. And, as noted above, the pre-analytical vision of a theoretical concept derives itself from earlier research.

The point of factor analysis is to describe an observable variable, or set of observable variables, in terms of its underlying constructs. Factor analysis is a maximum variance approach. This means that it is designed to delineate observed variables in terms of its latent constructs to maximally reproduce the correlations, or to have the maximum amount of variability of the observable variables to be explained by the underlying latent factors. The basic factor analysis model may described by the equation:

$$z_i = a_{i1}F_1 + a_{i2}F_2 + \ldots + a_{ik}F_k + e \tag{9.1}$$

where:
$z_i$ = observable dependent variable.
$F_i$ = represents (where $i = 1$ to $k$) latent factors which account for the correlation among the variables.
$a_j$ = the factor loadings (described in more detail below).
$e$ = accounts for the remaining variance in the dependent variable not explained by the latent factors.

   The factor loadings are the correlation coefficients between the observed dependent variable and the independent latent factors. Thus, as with all correlation coefficients, the factor loadings can be squared, which would be interpreted as the percentage of the variance in the observable dependent variable that is explained by the latent factor. As a general rule of thumb, a factor loading of 0.7 or greater is used to determine the significance of a latent factor. The cut-off of 0.7 as a general rule is because 0.7 squared is 0.49; this result is interpreted as roughly half of the variability exhibited in the observable variables is explained by an underlying factor. However this is just a rule of thumb, and in practice lower factor loadings may be perfectly acceptable depending upon the research undertaken. Now, the sum of squares of the factor loadings is equal to the total variability of an indicator variable explained by the model.
   What has just been described is the general idea of factor analysis. However factor analysis is subdivided into confirmatory factor analysis and exploratory factor analysis, detailed below.

**Confirmatory and Exploratory Factor Analysis**

Typically social science researchers do not start from scratch when developing a theory or illustrating a concept. Current research is typically an extension of previous research, and therefore investigations of the many relationships between causal mechanisms and their underlying structures can be guided by previous research. Thus, heterodox researchers employing critical realist and grounded theory techniques would typically start with confirmatory factor analysis. The goal of confirmatory factor analysis is to confirm whether a hypothesized set of latent variables fit to a covariance matrix. The main result of factor analysis (whether exploratory or confirmatory) is to show the factor pattern, or the values and the paths of latent variables and observed variables (Loechin 1998, p. 92). Once a factor pattern has been confirmed to fit a group of data, the scope of the factor relationship can be tested against different groups to determine the robustness of the theoretical relationships described. It is best to describe this technique by way of a hypothetical example.
   I will take a hypothetical example of a first-order model. The process described in this section is adapted from Byrne (2009, Ch. 2). The interested reader is encouraged to consult Byrne (2009) for a more complete discussion of CFA models and SEM in general

as she provides one of the best introductions to SEM and computer applications to conduct factor analysis.

I now proceed with my generic example regarding anomie described above. Let us say that it is hypothesized from previous research that anomie, which is the breakdown of social bonds between an individual and their community, is revealed by a three-latent-factor model. Call these latent factors: economic bonds (which could describe the unobservable social bonds an individual has to their place of employment, including self-identifying with a profession), household bonds (unobservable bonds to family members), and community bonds (social bonds to the community and its members). The three bonds constitute latent factors that underlie observable characteristics. For sake of example assume that each latent factor is measured by three observable variables. The CFA model can be represented graphically by the path diagram in Figure 9.1.

The CFA model depicted in Figure 9.1 is a first-order model. The CFA model states that the concept of anomie can be broken down into three latent constructs, each linked to three observable variables and their associated error. When CFA models are described graphically like this one, it is called a path diagram. Putting the path diagram into equations would generate:

$$\textit{Observed Economic Variable } 1 = a_1 \textit{EconomicBonds} + e_1$$

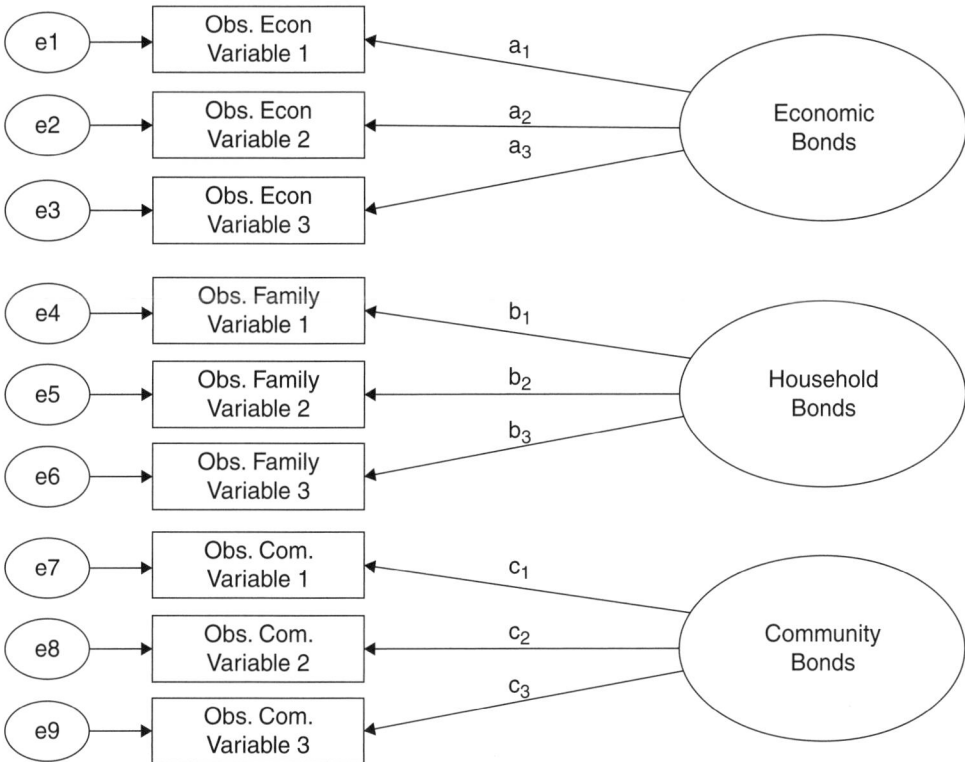

*Figure 9.1 Hypothetical path diagram for confirmatory factor analysis*

*Table 9.1   CFA factor loadings*

| Variable | Economic bonds | Family bonds | Community bonds |
|---|---|---|---|
| *Obs. Econ Var 1* | 0.78 | – | – |
| *Obs. Econ Var 2* | 0.88 | – | – |
| *Obs. Econ Var 3* | 0.93 | – | – |
| *Obs. Family Var 1* | – | 0.88 | – |
| *Obs. Family Var 2* | – | 0.87 | – |
| *Obs. Family Var 3* | – | 0.90 | – |
| *Obs. Community Var 1* | – | – | 0.94 |
| *Obs. Family Var 2* | – | – | 0.91 |
| *Obs. Family Var 3* | – | – | 0.78 |

*Observed Economic Variable 2 = $a_2$EconomicBonds + $e_2$*
*Observed Economic Variable 3 = $a_3$EconomicBonds + $e_3$*
*Observed Family Variable 1 = $b_1$HouseholdBonds + $e_4$*
*Observed Family Variable 2 = $b_2$HouseholdBonds + $e_5$*
*Observed Family Variable 3 = $b_3$HouseholdBonds + $e_6$*
*Observed Community Variable 1 = $c_1$CommunityBonds + $e_7$*
*Observed Community Variable 2 = $c_2$CommunityBonds + $e_8$*
*Observed Community Variable 3 = $c_3$CommunityBonds + $e_9$*

The coefficients $a_1$, $a_2$, $a_3$, $b_1$, $b_2$, $b_3$, $c_1$, $c_2$, $c_3$ are called the factor loadings, and the $e_i$ are the error terms. Let us examine the interpretation of the factor loadings and residuals closer. Rather than using variables, let us say that we estimate the model, and estimates of the factor loadings yield the results in Table 9.1.

The first thing to note is that all the factor loadings exceed the 0.70 level, because the factor loadings represent correlations (whose values range between −1 and 1). The factor loadings tell the researcher how much the variable correlates with the underlying latent factor that it is mapped to. As with correlation coefficients, squaring the factor loadings will tell the researcher how much of the variance can be accounted for based upon the underlying factor. So examining just the first observation, we see that the factor loading on economic bonds is equal to 0.78. Squaring this number we get 0.61. Thus the result can be interpreted as: 61 percent of the variability of *Observed Economic Variable 1* is accounted for on the basis of the underlying structure 'economic bonds'. The remaining factor loadings can be squared and the results similarly interpreted. The error factors in the model represent uncontrolled variability and/or sources of error within the data that is beyond the control of the researcher (Sheskin 2003, p. 833). The only thing left to do for the researcher is to examine the overall fit of the three-factor structure for a given group. Traditional model fit statistics are interpreted such as the chi-square test, the root mean square error (RMSE), Akaike Information Criterion (AIC), and Bayesian information criterion (BIC). (For a more complete analysis of model fit for factor analysis please see Byrne 2009, Ch. 3.)

By now, the connection between grounded theory, critical realism, and confirmatory factor analysis is probably obvious. Grounded theory concerns itself with the investigation and categorization of observable data. Critical realism concerns itself with identifying observable data and their relationship to underlying structures. Factor analysis helps to flesh out common traits in each category and extract latent constructs. Further, because neither grounded theory nor critical realism provides a method for estimating the variability found in observable phenomena that is explained by the underlying structure, factor analysis is highly useful for moving critical realist and grounded theory research methods forward.

In the event that little is known about the theoretical relationship, or if the researcher wishes to just begin constructing a theory from scratch, then exploratory factor analysis may be used to build the theory. Once the theoretical relationships are described, they can then be confirmed with existing groups of data. It is best to illustrate these approaches by way of an example.

Song et al. (2008) study the relationship between different types of businesses and the development of latent capabilities in marketing, market linking, information technologies, and capabilities to implement innovation strategies (p. 1). Businesses are classified as 'prospectors', which are industry leaders; 'defenders', which maintain and secure a market niche; 'analyzers', which display qualities of both; and 'reactors', which lack long-term plans and a consistent strategy (pp. 7–8). Specifically, strategic types differ in the rate at which they change products and markets in response to environmental changes (Song et al. 2008, p. 7). Regardless of the type of strategy a business employs, it must have organizational capabilities to sustain economic value. Song et al. (2008) cite the early work of Miles et al. (1978) and three decades of supporting studies which link a strategic business unit to the environment in which they operate.

Next, Song et al. (2008) describe four general, yet unobservable, types of business capabilities: market-linking capabilities, technical capabilities, marketing capabilities, and IT capabilities. Because they are unobservable, these underlying capabilities may be represented by actual observable economic phenomena. However, the relationships between these observable variables and latent structures on capabilities are unknown a priori and must therefore be derived. In this situation the researcher must utilize exploratory factor analysis, which is how the authors proceeded.

There are two different ways to identify the mapping of observable phenomena to latent constructs when there is no prior knowledge or theory to guide the analysis. The first method is through factor analysis. First, map each of the observed variables to every latent construct. Next, estimate the factor loadings and pair the observed variables to the latent constructs. If the factor loadings are greater than 0.7, then those factors are said to sufficiently explain the variability in the mapped observed factor. Proceed with mapping observable variables to factors which have a factor loading of 0.7 or higher, and eliminate the rest. Once this is completed and all observable variables are mapped to their appropriate factor, then re-run the analysis. This is the method employed by Byrne (2005).

Alternatively, the researcher can utilize the method called principal component analysis (PCA) to identify the number of underlying latent factors and pair data to the latent factors. This is the method conducted by Song et al. (2008). The mathematical procedure will not be elaborated here; instead I will offer a brief explanation of the principal component approach. It is a statistical procedure which converts correlated observable variables into uncorrelated principal components, where the number of principal components will be less than the number of observable variables. The transformation is defined in a

*Table 9.2   Principal component analysis of market-linking capabilities*

| Market-linking capabilities (latent factor) | Principal component |
| --- | --- |
| Market-sensing capabilities | 0.85 |
| Customer-linking capabilities (i.e., creating and managing durable customer relationships) | 0.80 |
| Capabilities of creating durable relationships with our suppliers | 0.81 |
| Ability to retain customers | 0.79 |
| Channel-bonding capabilities (creating durable relationships with channel members such as wholesalers and retailers) | 0.65 |

*Source:* Song et al. (2008, Table 1). Reproduced with permission of the authors.

way so that the first principal component accounts for the greatest degree of variability in the observable data. For an illustration of principal component analysis, see Table 9.2, which reproduces the PCA results for the latent factor market-linking capabilities in Song et al. (2008).

Table 9.2 transformed the observed variables into the principal components in order to determine the level of variability explained by the factor for each independent variable. Examining Table 9.2 further, the 'Principal component' column identifies the variance of each component explained by the latent factor. The components are ranked in order of variance explained. Thus we see from Table 9.2 that the latent factor 'market-linking capabilities' can be mapped to five observable variables.

Principal component analysis is a data mining tool. All it does is to help the researcher identify the appropriate number of latent factors for a given theoretical concept, and the number of observable variables that can be mapped to each latent variable. In other words, all PCA accomplishes is that it provides a starting point for the researcher to identify the appropriate number of factors, identify which observable variables are explained by the latent factors, and then the researcher can use this information to build the measurement model (see Figure 9.1) and then proceed to estimate the factor loadings.

However, as stated, in practice EFA would seldom be employed as a method to map out the causal structure of a theoretical concept. Normally, the researcher would have prior knowledge of the causal mechanisms and underlying structures from previous research.

## 9.7   CLUSTER ANALYSIS

Before concluding, cluster analysis and its relationship to factor analysis and heterodox research methods must be briefly discussed. Cluster analysis is an exploratory technique. Cluster analysis identifies and partitions data into various groups based upon homogenous traits. Unlike factor analysis, which categorizes data and identifies latent underlying constructs, cluster analysis simply categorizes data so that within each cluster the individuals have similar traits and across clusters there is heterogeneity. No identification of latent constructs is made. It is simply a grouping mechanism. Further, cluster analysis does not require any special assumptions like factor analysis (which assumes asymptotic normality).

There are three different procedures for conducting cluster analysis: hierarchical cluster analysis, k-means cluster analysis, and two-step cluster analysis. Which method to conduct depends upon the data set that is to be categorized. If the data set is small and contains numeric data, then hierarchical cluster analysis could be used. If the data set is of moderate size and the number of grouping clusters are known, then k-means can be employed. If the data set is very large or contains both categorical and numerical data, then the two-step method of formulating clusters is preferable.

The first technique is hierarchical clustering methods. Hierarchical clustering methods can be subdivided into agglomerative and divisive hierarchical methods. Agglomerative clustering is a bottom-up approach. It begins with individual clusters (meaning, clusters of one) and works in an iterative method combining clusters. This is in contrast to divisive clustering which is a top-down approach. It begins with one large cluster, breaking down into smaller clusters. The researcher must specify criteria on which clusters to split up. Hierarchical clustering categorizes clusters based on Euclidean distance (a measure of how far apart two objects are) and similarity (a measure of how similar variables are). Hierarchical clustering is by far the simplest technique, but in most cases it does not provide meaningful clusters when data sets grow.

The second technique of clustering is k-means clustering. K-means clustering requires that the number of clusters be specified a priori (where 'k' is the number of clusters). Further, like hierarchical clustering, k-means clustering works well with either numerical or categorical data (but not both). The clustering starts with an initial set of means and classifies clusters based upon their distance to their means. Then the process is repeated. The aim is to partition the data into k groups so that the differences within each cluster are minimized and the differences across clusters are maximized. Immediately we can see one drawback of k-means clustering is its inability to handle outliers. Typically, if k-means clustering is to be utilized, then outliers must be removed from the analysis prior to formulating clusters.

However, the central problem with the hierarchal and k-means clustering algorithms is that they treat every attribute like a single entity and ignore their interrelationships. 'For example, the person with high incomes may always live in a costly residence, drive luxurious cars, and buy valuable jewelry . . . and so on' (Shih et al. 2010, p. 13). The problem is that clustering algorithms work well with purely quantitative or purely qualitative data; but do poorly when the data exhibits both types. A two-step procedure can correct for this problem. The first step is to find the similarities among the categorical attributes based on the ideas of co-occurrence. Then all the categorical attributes are converted into numeric attributes based upon the relationships that are constructed. Finally, since the categorical data are converted into numeric data, then either of the two previous methods can be applied (Shih et al. 2010).

## 9.8   CONCLUSION

Heterodox research methods must rely on factor analytic models because heterodox economic analysis seeks to understand the relationships between observable phenomena and the underlying latent social structure. The factor analysis method delineates those relationships and seeks to explain the degree of variation exhibited in observable phenomena caused by latent structures. Factor analysis relates directly to both critical realism and grounded theory. Critical realists set out to explain socio-economic phenomena in terms of causal mechanisms and latent structures. Grounded theory provides a framework for coding and categorization of data. Factor analysis takes grounded theory one step further by providing a toolkit with which to categorize observable data, identify latent factors, and quantify the degree to which latent factors explain observed variability. Further, factor analysis has the potential to test the robustness of a theory by testing the fit of the hypothesized theory on new groups. Lastly, factor analysis can incorporate the dynamics of real-world latent structures and causal mechanisms. If society transforms social structures, the researcher can employ an EFA approach and investigate first-hand the relationships between the new social structures and the creation or modification of causal mechanisms. This chapter shows that employing the tools of factor analysis within the critical realist–grounded theory approach amplifies the ability to construct heterodox economic theory which explains real-world phenomena.

## NOTE

1. The Center for Epidemiologic Studies (CESD) score is used by psychologists as a measure of depression. For more details, see http://cesd-r.com/cesdr/.

## REFERENCES

Baranzini, Mauro and Roberto Scazzieri (1986), *Foundations of Economics: Structures of Inquiry and Economic Theory*, Oxford: Blackwell.
Bowerman, Bruce L. and Richard T. O'Connell (1990), *Linear Statistical Models: An Applied Approach*, Belmont, CA: Duxbury Press.
Byrne, Barbara (2005), 'Factor analytic models: viewing the structure of an assessment instrument from three perspectives', *Journal of Personality Assessment*, **85** (1), 17–32.
Byrne, Barbara (2009), *Structural Equation Modeling with AMOS: Basic Concepts, Applications, And Programming*, 2nd edn, Danvars, MA: Taylor & Francis.
Cureton, Edward E. and Ralph B. D'Agostino (1993), *Factor Analysis: An Applied Approach*, Hillsdale, NJ: Lawrence Erlbaum Associates.
Glaser, B.G. and A.L. Strauss (1967 [2012]), *The Discovery of Grounded Theory: Strategies for Qualitative Research*, reprinted 2012, Chicago, IL: Aldine Transaction.
Heilbroner, Robert L. and William S. Milberg (2012), *The Making of Economic Society*, Upper Saddle River, NJ: Pearson.
Lawson, T. (1997), *Economics and Reality*, London: Routledge.
Lawson, T. (2003), *Reorienting Economics*, London: Routledge.
Lee, Frederic S. (2003), 'Theory foundation and the methodological foundations of post-Keynesian economics', in Paul Downward (ed.), *Applied Economics and the Critical Realist Critique*, London: Routledge, pp. 170–93.
Lee, F.S. (ed.) (2013), *Markets, Competition, and the Economy as a Social System*, Hoboken, NJ: Wiley-Blackwell.
Loechin, John C. (1998), *Latent Variable Models: An Introduction to Factor, Path, and Structural Equation Analysis*, Mahwah, NJ: Lawrence Erlbaum Associates.
Lowe, Adolph (1951), 'On the mechanistic approach in economics', *Social Research*, **18** (4), 403–34.
Miles, R.E., C.C. Snow, A.D. Meyer, and H.J. Coleman, Jr (1978), 'Organizational strategy, structure and process', *Academy of Management Review*, **3** (3), 546–62.
Murray, M.J. (2013), 'Effective demand, technological change, and the job guarantee program', in M.J. Murray

and M. Forstater (eds), *The Job Guarantee: Toward True Full Employment*, New York: Palgrave Macmillan, pp. 95–124.

Nell, E.J. (1998), *The General Theory of Transformational Growth: Keynes After Sraffa*, Cambridge: Cambridge University Press.

Nell, Edward J. (2004), 'Critical realism and transformational growth', in Paul Lewis (ed.), *Transforming Economics: Perspectives on the Critical Realist Project*, Oxford: Routledge, pp. 76–95.

Nell, Edward J. and D. Gualerzi (2010), 'Transformational growth in the 1990s: government, finance and hi-tech', *Review of Political Economy*, **22** (1), 97–117.

Nelson, Richard R. and Sidney G. Winter (1982), *An Evolutionary Theory of Economic Change*, Cambridge, MA: Harvard University Press.

Robinson, Joan (1962), *Essays in the Theory of Economic Growth*, London: Macmillan.

Sayer, A. (1992), *Method in Social Science: A Realist Approach*, 2nd edn, London: Routledge.

Scazzieri, Roberto (1997), 'Analytical descriptions and theoretical pluralism in economics', in Andrea Salanti and Ernesto Screpanti (eds), *Pluralism in Economics: New Perspectives in History and Methodology*, Cheltenham, UK and Lyme, NH, USA: Edward Elgar, pp. 158–69.

Schumpeter, J.A. (1954), *History of Economic Analysis*, New York: Oxford University Press.

Sheskin, David (2003), *Handbook of Parametric and Nonparametric Statistical Procedures*, 3rd edn, London: Chapman & Hall/ CRC Press.

Shih, Ming-Yi, Jar-Wen Jhenh, and Lien-Fu Lai (2010), 'A two-step method for clustering mixed categorical and numeric data', *Tamkang Journal of Science and Engineering*, **13** (1), 11–19.

Song, Michael, Robert W. Nason, and C. Anthony Di Benedetto (2008), 'Distinctive marketing and information technology capabilities and strategic types: a cross-national investigation', *Journal of International Marketing*, **16** (1), 4–38.

Thurstone, L.L. and T.G. Thurstone (1941), *Factorial Studies of Intelligence*, Chicago, IL: University of Chicago Press.

Williamson, Stephen D. (2012), *Macroeconomics*, Toronto: Pearson Canada.

# 10 Regression analysis: a review
## *Paul Downward*

## 10.1  INTRODUCTION

This chapter presents a heterodox critique of regression analysis in economics but proceeds with a couple of important caveats. The first is that it does not intend to be exhaustive in terms of its discussion of the full range and technical details of regression techniques. Rather, its aim is to provide an overview of broad movements in the application of regression techniques highlighting aspects of a similar core structure. The second is that it does not draw upon a readily accepted view of what constitutes heterodox economics, as this is debated (see Backhouse 2004; Colander 2009; Davis 2009; Dequech 2007; Lawson 2003, 2006, 2009). Consequently it draws upon the author's own previous reflections, in connection with co-authors, on how critical realism, as a philosophical approach that has found resonance in heterodox economics, raises challenges for the application of regression analysis. However, unlike, for example, Lawson (1997), this chapter argues that researchers should seek to retain regression analysis as part of the inferential apparatus of economics.[1]

The chapter proceeds as follows. Section 10.2 provides a review of broad approaches to econometric analysis, the vehicle by which regression analysis is both introduced to economics researchers and applied by them. The section begins with a brief overview of 'textbook econometrics' and its antecedents before moving on to a discussion of more recent time-series and then (essentially) cross-section approaches to analysis in the context of the search for causes.[2] Section 10.3 briefly introduces critical realism and then presents a stylized overview of critical realist concerns with the use of regression analysis, focusing on both measurement and inference. Section 10.4 then suggests a modified role for regression analysis within economics. Conclusions then follow in section 10.5.

## 10.2  REGRESSION AS ECONOMETRICS[3]

The standard textbook approach to econometrics (see, e.g., Gujarati 2003) typically presents a (population) regression function of the form of equation (10.1):

$$Y_i = \beta_1 + \beta_2 X_{2i} + \beta_3 X_{3i} + \cdots + \beta_k X_{ki} + \upsilon_i \tag{10.1}$$

where $Y$ is the dependent variable, $X_{1 \text{ to } k}$ are independent variables, $\beta_{1 \text{ to } k}$ are parameters to be estimated and $\upsilon_i$ is a random error term. $i$ represents the index of observation to which values of the variables are attached. The error term $\upsilon_i$ presents random influences on the dependent variable $Y$ and consequently converts the mathematical model linking $Y$ to the $X$s into a stochastic or statistical model representing the population of interest. In this respect the approach implicitly assumes a 'correct' representation of economic theory, as given by the variables $Y$ and the $X$s, with a maintained hypothesis that the $X$s cause $Y$. The econometric strategy then is to estimate this model based upon the correct structure. Both the form and specification of the model to be estimated are driven by theory (Bond and Harrison 1992).[4]

Key assumptions that support the estimation of the model are that: the $X$s are non-random and the variables are not subject to perfect multicollinearity; the expected value of the error terms is 0; the error term and the $X$s are not correlated; and the variance is constant irrespective of observation, that is, no heteroskedasticity is present in cross-sectional data nor autocorrelation in time-series data. It is assumed that the random error (and hence $Y$) follows a normal distribution.

Based upon a sample of data the sample regression function form of the population regression function given in equation (10.1) is estimated, for example, by ordinary least squares (OLS) in which the sum of squared residuals, as sample representations of the error term, are minimized. Under such assumptions the OLS estimator of the model provides unbiased estimates of the parameters that have minimum variance.[5] Theoretically the model is the best representation of the data possible and the underlying theory can then be assessed through tests on the sign and significance of specific parameters as well as groups of parameters as implied in goodness of fitness tests like $R^2$. If tests support the model then it follows that the actual estimate of the sample regression function given in equation (10.2) indicates that 'on average' (that is, the expected value of $Y$ conditional on $X$) the model is 'correct'. The approach is consequently often referred to as the 'average economic regression' approach (Gilbert 1986). In equation (10.2), the $b$s represent sample estimates of parameters:

$$E(Y_i|X) = b_1 + b_2X_{2i} + b_3X_{3i} + \cdots + b_kX_{ki} \qquad (10.2)$$

This aspiration to obtain a correct representation of the model means that the bulk of econometric textbooks and teaching focuses on adjusting estimates to cope with failures of the assumptions to hold. Non-normality can be dealt with by transformation of the measurement of variables, or controlling for outliers. Corrections to variance–covariance matrices and generalized least squares transformations of the OLS model are presented to solve estimation and testing problems raised by heteroskedasticity and autocorrelation. Further, instrumental variable estimation (see further below) is advocated if the $X$s are correlated to the error term, which might be a result of simultaneity of the determination of $Y$ and $X$, that an omitted variable means that a confounding variable linked to both $Y$ and $X$ is not controlled for, or that some measurement error is present in the $X$s. Typically, multicollinearity is presented as a problem of data (Gujarati 2003).

This textbook approach emerged out of arguments by Haavelmo (1944) and, more generally, the Cowles Commission, in which a concerted effort was made to approach econometrics in such a way as to use theory and the refinement of estimates to identify causal structures. This was because of concern that regression techniques lacked the ability to identify invariant structures in the data.

Identification in econometrics is typically discussed as a concern with recovering structural – that is, behavioral – parameters from estimates. In other words, based on a sample of data an estimated relationship, for example of $b_2$ from equation (10.2), may not yield information about the underlying impact of $X_2$ on $Y$, because the former might also be influenced by the latter. The analysis of identification consequently asks if one can deduce the unknown value of the parameter from the distribution of the observed data. If the answer is 'yes' then the underlying structure generating the observed data can be established. Identification is thus directly linked with cause in econometric discussion in as much that exogenous influences on observed relationships are uncovered. Of course the theoretical narrative that accompanies the uncovered statistical relationships can still vary as discussed further in the last section.

These concerns had been discussed by Keynes (1939), but also by others such as Frisch (1938). The former's argument was more (onto) logical in orientation and concerned the application of regression to non-homogenous social material. The latter emphasized the difficulty of establishing measurement without error and hence the causality implied in a regression equation. Essentially, reordering the model could produce entirely different, or in Keynes's terminology a 'free choice' of, parameter estimates. Significantly, Frisch (1948) expressed his concerns as arising from the presence of multicollinearity. This suggests that originally multicollinearity was an issue of theory selection connected with identification, rather than simply being a problem with the data. For Frisch, the response to some of these concerns lay in more data descriptive analysis, setting out in 'confluence analysis' a set of 'bunch maps' of the relationships that could be identified. These were constructed by minimizing the errors on each variable sequentially and using more qualitative means to interpret them, even relying on interviews.[6]

Despite the textbook model, more recent recognition of need to modify econometric strategy has been documented in a variety of contexts, and has included both theoretical concerns, for example raised by the Lucas critique (Lucas 1976), and a more general concern that econometric analysis, despite the rhetoric of theory testing, had descended into data-mining. Researchers in practice focused on adjusting their regression specification and functional form to 'identify' significant parameters that suited their motives but may reflect spurious correlation, rather than true underlying structure (Hoover and Perez 2000). Cooley and LeRoy (1981), for example, provide an extensive discussion of such strategies and argue that incentives exist for researchers to become advocates for their theories. In one sense, it might be argued that there is nothing inherently wrong in such activity, because academic freedom suggests that opportunity exists for challenges to accepted wisdom. However, the sociology of knowledge warns of the dangers of limited paradigm change or degenerating research programs (Kuhn 1962; Lakatos 1978), and there is strong evidence that the neoclassical theories that dominate economics reflect a lack of desire to engage with a plurality of theory and, more seriously, a lack of opportunity to challenge existing wisdom within the economics profession and academy (Lee 2007). Nonetheless, two econometric responses to these issues are now discussed as they have arisen to confront the issue of 'identification', which is central to the econometrician's concept of cause.

**Time Series Responses**

One response to the increasingly recognized ad hoc nature of identification in econometrics is vector auto regression (VAR) analysis, which was originally popularized by Sims (1980, 1982). In this context a series of variables are regressed upon their own lagged values and lags of the other variables as well. The idea is to let theory decide which variables enter the analysis, but testing the lag structures determines the form of relationship that exists. Consequently, no exogenous variables or identifying restrictions are imposed and the approach has been described as atheoretical (Cooley and LeRoy 1985; Pesaran and Smith 1992). Equations (10.3) and (10.4) illustrate the model for two variables and $p$, $q$ lags, where $t$ refers to the time period:

$$Y_t = \alpha_0 + \sum_{i=1}^{p} \alpha_i Y_{t-i} + \sum_{i=1}^{q} \beta_i X_{t-i} + \varepsilon_{1t} \tag{10.3}$$

$$X_t = a_0 + \sum_{i=1}^{p} a_i Y_{t-i} + \sum_{i=1}^{q} b_i X_{t-i} + \varepsilon_{2t} \tag{10.4}$$

Following Granger (1969), significant $\beta$ and $a$ parameters suggest two-way causality. In contrast, significance in either of the $\beta$ and $a$ parameters only suggests that causality runs from the particular right-hand-side variable connected with the significant parameters. Causality in this sense is linked to the temporal ordering of events as a source of exogenous influence. Following Engle and Granger (1987), equation (10.3) (or 10.4), can be also be reparameterized as equation (10.5):

$$\delta Y_t = \alpha_0 + \sum_{i=1}^{q} \beta_i \delta X_{t-i} - \gamma (Y_{t-1} - \phi X_{t-1}) + \varepsilon_{1t} \tag{10.5}$$

This equation indicates that changes in a given variable ($Y$) are related in the short run to changes in the other variables ($X$), but that in the long run, as indicated by the third term, the series are cointegrated such that the structure of differences between them does not persist over time. For example, as $Y$ begins to exceed $X$, this has a negative effect on the changes in $Y$.[7]

Equation (10.5) has been readily interpreted as capturing elements of neoclassical economic theory, as tests for cointegration could imply forces for equilibrium being observed.[8] More generally, Hendry (1993) has allied this time-series approach, in the 'LSE school', to one in which testing competing theories should take place by encompassing alternatives within a general model, and then reducing this to a more specific form through testing, which may or may not be indicative of a particular theory. This is referred to as 'general to specific' modeling. At its core lies the concept of a data generating process, which is the joint probability of all of the data, and whose representation is the objective of modeling which can encompass a number of alternative empirical models. These empirical models in turn may not be connected uniquely to a theoretical model. In this sense, as indicated earlier, there remains a fundamental problem of identification in econometrics. Hansen (1996), moreover, has also argued that an aspiration of nesting all relevant empirical models and testing between them is unsustainable.

## Cross-Section Responses[9]

The requirement for identification has also been emphasized, most recently in the context of a desire to evaluate the impact of policy more appropriately, as the impact of 'treatment' on 'outcomes' (Morgan and Winship 2007; Angrist and Pischke 2008). The broad context of these discussions is cross-sectional relationships, or at least having relatively large sets of cases $n$ compared to time periods $t$ in panel data. The policy evaluation problem can be presented as in equations (10.6) and (10.7) in which the average treatment effects for the treated (ATT) and average treatment effects for the controlled (ATC) are presented. $Y$ is an outcome variable of interest, and $D$ a treatment that if applied is scored 1 and if not is scored 0.[10] The subscripts on the outcome variable indicate their state according to whether or not the treatment has been applied:

$$ATT{:}E(Y_1 - Y_0|D = 1) = E(Y_1|D = 1) - \boldsymbol{E(Y_0|D = 1)} \tag{10.6}$$

$$ATC{:}E(Y_1 - Y_0|D = 0) = \boldsymbol{E(Y_1|D = 0)} - E(Y_0|D = 0) \tag{10.7}$$

These two equations reveal an important feature of evaluation which is that if the treatment is applied to an individual you cannot observe what the behavior of $Y$ might have been without the treatment (see the last term of equation 10.6, in bold). Alternatively, if the treatment is not applied to an individual you cannot observe what the behavior of $Y$ might have been with the treatment (see equation 10.7, in bold). These are counterfactual influences which need to be controlled for in establishing the causal impact of a treatment. Whilst accounting for these effects at the individual level is simply not possible as the treatment is either assigned to an individual or not, accounting for their impacts at the average level as expressed in the equations is possible. With non-experimental data, moreover, the non-random assignment of treatment to (samples of) individuals needs to be analyzed because if this is related to outcomes then causal effects are not established.

Blundell and Dias (2002, 2008) outline a variety of empirical strategies relevant for analyzing non-experimental data in the evaluation context to identify causal effects. These include the difference-in-difference approach, discontinuity design methods, the control function approach, instrumental variables, and matching.[11] The difference-in-difference approach compares mean differences in outcomes from a comparison of a treatment group and a control group both before and after a treatment is assigned. The discontinuity design and control function approaches, in contrast, explicitly model the selection of individuals into the treatment group.[12] In the former case analysis focuses on observing treatment effects when a discontinuous change in the probability of treatment being applied occurs, for example through eligibility for a policy. The control function approach explicitly models assignment to the treatment as a 'selection' problem. The instrumental variables approach makes use of variables that are assumed to affect outcomes only indirectly but are correlated to the treatment. This approach relies on having exogenous information to assign the treatment between groups in order to identify the treatment effects, and was a central feature of the discussion on how to identify causal effects in the Cowles Committee. Finally, matching analysis relies on identifying groups of individuals that are as alike as possible in observed characteristics other than the treatment, upon which to base comparisons. The aim is to ensure that the observations are what the treated would have been if untreated. In this sense a propensity score is often used to allocate matches, which is a form of regression.

## 10.3   CRITICAL REALISM

Critical realism is a philosophical position that developed a foundation in the social sciences with Bhaskar (1975, 1987, 1989) and has been further developed and applied to economics through the work of Tony Lawson and contemporaries (Lawson 2003, 2006, 2009). The aim of much of this work has been to subject economic analysis to ontological scrutiny. On this basis a critique of neoclassical economics and econometrics has been offered, as well as discussion connected with the formulation of an alternative heterodox approach to economics.

Critical realism adopts the ontological position that reality is a structured open system comprising three interrelated but relatively distinct domains. Reality is stratified to comprise actual events that occur, the real causes of those events, and our empirical understanding of events. In this regard critical realism argues that both the natural and social spheres can, in principle, be understood in the same way.

Because reality is an open system, critical realism argues that these domains are not perfectly synchronized and consequently causes of events can act transfactually in their natural setting. This means that actual events may emerge out of the action of a multitude of causal mechanisms, some of which may not always be triggered in any given context.[13] Observations of the same phenomena may not, therefore, be reducible to the same causal mechanism; that is, the triggering of some power to produce change. Moreover, the observation of events and their causes are only understood through the sense experiences of the empirical domain. Hermeneutic moments – that is, the interpretation of evidence through both the individual researcher's consciousness and the social context of the research – will influence the researcher's understanding of the causes of events. It follows that providing a causal explanation of phenomena is not only both difficult but also requires ontological depth and the recognition that deeper causal mechanisms act through the exercise of their power to change phenomena which then emerge into actual events taking place.

The logic of inference required to formulate causal explanations espoused by critical realism is retroduction. This is as opposed to deduction or induction or their combination in, for example, the hypothetico-deductive model. The causal narrative in these latter modes of reasoning, it is argued, relies on the constant conjunction of events as sets of observations to be generalized from, or theoretical predictions of events to be tested. Lawson (1997) describes these approaches as 'empirical realism'. There is the implicit invocation of a closed system which has the consequence of producing an 'epistemic fallacy'. There is a closed system because of the intrinsic condition of closure (ICC), that every cause has the same effect; and the extrinsic condition of closure (ECC), that every effect has the same cause. This can be illustrated in equations (10.8) to (10.10) below:

$$Y_i = Y_i(X_i, \varepsilon_i) \tag{10.8}$$

$$Y_i \leftarrow Y_i(X_i, \varepsilon_i) \tag{10.9}$$

$$Y_i \rightarrow Y_i(X_i, \varepsilon_i) \tag{10.10}$$

In equation (10.8) a generalized representation of all of the regression models discussed above is provided. Equation (10.9) indicates the intrinsic condition of closure, and equation (10.10) the extrinsic condition of closure. Cause and effect are logically and completely, though subject to stochastic error, contained symmetrically in equation (10.8). Presupposing that the mechanisms that are at work between variables $Y$ and $X$ are actually captured in the empirical analysis of the variables assumes that the objects that are investigated, and our subjective understanding of them, are conflated. As this cannot be the case in a non-experimental context then regression analysis can be viewed as being part of an inherently logically flawed method of inference, however the specifics of the analysis are expressed. Moreover, it can be argued that because the social world is not a closed system, this is why there is a problem of identification in economics and why various identification strategies ultimately do not resolve this problem.

## 10.4   A ROLE FOR ECONOMETRICS

There are three senses in which one might argue that abandoning the use of regression analysis in economic research might be too drastic a scenario. Two of these concern more technical features of regression analysis and one is concerned with more hermeneutic matters.

Ultimately the ICC suggests that there is invariance in the relationships between causes and effects and their measurement as variables. In the sense that all forms of realist analysis look to explore generalizable phenomena in society (without conflating this with universalization), then the identification of common understanding and categorization of phenomena across different contexts is an integral part of the process. This suggests that there is nothing essentially distinct about what regression analysis contributes to analysis when it is viewed as an approach presenting variables as relatively enduring and stable measurements of relatively enduring and stable underlying phenomena. Moreover it is clear that regression analysis can proceed with a wide variety of assumptions connected with both the measurement of the variables and how they are combined. For example, variables could be measured as being nominal, ordered, intervals, and ratios, and presented as parts of more generalized combinations (see the Appendix). It is, of course, true that regression analysis is a highly formal manifestation of this reasoning and thus less malleable as a narrative, but, as argued earlier, explicitly using a variety of (forms of) regression analyses to explore the robustness of insights about the relationships between variables by comparing results increases this malleability and necessarily sensitizes the results to context.

Such a strategy in the use of regression analysis would also help to address concerns raised by the ECC. The discussions above illustrate the difficulties and problems associated with relying on point estimates of single parameters, perhaps from one reported model, as is typically the case in neoclassical economics. However, exploring how sets of relationships and combinations of variables may be bounded helps to explore how phenomena are possibly linked. Exploring these in a contrastive way across time periods and units of analysis without a presupposition that generalities should be the norm is to respond to concern that because of their manifestation in an open system, data regularities will be expected to break down. In this way both descriptive presentation of results, or building statistical inference upon (what are in essence assumed to be immutable) probability distributions can take place, but should be done with explicit recognition that only during periods of stability may regular patterns of behavior and outcomes be identified, but these cannot be known a priori and if observed may be expected to fail. In other words all of the estimates are (ontologically) conditional upon a stability that we cannot assume to persist.

Adopting this approach to regression is to explicitly recognize that regression analysis does not provide a basis for a test of a specific theoretical position. The discussions above highlight this clearly, and suggest that this logically can never be. Despite the collective narrative of the econometric strategies above that implicitly retain the claim that at least aspects of a 'true' theory can be uncovered, this is to ignore the obvious point that the econometric analysis simply tests whether sample characteristics correspond or not to assumed population characteristics under the proviso that the underlying structures generating events are relatively stable and enduring. Postulating why the variables might be linked at all is simply a maintained and prior theoretical conjecture. For example, observing a negative parameter between being female and labor force participation could be 'explained' with reference to a neoclassical time allocation theory, and the preferences of individual females for home rather than market work. It could, however, be symptomatic of 'patriarchy' in the labor market. Viewed in this way the statistical inference remains fundamentally descriptive. The explanation for the phenomena must reside in other postulated mechanisms than are captured in the data and which ultimately, if implicitly in much neoclassical econometric analysis, leads to the search for regularities in the first place. Making clear this hermeneutic practice and exposing the basis of the arguments that lead to the conjectures of causes whose implications need to be understood could clearly be part of a retroduction exercise. As Downward and Mearman (2007) argue, the triangulation of insights would seem to be essential for retroduction. Methods of analysis like regression could codify more general behavior which may then be linked to insights from a plurality of methods of analysis like interviews, focus groups, participant observation, and documentary analysis that are, perhaps, more suitable for suggesting the actual processes that cause events to happen. Collectively the shared insights might provide a basis for investigating the production and relative generality of events that can then form the basis of theoretical evaluation and policy discussion. It is interesting to close this discussion by noting that this idea resonates with Frisch's (1948) earlier arguments.

## 10.5  CONCLUSION

This chapter presents a heterodox critique of regression analysis in economics in the sense that it reviews whether critical realist concerns should lead to the abandonment of regression analysis. A review is provided of the textbook account of regression analysis in econometrics before discussing different ways in which econometrics has tried to cope with the generally agreed difficulties of identification. From an econometric perspective identification is concerned with uncovering the structure that generates the data being observed. The critical realist position is then examined, and its arguments that the general econometric approach is indicative of an ontologically illegitimate application of a closed system to a structured open system. The chapter closes by arguing that set within the context that causes of events might be relatively enduring, but are subject to change, regression analysis, and particularly sets of results being compared, provides a basis for exploring the potential generality of events that can be linked to underlying causes that are more fully articulated with reference to other forms of evidence. In this way the problem with regression analysis is that it has been assumed in neoclassical economics both to give too much precision to the measurement of, and to be solely wedded to a singular view of, behavior. Consequently, critical theoretical discussion, as opposed to the technical exposition of a *specific* theory, is now ignored in economic analysis. Attempts to reform econometrics thus remain primarily linked to the aspiration of improving the precision with which to add to this technical exposition. The logical difficulty in doing this explains why different practices exist in econometrics.

## NOTES

1. In this regard the chapter draws heavily on previously published material, particularly that authored with Andrew Mearman. See, for example, Downward (2003, 2007), Downward et al. (2002), and Downward and Mearman (2002, 2003a, 2003b, 2004, 2007, 2008).
2. Elements of both of these sections easily combine into the panel data context in which large $n$ and small $t$ is typically contrasted with small $n$ and large $t$ for the primarily cross-section or time-series nature of the data respectively.
3. This section does not discuss the Bayesian approach to econometrics which was championed by Leamer (1983) in recognition of the problems facing the textbook (*American Economic Review*, AER) approach. A review of this work is available in Gilbert (1998) and Keuzenkamp (2000).
4. It is worth noting at this point that the linear regression model theoretically represents an attempt to capture how a set of variables have independent effects on $Y$, whose behavior, alternatively, can be decomposed into its distinct constituents. Consequently, interpretation and testing from a neoclassical economics perspective has a 'natural' focus upon individual estimated parameters or 'marginal effects' upon $Y$ following unit changes in a particular $X$ *ceteris paribus*.
5. A best linear unbiased estimate (BLUE) is obtained.
6. Such arguments coincided with the development of other data descriptive approaches such as factor analysis.
7. The third term represents the residuals of a regression equation such as equation (10.1), and unit root tests on these residuals can be used to test for cointegration; that is their stationarity. Multivariate versions of the test are discussed in Johansen (1995).
8. In reality, of course, all that the model suggests is that some mechanism might prevent the variable's time paths being too divergent. As many time-series econometric models are estimated in logarithms as well, it is not necessary to think of cointegration as equivalent to equilibrium in the levels of variables as implied in neoclassical theory.
9. More generally, econometrics has developed wide-ranging sets of estimators to deal with survey data and discrete outcomes including the censoring and truncation of dependent variables and also binary, multinomial, and ordered as well as count outcomes. This reflects a serious (ontological) concern of econometricians to measure the properties of phenomena adequately. The Appendix presents one way of summarizing these latter, discrete-choice models.
10. Treatment in this sense could refer to an actual policy intervention being evident, or simply to represent a characteristic, whose effect upon $Y$ is being investigated.
11. In each of these cases conditional means of $Y$ on sets of observed characteristics or variables $X$ typically apply.
12. This includes using a variable in the treatment assignment equation that is not included in the outcome equation as an instrumental variable (see below). The methods are thus not mutually exclusive.
13. For example, in a twin-engined plane, one engine might be all that is needed to cause a plane to fly in the sense that it provides forward momentum upon which the lift from aerodynamics can operate.

# REFERENCES

Angrist, J.D. and J. Pischke (2008), *Mostly Harmless Econometrics: An Empiricist's Companion*, Princeton, NJ: Princeton University Press.

Backhouse, R. (2004), 'A suggestion for clarifying the study of dissent in economics', *Journal of the History of Economic Thought*, **26** (2), 261–71.

Bhaskar, R.A. (1975), *A Realist Theory of Science*, London: Verso.

Bhaskar, R.A. (1987), *Scientific Realism and Human Emancipation*, London: Verso.

Bhaskar, R.A. (1989), *Reclaiming Reality: A Critical Introduction to Contemporary Philosophy*, London: Verso.

Blundell, R. and M. Costa Dias (2002), 'Alternative approaches to evaluation in empirical microeconomics', Cemmap working paper, CWP 10/02.

Blundell, R. and M. Costa Dias (2008), 'Alternative approaches to evaluation in empirical microeconomics', accessed August 7, 2014 at http://www.ucl.ac.uk/~uctp39a/Blundell-CostaDias-27-09-2008.pdf.

Bond, D. and M.J. Harrison (1992), 'Some recent developments in econometric model selection and estimation', *Statistician*, **41** (3), 315–25.

Colander, D. (2009), 'Moving beyond the rhetoric of pluralism: suggestions for an "inside-the-mainstream" heterodoxy', in R. Garnett, E. Olsen, and M. Starr (eds), *Economic Pluralism*, London: Routledge, pp. 36–47.

Cooley, T.F. and S.F. LeRoy (1981), 'Identification and estimation of money demand', *American Economic Review*, **71** (5), 825–44.

Cooley, T.F. and S.F. LeRoy (1985), 'A theoretical macro econometrics: a critique', *Journal of Monetary Economics*, **16** (3), 283–308.

Davis, J. (2009), 'The nature of heterodox economics', in Edward Fullbrook (ed.), *Ontology and Economics: Tony Lawson and his Critics*, London and New York: Routledge, pp. 83–92.

Dequech, D. (2007), 'Neoclassical, mainstream, orthodox and heterodox economics', *Journal of Post Keynesian Economics*, **30** (2), 279–302.

Downward, P.M. (2003), 'Econometrics', in John King (ed.), *Elgar Companion to Post Keynesian Economics*, Cheltenham, UK and Northampton, MA, USA: Edward Elgar, pp. 96–101.

Downward, P.M. (2007), 'Empirical analysis and critical realism', in M. Hartwig (ed.), *A Dictionary of Critical Realism*, London: Routledge.

Downward, P.M., J. Finch, and J. Ramsay (2002), 'Critical realism, empirical methods and inference: acritical discussion', *Cambridge Journal of Economics*, **26** (4), 481–500.

Downward, P.M. and A. Mearman (2002), 'Critical realism and econometrics: constructive dialogue with Post Keynesian economics', *Metroeconomica*, **53** (4), 391–415.

Downward, P.M. and A. Mearman (2003a), 'Critical realism and econometrics: interaction between philosophy and post Keynesian practice', in P.M. Downward (ed.), *Applied Economics and the Critical Realist Critique*, London: Routledge, pp. 111–28.

Downward, P.M. and A. Mearman (2003b), 'Presenting demi-regularities: the case of post Keynesian pricing', in P.M. Downward (ed.), *Applied Economics and the Critical Realist Critique*, London: Routledge, pp. 247–65.

Downward, P.M. and A. Mearman (2004), 'Presenting "demi-regularities" of pricing behaviour: the need for triangulation', in L.R. Wray and M. Forstater (eds), *Contemporary Post Keynesian Analysis*, Cheltenham, UK and Northampton, MA, USA: Edward Elgar, pp. 285–300.

Downward, P.M. and A. Mearman (2007), 'Retroduction as mixed-methods triangulation in economic research: reorienting economics into social science', *Cambridge Journal of Economics*, **31** (1), 77–99.

Downward, P.M. and A. Mearman (2008), 'Reorienting economics through triangulation of methods', in E. Fullbrook (ed.), *Ontology and Economics: Tony Lawson and his Critics*, London: Routledge, pp. 130–41.

Engle, R.F. and C.W.J. Granger (1987), 'Co-integration and error correction: representation, estimation and testing', *Econometrica*, **55** (2), 251–76.

Frisch, R. (1938), 'Statistical versus theoretical relations in economic macrodynamics', Mimeo in Memorandum of 6/11/48 entitled, 'Autonomy of economic relations', Oslo, Norway: Universitets Okonomiske Institutt.

Frisch, R. (1948), 'Repercussion studies at Oslo', *American Economic Review*, **38** (3), 367–72.

Gilbert, C. (1986), 'Professor Hendry's econometric methodology', *Oxford Bulletin of Economics and Statistics*, **48** (3), 283–305.

Gilbert, C. (1998), 'Econometric methodology', in J.B. Davis, D. Wade, and U. Mäki (eds), *The Handbook of Economic Methodology*, Cheltenham, UK and Lyme, NH, USA: Edward Elgar, pp. 211–16.

Granger, C.W.J. (1969), 'Investigating causal relations by econometric models and cross-spectral methods', *Econometrica*, **37** (3), 424–38.

Gujarati, D.N. (2003), *Basic Econometrics*, New York: McGraw-Hill.

Haavelmo, T. (1944), 'The probability approach in econometrics', *Econometrica*, **12** (Supplement), 1–118.

Hansen, B.E. (1996), 'Review article, methodology: alchemy or science?', *Economic Journal*, **106** (9), 1398–1413.

Hendry, D. (1993), *Econometrics: Alchemy or Science? Essays in Econometric Methodology*, Oxford: Blackwell.

Hoover, K.D. and S.J. Perez (2000), 'Three attitudes towards data mining', *Journal of Economic Methodology*, **7** (2), 195–210.
Johansen, S. (1995), *Likelihood-Based Inference in Cointegrated Vector Autoregressive Models*, Oxford: Oxford University Press.
Keuzenkamp, H. (2000), *Probability, Econometrics and Truth: The Methodology of Econometrics*, Cambridge: Cambridge University Press.
Keynes, J.M. (1939), 'Professor Tinbergen's method', *Economic Journal*, **49**, 558–68.
Kuhn, T.S. (1962), *The Structure of Scientific Revolutions*, Chicago, IL: University of Chicago Press.
Lakatos, I. (1978), *The Methodology of Scientific Research Programmes: Philosophical Papers*, Vol. 1, Cambridge: Cambridge University Press.
Lawson, T. (1997), *Economics and Reality*, London: Routledge.
Lawson, T. (2003), *Reorienting Economics*, London: Routledge.
Lawson, T. (2006), 'The nature of heterodox economics', *Cambridge Journal of Economics*, **30** (4), 483–505.
Lawson, T. (2009), 'Heterodox economics and pluralism: reply to Davis', in E. Fullbrook (ed.), *Ontology and Economics: Tony Lawson and his Critics*, London: Routledge, pp. 93–129.
Leamer, E. (1983), 'Let's take the con out of econometrics', *American Economic Review*, **73** (1), 31–43.
Lee, Frederic S. (2007), 'The research assessment exercise, the state and the dominance of mainstream economics in British universities', *Cambridge Journal of Economics*, **31** (4), 309–25.
Lucas, R. (1976), 'Econometric policy evaluation: acritique', in K. Brunner and A. Meltzer (eds), *The Phillips Curve and Labor Markets*, New York: Elsevier, pp. 19–46.
Morgan, S.L. and C. Winship (2007), *Counterfactuals and Causal Inference: Methods and Principles for Social Research*, Cambridge: Cambridge University Press.
Pesaran, M. and R. Smith (1992), 'The interaction between theory and observation in economics', *Economic and Social Review*, **24** (1), 1–24.
Sims, C.A. (1980), 'Macroeconomics and reality', *Econometrica*, **48** (1), 1–48.
Sims, C.A. (1982), 'Scientific standards in econometric modelling', in M. Hazewinkel and A.H.G. Rinnooy-Kan (eds), *Current Developments in the Interface: Economics, Econometrics, Mathematics*, Dordrecht: D. Reidel, pp. 317–37.

# APPENDIX 10A.1   GENERALIZED LINEAR MODELS (GLM)

In generalized linear models (GLM), the transformed expectation of the dependent variable $Y$ is modeled as in equation (10A.1). In this way an underlying linear relationship is used to inform how factors affect a dependent variable that has a discrete or non-continuous form:

$$gE(Y_i) = b_1 + b_2 X_{2i} + b_3 X_{3i} \qquad (10A.1)$$

Importantly, the model is comprised of three components. First there is a random component indicating the conditional distribution of $Y_i$ given $X_i$. This might include exponential forms as in the binomial, Poisson, and multinomial cases, but also non-exponential forms such as the negative binomial case. Second, there is a linear predictor as indicated in equation (10A.2) which captures the influence of independent variables:

$$\eta_i = b_1 + b_2 X_{2i} + b_3 X_{3i} \qquad (10A.2)$$

Finally, there is a link function $g(\cdot)$ which transforms the expectation of the dependent variable $\mu_i \equiv E(Y_i)$, to the linear predictor as in equation (10A.3):

$$g(\mu_i) = g(E(Y_i)) = \eta_i = b_1 + b_2 X_{2i} + b_3 X_{3i} \qquad (10A.3)$$

In such models the estimated parameters have effects on the dependent variable through changes in the relevant independent variable, but also the other variables. Consequently, marginal effects need to be calculated to isolate the influence of a particular variable.

# 11 Critical realism, econometrics, and heterodox economics
## Nuno Ornelas Martins

## 11.1 INTRODUCTION

Econometrics, understood as the measurement of quantities relevant to economic analysis, has a long tradition in economics, which goes back at least to the authors that Joseph Schumpeter (1954 [1994], pp. 209–43) called the early 'econometricians', such as William Petty, Richard Cantillon, and François Quesnay. However, the approach adopted by those authors, who were the initiators of classical political economy, is very different from that of the contemporary econometricians. For classical political economists like Petty, Cantillon, and Quesnay, economic science was the study of the production and distribution of the surplus. To study this process, they developed arithmetical methods of measuring the surplus, taking into account quantities which can be objectively observed and measured, such as the quantity of land and quantity of labor time employed in the production process.

The classical surplus approach developed by those authors, which was continued by Smith, Ricardo, and Marx, was abandoned by the more influential schools of thought after the marginal revolution (and was already being abandoned after Ricardo). The introduction of differential calculus into economics played an important role here, as the emphasis was switched from the process of production and distribution of the surplus as a whole, focusing on aggregate quantities measured through arithmetic methods, towards marginal changes studied through differential calculus.

After the marginal revolution, the relationship between prices and quantities started to be studied in terms of marginal changes represented by supply and demand curves, and economics became increasingly concerned with the relation between the increment of a given quantity $X$ and the increment of another quantity $Y$, while assuming everything else constant. Although this mode of reasoning emerged in the nineteenth century, it became more dominant than ever throughout the twentieth century, within neoclassical economics. In this context, econometrics emerged as an autonomous field within the mid-twentieth century, focusing on how changes in one variable affect another variable, while isolating the studied variables from everything else. The measurement of aggregate quantities taking into account the whole system, which was the method adopted by the classical authors, was relegated to the study of national accounts, and considered less scientific than the study of constant conjunctions of the form 'if event X then event Y'.

Critical realism in economics emerged as a critique of the use of methods which presuppose systems characterized by constant conjunctions of the form 'if event X then event Y', systems which are defined in critical realism as closed systems. In so doing, critical realism engaged in a critique of mainstream economics, including mainstream econometrics, due to its use of methods that presuppose closed systems. Critical realism both observes that constant conjunctions of the form 'if event X then event Y' are not ubiquitous, and indeed are rare, and also emphasizes that the socio-economic realm is an internally related open system in process.

But critical realism constitutes a philosophical perspective, and does not engage in substantive theorizing. Rather, it has been concerned with philosophically under-laboring for a more relevant economic theory and method, which does not presuppose a priori the existence of closed systems, and focuses on the reproduction of socio-economic structures as a whole, as the classical political economists and Marx had done. Critical realism advances a transformational conception of social activity, in which social structures are the condition of possibility of human agency, which in turn not only reproduces but also transforms social structures.

The set of substantive contributions that fall within the conception advocated by critical realism is the set of contributions often designated as 'heterodox economics'. The substantive theories developed within heterodox economics have been concerned with the reproduction of socio-economic structures as a whole, paying close attention to social provisioning in this context.

In so doing, heterodox economics engaged in a return to the surplus approach, since the study of the process of social provisioning is essentially a study of the distribution of the surplus, which was the central topic of the classical political economists who Schumpeter called the first 'econometricians'. The latter authors focused on the theory of value and price formation (a topic addressed today within what is called microeconomics), and when engaging in measurement focused on aggregate quantities in order to explain the production and distribution of the surplus (as heterodox macroeconomists have done since Kalecki and Keynes), rather than on correlations between increments in variable $X$ and increments in variable $Y$, as mainstream economists and econometricians do while presupposing closed systems.

## 11.2   NEOCLASSICAL ECONOMICS AND MAINSTREAM ECONOMETRICS

As Schumpeter (1954 [1994], p. 209, fn. 2) notes, the term 'econometrics', coined by Ragnar Frisch, emerges in the mid-twentieth century in order to designate a research program which entails much more than mere measurement of observable quantities. The emergence of the field of econometrics in the twentieth century, together with the distinction between microeconomics and macroeconomics also stressed by Frisch, led to the structure of modern mainstream economics, typically divided into these three subfields: microeconomics, macroeconomics, and econometrics.

Schumpeter (1954 [1994], pp. 209–43) argues, however, that if 'econometrics' means the measurement of quantities relevant to economic analysis, then econometrics is a field which goes back into the very emergence of classical political economy, when authors such as Petty, Cantillon, and Quesnay developed arithmetical methods for measuring objective and observable quantities relevant to economic analysis. But in so doing, Petty, Cantillon, and Quesnay adopted an integrated approach, rather than separating economic analysis into microeconomics, macroeconomics, and econometrics.

The approach of the early classical political economists was macroeconomic in the sense that they focused on the study of the reproduction of the economy and society as a whole. The unit of analysis they used, which was also used by those who followed their approach such as Smith, Ricardo, and Marx, was the social class, rather than the isolated individual presupposed in mainstream microeconomics. The approach of those authors, designated by Marx as 'classical political economists', consisted of studying the production and distribution of the surplus throughout the various social classes.

For the classical political economists, the need to engage in economic measurement emerged initially in the context of a theoretical problem, concerning the definition of the surplus. In order to define the surplus, it is necessary to know how to value outputs and inputs in the production process, so that the surplus can be defined as the difference between the aggregate quantity of outputs and the aggregate quantity of inputs. The key production inputs considered by the classical authors were land and labor. Political arithmetic, to use the term employed by Petty, consisted thus in the measurement of value focusing on objective and observable entities such as quantity of labor time and quantity of land. Karl Marx (1867 [1999]) uses the term 'classical political economy' to designate the approach running from Petty to Ricardo, in order to distinguish it from the approach of Nassau William Senior and John Elliot Cairnes, in which subjective elements such as 'abstinence' and 'sacrifice' start to play a key role in the explanation of the cost of production.

The contribution of Menger, Jevons, and Walras constitutes for many a break with classical political economy, where subjective elements start to play a key role in the explanation of demand too. Marshall (1890 [1920]), however, argued that his approach was in continuity with classical political economy, which he interprets as an approach centered on supply and demand analysis, rather than on the reproduction and distribution of the surplus with value explained in objective terms. In Marshall's (1890 [1920]) framework, the cost of production includes subjective elements such as Senior's 'abstinence' (which Marshall prefers to call 'waiting') or Cairnes's 'sacrifice', which are represented through a supply curve. The demand curve, in turn, represents subjective marginal utility, in line with the marginalist authors. Marshall used supply and demand curves so construed in order to explain the mutual determination of prices and quantities.

Marshall faced a methodological problem when using supply and demand curves, namely the fact that those curves cannot move independently. Moving one curve triggers a sequence of events that leads to changes in the other curve, as Sraffa (1925, 1926) was later to show. Thus, in order to use supply and demand curves when determining prices and quantities, Marshall (1890 [1920]) assumed that everything else remains constant, for a time, in a pound called *ceteris paribus*.

Marshall (1919 [1923]) found a methodological justification for this procedure in Newton's and Leibniz's differential calculus, who noted that when looking at small changes, we can focus on the direct effect of a change in one variable $X$ on another variable $Y$, while assuming that the indirect effects (the effect of a change on variable $X$ on some variable $Z$ which in turn influences variable $Y$) are negligible, since they will be a very small thing of a very small thing. This, of course, presupposes that changes are infinitesimally small, so that the product of an infinitesimally small quantity (the change in $Z$ caused by a change in $X$) by another infinitesimally small quantity (the change in $Y$ caused by a change in $Z$) can be neglected (so that we can focus on the direct effect that a change in $X$ has on $Y$).

Marshall (1890 [1920]) explains that his use of differential calculus was influenced by Augustin Cournot and Johann Heinrich Von Thünen, who used differential calculus before the marginal revolution. The procedure Marshall adopts is, of course, highly problematic, since in economics we are not dealing with infinitesimally small changes, and so indirect effects cannot be ignored, as Sraffa saw early on; see Martins (2013, Ch. 2) for a discussion of this issue with reference to Sraffa's unpublished papers.

The Marshallian neoclassical method stands in stark contrast to the method adopted by the classical political economists from Petty to Ricardo, who focused instead on the reproduction of the economic system as a whole. While the classical authors relied merely on arithmetic while focusing on aggregate quantities, neoclassical economics drew heavily upon differential calculus in order to explain the direct effect of changes in a given variable $X$ on another variable $Y$ while assuming that indirect effects can be neglected, that is, everything else remains constant.

The mathematization of economics advanced rapidly with the development of general equilibrium theory by Kenneth Arrow, Gérard Debreu, and Lionel McKenzie, and the development of game theory by John Von Neumann, Oskar Morgenstern, and John Nash. At this stage, fixed point theorems play a key role in the development of general equilibrium theory and game theory. But the use of differential calculus plays a central role in the development of mainstream economics at this stage too, so much so that Paul Samuelson (1970) focuses on the 'maximum principle' in his Memorial Nobel Prize Lecture. In his lecture, Samuelson refers also to the importance that differential calculus had to Marshall's *Principles of Economics*, which Samuelson describes as the dominant economics treatise in the 40 years following its publication (and was replaced by Samuelson's own textbook as the dominating economics treatise), while referring also to Cournot's pioneering contribution to differential calculus.

The program known as 'econometrics', led by authors such as Ragnar Frisch and Jan Tinbergen, is part of this increasing mathematization of economics in the mid-twentieth century, where differential calculus plays a central role. The research program of mainstream econometrics is centered on the formulation of an econometric model in which a given variable (or set of variables) $X$ influences a given variable (or set of variables) $Y$. The econometric model focuses only on the direct effects of $X$ on $Y$, which are expressed in terms of the regression coefficients associated with each variable $X$, leaving other aspects as part of a residual term.

In order to estimate the regression coefficients various methods are used, such as the least squares method, the method of maximum likelihood, or the generalized method of moments. All these methods consist of an optimization procedure drawing upon differential calculus, focusing on the variables which are selected, while assuming that everything else remains constant (or constitutes a mere residual which has a negligible influence on the econometric model).

The methodology employed in econometrics was criticized early on by John Maynard Keynes, who noted how it presupposes atomism; that is, presupposes that we can focus on the effect of a given variable on another variable while assuming it to be isolated from everything else. Keynes's critique of econometrics is part of his critical approach to symbolic mathematics in general, which can be seen for example in his critique of the use of differential calculus by Marshall and Pigou. According to Keynes econometrics, like differential calculus, presupposes strict independence between the various factors involved, and loses all its applicability if there is no strict independence between the variables being analyzed and the rest of reality; see, for example, Keynes's (1936, pp. 297–8) discussion of symbolic mathematics.

The problem at stake here is connected to the use of differential calculus, which led Marshall and neoclassical economics to focus on the effect of an increment in a given variable $X$ on another variable $Y$ while assuming everything else constant, in contrast with the classical method which focused instead on the arithmetic analysis of aggregate quantities. Keynes's (1936) own approach consists of a return to the study of macroeconomic aggregate quantities, which can be studied through basic arithmetic. Thus, Keynes's perspective can be seen as a return to the classical method of focusing on macroeconomic aggregate quantities.

Keynes's approach is quite compatible not only with the classical method, but also with classical theory. Keynes seems to have taken seriously Marshall's claim to be in continuity with classical political economy. Thus, when Keynes claims he is criticizing 'classical' theory, he is in truth criticizing the 'neoclassical' theory, as developed by Marshall and Pigou. But once we distinguish between classical political economy and vulgar economy, as Marx did, we see quite clearly that Keynes's theory is quite compatible with classical political economy, understood as a study of the circular process of reproduction while focusing on macroeconomic aggregate quantities; see Martins (2013, Ch. 4) for a discussion.

## 11.3   CRITICAL REALISM IN ECONOMICS

Critical realism in economics engaged in a critique of mainstream economics, including mainstream econometrics. Lawson's contribution, which is central to the development of critical realism within economics, was inspired by Keynes's methodological critique of the use of mathematical methods that presuppose atomism, as well as by the contributions of many other heterodox economists. The philosophy of critical realism, led by Roy Bhaskar, helped in systematizing the contributions of those various heterodox economists.

The conception reached within critical realism in economics is one in which human agents and social structures are in a continuous process of reproduction and transformation. The focus on the reproduction and transformation of social structures in critical realism goes back to Marx's contribution, which is explicitly acknowledged by Bhaskar and Lawson. Bhaskar's critical realism was especially influenced by the way in which Louis Althusser developed Marx's perspective, while Lawson's approach is influenced by other heterodox economists who also focused on social reality as a whole; see Martins (2013, Ch. 7).

A central notion in critical realism is the notion of 'internal relation', which can be defined as a relation which is constitutive of its parts. The notion of internal relation is present in Marx's philosophy, and is connected to the influence of Friedrich Hegel on Marx. Even if we accept Althusser's (1965 [2005]) thesis that there is an epistemological break in Marx's thinking after which Hegelianism is dropped, the notion of internal relation remains central to Marx's mature thinking.

However, if everything is internally related, we cannot have complete knowledge by focusing on a given part. If we focus only on a given part, we are missing the other parts, in a context where the relations to those parts are constitutive of the part we want to study. Drawing upon Bertell Ollman's (1993) interpretation of Marx's method, Lawson (1997) makes a distinction between abstraction and isolation in order to address this problem (which is the same problem faced by Marshall, and which Keynes pointed out when criticizing mainstream econometrics and the use of differential calculus). To abstract means to focus on a given part without supposing that the part is independent from the other parts we are abstracting from. This means that when looking at a given part, there is always uncertainty due to the existence of other parts we are abstracting from. To isolate, in contrast, means to focus on a given part while assuming that the part is not related to the other parts we are isolating it from.

Like Marx, Marshall was also influenced by Hegel and perceived the problem of internal relations early on. Marshall's use of differential calculus was a way to avoid the problem raised by internal relations, in order to focus on a given part of reality. Marshall acknowledged the existence of internal relations, but assumed that we could focus on direct effects only in order to study the conditions for partial equilibrium, while assuming indirect effects to be negligible.

Marshall's assumption that indirect effects are negligible, for a given time at least, was an attempt to avoid the uncertainty that occurs when abstracting. Bertrand Russell was so troubled by this uncertainty that he adopted the method of isolation instead, since only isolation guarantees that knowledge of a given part is not disturbed by other parts of reality. But isolation presupposes that each part is a self-sufficient atom, in the sense that it remains undisturbed by other parts of reality. Thus, Russell embraced atomism, breaking with the Cambridge philosophical tradition where internal relations were always a central notion.

In short, abstracting and isolating are two different procedures, which lead us to focus on a given part of reality. If we abstract from other parts which are internally related to the part we are focusing on, we reach knowledge of a given part which comes to us under a given degree of uncertainty and vagueness. This is why Keynes (1936, pp. 297–8) argues that ordinary discourse is a more appropriate method for describing reality than symbolic mathematics. Keynes (1936, pp. 297–8) notes that when engaging in ordinary discourse, we are using words which are part of a broader semantic context, and so we can keep at the 'back of our heads' the necessary qualifications related to the other parts we are abstracting from, taking into account internal relations. Mathematical symbols, in contrast, indicate exact rules which must not contain any uncertainty or vagueness, and presuppose that the part of reality we are focusing on is isolated from everything else.

The positivist attempt to find laws of the form 'if X then Y' is an attempt to find the connections between isolated parts, while ignoring other interactions that X and Y may have with other entities Z. Lawson (1997, 2003) defines closed systems as systems characterized by constant conjunctions of the form 'if event X then event Y', while open systems are systems in which those constant conjunctions need not occur. Lawson (1997, 2003) defines deductivism as a form of explanation which presupposes closed systems, that is, it presupposes constant conjunctions of the form 'if event X then event Y'. Critical realists criticize mainstream economics, including mainstream econometrics, due to its ubiquitous use of mathematico-deductivist methods; that is, methods that presuppose closed systems.

Mathematical methods were applied successfully in natural sciences such as physics. However, this is because closed systems are created artificially under controlled laboratory conditions, so that exact regularities are sometimes obtained, and mathematical methods can be applied successfully. Of course, in fields such as astronomy, exact regularities can be found without laboratorial manipulation. In fact, Newton developed differential calculus (which he called the 'method of fluxions') at the same time as he was studying celestial mechanics. Gauss developed regression analysis in order to study celestial mechanics too.

Techniques widely used in mainstream economics, such as differential calculus and regression analysis, proved to be very useful when applied to closed systems, be it celestial mechanics, or the systems artificially generated in the laboratory. The use of those methods indeed presupposes closed systems. Thus, if we apply those methods to social reality we are presupposing, a priori, that social reality must be characterized by closed systems, or atoms, as Keynes noted early on in his critique of econometrics.

## 11.4   REALISM, INSTRUMENTALISM, AND CAUSATION

Trygve Haavelmo tried to address the implications of the problems raised by Keynes, and pointed out the need of using joint probability density functions, to take into account that reality is deeply interconnected, as Keynes argued it is. David Hendry (2000) developed a methodology in which one starts from such an assumption, and then one tries to find reduced-form models where we can identify a given variable (or set of variables) $X$ as an exogenous or independent variable. After this is done, one can then follow the usual procedure undertaken within mainstream econometrics, which is to assume that a given variable (or set of variables) $Y$ is a dependent or endogenous variable, in the sense that it is explained in terms of the variable (or set of variables) $X$, which is typically taken to be independent or exogenous. But the variable which is supposed to be independent or exogenous is often actually endogenous too, and correlated with the error term, leading to inconsistent estimates.

There are, of course, various attempts within mainstream econometrics to circumvent these problems. One is the use of the method of instrumental variables, which can be interpreted also as a least squares method undertaken in two steps. In the first step, we find a variable $Z$ which is not correlated with the error term, but is correlated with the variable $X$. We can then estimate $X$ using $Z$, and afterwards use the estimates of $X$ which do not suffer from endogeneity since we are actually using a linear combination of $Z$ which is not endogenous.

The use of instrumental variables implies, of course, the use of variables which may have no theoretical connection to the variables we intend to explain. This is why the former are called 'instrumental' variables. In mainstream econometrics, the aim is often to find some correlation regardless of theory. The Cowles Commission, which contributed much to the establishment of mainstream econometrics, stressed the need to combine measurement with theory. But given the difficulties of engaging in measurement in the context of open systems, a tendency emerged where the aim is simply to find correlations.

This is clear in the widespread use of the method of instrumental variables, but it is also clear in the methodological position adopted by Milton Friedman (1953 [1970]), often designated as 'instrumentalism'. According to Friedman's position, economic models need have no connection to reality, as long as they predict. Friedman's position was challenged by mainstream economists such as Paul Samuelson (1963), who argued that models must be used to find an underlying structure. But whatever methodological position is explicitly supported, mainstream economics is characterized by the use of a deductivist methodology which presupposes implicitly that reality is constituted by closed systems. Friedman's instrumentalism is a more honest rendering of what is actually being done in mainstream economics, and the use of instrumental variables is often a way to simply find a correlation, even if the proposed aim of the instrumental variable method is to avoid problems of endogeneity in the explanatory variables.

The 'endogeneity' of the explanatory variables, which should be exogenous instead in order to avoid inconsistent estimators, is simply a consequence of the fact that the data generating process – that is, social reality – is an internally related open system, and so it becomes impossible to find constant conjunctions of the form 'if X then Y', and *X* cannot be seen as an independent and exogenous variable. In order to avoid this problem, Christopher Sims adopted a methodology which consists simply in assuming that all variables are endogenous, and correlating a vector of such variables with themselves at different time periods, leading to a methodology known as a VAR (vector auto regression) model. The VAR methodology is supposed to be completely atheoretical, since we are only searching for correlations, without any regard for the underlying theory.

Without an underlying theory, we are faced with the problem of causal explanation. As critical realists explain, natural scientists identify causal mechanisms because different experiments are conducted, in order to find the conditions under which causal mechanisms are triggered. If the social realm is an open system which cannot be subject to experimental control in the same way as the natural realm, we cannot identify causal mechanisms in the same way as in the natural realm. For this reason, Lawson (2003, Ch. 4) develops a methodological procedure termed 'contrast explanation', where instead of producing a given outcome in a closed system, we must wait until scientifically interesting surprising contrasts appear in socio-economic reality. While a laboratory experimental activity is forward-looking, since it deliberately produces situations where surprising contrasts become manifest and causal powers and structures are identified, contrast explanation is backward-looking, since in contrast explanation we typically look at historical data or case studies and try to find surprising contrasts that may arise in an open system.

If the social realm were a closed system, as presupposed in mainstream economics, we could find constant conjunctions of the form 'if X then Y'. However, without being able to artificially construct several experimental arrangements in order to identify the conditions which trigger specific causal mechanisms, we would be unable to find what causes what. Causes are identified when contrasting situations are observed, where in some situations causal powers are triggered, and in other situations causal powers are not triggered.

This shows that Friedman's (1953 [1970]) instrumentalist methodology is much more consistent with the deductivist methods used in mainstream economics, which presupposed closed systems. If the world is a closed system, we simply observe correlations, without being able to identify causality, since we cannot identify contrasting situations in order to find which underlying conditions trigger causal powers. All that we would be able to achieve is prediction of events based on our model, without being able to explain the real underlying causes.

## 11.5   THE MAINSTREAM ECONOMETRICIANS' CRITIQUE OF CRITICAL REALISM

Clive Granger developed a notion of causality which shows what causality means in a context of closed systems. 'Granger causality' is a conception where causality means merely whether one variable is useful for forecasting another model in the context of an econometric model. Granger (2004) criticizes critical realism for failing to note that many statistical tools developed within contemporary econometrics address the problems raised by critical realism, focusing for example on time-varying parameters, and argues that there are some examples of successful prediction in econometrics, such as that undertaken in Ramanathan et al. (1997).

As Lawson (2003) notes, his critique does not imply that closures never occur, but merely that they do not always occur, and so the insistence on always using methods that presuppose closed systems leads to a great waste of energy and effort. The problem identified in critical realism is not the use of mathematics, but rather the belief that the use of mathematico-deductivist methods is the only scientific way to undertake valuable economic research. Scientifically interesting closures are rare, and so the insistence on the use of methods that presuppose them is misplaced. Concerning time-varying parameters, which is another point raised by Granger, Lawson (2003) notes that those parameters are often described in terms of other mathematical constants, and thus the assumption of exact closure appears at another level.

Hendry (1983) criticized Lawson (1981) for failing to note that many econometricians do take into account the issues raised by Lawson; see Stephen Pratten (2005) on the debate between Hendry and Lawson. Hendry, like other econometricians such as Robert Engle, has been much concerned with the problem of endogeneity. Hendry, like Haavelmo, notes that we must start from a joint probability density function, in order to take into account the fact that reality is interconnected, and so we cannot take for granted the exonegeity and independence of the explanatory variables.

However, even if we start from a joint probability density function, we still must know which probability density function we should choose in order to describe the data generating process. The central limit theorem is sometimes pointed out as a justification for the use of normal (or Gaussian) probability functions. The central limit theorem states that the arithmetic mean of a sufficiently large number of independent and identically distributed random variables will follow approximately the normal distribution. But the central limit theorem, as usually formulated in most statistics and econometrics textbooks, presupposes independence between the various variables, which means that it presupposes isolation again. Even if dependence concepts are developed, so that the central theorem can be applied to cases where dependence exists, it must presuppose constants at some level, as all mathematics does.

Of course, other probability functions can be tested, until we find the correct one. The problem is that all probability functions must presuppose constants at some level, and the only thing which is constant in economic reality is change. The data we may want to analyze are typically not stationary, nor even ergodic, which means that we cannot assume that the study of a given time period gives us any guidance to understanding other time periods. That is, even basic concepts such as the mean, variance, or covariance may not be constants; see Paul Davidson (1994) on how Keynes's critique applies to all approaches that presuppose ergodicity. As Granger (2004) argues when criticizing critical realism, contemporary econometrics allows for time-varying parameters. But constants, and thus closure, must be found at some level so that mathematico-deductivist tools can be successfully employed.

Edward Leamer (1985) recognized the need for robust relations between variables if econometric methods are to be of any use. Thus, he developed a procedure of sensitivity analysis, often called 'extreme bounds analysis', which consists in, when studying the relationship between variables $X$ and $Y$, changing a set of variables $Z$, and see how the relationship under study (between $X$ and $Y$) is affected by those changes in variables $Z$. The relationship between variables $X$ and $Y$ is said to be robust if it is not significantly affected by the changes in $Z$. If the coefficients of a regression of $Y$ on $X$ do not remain sufficiently stable when changes in another set of variables $Z$ occur, we may wonder why we are trying to measure with precision something which is not precise at all. The same can be said of other mathematical constants we may want to find in order to describe time-varying parameters.

The point can be illustrated by imagining a graph which shows the relationship between two variables $X$ and $Y$. The points in the graph, which represent each observation, may be disposed across an exact straight line, or may be led to do so after appropriate transformations (for example logaritmization, or taking differences) are performed. In that case, we are clearly in the presence of a closed system, and it becomes important to measure exactly the slope of the line, and its intercept with the $Y$ axis, measured by the regression coefficients.

But it may also happen that the points in the graph show no exact line, or no line at all, even if they appear to indicate a more or less vague positive or negative correlation between $X$ and $Y$. Under such a situation, it often happens that adding a new observation, or removing one, significantly changes the coefficients of any regression analysis that we may perform. Under such a situation, do we gain anything by adding a regression line to the set of points represented in the graph? The coefficients we obtain under those situations are highly fragile, as Leamer (1985) points out, and the regression line only gives a false sense of precision. Probably graphical inspection of the dots on the graph, with no regression curve added, gives us a better description of the situation, since it gives us a sense of the various tendencies at stake, and of how uncertain the situation is.

A similar case occurs with supply and demand curves. As Pierangelo Garegnani (1998) explains, the classical economists did not resort to supply and demand curves in order to explain prices. For the classical authors, the gravitation of the market price around the natural price was a vague process, which is best described by a series of points in a graph which conveys the vague character of the process, as Garegnani (1998) does when representing gravitation graphically, rather than by supply and demand curves which give a false idea of precision. As Aristotle argued, we cannot aim at more precision than the precision that the subject matter allows for. If we are analyzing a closed system, mathematical methods that presuppose such systems are most appropriate. If we are analyzing an open system, a description of the system that does not presuppose closure is more appropriate.

## 11.6   HETERODOX ECONOMICS AND THE SOCIAL SURPLUS APPROACH

Since scientifically interesting closures are not found easily, we often find mainstream econometricians torturing the data until the data fit into the model, leading Leamer (1983, p. 37) to point out that in mainstream econometrics 'hardly anyone takes anyone else's data analysis seriously', as Lawson (2003, p. 11) also notes.

The problem faced by mainstream econometrics is that it engages in what Lawson (1997) calls 'isolation', by focusing on models that attempt to establish correlations between variables while assuming everything else remains constant. Lawson argues that while mainstream economics is characterized by the use of mathematico-deductivist methods that presuppose an ontology of closed systems, heterodox economics is best defined in terms of a concern with a social reality understood as an internally related open system in process. In the latter situation, the best methodological procedure available is a combination of abstraction and contrast explanation, which requires using words in the context of a narrative, rather than mathematico-deductivist methods, and thinking dialectically.

Mary Morgan (2002) suggests combining models with narrative stories when explaining reality. The question is whether the model adds anything to the narrative. When facing partial regularities represented in a graph showing several dots that do not follow an exact pattern, do we gain anything by adding a regression equation, whose coefficients are fragile enough to change significantly as new data arises? Most econometricians would argue that any good econometrician would not do so. But as Leamer (1983) and Hendry (2000) acknowledge, this is often done in fact. And the reason it is done is because whatever is perceived as mathematical complexity is immediately if erroneously equated with science. Thus, unrealistic econometric models are developed even when they bring little added value, in order to conform to what is perceived as 'proper practice' or science.

In order to engage in abstraction, rather than in isolation, the most useful mathematics is the mathematics that can be more easily explained in words, which enables us to keep in mind the various tendencies at play. And the mathematics that can be more easily explained in words is a simpler type of mathematics, rather than a too-complex analysis which presupposes closed systems while making us lose sight of the fact that an isolation, rather than an abstraction, is being made. Words are a better tool for engaging in abstraction since, as Keynes (1936, pp. 297–8) notes, when using words we can keep in mind the connections of the objects we are focusing on to the rest of reality, in a way that we cannot when using differential calculus.

The tendency to admire the mathematical tools developed within advanced physics often leads economists to forget that science is characterized not by a specific method, but rather by a concern with underlying structures and mechanisms, and with using the best methods to identify them under each context. Even in physics, the use of mathematical methods often fails to take uncertainty into account; I discuss this issue together with a physicist colleague in Rodrigues and Martins (2014). The best methods, which bring more insight into underlying structures, are not necessarily the most complicated ones, but the ones which are more appropriate given the nature of reality.

Paul Downward and Andrew Mearman (2009) suggest the use of a wider range of mathematical techniques in combination with the critical realist methodology; see Lawson (2009) for a reply. Consideration of different methods is indeed important, as Downward and Mearman (2009) argue, but the key issue at stake concerns the appropriateness of those methods used given the nature of reality. When criticizing Lawson's (1997) critique of econometrics, Kevin Hoover (2002) provides various examples that he identifies as useful econometrics. Quite significantly, the examples he points out refer to quite elementary procedures of data analysis, which Hoover (2002, p. 166) names 'primitive econometrics'. When using more elementary procedures, the underlying presuppositions can be taken into account more easily, and it becomes easier to engage in abstraction rather than in isolation.

John Finch and Robert McMaster (2002) advocate the use of categorical variables and non-parametric techniques, and suggest also an important distinction between 'econometrics mainly-as-regression' and 'econometrics-as-measurement'. If econometrics consists mainly in regression analysis, then 'econometrics' consists in the mainstream project that emerged in the mid-twentieth century, developed by authors such as Ragnar Frisch and Jan Tinbergen. If econometrics consists mainly in measurement, then it goes back to Petty, Cantillon, and Quesnay, as Schumpeter argues. Within heterodox economics, econometrics can be best interpreted as an attempt to measure quantities which are relevant to economic analysis, as was the case for the classical economists.

The quantities which are relevant for heterodox economists are the aggregate quantities that help us to explain the process of social provisioning, and those quantities help us to explain the production and distribution of the surplus, which were also studied by the early classical political economists. But the more adequate method to employ when studying those magnitudes is a method which provides a description of those magnitudes that can be used when formulating an economic theory, rather than a method that attempts to predict events while presupposing closed systems.

The approach of the classical political economists, the early 'econometricians', consisted of very elementary arithmetic. But it was an approach that enabled them to develop a theory of the process of production and distribution of the surplus as a whole, unlike the contemporary mainstream models, which by presupposing isolation rather than abstraction, end up distracting from (or indeed preventing) the development of a theory of the production and distribution of the surplus, and of the process of social provisioning.

As noted above, the classical authors focused on the description of aggregate quantities through arithmetic in order to study the economy as a whole, rather than focusing on marginal changes in a given a part of reality which is assumed to be isolated from everything else. The central core of economic reality, for the classical economists, was the process of production and distribution of the surplus. But even the description of such a core was conducted using a narrative that takes into account the connections of such an abstract core to the remaining aspects of reality.

The emphasis on the surplus is also a central concern of heterodox economists today. Heterodox economists have been concerned with the process of social provisioning; see

Lee (2009). When focusing on such a process, the central aspect to be addressed is the surplus, and the way in which it is distributed; see Lee (2012) and Lee and Jo (2011). The distribution of the surplus through social provisioning is, of course, a process which cannot be described only in mathematical terms, much less predicted through econometric analysis. The distribution of the surplus through social provisioning must be explained using a narrative that integrates ethical and political aspects. The Cambridge controversies in the theory of capital were an important refutation of the attempt to reduce distribution to a mathematical exercise; see Martins (2013, Ch. 2). And even when a model is provided, it must be a model grounded on empirical facts, driven by a concern with reality, rather than with modeling per se; see the contribution by Lee, Chapter 14 in this *Handbook*.

## 11.7   CONCLUDING REMARKS

According to critical realism in economics, the social realm is an internally related open system, where scientifically interesting closures are rare. Thus, the best methodological procedure available is abstraction aimed at reaching a theory of the reproduction of the socio-economic system, rather than isolation aimed at reaching a model while assuming everything else remains constant.

If we are in the presence of a closed system, there are constant conjunctions of the form 'if X then Y' to be found, and mathematico-deductivist techniques can be most useful. If we are in the presence of an open system, where events are co-produced by a multiplicity of structures, powers, mechanisms, and tendencies, the best methodological procedure for identifying causal factors consists in the identification of surprising contrasts that reveal causal powers at play. But those contrasts become manifest in partial and inexact regularities, rather than in exact regularities such as the one we find in celestial mechanics or laboratory situations.

When studying partial and inexact regularities, simple descriptive mathematics usually provides a more adequate guidance for causal explanation, which can be more easily combined with ordinary discourse which, in turn, is a more adequate language for engaging in abstraction while taking into account internal relations. Those were the methods used by the classical political economists, which enabled them to engage in the first systematic and objective analysis of the production and distribution of the surplus. Such an analysis of the production and distribution of the surplus is essential in order to study the process of social provisioning, which is the central aspect studied by heterodox economists.

As critical realists point out, human knowledge is a permanently reproduced means for further knowledge, and scientists are permanently under a given theoretical and methodological paradigm. Mainstream economics is a paradigm that can be best defined methodologically, as an insistence on the use of mathematico-deductivist methods. Heterodox economics, in contrast, can be best defined ontologically, in terms of a concern with the nature of reality, and the methods used are seen as more or less appropriate depending on the nature of reality.

The term 'econometrics' constitutes a philological error too, since '*nomos*' should not be separated, and so it ought to have been either suppressed so that it reads 'ecometrics', or maintained so that it reads 'economometrics'. Just as the name 'econometrics' shows a lack of concern with its classical linguistic roots, so does the research program it designates show a lack of concern with the method followed by the classical authors who Schumpeter named the first 'econometricians', and were not the precursors of mainstream economics and its reliance on methods that presuppose closed systems, but rather the precursors of those who focus on the production and distribution of the surplus in the context of social provisioning, that is, heterodox economists.

# REFERENCES

Althusser, L. (1965 [2005]), *For Marx*, reprinted 2005, London: Verso.
Davidson, P. (1994), *Post Keynesian Macroeconomic Theory: A Foundation for Successful Economic Policies for the Twenty-first Century*, Aldershot, UK and Brookfield, VT, USA: Edward Elgar.
Downward, P.M. and A. Mearman (2009), 'Reorienting economics through triangulation of methods', in E. Fullbrook (ed.), *Ontology and Economics: Tony Lawson and his Critics*, London: Routledge, pp. 130–41.
Friedman, Milton (1953 [1970]), 'The methodology of positive economics', in Milton Friedman (1970), *Essays in Positive Economics*, Chicago, IL: University of Chicago Press, pp. 3–43.
Garegnani, P. (1998), 'Sraffa: the theoretical world of the "old classical economists"', *European Journal of the History of Economic Thought*, **5** (3), 415–29.
Granger, C. (2004), 'Critical realism and econometrics: an econometrician's viewpoint', in P. Lewis (ed.), *Transforming Economics*, London: Routledge, pp. 96–106.
Finch, J.H., and R. McMaster (2002), 'On categorical variables and non-parametrics statistical inference in the pursuit of causal explanations', *Cambridge Journal of Economics*, **26** (6), 753–72.
Hendry, D. (1983), 'On Keynesian model building and the rational expectations critique: a question of methodology', *Cambridge Journal of Economics*, 7 (1), 69–75.
Hendry, D. (2000), *Econometrics: Alchemy or Science?*, Oxford: Oxford University Press.
Hoover, K.D. (2002), 'Econometrics and reality', in U. Mäki (ed.), *Fact and Fiction in Economics: Models, Realism and Social Construction*, Cambridge: Cambridge University Press, pp. 152–77.
Keynes, J.M. (1936), *The General Theory of Employment, Interest and Money*, London: Macmillan.
Lawson, T. (1981), 'Keynesian model building and the rational expectations critique', *Cambridge Journal of Economics*, **5** (4), 311–26.
Lawson, T. (1997), *Economics and Reality*, London: Routledge.
Lawson, T. (2003), *Reorienting Economics*, London, Routledge.
Lawson, T. (2009), 'Triangulation and social research: reply to Downward and Mearman', in E. Fullbrook (ed.), *Ontology and Economics: Tony Lawson and His Critics*, London, UK and New York, USA: Routledge, pp. 142–57.
Leamer, E. (1983), 'Let's take the con out of econometrics', *American Economic Review*, **73** (1), 31–43.
Leamer, E. (1985), 'Sensitivity analysis would help', *American Economic Review*, **75** (3), 308–13.
Lee, Frederic S. (2009), *A History of Heterodox Economics: Challenging the Mainstream in the Twentieth Century*, London: Routledge.
Lee, Frederic S. (2012), 'Heterodox surplus approach: production, prices, and value theory', *Bulletin of Political Economy*, **6** (1), 65–105.
Lee, Frederic S. and T-H. Jo (2011), 'Social surplus approach and heterodox economics', *Journal of Economic Issues*, **45** (4), 857–75.
Marshall, A. (1890 [1920]), *Principles of Economics*, reprinted 1920, London: Macmillan.
Marshall, A. (1919 [1923]), *Industry and Trade*, reprinted 1923, London: Macmillan.
Martins, N. (2013), *The Cambridge Revival of Political Economy*, London: Routledge.
Marx, K. (1867 [1999]), *Capital*, reprinted 1999, Oxford: Oxford University Press.
Morgan, M. (2002), 'Models, stories, and the economic world', in Mäki, U. (ed.), *Fact and Fiction in Economics: Models, Realism and Social Construction*, Cambridge: Cambridge University Press, pp. 178–201.
Ollman, B. (1993), *Dialectical Investigations*, London: Routledge.
Pratten, S. (2005), 'Economics as progress: the LSE approach to econometric modelling and critical realism as programmes for research', *Cambridge Journal of Economics*, **29** (2), 179–205.
Ramanathan, R., R. Engle, C. Granger, F. Vahid-Araghi, and C. Brace (1997), 'Short-run forecasts of electricity loads and peaks', *International Journal of Forecasting*, **13** (2), 161–74.
Rodrigues, A.F. and N. Martins (2014), 'Numerical uncertainty and its implications', *Journal of Applied Mathematics and Physics*, **2** (1), 33–44.

Samuelson, P.A. (1963), 'Problems of methodology: discussion', *American Economic Review*, **53** (2), 231–6.
Samuelson, P.A. (1970), 'Maximum principles in analytical economics', Nobel Memorial Lecture, December 11.
Schumpeter, J. (1954 [1994]), *History of Economic Analysis*, reprinted 1994, London: Routledge.
Sraffa, P. (1925), 'Sulle relazioni fra costo e quantita prodotta', *Annali di economia*, **2**, 277–328.
Sraffa, P. (1926), 'The laws of returns under competitive conditions', *Economic Journal*, **36**, 535–50.

# 12 Social network analysis
## Bruce Cronin

## 12.1 INTRODUCTION

A key consideration in heterodox economics is the situating of economic activity in a social context. Where classical and neoclassical economics abstracts away from social relationships to a foundation of atomized rational egoists optimizing choices in conditions of scarcity, heterodox traditions focus on the variety of social interactions involved in people meeting their material needs, emphasizing the social embeddedness of economic decisions and particularly power disparities within this (Polanyi 1944). But even within this tradition, the extent to which economic decisions are subject to social or individual determination remains grist to a large, philosophical and politically polarized mill (Granovetter 1985).

Social network analysis (SNA) provides a set of powerful techniques for the study of social interactions empirically. It is thus well placed to provide concrete evidence illuminating the polarized and historically abstract structure–agency debate. For example, SNA has been used to identify extensive interlinks between firms formed by their sharing directors, and persistent links between contracting firms and contractors, both undercutting assumptions that firms act independently of one another (Eccles 1981; Useem 1979). It has provided important tools to move beyond the neoclassical 'black box' of the firm and explore Penrose's (1959) notion of the firm as a bundle of resources and knowledge and the micro-power relations associated with this (Burt 1992; Ferlie et al. 2005; Kogut 2000; Kondo 1990). It has contributed to the understanding of team dynamics and conflict (Brass 1992; Burt and Ronchi 1990; Ibarra 1992), matching problems underpinning imperfect labour markets (Calvó-Armengol and Jackson 2004; Granovetter 1974). And there have been many applications of social network analysis in the field of decision-making, contrasting rational decision assumptions, particularly the influence of interest groups on government policy (Knoke 1990; Laumann and Knoke 1987; Sabatier 1987).

This chapter provides an introduction to social network analysis, and ways in which this methodological and theoretical approach might contribute to heterodox economic analysis. It considers first the notion and visualization of social networks, next important data considerations, then the principal analytical methods in the field. These include individual positions within the network, the concepts of closure and brokerage, subgroups and characteristics of the network as a whole. Finally, issues related to hypothesis testing with network data are considered, and conclusions are drawn.

## 12.2 SOCIAL NETWORKS AND THEIR VISUALIZATION

Social network analysis comprises a set of techniques for the quantification and interpretation of relationships among social entities. Social entities may be single individuals or

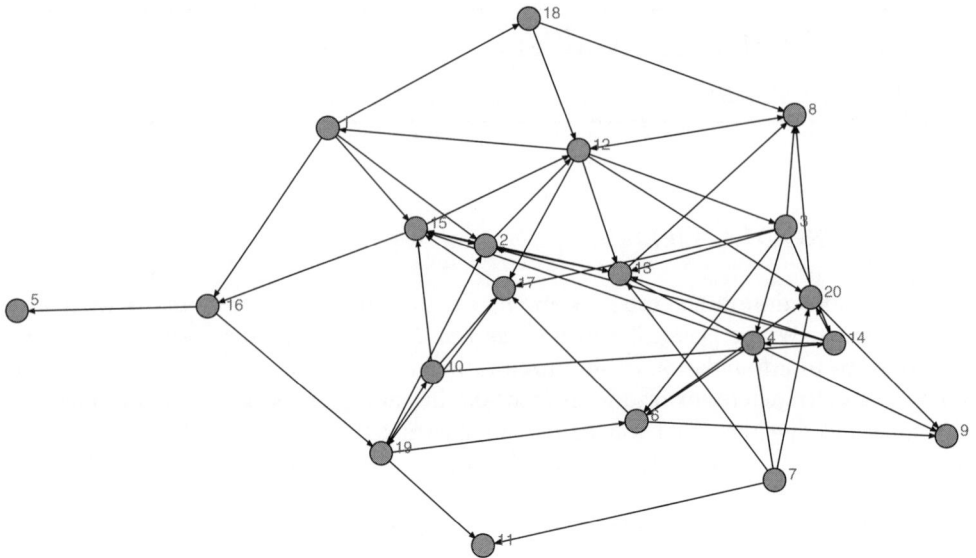

*Figure 12.1   Network graph*

organizations; groups of individuals such as teams, communities, or alliances; and social constructions such as artefacts, texts, databases, or processes. The focus on social entities reflects the origins of the field in sociology and anthropology and the theoretical assumptions it draws on in terms of the interpretation of relationships. But many of the analytic techniques, drawing from the mathematics of graph theory, are common to applications of networks in physical fields such as computing, engineering, and physiology.

A characteristic tool of SNA is visualization. Network visualization allows social relationships to be portrayed simultaneously at individual and global levels providing rich context for each. Network graphs such as Figure 12.1 (alternatively described as 'social graphs' or 'sociograms') communicate complicated data powerfully. In this graph, each circle (alternatively described as a 'node' or 'vertex') represents a social entity, such as an individual staff member in a workplace, a group, an organization, or even a social artefact such as a text.

Each line in the graph (alternatively described as 'tie', 'edge', or 'arc') represents a relationship between two nodes, such as the provision of information. Each node is distinctly identified and is labelled by a number in this case, but names could also be used. The arrows indicate a direction to the relationship; node 7 is providing something (say information) to node 11 but not vice versa. Non-directional relationships can also be plotted, such as where two individuals share an office (formally, 'arcs' refer to directional relationships while 'edges' refer to non-directional relationships). Finally, the relative importance or value of a node or the strength of a relationship can be represented by differences in the size of the node or width of a line.

One of the powerful communicative features of a network visualization is that it simultaneously presents both specific and general data. Taking node 20, for example, there are specific data about its information flows: 20 receives information from nodes 12, 7, 6, and 14 while it provides information to nodes 8 and 9 and reciprocates with 14. At the same time, the visualization illustrates the flow of information among the workplace as a whole, a lot of information flows being concentrated in the region encompassing nodes 20, 14, and 4; and 15, 2, 12, 17, and 10. Finally, the relative position of node 20 compared to other nodes and the network as a whole is readily apparent. The visualization of the network thus provides a much richer representation of the data than traditional social science approaches utilizing bivariate or multivariate comparisons.

## 12.3   WHERE DO THE LINES COME FROM?

Early social network analysis was predominantly undertaken on a small-scale basis via personal interviews. In the example network, a researcher would interview each person in the workplace, asking each in this case, 'Who in this workplace provides you with information important to complete your work?' The responses are plotted, with a nomination being represented as a line to the nominator from the person nominated. The complete network of relationships emerges from the triangulation of the responses of all the participants.

Alternative approaches to small-scale data collection include ethnography, where a researcher is located in a social environment and observes and records interactions; and expert panels, where people familiar with an organizational setting are asked to describe interactions they are aware of. For larger personal networks, structured questionnaires are widely used, increasingly web-based, to reach distant or dispersed participants. Structured questionnaires normally employ a roster of all members of the social environment of interest, prompting each participant to consider their relationship with each of the other members. This helps to overcome recall bias, where respondents typically do not recall their strongest relationships but rather the most salient, those that have had a recent unusual impact on them; without prompting, respondents normally will not cite partners, best friends, or long-standing colleagues (Bernard et al. 1982).

With the rapid growth in the availability of online communication logs, databases, and documentary archives, archival sources and data-mining approaches have become increasingly popular in social network analysis. There is a long tradition of mining official company registers to identify interlocking directors between firms. More recently SNA has been applied to analyse very large data sets of patent registrations to examine collaboration in research and development; publication citations to study scientific collaboration more generally; hyperlinks between websites to map the World Wide Web and groups within it; and social media interactions such as tweets. Mining of large economic data sets include inter-country and inter-industry trade data to examine core–periphery structures (Smith and White 1992); financial transactions; and news data to study contagion in financial markets (Kyriakopoulos et al. 2009). More traditional archival sources may also provide data for heterodox economic applications; John Padgett has mined parchments to map the social networks underpinning the economy of Renaissance Florence (Padget and Ansell 1993).

Outside very small numbers of nodes, it is difficult to manually and systematically visualize and otherwise analyse social networks, so computer software is employed to analyse network data. For decades, the most widely used SNA software package has been UCINET, originally developed at UC Irvine and Boston College, USA and the

University of Greenwich, UK. It maintains its popularity in a similar manner to SPSS in the social sciences more generally; a reasonably accessible user interface, continuous integration of new routines as these are developed in the field, and its ability to readily explore many facets of networks of up to about 5000 nodes.

There are a growing number of alternative packages, generally free and optimized for a specific type of network analysis. For example, Pajek emphasizes its ability to analyse very large networks (billions of nodes), ORA is designed to analyse multiple networks, Siena is optimized for longitudinal data, NodeXL for social media, Gephi for customized visualizations. Recently there has been a proliferation of SNA program libraries for program languages, principally for R, but also Python, allowing advanced users to develop highly customized routines for specific analyses (see the SNA library for R and the NetworkX library for Python). All of these packages are readily accessed through a web search.

Whichever software is used for the analysis, there is a common step in preparing the data collected for analysis in such a manner that it can be interpreted as relational data, that is, each data item comprises two nodes and a relationship between them (or not). For all but very large data sets (more than 1 million nodes), this is readily undertaken in a spreadsheet such as Excel. Table 12.1 presents the initial rows of the spreadsheet containing the data used to generate the network graph in Figure 12.1. This is known as an 'edgelist' as it comprises a list of the edges (lines) between nodes in the network. Each row represents an edge between the two nodes listed in columns A and B. More precisely, these are arcs from the node in column A to the node in column B.

This particular way of collecting and recording network data is very simple, versatile, and eases error-checking. In particular, there is normally no need to record the absence of ties, such as between nodes 16 and 10; the nodes listed in the spreadsheet are those with ties, those not listed do not have ties. By default, such a tie is assumed by UCINET to have a value of 1; this value could be recorded in column C and pairs of nodes could be added with a value of 0 representing no tie, but as explained, there is no need to be so pedantic. However, column C can be used to hold information about the strength of the relationship; this might record the number of times information was transferred between nodes in a week, for example, or the value of transactions between two firms. That value can then be used as the basis for the width of the edges in the visualization.

With the data in this format in Excel, it is easy to order them in various ways and use spreadsheet functions to clean the relational data and associated information. For example, Excel's pivot table tool can be used to extract a list of each unique node, stored in a second worksheet alongside various characteristics or attributes of the nodes. Table 12.2 illustrates a node attributes list. The first column lists the node label from the edgelist and the subsequent columns contain information on three attributes of the node; there can be any number of columns. Thus row 3 concerns the attributes of node 5; it is not female (0), has a salary of 25500 and is in department 1. The values of attributes in this example are all numeric, normally a requirement of SNA software. Note the contrast with the format of the edgelist in Table 12.1: an edgelist holds data about the relationships between pairs of nodes; a node attribute list holds data about the characteristics of each node.

Most SNA software has easy methods for importing data in the formats above, sometimes involving a conversion program. Once imported into SNA software, the network can be quickly visualized and various metrics of the network calculated.

*Table 12.1   Edgelist example*

|   | A | B | C |
|---|---|---|---|
| 1 | 16 | 5 | |
| 2 | 1 | 16 | |
| 3 | 15 | 16 | |
| 4 | 16 | 19 | |
| 5 | 1 | 15 | |

*Table 12.2   Node attributes example*

|   | A | B | C | D |
|---|---|---|---|---|
| 1 | Node | Female | Salary | Department |
| 2 | 1 | 1 | 23 000 | 1 |
| 3 | 5 | 0 | 25 500 | 1 |
| 4 | 15 | 1 | 23 500 | 2 |
| 5 | 16 | 1 | 27 000 | 3 |
| 6 | 19 | 0 | 21 500 | 3 |

## 12.4   DATA CONSIDERATIONS

Collecting relational data raises a range of data considerations outside those normally faced by traditional social science. First, the consistency of the relationship is critical in SNA. Second, there are some particular ethical considerations involved in the collection of data for SNA. Finally, there are a series of important considerations, differing from standard social science approaches, in terms of the boundaries of the sample, the method of collecting the sample, and the response rate.

To analyse a network, the relational data must be consistent: that is, the relationship being measured between nodes 1 and 2 must be the same relationship as the relationship being measured between nodes 2 and 3 and all other nodes in the network. For example, we might ask someone to tell us who they get information from and who they get advice from; while these sound similar it is important not to conflate the two. When information networks and advice networks are mapped separately, they typically have quite different structures; the relationships are related, but distinct (Cross and Parker 2004). Multiple distinctive relationships are typically analysed by superimposing the visualization of one network on top of another or regressing the variations.

While distinctions between relationships are relatively straightforward to deal with when using archival sources, through the use of explicit and consistent definitions of relevant data, it is more problematic for the design of network questions as respondents may have quite different interpretations of categories being employed. For example, respondents are likely to define 'friend' differently; some will define this as very close relationships while others may include passing acquaintances. Respondents may employ different time periods, for example including a first meeting as important information, while others may focus on information in the last week. Respondents may be reluctant to discuss some relationships; trust is a relationship theorized as important to many economic transactions but in survey situations respondents are often unwilling to reveal who they do or do not trust. Network questionnaires thus need careful design and piloting; questions should be specified within a particular context and time period, for example, 'How many times in the last week did this person provide you with information important to your work?' (Laumann et al. 1983).

The sensitivity of network analysis to the specific questions asked in questionnaires highlights another difficulty in data collection: the heightened intrusiveness of the questions. People are not normally asked by social scientists to specify their close personal relationships. Because of this heightened intrusiveness, together with the relative novelty of the techniques, negotiating access to respondents is typically more involved than in traditional social science research. In particular, comprehensive buy-in is needed from the principal decision-makers in organizational settings. There have been numerous cases where data collection has been disrupted by the late intervention by a senior decision-maker who was not sufficiently briefed during the establishment of a project (Cross and Parker 2004).

The heightened intrusiveness also raises a particular range of ethical challenges, as Borgatti and Molina (2003) discuss. Firstly, unlike in most social science research, in SNA it is not possible to offer respondents anonymity because specific personal relationships are the object of study; we are interested in the relationship between 'Tom' and 'Joan', rather than the relationship between any X and Y. Secondly, respondents may cite relationships with third parties who may not wish to participate in the study. While respondents are reporting their own perception, they are also reporting shared information: the fact that a relationship exists. Thirdly, it is difficult to offer confidentiality as participants may deduce the identity of individuals from a network position, even when presented in a sociogram with anonymous identifiers. Lastly, obtaining informed consent is difficult because the techniques are new and participants are unlikely to fully anticipate the implications of the information they provide, as compared to a standard questionnaire. These ethical considerations extend to archival sources as well as survey data. When people make use of a social media site or submit forms to a registry they are unlikely to understand that their location in the communication network can be identified and highlighted.

Accordingly SNA researchers need to consider particular methods of protecting the subjects of research from harm, most likely reputational. Some means of mitigating the concerns about social network data are to provide participants with more information than would normally be provided about the techniques before data is collected; pre-collection workshops or extended briefings are effective. This allows participants to judge what sort of information they want to provide and decide how to respond to questions; it allows third parties a greater chance to remove themselves from the study if they wish. Lastly, sociograms should be used judiciously; if the network has very prominent nodes, the data might best be presented differently, such as by numerical tables.

A further important data consideration is the specification of the network boundary. In one sense, everything in society is connected, but for social analysis we need to isolate parts of society for meaningful examination. But where does the network of interest end? Geographic or organizational boundaries may overlook important relationships;

for example, customers external to the firm often influence what happens within a firm; transactions among firms in one country may be influenced by their dealings with government agencies and banks in other countries. Cut-off points are often arbitrary; many early studies of interlocking directors examined only the largest 100 or 200 listed firms but these networks look quite different when 500 or 1000 firms or when non-listed companies are included. Using participants' own definitions of boundaries, such as nominating their most important customers, is vulnerable to the subjectivity problems discussed earlier. The answer to the boundary definition problem is in the underpinning research design; the boundary needs to have theoretical significance (Laumann et al. 1983).

The sampling strategy also affects the outcome of the analysis; typically positional, reputational, or event approaches are used. Firstly, a positional strategy selects all participants occupying a defined position in a research setting, such as the chief executive officers (CEOs) of the 100 largest firms or all small businesses in Bristol. The limitation of this approach is the boundary definition problem discussed above. Secondly, a reputational strategy selects participants based on an expert panel – knowledgeable informants – who nominate the key people in the research setting. Alternatively, the sample could be selected by snowballing from an initial contact or recommendation, asking these to nominate others for inclusion, who then nominate others. The limitation of the reputational approach is that it tends to overstate connectedness; respondents are likely to nominate the people they know the best. Thirdly, an event strategy selects respondents who participate in important events. This overcomes the limitations of the other two approaches, but issues remain with selecting the correct event and handling otherwise important participants who may have missed the event for particular reasons (Laumann et al. 1983).

Whichever sampling strategy is adopted, SNA needs high response rates. Unlike statistical social science approaches, completeness of data is important; SNA does not generally use representative samples because the distributions of ties in networks vary greatly.[1] Missing data and false positives can have a large impact on the network structure if this concerns highly connected nodes. Figure 12.1 would look quite different if node 12 was missing. Archival data, in particular, normally need a great deal of cleaning and checking to make sure that nodes are identified correctly and consistently. When identifying directors who serve on multiple company boards, for example, the challenge is to ensure that 'J. Smith' listed on one board is the same person as the 'J. Smith' listed on another, and to determine whether this is the same person as 'J.S. Smith' or 'John Smith' on another; birthdates can help but are not foolproof. Where these are incorrectly identified as the same, a false positive, that part of the network will be erroneously dense; if incorrectly identified as different, a false negative, there will be erroneous gaps in the network. While an entire field of prosopography has developed around these questions (Stone 1971), the key task is to use clearly documented protocols to ensure identification methods are consistent and rigorous.

Survey data for SNA, where non-response is more likely, typically requires much higher response rates than statistically based social science approaches, but, given this, is reasonably robust to missing data where reciprocation is not required: that is, a tie is assumed if node 1 nominates node 2 even without a response from node 2. Here a 60–70 per cent response rate has been found to provide robust results with $< 0.1$ error, generally underestimating the number of connections and clusters and overestimating the number of steps between each pair of nodes (Kossinets 2006). For SNA metrics more dependent on the network structure, such as closeness and betweenness (discussed below), even 80 per cent response rates would produce error rates of 0.15 and 0.25 respectively (Costenbader and Valente 2003). However, low response rates are not associated with great errors in the ranking of nodes within these metrics; that is, it is possible to robustly identify the nodes within the highest 10 per cent of scores on a wide range of network metrics, even with response rates of 60–70 per cent (Borgatti et al. 2006).

## 12.5   CENTRALITY

Once an edgelist has been imported into SNA software, the network can be quickly visualized, a wide range of network metrics automatically calculated, and analysis commenced. One of the most intuitive steps in this analysis is to consider which nodes have important positions in the network. Looking at Figure 12.1 there are a number of nodes that appear prominently in the visualization, seeming to be more central to the network than others: nodes 13, 2, 12, 17 and perhaps 15 and 4. However, we can go beyond this intuitive, visual impression and analyse this in a more rigorous, mathematical manner.

First, we can count the number of ties each node has, a metric known as degree centrality, on the basis that the node with the most ties (degree count) to other nodes is likely to be more at the centre of what is going on in that network. Node 12 has the most, with nine ties, followed by nodes 13 and 15, with eight ties each. As the ties in this network are directional, representing provision of information, we can distinguish nodes providing information, arrows pointing out or outdegree centrality from those receiving information, arrows pointing in or indegree centrality. Nodes 12 and 6 have the greatest centrality in terms of outdegree, each providing information to six nodes. Node 13 has the greatest indegree, receiving information from six nodes. In an organizational setting, node 13 might be a supervisor or manager receiving reports.

But these simple counts of ties do not seem to explain the apparent centrality of nodes such as 2, 15, 17, and 4, which seem to be in influential positions in the network. These nodes are one step away from those with high degree centrality, they are connected to well-connected positions, in which case they have access to the major information flows in the organization. This position is known as eigenvector centrality, which is degree centrality, weighted by the degree of the nodes connected to; this is a complex calculation best left to the software (see Freeman (1978) for an extended discussion and definitions of this and other forms of centrality). In Figure 12.1 the nodes with the greatest in- and outdegree centrality, 12 and 13, also have the greatest eigenvector centrality, but node 15 comes third and nodes 4 and 2 come fourth and fifth. Nodes 12, 13, and 15 also have the greatest 'closeness centrality'. Closeness is the minimum number of steps to reach all other nodes by the shortest path. There are 31 steps between these nodes and each of the other nodes, another calculation best done by the software.

So far, the nodes and some of the mathematical properties of the nodes in the middle of the network have been considered, but there are some nodes towards the perimeter of the network, not yet considered, that are contributing to its structure. Node 19, for example, seems to have an important intermediary position between the nodes around node 16 and those around node 6; without it there would be a large gap in the network. This node has high betweenness centrality, that is, it is on the shortest path between more

*Table 12.3    Centrality metrics, selected nodes*

| Node | Degree | OutDegree | Indegree | Eigenvector | Closeness | Betweenness |
|------|--------|-----------|----------|-------------|-----------|-------------|
| 2 | 6 | 2 | 5 | 0.263 | 34 | 23.7 |
| 4 | 7 | 3 | 4 | 0.273 | 33 | 17.8 |
| 6 | 6 | 3 | 3 | 0.213 | 35 | 15.9 |
| 12 | **9** | **6** | 4 | **0.359** | **31** | **108.1** |
| 13 | 8 | 4 | **6** | 0.345 | **31** | 29.4 |
| 15 | 8 | 4 | 5 | 0.315 | **31** | 58.9 |
| 17 | 6 | 2 | 4 | 0.246 | 34 | 36.0 |
| 19 | 6 | 4 | 3 | 0.169 | 34 | 52.9 |

*Note:*   Most central nodes on each metric in bold.

pairs of nodes than any other barring nodes 12 and 15. Taking the direction of the ties into account, that is, the flow of information in this case, node 17 has the next-highest betweenness.

Table 12.3 summarizes the metrics for these prominent nodes (demonstrating that it is possible to report network characteristics avoiding the ethical risks associated with the use of sociograms). As these are identifying influential positions within the social network, they can be interpreted as indicators of social capital (Burt 1992; Lin 2001).

## 12.6   CLOSURE AND BROKERAGE

The contrast between network metrics that emphasize the cohesive centre of the network (degree, eigenvector, and closeness centrality) and those focused on bridging different parts of the network (betweenness centrality) underpins an important distinction in social network analysis: closure and brokerage. Closed, cohesive groups have long been seen to underpin trust and reciprocation that provide foundations for efficient, non-transactional, reinforcing economic activity, such as Italian industrial districts, the gift economy, and micro-finance (Macaulay 1963; Uzzi 1996). But highly cohesive groups can become stuck in their ways, slow to react to external change, overdependent on the central nodes of the group, and become inefficient over time. By contrast, ties that bridge one cohesive group to another provide access to different information and practices that can stimulate creativity and change. This is the classic entrepreneurial situation: combining resources in novel combinations. The nodes located between cohesive groups have brokerage power; information or other resources can only be transferred by means of the broker, for which they can draw a rent. Hansen et al. (2001) note how the distinction echoes March's (1991) contrast between exploration and exploitation: tight reinforcing networks (closure) facilitate economies of scale and exploitation of ideas and resources, while looser more diverse links with other groups (brokerage) facilitate exploration of new ideas.

The distinction between closure and brokerage has some dynamic implications. Relationships within a cohesive group are likely to be strong, reinforcing, and overlapping, while those in a brokering situation are more weak, transitory, and vulnerable. But what sort of ties are more valuable: strong or weak ties? In his doctoral thesis, Mark Granovetter (1974) explored how people find jobs, finding that this was not normally a rational search of vacancy listings but rather, perhaps not so surprisingly, through personal referrals. But what was more surprising was that these referrals were not from close ties, such as friends or family. People found jobs through referrals from weak ties: friends of friends and family associates. Granovetter reasoned that cohesive groups of strong ties are likely to know each other's information already; the source of novel information is outside the closed group, provided by the weak ties. He famously summarized this theory as 'the strength of weak ties' (Granovetter 1973).

Burt (1992) built on this information theory to argue that it was not the brokerage position per se but the act of creating the link between otherwise disconnected groups that introduced new resource and informational combinations. Disconnected or less connected groups within a network implied there were 'structural holes' that could be potentially bridged. Burt (2004) found that individuals who forged bridging ties were more creative (exposed to novel information and combinations), paid more, promoted more quickly, and happier in their work. But at the same time, the act of creating new ties was to close the hole, creating closure, underpinning a fundamental dynamism to networks.

## 12.7   SUBGROUPS

We have seen that network analysis simultaneously provides information about individual nodes and the network context in which they are located. An intuitive second step after identifying particularly prominent nodes is to identify the 'core' of the network, the group of nodes that seem to dominate the network structure and around which the others revolve and the most distant nodes form a periphery. A fruitful approach to this is to identify the nodes belonging to the highest 'k-core', a subgroup where all nodes are connected to each other by a degree of k or more (Seidman 1983). In Figure 12.1 all nodes are connected and have a degree of at least 1, all but node 5 are connected and have a degree of at least 2, and so on. Figure 12.2 highlights the highest k-core: k is 4.

Within the core it is possible to distinguish particularly closely connected groups. In Figure 12.1 there appear to be a large number of connections within the group of nodes 15, 2, 13, and 17 and the group of nodes 4, 14, 2, and 20, and together these more connected groups appear to be important to the structure of the network. Much early SNA undertaken by anthropologists and sociologists concentrated on identifying such stable substructures with larger networks, broadly known as 'clique analysis' (see Scott 2013 for an overview). This draws on the notion that the minimal social structure to exhibit network characteristics – that is, beyond the dyadic relationship possible between two individuals – is a triad: relationships among three individuals. Heider (1958) theorized that triadic relationships such as that among nodes 5, 16, and 19 were relatively unstable: because node 16 is providing information to 5 and 19, it is likely that 5 and 19 will find something in common and eventually form a relationship, a process known as triadic closure. Similarly, the relationship among nodes 1, 15, and 16 is unstable as 1 is providing a lot and 16 is providing nothing to the triad. By contrast, the relationship between nodes

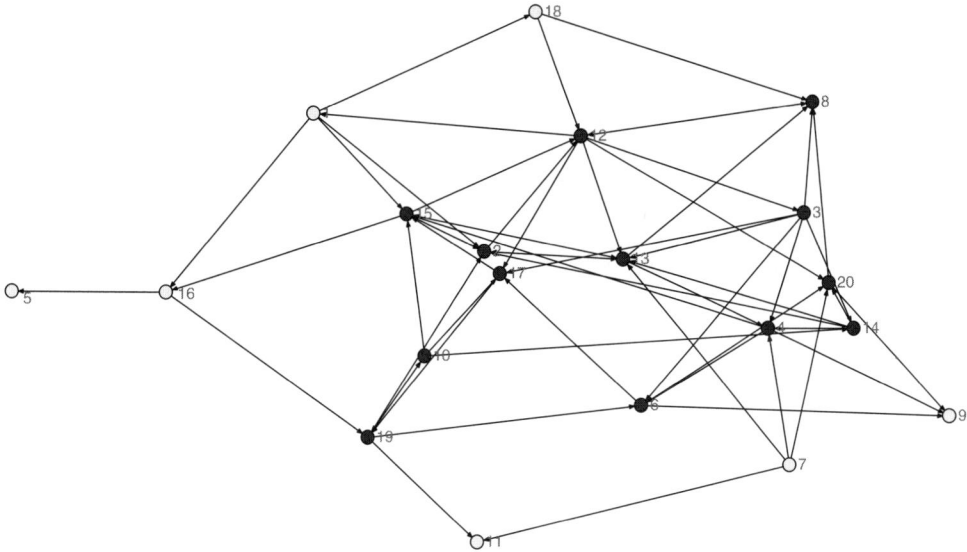

*Figure 12.2   k-cores*

12, 1, and 18 would be characterized as highly stable, a strong triad, because the relationship is reinforcing. So this structural analysis allowed predictions about the dynamics of the network, which has been applied to the analysis of business groups (Rowley et al. 2005). SNA software has extensive capacity to analyse all manner of variations of triads or larger substructures. A difficulty in this approach, however, is that it is difficult to isolate particularly important subgroups as they overlap widely with others. The 12, 1, 18 triad overlaps with two other strong triads – 1, 15, 12 and 1, 2, 12 – and several weaker triads. But the software can produce a list of all combinations.

   An alternative approach is to use cluster analysis to separate groups of nodes that are most similar from those that are most dissimilar. Because networks are highly interdependent, attempts to apply hierarchical clustering analysis (discussed in Chapter 9 in this *Handbook*) generally only separate a few peripheral nodes from the bulk of the network. More recent developments have focused on 'community detection', employing algorithms that first separate small differences in the core such as between the group 15, 2, 13, 17 and the group 4, 14, 20. Figure 12.3 presents the results of one of these community detection algorithms, Girvan–Newman (Girvan and Newman 2002). This suggests that nodes 5 and 11 are peripheral, that the groups initially identified visually as related are central to somewhat larger groups, and that a third group (17, 10, 19) can be distinguished. Note that nodes 17, and 13, identified visually as close to 15 and 2, are grouped elsewhere by this algorithm.

## 12.8   NETWORK CHARACTERISTICS

Not only does SNA provide metrics for characterizing the positions of nodes within networks, methods for identifying subgroups, but there are a range of metrics for

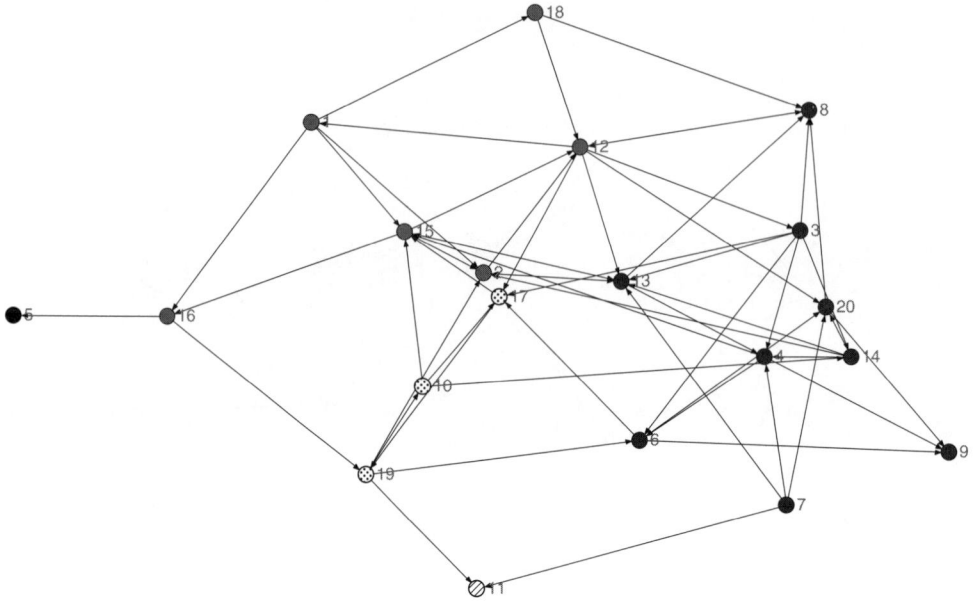

*Figure 12.3    Girvan–Newman clusters*

distinguishing networks from each other, essentially indicators of network cohesion or 'knittedness' (Borgatti et al. 2013). Traditionally, network density has been widely used as an indicator of cohesion, defined as the number of ties divided by the total possible number of ties. But it is difficult to compare densities of greatly different-sized networks; it is possible that all 20 nodes in our example could be connected to each other, but unlikely that this would occur with 100 nodes, so larger networks tend to have lower densities. So more recently, networks have tended to be compared on multiple measures including average degree, the mean degree of all nodes; average path distance, the mean number of steps for each node to connect to each other; degree centralization, the extent to which the network centres on a single node; compactness, the mean reciprocal of the shortest paths between each pair of nodes; connectedness, the proportion of pairs of nodes that can reach each other (where parts of a network are disconnected); reciprocity, the proportion of directional ties between pairs of nodes that are reciprocated; and transitivity, the proportion of nodes in complete triads 1-2-3-1 (also known as the overall clustering coefficient). Table 12.4 reports these metrics for the example network.

A supplementary approach to characterizing networks as a whole draws from the subgroup characteristics discussed above. A 'triad census' measures the distribution of different types of triadic relationships in a network, highlighting the preponderance of stronger or weaker substructures. The distribution is based on the assumption that any three nodes can be connected in 16 different ways, ranging from no connection at all to three reciprocated ties (Holland and Leinhardt 1970). Triad censuses are readily calculated by major SNA software packages.

*Table 12.4   Network cohesion metrics*

| Metric | Value |
| --- | --- |
| Average degree | 2.85 |
| Degree centralization | 0.19 |
| Density | 0.15 |
| Connectedness | 0.81 |
| Average path distance | 2.54 |
| Compactness | 0.40 |
| Arc reciprocity | 0.14 |
| Transitivity | 0.20 |

## 12.9   HYPOTHESIS TESTING

The analytic techniques discussed above are largely descriptive, though many provide data for specialized micro-sociological theorizing, such as the dynamic implications of reciprocity, closure, and brokerage, and various triad configurations. But two questions typically remain outstanding from a descriptive analysis of network structure or network positions: is the observed network structure or network position atypical? And is this structure or position related to other observations? For example, interlocking director networks are highly centralized and banks are very central within these; given the number of nodes and the number of interlocks, is this different from similarly sized networks in other fields? And, given that centrality in such a network is likely to provide informational advantages, is network centrality of these firms related to financial performance?

Traditional statistical techniques used in the social sciences (see Chapter 10 in this *Handbook*) cannot be used to answer such questions because the distributions of network connections are highly variable, highly sensitive to small changes in parameters, and thus unstandardized, to date. So the standard statistical technique of comparing observed data to standardized distributions (normal, Poisson, and so on) cannot be used to identify atypical phenomena. Secondly, standard regression techniques assume independence of variables, whereas network data is inherently interdependent: connections among nodes are likely to be maintained and reinforced over time through network effects such as popularity and reciprocity. Attempts to employ standard statistical techniques to network data are prone to the identification of spurious associations, generally overstating the effects of connectivity (Borgatti et al. 2013; Snijders et al. 2010).

However, a range of permutation-based regression techniques can be employed to address the limitations of standard statistical techniques when dealing with network data, as no assumptions are needed about the distribution of observations. Standard ordinary least squares (OLS) regression techniques provide the coefficients. But instead of comparing observed data to standardized distributions to determine statistical significance, permutation techniques are used to compare observed data to thousands of random permutations of the observed values (typically 10 000). Statistical significance is attributed to observations that persistently differ from the randomly generated network data (Borgatti et al. 2002). Quadratic assignment procedure (QAP) regression is a powerful set of these techniques; exponential random graph models (ERGM) and stochastic actor-oriented models (SAOM) are also widely used. In interlocking directorship studies, there have been mixed results from statistical examinations of the relationship between interlocks and the financial performance of firms. Early OLS-based approaches suggested some relationship between director interlocks and firm financial performance in particular circumstances (Richardson 1987; Mizruchi and Stearns 1994; Cronin and Popov 2005). But Robins and Alexander (2004), employing ERGM techniques, found the structure of director interlock networks not atypical of random networks of similar size. QAP regression techniques, however, have found a variety of firm financial indicators associated with director interlocks, again in particular circumstances (Cronin 2012, 2013).

## 12.10   CONCLUSION

Social network analysis, then, provides a rich methodological toolkit for the study of social relationships, relationships that are often at the heart of questions of interest to heterodox economics. It is used to uncover the meso-level social interactions that are normally elided by structural or agency constructs.

SNA visualization techniques have proved useful in conveying complex data highly effectively, and in facilitating preliminary analysis of specific and general data simultaneously. With the increasing availability of larger data sets of relational data, however, visualization has been increasingly superseded by analysis of the network metrics, with visualization reserved for the examination of particular micro-interactions. This has been reinforced by methodological advances and the computational power increasingly available to researchers.

Data collection for SNA involves a distinct set of considerations from those usually faced in the social sciences. These include relationship consistency, relational questionnaire design, careful negotiation of access, ethical challenges, boundary specification, sampling strategies, and completeness. Clearly documented protocols for data collection can save a great deal of time and reduce the need for rework.

A range of node-level metrics allow the consideration of individual positions within a network as a whole. These draw principally from micro-sociological theories of social exchange and social capital, but are useful in developing and testing a wide range of propositions about social dynamics, such as the strength of weak ties and the dynamics of brokerage and closure.

Similarly, micro-sociological theory provides the basis for a set of metrics about the presence and significance of subgroups within a network. Not only do triadic and clique-like micro-structures highlight groups of influential nodes, but in constituting the endoskeleton of a network they influence the social dynamics within the network. Larger groupings of related nodes can be identified by a range of community detection algorithms.

At the macro-network level, a further set of metrics consider the characteristics of the network as a whole, essentially its cohesiveness. These provide a basis for comparing different networks or for considering network change over time. A denomination of the endoskeleton of subgroup structures via a triad census provides a further DNA-type comparator.

Finally, emergent statistical techniques are providing a firmer basis for hypothesis testing with network data than earlier attempts to apply standard statistical approaches in violation of their basic assumptions. QAP regression, ERGM and SAOM modelling provide much more rigorous methods for testing associations involving network data, with further methods regularly being deployed.

SNA is still a rapidly evolving field, methodologically and theoretically. It is reminiscent of the early days of astronomy, where relatively crude instruments first revealed a vast set of hitherto unknown phenomena; as the instruments have improved, more and more phenomena have been revealed and the theories of how these have come to be have developed greatly. The universe of social relations awaits deep exploration and with their central focus on social relationships, heterodox economic approaches are bound to contribute much to this.

## NOTE

1.  There are, however, emerging statistical techniques enabling controlling for missing data. These involve the comparison of observed network data against what would be expected to be found in randomly generated networks of the same size (see Scott and Carrington 2011).

## REFERENCES

Bernard, H.R., P.D. Killworth, and L. Sailer (1982), 'Informant accuracy in social-network data V. An experimental attempt to predict actual communication from recall data', *Social Science Research*, **11** (1), 30–66.

Borgatti, S.P., K.M. Carley, and D. Krackhardt (2006), 'On the robustness of centrality measures under conditions of imperfect data', *Social Networks*, **28** (2), 124–36.

Borgatti, S.P., M.G. Everett, and L.C. Freeman (2002), 'Ucinet 6 for Windows: software for social network analysis', Harvard, MA: Analytic Technologies.

Borgatti, S.P., M.G. Everett, and J.C. Johnson (2013), *Analysing Social Networks*, London: Sage.

Borgatti, S.P. and J.L. Molina (2003), 'Ethical and strategic issues in organizational social network analysis', *Journal of Applied Behavioral Science*, **39** (3), 337–49.

Brass, D.J. (1992), 'Power in organizations: a social network perspective', in G. Moore and J.A. Whitt (eds), *Research in Politics and Society*, Greenwich, CT: JAI Press, pp. 295–323.

Burt, R.S. (1992), *Structural Holes: The Social Structure of Competition*, Cambridge, MA: Harvard University Press.

Burt, R.S. (2004), 'Structural holes and good ideas', *American Journal of Sociology*, **110** (2), 349–99.

Burt, R.S. and D. Ronchi (1990), 'Contested control in a large manufacturing plant', in J. Wessie and H. Flap (eds), *Social Networks Through Time*, Utrecht: ISOR, pp. 121–57.

Calvó-Armengol, A. and M.O. Jackson (2004), 'The effects of social networks on employment and inequality', *American Economic Review*, **94** (3), 426–54.

Costenbader, E. and T.W. Valente (2003), 'The stability of centrality measures when networks are sampled', *Social Networks*, **25** (4), 283–307.

Cronin, B. (2012), 'National and transnational structuring of the British corporate elite', in J.P. Scott and G. Murray (eds), *Financial Elites and Transnational Business: Who Rules the World?*, Cheltenham, UK and Northampton, MA, USA: Edward Elgar, pp. 177–92.

Cronin, B. (2013), 'The value of corporate political connnections', paper presented to the International Network for Social Network Analysis Conference, Hamburg University, 23 May.

Cronin, B. and V. Popov (2005), 'Director networks and UK corporate performance', *International Journal of Knowledge, Culture and Change Management*, **4** (1), 1195–1205.

Cross, R. and A. Parker (2004), *The Hidden Power of Social Networks: Understanding How Work Really Gets Done in Organizations*, Boston, MA: Harvard Business School Press.

Eccles, R. (1981), 'The quasifirm in the construction industry', *Journal of Economic Behavior and Organization*, **2** (4), 335–57.

Ferlie, E., L. Fitzgerald, M. Wood, and C. Hawkins (2005), 'The nonspread of innovations: the mediating role of professionals', *Academy of Management Journal*, **48** (1), 117–34.

Freeman, L.C. (1978), 'Centrality in social networks: conceptual clarification', *Social Networks*, **1** (1), 215–39.

Girvan, M. and M.E.J. Newman (2002), 'Community structure in social and biological networks', *Proceedings of the National Academy of Sciences of the United States of America*, **99** (12), 7821–26.

Granovetter, M. (1973), 'The strength of weak ties', *American Journal of Sociology*, **78** (6), 1360–80.

Granovetter, M. (1974), *Getting a Job: A Study of Contacts and Careers*, Chicago, IL: Chicago University Press.

Granovetter, M. (1985), 'Economic action and social structure: the problem of embeddedness', *American Journal of Sociology*, **91** (3), 481–510.

Hansen, M.T., J. Podolny, and J. Pfeffer (2001), 'So many ties, so little time: a task contingency perspective on corporate social capital in organizations', *Social Capital in Organizations*, **18**, 21–57.

Heider, F. (1958), *The Psychology of Interpersonal Relations*, New York: John Wiley & Sons.

Holland, P.W. and S. Leinhardt (1970), 'A method for detecting structure in sociometric data', *American Journal of Sociology*, **76** (3), 492–513.

Ibarra, H. (1992), 'Homophily and differential returns: sex differences in network structure and access in an advertising firm', *Administrative Science Quarterly*, **37** (3), 422–47.

Knoke, D. (1990), *Political Networks: The Structural Perspective*, New York: Cambridge University Press.

Kogut, B. (2000), 'The network as knowledge; generative rules and the emergence of structure', *Strategic Management Journal*, **21** (3), 405–25.

Kondo, D.K. (1990), *Crafting Selves: Power, Gender and Discourses of Identity in a Japanese Workplace*, Chicago, IL: University of Chicago Press.

Kossinets, G. (2006), 'Effects of missing data in social networks', *Social Networks*, **28** (3), 247–68.

Kyriakopoulos, F., S. Thurner, C. Puhr, and S.W. Schmitz (2009), 'Network and eigenvalue analysis of financial transaction networks', *European Physical Journal B*, **71** (4), 523–31.

Laumann, E.O. and D. Knoke (1987), *The Organizational State: Social Choice in the National Policy Domains*, Madison, WI: University of Wisconsin Press.

Laumann, E.O., P.V. Marsden, and D. Prensky (1983), 'The boundary specification problem in network analysis', in R.S. Burt and M.J. Minor (eds), *Applied Network Analysis*, Beverly Hills, CA: Sage, pp. 18–34.

Lin, N. (2001), *Social Capital: A Theory of Social Structure and Action*, Cambridge: Cambridge University Press.

Macaulay, S. (1963), 'Non-contractural relations in business: a preliminary study', *American Sociological Review*, **28** (1), 55–70.

March, J.G. (1991), 'Exploration and exploitation in organizational learning', *Organization Science*, **2** (1), 71–87.

Mizruchi, M.S. and L.B. Stearns (1994), 'A longitudinal study of borrowing by large American corporations', *Administrative Science Quarterly*, **39** (1), 118–40.

Padgett, J.F. and C.K. Ansell (1993), 'Robust action and the rise of the Medici, 1400–1434', *American Journal of Sociology*, **98** (6), 1259–1319.

Penrose, E.T. (1959), *The Theory of the Growth of the Firm*, Oxford: Oxford University Press.

Polanyi, K. (1944), *The Great Transformation: the Political and Economic Origins of Our Time*, New York: Farrar & Rinehart.

Richardson, R.J. (1987), 'Directorship interlocks and corporate profitability', *Administrative Science Quarterly*, **32** (3), 367–86.

Robins, G. and M. Alexander (2004), 'Small worlds among interlocking directors: network structure and distance in bipartite graphs', *Computational and Mathematical Organization Theory*, **10** (1), 66–94.

Rowley, T.J., H.R. Greve, H. Rao, J.A.C. Baum, and A. Shipilov (2005), 'Time to break up: social and instrumental antecedents of firm exits from exchange cliques', *Academy of Management Journal*, **48** (3), 499–520.

Sabatier, P.A. (1987), 'Knowledge, policy-oriented learning, and policy change: an advocacy coalition framework', *Science Communication*, **8** (4), 649–92.

Scott, J.P. (2013), *Social Network Analysis: A Handbook*, 3rd edn, London: Sage.

Scott, J.P. and P.J. Carrington (eds) (2011), *The SAGE Handbook of Social Network Analysis*, London: Sage.

Seidman, S. (1983), 'Network structure and minimum degree', *Social Networks*, **5** (3), 268–87.

Smith, D.A. and D.R. White (1992), 'Structure and dynamics of the global economy: network analysis of international trade 1965–1980', *Social Forces*, **70** (4), 857–93.

Snijders, T.A.B., G.G. van de Bunt, and C.E.G. Steglich (2010), 'Introduction to stochastic actor-based models for network dynamics', *Social Networks*, **32** (1), 44–60.

Stone, L. (1971), 'Prosopography', *Daedalus*, **100** (1), 46–71.

Useem, M. (1979), 'The social organization of the American business elite and participation of corporation directors in the governance of American institutions', *American Sociological Review*, **44** (4), 553–72.

Uzzi, B. (1996), 'The sources and consequences of embeddedness for the economic performance of organizations: the network effect', *American Sociological Review*, **61** (4), 674–98.

# 13 Agent-based computational economics: simulation tools for heterodox research
*Jonathan F. Cogliano and Xiao Jiang*

## 13.1  INTRODUCTION

This chapter introduces agent-based modeling (ABM) as a research tool that possesses advantages for current heterodox research programs. An agent-based model (ABM) consists of a computer simulation of many interacting heterogeneous agents that produces economic phenomena of interest. The purpose of producing, or generating, economic phenomena with an ABM is to develop an account of how the phenomena in question are generated and to study the processes through which these phenomena evolve. The dynamics produced by ABMs are often complex and the ABM approach in general overlaps with complexity approaches to economics.[1] ABMs are extremely flexible in their construction and can incorporate many aspects of economic behavior and socio-economic situations that are of paramount interest to heterodox economists.

The general approach of ABM and how it might be applied to existing heterodox research programs is introduced in four steps. First, the uniqueness of ABM, which lies primarily in the flexibility to incorporate vastly heterogeneous agents and to address models with high degrees of freedom, is presented and discussed. Second, it is argued that the flexibility of ABMs makes them an appropriate tool for the questions raised by classical and (post)-Keynesian economists. This argument is demonstrated by briefly sketching two existing ABMs: one which constructs an environment that captures the classical-Marxian processes of gravitation, thereby opening new pathways in value theory; and another which presents a nuanced analysis of Keynesian effective demand problems and the existence of chaotic cycles in a capitalist economy. The last section revisits the flexibility of ABMs in order to discuss the open possibilities of applying the ABM toolset to different visions from across the variety of heterodox bodies of thought.

## 13.2  WHY ABM?

Agent-based modeling (ABM) presents a framework and set of tools that hold promise for advancing research within bodies of heterodox economics. To address the pertinent question of 'Why should heterodox economists be interested in agent-based models?' a brief, and abstract, sketch of the basic features of an agent-based model (ABM) is presented below and discussed in relation to current research programs. Detailed introductions to the construction of ABMs in general can be found in Railsback and Grimm (2012) and Salamon (2011). The exact choice of programming language or the software in which an ABM is developed depends on the researcher. NetLogo (Wilensky 1999) is a popular package that is easy to become acquainted with and has free introductions available online.[2] Other languages and software packages that are used in developing ABM are Mathematica, Swarm, and Repast. These are more difficult to pick up without any prior background in computer programming, but they can be more computationally powerful than NetLogo. For instance, if an ABM is built in Mathematica it is possible to use the software to analytically study the properties of the model.

**The Basics of ABM**

The first thing to consider when constructing an ABM is the design of a set of agents. The agents are heterogeneous to varying degrees, depending on what is desirable for the model being constructed, and a single model can feature multiple sets of agents, for example: consumers, households, firms, government, financial institutions, and/or other institutions. Consideration of heterogeneous agents is not new to heterodox economics, but the capability to work with heterogeneous agents is one way in which ABM could be appealing to those working in the different heterodox branches. Once the 'taxonomy of agents' (LeBaron and Tesfatsion 2008, p. 246) is decided upon, the agents are then given a set of characteristics appropriate for the model at hand. These characteristics could be endowments of commodities, preferences, a production technology, and/or abilities to process information.

Next, the agents must also be given rules through which they interact. The interactions can range from simple to complex, or from one-off to repeated interactions, and anything in between. Examples of possible interactions could be exchange, wage bargaining, competition between firms, management–employee interactions, and/or interactions between individual members of a household. The benefit of an ABM is that it can capture many of these interactions, and others, between heterogeneous agent sets within one model.

Lastly, the 'scale of the model must be suitable for the particular purpose at hand' (LeBaron and Tesfatsion 2008, p. 246). Stated another way, the agents must be situated within a world that makes sense for the problem being investigated, and the number of agents should be appropriately large enough. Similarly, when dealing with heterogeneous sets of agents, the proportions of different agent types should fit the problem or phenomena being investigated.

Broadly speaking, ABMs fit into what can be described as a 'generativist' methodology (Epstein 2006a). The purpose of a generativist methodology is to develop a micro-specification (the agents and their rules of interaction) that grows some type of more macro-level phenomenon through the interaction(s) of the many agents. Thus, some type of macro-behavior, or regularity, is generated from the micro-specification of the model and the model itself provides an account of how the macro-behavior is attained. As an ABM simulation unfolds the micro-specification generates macrostructures, which feed back into how the micro-specification updates and produces future macrostructures, thus the micro and macro 'co-evolve' (Epstein 2006a, p. 6). The focus on the formation of macro-behavior or a 'macrostructure' (Epstein 2006a, p. 8) should not be taken to mean that all ABMs are macroeconomic models; it simply means that ABMs are focused on economic phenomena that cannot be explained at the level of an individual agent. Stated differently, ABMs focus on phenomena that are the collective result of interacting agents as opposed to the direct outcomes of isolated individual agents. According to Epstein (2006a), ABMs 'provide computational demonstrations that a given microspecification is in fact *sufficient to generate* a macrostructure of interest', and the account of this genera-tion is how ABMs explain economic phenomena (Epstein 2006a, p. 8).

In the context of discussing how ABMs are built and explain economic phenomena it should be noted that, while ABMs are built around individual agents, these agents are not representative agents. One can examine a particular agent in an ABM over the course of a simulation, but the state of this agent over the simulation may or may not provide any information regarding the aggregate behavior of the model. In many ways, ABMs inherently accept Kirman's (1992) point that the representative agent is unjustified, and attempt to move beyond this modeling convention. Furthermore, the micro-specification of an ABM is not the same as the microfoundations found in many economic models. The micro-specification of an ABM sounds suspiciously similar to the microfounda-tions found in many neoclassical macroeconomic models, but the interaction of the agents in an ABM provides a degree of freedom between the micro-specification and the macrostructure that emerges from the simulation.

**The Advantages**

The advantages of using ABM come in several forms. As Tesfatsion (2006) notes, ABMs are particularly well adapted to incorporate asymmetric information, strategic interac-tions or choices, learning behavior, and the existence of multiple equilibria. The ability to incorporate the aforementioned features stems from the heterogeneity of the agents and the flexibility in their construction. ABMs are flexible in construction to the point that it is theoretically possible to include all of the characteristics mentioned by Tesfatsion (2006) in a model that demonstrates highly complex behavior. Similarly, this flexibility can allow ABMs to be 'tuned' (or 'calibrated' if one prefers) to replicate multiple empiri-cally observable behaviors in the same model; something that can be difficult with more traditional modeling techniques. Arguing the point further, Dosi et al. (2010) remark on the fact that an ABM's construction allows it to be 'empirically quite robust' because it can account 'for a large number of empirical regularities' rather than just a few moments or stylized facts observable in time series data (Dosi et al. 2010, p. 1759).

It is not uncommon for proponents of ABM to stress that the purpose of an ABM is to grow or have it produce some empirically observable pattern(s) in economic data. There is language to this effect in Dosi et al. (2010), Epstein (2006a), LeBaron and Tesfatsion (2008), and Tesfatsion (2006). The desire for ABMs to be empirically applicable and robust raises the question of how abstract the micro-specification of the models should be in order to be applicable to the real world. In theory an ABM could be built upon sets of agents and assumptions that are highly abstract and consistent with typical textbook approaches to economics, however, this approach would not be taking advantage of ABM's potential. Thus there is reason for the foundation of ABMs to be built upon the type of reasonable and grounded assumptions that are more characteristic of heterodox economics. The larger questions of which assumptions are the right assumptions and what is the correct degree of abstraction from the real world for ABMs are beyond the scope of this current endeavor.

While the empirical robustness aspect of ABM is of great importance for further estab-lishing ABM as an acceptable modeling choice, the benefits of ABMs do not lie exclu-sively in their ability to mimic empirical data. ABMs can contribute to the development of economic theory by: (1) allowing exploration of complex model set-ups that cannot be solved with traditional techniques; and (2) extending existing theory through adding to our understanding of how relevant phenomena are produced within the theory (Arthur 2006). Point (2) is particularly so in the case of classical and Marxian political economy, as shown in section 13.3, and in the case of the macro-dynamics explored in section 13.4.

Agent-based modeling holds promise for heterodox economics because of the inherent flexibility in construction. As discussed above, the flexibility can be how agents are designed and granted capabilities to process (or not process) information, how the interaction of agents is set up, the possible array of agents present in the model, and the complexity of agent interactions. This flexibility can allow the further development of both theory and modeling in some of the major heterodox traditions. This particular point is discussed further in the remaining sections.

### ABMs of Interest

Agent-based modeling already has some history in economics, with examples dating back roughly 20 years. However, many aspects of ABM are still underdeveloped, particularly its possible applications to existing research programs in the heterodox traditions. One of the earliest instances of an economic model built around interacting agents can be found in Albin and Foley (1992). Other early examples of agent-based modeling, simulation with heterogeneous agents in mind, or thinking of the economy as a complex system, can be found in Anderson et al. (1988), Arthur et al. (1997), and Lee (1996), with the contributions by Kirman (1997) and Tesfatsion (1997) speaking directly to the modeling of economies as systems of interacting agents. Lee (1996) explores the theoretical issues at the heart of considering multiple pricing strategies on the part of firms and corresponding issues of convergence in real-world pricing. There is also a growing number of collected volumes containing a variety of examples of agent-based models of economic phenomena. Notable among these are Epstein (2006b) and Tesfatsion and Judd (2006). ABMs, including the plea for more attention to the benefits of ABM, have also found their way into some academic journals. LeBaron and Tesfatsion (2008), for instance, is in the *American Economic Review*, and presentations of ABMs have been published in the *Journal of Economic Behavior and Organization*, *Journal of Economic Dynamics and Control*, and *Advances in Complex Systems*, and the *Journal of Economic Interaction and Coordination* was founded with the express purpose of furthering the development of ABMs.

Recent ABMs that may prove interesting for heterodox researchers to consider, some of which could be considered heterodox in their own right, can be found in the following works: Axtell (2010), Carvalho and Di Guilmi (2014), Delli Gatti et al. (2004), Di Guilmi and Chiarella (2011, 2013), Di Guilmi et al. (2012), Dosi et al. (2006), Dosi et al. (2010), Foley (2010), Gintis (2007, 2012), Kinsella et al. (2011), LeBaron (2006), Ussher (2008), and Wright (2008, 2011a).

The models presented in Axtell (2010) and Delli Gatti et al. (2004) study the distribution of firm size and the associated dynamics over business cycles. In Axtell's (2010) case an ABM is developed to replicate the distribution of firm size that is observable in economic data because the neoclassical theory of the firm is lacking in its ability to speak to empirically observable aspects of firms. Continuing with the more micro-oriented of the aforementioned models, Foley (2010) and Gintis (2007, 2012) present models of exchange processes in the general equilibrium tradition, but with a distinctly non-Walrasian flavor. Instead of employing a Walrasian auctioneer or having agents always trade at equilibrium prices, Foley (2010) and Gintis (2007, 2012) have the agents discover the equilibrium through their exchanges. Ongoing work by LeBaron (2006) and Ussher (2008) furthers understanding the behavior of financial markets in terms of the interaction of economic agents. Wright's (2008, 2011a) contributions situate classical-Marxian political economy in an agent-based environment in order to construct models that demonstrate the emergence of the labor theory of value of the classical-Marxian tradition. The model presented in section 13.3 is heavily influenced by Wright's pioneering contributions.

The remaining models listed above are more macro-oriented, although Delli Gatti et al. (2004) span both groups. Dosi et al. (2006) and Dosi et al. (2010) develop an ABM built around a Schumpeterian engine of technical change and economic growth that eventually incorporates Keynesian demand management (see Dosi et al. 2010) in order to study the potential positive effects of complementary creative destruction and demand management policies. Di Guilmi et al. (2012) further explore and develop analytical techniques for ABMs, and Di Guilmi and Chiarella (2011, 2013) explore financial instability, with Di Guilmi and Chiarella (2013) focusing on Minskyan dynamics, and transmission mechanisms of financial stress and instability to the real economy. Kinsella et al. (2011) develop an agent-based macro-model based on the stock-flow consistent approach to macroeconomics found in Godley and Lavoie (2007), which replicates a number of distribution patterns found macroeconomic data, for example, distributions of firm size and income. Carvalho and Di Guilmi (2014) study macroeconomic instability and financial fragility brought about by financialization and heterogeneous firm investment decisions in an agent-based stock-flow consistent environment. The contributions by Carvalho and Di Guilmi (2014) and Kinsella et al. (2011) may be of particular interest to those working in heterodox macroeconomics.

This is just a sample of the burgeoning literature on ABMs that may be of interest to heterodox researchers in further developing their own research programs. In the remaining sections of this chapter the application of ABM to specific heterodox bodies of thought is explicitly discussed.

## 13.3   ABM FOR CLASSICAL-MARXIAN VALUE THEORY

One thread of heterodox research that benefits from an agent-based setting is classical-Marxian value theory. The complementarity between classical-Marxian value theory and ABM becomes clear when reading Marx and the classicals (Smith and Ricardo) as employing a long-period method[3] in their development of the labor theory of value. This particular reading also treats the classicals (Smith and Ricardo in particular) and Marx as viewing capitalist economies to be complex systems (Foley 2003). The long-period method is briefly reconstructed below, with specific focus on Marx, in order to present the characteristics that make it a natural choice for an agent-based framework.

Marx's long-period method, as developed in Foley and Duménil (2008a, 2008b) and Foley (2011), begins with an abstraction in which there are a large number of commodity producers, with access to very low-cost means of production, laboring across many lines of production to create commodities. These producers are also taken to be mobile across lines of production. The producers then engage in direct exchange with one another and the prices of commodities that emerge are proportional to the labor-time required for their production. If prices are not proportional to labor-time requirements then the producers will migrate across lines of production until prices are once again proportional to labor-time requirements. This movement of producers across industries is conceived to be ongoing, thus the equilibrium at which prices are exactly proportional to labor-time requirements – or prices are proportional to values – emerges as a center of gravity for the constant oscillations of prices and the allocation of producers across lines of production.

The abstraction outlined above is referred to as the 'commodity law of exchange' (Foley and Duménil 2008a; Foley 2011) and can be expanded to include ownership of means of production and costly capital goods. As a result of including costly capital goods, the prices that form become prices of production (Marx 1981, pp. 297–8). The expanded abstraction is referred to as the 'capitalist law of exchange' (Foley and Duménil 2008a; Foley 2011) and 'transcends' (Foley 2011, p. 22) the commodity law of exchange so that the mobility of producers becomes the mobility of labor and capital across lines production. The mobility of labor and capital then entail that the relevant central tendencies of the capitalist law of exchange are the independent equalization of rates of surplus value across sectors (Cogliano 2013) and the equalization of profit rates.

The focus of classical-Marxian value theory on the emergence of centers of gravity (or central tendencies) lends itself to an agent-based approach, which has the flexibility to capture the type of open-ended oscillations described above. The ABM approach carries the additional benefit of allowing for detailed study of the exchange process taking place in the commodity or capitalist laws of exchange; a story that is largely absent from presentations of the classical-Marxian theory of value. Examples of recent work that situates the labor theory of value in an ABM can be found in Cogliano (2013) and Wright (2008, 2011a, 2011b). The approach and main results of Cogliano (2013) are presented below to demonstrate the advantages of an ABM approach to the study of classical-Marxian value theory.

**The Beaver–Deer World**

The flexibility of ABM to capture the open-ended processes of gravitation described by Marx can be demonstrated with the simple two-commodity model of the commodity law of exchange initially presented by Cogliano (2013). This particular model can be viewed as a version of Smith's beaver–deer thought experiment through which he develops the basic insights of the labor theory of value (Smith 1776 [2000]). This model lacks certain features of Marx's theory of value yet still holds insight for Marxian political economy given Marx's acceptance and approval of Smith's abstract approach to developing the labor theory of value.[4]

The model consists of a set of $N$ agents similar to the producers in the commodity law of exchange within a two-commodity world and occurs in discrete time steps $t$ for some total length of time $T$. The commodities held by the agents are denoted by $x_1$ and $x_2$. The agents produce commodities, trade with one another, consume commodities, and decide where to allocate their productive capacity. Commodities are produced with labor as the only input in order to capture the open access to means of production in the commodity law of exchange. The output of each agent during one time step of the model is given by $x_i = 1/l_i$ with $l_i$ denoting the labor value or labor-time requirement of producing commodity $i$. With $l_i \in (0, 1]$ for all $i$, the speed of production can be fairly rapid, with each agent producing at least one commodity during each time step of the simulation. Each agent produces one of the two commodities at a time but consumes a fixed proportion of their holdings of both during each time step of the model.

Once the agents have produced their commodities, they enter the market to exchange for the commodity they do not produce. There is no money in the model since the presence of money in a two-commodity world does not add to the story,[5] thus all exchanges take place via barter. The agents enter the market and determine their initial offer prices from a Cobb–Douglas utility function $u[x_1, x_2] = x_1^\alpha x_2^\beta$ with $\alpha = \beta$. Using a utility function to capture agents' willingness to trade is one possible way to construct this model. While the utility function has mathematical properties that are accommodating to this model, it would be of interest to heterodox economics to explore possible alternatives and incorporate other specifications of agents' willingness to trade that do not rely on utility functions.

With the above Cobb–Douglas utility function, the agents' willingness to trade is given by their marginal rate of substitution between the two commodities.[6] Hence, with $x_2$ as the numéraire, the initial offer prices are given by:

$$p = \frac{\partial u[x_1, x_2]/\partial x_1}{\partial u[x_1, x_2]/\partial x_2} = \frac{\alpha x_2}{\beta x_1} = \frac{x_2}{x_1} \tag{13.1}$$

The agents in each sector are then randomly matched with agents in the other sector and they determine a final exchange price as the geometric mean of their offer prices, for example: for some pair of agents $j$ and $k$ in sectors 1 and 2 respectively, their exchange price will be $\rho = (p_{1,j} \cdot p_{2,k})^{1/2}$. Once an exchange price $\rho$ is struck between the agents, they exchange a given quantity of the numéraire good and an appropriate amount of $x_1$ based on the exchange price: $x_1 = \bar{x}_2/\rho$.

Agents can engage in multiple exchanges during each time step of the model, thus multiple exchange prices manifest during each time step $t$ and exchanges continue to take place until the average offer prices across the two sectors are close. The exact exchange prices and the allocation of commodities across agents depends on the path taken to reach the equilibrium and varies over each iteration of the model. This type of exchange procedure and the corresponding equilibrium it reaches are referred to as 'catallactic' (Foley 2010; Julius 2013), which entails that 'agents who have identical preferences and endowments may have different commodity bundles and utility levels' (Foley 2010, p. 119) even in equilibrium.[7]

After the exchange procedure finishes, agents consume a fixed proportion of their holdings of both commodities and decide whether or not to reallocate their productive capacity across sectors in response to how they fared in exchange. Agents make this decision by comparing a moving average of the prices at which they exchanged to the average exchange price in the other sector. For example, an agent $j$ in sector 1 producing $x_1$ will compare a moving average of their $\rho_j$ to the average price in sector 2 given by $\bar{\rho}_2$. The comparison is made with a logistic function that takes the following form for an agent currently engaged in sector 1:

$$\Theta = \frac{1}{1 + e^{\gamma\left(\varepsilon(\bar{p}_2 - p_t) + (1-\varepsilon)\left(\frac{x_2}{x_1}\right)^{-1}\right)}} \qquad (13.2)$$

The $\varepsilon$ is a binary term that denotes whether or not the agent successfully completed an exchange in the market. If the agent did not exchange then $\varepsilon = 0$ and the agent could switch sectors if their offer price becomes small enough (or large enough in the case of agents in sector 2). The $\gamma$ term in equation (13.2) is a damping parameter. Equation (13.2) can be interpreted as yielding the inverse probability of an agent switching sectors. This probability $\Theta$ then updates the following equation:

$$s_t = s_{t-1} + \theta(\Theta - s_{t-1}) \qquad (13.3)$$

The agent then compares $s_t$ to a number that is drawn randomly from a normal distribution with $\mu = 0$ and $\sigma = 0.75$. If the number drawn is greater than $s_t$ then the agent will switch sectors and produce the other commodity in the next time step of the model. The result of equation (13.2) is fed into equation (13.3) in order to make each agent's decision to switch a gradual one based on some history of their experience in production and exchange.

The movement of producers across sectors in response to price signals occurs during each time step of the model. Thus the prices that emerge from the market during one time step $t$ will determine the allocation of producers across sectors in the next time step $t + 1$, which effectively determines the available supply of commodities. The available supply of commodities, in large part, determines the prices that emerge from the market in $t + 1$, which then determines the allocation of producers in $t + 2$.[8] Hence, the relative price and the allocation of producers across sectors co-evolve and the labor theory of value equilibrium emerges as a center of gravity as the simulation unfolds.

### Results and Considerations

Figure 13.1 demonstrates the co-evolution of relative price and producer allocation for a typical run of the model that begins out of equilibrium with $l_1 = l_2$. Figure 13.2 demonstrates how the deviations of relative price and the allocation of producers from the equilibrium fit a tight pattern about the equilibrium for a longer period of time.[9]

The gravitation of price and producer allocation about the equilibrium continues for any length of time $T$ without settling down or converging to the equilibrium. This model helps frame the labor theory of value not only as a theory of price formation, but also as a theory of the allocation of productive labor across sectors of an economy; an important nuance of the labor theory of value emphasized by Cogliano (2013). Thus this simple ABM captures the open-ended processes of gravitation that are a central aspect of the classical-Marxian vision.

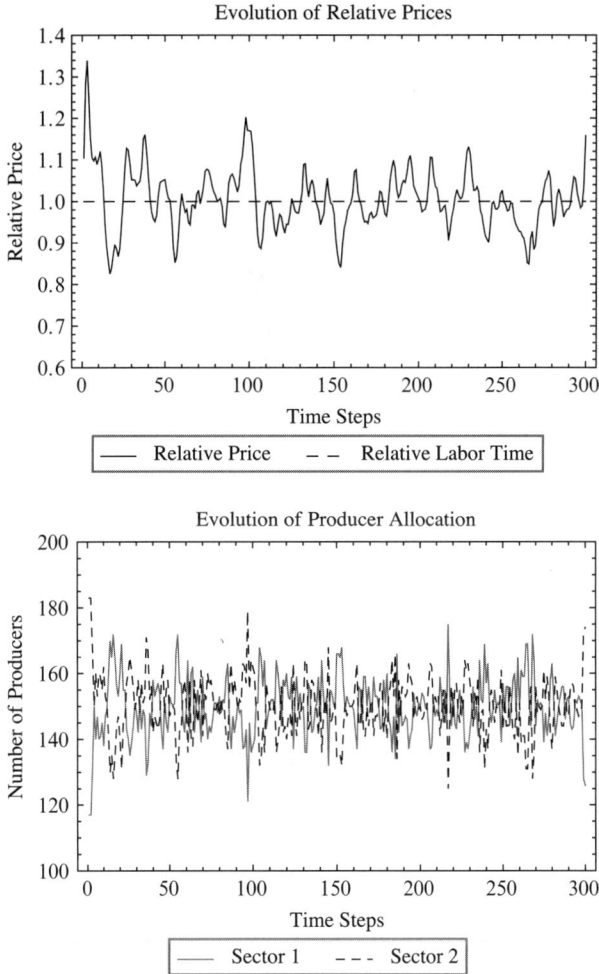

*Figure 13.1    Evolution of relative price and allocation of producers for: N = 300 and* $l_1$ = $l_2$ = *0.20 for 300 time steps*

## 13.4   ABM FOR (POST)KEYNESIAN MACRO-DYNAMICS

This section introduces a firm-level agent-based simulation model that is capable of generating chaotic cycles endogenously from an artificial economy. This model is particularly heterodox in the sense that it is a circuit of capital model in the Marxian tradition, and, at the same time, it imports various insights from Keynesian and post-Keynesian macroeconomics. Perhaps more importantly, this section also intends to show that the method of **ABM** is particularly useful in addressing some research questions that are quite heterodox in nature, such as: 'What are the dynamics implied by complex interactions of profit-seeking firms?' and 'What are the structural causes of growth and instability in a capitalist economy?'

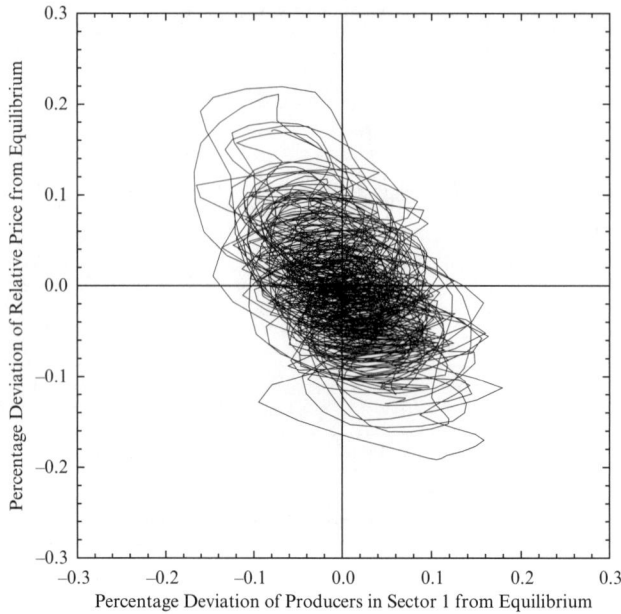

*Figure 13.2*   *Percentage deviation of relative price and allocation of producers from equilibrium for: $N = 300$ and $l_1 = l_2 = 0.20$ for 900 time steps (excludes initialization period)*

## An Overview of the Structure of the Circuit of Capital

Marx's circuit of capital model[10] was an attempt to conceptualize the economy as a whole by studying the macroeconomy in a way that is stock and flow consistent and compatible with the labor theory of value. The circuit of capital was originally written down by Marx (1978) as $M - C \dots P \dots C' - M'$. Money (or financial capital) $M$ is first transformed into commodities $C$ through advancing capital outlays, with $C$ taking on the form of constant and variable capital.[11] $C$ is then thrown into the production process $P$ and is transformed into a new commodity $C'$, which contains surplus value. Finally, this commodity is sold in the market and transformed back into money $M'$, with $M'$ being greater than the money value $M$ that began the circuit. The increase of $M' > M$ presupposes that $M'$ contains realized surplus value.

## An Agent-Based Circuit of Capital Model

Rooted in Marx's circuit of capital and the formal model developed by Foley (1982, 1986), this model of an artificial economy consists of $n$ profit-seeking firms, each owning two stocks: financial capital ($M$) and productive capital ($X$); and two flows: sales ($S$) and capital outlays ($C$). In the beginning, each firm is endowed with some amount of initial financial and productive capital and they have to first make investment, lending, and borrowing decisions. These decisions are modeled with an investment function in the post-Keynesian tradition:

$$C_{i,t+1} = C_{i,t} + a[m_{i,t}, i_t - r_{i,t}]C_{i,t}, \quad C_m > 0, \ C_{i-r} < 0 \tag{13.4}$$

In equation (13.4), $m$ is the liquidity ratio, which is the ratio between financial capital and productive capital ($M/X$). There is a positive relation between the growth rate of capital outlays ($a[m, i - r]$) and $m$ because higher liquidity will encourage greater investment on the part of firms. The growth rate of capital outlays also depends on the difference between the interest and profit rates ($i - r$). The higher the difference, the more a firm is inclined to lend its money to banks to earn interest rather than investing in real production to earn a profit, and vice versa.

The next step is the introduction of the demand closure. Assuming a portion of capital outlays of each firm goes to wages, and wages are spent instantaneously, then firms' capital outlays in the form of means of production and means of consumption must be shared across all other firms in the form of sales. This model further assumes that there is no capitalist consumption, hence there is no leakage from the sales. These constructs therefore yield (13.5): the sum capital outlays equals to the sum of sales; in other words, total effective demand always meets total supply:

$$\sum_{n=1}^{N} C_{n,t} = \sum_{n=1}^{N} S_{n,t} \tag{13.5}$$

The specific way in which capital outlays and sales match on the firm level in this system depends on the construction of the matrix $A$. Let $A$ be an $n \times n$ transition matrix of coefficients with its columns summing to one. Right-multiplying it by the vector of capital outlays $C$ will result in the vector of sales $S$:

$$A \cdot C = S \tag{13.6}$$

The $A$ matrix essentially distributes capital outlays across firms as their sales. In fact, the shape of the $A$ matrix is what makes this model 'agent-based' because it determines the heterogeneity of the firms. The $A$ matrix creates a network of supply and demand (capital outlays and sales) amongst the $n$ firms in the same way as a typical input–output matrix. Although equation (13.5) must hold in the aggregate, at the individual level each firm might have its capital outlays (supply) above or below the sales (demand from the rest of the firms). In other words, the Keynesian problem of effective demand arises at the individual firm level. The effective demand problem is modeled by the $A$ matrix with each column summing to 1, but each row sums to a number that is either above or below 1 (and yet the sum of column sums and the sum of row sums are kept equal, so equation 13.5 still holds).

For each firm, its pre-profit sales plus a mark-up minus capital outlays is its profit, and the share of profit out of sales is represented by the profit margin $q$. The accounting framework of this model deducts sales after profit, therefore, while updating the productive capital, the profit margin is discounted:

$$X_{i,t+1} = X_{i,t} + C_{i,t+1} - S_{i,t+1} \cdot (1 - q_i) \tag{13.7}$$

Equation (13.7) states that a firm's capital outlays add to its productive capital, and its sales (discounted by its profit margin) reduce its productive capital. Next, a firm's financial capital is updated in a similar fashion given by equation (13.8) below:

$$M_{i,t+1} = (1 + i_t)M_{i,t} - C_{i,t+1} + S_{i,t+1} \tag{13.8}$$

A firm receives (or pays out) interest on its financial capital first. Capital outlays reduce a firm's financial capital and sales increases the firm's financial capital. Finally, the firm's profit rate is determined as follows:

$$r_{i,t+1} = (q_i \cdot S_{i,t})/X_{i,t} \tag{13.9}$$

There is a central bank that determines a single new interest rate for all firms by looking at the average liquidity ratio $(\overline{m})$ of the entire economy. The central bank issues a lower interest rate when the average liquidity is high, and vice versa. The determination of the interest rate is expressed by equation (13.10) below:

$$i_{t+1} = \phi[\overline{m}_t], \ i_m < 0 \tag{13.10}$$

Once the interest rate is determined, the round of interaction ends and the new round starts with updated variables.

**Simulation Results**

For the purposes of simulation, the equations in the system are parameterized, the $A$ matrix is generated with desired properties as discussed in the last subsection, the number of firms and the uniform profit margin are again set to be 200 and 0.4 respectively, and finally, the initial values for each firm's stock variables are randomly assigned from a uniform distribution bounded between 0 and 200. The simulation is carried out using Mathematica.

Since the model itself is an artificial economy, some measure of gross domestic product (GDP) can be constructed similarly to how GDP is computed in actual economies. For this particular economy GDP can be measured using the income approach. In this model, there are only two sources of income: wages and profit. Wages in this model are specified as a portion of capital outlays and all wages are spent instantaneously. Profit is equal to sales multiplied by the profit margin, as stated in part of equation (13.9), but profit is claimed by firms after goods are sold, which is one period after wages are paid and consumed. Therefore, the GDP in this model is calculated by following equation:

$$GDP_t = kC_{t-1} + qS_t \tag{13.11}$$

With the proportion of capital outlays that goes to wages set at 30 percent, the growth rate of GDP in the simulation is illustrated in Figure 13.3. The growth rate of GDP in this model fluctuates within a range of 1 percent and displays a great deal of irregularity. In fact, disregarding the scale of the model,[12] the GDP growth rate trajectory of this system is strikingly similar to the actual US GDP growth rate path. It is worth noting that

Rate of Growth

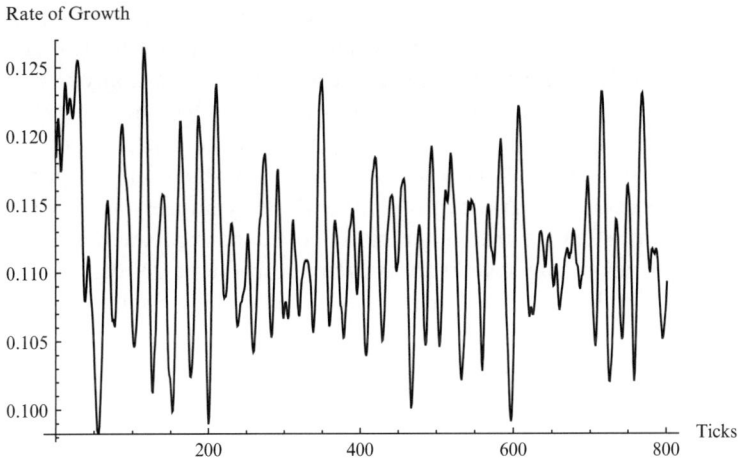

*Figure 13.3   GDP growth rate, 400 ticks*

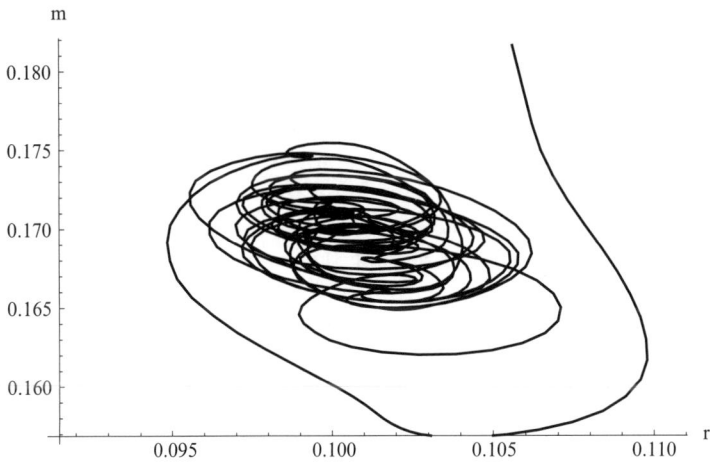

*Figure 13.4   Liquidity–profit rate, 500 ticks*

the cycles and turbulence appearing in the simulated GDP growth rate path are results of the nonlinear deterministic interactions of agents rather than random exogenous shocks. This in turn raises the important methodological question of how macroeconomic outcomes should be assessed and studied.

Shifting focus to the average liquidity ($m$) and profit rate ($r$), this model is able to generate chaotic average liquidity–profit rate cycles, which can be seen in Figure 13.4. Similar to Foley (1987), the basic cycles in this model are generated via accelerator-multiplier effects in the tradition of Hicks (1950), Kalecki (1969), and Goodwin (1982) with the major distinction being that this model generates accumulation cycles endogenously rather than exogenously; although, differing from Foley (1987), cycles in this model exhibit chaotic patterns that are qualitatively similar to the Goodwin cycles that have been empirically estimated by several authors.[13] In fact, what is shown in Figure (13.4) is a projection of a multidimensional orbit into two dimensions. Hence, the qualitative similarity between the output in Figure 13.4 and previous empirical studies interestingly suggests that the observed patterns of macroeconomic fluctuations can very well be generated by a high-dimensional nonlinear deterministic system rather than a stochastic process.

This model can also be solved analytically for its steady states and it can be shown that the steady states are centers of gravitation for the whole dynamic system. Mathematically, this set of steady states forms a trapping region in the dynamic system which ensures that the chaotic trajectories of the system always remain in the neighborhood of the steady state (global stability). In economic terms, they are essentially a set of long-period positions, as can be found in classical and Marxian political economy. Since the relationship between the long-period method and ABM was one of the emphases of section 13.3, it will not be further discussed here.

**Discussion**

A key feature of this model is that, as a deterministic model, it is able to produce chaotic trajectories that qualitatively resemble what one often observes in actual macroeconomic data. In fact, such a capability comes from the construction of the capital outlays–sales matrix ($A$) that models the Keynesian problem of effective demand at the individual level. It has been shown elsewhere[14] that the same model, but without the Keynesian problem of effective demand, will produce cycles and fluctuations that are regular rather than chaotic. Hence, this model provides a heterodox interpretation of the chaotic characteristic of capitalist accumulation. As soon as firms fail to coordinate their sales and capital outlays in a way that the effective demand is correctly met for each firm, the size of the firms (measured by their stock variables) becomes very different, hence this model becomes one with multiple heterogeneous agents, and the trajectories of the system become chaotic due to the fact that the system goes through numerous bifurcations as the agents interact.

The immediate political economy implication is that cycles and chaos in capital accumulation are due to neither 'mistakes' that firms make nor mysterious shocks from outside the system. Instead, they are embedded in the logic and structure of the circuit of capital: a decentralized system of production and distribution conceptualized from the perspective of profit-seeking enterprises. It is also worth emphasizing that, although the model is highly abstract at the present stage, what is not being abstracted from in building this model is the coexistence of individualistic profit-seeking actions (the heterogeneous micro-behavior of the firms) and the interdependence of the firms within a network of supply and demand (the $A$ matrix). Such coexistence is in fact an important feature of capitalism and it is precisely due to the dialectical tensions generated from such coexistence that the system under investigation is dynamic and complex in nature, which in turn demands methodologies such as nonlinear dynamics and ABM.

## 13.5   HETERODOX VISIONS, ABM METHODOLOGY, AND THE ROAD AHEAD

This section discusses the possibilities of ABM being applied to different dimensions of the broad variety of heterodox research programs. Heterodox economics is an umbrella term that covers various approaches, schools, or traditions, for example Marxian (Smith, Ricardo, and Marx), post/Keynesian, feminist, institutionalist, and Austrian. Despite its much-celebrated diversity, heterodox economics tends to share one theoretical commonality: that is, economic outcomes are, to a large extent, determined by the relation(s) between socio-economic structure and the agents who reside in it. In critical realist literature this is referred to as the structure–agency relation, a topic that has generated waves of theoretical debate.[15] Surveying the details of this line of debate is beyond the scope of this chapter, but it is important to emphasize here that these debates are concerned with the exact ways through which agency and structure relate to one another. As in most heterodox lines of thought, the importance of structure is never questioned in these debates. This section will argue that this theoretical commonality among heterodox schools of thought makes ABM a particularly useful research method for heterodox economics.

Take capital–labor relations in Marxian political economy as an example. The socio-economic structure of capitalism produces two distinct classes of agents: wage-laborers and capitalists. Agents from each class have distinct (and often conflicting) intentions and patterns of behavior, and their interactions generate various economic outcomes, such as increasing inequality, the falling rate of profit, and global expansion of capital. A parallel to the capital–labor relations is the gender relations emphasized by feminist economics. Socially constructed gender differences endow economic agents with gender-biased roles in economic life, and agents endowed with gender-biased roles interacting in a market economy results in a series of economic phenomena of central concern to feminist economists. Among these concerns are gender segregation, feminization of global production, and the widening and persistence of gender wage gaps. 'Institutions' are either products of some socio-economic structures, for example, labor unions, international organizations, and healthcare systems; or subsets of some socio-economic structures, which could be but are not limited to the market system, marriage, property rights, and the legal system.[16] Institutions shape the behaviors of economic agents, and economic agents' behavior in turn influences the evolution of institutions. Moreover, the importance of institutions has also been stressed by Austrian economists in their attempts to understand market order. To them, the study of market order is fundamentally about exchange behavior and the institutions within which exchanges take place. Finally, the relation between socio-economic structure and individual agents plays a central role in the Keynesian and post-Keynesian line of thought. The capitalist structure of production and distribution determines the behaviors of economic agents in the system, and a set of macroeconomic phenomena emerge out of the interactions amongst those agents as unintended consequences; for example, inflation, unemployment, cycles, and fluctuations.

The previous paragraph is intended to show that heterodox schools of thought tend to share a theoretical commonality; that is, many economic processes happen to be conceptualized as the interplay amongst different economic agents and the socio-economic structure in which they reside. Although this theoretical commonality cannot and should not be generalized to all of heterodox economics, it is not a stretch to see it as an important characteristic that brands of heterodox economics happen to share. ABM holds some unique advantages to modeling this characteristic as it appears in the different bodies of heterodox thought. Chief among these advantages are ABM's flexibility in construction and the heterogeneity of agents (as mentioned in 'The Advantages' in section 13.2). Socio-economic structures can be modeled as either a general environment that agents have to respond to, or characteristics that agents take on. For example, in the model introduced in section 13.3, the structure of production and distribution that characterizes the commodity law of exchange was constructed by building the beaver–deer world which endows a set of behavioral rules on the agents. In the model in section 13.4, the productive and distributive outcomes of the system depend on the structure of the circuit of capital and the network of supply and effective demand.

Furthermore, given the flexibility of ABM, gender- and social class-differentiated behavioral traits can be easily built into agents' behavior. With well-specified behavioral rules that are consistent with the relevant socio-economic structures, interactions amongst those agents will be capable of producing fruitful results that help the understanding of human (gender and/or capital–labor) relations. Institutions can be modeled as individual agents, such as the state, the central bank, and the labor union, that directly interact with economic agents; or as behavioral rules economic agents might follow – examples of such rules could be: to get married, to emulate others, to sell labor power, and to file lawsuits. More importantly, with the 'generativist' nature of ABM, the modeled institutions are capable of self-evolving via the feedback mechanism(s) between the macrostructure and the micro-specification (as mentioned in 'The Basics of ABM' in section 13.2). Finally, the heterogeneity of agents and high flexibility in agent construction make ABM an extremely useful methodology for some important Keynesian and post-Keynesian research programs involving the explorations of emergent macroeconomic properties, unintended consequences, and the fallacy of composition.

Finally, it is important to point out here that this chapter argues that ABM is a useful methodology for heterodox economics, given its unique advantages. This chapter should not be taken as arguing the superiority of ABM over other research methods for heterodox economics. ABM cannot replace formal mathematical modeling, empirical research, and nuanced qualitative analysis. While ABM is particularly well suited for exploring ways to model human interactions and the relationship(s) between micro-behaviors and macro-outcomes, at the same time, given its shortcomings,[17] it might very well be impotent in many other areas of research taken up by heterodox economists. After all, it is the research question itself that demands the right methodology, not the other way round. Thus, the toolset provided by ABM should be viewed as a valuable complement to the already vibrant research programs in the heterodox traditions.

## NOTES

1.  Discussions of complexity theory and economics that may be of interest to heterodox economists can be found in the volumes by Colander (2000) and Rosser (2009), as well as in the work of Kirman (2004) and Rosser (1999, 2008). In a similar thread, Holt et al. (2011) describe the recent emergence of what they deem to be the 'complexity era' of economics.
2.  http://ccl.northwestern.edu/netlogo/.

3. See Garegnani (1970, 1976, 1984).
4. The closeness of Smith and Marx on the development of the labor theory of value is discussed in detail by Cogliano (2013) and the passages in Marx's own work can be found in Volume 3 of *Capital* (Marx 1981, pp. 241–2), the introduction to the *Grundrisse* (Marx 1973, p. 104), and *Theories of Surplus Value* (Marx 1988, pp. 376–411).
5. A further developed version of this model that considers more sectors could benefit from the addition of money. The possibility of considering state-issued money that could introduce its own set of dynamics into the model would be ripe for consideration as well.
6. This type of trading procedure can first be found in one of the early agent-based exchange procedures developed by Albin and Foley (1992).
7. Axtell (2005), Fisher (1983), and Smale (1976) study exchange processes with a similar non-Walrasian flavor, while Gintis (2007, 2012) develops an exchange procedure in an agent-based setting that is also non-Walrasian.
8. The other factor in determining the price(s) that manifest in the market is the particular path that producer trades take from the starting point to the equilibrium.
9. Figure 13.2 features the deviation in the number of producers in sector 1 from the equilibrium because the number of producers in one sector provides information regarding the overall allocation across sectors since the model is built with two sectors.
10. First appearing in its developed form in Volume 2 of *Capital* (Marx 1978).
11. It is important to note here that one of the $C$ commodities is labor-power.
12. A model as such can be calibrated and scaled while its dynamics are still preserved, but the discussion of scaling and calibrating is beyond the aims of the current chapter.
13. See Barbosa-Filho and Taylor (2006), Tarassow (2010), and Rezai (2012).
14. See Jiang (2013).
15. For examples see Chapter 1 of the present *Handbook* as well as Archer (1995), Porpora (1987), and Wight (2006), among others.
16. Judging whether an institution is a product or a part of a particular socio-economic structure is an extremely controversial task, and it is beyond the scope of this chapter. The key is to show that institutions are inseparable from the notion of socioeconomic structure.
17. Some of the limitations of ABM are discussed by Arthur (2006), Epstein (2006a), LeBaron and Tesfatsion (2008), and Tesfatsion (2006).

# REFERENCES

Albin, P.S. and D.K. Foley (1992), 'Decentralized, dispersed exchange without an auctioneer', *Journal of Economic Behavior and Organization*, **18** (1), 27–51.
Anderson, P.W., K.J. Arrow, and D. Pines (eds) (1988), *The Economy as an Evolving Complex System*, Redwood City, CA: Addison-Wesley.
Archer, Margaret (1995), *Realist Social Theory*, Cambridge: Cambridge University Press.
Arthur, W.B. (2006), 'Out-of-equilibrium economics and agent-based modeling', in K.L. Judd and L. Tesfatsion (eds), *Handbook of Computational Economics, Volume 2*, Amsterdam: Elsevier, pp. 1551–64.
Arthur, W.B., S.N. Durlauf, and D.A. Lane (eds) (1997), *The Economy as an Evolving Complex System II*, Reading, MA: Perseus Books.
Axtell, R. (2005), 'The complexity of exchange', *Economic Journal*, **115** (504), F193–F210.
Axtell, R. (2010), 'Many agent firms', Working Paper, Washington DC: Center for Social Complexity, Krasnow Institute for Advanced Study, George Mason University, July.
Barbosa-Filho, N.H. and L. Taylor (2006), 'Distributive and demand cycles in the US economy: a structuralist Goodwin model', *Metroeconomica*, **57** (3), 389–411.
Carvalho, L. and C. Di Guilmi (2014), 'Macroeconomic instability and microeconomic financial fragility: a stock-flow consistent approach with heterogeneous agents', unpublished manuscript, January 24, 2014.
Cogliano, J.F. (2013), 'New directions in political economy: value theory, agent-based computational modeling, and the dynamics of labor mobility', PhD thesis, New School for Social Research.
Colander, D. (ed.) (2000), *Complexity and the History of Economic Thought*, London: Routledge.
Delli Gatti, D., C.D. Guilmi, E. Gaffeo, M.G. Gianfranco Giulioni, and A. Palestrini (2004), 'Business cycle fluctuations and firm size distribution dynamics', *Advances in Complex Systems*, **7** (2), 223–40.
Di Guilmi, C. and C. Chiarella (2011), 'The financial instability hypothesis: a stochastic microfoundation framework', *Journal of Economic Dynamics and Control*, **35** (8), 1151–71.
Di Guilmi, C. and C. Chiarella (2013), 'A reconsideration of the formal minskyan analysis: microfoundations,

endogenous money and the public sector', in G.I. Bischi, C. Chiarella, and I. Sushiko (eds), *Global Analysis of Dynamic Models in Economics and Finance*, Heidelberg: Springer, pp. 63–81.

Di Guilmi, C., M. Gallegati, S. Landini, and J.E. Stiglitz (2012), 'Towards an analytical solution for agent based models: an application to a credit network economy', in M. Aoki, K. Binmore, S. Deakin, and H. Gintis (eds), *Complexity and Institutions: Markets, Norms and Corporations*, London: Palgrave Macmillan, pp. 63–8.

Dosi, G., G. Fagiolo, and A. Roventini (2006), 'An evolutionary model of endogenous business cycles', *Computational Economics*, **27** (1), 3–34.

Dosi, G., G. Fagiolo, and A. Roventini (2010), 'Schumpeter meeting Keynes: a policy-friendly model of endogenous growth and business cycles', *Journal of Economic Dynamics and Control*, **34** (9), 1748–67.

Epstein, J.M. (2006a), 'Agent-based computational models and generative social science', in J.M. Epstein (ed.), *Generative Social Science: Studies in Agent-Based Computational Modeling*, Princeton, NJ: Princeton University Press, pp. 4–46.

Epstein, J.M. (ed.) (2006b), *Generative Social Science: Studies in Agent-Based Computational Modeling*, Princeton, NJ: Princeton University Press.

Fisher, F.M. (1983), *Disequilibrium Foundations of Equilibrium Economics*, Cambridge: Cambridge University Press.

Foley, D.K. (1982), 'Realization and accumulation in a Marxian model of the circuit of capital', *Journal of Economic Theory*, **28** (2), 300–319.

Foley, D.K. (1986), *Money, Accumulation and Crisis*, Chur, Switzerland: Harwood.

Foley, D.K. (1987), 'Liquidity-profit rate cycles in a capitalist economy', *Journal of Economic Behavior and Organization*, **8** (3), 363–76.

Foley, D.K. (2003), *Unholy Trinity: Labor, Capital, and Land in the New Economy*, New York: Routledge.

Foley, D.K. (2010), 'What's wrong with the fundamental existence and welfare theorems?', *Journal of Economic Behavior and Organization*, **75** (2), 115–31.

Foley, D.K. (2011), 'The long-period method and Marx's theory of value', in V. Caspari (ed.), *The Evolution of Economic Theory: Essays in Honour of Bertram Schefold*, Abingdon: Routledge, pp. 15–38.

Foley, D.K. and G. Duménil (2008a), 'Marxian transformation problem', in S.N. Durlauf and L.E. Blume (eds), *The New Palgrave Dictionary of Economics*, Basingstoke: Palgrave Macmillan, accessed January 28, 2010 at http://www.dictionaryofeconomics.com/article?id=pde2008_M000400.

Foley, D.K. and G. Duménil (2008b), 'Marx's analysis of capitalist production', in S.N. Durlauf and L.E. Blume (eds), *The New Palgrave Dictionary of Economics*, Basingstoke: Palgrave Macmillan, accessed January 28, 2010 at http://www.dictionaryofeconomics.com/article?id=pde2008_M000399.

Garegnani, P. (1970), 'Heterogeneous capital, the production function and the theory of distribution', *Review of Economic Studies*, **37** (3), 407–36.

Garegnani, P. (1976), 'On a change in the notion of equilibrium in recent work on value and distribution: a comment on Samuelson', in M. Brown, K. Sato, and P. Zarembka (eds), *Essays in Modern Capital Theory*, Amsterdam: North-Holland, pp. 25–45.

Garegnani, P. (1984), 'Value and distribution in the classical economists and Marx', *Oxford Economic Papers*, **36** (2), 291–325.

Gintis, H. (2007), 'The dynamics of general equilibrium', *Economic Journal*, **117** (523), 1280–1309.

Gintis, H. (2012), 'The dynamics of pure market exchange', in M. Aoki, K. Binmore, S. Deakin, and H. Gintis (eds), *Complexity and Institutions: Markets, Norms, and Corporations*, Basingstoke: Palgrave Macmillan, pp. 33–62.

Godley, W. and M. Lavoie (2007), *Monetary Economics: An Integrated Approach to Credit, Money, Income, Production and Wealth*, Basingstoke: Palgrave Macmillan.

Goodwin, R.M. (1982), *Essays in Economic Dynamics*, London: Macmillan.

Hicks, J.R. (1950), *A Contribution to the Theory of the Trade Cycle*, Oxford: Clarendon Press.

Holt, R.P., J.B. Rosser, and D. Colander (2011), 'The complexity era in economics', *Review of Political Economy*, **23** (3), 357–69.

Jiang, X. (2013), 'From limit-cycle to chaos: an inquiry into the macro-dynamics of a profit-seeking economy through the lens of circuit of capital', unpublished manuscript.

Julius, A.J. (2013), 'Class in catallaxy', in L. Taylor, A. Rezai, and T. Michl (eds), *Social Justice and Economics: Economics Essays in the Spirit of Duncan Foley*, Abingdon: Routledge, pp. 85–100.

Kalecki, M. (1969), *Studies in the Theory of Business Cycles: 1933–1939*, Homewood, IL: Irwin.

Kinsella, S., M. Greiff, and E.J. Nell (2011), 'Income distribution in a stock-flow consistent model with education and technological change', *Eastern Economic Journal*, **37** (1), 134–49.

Kirman, A.P. (1992), 'Whom or what does the representative individual represent?', *Journal of Economic Perspectives*, **6** (2), 117–36.

Kirman, A.P. (1997), 'The economy as an interactive system', in W.B. Arthur, S.N. Durlauf, and D.A. Lane (eds), *The Economy as an Evolving Complex System II*, Reading, MA: Perseus Books, pp. 491–532.

Kirman, A.P. (2004), 'Economics and complexity', *Advances in Complex Systems*, **7** (2), 139–55.

LeBaron, B. (2006), 'Agent-based financial markets: matching stylized facts with style', in D. Colander (ed.), *Post Walrasian Macroeconomics*, Cambridge: Cambridge University Press, pp. 22–38.

LeBaron, B. and L. Tesfatsion (2008), 'Modeling macroeconomies as open-ended dynamic systems of interacting agents', *American Economic Review*, **98** (2), 246–50.

Lee, Frederic S. (1996), 'Pricing, the pricing model and Post-Keynesian price theory', *Review of Political Economy*, **8** (1), 87–99.

Marx, K. (1973), *Grundrisse*, New York: Penguin Group.

Marx, K. (1978), *Capital: Volume II*, New York: Penguin Group.

Marx, K. (1981), *Capital: Volume III*, New York: Penguin Group.

Marx, K. (1988), *Collected Works*, Vol. 30, New York: International Publishers.

Porpora, D. (1987), *The Concept of Social Structure*, New York: Greenwood Press.

Railsback, S.F. and V. Grimm (2012), *Agent-Based and Individual-Based Modeling: A Practical Introduction*, Princeton, NJ: Princeton University Press.

Rezai, A. (2012), 'Goodwin cycles, distributional conflict and productivity growth', *Metroeconomica*, **63** (1), 29–39.

Rosser, J.B. (1999), 'On the complexities of complex economic dynamics', *Journal of Economic Perspectives*, **13** (4), 169–92.

Rosser, J.B. (2008), 'Econophysics and economic complexity', *Advances in Complex Systems*, **11** (5), 745–60.

Rosser, J.B. (ed.) (2009), *Handbook of Research on Complexity*, Cheltenham, UK and Northampton, MA, USA: Edward Elgar.

Salamon, T. (2011), *Design of Agent-Based Models: Developing Computer Simulations for a Better Understanding of Social Processes*, Repin, Czech Republic: Tomas Bruckner.

Smale, S. (1976), 'Exchange processes with price adjustment', *Journal of Mathematical Economics*, **3** (3), 211–26.

Smith, Adam (1776 [2000]), *An Inquiry into the Nature and Causes of the Wealth of Nations*, reprinted (2000) as *The Wealth of Nations*, New York: Random House.

Tarassow, A. (2010), 'The empirical relevance of Goodwin's business cycle model for the US economy', MPRA Paper No. 22271.

Tesfatsion, L. (1997), 'How economists can get alive', in W.B. Arthur, S.N. Durlauf, and D.A. Lane (eds), *The Economy as an Evolving Complex System II*, Reading, MA: Perseus, pp. 533–64.

Tesfatsion, L. (2006), 'Agent-based computational economics: a constructive approach to economic theory', in L. Tesfatsion and K.L. Judd (eds), *Handbook of Computational Economics*, Vol. 2, Amsterdam: Elsevier, pp. 831–80.

Tesfatsion, L. and K.L. Judd (eds) (2006), *Handbook of Computational Economics*, Vol. 2, Amsterdam: Elsevier.

Ussher, L.J. (2008), 'A speculative futures market with zero-intelligence', *Eastern Economic Journal*, **34** (4), 518–49.

Wight, C. (2006), *Agents, Structures, and International Relations: Politics as Ontology*, New York: Cambridge University Press.

Wilensky, U. (1999), *Netlogo*, Evanston, IL: Center for Connected Learning and Computer-Based Modeling, Northwestern University, accessed August 27, 2014 at http://ccl.northwestern.edu/netlogo/.

Wright, I. (2008), 'The emergence of the law of value in a dynamic simple commodity economy', *Review of Political Economy*, **20** (3), 367–91.

Wright, I. (2011a), 'Classical macrodynamics and the labor theory of value', Open Discussion Papers in Economics, no. 76, Milton Keynes: Open University.

Wright, I. (2011b), 'Convergence to natural prices in simple production', Open Discussion Papers in Economics, no. 75, Milton Keynes: Open University.

# 14 Modeling as a research method in heterodox economics*
## Frederic S. Lee

## 14.1 INTRODUCTION

Heterodox economists are divided into three camps regarding modeling and its significance for theorizing. One position argues that theorizing without modeling is the only way to proceed since models are viewed as mathematically overly complex and have no relationship to the real world. A second position is that the use of complex mathematical models that have little grounding in the real world but are based on heterodox economic theory (which may or may not have empirical grounding) is the way to proceed. The third position is that modeling, when it is empirically grounded, contributes to the development of heterodox theory and its properties and outcomes. Theorizing and analysis that entirely exclude modeling have never existed in economics and certainly do not exist today. That is to say, representing in the form of an analytical, abstract diagram as schema and modeling in the form of diagrams, sets of accounts, or mathematical equations as a way to conduct economic theorizing are found as far back as Quesnay's 1758 *Tableau Economique* or A.N. Isnard's 1787 two-sector model of the economy (Jaffe 1969), although their general use by economists dates back only to the 1930s. The early 'models' were often just schemas based on objective, measurable quantities and prices that actually existed in the economy, such as Marx's simple reproduction schema of the circuit of commodity capital (Marx 1971, Chs 3, 20), shown in Figure 14.1

However, starting in the 1930s, and certainly by the 1950s, mathematical modeling relative to schemas had become dominant, with the important difference that economists no longer constrained their the models (and their mathematics) by the actual economy, with the outcome that most models became mathematically highly developed. In addition, the

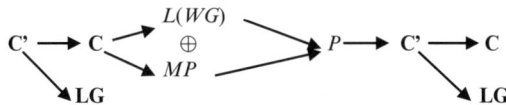

*Notes:*
C' is a vector of length $n$ outputs;
C is a vector of length $m$ of wage goods (*WG*) that sustains the quantities of the differentiated array of labor power (*L*) and quantities of differentiated means of production (*MP*) that replace the *MP* used up in production;
**LG** is a vector of length $n - m$ of quantities of luxury goods consumed by capitalists and constitutes the physical surplus of the economy;
*P* stands for the act of production; and
$\oplus$ means both labor power and produced means of production inputs are used to produce the output.

*Figure 14.1   Marx's simple reproduction schema*

neoclassical mainstream theory which formed the conceptual-theoretical background for the models was (and is) itself theoretically incoherent and unconnected to the real economy. This has had the outcome of further distancing the economic models from the real world.

The separation of the real world from the model has progressively shaped how economists generally view models and what it means to be engaged in modeling. One view is to see the model as an investigative artifact created independently of the theory and the world for the purpose of testing the theory through mimicking the real world; and a second is to conflate the theory with the model, so that the model is the theory and the theory is the model and neither is directly connected to the real world. What is evident now in economics is that these two views have merged into a single view in which the theory as modeling is a self-contained, empirically ungrounded, theoretical entity. This theory-model contains deliberate fictions and falsehoods, and hence is completely separate from the real world. Consequently, theorizing about the world consists of examining the world within the model and testing the theory-model by comparing the model outcomes to real-world data, as for example is done in real business cycle theory. What is clearly recognized by all is that the structures and causal mechanisms producing the real-world data are not actually embedded within the model. Therefore, to remedy the appearances of unworldliness, a diffused literature has emerged addressing the following concerns:

1. What constitutes 'credible models'?
2. Is surrogate modeling legitimate?
3. Can inferences be made from the model to the real world and vice-versa?

This leads to the central issue of this chapter: what is the role of modeling in heterodox economics? As noted in Chapter 2 in this *Handbook*, a critical realist–grounded theory (CR–GT) is a historical, analytical explanation of the actual economic events represented in the data. The theory is predicated on structures and causal mechanisms with their acting persons – that is, agency – and both are relatively enduring. Structures can be represented by an analytical, abstract diagram or schema, as in Figure 14.1; or the structures and causal mechanisms can be delineated as a model, that is, as a mathematical system of equations with standardized and formal conventions to denote their phenomena of interest that relate measurable quantities and involve causal mechanisms as agency (Morgan 2012). To construct a CR–GT schema or model, it is necessary to identify its structures and determine how they are linked to each other, and what outcomes emerge when agency as decisions are made. Thus, a schema or a model is a way to concretely identify and quantitatively and mathematically relate particular structures to theory; so they assist in 'structuring' the theory but they are not the theory itself. Moreover, through the use of agency manipulation, it is possible to examine variations in the outcomes. This enables the narrative of the model and the emerging theory to be enriched and comprehensive, or to discover problems with it as well, which permits a form of structural robustness analysis in which hypothetical-exploratory variations in structures leading to different outcomes can be compared and critically evaluated. In this manner, modeling is a research method that contributes to theory construction and development.

With modeling as a method, the issues that shape the rest of the chapter are: what is a model, and how can it be a research method? Section 14.2 deals with issues of the real world and the model, starting with a comparative analysis of heterodox and mainstream modeling, next dealing with credible versus real-world models, and finishing with a discussion of the kind of mathematics that is relevant for heterodox modeling. Section 14.3 introduces heterodox modeling in four steps: first by distinguishing between representing and modeling the subject matter, then introducing the model as a theorizing tool, followed by building the world into the heterodox model, and ending with 'working the model'. Section 14.4 concludes the chapter with a discussion of good and bad heterodox models and their impact on heterodox economics.

## 14.2   THE REAL WORLD AND THE MODEL

**Heterodox versus Mainstream Modeling**

From a critical realist perspective, the real economic world is a structural-causal analytical narrative, and because of this, it is also a historical analytical narrative. As part of the overall narrative there can be a schema and, more specifically, a model that represents some structures in terms of quantitative-mathematical relationships and includes causal mechanism agency. In this regard, because the real world consists of structures and causal mechanisms, it contains schemas and models, or there are models in the world (see Chapters 1 and 2 in this *Handbook*). Consequently, to engage in modeling, it is necessary to create the world in the model that is empirically grounded from the real world, that is, it has the same structures, causal mechanisms, and agency that exist in the real world. In this case, through the use of the method of grounded theory, the model in the world becomes the world in the model. So heterodox economists work with CR–GT models where the real world 'constrains' the model (and the types of mathematics used in the model); that is to say, heterodox economists require that their CR–GT abstractly, directly represent models to abstractly, directly represent the actual structures and causal mechanisms with their agency of the phenomenon under analysis to generate outcomes that are part of the real world, which can be predictions or simply accurate explanations of the real world. In this manner, a heterodox CR–GT and abstract, direct representation (ADR) modeler aims to create a model that is a complete real-world representation of the phenomenon under analysis which contains no fictitious components.[1] Such an approach to modeling is quite distinct from the approach used by mainstream economists (Weisberg 2007).

In contrast to taking the model in the world and putting it in the world in the model, mainstream economists create models that have their own world and hence are not constrained by the real world.[2] With no constraints, the representation of the world and its structures and causal mechanisms in the model may be anything. Consequently, it is possible to create models via analogies, metaphors, through idealization, or by imagination. Common to these models is that their worlds are deliberately not grounded in or otherwise directly connected to the real world. In a metaphor-analogy model, a metaphor, for example, is first used to derive the world as a model of the economic phenomenon under investigation; and then it is claimed that the metaphor model is analogous to (but not the same as) the actual phenomenon. So the outcome is that the model and its world is completely separate from the actual world and has no capability of understanding how the actual world operates. Similarly, using idealization or the imagination to construct the world in the model is a deliberate strategy to separate the model from the actual world. The outcome is a model that can be manipulated via agency as simulations or shifting structures (exogenous shocks) to generate outcomes that 'logically' (as opposed to 'empirically') emerge from the model. However, since the model and the actual world are separate, the outcomes do not constitute knowledge of the actual world, but are a form of pseudo-knowledge or, at best, knowledge of other worlds. Faced with such a conclusion, mainstream economists argue that the model and its fictitious world can provide an understanding of the actual world if there is a reasonable correlation between the outcome of the model and real-world data. This is a form of inductive inference based on subjective judgments of what constitutes an adequate or benchmark comparison that defines how close the comparison must be to be credible. If it meets and/or exceeds the benchmark, the model is credible and so its results can be used to make statements about the actual world. Yet this outcome suffers from a basic problem: the outcomes of the model are not established as identical to the outcomes of the real world. So there is no warrantable assertability beyond simple belief to claim that the model can actually say anything about the real world (Morgan 2012).

**Credible Models**

The substantive issue is whether it is reasonable for an economic model to be in a world of its own; or must it be of the real world? For the former to be reasonable, an argument has to be made about how the outcomes are generated within the model relative to the issues in the real world that it purports to deal with. That is, what degree of dependence on the real world must a model achieve in order to be credible? For if the model via its structures and causal mechanisms has no empirical grounding in the real world, then to what extent can it say anything about the real world? The question of model-derived knowledge is important. For mainstream economists, models need only to be credible in order to produce knowledge.

Credible models are models that succeed in capturing something of an observed pattern of the real-world phenomenon being investigated. But since such models contain fictitious worlds, they are parallel to the real world and this gap has to be crossed through inductive inference based on subjective judgments. However, is it really possible to make inferences from a fictitious model to the real world? In addition, what does it mean to make an inference from something that is fictitious to something that is real? Moreover, is it possible to have an objective (versus subjective) benchmark through which to determine whether a fictitious model is credible or not? And finally, if the model and the real world are similar (but the former is not empirically grounded) to some degree, is it possible for the causal mechanisms in the model to be the same (not just similar) to the one in the real world? To resolve these issues, mainstream economists intuitively – that is, delusively – believe their fictitious models support their conjectures about the real world, and they want to communicate them in a convincing way; that is, they believe that making inferences is reasonable and there is an 'objective' basis for distinguishing between creditable and non-credible models. The problem here is the issue of belief because, from a heterodox perspective, it is not possible for a fictitious model to say anything about the real world, and believing that it can does not constitute scientific knowledge.[3] Therefore heterodox economists do not entertain the possibility of credible models since all models must be grounded in the real world; and do not engage in making inferences from fictitious models to the real world. From a heterodox perspective, working inside of a fictitious world in the model to help theorize about the real world's social provisioning process is a process of destroying theory; that is, destroying an accurate explanation of how the provisioning process works, if the model is not empirically grounded (Sugden 2002, 2009).

**Mathematics**

The heterodox and mainstream modeling strategies have different implications for the kind of mathematics used since a modeling strategy enables the modeler to use types of mathematics appropriate to the model; that is, appropriate to the world within the model. Hence how the world in the model is created matters with regard to the mathematics used. Because the mainstream approach to modeling involves creating fictitious worlds, there is no constraint on the type of mathematics used. In fact, the more fictitious and convoluted the imagined world is, the more involved mainstream economists often (but not always) make the mathematics.[4] Moreover, at times the mathematics is used to construct the world as opposed to emanating from the world itself, such as assuming that all economic problems must be formulated in terms of constraint optimization (Samuelson 1947). Consequently, mainstream modeling appears overly mathematically complex.[5]

The heterodox CR–GT-ADR modeling approach, on the other hand, has the world in the model grounded in the real world. Hence the mathematics in the model is constrained by the real world. That is, model building involves converting the relevant empirically grounded structures and causal mechanism (which embody accurate measurements and observations) in the real world into a system of mathematical equations and language. As a result, the mathematical form of the model is determined and constrained by the empirically grounded structures (such as the input structures of an input–output model) and causal mechanisms (such as investment decisions by business enterprises), and hence is isomorphic with its empirical data (as well as the theory), which means it is intrinsically closed but externally open via the causal mechanism. The requirement that the mathematics be constrained by the real world means that only certain types of mathematics, such as arithmetic and linear-matrix algebra (especially when used in an arithmetical mode), can be used and that the measurable and observable outcomes of the model are determined, constrained, and real (as in the real world).[6] Hence, the model generates non-logical empirically grounded outcomes that are in the real world although not necessarily equivalent with the actual outcomes of the real world; and that is because the mathematics of the model is of the world itself. When this is the case, the model and its outcomes are characterized as rigorous and non-deductive. This is similar to the late nineteenth century view that mathematical rigor is established by basing the mathematics on physical reasoning resulting in physical models. However, the difference for heterodox modeling is that rigor results when the mathematical model is based on social reasoning represented by the CR–GT-ADR approach (Weintraub 1998a, 1998b, 2001, 2002; Israel 1981, 1991; Morgan 2012; Martins 2014; Chapter 11 in this *Handbook*).

## 14.3   HETERODOX MODELING

### Representing and Modeling

Representing and modeling a subject matter, such as the circuit of production schema, are distinct yet hierarchical activities. Representing has historically taken the form of an analytical, abstract diagram or schema that focuses primary attention on the quantitative relationships of the core concrete structures that clarify the complex relationships associated with the subject matter. Being empirically grounded, a schema establishes relationships between quantities that in turn facilitate the modeling and theorizing of the subject matter. What is significant about a schema is its claim to abstractly, directly represent the relatively enduring structural relationships among the quantities under investigation, thus restricting the kind of modeling and theorizing that is possible. In short, a schema establishes, from the beginning, the analytical limits of how the subject matter can be understood, theorized about. For example, the circuit of production concerns the economy as a whole; hence its schema, such as Marx's simple reproduction schema in Figure 14.1, portrays the 'structural law-like composition of quantity relations of the market economy as a whole' (Burchardt 1931, p. 529 [2013, p. 8]).[7] Consequently, the schema not only establishes and makes directly visible the ontological vision of the quantitative structures of the economy as a whole, but also constitutes the conceptual foundation upon which all other theories, such as theories of price and output, are developed. A schema can also represent aspects of the economy that are less than the economy as a whole, such as an integrated sector of the economy as delineated by Lowe (1976, p. 32) or the direct production of an output at the level of the business enterprise. In this case, the production schema can have the form in Figure 14.2.

This schema is to be interpreted as follows. In order to produce $Q$ units of output, the enterprise needs to assemble and combine the amounts of $C$ (intermediate inputs), $R$ (resources), $M$ (investment goods), and $L$ (labor) respectively. The production schema at the level of the enterprise also makes directly visible the ontological vision of production at the micro level in that it can only take place through the combination of distinctly different types of inputs, so that depicting production as utilizing only one type of input (labor for example) is not simply wrong, it, more significantly, violates the way in which production is conceptualized in the schema.

A schema does not, however, need to represent just relatively enduring structural relationships among the quantities. From a critical realist perspective in which structures and causal mechanisms and their agency form an integrated whole, a schema can include both. In this case, the relatively enduring relationship among quantities is expanded to include causal mechanisms, so that they become constituent components of the schema. Consequently, the ontological vision of the schema includes both structures that may include quantities, institutionalized flows of information such as data and hierarchical administrative directives (representing power relationships), and agency, meaning that an economic issue which involves agency but which is excluded when it comes to modeling,

$$C \oplus R \oplus M \oplus L \rightarrow Q$$

*Figure 14.2   Production schema for a single output*

Production Schema   →   Accounting Information   →   Pricing Committee   →   Outcome
                          Flows

$C \oplus R \oplus M \oplus L \rightarrow Q$   →   Costs   →   Costing   →   Price
                          Sales   →   Profit Mark-up

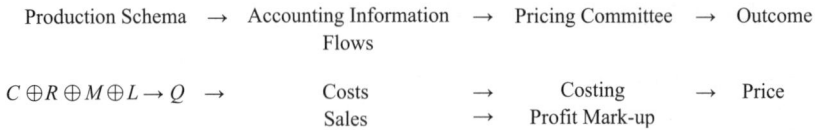

*Figure 14.3   Business enterprise pricing schema for a product line*

for example, violates the schema and its vision. An example of a schema that depicts quantitative and other structures along with causal mechanisms agency is the one for pricing of a product line by the business enterprise. The structures consist of the production schema and the accounting information flows of costs and sales (which consist of numerical amounts, that is, quantities) and the causal mechanism is the pricing committee in which its members (agency) draw upon the structures to cost the product and to determine the profit mark-up. The outcome of this interaction of structures and causal mechanism is the price of the product. The pricing schema is represented in Figure 14.3.

Within the CR–GT-ADR approach, the schema must represent the ontological vision and the substantive nature or relatively enduring relationships of the economic event under examination. Thus, the schema provides the empirical foundation of the model which it cannot exceed. Models are generally seen as mathematical relationships between quantities; thus they are associated with schemas that represent only structures as in Figures 14.1 and 14.2; but they can be integrated into schemas such as Figure 14.3 so that causal mechanisms agency become part of the model, that is, the model is open and hence need not have a solution based solely on structures. Once created, the model must be capable of being 'manipulated' by the modeler or the agents associated with the model via the subject matter under investigation. In this manner, the narrative explanation of the subject matter is worked out in conjunction with the model and its underlying schema. As a result the subject matter is directly embedded in the schema model and the schema model is in the subject matter: the world in the model and the model in the world. This simultaneous relationship means that the narrative explanation of the subject matter is ultimately constrained by the schema's structural, relatively enduring relationships so that different schemata of the same subject matter generate paradigmatically different theoretical narratives (Boumans 2005: 21–3; Burchardt 1931: 528–32 [2013: 5–11]; Morgan 2012).

**Model as a Theorizing Tool**

Models have a dual role in heterodox theory. Firstly, a model can be used to assist in developing the narrative of the heterodox theory. In this case, the model is an analytical exploratory tool that starts with empirically grounded structures and causal mechanisms and ends with rigorous outcomes. For example, if the empirical data that are being used to develop the theoretical narrative suggest a particular quantitative relationship between a set of variables, then attempting to model and hence evaluate the relationship is one way to help develop the narrative. Thus heterodox models are integral to the construction of heterodox theory. The outcome is that models are directly embedded in the theoretical narrative rather than having a narrative of their own.[8] Secondly, once the models and narrative are developed, they can be used to evaluate new data or explore the robustness of the narrative under different hypothetical conditions (which is discussed below). In this case, heterodox models contribute to the filling out of the narrative as well as assisting it to adapt to new data and slowly changing structures and causal mechanisms. A CR–GT–ADR model also has a role in examining and evaluating theoretical propositions associated with different heterodox theories. Hence a proposition, which is articulated in a manner that can be modeled and that is asserted to be true, can be examined by an empirically grounded model. The outcome of such a 'modeling examination' provides support or not for the proposition. For example, the Kaleckian proposition of wage-led growth is often asserted, but when introduced into an integrated, disaggregated output–employment and price model, the proposition is not supported, which in principle should promote its re-evaluation.

**Building the World in the Model**

As noted in Chapter 2 in this *Handbook*, the method of grounded theory compacts the scale of reality and therefore the degree of detail and specificity required of the narrative. That is, the structures and causal mechanisms that constitute the narrative are neither too aggregated to eliminate variations in the structures and eliminate agency nor too disaggregated to make the variations and agency so idiosyncratic that they are irrelevant for developing theoretical narratives. When applied to model construction, the world in the model is also compact as well as empirically grounded. Consequently, the model is small enough to examine the issue at hand while maintaining the diversity of structures and its manipulability through the agency embedded in the causal mechanisms by the modeler.[9]

The starting point of building a model is the array of structural relationships and causal mechanisms to be examined relative to particular outcomes. The next step is then to determine what real-world structures should be used to frame the model and what causal mechanisms with particular types of agency need to be included. Moreover, the empirically grounded structures must be relatively enduring and the agency via the acting person[10] working through the causal mechanism must also be relatively enduring and make the decisions that generate the rigorous outcomes emanating from the model (as discussed above). The result is a model that abstractly and directly represents the real world under examination, rather than being similar to, a surrogate of, an imitation of, analogous to, a mimic of, or an outright falsification of the real world.[11] Because of the acting person, who can make a great variety of decisions, the model is open to different rigorous outcomes, as opposed to a single deterministic outcome. Hence, it is possible for the modeler to develop different analytical narratives for different decisions as a way to examine the structural properties of the model.

With the world built into the model (at least that is the aim), the evaluation of the model consists of two distinct components: the model itself and its output. The former, which is the most important, concerns how closely the internal structures and causal mechanisms of the model match those in the real world; that is to say, how close the model's ADR of the real world is to the actual real world. Admittedly, the evaluation is, to at least some degree, subjective, but the point is that the ADR of a model is open to questioning and examination so that the 'acceptability' of a model is judged not solely on its outcomes. This means that it is possible to reject a model based on what it is – that is, on its empirical grounding and ADR – prior to any evaluation of its output.[12] The latter involves evaluating the differences between the rigorous outcomes which are grounded in the real world with the actual real-world outcomes. This again has a subjective element, but in both cases criteria can be developed to determine whether the differences are tolerable or not. Because the ADR of the real world of a CR–GT model is high in any case, the differences between its rigorous real-world output and the actual real world are small, hence minimally adequate to begin with.[13] As long as the issues under examination are part of developing a theoretical narrative of a particular issue, then the model's rigorous real-world output does not need further examination. But if the 'closeness' of the rigorous output to the actual real-world output is relevant, such as in the case of developing a narrative of an actual economic event or when making policy recommendations, then evaluating the closeness becomes important; thus the 'adequacy' of the model requires that both ADR and the output are more than 'adequate' (Weisberg 2007).

**Working the Model**

Working the CR–GT-ADR model is a form of theoretical exploration or, more specifically, a research method for developing and extending heterodox economic theory. This is done in a number of ways. Starting with the empirically grounded model that has been developed, and its relatively enduring structures and causal mechanisms, the working of this 'core' model consists of focusing on agency within the primary and secondary causal mechanisms because it can make decisions. In this manner, it is possible to see the different kinds of rigorous outcomes that are produced through the structures and causal mechanisms of the model. While appearing as a form of comparative statics, it is not because it does not involve changes in the structures and causal mechanisms (that is, the 'givens' of the model) but only changes in agency decisions that are consistent with their embeddedness in their causal mechanisms.[14] Thus, the variations in the core model's rigorous outcomes do represent plausible outcomes in the real world if the same decisions are made. Hence, we have reasoning within the model and through the model to the real world. The modeler could, upon reflecting on different theoretical arguments, also institute specific demands on the model to see what the rigorous outcomes would be relative to the core model. This could involve imposing uniform decisions on the agents or emphasizing the agency of a secondary causal mechanism over the agency of the primary causal mechanism. In both cases, the outcomes will provide the modeler with a better theoretical understanding of the core model and its contribution to the development of heterodox theory.

Historical change takes place through the interactive changes in structures and causal mechanisms, which implies changes in how agency is carried out. To explore the world of historical change and begin thinking of different possible analytical ways of narrating it, the core model can be explored – that is, manipulated – to provide different possible outcomes and hence narratives that can be compared to the core model's output and its narrative. This can be done by varying the structures and causal mechanisms independently or both together. The core model's variations include emphasizing secondary structures or causal mechanisms over the primary ones, reducing the causal mechanisms to a single one, altering structures and causal mechanisms, having agency decisions affect structures, having the changing structures affect causal mechanisms and hence agency decisions, all of which affect the outcomes which can be compared and analyzed relative to the core outcomes. In all cases, the variations must be empirically plausible if not to some degree empirically grounded, as opposed to outright empirical fictions, although there may be a fine dividing line between the two which would be open to debate. Through the variations and the subsequent comparing of the outcomes with the outcomes of the core model, it is possible to determine which structures and causal mechanism of the core CR-GR-ADR model are the ones that give it its essential properties and hence its theoretical identity, and the ones that contribute little or may even contradict its essential properties. This helps the modeler to strengthen the core model and the analytical narrative that goes along with it as well as providing an insight to identify historical change when it is occurring.[15]

## Two Examples of Working the Model[16]

Consider the following pricing model of the economy:

$$[R_d][Z_d][Mp_t + l*w + d] = p_{t+1} \qquad (14.1)$$

where:
$R_d$ is a $m \times m$ diagonal matrix of profit mark-ups with $(1 + r_i)$ being the $i$th profit mark-up along the principal diagonal;
$Z_d$ is a $m \times m$ diagonal matrix of overhead mark-ups with $(1 + z_i)$ being the $i$th overhead mark-up along the principal diagonal;
M is a $m \times n$ matrix of material pricing coefficients that are invariant with respect to short-term variations in output;
$l*$ is a $m \times z$ matrix of labor pricing coefficients that are invariant with respect to short-term variations in output;
w is a $z \times 1$ vector of wage rates;
d is a $m \times 1$ vector of depreciation pricing coefficients;
$p_t$ is a $n \times 1$ vector of basic goods input prices at time t; and
$p_{t+1}$ is a $m \times 1$ vector of output prices at time t + 1 where the first n prices are for the basic input goods and the last $m - n \times 1$ prices are for the non-basic surplus goods.

Given the pricing equations as structures – that is, some form of overhead and profit mark-ups on costs to set the price – and the causal mechanism as pricing committee (see Figure 14.3), the agency in the model consists of the modeler as $m$ pricing committees making decisions about wage rates and profit mark-ups to set the price. The modeler can start with any initial set of wage rates and profit mark-ups and through an iterative process will find out whether input prices converge to their output prices; or the modeler can use the inversion process to achieve the same outcome. The modeler will discover that for both processes to generate a positive solution set of prices the profit mark-ups are constrained; that is, the modeler cannot set any profit mark-ups they want, which is a very interesting property of the pricing model. Starting with this set of solution prices, the modeler could increase each wage rate by the same percentage to see what happens to prices, and the result will be that output prices will increase by the same percentage (actually slightly less, due to the depreciation term). The modeler could continue exploring the pricing model by altering the proportions of the various pricing equations in the model, by having only one pricing equation represented in the model, or by introducing a frequency of price change variable to see what happens to output prices and how long they take to converge to solution prices. Finally, the modeler could connect each decision to consider a price change with the change of some wage rates and profit mark-ups to examine the convergence process. All of these activities of the modeler are about working with the price model in order to get a better understanding of it and the narrative that goes along with it (Lee 1996).

A second example of working the model involves the output–employment model of the economy. Starting with an economy that consists of basic and non-basic sectors, and presuming that the surplus emanating from the basic sectors is used up in the production of the non-basic goods with the latter constituting the surplus, the output–employment model is the following:

| | | |
|---|---|---|
| Output: Basic Goods Sector | $\mathbf{Q}_1 = [\mathbf{I} - \mathbf{A}_{11}^{\mathsf{T}}]^{-1}\mathbf{A}_{21}^{\mathsf{T}}\mathbf{S}$ | (14.2) |
| Output: Surplus Goods Sector | $\mathbf{S} = \mathbf{Q}_{2G} + \mathbf{Q}_{2C} + \mathbf{Q}_{2I}$ | (14.3) |
| Total Employment | $\mathbf{L}^* = l_1^{\mathsf{T}}[\mathbf{I} - \mathbf{A}_{11}^{\mathsf{T}}]^{-1}\mathbf{A}_{21}^{\mathsf{T}}\mathbf{S} + l_2^{\mathsf{T}}\mathbf{S}$ | (14.4) |

where:
$\mathbf{A}_{11}$ is a $n \times n$ matrix of intermediate material production coefficients inputs used in the production of $\mathbf{Q}_1$, a strictly positive $n \times 1$ vector of basic intermediate goods and services;
$\mathbf{A}_{21}$ is a $m{-}n \times n$ matrix of intermediate material production coefficients used in the production of $\mathbf{S}$ a strictly positive $m{-}n \times 1$ vector of final or surplus goods and services for government, consumption and investment use and $\mathbf{Q}_{2G}$, $\mathbf{Q}_{2C}$ and $\mathbf{Q}_{2I}$ are semi-positive;
$l_1$ is a $n \times z$ matrix of labor production coefficients used in the production of $\mathbf{Q}_1$;
$l_2$ is a $m{-}n \times z$ matrix of labor production coefficients used in the production of $\mathbf{S}$; and
$\mathbf{L}^*$ is a $z \times 1$ vector of the total labor of the z different skills employed in the economy.

Because the maximum eigenvalue of $\mathbf{A}_{11}$ is less than 1, any positive vector of $\mathbf{S}$ will generate positive vectors of $\mathbf{Q}_1$ and $\mathbf{L}^*$. Moreover, the modeler can argue that whatever decision-making process that governs the decisions of the state and the business enterprises about how much government and investment goods to demand and how much consumption goods to produce, the outcome will always be that there is no constraint on the quantities produced and that they are produced independently of each other; for example, increasing the production of investment goods does not mean the reduction of the production of consumption and government goods. In addition, the modeler could examine the theoretical implications arising from the decline of the maximum eigenvalue of $\mathbf{A}_{11}$ due to the decline of the material production coefficients when $\Delta\mathbf{S} > 0$ (which implies that the real cost of producing the surplus is declining, as opposed to increasing as in mainstream economics). Finally, the modeler can show that the composition of total employment and total employment itself depend on what kind of surplus is produced. Again, through working with the model, the modeler can get a better understanding of it and the narrative that goes along with it.

## 14.4   CONCLUSION

As a research method, heterodox modeling has a great deal to offer heterodox econo-mists for the development of heterodox economic theory. But this will not happen if poor heterodox models continue to dominate heterodox economics and serve as the rep-resentative modeling method. Because of its CR–GT-ADR foundation, the model must consist of empirically grounded structures that are represented in terms of quantitative-mathematical relationships and empirically grounded causal mechanisms (that will also have structures as mathematical relationships) which include agency. With the world in the model coming from the model in the world and resulting in a model of the world, it is easy to differentiate between good and bad heterodox models. The latter will contain fictions, under-represent structures and omit causal mechanisms. For example, many aggregate post-Keynesian macroeconomic models and stock-flow consistent models omit circular production and the use of produced intermediate inputs, have only a single output, do not include any agency and assume a stationary state or a steady-state growth rate. Other models only have structures and no causal mechanisms, such as Sraffian price models, and there are models which under-represent causal mechanisms, such as omitting the state as a causal mechanism in determining the surplus or in the creation of money and financial assets in the economy. In contrast, a good model is one whose ADR is more accurate in that its structures and causal mechanisms come close to matching their real-world counterparts. Discriminating between good and bad models is important because when manipulating a CR–GT-ADR model, the modeler is also in a sense manipulating the real world: model in the world → world in the model → model of the world. That is, the structures and causal mechanisms as model that are in the real world become the world in the model, which in turn makes the model of the real world. Therefore, a poor model provides a poor if not false understanding of how the real world really works, and hence very much hinders the development of heterodox economic theory.

As a research method, building good heterodox models, such as the use of other research methods including surveys, ethnographic studies, oral histories, and case studies, is a very time-consuming activity, much more so than building poor models, because the modeler really does have to know a great deal about the real world to build one. Moreover, using them as a research method to contribute to theory development, to evaluate new data, or to explore the robustness of the narrative under different empiri-cally plausible hypothetical conditions, requires more diligence, not just because of what is at stake in the development of heterodox theory, but because just believing in the model and creating a fictional narrative for it is not good enough. A CR–GT-ADR model must actually be empirically sound and have a narrative that is grounded in the real world and which is part of the larger empirically grounded analytical narrative or theory. Heterodox economists need to utilize an array of research methods to develop theory and carry out applied and policy research. Modeling is one such method that can make a vital contribution to heterodox economics.

## NOTES

* I am grateful for the comments by Tae-Hee Jo, Drew Westberg, Nicola Matthews, Matthew Berg, Andrew Johnson, and Neal Wilson on previous drafts of the chapter.
1. 'Abstract', in this context, means to 'summarize' or directly represent the actual structures and causal mechanisms in the real world, much like an abstract of a book or article. This is in contrast to the use of 'abstract' by mainstream economists. They use it as a way to remove the real world from the model so to be able to introduce fictional concepts into it. In order to differentiate the two uses of abstract, I use 'direct representation' to denote the former meaning of abstract.
2. Some heterodox economists also create models which have their own world and hence are indistinguishable from mainstream modelers in terms of modeling.
3. This statement is distinct from the various ways in which the ideas that underpin it are arrived at, such as a combination of ungrounded conjunctures followed by empirical grounding. The point is that the end result – that is, the model itself – is empirically grounded and does not contain any fictitious components.
4. To facilitate their inclinations to deal with fictions as opposed to the real world, mainstream economists adopted the Cartesian approach to mathematics in which reality can be neglected; see Martins (2014, pp. 123–59).
5. Some heterodox economists have accepted the mainstream modeling strategy as the only possible strategy, and hence view the complex mathematics associated with the strategy as natural. In particular, because they fail to distinguish between modeling strategy and the use of mathematics, they attack the mathematics and the formalism it represents, while at the same time leaving unexamined the modeling strategy. Thus it can appear that heterodox economists reject 'mathematical modeling'. However this is not the case; see Lawson (2009, pp. 197–202, 2013, pp. 973–4).
6. Other types of mathematics could be used if the structures and causal mechanisms warranted it.
7. In critical realist terminology, structural law can be interpreted as 'relatively enduring'.
8. This is in contrast to mainstream economics where the special narrative accompanying the model is designed to legitimate it because the model is not at all grounded in the real world and hence has no inherent plausibility.
9. One outcome of a grounded theory, compacted model is that it is not identical to the real world; hence the model and the world are not the same.
10. The acting person represents the agency of individuals embedded in organizations and institutions, such as the business enterprise, the state, households, market governance organizations, and trade unions. Thus, as the individuals make decisions, so do their organizations and institutions.
11. See Morgan (2012) and Boumans (2005) for such models.
12. Many modelers find this mode of evaluation unacceptable because it prevents them from using their outcomes to legitimize the model that produced them.
13. For a CR–GT–ADR model, it is not acceptable to arbitrarily adjust the givens that constitute the structures in order to make the output of the model approach the actual real-world outcomes. This is similar to the issue of calibration in economics which rests on the position that an economic model is an artifact completely divorced from the real world. Although a CR–GT–ADR model is grounded in the real world, some (but not all) calibration issues may be relevant for heterodox economists to at least consider as they further develop their modeling research method (Boumans 2005, pp. 119–28).
14. For a similar form of modeling, see Setterfield (2003).
15. This is similar to 'robustness analysis', with the difference that its core model can be completely fictitious. Still, some of the issues raised in robustness analysis might be relevant to heterodox economists as they work their core models (Weisberg 2006; Kuorikoski et al. 2010).
16. For the mathematics of the two models, see Pasinetti (1977, Mathematical Appendix) and Berman and Plemmons (1994, Chs 2, 6, and 9).

## REFERENCES

Berman, A. and R.J. Plemmons (1994), *Nonnegative Matrices in the Mathematical Sciences*, Philadelphia, PA: SIAM.
Boumans, M. (2005), *How Economists Model the World into Numbers*, London: Routledge.
Burchardt, F. (1931 [2013]), 'Die schemata des stationaren kreislaufs bei Böhm-Bawerk und Marx (part I)', *Weltwirtschaftliches Archiv*, **34**, 525–64; transl. in C. Spanberger and F.S. Lee (eds) (2013), 'The schemata of the stationary circuit in Böhm-Bawerk and Marx', unpublished manuscript.

Israel, G. (1981), '"Rigor" and "axiomatics" in modern mathematics', *Fundamenta Scientiae*, **2**, 205–19.
Israel, G. (1991), 'Volterra's "Analytical mechanics" of biological associations', *Archives Internationales d'Histoire des Sciences*, **41** (1), 307–52.
Jaffe, W. (1969), 'A.N. Isnard: progenitor of the Walrasian general equilibrium model', *History of Political Economy*, **1** (1), 19–43.
Kuorikoski, J., A. Lehtinen, and C. Marchionni (2010), 'Economics as robustness analysis', *British Journal for the Philosophy of Science*, **61** (3), 541–67.
Lawson, T. (2009), 'On the nature and roles of formalism in economics: reply to Hodgson', in E. Fullbrook (ed.), *Ontology and Economics: Tony Lawson and his Critics*, London: Routledge, pp. 189–231.
Lee, Frederic S. (1996), 'Pricing, the pricing model and Post-Keynesian price theory', *Review of Political Economy*, **8** (1), 87–99.
Lowe, A. (1976), *The Path of Economic Growth*, Cambridge: Cambridge University Press.
Martins, N. (2014), *The Cambridge Revival of Political Economy*, London: Routledge.
Marx, K. (1971), *Capital: A Critique of Political Economy*, Vol. II, *The Process of Circulation of Production*, F. Engels (ed.), Moscow: Progress Publishers.
Morgan, M.S. (2012), *The World in the Model: How Economists Work and Think*, Cambridge: Cambridge University Press.
Pasinetti, L.L. (1977), *Lectures on the Theory of Production*, New York: Columbia University Press.
Samuelson, P.A. (1947), *Foundations of Economic Analysis*, Cambridge, MA: Harvard University Press.
Setterfield, M. (2003), 'Critical realism and formal modelling: incompatible bedfellows?', in P. Downward (ed.), *Applied Economics and the Critical Realist Critique*, London: Routledge, pp. 71–88.
Sugden, R. (2002), 'Credible worlds: the status of theoretical models in economics', in U. Maki (ed.), *Fact and Fiction in Economics: Models, Realism and Social Construction*, Cambridge: Cambridge University Press, pp. 107–36.
Sugden, R. (2009), 'Economic models as credible worlds or as isolating tools?', *Erkenntnis*, **70** (1), 3–27.
Weintraub, E.R. (1998a), 'From rigor to axiomatics: the marginalization of Griffith C. Evans', in M.S. Morgan and M. Rutherford (eds), *From Interwar Pluralism to Postwar Neoclassicism*, Durham, NC: Duke University Press, pp. 227–59.
Weintraub, E.R. (1998b), 'Controversy: axiomatisches mißverstandis', *Economic Journal*, **108** (451), 1837–47.
Weintraub, E.R. (2001), 'Measurement, and changing images of mathematical knowledge', in J.L. Klein and M. S. Morgan (eds), *The Age of Economic Measurement*, Durham, NC: Duke University Press, pp. 303–12.
Weintraub, E.R. (2002), *How Economics Became a Mathematical Science*, Durham, NC: Duke University Press.
Weisberg, M. (2006), 'Robustness analysis', *Philosophy of Science*, **73** (5), 730–42.
Weisberg, M. (2007), 'Who is a modeler?', *British Journal for the Philosophy of Science*, **58** (2), 207–33.

# 15 Multiple and mixed methods research for economics
## Bruce Cronin

## 15.1 INTRODUCTION

Where economics is dominated by a monolithic methodology of axiomatic theorizing and econometric analysis of secondary data sets, multiple and mixed methods research offers a much richer toolkit to examine economic problems from a variety of perspectives with custom methods suited for the particular task. Rather than limiting analysis to the application of approved methods to an approved data set, with little consideration of its content, a multiple or mixed methods approach inherently interrogates choices and limitations of data and methods from the outset.

Multiple and mixed methods research is of particular value to heterodox economics because heterodox concerns are broader than those of orthodox economics; explaining and advocating change in the social provisioning process in general including institutions, power and ideology. As argued in Part I of this *Handbook*, the critical realist ontological foundations of heterodox enquiry demand a research strategy consistent with this, one that embraces contestation, plurality, emergence and interdisciplinarity. Thus heterodox economics inherently rejects any preference for particular method or data and must be open to multiple and mixed methods.

But openness to multiple and mixed methods is insufficient in itself to advance a heterodox research agenda. A learned understanding of multiple and mixed methods design is needed to select appropriate tools to investigate particular problems, to use them well and appropriately combined with other tools, and to clearly understand the limitations of orthodox approaches. This chapter aims to equip readers with a grounding in the principles of multiple and mixed methods research and to consider benefits and limitations of triangulation of methods, issues in research design, choices of methods and their integration, and issues of validity and ethics.

## 15.2 THE MIXED METHODS PARADIGM

The use of multiple sources of evidence to support arguments is a long-standing characteristic of the humanities and the social sciences, notably in history, anthropology and sociology but also prominent in classical economics. In psychology, the famous Likert (1932) scale is a method of quantifying qualitative data. But advocacy of the use of multiple techniques as a method *itself* for the social sciences emerged in the use of multiple methods to reveal a variety of perspectives on a research problem and to try to offset known biases characteristic of each method, which can be traced back to Jahoda et al. (1933 [1971]) and the later formalization of the notion of 'triangulation': the claim that corroboration of results from multiple perspectives enhanced their validity (Campbell and Fiske 1959; Garner 1954; Boring 1953; Webb et al. 1966; Deising 1971; Sieber 1973).

Despite the avowed benefits of corroborated evidence from independent sources, concerns about incommensurability of results derived from greatly different methods underpinned the quantitative–qualitative divide that emerged from the 1970s. As discussed by Pickbourn and Ramnarain in Chapter 4 of this *Handbook*, strongly advocated preferences for particular ontological and methodological preferences in publishing, funding and hiring decisions institutionalized the divide, particularly evident in economics. Each stream emphasized the advantages of their approach over the weaknesses of the other: quantitative approaches criticized for their reductionism, formalism and insufficient attention to subjective interpretation; qualitative approaches criticized for limited generalizability, limited rigour and vulnerability to researchers' subjective biases.

From the late 1980s, 'mixed methods research', active combination of multiple methods, was advanced as a means of overcoming the qualitative–quantitative divide. Tashakkori and Teddlie (1998) argued that an ontological grounding of mixed methods research in pragmatism gave the approach a paradigmatic status as distinctive as qualitative or quantitative approaches themselves. In particular, Howe (1988) and Brewer and Hunter (1989) emphasized the pragmatist position that plurality of views, respectful dialogue and the search for workable solutions generates high-quality decision-making and thus the advancement of knowledge. Enquiry was thus agnostic in terms of particular methods and approach (inductive, deductive and abductive), other than that the methods combined should be those most useful to address the particular research question, and complementary rather than overlapping (Brewer and Hunter 1989; Johnson and Turner 2003). The pragmatic stance allowed rejection of a dichotomy between deductive and inductive approaches to research. Krathwohl (1993) envisaged a chain of reasoning from observations via induction to generalization and abstraction, to prediction and deduction tested by observations, with research starting at any point in the cycle.

The rise of the mixed methods paradigm generated wide interest in part because of the transformative or liberatory potential it offers. Qualitative methods counteract the institutional power of imposed meanings via standardized instruments (Harding 1986). In economics, where the highly standardized quantitative approach tests given phenomena within an assumed closed system, the addition of qualitative methods allows more open interrogation of these assumptions and given power structures (Downward and Mearman 2007). Engagement of stakeholders in decisions on methods, particularly stakeholders normally under-represented, sensitizes research to power imbalances, builds trust of research participants, and so leads to higher-quality data collection and generates results more likely to lead to social change (Berik 1997; Mertens 1999). Specifically with regard to mixed methods, Hesse-Biber (2010) argues that the combination of quantitative techniques to locate traditionally less-accessible groups then allows qualitative methods to give the under-represented 'voice'.

The transformative agenda in the use of mixed methods has drawn more from critical realist than from pragmatic ontologies. In contrast to an inductive/deductive cycle, this approach has employed 'retroduction', inferring mechanisms that must be in place for observed events to occur (Sayer 1992; see also Chapter 1 of this *Handbook*). Downward and Mearman (2007) argue that retroduction necessarily entails mixed methods. Firstly, qualitative and quantitative methods are not ontologically distinct; each contains quantitative and qualitative elements. Secondly, the demi-regularities in open systems that critical realism uses to infer causal mechanisms are best captured by quantitative methods, while the openness of these systems is best captured by qualitative methods.

The defining character of the 'mix' in mixed methods is the combination of qualitative and quantitative methods. It is argued that consideration of qualitative and quantitative methods in combination can put the respective limitations of each in perspective and thus offset their respective weaknesses (Tashakkori and Teddlie 1998; Creswell and Plano Clark 2007). This has been the basis of a great growth in 'mixed methods' as a methodological descriptor in the early twenty-first century, including the establishment of a journal of this name in 2007.

It has been argued, however, that, ironically, the restricted definition of mixed methods as the mixing of qualitative and quantitative methods tends to reinforce the supposed incommensurability of these paradigms and overstates the 'purity' and consistency of the methods grouped under these labels (Gorard 2004). As discussed in Chapter 4 in this *Handbook*, these categories are far less distinctive than is normally suggested, with open-ended data often subject to quantitative analysis in various forms, and closed-ended data influenced by subjective interpretation in construction, during collection and in analysis. Yin (2006) advocates use of a diversity of methods to generate rich, meaningful descriptions, thereby avoiding the quantitative–qualitative dichotomy (see also Brewer and Hunter 1989).

Howe (2004) further argues that mixed methods research tends to diminish the value of qualitative methods as interpretative tools, restricting these to exploratory uses, subservient to the alleged confirmatory power of quantitative methods, and reducing the potential for active engagement with research participants, relegating them to the role of research subjects; mixed methods in practice essentially amounts to 'positivism dressed in drag' (Giddings 2006). Bryman (2006a) found 63 per cent of mixed methods studies were cross-sectional and 57 per cent used a combination of a survey instrument and qualitative interviewing. While there are many examples of qualitative methods predominating over quantitative methods in mixed studies (Johnson and Onwuegbuzie 2004; Creswell et al. 2006; Mason 2006), mixed methods research remains predominantly quantitatively led, with minor qualitative illustration (Torrance 2013; Morse 2015).

## 15.3   MULTI-METHOD RESEARCH

Studies making use of multiple research methods within the same 'qualitative' or 'quantitative' paradigm or not involving systemic mixing or integration of these methods has been distinguished from 'mixed methods' as 'multi-method' research, with an emphasis on broadness and openness of method choice. The complementary criterion in methods choice remains; weaknesses should be non-overlapping (Brewer and Hunter 1989; Bryman 2006b, 2007; Yin 2006).

Mark (2015) argues that much social science research involves multi-method design even if this is not pursued consciously. He suggests that qualitative methods are particularly useful for generating research questions, via interpretative and discursive mechanisms and stakeholder engagement (Bryk 1983). While qualitative methods are often used to generate or collect these inputs, quantitative techniques to collect and report data are not precluded. Operationalizing research questions often involves the quantification of qualitative data. Pilot testing is a common qualitative method used to refine research instruments, whether qualitatively or quantitatively oriented. Qualitative interviews are widely used in combination with quantitative survey methods. Qualitative insight often informs the selection of quantitative analytical technique and the interpretation of results; the use of advisory boards can make the qualitative input more systematic (Campbell 1984; Cook 1985). But, while noting the widespread multi-method practice, Mark (2015) offers no guidance on selection beyond using what is needed, noting Cook's (1985) observation that no algorithm for selection exists.

Creswell and Plano Clark (2007) advocate explicit statements of the rationale for selection of particular combinations of methods in research design and detailed specification of the ways in which the methods are used and impact on each other in the design. Patai and Koertge (1994) criticize uncritical appropriation of methods from other fields as 'interdisciplinary opportunism'; Mutch (2009) as 'methodological eclecticism' or superficiality (Giddings and Grant 2007). A major limitation in mixing methods is the great specialized knowledge that may be required to use a particular method, such as discourse analysis or complex econometric modelling. This may lead to a division of labour in analysis without any of those in a research team having sufficient understanding to integrate the results effectively (Bryman 2007; Hesse-Biber and Leavy 2008; O'Cathain et al. 2008; Sandelowski 2014).

## 15.4 TRIANGULATION

One of the major benefits of multiple and mixed methods research is the increased confidence in the results of one method that comes when these results are corroborated by another method. This 'triangulation', the convergence of results or a 'confidence interval' range of results from multiple methods, is seen to reduce the likelihood that a result is affected by method choice or researcher bias (Campbell and Fiske 1959; Denzin 1970; Cook 1985; Mark and Shotland 1987). In multiple methods research compatible results are interpreted as increasing the validity of the results, while divergent results can alert researchers to the need for further analysis and cautious interpretation (Brewer and Hunter 2006).

Where triangulation is used to offset biases inherent in a particular method, the multiple methods must be implemented independently and simultaneously to avoid introducing further biases (Greene and McClintock 1985). Triangulation can be 'within-method' (Glaser and Strauss 1965) or 'between-methods' (Denzin 1970), the latter also known as 'across-methods'. Within-method triangulation involves multiple techniques or multiple comparison groups within a qualitative or quantitative approach serving as a form of internal consistency. Across-methods triangulation uses a qualitative method to provide external validity for a quantitative method or vice versa.

A problem with the concept of triangulation as a validation mechanism is that corroboration of two or more inaccurate methods or variations of the same method is not superior to the evidence from a single accurate instance of a single method (Denzin 1970). Different methods do not offset biases when they are biased in the same direction, or ask different questions (Rohner 1977; Mark and Shotland 1987). And when results from different methods do not converge, there are often considerable challenges in reconciling these (Cook 1985).

Results from multiple methods are likewise unlikely to converge where they ask sufficiently different questions. Disparate methods may not provide meaningful insights of relevance to each other and may simply generate more unanswered questions or invite a revisit of the implementation of the methods used (Mark and Shotland 1987; Cook 1985). In addition, the very act of undertaking multiple analyses of a set of data are likely to produce some results, simply because the chance of encountering something increases with more encounters (Stigler 1987). Such analytical 'fishing' is a well-known ethical problem in econometrics and has been considered in terms of 'principled discovery' in mixed methods research (Mark et al. 1998).

Jick (1979) highlights benefits of triangulation beyond validation, providing a fuller, more rounded, contextful picture, illuminating otherwise undetected variance, eliciting novel perspectives and enriching and deepening understanding, and facilitating the integration of or test of theories. Mark and Shotland (1987) highlight the value of complementarity of methods as the source of superiority of mixed methods over mono-method approaches. So qualitative interviews provide richness and insight into complexities of a situation that closed-ended survey questions cannot; but closed questions can be used to systematically detect the effects of particular theoretical propositions in a way that open-ended interviews may miss. Mark and Shotland (1987) see complementarity arising where one method adds additional insight or clarity to another, where distinct methods address different parts of a problem or different levels of analysis, or where a method helps to determine the plausibility of threats to the validity of another. Richardson and St Pierre (2003) reject the trigonometric metaphor of triangulation as offering precision, seeing the strength of mixed methods lying in the montage of views. Morse (1991) argues that triangulation does not rely on confirmation in the manner of a weighted comparison of the results of each method, but should be seen more as a process akin to fitting pieces to a jigsaw puzzle.

## 15.5   MIXED METHODS RESEARCH DESIGN

In an influential typology, based on a meta-analysis of mixed methods studies in policy evaluation, Greene et al. (1989) identify five major uses of mixed methods research, with complementary and expansion being most frequent (see also Bryman 2006a):

1. Triangulation – seeking convergence or corroboration in results.
2. Complementarity – elaboration, enrichment of understanding.
3. Initiation – discoveries that reframe research questions.
4. Development – apply a method because of the findings from another method.
5. Expansion – add breadth to the results of another method.

In a meta-analysis of 57 mixed method evaluation studies, Green et al. (1989) found each of these uses employing distinctive research designs, as summarized in Table 15.1. Mixed method studies seeking triangulation tended to apply different methods to the same phenomena, drawing from the same paradigm, giving both paradigms equal status, implementing these methods concurrently and independently. By contrast, studies

*Table 15.1   Mixed-method designs by purpose*

| Purpose: | Triangulation | Complementarity | Initiation | Development | Expansion |
|---|---|---|---|---|---|
| Methods | Different | Different | Different | Somewhat different | |
| Phenomena | Same | Similar | Somewhat different | Similar | Different |
| Paradigms (qualitative or quantitative) | Same | Same | Different | Same | |
| Status of paradigms | Equal | Equal | Equal | Equal | |
| Independence | Independent | Interactive | Interactive | Interactive | |
| Timing | Simultaneous | Simultaneous | | Sequential | |

*Source:*   Adapted from Greene et al. (1989).

seeking complementarity operated with similar rather than identical phenomena, and interaction among methods tended to be allowed. Studies seeking initiation tended to explore more distinctive phenomena and employ different paradigms interactively. Studies with development purposes tended to employ less distinctive methods sequentially. Studies with expansion purposes typically explored differing phenomena. The results suggest that the purposes to the left of the table benefit from more constrained research designs, and those to the right, from more open designs.

In a review of 13 classificatory systems in mixed methods research, Creswell et al. (2003) distinguish three major designs, while Tashakkori and Teddlie (1998) provide a fourth.[1] These are presented with a notation developed by Morse (1991), with the methods abbreviated, the major method capitalized, the minor in lower case, + indicating parallel timing, and → indicating sequence.

1. Convergent, 'concurrent' or 'parallel' design: the outputs of separate quantitative and qualitative analyses are compared; QUAL + *quan* or QUAN + *qual*. This design tends to be used for triangulation purposes.
2. Explanatory sequential design: deploy a quantitative method and then follow up with a qualitative method; QUAN→*qual*. This provides context or elaboration to complement, expand or develop a conventional quantitative analysis.
3. Exploratory sequential design: a qualitative analysis is followed by a quantitative analysis; QUAL→*quan*. This may quantitatively test some propositions developed in the qualitative component and is normally deployed iteratively in response to the qualitative findings for initiation, development or expansion purposes.
4. Multilevel design: while this may have the form of any of the other above types, one method is used at the class level and another at the sub-class level as, for example, qualitative analysis of chief executive officer (CEO) characteristics and quantitative analysis of individual firm performance.

Because design decisions should be appropriate for the research purpose, Creswell and Plano Clark (2007) advocate defining the research question in mixed methods terms; the role of each method and their relationship should be explicit in the research question asked. Key considerations in research design are then the sequencing of the research, the primacy given to either method, and the actual interaction of the methods during the study. A paragraph at the start of a methodological discussion providing a statement of purpose and an overview of the research design provides valuable orientation.

Hesse-Biber et al. (2015) argue that mixed methods studies have a different character where they are primarily qualitatively or quantitatively driven. When qualitative methods have primacy (QUAL), the research is said to have the exploratory, iterative, theory-building dimensions characteristic of grounded theory, but also transformatory and liberatory effects are heightened. Qualitative research (QUAL) may be enhanced by use of quantitative (*quan*) random selection to draw a sample for study that is representative, generalizable, comprises particular characteristics of interest or emerges as outliers (*quan*→QUAL). The reliability and validity of qualitative results can be assessed by exploring any differences to those from a similar investigation using quantitative methods or formally tested with quantitative techniques (QUAL→*quan*). Qualitative results (QUAL) may be enriched or extended (*qual*) by contrasting these with the results of quantitative investigation of other questions (QUAL→*quan*→*qual*). Extended chains of these approaches are typically developed iteratively.

Morse (1991, 2003), however, contends that it is important to restrict the mixed methods classification to studies that are 'one-and-a-half', that is, where a core QUAL or QUAN project is supplemented by a secondary *quan* or *qual* method, rather than a long, iteratively developed chain. The core project may be complete or publishable in its own right but is enriched or elaborated by the secondary questions, which are insufficient to be considered complete projects in their own right. The scope of the supplementary project is to provide certainty, a minimal threshold, about the secondary research question, rather than saturation to the point of a comprehensive account (Morse and Maddox 2014). Designs may include multiple supplementary projects such as concurrent QUAL + *quan* + *quan* designs or sequential QUAN→*qual*→*quan* ones, but the extensions must remain secondary. Thus, the 'one-and-a-half' criterion means that equal-weight studies QUAL + QUAN are not possible; these would comprise two studies. Likewise, *qual*→QUAN designs are misconceived; if the qualitative element is so defining, then this is actually a QUAL→*quan* design. And studies with more than one core element such as QUAL→*quan*→QUAL exceed the 'one-and-a-half' criterion and so amount to multiple methods studies (Morse 2015).

## 15.6   DIAGRAMMING

The relatively complicated natures of multiple and mixed methods studies greatly benefit from diagrammatic representation of research design (Creswell et al. 2003; Hesse-Biber 2010; Morse 2003; Morse and Maddox 2014). A flow diagram, such as the example in Figure 15.1, allows the relationship between the major and secondary research question to be visualized and the relationships between these and each data source, methods of data collection and analysis to be specified and, perhaps most importantly, demonstrates how the results of each method will be integrated to inform the research narrative. This can be particularly useful at iteration points where consideration may be given to adding

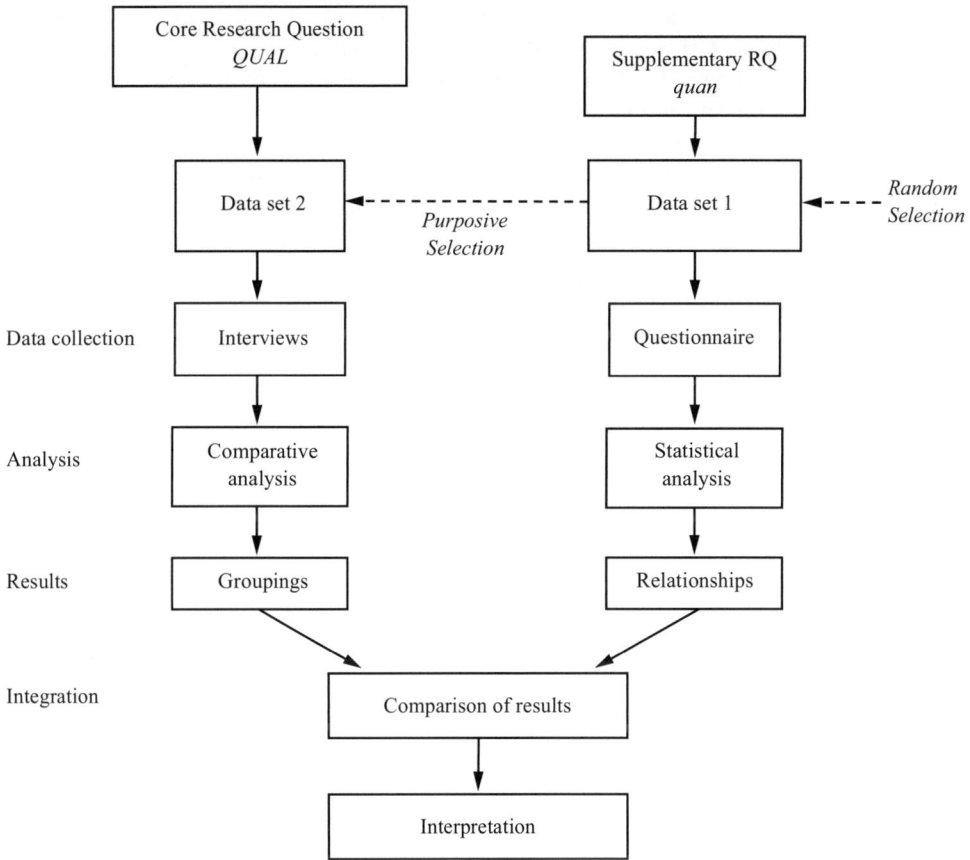

*Figure 15.1    Diagrammatic representation of a concurrent mixed methods study*

a further supplementary method; revising the diagram at this point to include the additional method can help to optimize choices.

Of course, such visualizations are highly stylized and do not capture the constant to-and-fro iterations between stages that occur in research in practice. Data collection techniques are adapted to particularities of the available data and data sets are revisited as limits of data collection tools are encountered, and so forth, suggesting that the dialogue between methods underpinning the potential power of mixed methods is not reserved to the formal integration stage alone (Maxwell and Loomis 2003).

## 15.7   MIXED METHODS INTEGRATION

Despite the perceived benefits of integrating different methods, there is little actual integration in much published mixed methods research. Greene et al. (1989) found integration absent in 44 per cent of the mixed methods studies they examined, with the remainder predominantly integrating methods only at the final interpretation stage. Interviews with practitioners suggest a preference to concentrate on the method they are most familiar with, often reinforced by the original research design and the locus of 'interesting' results, difficulties in developing effective dialogue with specialists in other methods, and perceptions of suitable publication outlets (Bryman 2007).

To overcome these limitations, Greene and Caracelli (1997) advocate a dialectical interaction of methods where researchers consider the contributions and limitations from each method alone, and then the distinctive benefit or loss from their combination (see also Greene and Hall 2010). Ahmed and Sil (2012, p. 948) argue that this can be achieved via 'cross-cultural communication' among mono-method specialists.

Caracelli and Greene (1993) identify four main strategies used to integrate mixed methods in analysis, while Cronin et al. (2008) offer a fifth:

1. Data transformation. There has been a long history of coding non-numeric data into countable categories via scaling techniques (Smith 1975), alongside simple descriptive statistics; Miles and Huberman (1994) dub this 'quantitizing'. By contrast, qualitatively categorizing quantitative data or describing this narratively can be considered 'qualitizing'. Narrative profile formation comprises narrative descriptions of the characteristics or themes of the modal or mean cases, the data as a whole, comparisons among groups, or with external norms (Tashakkori and Teddlie 1998).

2. Data consolidation. A data set is constructed with variables from different data types. Data are presented in a manner that allows comparison between the different approaches, typically in 'joint display'. This comprises tables with thematic rows and comparative qualitative and quantitative columns, or results from one method as rows and the other as columns (Miles and Huberman 1994). This can be used for triangulation to test for convergence or divergence, or to draw out and code themes.

3. Typology development. A typology is derived from one data type and this is used to categorize and analyse data of another type. Categories may be pre-existing, or emerge from the interpretation of themes or factor analysis in qualitative data, or from an analysis of covariance in quantitative data (Tashakkori and Teddlie 1998).

4. Extreme-case analysis. Contrasting cases are identified from one data type, such as high residuals in a regression analysis of quantitative data or from constant comparative analysis of qualitative data. The explanation for extremes is tested or refined with analysis of the other data type.

5. Following a thread. Themes and issues for exploration are drawn from each method, then a theme from one method is selected because of its salience for the research question. This is then followed across the results from the other method(s) to create an assembly of related findings which are further interrogated. These steps are repeated for other themes (Cronin et al. 2008).

Pearce (2015) suggests that some quantitative methods themselves, such as cluster analysis, exploratory factor analysis, data mining, qualitative comparative analysis, and others, invite inductive and exploratory treatment and that the sum is greater than the parts when doing so in a 'person-centred' rather than 'variable-centred' manner. Such methods bring out differences in data rather than reducing data to mean trends. Onwuegbuzie and Combs (2010) argue that such methods can be formalized as 'crossover mixed analysis', the analysis of qualitative data with quantitative techniques, or vice versa, offering greater

*Table 15.2*   *Examples of increasing levels of integration in mixed analysis*

| Level of integration | QUAL-dominant designs | QUANT-dominant designs |
|---|---|---|
| Low | Descriptive statistics of qualitative data | Inferential analysis of word counts |
| | Inferential statistics of qualitative data | Narrative profile formation |
| | Cluster analysis | Constant comparison analysis |
| | Exploratory factor analysis | Hierarchical linear modelling |
| | Structural equation modelling | Interpretative phenomenological analysis |
| | Path analysis | |
| | Correspondence analysis | Social network analysis |
| | Qualitative comparative analysis | Bayesian analysis |
| High | Micro-interlocutor analysis | Spatial analysis* |

*Note:*   * Onwuegbuzie and Combs (2010) suggest spatial analysis is sufficiently flexible for mixed designs of equal status rather than QUANT-dominant designs but the same could be said about the clustering techniques within social network analysis; the general conceptual orientation of both is quantitative.

*Sources:*   Tashakkori and Teddlie (1998) and Onwuegbuzie and Combs (2010).

integrative potential than simply comparing the separately applied outputs of qualitative and quantitative analyses (see also Greene 2007, 2008; Onwuegbuzie and Teddlie 2003). Some examples of crossover mixed analysis are presented in Table 15.2.

Sandelowski et al. (2009), however, warn that the concept of transforming one data type to another is more problematic than computer-aided pragmatic considerations suggest. The act of selecting and abstracting phenomena as data is a social activity, and whether these are abstracted in quantitative or qualitative form is influenced by disciplinary values. 'Quantitizing', converting from qualitative expression to quantitative expression, may be undertaken to assist pattern recognition, thereby retaining much of the data's diversity. Alternatively, it may be undertaken to make data amenable for formal quantitative analysis such as inferential statistics, that is, to reduce the diversity of data in order to assimilate with already quantitatively expressed phenomena (Maxwell 1992). The process of reducing qualitative data to numbers, such as by means of counting, is again a socially influenced interpretative act (Martin 2004). Even when carefully quantitized to explicit criteria, it is rare for the quantitative results to have the precision or replicability of quantitative data from other sources and so care should be taken in attributing these quantitative forms ordinal or interval properties. Even simple numerical categorization such as presence–absence (1–0) is subject to classifiers' expectations of what should be present. Because of these limitations and the great data loss involved in the quantitative reduction of qualitative data, mixed methods researchers need to clearly justify why they take any quantitizing step.

For Morse and Neihaus (2009), integration of methods is ultimately synthesized in the results narrative (the results and integration steps in Figure 15.1), requiring 'a capacity to organize materials within a plausible framework' (Weiss 1968, p. 349). A common error is to leave this for the discussion (interpretation) step, but the main contribution of a mixed methods approach is the integration of methods and therefore this needs specific attention. The separate discussion section is of the usual form, relating the results to previous research, limitations and implications, but should also include the contribution of the mix: to what extent does the secondary method strengthen the core study?

Creswell (1994), however, notes that integration of methods occurs throughout the process of a research study as questions, data, procedures and results are revisited iteratively from start to finish; researchers describe and classify data – that is, they interpret it – as they measure it, and so engagement in data collection itself is a particularly important integrative task for mixed methods research (Maxwell and Loomis 2003; see also Glaser and Strauss 1965; Yin 2006). Greene (2007) similarly emphasizes the value of researchers explicitly stating their ontological and epistemological assumptions as indicators of the integrative processes likely to have been used throughout a project.

## 15.8  VALIDITY IN MULTIPLE AND MIXED METHODS RESEARCH

Assessing the validity of multiple and mixed methods research is more complicated than mono-method studies because the validity of each method must be reviewed alongside standard validity considerations. Ioannidis et al. (2004) provide a useful summary checklist to assess the validity of a research project. Mixed methods research presents additional validity challenges as qualitative and quantitative approaches employ different mechanisms to assess internal validity. While quantitative methods assess inferred relationships against disciplinary evidential standards, such as norms for acceptable statistical probability, qualitative inferences are assessed in terms of credibility to participants and users of the research (Lincoln and Guba 1985). These are not so far apart as they may seem, as the disciplinary evidential standards of quantitative methods can also be seen as meeting a credibility criterion (Henry 1990).

Tashakkori and Teddlie (1998) suggest that the quality of mixed methods research can be evaluated in terms of its inference quality and interpretive rigour. Inference quality comprises the appropriateness of the research design for the research question and the extent to which the methods are applied appropriately and rigorously, including threats to validity in data collection. These might include differences in questions addressed by each method, appropriateness of samples, sample selection and size differences, and differences in response biases. Interpretative rigour comprises the quality of inferences drawn from the mixing of the methods, their relevance to the research question and the existing literature, their credibility and distinctiveness compared to mono-method approaches.

In convergent designs, validity issues include the independence and concurrency of the methods, to what extent samples and constructs differ, and to what extent divergences are accounted for. In sequential designs, validity issues centre on the extent to which the qualitative and quantitative procedures are compatible, such as use of psychometric scales in operationalizing qualitative variables and the extent to which weak results from one method were followed up by the other(s) (Creswell and Plano Clark 2007).

## 15.9  ETHICAL CONSIDERATIONS

As with most distinctive research approaches, multiple and mixed methods research raises some particular ethical considerations, arising from the extended procedures and their interactions. In an extensive discussion, Preissle et al. (2015) traverse three areas of particular ethical concern for multiple and mixed methods research.

First, the value added from supplementing existing approaches with further procedures needs to be clear in order to justify the additional resources used; the results of mixed methods designs are often only weakly integrated, for example (Bryman 2007). Does the team have sufficient skills to use and integrate the variety of methods effectively? Is the potential unique insight from multiple methods actually realized and used? Complicated procedures may be of questionable value if stakeholders do not make use of the findings (Weiss 1977).

Second, use of multiple methods implies an increased burden on participants in terms of information provided and, in sequential designs, the length of time involved. How is attrition of the population over time dealt with? Are participants fully informed of the burden of engagement and what triangulation of methods may reveal about them? What measures are taken to protect participants from any potentially harmful consequences of unanticipated revelations?

Third, the use of multiple methods requires consideration of the ethical implications of each, and in combination; are the sampling strategies appropriate for the specific requirements of each method, are random and purposive sampling related effectively, for example? The iterative character of sequential designs demands candour and transparency, with additional reporting implications in footnotes or appendices, in the interests of integrity and replicability.

## 15.10  CONCLUSION

Multiple and mixed methods research provides a means of investigating social reality in the heterodox spirit of contestation, plurality, emergence and interdisciplinarity. Multiple methods are useful in expanding the range of perspectives available in interrogating a problem, offering a richer understanding than that provided by mono-method approaches and cautioning against premature theoretical closure. But there is a danger of eclecticism where methods are combined without clear reasoning, potentially obscuring instead of enlightening, if not reinforcing dominant quantitative approaches with qualitative window-dressing.

Within the broad multiple methods approach, the mixed methods paradigm has emerged over the last three decades with a strong set of operational principles that allow heterodox researchers to engage in rigorous economic research on a critical realist foundation. Careful mixing of qualitative and quantitative methods in a manner appropriate to the research question at hand allows a much richer analysis of a problem than the highly restricted mono-method approaches that dominate economics in general. This offers greater rigour than mainstream approaches, but also the ability to tackle important issues of institutions, power and ideology in the social provisioning process.

Rigorous mixing of methods requires a clear understanding of the purpose for the mix, with triangulation actually being less common than complementarity and expansion purposes. From clear purpose can follow appropriate design, with diagramming providing useful support. Of critical importance to a rigorous mixes method design is careful attention to the integration of the methods; this is the point of make or break in a mixed methods study and is a challenging skill to develop. Clear purpose, design and planned execution provide the grounds for a valid and ethically justified study, easily superior to the uncritical adoption of a standard mono-method that so characterizes mainstream economics today.

## NOTE

1.  In a review of 13 classificatory systems in mixed methods research, Creswell et al. (2003) additionally included an 'embedded' or 'nested' design QUAN(*qual*) or QUAL(*quan*), providing support for the major method. However, these can be readily considered as variations of the original three design types (see Morse 2003).

## REFERENCES

Ahmed, A. and R. Sil (2012), 'When multi-method research subverts methodological pluralism – or, why we still need single-method research', *Perspectives on Politics*, **10** (4), 935–53.
Berik, G. (1997), 'The need for crossing the method boundaries in economics research', *Feminist Economics*, **3** (2), 121–5.
Boring, E.G. (1953), 'The role of theory in experimental psychology', *American Journal of Psychology*, **66** (2), 169–84.
Brewer, J. and A. Hunter (1989), *Multimethod Research: A Synthesis of Styles*, Newbury Park, CA: Sage.
Brewer, J. and A. Hunter (2006), *Foundations of Multimethod Research: A Synthesis of Styles*, Thousand Oaks, CA: Sage.
Bryk, A.S. (ed.) (1983), *Stakeholder-based Evaluation*, San Francisco, CA: Jossey-Bass.
Bryman, A. (2006a), 'Integrating quantitative and qualitative research: how is it done?', *Qualitative Research*, **6** (1), 97–113.
Bryman, A. (2006b), 'Paradigm peace and the implication for quality', *International Journal of Social Research Methodology*, **9** (3), 111–26.
Bryman, A. (2007), 'Barriers to integrating quantitative and research', *Journal of Mixed Methods Research*, **1** (1), 8–22.
Campbell, D.T. (1984), 'Can we be scientific in applied social science?', in R.F. Conner, D.G. Altman and C. Jackson (eds), *Evaluation Studies: Review Annual*, Vol. 9, Beverly Hills, CA: Sage, pp. 26–48.
Campbell, D.T. and D.W. Fiske (1959), 'Convergent and discriminant validation by the multitract-multimethod matrix', *Psychological Bulletin*, **56** (2), 81–105.
Caracelli, V.J. and J.C. Greene (1993), 'Data analysis strategies for mixed-method evaluation designs', *Educational Evaluation and Policy Analysis*, **15** (2), 195–207.
Cook, T.D. (1985), 'Postpositivist critical multiplism', in R.L. Shotland and M.M. Mark (eds), *Social Science and Social Policy*, Beverly Hills, CA: Sage, pp. 21–62.
Creswell, J.W. (1994), *Research Design: Qualitative and Quantitative Approaches*, Thousand Oaks, CA: Sage.
Creswell, J.W. and V.L. Plano Clark (2007), *Designing and Conducting Mixed Methods Research*, Thousand Oaks, CA: Sage.
Creswell, J.W., V.L. Plano Clark, M. Gutmann and W. Hanson (2003), 'Advanced mixed methods research designs', in A. Tashakkori and C. Teddlie (eds), *Handbook of Mixed Methods in Social and Behavioral Research*, Thousand Oaks, CA: Sage, pp. 209–49.
Creswell, J.W., R. Shope, V.L. Plano Clark and D.O. Green (2006), 'How interpretive qualitative research extends mixed methods research', *Research in the Schools*, **13** (1), 1–11.
Cronin, A., V.D. Alexander, J. Fielding, J. Moran-Ellis and H. Thomas (2008), 'The analytic integration of qualitative data sources', in P. Alasuutari, L. Bickman and J. Brannen (eds), *The SAGE Handbook of Social Research Methods*, London: Sage, pp. 572–84.
Deising, P. (1971), *Patterns of Discovery in the Social Sciences*, Chicago, IL: Aldine-Atherton.
Denzin, N.K. (1970), *The Research Act: A Theoretical Introduction to Sociological Methods*, New York: McGraw-Hill.
Downward, P. and A. Mearman (2007), 'Retroduction as mixed-methods triangulation in economic research: reorienting economics into social science', *Cambridge Journal of Economics*, **31** (1), 77–99.

Garner, W.R. (1954), 'Context effects and the validity of loudness scales', *Journal of Experimental Psychology*, **48** (3), 218–24.

Giddings, L.S. (2006), 'Mixed methods research: positivism dressed in drag?', *Journal of Research in Nursing*, **11** (3), 195–203.

Giddings, L.S. and B.M. Grant (2007), 'A Trojan horse for positivism?', *Advances in Nursing Science*, **30** (1), 52–60.

Glaser, B.G. and A.L. Strauss (1965), 'Discovery of substantive theory: a basic strategy underlying qualitative research', *American Behavioral Scientist*, **8** (1), 5–12.

Gorard, S. (2004), 'Scepticism or clericalism? Theory as a barrier to combining methods', *Journal of Educational Enquiry*, **5** (1), 1–21.

Greene, J.C. (2007), *Mixed Methods in Social Inquiry*, San Francisco, CA: Jossey-Bass.

Greene, J.C. (2008), 'Is mixed methods social inquiry a distinctive methodology?', *Journal of Mixed Methods Research*, **2** (1), 7–22.

Greene, J. and V. Caracelli (1997), 'Defining and describing the paradigm issue in mixed-method evaluation', *New Directions for Evaluation*, **74**, 5–17.

Greene, J.C., V.J. Caracelli and W.F. Graham (1989), 'Toward a conceptual framework for mixed-method evaluation designs', *Educational Evaluation and Policy Analysis*, **11** (3), 255-74.

Greene, J.C. and J.N. Hall (2010), 'Dialectics and pragmatism: being of consequence', in A. Tashakkori and C. Teddlie (eds), *SAGE Handbook of Mixed Methods in Social and Behavioral Research*, 2nd edn, Thousand Oaks, CA: Sage, pp. 119–44

Greene, J.C. and C. McClintock (1985), 'Triangulation in evaluation: design and analysis issues', *Evaluation Review*, **9** (5), 523–45.

Harding, S. (1986), *The Science Question in Feminism*, Ithaca, NY: Cornell University Press.

Henry, G.T. (1990), *Practical Sampling*, Newbury Park, CA: Sage.

Hesse-Biber, S.N. (2010), *Mixed Methods Research: Merging Theory with Practice*, New York: Guilford Press.

Hesse-Biber, S.N. and P.L. Leavy (eds) (2008), *Handbook of Emergent Methods in Social Research*, New York: Guilford Press.

Hesse-Biber, S.N., D. Rodriguez and N.A. Frost (2015), 'A qualitatively driven approach to multimethod and mixed methods research', in S.N. Hesse-Biber and R.B. Johnson (eds), *The Oxford Handbook of Multimethod and Mixed Methods Research Inquiry*, Oxford: Oxford University Press, pp. 3–20.

Howe, K.R. (1988), 'Against the quantitative–qualitative incompatibility thesis or dogmas die hard', *Educational Researcher*, **17** (1), 10–16.

Howe, K.R. (2004), 'A critique of experimentalism', *Qualitative Inquiry*, **10** (1), 42–6.

Ioannidis, J.P.A., S.J.W. Evans, P.C. Getzsche, R.T. O'Neill, D.G. Altman, K. Schulz and D. Moher (2004), 'Better reporting of harms in randomized trials: an extension of the CONSORT statement', *Annals of Internal Medicine*, **141** (10), 781–88.

Jahoda, M., P.F. Lazarsfeld and H. Zeisel (1933 [1971]), *Marienthal: The Sociography of an Unemployed Community*, Chicago, IL: Aldine Atherton.

Jick, T.D. (1979), 'Mixing qualitative and quantitative methods: triangulation in action', *Administrative Science Quarterly*, **24** (4), 602–11.

Johnson, R.B. and A.J. Onwuegbuzie (2004), 'Mixed methods: a research paradigm whose time has come', *Educational Researcher*, **33** (7), 14–26.

Johnson, R.B. and L.A. Turner (2003), 'Data collection strategies in mixed methods research', in A. Tashakkori and C. Teddlie (eds), *Handbook of Mixed Methods in Social and Behavioral Research,* Thousand Oaks, CA: Sage, pp. 297–319.

Krathwohl, D.R. (1993), *Methods of Educational and Social Science Research: An Integrated Approach*, White Plains, NY: Longman.

Likert, R. (1932), 'A technique for the measurement of attitudes', *Archives of Psychology*, **140**, 1–55.

Lincoln, Y.S. and E.L. Guba (1985), *Naturalistic Inquiry*, Beverly Hills, CA: Sage.

Mark, M.M. (2015), 'Mixed and multimethods in predominantly quantitative studies, especially experiments and quasi-experiments', in S.N. Hesse-Biber and R.B. Johnson (eds), *The Oxford Handbook of Multimethod and Mixed Methods Research Inquiry*, Oxford: Oxford University Press, pp. 21–41.

Mark, M.M., G.T. Henry and G. Julnes (1998), 'A realist theory of evaluation practice', *New Directions for Evaluation*, **78**, 3–32.

Mark, M.M. and R.L. Shotland (1987), 'Alternative models for the use of multiple methods', *New Directions for Program Evaluation*, **35**, 95–100.

Martin, A. (2004), 'Can't any body count? Counting as an epistemic theme in the history of human chromosomes', *Social Studies of Science*, **34** (6), 923–48.

Mason, J. (2006), 'Mixing methods in a qualitatively driven way', *Qualitative Research*, **6** (1), 9–25.

Maxwell, J.A. (1992), 'Understanding and validity in qualitative research', *Harvard Educational Review*, **62** (3), 279–300.

Maxwell, J.A. and D.M. Loomis (2003), 'Mixed methods design: an alternative approach', in A. Tashakkori and C. Teddlie (eds), *Handbook of Mixed Methods in Social and Behavioral Research*, Thousand Oaks, CA: Sage, pp. 241–71.
Mertens, D.M. (1999), 'Inclusive evaluation: implications of transformative theory for evaluation', *American Journal of Evaluation*, **20** (1), 1–14.
Miles, M.B. and A.M. Huberman (1994), *Qualitative Data Analysis: An Expanded Sourcebook*, 2nd edn, Thousand Oaks, CA: Sage.
Morse, J.M. (1991) 'Approaches to qualitative–quantitative methodological triangulation', *Nursing Research*, **40** (2), 120–23.
Morse, J.M. (2003), 'Principles of mixed and multi-method research design', in A. Tashakkori and C. Teddlie (eds), *Handbook of Mixed Methods in Social and Behavioral Research*, Thousand Oaks, CA: Sage, pp. 189–208.
Morse, J.M. (2015), 'Issues in qualitatively-driven mixed-method designs: walking through a mixed-method project', in S.N. Hesse-Biber and R.B. Johnson (eds), *The Oxford Handbook of Multimethod and Mixed Methods Research Inquiry*, Oxford: Oxford University Press, pp. 206–22.
Morse, J.M. and L. Maddox (2014), 'Analytic strategies with qualitative components in mixed method research', in U. Flick (ed.), *The SAGE Handbook of Qualitative Data Analysis*, London: Sage, pp. 524–39.
Morse, J.M. and L. Niehaus (2009), *Mixed Method Design: Principles and Procedures*, Walnut Creek, CA: Left Coast Press.
Mutch, C. (2009), 'Mixed method research: methodological eclecticism or muddled thinking?', *Journal of Educational Leadership, Policy and Practice*, **24** (2), 18–30.
O'Cathain, A., E. Murphy and J. Nicholl (2008), 'Multidisciplinary, interdisciplinary, or dysfunctional? Team working in mixed-methods research', *Qualitative Health Research*, **18** (11), 1574–85.
Onwuegbuzie, A.J. and J.P. Combs (2010), 'Emergent data analysis techniques in mixed methods research: a synthesis', in A. Tashakkori and C. Teddlie (eds), *SAGE Handbook of Mixed Methods in Social and Behavioral Research*, 2nd edn, Thousand Oaks, CA: Sage, pp. 397–430.
Onwuegbuzie, A.J. and C. Teddlie (2003), 'A framework for analyzing data in mixed methods research', in A. Tashakkori and C. Teddlie (eds), *Handbook of Mixed Methods in Social and Behavioral Research*, Thousand Oaks, CA: Sage, pp. 351–83.
Patai, D. and N. Koertge (1994), *Professing Feminism: Cautionary Tales from the Strange World of Women's Studies*, New York: Basic Books.
Pearce, L.D. (2015), 'Thinking outside the q boxes: further motivating a mixed research perspective', in S.N Hesse-Biber and R.B. Johnson (eds), *The Oxford Handbook of Multimethod and Mixed Methods Research Inquiry*, Oxford: Oxford University Press. pp. 42–56.
Preissle, J., R.M. Glover-Kudon, E.A. Rohan, J.E. Boehm and A. DeGroff (2015), 'Putting ethics on the mixed methods map', in S.N. Hesse-Biber and R.B. Johnson (eds), *The Oxford Handbook of Multimethod and Mixed Methods Research Inquiry*, Oxford: Oxford University Press, pp. 144–62.
Richardson, L. and E.A. St Pierre (2003), 'Writing: a method of inquiry', in N.K. Denzin and Y.S. Lincoln (eds), *The Sage Handbook of Qualitative Research*, 3rd edn, Thousand Oaks, CA: Sage, pp. 959–78.
Rohner, R.P. (1977), 'Advantages of the comparative method of anthropology', *Cross-Cultural Research*, **12** (2), 117–44.
Sandelowski, M. (2014), 'Unmixing mixed-methods research', *Research in Nursing and Health*, **37** (1), 3–8.
Sandelowski, M., C.I. Voils and G. Knafl (2009), 'On quantitizing', *Journal of Mixed Methods Research*, **3** (3), 208–22.
Sayer, A. (1992), *Method in Social Science: A Realist Approach*, London: Routledge.
Sieber, S.D. (1973), 'The integration of fieldwork and survey methods', *American Journal of Sociology*, **78** (6), 1335–59.
Smith, H.W. (1975), *Strategies of Social Research: The Methodological Imagination*, Englewood Cliffs, NJ: Prentice Hall.
Stigler, S.M. (1987), 'Testing hypotheses or fitting models: another look at mass extinction', in M.H. Nitecki and A. Hoffman (eds), *Neutral Models in Biology*, Oxford: Oxford University Press, pp. 145–9.
Tashakkori, A. and C. Teddlie (1998), *Mixed Methodology: Combining Qualitative and Quantitative Approaches*, Thousand Oaks, CA: Sage.
Torrance, H. (2013), 'The practice of educational and social research: running a small research institute', *International Review of Qualitative Research*, **6** (3), 323–36.
Webb, E.J., D.T. Campbell, R.D. Schwartz and L. Sechrest (1966), *Unobtrusive Measures: Nonreactive Research in the Social Sciences*, Chicago, IL: Rand McNally.
Weiss, R.S. (1968), 'Issues in holistic research', in H.S. Becker, B. Geer, D. Riesman and R. Weiss (eds), *Institutions and the Person*, Chicago, IL: Aldine, pp. 342–50.
Weiss, C.H. (ed.) (1977), *Using Social Research in Public Policy Making*, Lexington, MA: D.C. Heath.
Yin, R.K. (2006), 'Mixed methods research: are the methods genuinely integrated or merely parallel?', *Research in the Schools*, **13** (1), 41–7.

# PART III

# APPLICATIONS

# 16 A mixed methods approach to investment behavior
### *Armağan Gezici*

## 16.1 INTRODUCTION

Empirical testing of alternative theories of investment has been a challenge as competing theories often end up using similar variables. In selecting among this mélange of possible empirical specifications, researchers from different perspectives can pick and choose among variables to get desired results. Deploying solely quantitative methods such as econometric tests of correlations between firm-level variables does not quite help us to acquire a holistic understanding of why and how firms undertake investment projects in a particular context with certain circumstances. A more multifaceted investigation can be accomplished by utilizing both qualitative and quantitative data in the framework of a case study. By providing information from a number of different data sources over a period of time, a case study permits a more holistic study of structures and causal mechanisms of investment decisions of companies.

In this chapter, I present a case study examining the patterns and determinants of firm-level investment in the Turkish economy after the opening of the capital account in 1989. Since the beginning of the 1990s, the Turkish economy followed a pattern of boom–bust cycles, with major crises in 1994 and 2001, which created greater instability.[1] Despite a relatively stable period over the last decade, the investment performance of the Turkish economy has been far from impressive: the total investment as a share of gross domestic product (GDP) was 23 percent in 2011, two percentage points lower than it was in 1986. While such poor investment performance has been studied, existing empirical literature provides only aggregate estimations that produce broad correlations between macroeconomic variables and investment.[2] What is unclear in these studies is how firms respond to their macroeconomic environment. To examine particular channels through which investment is induced and/or curbed, a firm-level microeconomic analysis is needed.

Challenges of using only quantitative data to analyze investment behavior of companies are further aggravated in the context of a developing country, such as Turkey. Quantitative firm-level data utilized in investment studies are typically derived from balance sheets and income statements of publicly listed companies. The absence of a firm-level data set with continuous coverage over a long enough time period has been an important obstacle for undertaking firm-level investment studies in a developing-country context. For instance, the widely used Worldscope database[3] could not be used for a long-term analysis of investment patterns, since it provides observations on only 23 firms in Turkey, beginning from the early 1990s. Even with available data for later years, the lack of full inflation accounting poses a specific problem for studies of investment in highly inflationary countries, as various components of capital stock are disproportionally affected by inflation.[4] For these reasons, quantitative data from developing economies may be either not available or not reliable in most cases.

The case study presented in this chapter examines firm-level investment behavior by 'mixing' quantitative firm-level data with qualitative insights from fieldwork. Approaches taken to defining 'qualitative' and 'quantitative' have long been associated with different paradigmatic approaches to research: different assumptions about the nature of knowledge (ontology) and the means of generating it (epistemology).[5] From another angle, it is generally suggested that qualitative research questions are exploratory, while quantitative research questions are confirmatory. With these features, qualitative research involves more theory generation, and quantitative research involves more theory verification. When the purpose is to do both, as in the case of the present study, mixing these methods is especially useful. In this chapter, qualitative research is deployed to explore the determinants of investment and to generate a framework of investment in the context of a developing country, prone to boom–bust cycles of growth. Then quantitative methods and data are used to see if the framework emerging from the qualitative part is valid. Qualitative data from fieldwork will further allow us to interpret correlations in quantitative data by revealing the motivations behind firms' investment behavior, and help us identify the constraints and impediments to investment in a realistic manner. Such use of qualitative findings to move backward from an observation of correlation to the causes of that observation is known as retroduction and has an important role in 'triangulation' of research methods as argued by Downward and Mearman (2007).

In section 16.2 of the chapter, I provide a review of various investment models that inform the qualitative fieldwork to follow. The goal of this review is to identify the main threads across competing models, upon which the framework and the questions of the fieldwork will be designed. Section 16.3 introduces and presents the qualitative findings from the fieldwork on investment behavior of the Turkish manufacturing firms. Section 16.4 provides a statistical examination of investment behavior based on a quantitative firm-level data set of the Turkish manufacturing firms. Lastly, section 16.5 concludes.

## 16.2    WHAT DO WE KNOW ABOUT INVESTMENT?

Prior to the mid-1980s, the mainstream models of Jorgenson, the accelerator model, and the q model constituted the main theoretical foundations of empirical investment studies.[6] More recently, issues such as internal funds, uncertainty, and irreversibility have become prominent.

Accelerator models focus on output growth as the key determinant of investment decisions and are usually seen as 'Keynesian' due to their focus on quantity adjustments and extrapolations of current levels to develop future expectations. Simple accelerator models include only one output growth term within their specifications and imply that the capital stock reaches its desired level in each period of time. In flexible accelerator models (Chenery 1952), developed later, adjustment to the desired capital stock is assumed to take place over many periods and is represented by a distributed lag structure.

From a neoclassical perspective, critics of accelerator theory propose that investment is driven by profit maximization behavior of business; thus cost variables should have an impact on investment. Jorgenson's model is an example of this approach. In Jorgenson's (1963) model, investment is described as a process of optimal capital stock adjustment, through which capital–labor ratios adapt to relative factor price changes, where the relative factor price of capital is measured as the user or rental cost of capital. Following widespread criticism, ad hoc lags are introduced into later specifications of Jorgensonian models to capture expectations.

The estimated lag parameters *à la* Jorgenson are difficult to interpret because the influence of expectations cannot be separated from the other factors captured by the lag structure, such as delivery, adjustment, and installation lags.[7] Attempts to better introduce expectations led to the development of the q theory of investment and Euler equation models, which include dynamic elements and expectation parameters that appear explicitly in the optimization problem. The q theory of investment, established by Brainard and Tobin (1968), uses information in financial markets to relate expectations about future. Euler equations, on the other hand, are derived from firms' maximization problems and equate the marginal cost of investing today to the discounted marginal cost of postponing investment until tomorrow. While q theory is not quite useful for countries with less-developed stock markets, the Euler equation framework has been criticized for its over-reliance on the assumption of rational expectations.[8] Moreover, as the Euler method examines investment decision at the margin, the possibility of not investing at all is not handled in this framework. The literature on financing constraints of the post-1980s has shown that financially constrained firms may either postpone or abandon investment projects, displaying a lumpy investment behavior.[9]

This new focus on financing constraints emerged from the research agenda of New Keynesian economics that placed emphasis on asymmetric information and incomplete contracts as sources of market imperfections.[10] This approach suggests that in a perfect world, investment should not depend on the availability of internal funds; yet when a firm is credit-rationed due to problems of asymmetric information, investment spending is affected by internal funds.[11] Incorporating a cash flow variable in the investment specification has been viewed as one way of capturing the constraint.[12]

Following the literature on financing constraints, the 1990s saw new developments in investment literature emphasizing the issues of irreversibility and uncertainty. Developed by Dixit and Pyndick (1994), among others, this emphasis laid the main theoretical foundation for what is known as option value theory. This approach treats not-yet-committed investment projects as having a 'perpetual call option' value. This value is determined by the value of future investment opportunities; increasing uncertainty increases the value of the option to delay investment. While welcomed by many researchers for its novelty in introducing uncertainty into decision-making, the option value models were seen as flawed by some, as the framework required a stable and predictable uncertainty variable in its structure. Among those criticizing the option value model's treatment of uncertainty, scholars of post-Keynesian origins stand out with their own distinct theory of investment. As the approach of this chapter is grounded in post-Keynesian theory, in what follows I briefly present an overview of a post-Keynesian investment framework.

In most studies of post-Keynesian theory the primary objectives of a firm are depicted as growth and acquisition of power, as opposed to the profit or market value maximization motive of neoclassical theory (Lavoie 1992). Hence investment spending is not derived from the optimization of a typical profit function, as it is in the case of neoclassical models.[13] The consensus opinion among post-Keynesians is that profits are means which allow firms to finance growth. The relationship between profits and growth in the post-Keynesian firm is based on the hypothesis that firms will borrow only to the extent that they have been accumulating inadequate internal funds to finance investment.[14] Similarly, banks will grant loans to firms only to the extent that their customers have been profitable in the past. The fact that a firm is willing to borrow only limited amounts, related to its previously accumulated internal funds, is known as Kalecki's principle of increasing risk. In general, the higher the proportion of outside funds financing investment, the stricter the limits the management of the firm will self-impose, becoming more cautious in its borrowing. Based on the conventions in their own industries and their own perceptions, managers conceive a 'safe' level of leverage to which they would get 'too close' with new borrowing. This concern of management over the safety of the firm has implications of nonlinearity in the response of the management to leverage.[15]

Hence, a finance constraint is a crucial and intrinsic aspect of post-Keynesian investment theory, but the interpretation is different from that of the literature on financing constraints, discussed above. In the post-Keynesian framework, firms are always constrained by availability of finance. A positive relationship does not indicate the presence of supply-side credit constraints caused by asymmetric information problems, but can be interpreted as a demand-side constraint without any implications for the functioning of financial markets and the inherent problems of information asymmetries plaguing them. Even if there are supply-side credit constraints imposed on the firm, they may have more to do with overall credit availability in the economy rather than asymmetric information problems that individual firms face.

The crucial assumption that allows this different interpretation of finance constraints is the combination of fundamental uncertainty and irreversibilities prevailing in the decision-making environment. Regarding investment decisions, future financial commitments to creditors are relatively certain while expected profits are not. The unknown aspect of future cash flows makes managers cautious about their reliance on financial markets and leads to a preference for internal funds. For post-Keynesians, the role of managerial perceptions and the notion of 'degree of confidence' are key to understanding investment behavior: a higher level of uncertainty is associated with a lower level of confidence in formed expectations and thus a lower level of investment.[16]

As revealed in this review, determinants of and impediments to investment are contentious issues in investment literature. Different investment theories have sometimes conflicting propositions on firm-level investment behavior that highlight different structures and causal mechanisms, as exemplified by the interpretation of the reliance on internal funds. The fieldwork presented in this chapter aims to gain a more in-depth understanding of investment decisions in a developing-country setting.

## 16.3   FIELDWORK ON INVESTMENT BEHAVIOR: A QUALITATIVE INVESTIGATION

The fieldwork project has two primary objectives. The first is to shed light on the conflicts among various theories of investment, with a focus on the relative importance of financing constraints and uncertainty. The second objective is to reveal how the role of these determinants changes under changing circumstances. With that in mind, I explore the

*Table 16.1  Composition of interviewed firms*

| Firm characteristics | % in firms interviewed |
|---|---|
| *Size* | |
| Small | 9 |
| Medium | 42 |
| Large | 49 |
| *Industries* | |
| Food, drinks and tobacco | 12 |
| Textiles, clothing, leather | 24 |
| Wood/furniture + paper/printing | 12 |
| Petroleum, plastic and rubber products | 12 |
| Cement, glass, ceramics | 9 |
| Basic metals | 9 |
| Machinery, metal goods + automotive | 21 |
| *Established after 1980* | 12 |
| *Median share of exports in sales* | 30 |
| *More than 10% foreign ownership* | 21 |

sources of uncertainty and the effect of financial crises on firm behavior and the firms' strategies to cope with crises.

The fieldwork was conducted through in-depth, semi-structured interviews with chief financial officers (CFOs) of manufacturing firms in Turkey in 2004. Only manufacturing firms were included in this study, since investment as physical capital accumulation is most prominent in the manufacturing industry (Table 16.1). Companies interviewed were among 108 manufacturing firms of the quantitative data set used in the following sections of this case study.[17] The Industrial Data Base kept by the Union of Chambers and Commodity Exchanges of Turkey (TOBB) was used for contact information and provided up-to-date information on 96 firms out of 108. Thirty-three CFOs accepted to be interviewed.[18]

The fieldwork was conducted over the period of September–October 2004 in eight cities, mostly located in the western part of Turkey. During the first three weeks, in addition to arranging the appointments with CFOs, face-to-face interviews with the representatives from Turkish Industrialists' and Businessmen's Association (TUSIAD) and TOBB were conducted. These preliminary interviews provided me access to previously undertaken survey results by these organizations and helped me revise the interview design. All interviews were conducted in Turkish. I obtained permission to use a voice recorder for eight interviews and took notes during the others. I also acquired company-specific documents, such as annual audit reports and feasibility reports for some of their investment projects.

In the first part of each interview, information on firm demographics, including the age of the firm, the number of employees, products made, market share, profit margin, export orientation, group affiliation, and foreign ownership was captured by closed questions. In the second part, CFOs were asked about the nature of specific investment projects undertaken within the last ten years. For these questions, a semi-structured interview design was adopted. The specific issues that were investigated were: sources of investment funding, determinants of investment, impediments to investment, sources of uncertainty, impact of the 2001 economic crisis, strategies to cope with uncertainty and instability in the post-crisis period.

**Findings on Firm Demographics**

The majority of firms are medium-sized or large with from 89 to 1864 employees.[19] This simply results from the fact that the firms interviewed are publicly traded on the Istanbul Stock Exchange. While the focus on large and medium-sized firms might reduce the firm heterogeneity in sampling, it should be noted that in 2005, medium-sized and large firms produced 93 percent of total output in Turkish manufacturing. As indicated by the 'age' of the firms, the majority of the firms interviewed are likely to have a good reputation and network connections in their market due to their longevity. This can also be observed in the market shares of firms, ranging from 5 percent to 85 percent in particular output markets. High market shares of these firms are an indication of oligopolistic structures in product markets.[20] Considering the substantial market power of these firms, the competitive product market assumption of various neoclassical investment models seems to be highly unrealistic. Another finding that might signal the relative market power of these firms is the issue of group affiliation. Nine out of 33 firms are owned by well-known holding companies, that is, Turkish conglomerates. Five of these nine firms are affiliated with a group that also owns the majority shares of a bank. While group affiliation tends to coincide with large size and longevity, affiliation with a bank-owning group might have implications for the funding of investment. In an institutional setting of relationship banking, banks owned by holding companies might provide access to cheaper and safer funds compared to other alternatives of external funding.[21]

While some firms might have advantages due to group affiliation, interviewed firms reflect the overall patterns of the Turkish manufacturing industry in other ways. For instance, as in the case of the distribution of the Turkish manufacturing output across different sectors, textiles and clothing emerge as the most important industry category, followed by machinery and equipment industries (see Table 16.1). Likewise, export orientation of firms interviewed is similar to the manufacturing industry trends: the median share of exports in total sales is 30 percent for the sample of firms interviewed, whereas the same figure for the whole manufacturing industry was 31.2 percent in 2003.

The last firm characteristic to focus on is the ownership structure of these firms. All firms are publicly traded; the average of shares traded in Istanbul Stock exchange is 20 percent and the median is 30 percent. Firms interviewed typically express their concern about losing their autonomy from equity markets by selling the majority of shares to the public. Gursoy (2005) provides evidence that Turkish firms have highly concentrated ownership structures and families have significant involvement in the governance of their firms. This also shows that unlike in most developed countries, the threat of stock market takeover does not exist and a 'shareholder revolution' has not happened for these manufacturing firms in Turkey. The lack of shareholder pressure has implications for the investment behavior of these firms. Away from shareholder pressure, managers might still have room to maximize long-term reproduction and growth of their firms instead of short-term stock market value, as suggested by post-Keynesian theory.

## Findings on Investment

In the second part, interviewees were asked about the nature of specific investment projects undertaken within the last ten years in a semi-structured interview design. The specific issues investigated were sources of investment funding, determinants of investment, impediments to investment, sources of uncertainty, and impact of the 2001 economic crisis. The following extracts are derived from these interviews, as well as previously undertaken surveys.

### Sources of funds

While various recent investment theories concur about the validity of the hierarchy of finance hypothesis of investment funds, there are theoretical disagreements on the underlying reasons for the hierarchy of finance. Interview results suggest internal funds are very important for financing investment projects, while external funds in the form of bank credit are also used in the event that internal funds are insufficient: 18 percent of firms use only bank credit to finance investment; 27 percent use only internal funds; and 55 percent use a combination of both.[22] No firm reported informal credit as a source of finance.

All firms that use solely internal funds to fund investment are either medium-sized or large (18 percent of sample). They use internal funds only, because their 'internal funds tend to be sufficient to fund large projects'. When explicitly asked about why they prefer internal funds, CFOs' answers range from 'cheaper' to 'safer'. It seems that the managers are risk averse in their behavior, as they want to avoid formal debt commitments in the future when possible. No small firm uses only internal funds to finance investment. Their funds are not enough to fund investment so they must borrow. Overall, I conclude that large firms with large internal resources rely on internal funds more than small firms do, although all firms prefer internal funds as a result of risk-aversive behavior of managers.

This conclusion seems to contradict size-based firm classifications suggested in the literature on financing constraints. In the framework of information asymmetries, the cash flow sensitivity of investment of small firms is expected to be higher than that of large firms, as small firms are assumed to face greater constraints in the credit markets. This interpretation of cash flow sensitivity as a sign of a constraint imposed by the credit market would lead to the unrealistic conclusion that in the Turkish manufacturing industry large firms are the ones facing greater constraints.

Interview results suggest that the preference for internal funds might be reversed in the case of firms with group affiliations, especially if the holding company is also affiliated with a bank. Firms with group affiliations mention that they prefer borrowing from the holding company or the group bank, since the terms of credit are 'favorable'. Although this type of credit is reported under debt accounts on the balance sheets, due to the nature of the borrowing relationship, it can be seen as a substitute for internal funds. Therefore in the case of firms with group affiliation, one can expect a lower cash flow sensitivity of investment, compared to that of those without group affiliations.

### Determinants of investment[23]

Sixty percent of firms that were interviewed reported that future demand conditions are the most important determinant of their investment decisions. In further conversations, firms mentioned that they follow current trends in sales to generate a forecast on future demand conditions.[24] However they do not rely solely on current trajectory of demand to generate the forecasts of expected demand. They also follow the key macroeconomic variables from business news, expert opinions in the media, and industry association publications. The process of forming expectations is embedded in social conventions due to the fundamental uncertainty surrounding future outcomes.

The second-highest ranked determinant of investment is the growth of firm's market share. This finding is reinforced by the observation that most product markets are oligopolistic. Investment and pricing decisions of these oligopolies are linked through the preservation of high profit margins.[25] Firms with market power conceive of investment as a way of sustaining or expanding their power. In line with the arguments of the post-Keynesian perspective on firm behavior, firms aim to grow in size and increase their market share to further increase their market power. Quality improvement, cost reduction, and product differentiation are factors ranked as secondary with almost equal importance.

**Impediments to investment**
Responses to the questions on impediments to investment can be categorized under two subcategories: (1) high cost of finance or insufficient funds; and (2) uncertainties in cost or demand conditions. Ninety-seven percent of firms report that uncertainties in either demand or cost conditions have become impediments to their investment projections. Only 20 percent of firms cite 'cost of finance' as the most important problem, while 'insufficient funds' are reported by 10 percent of firms. While there is no explicit pattern in these responses based on size or export orientation, none of the firms with group affiliation report cost and/or availability of funds as important impediments. Another interesting pattern is that all firms reporting insufficient funds as a problem are those that are in financial jeopardy as indicated by their accounting data.

A similar pattern emerges from the data provided in the Business Tendency Survey (BTS).[26] In 2003, 47 percent of firms report 'demand uncertainty' as the most important impediment to their investment project. 'Cost of financing' is mentioned by 25 percent, inadequate net present value by 13 percent, inadequate internal funds by 13 percent, and inadequate external funds by 1 percent of all firms. Uncertainty is again the prominent impediment to investment.

Another finding from interviews is noteworthy here: although the cost of external funds and the availability of internal funds matter, obtaining external funds is not perceived as the major problem in investment decisions. Firms do not perceive themselves as facing credit constraints in terms of quantity of credit.[27]

A last interesting finding is the relative insignificance of 'cost of labor' in investment projections. Among the responses to the question on the sources of uncertainty, 'uncertainty in wages' is mentioned by only one firm as the third important source of uncertainty, while the other firms do not even rank this factor. In further conversations, firms mention that they do not face problems with their labor force. Unions are present in all production sites with the exception of four firms. However, this should not be seen as a sign of strong unions. Instead, the declining trend of real wages since the crisis of 1994 might help to explain why in 2004 private manufacturing firms do not expect that uncertainty in industrial relations might play a negative role in their investment projections.

Weak unions, high unemployment, and the existence of informal labor markets with jobs that pay significantly less than formal employment all contribute to this result.

### Sources of uncertainty

When asked to rank potential sources of uncertainty, firms responded as follows: uncertainty in demand conditions, uncertainty in overall macro policies, uncertainty in input costs, uncertainty in inflation, uncertainty in interest rates.

The following observations were also gathered in further conversations about other sources of uncertainty. Firstly, in choosing 'uncertainty in macro policies' firms are mainly referring to the exchange rate and the interest rate policies of the government, as these policies are perceived as responsible for unanticipated changes in key macroeconomic variables including the exchange rates, interest rate, and the inflation rate. When firms rank policy uncertainty as the second important source, they might implicitly be referring to uncertainties in these three indicators, instead of ranking them separately. Secondly, uncertainty in input costs seems to be important through two channels. The most prevalent channel is the one caused by fluctuations in the exchange rate. Firms either directly import inputs or buy from domestic suppliers whose prices are sensitive to exchange rate fluctuations. Hence production and investment decisions are heavily influenced by volatility in input prices, as caused by exchange rate fluctuations. The second channel works through uncertainty in inflation. Sometimes contracts with suppliers require these firms to make payments adjusted for inflation. When actual inflation exceeds the level that they anticipated, firms lose money on these contracts. Finally, uncertainty in exchange rates also affects those firms that borrow in foreign currency, by making their debt commitments and the cost of finance uncertain.[28] Currency mismatch in financial structure poses a greater risk for firms with very low export shares. Firms with a mostly domestic market orientation have no means of generating revenues in foreign currency, hence they are expected to be more vulnerable to devaluations because of their highly dollarized liability structure.

### The impact of 2001 crisis on firms

In this section of the interviews, I asked open-ended questions about how the crisis in 2001 affected these firms. In 2001, with the most recent crisis of the Turkish economy, real GDP declined by 9.5 percent, and the Turkish lira was devalued in real terms by 45 percent. These extreme swings in domestic demand and exchange rate should have consequences for the performance of the firms in manufacturing industry.

Eighty-seven percent of all firms reported that they incurred losses for at least one year after the crisis because of the decline in domestic demand. The remaining 13 percent were able to find new international export markets as they already had a high share of exports in their sales.

Approximately half of all firms (45 percent) reported that they were 'caught unprepared' when the crisis of devaluation hit; they incurred losses due to devaluation.[29] The remaining 55 percent said that they had been careful about not having a short position in foreign currency as they were anticipating devaluation at some point. Firms in this group avoided a potential loss from currency mismatch in their balance sheets thanks to either their reluctance to borrow in foreign currency, or hedging in various ways. The majority of these firms also mentioned that they had substantial shares of exports in their sales, which apparently helped in matching debt commitments with revenues in foreign currency after the crisis.

For most firms, incurring unanticipated losses with the crisis made the decision-making process more 'conservative' or 'overly careful' for at least a year into the post-crisis era. As mentioned above, high volatility in key macroeconomic variables causes a decline of confidence in the ability to make reliable forecasts. When the volatility is extreme, as in the case of the 2001 crisis, firms find themselves in a 'crisis of confidence' where the belief that the future will look like the past extrapolated breaks down. Many interviewees mentioned that after the crisis, the time horizon for future planning got shorter, and no company in their industries can plan for a term longer than three years.

### An Investment Framework from Fieldwork

Interview results show that managers of these firms act as risk-averse agents in their investment decisions. This risk aversion follows from the fact that both investment and associated financial commitments in future are irreversible. There is no evidence in these interviews that the hurdle rate they follow in investment projections is stable over the long run. On the contrary, hurdle rates are highly sensitive to changes in expectations, as well as the degree of confidence that management places on them. The neoclassical assumptions of the reversibility of investment and risk-neutral behavior of managers seem to be in contradiction with interview results.

Interview results show that an important determinant of investment is internal funds, interpretation of which has been theoretically contentious. While post-Keynesian investment theory emphasizes 'demand-side' constraint imposed by the risk-averse managers, literature on financing constraints points to the information asymmetries in the credit markets and interprets this positive link as a 'supply-side' constraint imposed by creditors. Interviews tell us that larger firms that are expected to be less constrained in credit markets might rely more on internal funds, while smaller firms might be inclined to use external funds or a combination of both. These findings lead to the conclusion that the use of internal funds should not be seen as a sign of financing constraint caused by information asymmetries. It is possible that preference for internal funds is caused by Keynesian motives as firms themselves avoid debt to reduce risk.

Demand conditions and a desire for greater market share are the most important determinants of investment decisions. As in the accelerator theory of investment, firms consider current trend in sales as very helpful information in forecasting the future prospects of an investment project. As suggested by post-Keynesian perspective of firm behavior, firms aim to increase their market share to gain power and invest accordingly by considering extrapolated demand conditions as an important indicator of future revenue streams. The contrast with neoclassical theory is striking. Interview results show that firms treat future demand as an unknown to forecast carefully, while in Jorgensonian neoclassical theory, output (not demand) is derived via a production function based on the labor and capital employed.

The most important impediment to investment emerges as uncertainty, which is faced by all firms regardless of demographics. The cost of financing is secondary in importance and is experienced as an obstacle to investment only by certain firms.[30] Interview results also emphasize the role of 'confidence' in expectation formation, a variable missing from mainstream theories. Unexpected outcomes induce a decline in management's confidence in the validity of the forecasting process. The moments in which outcomes become the least predictable are the times the macroeconomic instability is at peak; that is, crises. When the volatility is extreme, as in the case of 2001 crisis, firms find themselves in a 'crisis of confidence' where the belief that the future will look like the past extrapolated breaks down. Extreme volatility causes not only a decline in confidence but also shorter time horizons for investment planning.

The interviews also imply that there might be differences in the sensitivity of investment to various determinants across different firm types. The following hypotheses are derived from interview results and will be quantitatively tested in the next section:

1.  Large firms might have a higher sensitivity of investment to internal funds than smaller firms.
2.  Well-established firms might rely less on internal funds than younger firms.
3.  The investment of firms with higher export orientation might be more sensitive to the sales variable than that of firms with domestic market orientation.
4.  The investment of firms with domestic market orientation might be more sensitive to the uncertainty variable compared with those firms with higher export orientation.

## 16.4  A QUANTITATIVE EXAMINATION OF INVESTMENT

Downward and Mearman (2002, p. 392) argue that: 'a degree of tension exists between the philosophical pronouncements of critical realism and the consequences of referring to empirical concepts in the practice of inference'. Deriving from the example of Gardiner Mean's post-Keynesian work on administered prices, Downward and Mearman (2002) make the point that even from a critical realist point of view, regression-based analysis can contribute to the specification of 'demi-regularities' as long as it draws upon more historical and qualitatively based analysis. Since retroduction should involve the 'triangulation' of types of empirical analyses, in what follows I proceed with a regression analysis of firm-level investment, deriving from our qualitative findings.

The findings from the fieldwork tell us that demand conditions, uncertainty, and internal funds are important determinants of investment, while the importance of each variable is expected to change with firm characteristics. An investment function with those variables is similar to accelerator models that emphasize demand conditions and post-Keynesian models that focus on expected demand, uncertainty, and the role of internal funds across different firm categories. The investment function is specified as:

*Investment = f(Uncertainty, Internal Funds, Sales, Past Investment)*

Uncertainty is expected to have a negative relation with investment. A rise in uncertainty does not necessarily imply that expected profits decline accordingly, since the change in the expected profitability forecast might be mean-preserving. However, as uncertainty increases, the confidence of the managers in the validity of their own forecast declines. As the state of confidence declines, *ceteris paribus* lower investment follows.

There are various methods in the empirical literature for constructing an uncertainty variable.[31] One approach is to incorporate some direct measure of uncertainty, generally from business surveys. This requires primary data collection at the firm level, which is expensive and difficult. A second approach is to compute the unconditional variance of a particular economic series (commonly demand, price, or cost-related variables derived from balance sheet items) which managers are presumed to be uncertain about. A third approach is to estimate a statistical model of the process – such as autoregressive conditional heteroskedasticity (ARCH), generalized autoregressive conditional heteroskedasticity (GARCH) or autoregressive integrated moving average (ARIMA) models – determining the conditional variance of the same related series and using this as a proxy for uncertainty. The computation of the conditional variance via such models requires high-frequency data which are not available in the case of Turkey. Since survey results suggest that the uncertainty in demand conditions is the most visible and important source of uncertainty for firms, the uncertainty measure in this chapter is constructed as the coefficient of variation in the firm-level sales-to-capital ratio. The standard deviation and the mean of sales variable are computed every year by using all available lagged values of the sales ratio.

While the expected sign for the coefficient of internal funds is positive, the reasons for this are not unique across firms. Some firms value their autonomy from creditors; others mention a choice dictated by the unfavorable terms of borrowing because of problems with their financial worth. The former motivation supports a demand-side explanation, as suggested by Crotty and Goldstein (1992), while the latter is in line with the New Keynesian concept of financing constraints, which could be imposed by credit markets. Hence, the fact that a firm uses external funds does not necessarily lead to the conclusion that the firm is financially constrained in credit markets.

Another issue in the interpretation of the investment–internal funds nexus is the fact that internal funds are highly correlated with current operating profits and may simply reflect future profitability. In order to control for the link between internal funds and future profitability, Love (2003) suggests a narrower definition of internal funds, derived from the most liquid assets of the firm, as shown under the accounts of 'cash and checks' and 'marketable securities' on the balance sheets. I adopt the same definition in this chapter. Survey findings indicate that there might be differences across firm categories in the borrowing terms these firms face. Hence, regardless of the theoretical explanations, I expect to find different sensitivities of investment to internal funds across these categories.

Sales represent growth opportunities for the firm. As future profits and demand conditions cannot be known under fundamental uncertainty, expectations about future conditions are formed on the basis of current and past sales performance. Investment is expected to be positively related to sales.

Past investment represents dynamic effects such as gestation lags and inertia. Investment projects can take longer than one year to complete; or investment behavior can be path dependent given the structural characteristics of firms or industries. The expected sign of this dynamic effect is positive.

The following empirical specification is designed to see whether the variables in the model have the expected relations with investment:

$$(I/K)_{it} = \beta_0 + \beta_1 U_{it} + \beta_2 (IF/K)_{it} + \beta_3 (S/K)_{it} + \beta_4 (I/K)_{it-1} + \alpha_t \qquad (16.1)$$

*Table 16.2  Descriptive statistics of firm level variables, 1985–2003*

| Variable | | Median | Std dev. | Min. | Max. | Observations |
|---|---|---|---|---|---|---|
| I/K | overall | 0.168 | 0.237 | −0.478 | 2.897 | N = 2005 |
| | between | | 0.09 | −0.019 | 0.746 | n = 165 |
| | within | | 0.221 | −0.493 | 2.760 | T-bar = 12.151 |
| S/K | overall | 1.873 | 5.163 | 0.001 | 138.205 | N = 2005 |
| | between | | 3.818 | 0.349 | 37.001 | n = 165 |
| | within | | 3.34 | −26.132 | 104.198 | T-bar = 12.151 |
| IF/K | overall | 0.077 | 0.371 | 0.000 | 3.862 | N = 2005 |
| | between | | 0.230 | 0.004 | 1.302 | n = 165 |
| | within | | 0.303 | −0.993 | 3.259 | T-bar = 12.151 |
| U | overall | 0.305 | 0.188 | 0.003 | 1.412 | N = 1830 |
| | between | | 0.157 | 0.076 | 0.772 | n = 165 |
| | within | | 0.110 | −0.232 | 1.167 | T-bar = 11.090 |

where $I$ is investment, $K$ is capital stock, $U$ is uncertainty based on sales variability, $IF$ is internal funds based on very liquid assets, $S$ is sales, $\beta$s are parameters, the $i$ subscript denotes the firm, and the $t$ subscript denotes the time period. A time dummy ($\alpha_t$) is included to capture the effect of time-specific factors common to all firms. All regression variables, except uncertainty, are adjusted by the beginning-of-period capital stock.

### Data and Variables

The data set used in this study is a firm-level unbalanced panel data set that is constructed from the balance sheets and income statements of 165 manufacturing firms in Turkey for the period of 1985–2003. The construction of an original data set is essential to the analysis in this chapter, given that proper conceptualization of determinants of investment requires an analysis over time. Data were collected from the publications of two different sources: the Capital Markets Board of Turkey (CMB) for the years 1985–88 and publications of the Istanbul Stock Exchange (ISE) for the period 1989–2003, in both electronic and paper format. The Appendix presents further details on the construction of variables. Descriptive statistics are given in Table 16.2.

### Estimation Technique and Results

An ordinary least square estimation of equation (16.1) may yield biased results, as firm-level dynamic investment models are likely to be prone to heterogeneity and endogeneity problems in estimation. Heterogeneity is a potential problem, because many firm-specific factors such as production technology and managerial abilities can lead to substantial differences in investment behavior across firms. Endogeneity is expected; the error term may be correlated with the explanatory variables since they would all be affected by technology shocks. The presence of the lagged endogenous variable for investment would cause further bias in coefficient estimates. The problem of heterogeneity can be eliminated by using a fixed-effects model in which all the variables are first-differenced. However, this would not solve the problem of endogeneity, since the first-differenced error term would no longer be orthogonal to the first-differenced regressors. Hence an instrumental variable technique is called for.

I utilize the generalized method of moments (GMM) estimation technique, widely used in the empirical literature with dynamic panel data models. After first-differencing explanatory variables to eliminate firm fixed effects, the lagged values of these right-hand-side variables are used as instruments. Two specification tests suggested by Arellano and Bond (1991) are used to test for the validity of the empirical model. The first is a Sargan test for overidentifying restrictions, which is used to test the validity of instruments. It tests the null hypothesis of no correlation between the instruments and the residuals. The second is a test for the presence of serial correlation in differenced residuals. Given the lagged dependent variable in the specification, first-order correlation is expected, while no second- or higher-order correlation should be present in the estimated regressions.

The investment specification above is estimated for all firms over 1985–2003, as well as for different firm categories. The results of the regression analysis for all firms are presented in Table 16.3.

The regression passes the specification tests: the instruments are valid, and the correlation structure is as expected, with no second-order serial correlation. The coefficients of all variables of the base model have the expected signs and are statistically significant. To have a clear picture of the determinants of investment in this base model, in what follows I calculate the elasticities based on sample variation and regression results. The

*Table 16.3   Estimation results, all firms*

| Dependent variable $(I/K)_{it}$ | |
|---|---|
| $(I/K)_{it-1}$ | 0.141** |
| | (0.000) |
| $(S/K)_{it}$ | 0.013*** |
| | (0.008) |
| $(IF/K)_{it}$ | 0.175*** |
| | (0.003) |
| $U_{it}$ | −0.463*** |
| | (0.002) |
| No. of obs | 1651 |
| No. of firms | 165 |
| m1 | −4.18 |
| | (0.000) |
| m2 | 1.21 |
| | (0.225) |
| Sargan test | 162.76 |
| | (0.998) |

*Notes:*
Values in parentheses are p-values that are based on robust standard errors.
Coefficients for the constant term and the time dummies are not reported.
* indicates statistical significance at 10 percent, ** statistical significance at 5 percent, and *** statistical significance at 1 percent.
'm1' and 'm2' are tests for first and second-order serial correlation, respectively. The Sargan test statistic is obtained from GMM two-step estimations.

*Table 16.4   Responsiveness of investment to its determinants*

| Determinants of investment | Associated change over the median level of investment ratio (%) |
|---|---|
| Past investment | +20 |
| Sales | +26 |
| Internal funds | +32 |
| Uncertainty | −30 |

*Note:*  Elasticities are calculated based on the assumption of one standard deviation increase in the respective determinant of investment. All standard deviations represent 'within-firm' variation.

*Source:*  Author's calculations from regression results in Table 16.3 and descriptive statistics in Table 16.2.

coefficient for past investment ratio is 0.141. The descriptive statistics in Table 16.2 tell us that investment ratio has a standard deviation of 0.221. If the lag of the investment ratio increases by 0.221 for a typical firm in the sample, the overall impact on the current investment ratio would be an increase of 0.032. Given that the median level of investment for the overall sample is 0.168, this change would correspond to a 20 percent increase in the median ratio of investment. Hence one standard deviation increase in the past investment ratio is associated with a 20 percent increase in the current investment ratio for the sample of all firms. Elasticities computed based on this method are reported in Table 16.4. Given the sample variation, the relative impact of internal funds on investment (+32 percent) is the highest among all determinants of investment. Firms base their forecast of future demand on the current trends in sales, while their decisions are also influenced by the volatility of sales (−30 percent). On the whole these results are very supportive of the post-Keynesian framework emerging from the qualitative fieldwork.

Firm categories used in regressions are size, export orientation, and age (the detailed of explanation for these categories are included in the Appendix). Due to the low number of small firms in the sample, small and medium-sized firms are grouped together in one category. The age of the firms is expected to distinguish between young firms with lower reputations versus well-established firms with possible group affiliations. This method was chosen, instead of a more direct measure of group affiliation, as the information on group affiliation is not transparently available for many companies.[32]

The results of the regression analysis for various firm categories are presented in Table 16.5. Results allow us to test the four hypotheses developed from interview results and infer further on the investment behavior of different types of firms. All regressions pass the specification tests: the instruments are valid, and the correlation structure is as expected, with no second-order serial correlation.

The effect of internal funds on investment is positive in all regressions and the first hypothesis about the higher sensitivity of investment to internal funds for large firms finds support in the regression results. Descriptive statistics show that large firms have a higher ratio of internal funds. One recent study by the Central Bank of Turkey (Kaplan et al. 2006) shows that the holdings of financial assets that correspond to the definition of internal funds I use tend to increase with the firm size for manufacturing firms in Turkey. Accordingly the interview results suggest that smaller firms need to borrow more due to the insufficiency of internal funds. This finding contradicts the expectation that smaller

*Table 16.5    Estimation results, firm categories*

Dependent variable $(I/K)_{it}$
(Robust standard errors are in parentheses for regression coefficients)

| | Large firms | Small-medium firms | Exporter firms | Domestic market oriented | Established firms | Young firms |
|---|---|---|---|---|---|---|
| $(I/K)_{it-1}$ | 0.091* | 0.054 | 0.101* | 0.067 | 0.146** | 0.018 |
| | (0.043) | (0.059) | (0.052) | (0.047) | (0.058) | (0.044) |
| $(S/K)_{it}$ | 0.010*** | 0.020** | 0.024** | 0.010*** | 0.023** | 0.009*** |
| | (0.002) | (0.007) | (0.010) | (0.001) | (0.009) | (0.002) |
| $(IF/K)_{it}$ | 0.096** | 0.010 | 0.027 | 0.096* | 0.034 | 0.116* |
| | (0.046) | (0.036) | (0.040) | (0.048) | (0.033) | (0.071) |
| $U_{it}$ | −0.403** | −0.262** | −0.179 | −0.537*** | −0.273** | −0.340** |
| | (0.198) | (0.125) | (0.138) | (0.166) | (0.152) | (0.187) |
| No. of obs | 950 | 701 | 701 | 950 | 865 | 786 |
| No. of firms | 88 | 77 | 73 | 92 | 83 | 82 |
| m1 | −2.99 | −3.01 | −2.79 | −3.30 | −3.04 | −2.88 |
| | (0.002) | (0.003) | (0.005) | (0.001) | (0.002) | (0.004) |
| m2 | 1.09 | −0.52 | −0.84 | 1.06 | 0.98 | −0.21 |
| | (0.277) | (0.606) | (0.399) | (0.288) | (0.328) | (0.834) |
| Sargan test | 65.28 | 70.17 | 40.91 | 66.39 | 65.64 | 69.04 |
| | (0.987) | (0.990) | (0.854) | (0.754) | (0.887) | (0.723) |

*Notes:*
Coefficients for the constant term and the time dummies are not reported.
* indicates statistical significance at 10 percent, ** statistical significance at 5 percent and *** statistical
significance at 1 percent.
'm1' and 'm2' are tests for first and second-order serial correlation, respectively. The Sargan test statistic is
obtained from GMM two-step estimations.

firms should rely more on internal funds, as they are a priori identified as financially
constrained. While they might not be constrained in credit markets, large firms prefer
internal funds since they value their autonomy from financial markets. This interpretation reaffirms the assumption of risk-aversive management, as suggested by the post-
Keynesian investment theory.

The statistical insignificance of internal funds for investment of well-established firms
gives support to the second hypothesis stated above. It is quite likely that the size of
investment projects for well-established firms is not constrained by the availability of
internal funds, since these firms can easily borrow money and pursue their growth objective without worrying about their autonomy from financial markets. They can also rely
on their network for funding investment. Likewise a statistically significant and positive coefficient of internal funds for young firms can be explained as the result of their
lacking reputation and network.

The third hypothesis about the higher sales sensitivity of investment for exporters is
supported by the regressions, as the coefficient of sales for exporters is more than twice
the size of that for firms selling in domestic markets. As suggested by interview results,

firms with high export orientation generally sell slightly differentiated products of higher quality in export markets. Substantial change in international demand requires them to invest in new technologies and production processes to be able to produce differentiated products.

Among other firm types, the sensitivity of investment to sales for well-established firms is worth noting. It is likely that well-established firms are dominant firms with higher market shares in more oligopolistic markets. As suggested by the industrial organization literature on dominant firms, capacity building to meet fluctuations in demand can be an important entry-deterring strategy for these firms to sustain their dominant position. As a result of this drive to sustain the dominant position in their respective markets, the investment of well-established firms might be more responsive to sales. On the other hand, they do not have to invest in cycle upturns as the necessary capacity has already been put in place.

The expected negative impact of uncertainty on investment is negative and statistically significant for all firm categories, except for firms with a higher export orientation. As suggested by the last hypothesis, firms selling mainly in domestic markets have the highest negative sensitivity of investment to uncertainty. The interview results show that due to currency mismatches in their balance sheets, firms with very low export shares tend to have a fragile financial structure. These firms have no means of generating revenues in foreign currency; hence they are expected to be more vulnerable to sudden devaluations that accompany financial crises because of their highly dollarized liability structure. When firms face fluctuation in demand in domestic markets, those that can export can still sell their product and invest accordingly, as long as domestic market fluctuations are not correlated with demand in export markets. On the other hand, firms that mostly sell in domestic markets are more prone to experience a negative impact from fluctuations in demand conditions.

## 16.5  CONCLUSION

In this chapter, I presented a case study of the determinants of firm-level investment in the Turkish economy. By mixing qualitative and quantitative methods of examination, this case study aims to provide an in-depth and contextualized analysis of firm-level investment in a developing country that experienced macroeconomic instability.

The absence of a comprehensive and reliable data set for the Turkish firms had created a critical void in the literature on the investment behavior in the Turkish economy. This study fills that gap, as the first empirical examination of firm-level investment that spans the 1990s and 2000s; and what makes this study possible is mixing of the qualitative and quantitative data sources.

Qualitative results pose a challenge to various assumptions of neoclassical investment models and give support to post-Keynesian insights about managerial decision-making and investment. As suggested by the latter, managers of these firms are risk-averse agents who make investment decisions to increase the firm's market share and power. In these decisions, extrapolated demand conditions are the most important indicator of future revenue streams from projects. The need to carefully forecast future demand is the reason why the most important impediment to investment is reported to be uncertainty, defined in various ways. Extremely uncertain conditions, such as financial crisis, cause not only a decline of confidence in ability to form expectations, but also shorter time horizons for investment planning.

Quantitative data and analysis confirm these qualitative findings as well as others on various firm characteristics. Through quantitative analysis, we see that internal funds are an important determinant of investment; yet a priori categories such as size or age are not useful predictors of financing constraints for investment. We also find export orientation to be a significant firm characteristic in determining responsiveness of investment to demand and uncertainty.

The mixing of qualitative and quantitative data has important implications for the policy-oriented literature on investment in developing countries. With the hope of achieving high and stable growth, economies of developing countries have been integrated into the world financial system by a series of reforms. While financial reform policies are expected to stimulate capital accumulation by helping to finance productive areas of investment, the experience of the last two decades of crises increased doubts about the potential benefits. And yet current policy proposals regarding the future of these economies – be they proposals regarding macroeconomic stability or those aimed at ensuring greater competitiveness – still focus on improving the investment environment. It is, then, particularly important that researchers of developing economies integrate qualitative and quantitative methods to acquire a more comprehensive and realistic understanding of specific institutional context, including firm and market characteristics and causal mechanisms underlying investment decisions.

## NOTES

1. The case of the Turkish economy resembles the experiences of developing countries that were adversely affected by economic and financial crises after opening their capital accounts to international flows.
2. Among these macro-level studies Rittenberg (1991), Uygur (1993), Guncavdi et al. (1999), and Cimenoglu and Yenturk (2005) particularly focus on the link between conditions of finance and investment.
3. Worldscope is the global company accounts database from Thomson Reuters and thus a key research resource for firm-level information. It is accessed through a variety of Thomson Financial software products, including Thomson One product, Datastream.
4. Full inflation accounting practices became mandatory for the publicly listed companies in Turkey only in 2004. Before that, a revaluation method based on current inflation was used to adjust for inflation. Certain balance sheet categories that represent stock items are more prone to the price-level changes than others and revaluating these items by the same ratio might cause distortions in the analysis. Furthermore revaluation rates used for this purpose might not closely follow the relevant inflation rate, derived from specific price indices.
5. The idea that one's paradigmatic view of the world might be related to the way one went about researching the world was prompted by Kuhn (1962).
6. Chirinko (1993) provides an excellent review of different investment modeling strategies, their empirical strengths, and policy implications. For an empirical comparison of different models, see also Kopcke and Brauman (2001).
7. Even in the versions with explicit adjustment costs, the problem remains of how to identify future marginal revenue products.
8. Among those, Davidson (1991), Crotty (1993), and Minsky (1975) suggest that businesses operate in a 'fundamentally uncertain' environment that is incompatible with rational expectations theory.
9. See Chirinko (1993) for a critique of the Euler equation method.
10. Hubbard (1998) presents a New Keynesian theory of asymmetric information and a comprehensive review of market imperfections and investment models.
11. In the seminal paper by Fazzari et al. (1988), the effects of cash flow on investment spending are assessed

by employing a Tobin's q model for fundamentals. Firms are sorted by retention ratios under the hypothesis that firms retaining a higher percentage of their equity income must face higher costs of external funds.

12. Among many, Laeven (2003) is an example of the studies utilizing the Euler technique to assess financing constraints by inserting cash flow variables into the investment equation. The use of cash flow sensitivities as a sign of financing constraints has been controversial. The findings of Kaplan and Zingales (2000) suggest that under certain assumptions investment–cash flow sensitivities may increase as financing constraints are relaxed and that investment–cash flow sensitivities are not necessarily monotonic in the degree of financing constraints. Almeida (1999) shows that firms with more liquid assets borrow more and therefore are more sensitive to profitability shocks because of the leverage effect. Less financially constrained firms then exhibit bigger investment–cash flow sensitivities than similar firms, which have less liquid assets, and are more financially constrained. Povel and Raith (2002) find a U-shaped relationship between cash flow and investment, further adding to the controversy about the interpretation of cash flow sensitivities. Critics of the use of the cash flow variable as a proxy for internal funds note that since cash flow might be closely related to operating profits and therefore to the marginal product of capital, it may not be picking up the desired liquidity effect but may be proxying either an accelerator effect or information about future investment opportunities not captured by variables of fundamentals. To circumvent this problem, a second set of studies has preferred including variables of net worth into the investment function to capture financing constraints. In the presence of information asymmetries, a firm's net worth is assumed to signal that the firm is a good borrower; hence the premium on external finance is assumed to be an inverse function of the firm's net worth, which is proxied by financial ratios such as leverage or interest coverage.

13. For instance, Robinson (1962, p. 38) notes: 'the central mechanism of accumulation is the urge of firms to survive and grow'. A similar view can be found in Kaldor (1978: xvi) for whom 'the individual enterprise – for reasons first perceived by Marx – must go on expanding so as to keep its share in the market'.

14. As pointed out by Kaldor (1978, p. xvi): 'Finance raised externally – whether in the form of loans or of equity capital – is complementary to, not a substitute for retained earnings.'

15. There might be a low range of leverage over which the management feels 'safe' up to a certain threshold beyond which borrowing would be 'threatening' to the management. See Crotty and Goldstein (1992) for an example. A similar perspective can be found in Keynes's *General Theory*:
'Two types of risk which affect the volume of investment have not commonly been distinguished. The first is the entrepreneur's or borrower's risk and arises out of doubts in his own mind as to the probability/minds of his actually earning the prospective yield for which he hopes. If a man is venturing his own money, this is the only risk, which is relevant. But where a system of borrowing and lending exists, by which I mean the granting of loans with a margin of real or personal security, a second type of risk is relevant and which we may call the lender's risk' (Keynes 1936, p. 44).

16. In his early work Keynes formulated this issue as the 'weight of an argument', while the concept gets translated later on in the *General Theory* by the 'state of confidence':
'The state of long term expectations, upon which our decisions are based, does not solely depend, therefore, on the most probable forecast we can make. It also depends on the confidence with which we make this forecast – on how highly we rate the likelihood of our best forecast turning out quite wrong' (Keynes 1936, p. 148).

17. Quantitative analysis in this chapter relies on an unbalanced firm-level data set with observations over the period of 1985–2003. Due to its unbalanced structure, the number of firms changes across years.

18. All of these firms are publicly traded on the Istanbul Stock Exchange and are therefore bound by public disclosure rules. Some CFOs declined interview requests regarding their financing and investment activities, with the claim that any further information disclosure might be harmful for the performance of the shares of their company in the market. Although this might have some correlation with the firm-specific conditions, such as an anticipation of a merger or an initial public offering (IPO) among many, no particular pattern was observed.

19. The size distribution categories adopted in this study follow the definitions in Central Bank of Turkey Sectoral Balance Sheets for 2003 and are based on the net sales of the firms.

20. See for instance Gunes et al. (1996). Metin-Ozcan et al. (2002) argue that, contrary to expectations, the processes of export orientation and overall trade liberalization since 1980 have not altered the highly concentrated structure in the Turkish industrial markets.

21. Some of these holding companies are owned by powerful and old families or coalitions of families; they produce many household brands and typically own a commercial bank. Being a member of these groups seems to be the most beneficial type of group affiliation. Other holding companies are more recently established and not as diversified across different industries. They have a heavier commerce orientation in their activities rather than industry and have gathered only a few firms under their roof for mainly legal reasons.

22. It should also be noted that respondents who chose the combination option add that they benefit from investment subsidies provided by the government, which require at least 20 percent contribution of internal funds in investment projections.
23. During the interviews, I provided the interviewees with a list of possible determinants of investment derived from different theories and asked them to rank these factors. In the evaluation of answers, I assigned points to these determinants based on the rankings by the firms. On a scale from 5 to 1, the factor that is reported as the first is given 5 points; the second is given 4 points, and so on, while the fifth factor's score is 1.
24. A similar result regarding the importance of current demand conditions was found in the survey by ICI in 1991. In this survey, 48 percent of all manufacturing firms mention the role of current demand conditions as highly important.
25. Eichner (1976) provides a theory of 'megacorp', in which oligopolistic pricing decisions are linked with investment decisions.
26. The Business Tendency Survey has been regularly conducted by the Central Bank of Turkey since December 1987. Monthly results are disseminated through the Central Bank website. Question #27 asks respondents to rank factors that might impede the investment projects that they are planning to undertake within the next 12 months.
27. Many firms mention that they have access to subsidized investment credit not only from the government of Turkey, but also from foreign sources. When investment projects involve the purchase of machinery and equipment, these capital goods are typically imported from European countries. In this case, the company generally has access to European EximBank credits, subsidized by the government of the exporter country.
28. Further conversations revealed that these firms refer to unanticipated devaluations in the value of domestic currency as exchange rate uncertainty. Given that the cyclical growth pattern of the Turkish economy is knotted with financial crises during which the domestic currency had huge losses in value over very short periods of time, this fear can easily be understood.
29. Two firms also mentioned that they incurred losses on forward options they were holding for hedging purposes.
30. The availability of credit is not ranked as a serious problem.
31. For a comprehensive review of these methods, see Carruth et al. (2000).
32. Many holding companies that are not listed in the Istanbul Stock Exchange do not disclose their subsidiaries and affiliations.

# REFERENCES

Almeida, H. (1999), 'Financial constraints, asset liquidity and investment', Working Paper, April, Chicago, IL: University of Chicago.
Arellano, M. and S. Bond (1991), 'Some tests of specification for panel data: Monte Carlo evidence and an application to employment equations', *Review of Economic Studies*, **58** (2), 277–97.
Brainard, W. and J. Tobin (1968), 'Pitfalls in financial model-building', Cowles Foundation Discussion Papers, 244, Princeton, NJ: Yale University.
Carruth, A., A. Dickerson, and A. Henley (2000), 'What do we know about investment under uncertainty?', *Journal of Economic Surveys*, **14** (1), 119–53.
Chenery, H. (1952), 'Overcapacity and the acceleration principle', *Econometrica*, **20** (1), 1–28.
Chirinko, R. (1993), 'Business fixed investment spending: modeling strategies, empirical results and policy implications', *Journal of Economic Literature*, **31** (4), 1875–91.
Cimenoglu, A. and N. Yenturk (2005), 'Effects of international capital inflows on the Turkish economy', *Emerging Markets Finance and Trade*, **41** (1), 90–109.
Crotty, J. (1993), 'Neoclassical and Keynesian approaches to the theory of investment', in P. Davidson (ed.), *Can The Free Market Pick Winners? What Determines Investment*, Armonk, NY, USA and London, UK: Sharpe.
Crotty, J. and J. Goldstein (1992), 'The investment decision of the post Keynesian firm: a suggested microfoundation for Minsky's instability thesis', Levy Institute Working Paper, 79.
Davidson, P. (1991), *Controversies in Post Keynesian Economics*, Aldershot, UK and Brookfield, VT, USA: Edward Elgar.
Dixit, A. and R. Pindyck (1994), *Investment under Uncertainty*, Princeton, NJ: Princeton University Press.
Downward, P.M. and A. Mearman (2002), 'Critical realism and econometrics: constructive dialogue with Post Keynesian economics', *Metroeconomica*, **53** (4), 391–415.

Downward, P.M. and A. Mearman (2007), 'Retroduction as mixed-methods triangulation in economic research: reorienting economics into social science', *Cambridge Journal of Economics*, **31** (1), 77–99.

Eichner, A. (1976), *The Megacorp and Oligopoly: Micro Foundations of Macro Dynamics*, White Plains, NY: M.E. Sharpe.

Fazzari, S., G. Hubbard, and B. Peterson (1988), 'Financing constraints and corporate investment', *Brookings Papers on Economic Activity*, **1988** (1), 41–195.

Guncavdi, O., M. Bleaney, and A. McKay (1999), 'The response of private investment to structural adjustment: a case study of Turkey', *Journal of International Development*, **11** (2), 221–39.

Gunes, M., A. Kose, and E. Yeldan (1996), 'Concentration trends in Turkish manufacturing industry in accordance with IO table's sectoral classification' (in Turkish), *Ekonomik Yaklasim*, **8** (26), 33–47.

Gursoy, G. (2005), 'Changing corporate ownership in the Turkish market' *Journal of Transnational Management*, **10** (2), 33–48.

Hubbard, G. (1998), 'Capital market imperfections and investment', *Journal of Economic Literature*, **36** (1), 193–225.

Jorgenson, D. (1963), 'Capital theory and investment behavior', *American Economic Review*, **53** (2), 247–59.

Kaldor, N. (1978), *Further Essays on Economic Theory*, New York: Holmes & Meier.

Kaplan, C., E. Ozmen, and C. Yalcin (2006), 'The determinants and implications of financial asset holdings of non-financial firms in Turkey: an empirical investigation', Working Papers 0606, Ankara, Turkey: Research and Monetary Policy Department, Central Bank of the Republic of Turkey.

Kaplan, S. and L. Zingales (2000), 'Investment–cash flow sensitivities are not valid measures of financing constraints', *Quarterly Journal of Economics*, **115** (2), 707–12.

Keynes, J.M. (1936), *The General Theory of Employment, Interest and Money*, London: Macmillan.

Kopcke, R. and R. Brauman (2001), 'The performance of traditional macroeconomic models of businesses investment spending', *New England Economic Review*, **2001** (2), 3–39.

Kuhn, T.S. (1962), *The Structure of Scientific Revolutions*, Chicago, IL: University of Chicago Press.

Laeven, L. (2003), 'Does financial liberalization reduce financing constraints?', *Financial Management*, **32** (1), 5–31.

Lavoie, M. (1992), *Foundations of Post-Keynesian Economics*, Aldershot, UK and Brookfield, VT, USA: Edward Elgar.

Love, I. (2003), 'Financial development and financing constraints: international evidence from the structural investment model', *Review of Financial Studies*, **16** (3), 765–91.

Metin-Ozcan, K., E. Voyvoda, and E. Yeldan (2002), 'The impact of the liberalization program on the price-cost margin and the investment of Turkey's manufacturing sector after 1980', *Emerging Markets Finance and Trade*, **38** (5), 72–103.

Minsky, H. (1975), *John Maynard Keynes*, New York: Columbia University Press.

Povel, P. and M. Raith (2002), 'Optimal investment under financial constraints: the roles of internal funds and asymmetric information', mimeo, Universities of Minnesota and Rochester.

Rittenberg, L. (1991), 'Investment spending and interest rate policy: the case of financial liberalization in Turkey', *Journal of Development Studies*, **27** (2), 151–67.

Robinson, Joan (1962), *Essays in the Theory of Economic Growth*, London: Macmillan.

Uygur, E. (1993), *Financial Liberalization and Economic Performance in Turkey*, Ankara: Central Bank of Turkey Publications.

## APPENDIX 16A.1    DEFINITION OF FIRM-LEVEL VARIABLES AND CATEGORIES

**Variables**

- *Capital Stock* (*K*). The item 'Tangible Fixed Assets' on the balance sheet, which includes accumulated depreciation. Specifically, it is the sum of machinery, plant, equipment, buildings, land, property, other tangible assets, and construction-in-progress.
- *Investment* (*I*). The change in capital stock by the end of the accounting year, net of depreciation. That is, $I_t = K_t - K_{t-1} - Depreciation_t$. (Depreciation in each year is calculated as the difference between the calculated depreciation of the current year and that of the previous year.)
- *Sales* (*S*). The item 'Net Sales', net of 'Sales Deductions'.
- *Internal Funds* (*IF*). The sum of 'Cash' and 'Marketable Securities' under 'Current Assets'.
- *Uncertainty* (*U*). The coefficient of variation in sales ratio, that is, the mean adjusted standard deviation.

**Size**

This is a time-invariant identifier for firms, based on net sales. It follows the definitions given in the Sectoral Balance Sheets published by Central Bank of Turkey. According to these definitions in 1999, firms with sales of less than 17 824 600 million TL are classified as small and medium-sized, while those with sales above this level are considered large. In the literature, the most common classification is a self-referential method based on the mean or the median of sales. However my sample is not randomly selected. It is possible that, over time, smaller firms enter the sample by issuing bonds in the capital markets or selling shares in the stock exchange. This pulls the median size levels down, causing a categorization of more firms as 'large', without any substantial change in the size of manufacturing firms in the overall economy. Hence I prefer this method to reflect the size of the firms in the overall economy.

**Export Orientation**

This is a time-invariant identifier for firms, based on the ratio of firms' foreign sales to their total sales. If the average of the foreign sales ratio over all the years that data are available is higher than 25 percent, the firm is classified as an exporter. If the average of the ratio is below 25 percent, the firm is considered to be domestic market oriented.

**Age**

The data on age are derived from company publications and firms' websites. The median and the mean of the age of firms in the sample are both 31. Firms that are younger than 31 are classified as young, while those which are older are considered as established firms.

# 17 Price stability
*Gyun Cheol Gu*

## 17.1 INTRODUCTION

The general methodological framework to be used in this chapter is the method of grounded theory, which is covered in Chapter 2 in this *Handbook*. There is a consensus among post-Keynesians that their economics has philosophical and methodological foundations that are different from the positivist, empirical realist, and deductivist foundations underpinning neoclassical economics. Based on critical realism they advocate various methodological guidelines, such as retroduction, Babylonian method, and empirically grounded method, to be utilized for creating and developing post-Keynesian theory. The method of grounded theory is consistent with critical realism and is a better and more developed set of guidelines for theory creation than the others (Lee 2002, 2005). That method paves the way to economic theories that are historical in structure, content and explanation because, '[t]he method of grounded theory can be described as a process in which researchers, or more specifically economists, create their theory "directly" developed from data; and in which data collection, theoretical analysis and theory building proceed simultaneously' (Lee 2002, p. 793). In other words, grounded theorizing is a method of undertaking economic research that aims at theoretical development and generalization rather than testing established theories; and it encompasses a set of procedures for analyzing data in a systematic and comparative manner (Finch 2002). A number of specific categories or analytical concepts and their associated properties stem from the relevant theoretical, empirical, and historical literature along with a collection of comparable data from economic events. Since the concepts and relationships are empirically grounded in detail, the researcher develops a theory explaining why and how the sequence of economic events represented in empirical data transpire. Hence, the method allows economists to develop a theory that explains historically contingent economic events analytically; each theory is empirically grounded in its data.

Let us now consider aspects of the grounded theory method in more detail based on Finch (2002), Goulding (2002), and Lee (2002, 2005). First, the collection of data is not only collecting the data themselves but also constantly comparing, analyzing, and interpreting the data collected while simultaneously organizing them into conceptual or generalized categories. The categories that emerge come from the process of collecting them. Consequently each category is tied to or empirically grounded in its data. Since the data lie in time and history, each category is related to a particular historical setting. The more properties a category has, the more realistic it is. Once the real, observable categories are delineated and grounded, the economist classifies some as economic structures and others as components of economic structures. Continuing the practice, other categories that center on human motivation and action and a set of the outcomes will be woven together into a causal mechanism. The resulting structures and causal mechanisms will be real and observable. Then, the economist will select, from the causal mechanisms identified, one as the central causal mechanism around which the structures and secondary causal mechanisms with their outcomes are arranged. Criteria for selecting the central causal mechanism are that it appears frequently in the data as a cause of the outcomes, that it has clear implications for a more general theory, and that it allows for complexity. The grounded economic theory that eventually emerges is a complex analytical explanation or interpretation of the actual economic events represented in the data. Economic theory centered on a single central causal mechanism is classified as a substantive economic theory since it is an explanation of a single basic economic process that occurs widely in the economy. From a number of substantive theories, a formal economic theory can be developed into a general or holistic theory where the relationship or pattern among the substantive theories is its analytical explanation. As in the process of grounding the substantive economic theory, the formal theory also has to be grounded.

Economic models based on mathematical language can be useful tools and instruments that help develop and clarify causal mechanisms and grounded theory. However, their use should be restricted, since '[t]he method of grounded theory prescribes that the type of mathematics used and economic models constructed are derived from (as opposed to being imposed upon via analogy or metaphor) the empirically grounded theories being developed' (Lee 2005, p. 106). In other words, the economic model is supposed to reflect the narrative of the grounded theory, while the mathematical form of the model is determined and constrained by the empirically grounded structures and causal mechanisms. To translate a grounded theory into an economic model, its structures and causal mechanisms have to be converted into mathematical language where each mathematical entity and concept is in principle unambiguously empirically grounded. In this manner, mathematical model-based analysis remains subjugated to the study of economic activity. Thus, while mathematics helps to illuminate aspects of the grounded theory and make clear what might be obscure, it does not add anything new to the theory, that is, it does not by itself produce new scientific knowledge (Lee 2005). In this vein, a mathematical model has to be a narrative about empirical evidence. A narrative mathematical model which reflects the empirical evidence on the relationship between labor productivity and unemployment is developed and delineated in this chapter as a practical example.

Section 17.2 of this chapter discusses the empirical evidence for countercyclical prices in the post-1945 period around the world and for acyclical prices in the post-1983 period in the United States. Section 17.3 establishes the causal mechanisms for price stability based on an empirically grounded model of costing and pricing procedures within a single pricing period and cost-base stabilization between two consecutive pricing periods. It shows that it is a structural change in the socially constructed labor productivity that brings about the price stability during the post-1984 period; in more detail, the cyclicality of the cost base has been weakened and thus prices have become less cyclical. Section 17.4 concludes this chapter.

## 17.2 EVIDENCE ON PRICE STABILITY IN THE US ECONOMY

For most of the twentieth century, economists believed that prices were clearly procyclical. Most of the development of business cycle theories was predicated on the assumption that the overall price level is procyclical, meaning that output and prices move in the same direction. In particular, new classical economists as well as 'bastard Keynesians' often interpret it as strong evidence for the importance of demand shocks in the aggregate supply and demand framework. Based on these studies, Lucas (1977) considers that prices are procyclical variables, leading to the monetary misperceptions model.

Some economists, however, started to suggest that prices turned out to be countercyclical after the Korean War, whereas they used to be procyclical during the period prior to World War I (Friedman and Schwartz 1982; Kydland and Prescott 1990; Backus and Kehoe 1992; Cooley and Ohanian 1991). The countercyclicality of prices has become a stylized fact since there is a great deal of aggregate and disaggregate empirical evidence that prices are decreasing as outputs are increasing. Consider the aggregate evidence: Barro and Tenreyro (2006) show that prices in four-digit manufacturing industries are negatively correlated with gross domestic product (GDP) per capita. Konstantakopoulou et al. (2009) observe that there is a negative correlation between prices and real output at both leads and lags for the majority of Organisation for Economic Co-operation and Development (OECD) countries using quarterly data from 1960 to 2004. The countercyclical behavior of price level is also shown in Webb (2003), Agresti and Mojon (2001), Stock and Watson (1999), Chadha and Prasad (1994), and Fiorito and Kollintzas (1994). Consider the microeconomic case studies. Chevalier et al. (2003) demonstrate that prices tend to fall in response to a positive demand shock for consumption goods such as beer, crackers, and tuna in a supermarket chain in Chicago. MacDonald (2000) finds that prices of groceries exhibit countercyclical behavior. Warner and Barsky (1995) show that appliances fall in price during Christmas. Indeed, the famous price wars in automobiles (Bresnahan 1987) and railroads (Porter 1983) occurred when demand was high.

The countercyclical pricing is inconsistent with the standard neoclassical model of production and cost, since a price should be procyclical as the marginal cost has to be increasing in principle. Thus, some economists have been trying to reconcile the anomaly and their theoretical frameworks based on supply shock. Kydland and Prescott (1990) exploit the countercyclicality of prices to argue that supply shocks (not demand shocks) must account for business cycle fluctuations as the countercyclical prices could not be reconciled with a model driven by demand shocks, leading to the real business cycle (RBC) models. Other studies have tried to address this issue predicated on the neoclassical monopoly model, particularly, possible changes in demand elasticity. For example, Plehn-Dujowich (2008) shows that the countercyclical movement stems from changes in the extent of competition if the income effect is decreasing in the price, as occurs when preferences are homothetic or demand is isoelastic. The controversy over price cyclicality is still among the most unsettled issues in economics.

Behavioral economists have also attempted to explain the countercyclical prices based on cost-base pricing procedure. While neoclassical economists continue to explain price movement over the cycle predicated on cyclical profit mark-up or elasticity of demand with the marginal cost constant or increasing, post-Keynesian economists argue that constant average direct costs and fixed indirect costs cause average total cost to fall as the output increases, while the *ex ante* profit mark-up does not vary significantly within the business cycle. In other words, they consider the countercyclical cost movement and the quasi-constant mark-up as the implicit reason for countercyclical price movement, with the labor hoarding effect lying at the center of their exposition of countercyclical productivity and prices. For instance, Blair (1974) proposes a short-run target return model to see whether prices move procyclically or countercyclically over the business cycle. He argues that prices tend to be countercyclical since unit labor and fixed costs are decreasing in the operating rate. That is, unit labor cost is decreasing in the output level due to the existence of hoarded labor, while fixed costs are spread out over the increased quantity produced thereby reducing average fixed costs. Prices tend to fall in expansion and rise in recession.

However, prices can be acyclical or stable over the business cycle even if there are still labor hoarding practices and/or fixed costs, as in the US economy during the post-1984 period. The price–output relationship began to change again in the US economy from the early 1980s. Based on monthly industrial production, the consumer price index, quarterly GDP and its deflator, Den Haan and Sumner (2004) observe that the correlation between the price index and the output gap has become much less negative – nearly close to zero – during the last two decades for the United States, while no substantial change is observed for the other G7 economies. Mumtaz et al. (2011) also find that annual consumer price index has become significantly less countercyclical along GDP from the pre-1984 to the post-1984 sample. Gu (2015) shows that correlation coefficients between output and price at the four-digit industry level reflect the robust weakening of the price countercyclicality in the post-1984 era.

## 17.3   CAUSAL MECHANISMS FOR PRICE STABILITY

The tradition of post-Keynesian pricing research has made an important contribution to the behavioral theory of the firm in terms of price stability by investigating and establishing costing and pricing procedures based on real-world accounting practices of the business enterprise as a going concern. Lee (1998) provides an empirically grounded foundation for post-Keynesian price theory based on more than 100 empirical studies conducted until early 1990s on costing and pricing, which allowed him to establish the appropriate analytical exposition of the costing and pricing procedures, price policies of the business enterprise, and price-setting market institutions. The essential scheme is that depending upon the costing procedures used by the enterprise, the pricing procedures will ensure that the costing margin or mark-up will cover overhead costs and produce profits with all of the costs estimated at a budgeted or standard level of output. Lavoie (2001) proposes cost-plus pricing and mark-up processes as essential parts of post-Keynesian price theory. While cost-plus pricing comes in several variants, firms fix prices based on some measure of full costs, rather than as a reaction to demand fluctuations.

Except for the case of a dramatic change in the prices of inputs such as energy costs, prices are stable at least during a pricing period – that is, remain unchanged – since they are determined alongside the firm's routine budgeting process and then are administered to the market during that period. In other words, price stability is inherent to the price-setting mechanism, which I name 'intrinsic price stability'. At the same time, it is obvious that prices may change for the next pricing period. The number of the consecutive pricing periods during which prices remain unchanged varies across products, industries, and countries. However, that difference cannot be explained by intrinsic price stability since the routine accounting and budgeting process is common to all the firms no matter what and where they produce. Rather, the persistence of unchanged prices beyond a pricing period depends on the frequency and magnitude of changes in profit mark-up and cost base. This form of price stability is named 'extrinsic price stability', which is a stability induced by a low degree of volatility of the cost base and/or a high rate of the profit mark-up's absorption of shocks and changes to the cost base as well as the change in the profit mark-up itself.[1] In this way, extrinsic price stability reinforces and extends intrinsic price stability.

## Intrinsic Price Stability

Managerial accounting textbooks mainly comprise compilations of common company practices such as costing and pricing. In contrast to the traditional theory of optimal pricing, managerial accounting offers a guide to accounting principles used in day-to-day costing and pricing. The most common real-world pricing practices include cost-based pricing, cost-plus pricing, and full-cost pricing. Although they come in a wide range of variation, they all base price on a calculation of an average total cost, which includes variable (direct), overhead (indirect), and sunk costs. In order to establish an empirically grounded pricing procedure, the first thing to do is to review new empirical studies which investigate the advances in accounting and managerial techniques. Since the late 1980s, business researchers have no longer tried to test neoclassical pricing theory, based on marginal cost and marginal revenue, because most surveys and empirical studies have continued to disprove this unrealistic assertion. Instead, they have investigated and classi-fied several pricing strategies in use in the field and also have identified pricing objectives and pricing strategy determinants. The growing concern with the subject has provided much empirical literature making use of survey, interview, and econometric analysis.[2] The grounded method allows the empirical findings to be collected cohesively and categorized systematically into an updated, comprehensive taxonomy for pricing procedures, which is supposed to provide an analytical scheme.

Pricing procedures refer to the specific formulas used in order to set a price. These for-mulas can range from highly sophisticated ones to rather simple ones. Lee (1998) suggests an empirically grounded pricing foundation for post-Keynesian price theory based on more than 100 empirical studies conducted until the early 1990s on costing and pricing to establish the appropriate analytical exposition of the costing and pricing procedures and price policies of the business enterprise and to delineate the properties of the prices. The essential scheme is that, 'depending upon the costing procedures used by the enterprise, the pricing procedures used by it will ensure that the costing margin or markup will cover overhead costs and produce a profit' (Lee 1998, p. 204), with all of the costs estimated at a normal or standard level of output. Lee (1998, p. 205) suggests three pricing methods as integrating categories: that is, labor and material-based mark-up pricing, normal cost pricing, and target rate of return pricing. Likewise, Lavoie (2001) advances cost-plus pricing and mark-up process as essential parts of post-Keynesian price theory.

However, both Lee (1998) and Lavoie (2001) have some limitations in that they fail to provide an organized classification of pricing procedures since their taxonomies do not differentiate between the two components of a pricing procedure: costing process and mark-up process. In other words, they presuppose that target rate of return pricing and normal-cost pricing can be posited in the same dimension. Yet, in fact, the former is concerned with mark-up process and the latter is predicated on costing process. In addition, they miss out on recent developments in costing and mark-up practices in the field since the 1980s. In order to revise their classifications based on new empirical studies which investigate the advances in accounting and managerial techniques, I propose two different taxonomies which can embrace not only the previous pricing taxonomy but also the newly accumulated empirical studies from the perspective of post-Keynesian microeconomics.

One group of the pricing procedures which they identify is predicated on different costing procedures, taking the rate of profit mark-up simply as given whatever the mark-up procedure may be, whereas the other group is defined according to the profit mark-up procedure, taking their relevant cost base as given whatever the costing procedure may be. Thus, it is necessary to differentiate between the two perspectives on pricing procedures and identify them as two different taxonomies: the costing-oriented pricing taxonomy and the mark-up-oriented pricing taxonomy, respectively. It should be noted that this does not mean that the previous pricing classifications are simply falsified; rather, they reflect the reality of their own time period in terms of pricing procedures which are supposed to be historically contingent. The two taxonomies suggested here are developed and extended from the previous perspectives, with the intention of taking into consideration recent developments in accounting system and pricing practices in the business world since the early 1990s. In Figure 17.1 the pricing procedures in bold incorporate the newly accumulated empirical data.

The costing-oriented pricing taxonomy is a pricing classification predicated primarily on various costing procedures, including both traditional and newly invented costing techniques. The pricing procedures in the costing-oriented taxonomy are budgeted direct cost pricing, total cost pricing, and activity-based costing (ABC) cost pricing. Their cost base always depends on budgeted output instead of actual or realized output. Direct cost pricing consists of marking up average direct cost based on the budgeted volume of output to set the price, with the mark-up being sufficient to cover overhead costs and produce profits. Total cost pricing has two forms: one is to mark up average direct costs (ADC) to cover overhead costs, which gives budgeted average total cost (ATC), and then apply a profit mark-up to ATC to set a price; the other applies the profit mark-up directly to ATC to set the price. As the most advanced pricing procedure, ABC cost pricing can be formulated in the following manner:

$$P = ADC \left[ 1 + \sum_{i=1}^{n} x_i \right] [1 + r] \qquad (17.1)$$

where $x_i$ is the mark-up to cover an allocated part of $i$-th overhead cost according to the product's consumption of the activity that causes the overhead cost, and $r$ is the mark-up for profits. It should be noted that the difference between total cost pricing and ABC cost pricing consists in the specific method by which to determine the mark-up for the overhead costs. With more than one product which a business enterprise produces, total cost pricing allocates the total amount of the overhead costs to each product based on each product's budgeted volume which may be irrelevant to the causes of the overhead costs, whereas ABC cost pricing utilizes each product's relative consumption of each overhead resource to allocate the total amount of the overhead costs among its products (Gu and Lee 2012).

**(1) Costing-oriented Taxonomy**

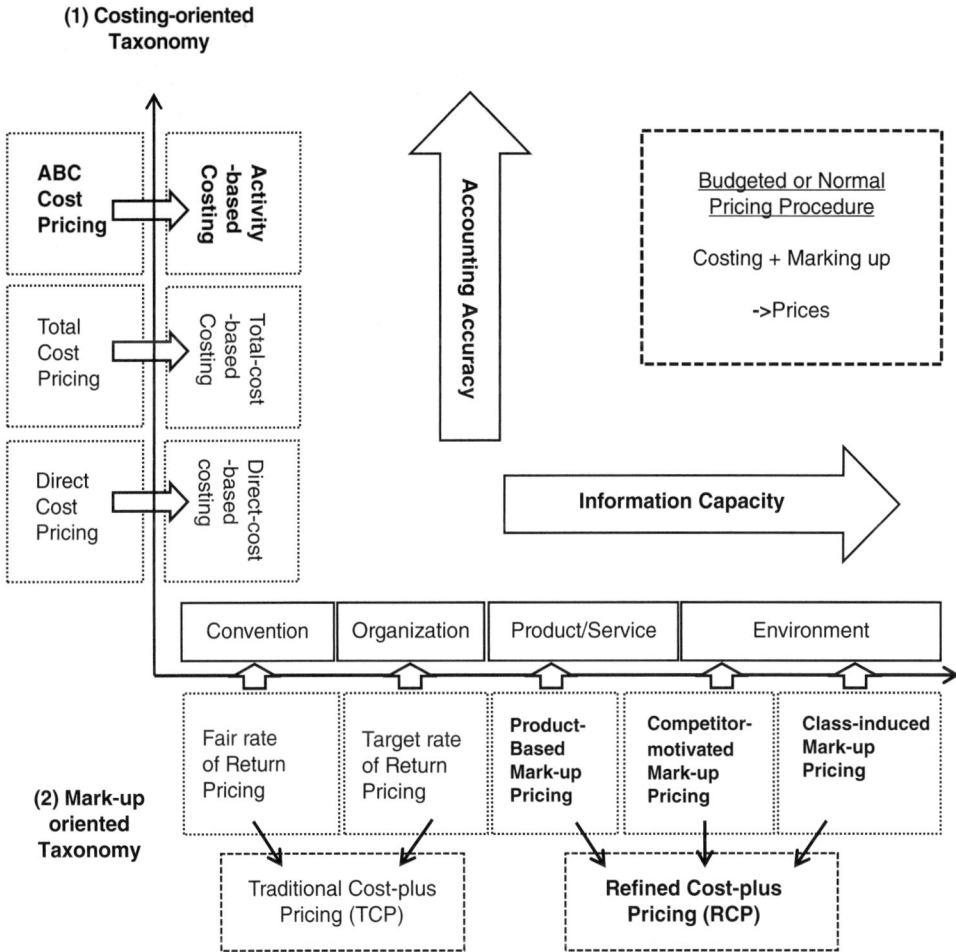

*Figure 17.1   Pricing procedures according to two taxonomy systems*

The mark-up-oriented pricing taxonomy is the other pricing classification, in which pricing procedures are differentiated according to a variety of profit mark-up procedures after presupposing a cost base such as ATC, regardless of what its costing procedure is. The best-known pricing procedures identified by this taxonomy are fair rate of return pricing and target rate of return pricing. In addition, there is also a refined pricing procedure, which can be divided into three subgroups: product-based mark-up pricing, competitor-motivated mark-up pricing, and class-induced mark-up pricing. The following are short explanations of each pricing procedure based on Gu and Lee (2012).

Fair rate of return pricing is a cost-plus pricing procedure in which the mark-up is predetermined by convention or a fair rate of profit, based on the industry norms, which are customs and practices established within an industry and with which firms must comply. Target rate of return pricing is a cost-plus pricing procedure in which the mark-up is determined exclusively by organizational conditions. Refined cost-plus pricing procedures take into account not only convention and organizational situation but also costly information on characteristics of the organization's products, strategies of its competitors, or the extent of willingess-to-pay by a target income class. They can be divided into three subgroups: product-based, competitor-motivated, and class-induced mark-up pricing procedures. Product-based markup pricing is a cost-plus pricing procedure in which the mark-up rate is predominantly adjusted to reflect the characteristics or life cycle of products. Competitor-motivated mark-up pricing is a cost-plus pricing procedure in which the mark-up rate is set mainly to be responsive to the strategies of competitors in the same industry. Lastly, class-induced mark-up pricing is a cost-plus pricing procedure in which the mark-up rate differs primarily according to the primary target class based on the same information on environment as the competitor-motivated one.

To recap, Table 17.1 summarizes the new system of two pricing taxonomies and the relations between the pricing procedures suggested from the perspective of post-Keynesian

*Table 17.1   Extended PK pricing taxonomies, pricing procedures, and pricing strategies*

| | | | |
|---|---|---|---|
| (1) Costing-oriented taxonomy | Traditional cost pricing | Direct cost pricing | Full-cost pricing |
| | Refined cost pricing | Total cost pricing<br>ABC cost pricing | Full-cost pricing<br>Full-cost pricing |
| (2) Mark-up-oriented taxonomy | Traditional cost-plus pricing | Fair-rate of return pricing | Cost plus pricing |
| | | | Fair return pricing |
| | | Target-rate of return pricing | Target return pricing |
| | | | Breakeven pricing |
| | Refined cost-plus pricing | Product-based mark-up pricing | Skimming pricing |
| | | | Premium pricing |
| | | | Economy pricing |
| | | | Penetration pricing |
| | | | Experience/learning curve pricing |
| | | | Price bundling or system pricing |
| | | | Complementary product pricing |
| | | Competitor-motivated mark-up pricing | Leader pricing |
| | | | Parity pricing |
| | | | Low-price supplier |
| | | | Opportunistic pricing |
| | | Class-induced mark-up pricing | Perceived-value pricing |
| | | | Second-market discounting |
| | | | Price signaling |
| | | | Image pricing |
| | | | Reference pricing |

behavioral economics as applied to firms and the pricing strategies reported in business literature. It should be noted that the complexity of pricing decisions imposes the need to adopt more than one pricing procedure. For example, a particular pricing strategy can be used in everyday pricing decisions, while another one may be adopted in some special circumstances (Monroe 2003). Moreover, it should be emphasized that sophistication of the pricing procedures does not imply that price change becomes more frequent, or that prices grow more flexible than with traditional procedures.

Given the normal costing process and the relative stability of the profit mark-up, it follows that prices remain unchanged at least for a single pricing period regardless of the number of sequential transactions. Consequently, administered prices are neither exchange-specific prices nor prices that reflect the impact of immediate variations in sales. This implies that markets that have stable, normal cost-based prices are not organized like auction markets or oriental bazaars, where the retailer engages in individual price negotiation for each transaction. Rather, an enterprise that desires to enter these unorganized markets must first announce a price for its product and then enter into direct buyer–seller interaction to obtain sales. Since buyer–seller interactions take place both simultaneously and through time, business enterprises find that stable prices are cost-efficient in terms of selling costs, reduce the threat of price wars, and facilitate the establishment of goodwill relationships with customers (Lee 1998; Downward 1999).

**Extrinsic Price Stability**

With a clearer understanding of how firms set their prices and why prices are stable at least during a pricing period, it is possible to analyze why some US industrial prices have become acyclical, that is, more stable over the cycle since the early 1980s. Another important property of administered prices is that they change over time in a series of discrete steps. The pricing administrators of business enterprises maintain pricing periods of three months to a year in which their administered prices remain unchanged; and then, at the end of the period, they decide on whether to alter them. The factors which are most important to the enterprises in this regard are changes in labor and material costs, changes in the mark-up for profit, and changes in normal output. Factors prompting the enterprises to alter their profit mark-ups include short-term and long-term competitive pressures, the stage that the product has reached in its life cycle, and the need for profit. Moreover, since normal output is administratively determined, it is possible for pricing administrators to alter it cyclically over the business cycle, resulting in the ATC increasing in the downturn and decreasing in the upturn. If the mark-ups for profit remain constant, then the pricing administrators would be setting countercyclical prices. Consequently, administered prices can change from one pricing period to the next in any direction, irrespective of the state of the business cycle. However, evidence does suggest that within short periods of time (such as two-year intervals), change in costs will dominate price changes; whereas over a longer period of time the change in the mark-up will play a more important role (Lee 1998; Downward 1999).

The change in the profit mark-up can be caused by long-term structural factors and short-term strategic factors. First, the most influential long-term factor is the heterogeneous industry life cycle. Some research on firm dynamics tracks entrants to determine their subsequent growth and mortality rates along the industry life cycle. Klepper (1996) lists

334 Handbook of research methods and applications in heterodox economics

the empirical regularities concerning how firms' entry and exit decisions vary along the degree of maturity of a technologically progressive industry. One of the stylized facts on the long-run effect of industry life cycle on firm dynamics is that the market share change rate of the largest firms declines and the leadership of the industry stabilizes, which implies that the profit mark-up is also stabilized within a certain range of percentage in the long run. As an industry matures, it establishes different kinds of market governance, which allows the price leader in the industry to stabilize its profit mark-up rate through implicit collusion. Second, the most decisive short-term factor to determine the profit mark-up is firm dynamics over the cycle. The profit mark-ups can fall because of new entry or the threat of entry in booms (Chatterjee et al. 1993). It is undoubtedly true that more new firms incorporate in booms. Net entry (measured as net business formation, that is, the difference between new incorporations and failures) and realized total profits co-move, and both are strongly procyclical (Bilbiie et al. 2007). The correlation between net entry and output (measured by real GDP) ranges over the interval 0.70–0.73 (Lewis 2006; Bergin and Corsetti 2005; Devereux et al. 1996).

   The difference in the cost base between two successive pricing periods depends not only on changes in the prices of labor, material inputs, and overhead costs, but also on changes in material and labor productivity. The wages of most workers – at least those who do not switch jobs – typically change only annually and are mediated by a complex set of institutions. Barattieri et al. (2010) find that the probability of a wage change is about 18 percent per quarter, thus implying an expected duration of wage contracts of 5.6 quarters in the US economy. Moreover, examining longitudinal microeconomic data (Panel Study of Income Dynamics, PSID dataset) on the distribution of annual nominal wage and salary changes of US workers who remain on the same job, Kahn (1997) finds that a significant fraction of workers receive the same nominal wage/salary in consecutive years and there is also evidence of downward nominal wage stickiness. More recently, the International Wage Flexibility Project (IWFP) – a consortium of more than 40 researchers with access to individual workers' earnings data for 16 countries including the United States (during 1970–97) – finds a high incidence of wage freezes and a lack of nominal wage cuts, and a tendency for workers' wage changes to clump in the vicinity of the expected rate of price inflation, which are taken as evidence of downward rigidity in nominal wages and downward real wage rigidity, respectively (Dickens et al. 2007). Using data for hourly nominal wages at industry level, Holden and Wulfsberg (2008) also show the prevalent existence of downward nominal wage rigidity on industry wages in 19 OECD countries over the period 1973–99. Those studies imply that there is little empirical evidence of cyclical ups and downs of nominal wages. In addition, since intermediate goods are seen as products by other firms in the input–output framework, the price cyclicality of intermediate goods is a result from some other factors which drive price cyclicality. Thus, the change in the cost base over the business cycle is accounted for much more by the change in productivity measures than the differences in wage rates and material input prices. Given that the profit mark-up absorbs only part of changes in the budgeted average total cost,[3] the lower cost base leads the price to drop while the degree of the price cut depends on the firm's pass-through policy. If the budgeted total average cost is countercyclical, then the price will also be countercyclical. Furthermore, most of the variation in the average total cost over the cycle stems from labor productivity fluctuations,[4] since material inputs tend to vary proportionally along with output changes.

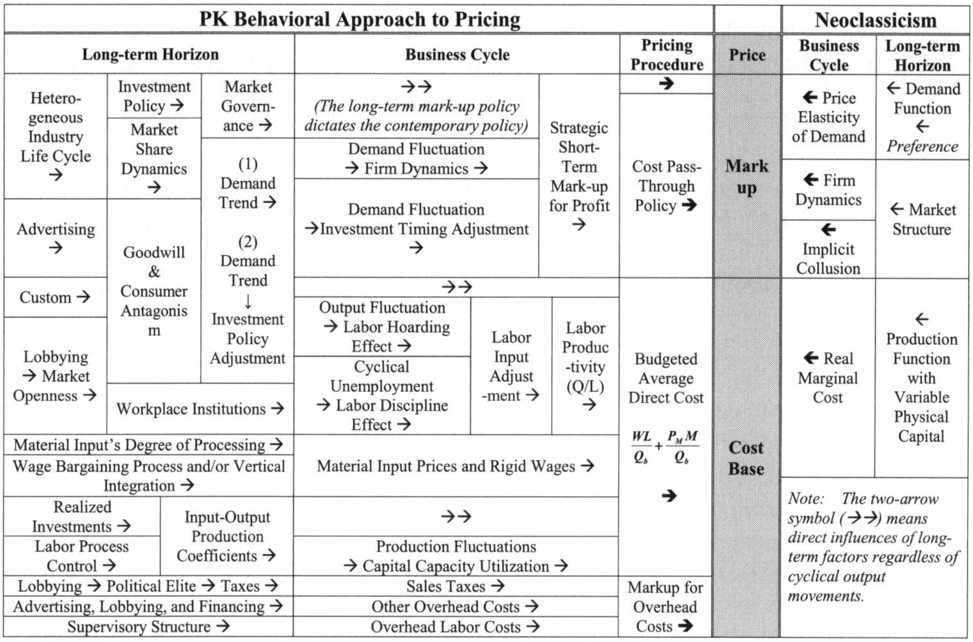

*Figure 17.2 Causal mechanisms for traditional and behavioral approaches to pricing*

Figure 17.2 shows all the possible causal mechanisms which have an effect on mark-ups, cost base, and/or cost pass-through policy from both neoclassical and post-Keynesian behavioral perspectives. According to neoclassicism, price cyclicality depends on the cyclicality of price elasticity of demand and/or the competitive condition associated with market structure, since cost base is simply marginal cost, which should be either increasing or constant. It is the cyclical movement of the profit mark-up that determines price cyclicality in an industry, while the cost base has no role in the process. Contrariwise, the post-Keynesian behavioral approach shifts the emphasis back to the cost base. True, profit mark-up itself can respond to demand shock, or change to a limited degree for the strategic short-term purpose. However, most of the profit mark-up fluctuation comes from the changes in incomplete cost pass-through policy. In other words, even if profit mark-up appears to change significantly over the business cycle, there are two aspects or factors of the appearance: one being pure mark-up change per se and the other being cost pass-through policy change.

When the extrinsic price stability is weakened over the cycle, we have more cyclical price movement. Extrinsic price stability is affected theoretically by changes in profit mark-up, cost base, and/or demand shock.

## A Mathematical Representation of the Causal Mechanism

As long as there is strong employment protection law, labor input will be varied, in part through cyclical changes in working rules and effort level. Labor productivity will fall with output during downturns (labor hoarding) and rise with output during upturns (labor dishoarding). During the expansion (recession), output per measured hour or worker may appear relatively high (low) due to unobserved increases (decreases) in hourly effort. As a consequence, output will change more than proportionately to total hours. True, until the mid-1980s, productivity growth rose and fell with output growth and labor input growth in the US. But some studies have started to note that since then the procyclical labor productivity has weakened, and it even moved in different directions in the mid-1980s from the macroeconomic perspective (Gali and Rens 2010; Zandweghe 2010; Barnichon 2010). That is, the cyclical behavior of labor productivity has changed since the mid-1980s. In about a year, for instance, the rolling correlation between labor productivity and unemployment switches swiftly from negative to positive values; quantitatively, a 0.5 percent rise in productivity is associated with a 0.2 percentage point increase in cyclical unemployment (Barnichon 2010).

A common explanation that does not involve supply shocks is the absence of labor hoarding caused by two structural changes. The first change is a decline in labor adjustment costs, that is, a decline in hiring and firing costs; and the second change pertains to firm-level uncertainty on firms' product demand, which has brought about intensified employment reallocation instead of temporary declines in employment in the recessions since the early 1980s (Zandweghe 2009). Another interpretation is that the neoliberal labor market reform has raised workers' effort during recession since unemployment plays as a discipline on workers and raises their work intensity as the structural change increases job insecurity and reduces unemployment benefits (Shapiro and Stiglitz 1984; Bowles 1985).

Both neoclassical and Marxian versions of theoretical models are based on optimization by an individual worker and a representative firm, where the worker determines their level of work effort according to the expected income loss. The worker seeks to maximize the present value of the expected future stream of income, which depends on the wage level received, the level of labor effort expended, the worker's rate of time preference, the likelihood that the worker will be dismissed, and the worker's fallback position if dismissed.

As an alternative model, an empirically grounded two-sector price–output–employment model can be utilized to explain the relationship. Consider the following two-industry model of the economy:

$$Q_m(l_m w_m)(1 + r_m) = Q_m P_m \tag{17.2}$$

$$Q_c(l_c w_c)(1 + r_c) = Q_c P_c \tag{17.3}$$

where $Q_m$ is the output of machines; $Q_c$ is the output of the consumption good; $l_m$ is the labor production coefficient for the machine industry; $l_c$ is the labor production coefficient for the consumption good industry; $w_m$ and $w_c$ are the wage rates in the machine and the consumption good industries; $r_m$ and $r_c$ are the profit mark-ups in the machine and the consumption good industries; and $P_m$ and $P_c$ are the prices of machines and the consumption good, respectively. Production in the model of production consists of machines with labor producing machines, and machines with labor producing consumption goods. In order for the economy to be productive, that is, to produce more machines than are used up in the production of machines, so that the surplus machines could produce consumption goods, the output–machine ratio for the machine industry ($q_{mm}$) must be greater than 1. On the other hand, the output–machine ratio for the consumption goods industry ($q_{cm}$) needs only to be greater than 0. Finally, total employment, $L$, is proportional to the output of machine and consumption goods: $l_m Q_m + l_c Q_c = L$. It is assumed that all the machines produced in the machine industry are entirely used up in the production of machines and consumption goods, thereby making the surplus of the economy consist entirely of consumption goods, $Q_c$. Thus the empirically grounded output–employment model of the economy is described with mathematical notations as below:

$$\left[ \frac{q_{mm}}{q_{mm}-1} \right] \left[ \frac{Q_c}{q_{cm}} \right] = Q_m \leftrightarrow aQ_c = Q_m \tag{17.4}$$

$$q_{cm} M_c = Q_c \tag{17.5}$$

$$l_m \left[ \frac{q_{mm}}{q_{mm}-1} \right] \left[ \frac{Q_c}{q_{cm}} \right] + l_c q_{cm} \left[ \frac{Q_c}{q_{cm}} \right] = L$$

$$\leftrightarrow l_m \left[ \frac{q_{mm}}{q_{mm}-1} \right] \left[ \frac{1}{q_{cm}} \right] + l_c = \frac{L}{Q_c}$$

$$\leftrightarrow a l_m + l_c = L/Q_c \tag{17.6}$$

where $Mc$ is the number of machines currently used in the consumption goods industry, and $a$ is $[q_{mm}/(q_{mm}-1)][1/q_{cm}]$ and constant since $q_{mm}$ is constant. Consider the gross national product ($Q_c$) has dropped by 10 percent from the trend in a recession. Since the production of $Q_m$ is in fixed proportion to $Q_c$, the intermediate machine industry also experienced 10 percent drop in its production. If the total employment ($L$) in the economy decreases less than 10 percent, then either or both labor production coefficients ($l_m$ and $l_c$) have to rise according to equation (17.6), which means a reduction to labor productivity. In this case, we have the negative relationship between unemployment and labor productivity growth in the aggregate data. If the total employment ($L$) dwindles more than 10 percent, then either or both labor productivity coefficients should fall according to equation (17.6), which indicates an improvement of labor productivity. In this case, we have the positive relationship between unemployment and labor productivity growth in the aggregated numbers. In short, the cyclicality of the cost base has been weakened and thus prices have become less cyclical. The structural change has led US industrial prices to move acyclically in the post-1984 period.

## 17.4   CONCLUSION

Neoclassical economists continue to explain price movement predicated on changes in profit mark-up or elasticity of demand with the marginal cost constant or increasing. Post-Keynesian economists had argued that constant average direct costs and fixed indirect costs cause average costs to fall as the output increases, while the *ex ante* profit mark-up does not vary significantly within the business cycle. In other words, they considered the countercyclical cost movement with the quasi-constant mark-up as the implicit reason for countercyclical price movement, with the labor hoarding effect lying at the center of their exposition of countercyclical productivity and prices.

The objective of this chapter is to refine the post-Keynesian framework for price stability and cyclicality based on the method of grounded theory. It shows that the grounded theorizing is critical for building a comprehensive and coherent theoretical system to provide an analytical framework for price stability. By examining the causal mechanisms for price setting which are supported by empirical evidence, the method is shown to shed light on the mechanisms through which price stability is properly secured.

## NOTES

1.  Dhyne et al. (2011) made a similar-looking, yet different distinction between intrinsic and extrinsic price rigidity, where a price is intrinsically rigid when it does not adjust, or only partially adjusts, to changes in demand and costs that have significant effects on the optimal price, whereas a price is extrinsically rigid when the price does not adjust because demand and costs are stable and the optimal price does not vary much.
2.  The marketing and management literature on pricing has been paying attention to the relationship between several alternative pricing objectives and the pricing strategies. However, in fact all the objectives end up being devised to serve the business enterprise's ultimate objective: its survival as a going concern. So it is much less relevant than it seems to be to differentiate between the sub-objectives and to associate them to pricing strategies, at least in the discipline of microeconomics, one of the main concerns of which is centered on a business enterprise's evolutionary aspects, that is, its active reaction and passive adaptation to market or institutional environment.
3.  Price acyclicality is also associated with incomplete cost pass-through policy. A firm's pass-through policy is a strategic variable where an agency can play its clear role. It is an interaction between changes in mark-ups and shocks to input price and productivity. A number of empirical studies document that shocks to input prices and productivity are not fully passed through to prices at the industry level. See, for example, Goldberg (1995) for the automobile industry, Kadiyali (1997) for the photographic film industry, Hellerstein (2004) for the beer industry, Nakamura and Zerom (2009) for the coffee industry, and Atesoglu (1997) for US economy as a whole.
4.  It is obvious that the level of labor productivity is determined by long-term factors such as technology improvement represented by input–output production coefficients. Still, labor productivity fluctuates around its trend over the cycle, which is enabled by short-term labor input adjustment.

## REFERENCES

Agresti, A-M. and B. Mojon (2001), 'Some stylized facts on the euro area business cycle', European Central Bank Working Paper, 95, Frankfurt: European Central Bank.
Atesoglu, H. (1997), 'A post Keynesian explanation of US inflation', *Journal of Post Keynesian Economics*, **19** (4), 639–49.
Backus, D. and P. Kehoe (1992), 'International evidence on the historical properties of business cycles', *American Economic Review*, **81** (4), 864–88.
Barattieri, A., S. Basu, and P. Gottschalk (2010), 'Some evidence on the importance of sticky wages', NBER Working Paper 16130, Cambridge, MA: NBER.
Barnichon, R. (2010), 'Productivity and unemployment over the business cycle', *Journal of Monetary Economics*, **57** (8), 1013–25.
Barro, R.J. and S. Tenreyro (2006), 'Closed and open economy models of business cycles with marked up and sticky prices', *Economic Journal*, **116** (511), 434–56.

Bergin, P. and G. Corsetti (2005), 'Towards a theory of firm entry and stabilization policy', NBER Working Paper Series 11821, Cambridge, MA: NBER.

Bilbiie, F., F. Ghironi, and M. Melitz (2007), 'Endogenous entry, product variety, and business cycles', NBER Working Paper Series 13646, Cambridge, MA: NBER.

Blair, J.M. (1974), 'Market power and inflation: a short-run target return model', *Journal of Economic Issues*, **13** (2), 453–78.

Bowles, Samuel (1985), 'The production process in a competitive economy: Walrasian, Marxian, and neo-Hobbesian models', *American Economic Review*, **75** (1), 16–36.

Bresnahan, T.F. (1987), 'Competition and collusion in the American automobile industry: the 1955 price war', *Journal of Industrial Economics*, **35** (4), 457–82.

Chadha, B. and E. Prasad (1994), 'Are prices countercyclical? Evidence from the G7', *Journal of Monetary Economics*, **34** (2), 239–57.

Chatterjee, S., R. Cooper, and B. Ravikumar (1993), 'Strategic complementarity in business formation: aggregate fluctuations and sunspot equilibria', *Review of Economic Studies*, **60** (4), 795–812.

Chevalier, J.A., A.K. Kashyap, and P.E. Rossi (2003), 'Why don't prices rise during periods of peak demand? Evidence from scanner data', *American Economic Review*, **93** (1), 15–37.

Cooley, T.F. and L.H. Ohanian (1991), 'The cyclical behavior of prices', *Journal of Monetary Economics*, **28** (1), 25–60.

Den Haan, W.J. and S. Sumner (2004), 'The comovements between real activity and prices in the G7', *European Economic Review*, **48** (6), 1333–47.

Devereux, M., A. Head, and B. Laphamb (1996), 'Aggregate fluctuations with increasing returns to specialization and scale', *Journal of Economic Dynamics and Control*, **20** (4), 627–56.

Dhyne, E., C. Fuss, H. Pesaran, and P. Sevestre (2011), 'Lumpy price adjustment: a microeconometric analysis', *Journal of Business and Economic Statistics*, **29** (4), 529–40.

Dickens, W., L. Goette,, E. Groshen, S. Holden, J. Messina, M. Schweitzer, J. Turunen, and M. Ward (2007), 'How wages change: micro evidence from the international wage flexibility project', *Journal of Economic Perspectives*, **21** (2), 195–214.

Downward, P. (1999), *Pricing Theory in Post Keynesian Economics*, Cheltenham, UK and Northampton, MA, USA: Edward Elgar.

Finch, J.H. (2002), 'The role of grounded theory in developing economic theory', *Journal of Economic Methodology*, **9** (2), 213–34.

Fiorito, R. and T. Kollintzas (1994), 'Stylized facts of business cycles in the G7 from a real business cycle perspective', *European Economic Review*, **38** (2), 235–69.

Friedman, M. and A.J. Schwartz (1982), *Monetary Trends in the United States and the United Kingdom: Their Relation to Income, Prices, and Interest Rates, 1867–1975*, Chicago, IL: University of Chicago Press.

Gali, J. and T. Rens (2010), 'The vanishing procyclicality of labor productivity', Kiel Working Paper, No. 1641.

Goldberg, P. (1995), 'Product differentiation and oligopoly in international markets: the case of the US automobile industry', *Econometrica*, **63** (4), 891–951.

Goulding, C. (2002), *Grounded Theory: A Practical Guide for Management, Business and Market Researchers*, London: Sage.

Gu, G. (2015), 'Why have U.S. prices become independent of business cycles?', *Metroeconomica*, **66** (4), 661–85.

Gu, G. and F.S. Lee (2012). 'Prices and Pricing', in J.E. King (ed.), *The Elgar Companion to Post Keynesian Economics*, Cheltenham, UK and Northampton, MA, USA: Edward Elgar Publishing, pp. 456–63.

Heil, O. and K. Helsen (2001), 'Toward an understanding of price wars: their nature and how they erupt', *International Journal of Research in Marketing*, **18** (1–2), 83–98.

Hellerstein, R. (2004), 'Who bears the cost of a change in the exchange rate? The case of imported beer', Federal Reserve Bank New York Staff Report, 179, New York: Federal Reserve Bank.

Holden, S. and F. Wulfsberg (2008), 'Downward nominal wage rigidity in the OECD', *The B.E. Journal of Macroeconomics*, **8** (1), 1–48.

Kadiyali, V. (1997), 'Exchange rate pass-through for strategic pricing and advertising: an empirical analysis of the US photographic film industry', *Journal of International Economics*, **43** (3–4), 437–61.

Kahn, S. (1997), 'Evidence of nominal wage stickiness from microdata', *American Economic Review*, **87** (5), 993–1008.

Klepper, S. (1996), 'Entry, exit, growth, and innovation over the product life cycle', *American Economic Review*, **86** (3), 562–83.

Konstantakopoulou, I., E. Tsionas and T. Kollintzas (2009), 'Stylized facts of prices and interest rates over the business cycle', *Economics Bulletin*, **29** (4), 2613–27.

Kydland, F.E. and E.C. Prescott (1990), 'Business cycles: real facts and a monetary myth', *Federal Reserve Bank of Minneapolis Quarterly Review*, **14** (1), 3–18.

Lavoie, M. (2001), 'Pricing', in Ric Holt and Steve Pressman (eds), *A New Guide to Post Keynesian Economics*, London: Routledge, pp. 21–31.

Lee, Frederic S. (1998), *Post-Keynesian Price Theory*, Cambridge: Cambridge University Press.

Lee, Frederic S. (2002), 'Theory creation and the methodological foundation of post Keynesian economics', *Cambridge Journal of Economics*, **26** (6), 789–804.

Lee, Frederic S. (2005), 'Grounded theory and heterodox economics', *Grounded Theory Review*, **4** (2), 95–116.

Lewis, V. (2006), 'Macroeconomic fluctuations and firm entry: theory and evidence', National Bank of Belgium Working Paper 103, Brussels: National Bank of Belgium.

Lucas, R.E. (1977), 'Understanding business cycles', in K. Brunner and A. Meltzer (eds), *Stabilization of the Domestic and International Economy*, Amsterdam: North Holland, pp. 7–29.

MacDonald, J.M. (2000), 'Demand, information, and competition: why do food prices fall at seasonal demand peaks?', *Journal of Industrial Economics*, **48** (1), 27–45.

Monroe, K. (2003), *Making Profitable Decisions*, 3rd edn, New York: McGraw-Hill/Irwin.

Mumtaz, H., S. Simonelli, and P. Surico (2011), 'International comovements, business cycle and inflation: a historical perspective', *Review of Economic Dynamics*, **14** (1), 176–98.

Nakamura, E. and D. Zerom (2009), 'Accounting for incomplete pass-through', NBER Working Paper 15255, Cambridge, MA: NBER.

Plehn-Dujowich, J.M. (2008), 'On the counter-cyclicality of prices and markups in a Cournot model of entry', *Economics Letters*, **99** (2), 310–13.

Porter, R.H. (1983), 'Optimal cartel trigger-price strategies', *Journal of Economic Theory*, **29** (2), 313–38.

Shapiro, C. and J. Stiglitz (1984), 'Equilibrium unemployment as a worker discipline device', *American Economic Review*, **74** (3), 433–44.

Stock, J.H. and M.W. Watson (1999), 'Business cycle fluctuations in US macroeconomic time series', in J.B. Taylor and M Woodford (eds), *Handbook of Macroeconomics*, Vol. 1, Amsterdam: Elsevier, pp. 3–64.

Warner, E. and R. Barsky (1995), 'The timing and magnitude of retail store markdowns: evidence from weekends and holidays', *Quarterly Journal of Economics*, **110** (2), 322–52.

Webb, R. (2003), 'The cyclical behavior of prices and employee compensation', *Economic Quarterly: Federal Reserve Bank of Richmond*, **89** (1), 69–83.

Zandweghe, W. (2010), 'Why have the dynamics of labor productivity changed?', *Federal Reserve Bank of Kansas City Economic Review*, **3** (1), 5–30.

Zeithaml, V., M. Bitner, and D. Gremler (2006), *Services Marketing: Integrating Customer Focus Across the Firm*, 4th edn, New York: McGraw-Hill.

# 18 Studying low-income households: challenges and issues
## *Lynne Chester*

## 18.1 INTRODUCTION

Research on family and domestic groups crosses a number of disciplines such as anthropology, economics, gender and cultural studies, history, and sociology. Much of that research focuses on the relationship between the changing forms of social provisioning and the domestic group through which the material needs of individuals are met. The study of households is important because it provides an intermediate analytical step between studies at the micro level of individuals and those at the macro level of socio-economic development.

A household is the locus of decision-making about meeting social needs. It is usually defined in economic or material terms and is analytically distinct from social relations that constitute a family. In itself, the concept of a household is not theoretically meaningful. It has, however, proven to be analytically useful within diverse theoretical traditions such as Marxist and related historical-structural approaches, the social-historical life cycle approach, and that of neoclassical economics exemplified by Gary Becker.

The household is also a common unit for the collection of empirical data by official statistical collections which provide a useful quantitative data source for secondary analysis. Nevertheless, official statistical collections and secondary analysis cannot answer all questions raised in theoretical or policy debates leading to the design of research to answer those questions, and questions that may concern the structure, characteristics, and behavior of households. Low-income households pose particular issues for research design.

Access to 'economically marginalized' populations to recruit research participants can be a challenge (Mammen and Sano 2012). Marginal populations are often referred to as 'hard to reach' populations (Hurley 2007). Low-income households are often labelled as marginal or 'hard to reach'. Although there is considerable ambiguity in the use of the latter term, it implies that it is some characteristic of the members of the group making them hard to reach suggesting the group holds a homogeneity which does not necessarily exist. Therefore, use of this term 'defines the problem as one within the group itself' (Brackertz 2007, p. 1). Low-income households may be information-poor; hold low literacy levels; be vulnerable due to long-term illness, disability, or age; suffer from domestic violence; or actively try to conceal their identity due to a fear of legal authorities because of issues with immigration, taxation, or illicit drug abuse; all of which reduce their accessibility for researchers (Shaghaghi et al. 2011).

This chapter discusses the challenges and issues in studying low-income households, drawing on a research project which investigated the impacts of rising energy prices on

Australian households. The study adopted a mixed methods approach to collect quantitative and qualitative data.

The chapter is structured as follows. Section 18.2 outlines the context and purpose of the Australian study. Section 18.3 discusses the reasons for the study using a mixed methods approach in order to access low-income households along with the advantages and disadvantages of the chosen research methods, which were an online survey, focus groups, and interviews. Section 18.4 details the quality of the data collected and the findings are illuminated to answer the research questions. Observations are drawn in section 18.5 about the use of intermediaries to recruit participants, the impact on the conduct of the research by ethics committee requirements, and the rewards provided for participation, before concluding with suggestions for methodological approaches which focus on low-income households.

## 18.2    CONTEXT AND PURPOSE OF THE STUDY

Most Australian households are able to choose the company to supply their electricity. If they do so, the prices paid are set by a market contract. If a household chooses to remain on a standard contract their electricity prices are set by state and territory government regulators. Some 40 percent of New South Wales (NSW) households, 30 percent of Victorian and Queensland, and 19 percent of South Australian households have chosen to remain on standard contracts, and thus pay regulated electricity prices (ESC 2012; ESCOSA 2013; IPART 2013). Regulated electricity prices are to be phased out subject to evidence of effective competition. There have been no regulated prices since 2009 for Victorian households, and since February 2013 for South Australian households, although electricity companies must provide standing-offer electricity prices to those households not on a market contract. The actual electricity prices paid, on average, by individual households under a market contract are not publicly available.[1] The changes in regulated prices, however, are reportedly similar to those on market contracts and thus are a strong indicator of the experience of all Australian households (ESC 2012).

During the five years to 2003–04, NSW regulated household prices showed no real change, although there were real increases of 5–11 percent in all other states and territories except South Australia, where prices stagnated before leaping 24 percent in real terms in 2003–04 (ESAA 2003). More substantive increases in regulated household prices have occurred in recent years as each regulator has sought to make prices cost-reflective of supply and 'consistent with the Government's policy aim of reducing customers' reliance on regulated prices' (IPART 2010, p. 11).

In the six-year period to mid-2013, the average increase in NSW regulated household electricity prices was nearly 108 percent. This compares to more than 80 percent in Victoria, Queensland, and Tasmania, and slightly less than 80 percent for households living in South Australia, Western Australia, and the Northern Territory (NT). Australian Capital Territory (ACT) households experienced the smallest increase of slightly less than 71 percent (Table 18.1).[2]

The average annual change may understate the actual increase experienced by a household as does the Consumer Price Index (CPI) Electricity Price Index for those who live in the eastern states (Table 18.2).[3] Nevertheless, this index shows (except for Canberra)

*Table 18.1   Nominal average increases in regulated household electricity prices, 2007–13*

| | Annual change | | | | | | Cumulative change | | |
|---|---|---|---|---|---|---|---|---|---|
| | 2007–08 (%) | 2008–09 (%) | 2009–10 (%) | 2010–11 (%) | 2011–12 (%) | 2012–13 (%) | 2007–08 to 2010–11 (%) | 2007–08 to 2011–12 (%) | 2007–08 to 2012–13 (%) |
| NSW | 7.5 | 7.5 | 20.2 | 10.0 | 17.3 | 15.7 | 52.8 | 79.5 | 107.9 |
| Victoria | 7.3 | 7.4 | 13.5 | 6.0 | 12 | 18.0 | 39.3 | 56.0 | 84.0 |
| Queensland | 11.4 | 9.1 | 11.8 | 13.3 | 6.6 | 11.5 | 54.0 | 64.1 | 83.0 |
| South Australia | 12.3 | 2.5 | 2.0 | 18.2 | 17.4 | 8.9 | 38.8 | 62.9 | 77.4 |
| Western Australia | 0.0 | 10.0 | 23.6 | 10.0 | 5.0 | 12.5 | 49.6 | 57.0 | 76.7 |
| Tasmania | 15.7 | 3.9 | 7.0 | 15.3 | 11.0 | 10.6 | 48.3 | 64.6 | 82.0 |
| NT | 4.4 | 3.4 | 18.0 | 5.0 | 2.8 | 30.0 | 33.7 | 37.5 | 78.7 |
| ACT | 16.7 | 7.1 | 6.4 | 2.4 | 6.4 | 17.7 | 36.2 | 44.9 | 70.6 |

*Sources*:   These average increases were calculated from the published price increases on the following state and territory government regulators' websites: http://www.economicregulator.tas.gov.au/domino/otter.nsf/elect-v/000; http://www.esc.vic.gov.au/Energy; http://www.escosa.sa.gov.au/electricity-overview/reporting-and-compliance.aspx; http://www.finance.wa.gov.au/cms/content.aspx?id=15096; http://www.icrc.act.gov.au/energy/electricity/; http://www.ipart.nsw.gov.au/Home/Industries/Electricity; http://www.qca.org.au/Electricity/Consumer/Electricity-Prices; http://www.utilicom.nt.gov.au/Electricity/Pages/default.aspx.

*Table 18.2    Comparative changes in regulated electricity prices, price indices and average*
*weekly earnings, 2007–12 (%)*

| 2007–08 to 2011–12 | Regulated household electricity prices | CPI electricity price index | All groups CPI | Average weekly earnings |
|---|---|---|---|---|
| NSW | 79.5 | 66.3 | 14.3 | 19.1 |
| Victoria | n.a. | 59.5 | 14.2 | 20.0 |
| Queensland | 64.1 | 49.7 | 16.0 | 26.7 |
| South Australia | 62.9 | 50.5 | 14.7 | 21.3 |
| Western Australia | 57.0 | 56.9 | 14.2 | 33.7 |
| Tasmania | 64.6 | 41.3 | 13.0 | 27.2 |
| NT | 37.5 | 34.9 | 15.2 | 32.3 |
| ACT | 44.9 | 22.5 | 14.4 | 27.1 |
| Australia | n.a. | 57.1 | 14.5 | 27.5 |

*Note:*   n.a. = not available; CPI figures are for each capital city and the weighted average for eight capital cities.

*Source:*   Table 18.1 and Australian Bureau of Statistics (2011b, 2011c).

electricity prices clearly outstripping CPI and average weekly earnings. During the same period the Pensioner and Beneficiary Living Cost Index (PBLCI) increased by 16 percent. The PBLCI informs decisions about pension indexation rates. Both indices substantively understate actual average electricity price movements for the majority of Australian households.

Around 3.5 million Australian households fall within the two lowest income quintiles (ABS 2011d). Poor households in advanced industrial economies, as in developing countries, spend higher proportions of their income and expenditure on energy (Jamasb and Meier 2010a; Khandker et al. 2010). In 2009–10, domestic fuel and power accounted for 2.6 percent of average weekly expenditure for all Australian households. Electricity costs accounted for 75 percent of this weekly expenditure (ABS 2011e).

This average, however, masks a distinct difference between income groups. As household disposable income rises, a steadily declining proportion is spent on domestic energy. The poorest 20 percent of households in 2009–10 spent 4 percent of average weekly expenditure on domestic energy costs, double that of the richest households (Table 18.3). The comparative weekly expenditure proportions in 2003–04 were 2.9 percent for the poorest and 1.5 percent for the highest income group (ABS 2006).

Table 18.3 also shows the disproportionate impact of energy costs by household income quintile. The poorest quintile, actually nearly 25 percent of Australian households, in 2009–10 spent, on average, 7 percent of equivalized disposable income on household energy costs. This is nearly three times the proportion spent by the wealthiest households and represents an upward shift since 2003–04 when the poorest quintile was found to be spending 2.4 times that of the wealthiest. It is also notable that the second-lowest quintile, and a little more than 18 percent of households, in 2009–10 spent twice the proportion spent by the wealthiest households.

Two cautionary notes need to be made about this data. First, all the energy expenditure proportions have been derived from the mean weekly income for each quintile. This

*Table 18.3   Average Australian household expenditure on energy, 2009–10*

| 2009–10 | Equivalized disposable household income quintile | | | | | | |
|---|---|---|---|---|---|---|---|
| | Lowest | Second | Third | Fourth | Highest | All | Second and third deciles |
| % of total households | 24.5 | 18.2 | 18.1 | 18.6 | 20.6 | 100 | 21.3 |
| Mean weekly income | $314 | $524 | $721 | $975 | $1704 | $848 | $429 |
| % of av. weekly expenditure on domestic fuel and power | 3.9 | 3.2 | 2.8 | 2.4 | 2.0 | 2.6 | 3.7 |
| % of av. weekly domestic fuel and power expenditure on electricity | 76.3 | 75.0 | 74.6 | 75.7 | 74.3 | 75.1 | n.a. |
| % of equivalised disposable income on domestic fuel and power | 7.0 | 5.3 | 4.3 | 3.7 | 2.6 | 3.8 | 6.5 |
| % of equivalised disposable income on electricity | 5.4 | 4.0 | 3.2 | 2.8 | 1.9 | 2.9 | n.a. |

*Source:*   Australian Bureau of Statistics (2011d, 2011f).

means that the derived figures will not be representative of all those within each income quintile and should be treated as indicative only. Second, these figures understate the current situation for low-income households because they do not include the effect of the substantial electricity prices increases since mid-2010 (as shown in Table 18.1).

These trends and data illustrate two critical points. Electricity price rises are causing low-income households to pay higher proportions of income and expenditure to meet energy bills. The severely disproportionate impact on the poorest Australian households is widening over time.

A low-income household's capacity to meet escalating energy costs will be influenced by the ability to change its energy demand and housing tenure. The condition of housing influences the demand for energy. Draughty, poorly insulated, inadequately ventilated, and older housing causing damp and mould growth, excess cold or excess heat, will directly influence energy use for space heating and cooling. Owner-occupiers may be more likely to make energy efficiency improvements given their greater level of control over the home. Many older owner-occupiers will, however, have insufficient financial resources for housing improvements to reduce their energy needs. Renters may not feel they have the responsibility or right to make housing improvements. Low-income renters also face the constraint of not being able to find alternative, affordable, and more energy-efficient housing. Low-income households have much less capacity to influence housing energy efficiency to reduce their energy demand and stem the growth of energy bills as prices rapidly rise.

The ability of low-income households to adjust their energy demand will also be influenced by the size, composition, and daily activities of the household, as well as the capacity to replace energy-inefficient appliances and adopt different household practices. A number of studies have found that the energy demand of low-income households is relatively price insensitive (IPART 2003; Jamasb and Meier 2010b). Consequently, higher electricity prices can be expected to shift low-income household expenditure patterns because greater proportions of disposable income are needed for energy bills and less will be available to meet other essentials.

There is limited understanding of the consequences for low-income Australian households of the substantive increases in electricity prices which have occurred during the last decade, and particularly since mid-2007. A 2004 report starkly described a range of physical and mental health effects, social exclusion, and deprivation experienced by 12 low-income South Australian households following an electricity price increase of around 30 percent in one year:

> all forgo at least one of the normal essentials of physical health, thermal comfort, adequate nutrition, social contact, access to education or entertainment, or freedom from financial insecurity and mental stress ... usually a combination of two or more of these unmet needs has emerged. (Laris and Associates 2004, p. 9)

Changed household expenditure patterns arising from electricity price increases were also found in 2004 amongst people receiving financial counselling. Half had reduced their spending on food and telephone, whereas 80 percent or more had cut expenditure on clothing, holidays, movies, and sport (UnitingCare Australia 2010). A few years later, more than 70 percent of financially stressed households were found to be making sacrifices to meet electricity price increases, and 10 percent were unable to meet the cost (Wesley Mission 2010). Electricity and gas bills have also been found to be the greatest cause of rental arrears (63 percent) in Victorian low-income households (Sharam 2007).

A not-for-profit organization, which distributes government vouchers to assist those having difficulty with the payment of energy bills, reported in 2008 that 80 percent of these were seeking assistance for electricity bills (Babbington and King 2008). Nearly 40 percent of the two lowest household income quintiles were unable to pay electricity, gas, or telephone bills on time during 2010.[4] The media also has reported cases of hardship such as parents going without food in order to pay energy bills.

There has been, however, no substantive contemporary evidence base to inform policy-making of the consequences for low-income households of escalating energy prices. Are increasing amounts of income needed to pay energy bills, and is expenditure being foregone on other essentials? Are escalating household energy bills, as found in the UK and Europe, contributing towards evidence of hardship such as inadequate nutrition, poor physical and psychological health, and social exclusion? What are the constraints on changes to energy use behavior and practices of these households? What is the impact of housing conditions on the energy use of low-income households? What is the extent of relief provided by government and energy company hardship programs? These are the questions which this study was designed to answer.

This study was designed to address these knowledge gaps. Specifically, the study sought to investigate: the affordability and payment of low-income household energy bills, the ability for low-income households to change their energy use, and the strategies adopted to manage higher energy bills, in order to determine the consequences for the well-being and lifestyle of rising energy prices for poorer Australian households.

## 18.3   THE STUDY'S RESEARCH DESIGN

### A Mixed Methods Approach

The study used a mixed methods approach to collect quantitative and qualitative data. Different views of reality are provided by different research methods. Each method provides a different 'slice' of reality (Denzin 1997): '[N]o single method can ever completely capture all the relevant features of that reality; consequently, [we] must learn to employ multiple methods in the analysis of the same empirical events' (Denzin 1989, p.13) to partially overcome the inherent weakness or bias inherent in single methods, data sources, perspectives, and observers. By utilizing both quantitative and qualitative methods, the study reduced the limitations of one technique or source and increased the validity of the empirical reality presented in the research findings. Also, different data types yield different aspects of the study's object, and 'a single, totally consistent picture' should not be expected (Patton 2002, p. 560). The advantage of using more than one research method and more than one data source is to deepen the interpretative base and ameliorate, as far as possible, the limitations of using a single method or data source.

Quantitative data was required to estimate the proportions of disposable income needed by low-income households to pay rising energy bills, and determine any correlation with household characteristics, geographic location, the condition of housing and household expenditure priorities.

Access to a sufficient number of low-income households to provide statistically significant data is difficult without considerable resources and the assistance of government agencies. One option was a reply-paid mail questionnaire distributed by Centrelink, the federal government agency responsible for income support payments such as the age and disability pensions, unemployment benefits, and family allowances. Those dependent on income support payments fall within the lowest income quintile. A mail questionnaire was ruled out because the risk of an insufficient response rate was considered high for the following reasons: a questionnaire may have been incorrectly perceived as a covert method by Centrelink to check on people's circumstances in order to cancel income support payments; and many low-income households have low literacy skills and are time-poor (Demi and Warren 1995). The study's limited funding was insufficient to meet the costs of a mail questionnaire on a scale to provide a statistically significant sample of all income support recipients (around 7.5 million Australians).

A sampling frame does not exist for low-income households, that is, a list of households from which a probability sample may be selected.[5] Therefore a random selection of participants was not an option and recruitment relied on some form of nonprobability sampling such as snowballing or self-selection, often through community agencies (Babbie 2007; Mammen and Sano 2012). Snowball (or accidental) sampling is suitable for small exploratory studies of marginalized groups such as the criminal or those suffering AIDS. The researcher relies on one subject providing the name of another subject, and so on. This method has a number of weaknesses, such as representativeness of the participants from which to draw generalizations from the findings, and the time and difficulty of finding a suitable number of participants. It is for these reasons that self-selection of participants was deemed more suitable to collect the quantitative data through the least costly method of an online survey.

Qualitative data was required to determine the impacts of rising energy bills on housing choices, health, social inclusion, and other determinants of well-being. A qualitative approach allows researchers to 'understand lived experiences and . . . interpret the understandings and shared meanings of people's everyday social worlds and realities' (Limb and Dwyer 2002, p. 6). Qualitative methods provide a fuller picture of how factors such as income and household structure are reflected in daily practices, understandings, and behavior (Barbour 2008). This picture was required to determine whether rising electricity bills impact on housing choices, health, social inclusion, and other determinants of well-being for low-income households. The study's qualitative methods were focus groups and in-depth interviews.

Face-to-face discussion is the most appropriate method to gain detailed and contextual insights into the well-being, health, and lifestyle of low-income households as a result of paying significantly higher energy bills. Focus groups tap into participants' perceptions, attitudes, and opinions. More than one focus group is necessary because of the serious risk that a single group 'will be too atypical to offer any generalizable results' (Babbie 2007, p. 309). In-depth semi-structured interviews allow for the probing of views and opinions to explore the subjective meanings that respondents ascribe to concepts or events, because 'interviewing offers researchers access to people's ideas, thoughts and memories' (Reinharz 1992, p. 19). Deeper information or knowledge can be obtained by interviews about lived experiences and situations which a focus group does not necessarily lend itself to, because some participants may dominate discussion, hide their real opinions, or be reluctant to participate.

**The Recruitment of Participants**

The study's target population was low-income households. The study defined low-income households as those with a weekly income equivalent to or less than the income quintile of the Federal Minimum Wage (FMW). FMW workers are strongly represented in the lowest income quintiles (Healy and Richardson 2006). Australian Bureau of Statistics data has consistently shown the FMW falling within the second household income quintile (ABS 2010, 2013).

The Australian Council of Trade Unions (ACTU) agreed to promote the online survey through unions which represent workers receiving the lowest level of wages, including those earning the Federal Minimum Wage. The Australian Council of Social Services (ACOSS) and its state-based organizations, the Council on the Ageing (COTA) and the Public Interest Advocacy Centre (PIAC) also agreed to promote participation in the study through their respective constituent member organizations and websites. These peak organizations were selected because of their roles concerning the provision of information to and advocacy on behalf of low-income households who are the focus of this research. ACOSS, the peak body of the community services and welfare sector, advocates on behalf of people affected by poverty and inequality; PIAC, a law and policy not-for-profit organization, is a long-standing consumer advocate on a range of public interest issues which include the provision of energy services; and the COTA advocates on behalf of older people to improve their well-being and circumstances. These organizations also have extensive networks of community agencies and organizations in direct contact with low-income households experiencing hardship and crisis, including those

---

BOX 18.1    INFORMATION PROVIDED TO PEAK ORGANIZATIONS TO
DISTRIBUTE ABOUT THE ONLINE SURVEY

**Survey of Low-Income Household Energy Use and Affordability**
The impact of higher energy bills for low-income households is being investigated by a researcher
from the University of Sydney. Why? There is no comprehensive picture of the pressures and circumstances of low-income households following substantial rises in electricity and gas prices. The findings will be used to develop policies to assist low-income households. [NAME OF ORGANIZATION]
will also have access to the findings for our own use.

An online survey is being used to collect information about household energy use, the size of
energy bills, the income needed to pay these bills, and the consequences for low income households of rising energy costs.

Participation is voluntary. The survey will take about 15–20 minutes to complete and is available
from 1 February.

We are seeking your assistance to encourage low-income households to complete the survey
and for them to tell their family and friends about the survey. Attached is a one-page sheet about
the survey which you may find useful to print out and make available to low income households with
whom you have direct contact.

Further details and the survey can be found at: www.householdenergyuse.com.

---

agencies that deliver assistance – on behalf of state governments – to those experiencing
difficulties with the payment of energy bills.

Details of the online survey were provided to ACOSS, ACTU, COTA and PIAC for
distribution through their member organizations and networks (Box 18.1).

A website was created at which the online survey was made available from February 1
to November 30, 2012.[6] The online survey was completed by 372 respondents, and 82
percent completed the survey in full.

Focus groups and in-depth interviews were conducted in the capital city of the four
most populous states of Queensland, New South Wales, Victoria and South Australia,
and the regional centres of Wagga Wagga (NSW), Toowoomba (Queensland), and Port
Augusta (South Australia). The Victorian regional centre of Bendigo was also selected.
However, no focus groups were conducted at this location due to recruitment issues
which are discussed below.

Covering the four largest states and including regional centres enabled determination
of the presence or influence of any significant locational differences. Low-income households have been found to have a higher representation in non-metropolitan locations and
their energy-impoverishment experience may differ from those located in capital cities
(ABS 2013).

Participants were recruited through local community agencies and organizations
located in inner and outer suburbs of the capital cities and which dealt with those on low
incomes and experiencing difficulties or hardship. Not all these agencies provided material aid in the form of food or emergency assistance. Some were referral agencies such as
the Redfern Legal Centre in inner Sydney and the Neighbourhood Justice Centre in the
inner Melbourne suburb of Collingwood.

Organizations were contacted by telephone to determine their willingness to volun-
tarily assist and were provided with A3 posters advertising the study and copies of a
one-page information sheet and the two-page Participation Information Statement,

which were displayed at front counters. Dates, times, and locations for the focus groups and interviews were also advised in advance to the organizations assisting. Low-income households who wished to participate could leave their details with the community organization or contact the research team on a 1800 number organized for this phase of the study.

All focus group discussions and interviews were conducted in October and November 2012, and held at the rooms of assisting organizations because these locations were familiar and accessible to participants. Each group discussion and interview lasted for about one hour and was audio-recorded for subsequent transcription. Each participant was provided with a $50 'essentials' supermarket voucher as an acknowledgement of their time and contribution to the study.[7]

The study's design allowed for a maximum of three focus groups to be conducted in each of the four capital cities, and one in a major regional centre of each state (16 focus groups in total). A maximum of 28 in-depth interviews (five per capital city, two per regional centre) was also set. Thus, depending on the willingness of low-income households to be involved and the effectiveness of recruitment, the study's design allowed for a maximum of 172 participants through focus groups and interviews. Across the four most populous states of Australia, 130 participants were recruited. Forty-eight (37 percent) participants were from South Australia, 35 (27 percent) from New South Wales, 24 (18 percent) from Victoria, and the remaining 23 (18 percent) were from South Australia.

The number of focus group discussions was lower than planned, which can be attributed to a number of factors. Some potential participants indicated their willingness to be involved but did not attend on the scheduled day. Many of the assisting organizations mentioned that their clients were very time-poor due to caring responsibilities or other circumstances, and held low-level literacy and/or English-language skills. Hence, to provide at least an hour to the project was often not possible and the two-page Participant Information Statement (required by the University of Sydney's Human Research Ethics Committee) was overwhelming for some others. Some regional community organizations did not wish to display the A3 poster so information about the study was made available only on a case-by-case basis at the discretion of the front counter worker. Other reasons offered by community workers for lower recruitment were: suspicion that the study was collecting information for taxation, immigration, public housing, or Centrelink purposes; embarrassment to admit to payment difficulties with household energy bills and more generally their living circumstances, especially when children were involved; and a reluctance to help as some past research projects had not shared findings with participants, so they believed participation would not change their circumstances. In the case of the Victorian regional centre of Bendigo, there was anecdotal evidence that potential participants had research fatigue from previous projects. It is also notable that Victorian households have not experienced the same rapid escalation in electricity prices as other states, are less reliant on electricity as a fuel source than other Australian households, and have access to more generous hardship assistance than in other state or territory jurisdictions.

In total, 99 people participated in focus group discussions. The size of focus groups ranged from two to 11 although the common group was seven or eight. Although the number of group participants was less than anticipated, the overall number and their geographic distribution provides sufficiently robust results from which to draw credible conclusions which are discussed in section 18.4.

Thirty-one participants were interviewed individually, either face-to-face or by telephone, which was three more than planned. It was decided to undertake these additional interviews to provide data for regional Victoria, given the difficulties experienced recruiting in Bendigo. The type of interview was determined by the availability of the interviewee to meet face-to-face. In the majority of cases (68 percent), caring responsibilities, medical conditions, limited transport access, or the hours of part-time or casual work meant that a telephone interview was preferred by the interviewee.

**The Online Survey**

An online survey provides a more cost-effective option compared to a mail questionnaire although this data collection method does not access the nearly 1.5 million low-income households who do not have home internet access (ABS 2011a). The representativeness of respondents is a particular issue for online data collection. A range of strategies were used to maximize responses from low-income households. The study's website explained the low-income household focus of the research and this was directly placed above the survey entry button. The survey was advertised through peak community and welfare organizations with extensive networks in direct contact with households experiencing hardship and crisis, including those agencies that deliver assistance – on behalf of state governments – to those experiencing difficulties with energy bills. Participants were given the opportunity to win a $50 supermarket voucher, which would have been of greatest interest to low-income households; and to reduce the possibility of non-Australian households responding, the survey website page discussed which households were eligible and the second survey question required provision of the household's residential postcode. If this question was not completed, survey completion was not possible.

The survey questions sought information about:

- characteristics of the household (such as location, how many people it comprised, how many children it contained);
- size and type of housing (such as how many rooms, what was the home constructed from);
- household energy use (such as the range of household appliances, the potential to reduce energy use);
- household energy bills and their impact (such as the cost, any payment difficulties, the impact on spending for other essentials).

The survey questions were prepared using SurveyMonkey, a minimal-cost online service which has a number of advantages: implementation and analysis costs are minimal; data are received in a predictable and consistent format; and responses can be generated very quickly (Mann and Stewart 2000: 70–74). To maximize the response rate and reliability of answers, the online questionnaire was designed to be easy to navigate and user-friendly, with a clear and logical question order, and answer options were placed under each question (Russell and Purcell 2009, pp. 120–21). Ethics approval for the online survey was obtained from the University of Sydney's Human Research Ethics Committee in December 2011.

A pilot survey was conducted during December 2011 to test the competency of the questionnaire, to gain feedback on the clarity of question wording and instructions, to determine if any important issues had been overlooked, and to verify the data collector settings provided by SurveyMonkey. The pilot was administered as a participatory survey; that is, respondents were informed that it was a pre-test of a full-scale survey. In addition to completing the questionnaire, respondents were asked to provide comments about the ease or difficulty in answering questions, the clarity of instructions, the length of time to complete, and if any other matters should be covered.

Thirty-two respondents completed the pilot survey. Respondents included the researcher's colleagues and their family and friends, located within the capital cities of Sydney and Melbourne, and regional Queensland. After reviewing the results of the pilot survey and respondent comments, some minor adjustments were made to the questions and instructions. A one-page information sheet about the survey and the Participant Information Statement were made available through the study's website.

**The Focus Groups and Interviews**

The interview is one of the principal methods to collect qualitative data, is very flexible as a data collection tool, and has many different types. The data collection requirements determine the type of interview which is most suitable (Fontana and Frey 1998). As Punch (2001, p. 176) states: 'different types of interview have different strengths and weaknesses, and different purposes in research. The type of interview selected should therefore be aligned with the strategy, purposes and research questions'.

A number of interview typologies are evident in social science research.[8] The key factors which differentiate types of interview are the degree of structure used and the extent to which the interview is standardized across interviewees. Structured interviews are often associated with survey research, with each person asked the same pre-established question in the same way, the interviewer's neutral role strongly promoted, little room for deviation from the interview schedule, and usually a limited set of response categories (Fontana and Frey 1998; May 2001; Punch 2001). This type of interviewing is claimed to permit comparability between responses, and the validity of responses is purportedly enhanced through the reliance upon a uniform structure. The semi-structured interview is a little more flexible, with the interviewer able to seek information beyond the answers given to pre-specified questions. The interviewer 'asks certain major questions the same way each time, but is free to alter their sequence and probe for more information' (Fielding and Thomas 2008, p. 256).

The endpoint of the interview typology is the unstructured interview which provides a greater breadth than the other types, given its open-ended character. The interviewer has a list of topics in outline form – an interview guide – but the sequence and wording of questions, about each topic, is decided during the course of the interview (Fielding and Thomas 2008; Patton 2002). This type of interview enables the interviewee to answer in their own words, their own frame of reference, as well as enabling a greater understanding of the interview focus from the interviewee's point of view. The unstructured interview allows the perspective of the person being interviewed to be taken into account (Bryman 1988) and the interviews remain fairly conversational. It is for these reasons that unstructured interviews were used for this study.

Ethics approval for the focus groups and interviews was obtained from the University of Sydney's Human Research Ethics Committee in September 2012. The focus group and interview questions sought to understand the pressures and circumstances that low-income households may be facing such as:[9]

- How has a household managed to pay higher energy bills?
- Has any assistance been sought to help pay energy bills?
- Are there household items which are not purchased, so that energy bills are paid?
- Has daily life been affected by rising energy bills? Have household members been affected?
- Does a household consider that their standard of living has changed?
- Are any difficulties faced in trying to reduce energy use at home?
- How is the affordability of energy bills viewed in relation to other household expenditures?

An interview guide was prepared prior to conducting the interviews (see Appendix 18A.1) and each participant was provided with the Participation Information Statement prior to signing the Participant Consent Form (see Appendix 18A.2).

A number of probes were also designed. 'Probing involves follow-up questioning to get a fuller response; it may be verbal or non-verbal . . . [because] our objective is to have a guided conversation' (Fielding and Thomas 2008, p. 260). Considerable care was taken to ensure that all probes were as neutral as possible, did not encourage a particular response from the interviewee, and hence did not lead to bias. The probes essentially were a reminder list of things to ask about for each of area of the interview guide.

The questions were open-ended and interviewees were encouraged to 'communicate their underlying attitudes, beliefs and values, rather than a glib or easy answer' (Fielding and Thomas 2008, p. 258), to respond in their own terms, their own length and depth. No particular sequence of questions was followed for each interview, the probes acting to ensure that all things were covered.

Given that the non-standardized format adopted for questions was discursive, it was important for the interviewer to establish rapport with each of the interviewees (Fontana and Frey 1998; Keats 1988; Minichiello et al. 1990; Patton 2002; Punch 2001). However, care was taken to ensure that the rapport established did not undermine the interviewer's neutrality. 'Rapport is a stance vis-à-vis the person being interviewed. Neutrality is a stance vis-à-vis the content of what the person says' (Patton 2002, p. 365). Rapport was established which conveyed understanding by the interviewer without passing judgement on the responses of interviewees. This was facilitated through the phrasing of questions, given the importance of questions to the structure and control of interaction in an interview (Minichiello et al., 1990). Both descriptive and structural questions were used, the latter allowing the interviewer to explore areas in greater depth.

The interviewer's communication and listening skills were also important, given the unstructured nature of the interviews (Keats 1988; Minichiello et al. 1990; Punch 2001), the importance of establishing rapport with each interviewee, and the need to ensure that the researcher found 'not the truth per se but rather the truth as the informant sees it to be' (Minichiello et al. 1990, p. 128).

Each focus group and interview was audio-taped and transcribed verbatim. The transcripts were read through several times to obtain an overall sense of the content. The data derived from the interviews provided the researcher 'with a means of analysing the ways in which people consider events and relationships and the reasons they offer for doing so' (May 2001, pp. 144–5). A picture was constructed from each interviewee's account and their experiences of it. A qualitative data analysis software package, Nvivo, was used which permitted the identification of trends and themes in the data.[10]

## 18.4   THE STUDY'S FINDINGS

There has been limited understanding of the impacts and consequences for low-income Australian households of the substantive increases in household energy prices since mid-2007. The average increase in Australian household electricity prices from 2007 to 2013 was nearly 83 percent, with the highest experienced by NSW households (108 percent) and the lowest average increase for those living in the ACT (71 percent). The study presented a substantive evidence base of the lived experiences of low-income households as a result of rapidly rising household energy bills. Survey respondents were highly representative of the Australian population in terms of location, income, dwelling type, and housing tenure. Focus group and interview participants were highly representative of the poorest 20 percent of households, the majority of which are dependent on pensions and allowances. Participants included indigenous Australians, those from a non-English-speaking background, full-time students, those with a disability or long-term illness, sole parents, the unemployed, and age pensioners.

There has been anecdotal reporting over the last decade of the deleterious effects of rising energy prices, from small-scale studies by the not-for-profit sector and the media. The findings of this study go beyond confirming the evidence of these past reports to provide strong substantiation of the embedded nature of the damaging effects. In addition, the study's findings show that these deleterious impacts are widespread and systemic and are not confined to a particular location or group of low-income households.

The well-being, health, and lifestyle of low-income Australian households are suffering from the cumulative effects of ever-increasing electricity bills over a sustained period of many years, which has compounded the circumstances of these vulnerable households. Never or rarely leaving home, using only one room, shorter (or occasionally, no) showers, watching less television, going to bed fully clothed (or early) to avoid the use of heating, families using a common sleeping room when cold, rarely having friends or extended family at home to avoid using cooking appliances, and/or the room temperature being uncomfortable – these are some of the 'strategies' that the study found that low-income households have adopted to 'manage' their energy use as they endeavour to control the size of bills. These actions are far more extreme than the commonly promulgated measures to improve household energy efficiency.

As a result of cutting expenditure on essentials such as food, reallocating expenditure on other items to be able to pay energy bills, and making relatively severe changes in household practices to reduce the size of energy bills, these households were found to be suffering physical discomfort, reduced physical and mental well-being, loneliness and social isolation, strains within household relationships, and distress about the social and emotional well-being of children.

The awareness of energy efficiency measures was found to be strong and nearly all households have tried to reduce their energy use in response to rising energy bills. Barriers to further reductions in energy consumption were found to be the lack of financial capacity to afford energy-saving appliances or household repairs and improvements (which is most problematic for renters), the need for health-related use of heating and cooling and life support equipment, and the presence of children. Households are loathe to cut heating or cooling too much in case it affects the health of children or exacerbates existing health vulnerabilities.

The study's quantitative findings also found that household energy expenditure as a proportion of disposable income is much higher for poorer households and declines as income rises. The findings also show the acute differential between the poorest and wealthiest households. This confirms the conclusions of past household income and expenditure studies which have relied on the use of static and dynamic econometric modeling (for example, Jamasb and Meier 2010b).

The dominant policy measures to assist low-income households with energy bills are rebates, concessions, and temporary financial assistance provided by state and territory governments, generally as an absolute amount (lump sum) rather than a proportion of a household energy bill, as is the case only in Victoria. At least 2.3 million low-income households are regularly receiving some form of concession or rebate on their electricity bill. Yet all states record a higher proportion of residential disconnections for the non-payment of bills in 2011–12 compared to 2007–08, which strongly signals the increasing ineffectiveness of these measures.

Payment plans and hardship policies are further types of assistance for households experiencing energy hardship. Under the new, and partially implemented, National Energy Customer Framework energy retailers are required to implement customer hardship programs, which are generally framed around payment arrangements for energy bills owing, ongoing use, and the avoidance of disconnection. Households who have used such plans to date generally considered the payments were unaffordable, being set too high, and did not reflect their capacity to pay.

Overall, the study's findings pose a number of critical issues for government and policy-makers. There is strong evidence of the inability of low-income households to become more energy efficient. Effort to reduce household energy use is widespread but has been highly concentrated on low-cost practices like the installation of low-energy light bulbs. The barriers to reducing energy consumption mean the scope for further and substantive improvements in the energy efficiency of these households is highly constrained. More minor changes to household energy behavior will not result in sufficiently significant changes to be reflected in lower energy bills, and will undoubtedly aggravate already diminished levels of health and well-being.

A problematic relationship between low-income households and energy retailers was also found by the study. This relationship is framed by companies providing customer information on websites, the use of 1300 or 1800 numbers for customers to make telephone contact, and the customer experience encountered when discussing payment difficulties or a payment plan. Nearly 1.5 million low-income households do not have home internet access. From January 1, 2015 calls from mobile phones to an 1800 number became free; until then, call costs posed a significant barrier to contact and information.

A further critical policy issue highlighted by the study is the purpose of energy bill assistance. Current assistance, the monetary value of which varies considerably across Australia, is reactive. Assistance is directed at the bill, which is the end-point of household energy use. Thus, this assistance does not help low-income households manage their energy use to achieve the maximum possible energy efficiency level for their circumstances. Measures for widespread, long-term improvements to the energy efficiency of housing occupied by low-income households are also non-existent. Energy efficiency measures are limited in scale and focus on household behavioral practices to reduce energy use.

Energy hardship is caused by a conjunction of factors: low income, energy prices, the condition of housing, and the capacity to adopt different household practices to manage energy use given its size, composition, and needs. This study provided strong evidence of the current extent of energy hardship and the need for current reactive policies to provide an improved level of assistance until preventative and remedial policies are successively implemented. The threshold question for policy-makers, which this study illuminated, is whether there is the political will to directly address and eliminate energy hardship, or whether the only form of assistance will remain reactive, fragmented, and increasingly ineffective.

## 18.5   OBSERVATIONS AND CONCLUDING COMMENTS

Low-income households are difficult to access for research because there is no sampling frame from which to randomly sample. However, there are approaches which can recruit sufficient numbers of participants to yield robust results from which to make generalized claims. As the Australian study of low-income households demonstrates, the use of an online survey combined with focus groups and interviews designed to cover the capital city and a regional centre in the four most populous states meant that representativeness was heightened.

The recruitment of participants through self-selection increases the possibility of bias, although this can be ameliorated, as in this study, by ensuring a wider geographic representation. Self-selection through community organizations also raises the possibility of bias. The Australian study chose a range of different welfare and community organizations with direct contact with low-income households. Some regional community organizations, however, did not wish to display the A3 poster so information about the study was made available only on a case-by-case basis at the discretion of the front counter worker. Hence recruitment was subject to an element of bias when staff exercised judgment as to whether someone may or may not be interested in participating in the study.

During the study's recruitment phase, many community organizations referred to past research projects which had not shared findings with participants, and thus suggested there may be a reluctance to participate again. The study asked participants if they wished to receive feedback, and a summary of findings was posted or emailed to all those wanting feedback. A full copy of the study's report was also provided to all organizations who assisted with study.

Ethics approval was required for the study by the University of Sydney's Human Research Ethics Committee. The approval mandated a two-page Participant Information Statement which many prospective participants found overwhelming. Low-income households have lower levels of literacy, cognitive, negotiation, and communication skills. Consequently, a researcher needs to give careful consideration to the potential impact on recruitment and retention of the materials used to promote participation.

The focus groups and interviews were held in locations easily accessible to the participants in terms of both public transport access and mobility, and in familiar facilities and meeting rooms. They were also conducted at times to suit participants, particularly those with caring responsibilities, and depending on the time of day, light lunches and morning or afternoon teas were provided. It was felt that these measures would assist the involvement of low-income households. Access to public transport and buildings, unfamiliar surroundings, and inconvenient appointments can each act as a barrier to participation.

Mention should also be made of the $50 supermarket voucher provided to focus group and interview participants, and a random draw of survey respondents. The vouchers (a prepaid plastic card) were provided as an acknowledgement of the time given by participants. Ethics approval required that the A3 poster promoting the focus groups and interviews made no mention of the voucher, although it was permitted for inclusion in the Participation Information Statement. When contacting community organizations about the study, the researcher referred to the voucher for each participant.

There is a considerable literature on participation rewards, their effect on response or participation rates, and whether they are coercive or exert undue influence. Incentives or rewards have been found to have a positive effect on response rates and pre-paid monetary incentives are more effective than promised in-kind incentives (Hansen 2006). Singer and Bossarte (2006) contend that incentives are never coercive but may exert influence in surveys on violence and injury. Careful consideration was given by the study to the amount of the participation reward and the form in which it was provided. It was concluded that an amount of $50 was a good balance between not being excessive and not being tokenistic. Some participants were noticeably more vocal than others, but there is no evidence that this can be attributed to the reward of the supermarket voucher.

In conclusion, studying low-income households poses a number of methodological issues. Nevertheless, there are a number of measures which a researcher can take to access 'hard to reach' low-income households using reliable and valid data collection instruments. Careful thought and attention to the potential barriers to participation by those on low incomes needs to inform the research design to ensure sufficient participation and representativeness, and reduce the possibilities of bias. The use of self-selection through community organizations, participation rewards, and data collection methods suitable to the task can yield robust findings to answer the research questions. By taking these issues into account, studies can be strengthened to provide strong insights for policy-makers into the circumstances and needs of low-income households.

# NOTES

1.  These price details are known only by the electricity supply company and the individual household.
2.  The only available Victorian data since 2009 are for average market contract prices. The average real increase for standing contract prices (tantamount to regulated prices) from 2006–07 to 2010–11 was 36 percent, which is comparable to the nominal change shown in Table 18.1 for regulated prices of nearly 40 percent in the four years to 2010–11 (ESC 2011).
3.  The average electricity price increases presented in Table 18.1 refer to all household consumers, whereas

the CPI electricity index covers only metropolitan households. This different coverage does not account for such a wide difference for so many households.
4. Prices for gas and telecommunications did not increase at the same rate as electricity during this period (ABS 2011g). Thus it was assumed that electricity bills were a significant contributor to this outcome.
5. A probability sample is one in which selection typically involves some form of random selection.
6. www.householdenergyuse.com.
7. An 'essentials' voucher can be spent on any supermarket item such as groceries, clothing, school supplies, household goods, and petrol, but not alcohol or tobacco. I consulted the welfare organizations assisting the project who advised that, from the range of available supermarket vouchers, an essentials voucher is of greatest benefit to low-income households.
8. Patton (2002) proposes three main types of open-ended interview: the informal conversational, the general interview guide approach, and the standardized open-ended interview. Standardized, semi-standardized, and non-standardized are the terms used by Fielding and Thomas (2008), whereas Minichiello et al. (1990) use a continuum based on the degree of structure involved, with the tighter structure and standardization on the left, and the opposite at the right-hand end. Fontana and Frey (1998) use a classification of structured, semi-structured, and unstructured.
9. A list of the focus group and interview topics and questions is in Appendix 18A.1.
10. For an overview on using this software for qualitative data analysis, see http://www.qsrinternational.com/.

# REFERENCES

Australian Bureau of Statistics (ABS) (2006), *Household Expenditure Survey Australia: Detailed Expenditure Items, 2003–04 (reissue)*, Cat. 6530.0, Canberra: ABS.
Australian Bureau of Statistics (ABS) (2010), *Household Income and Income Distribution Australia*, Cat. No. 6523, Canberra: ABS.
Australian Bureau of Statistics (ABS) (2011a), *Household Use of Information Technology: Australia 2008–09*, Cat. No. 8146.0, Canberra: ABS.
Australian Bureau of Statistics (ABS) (2011b), *Consumer Price Index, Australia, September 2011*, Cat. 6401.0, Canberra: ABS.
Australian Bureau of Statistics (ABS) (2011c), *Average Weekly Earnings, Australia, August 2011*, Cat. 63012.0, Canberra: ABS.
Australian Bureau of Statistics (ABS) (2011d), *Household Income and Income Distribution Australia*, Cat. 6523.0, Canberra: ABS.
Australian Bureau of Statistics (ABS) (2011e), *Household Expenditure Survey Australia, Summary of Results, 2009–10*, Cat. 6530.0, Canberra: ABS.
Australian Bureau of Statistics (ABS) (2011f), *Household Expenditure Survey Australia, Summary of Results, 2009–10*, Cat. 6530.0, Canberra: ABS.
Australian Bureau of Statistics (ABS) (2011g), *2010 General Social Survey: Summary Results, Australia*, Cat. 4159.0, Canberra: ABS.
Australian Bureau of Statistics (ABS) (2013), *Household Income and Income Distribution Australia*, Cat. 6523.0, Canberra: ABS.
Babbie, Earl R. (2007), *The Practice of Social Research*, 11th edn, Belmont, CA: Thomson Wadsworth.
Babbington, Sally and Sue King (2008), *Helping with the Cost of Energy*, Report of Anglicare Sydney's 2006 EAPA Data Collection, Policy Unit Research Paper, Sydney: Anglicare.
Barbour, Rosaline (2008), *Introducing Qualitative Research*, Thousand Oaks, CA: Sage.
Brackertz, Nicola (2007), 'Who is hard to reach and why?', ISR Working Paper, January, accessed October 10, 2012 at http://www.sisr.net/publications/0701brackertz.pdf.
Bryman, A (1988), *Quantity and Quality in Social Research*, London: Routledge.
Demi, Alice S. and Nancy A. Warren (1995), 'Issues in conducting research in vulnerable families', *Western Journal of Nursing Research*, **17** (2), 188–202.
Denzin, N.K. (1989), *The Research Act: A Theoretical Introduction to Sociological Methods*, Engelwood Cliffs, NJ: Prentice Hall.
Denzin, Norman K. (1997), 'Triangulation in educational research', in Jonathan P. Keeves (ed.), *Educational Research, Methodology, and Measurement: An International Handbook*, 2nd edn, New York: Pergamon, pp. 318–22.
Electricity Supply Association of Australia (ESAA) (2003), *Electricity Prices in Australia 2003/04*, Sydney South: ESAA.

Essential Services Commission (ESC) (2011), *Energy Retailers Comparative Performance Report – Pricing 2010–11*, December, Melbourne: ESC.

Essential Services Commission (ESC) (2012), *Energy Retailers Comparative Performance Report – Pricing 2011–12*, September, Melbourne: ESC.

Essential Services Commission of South Australia (ESCOSA) (2013), *Performance of the South Australian Retail Energy Market – Market Development, July–December 2012*, Adelaide: ESCoSA.

Fielding, Nigel and Hilary Thomas (2008), 'Qualitative interviewing', in Nigel Gilbert (ed.), *Researching Social Life*, 3rd edn, London: Sage, pp. 245–65.

Fontana, Andrea and James H. Frey (1998), 'Interviewing: the art of science', in Norman K. Denzin and Yvonna S. Lincoln (eds), *Collecting and Interpreting Qualitative Materials*, Thousand Oaks, CA: Sage, pp. 47–78.

Hansen, Kasper M. (2006), 'The effects of incentives, interview length, and interviewer characteristics on response rates in a CATI-study', *International Journal of Public Opinion Research*, **19** (1), 112–21.

Healy, Joshua and Sue Richardson (2006), *An Updated Profile of the Minimum Wage Workforce in Australia*, Research Report No.4/06, Melbourne: Australian Fair Pay Commission.

Hurley, Michael (2007), 'Who's on whose margins?', in Marian Pitts and Anthony Smith (eds), *Researching the Margins: Strategies for Ethical and Rigorous Research with Marginalised Communities*, Basingstoke: Palgrave Macmillan, pp. 161–89.

Independent Pricing and Regulatory Tribunal (IPART) (2003), 'Inclining block tariffs for electricity network services', IPART Discussion Paper 64, Sydney, IPART.

Independent Pricing and Regulatory Tribunal (IPART) (2010), *Review of Regulated Retail Tariffs and Charges for Electricity 2010–2013: Electricity – Final Report*, March, Sydney: IPART.

Independent Pricing and Regulatory Tribunal (IPART) (2013), *Review of Regulated Retail Prices for Electricity, From 1 July 2013 to 30 June 2016: Electricity – Final Report*, June, Sydney: IPART.

Jamasb, Tooraj and Helena Meier (2010a), 'Energy spending and vulnerable households', Cambridge Working Paper in Economics 1109, Cambridge: Faculty of Economics, University of Cambridge.

Jamasb, Tooraj and Helena Meier (2010b), 'Household energy spending and income groups: evidence from Great Britain', Cambridge Working Paper on Economics 1011, Faculty of Economics, Cambridge: University of Cambridge.

Keats, Daphne M. (1988), *Skilled Interviewing*, Hawthorn, Australia: Australian Council for Educational Research.

Khandker, Shahidur R., Douglas F. Barnes, and Hussain A. Samad (2010), 'Energy poverty in rural and urban India: are the energy poor also the income poor?', World Bank Policy Research Working Paper No. 5463, Washington, DC: World Bank.

Laris, Paul and Associates (2004), *Powering Poverty: A Report on the Impact of the 2002–03 Electricity Price Rises on 12 Low Income Households in South Australia*, Adelaide: Western Region Energy Action Group.

Limb, Melanie and Claire Dwyer (2002), *Qualitative Methods for Geographers*, London: Arnold.

Mammen, Sheila and Yoshie Sano (2012), 'Gaining access to economically marginalized rural populations: lessons learned from nonprobability sampling', *Rural Sociology*, **77** (3), 462–82.

Mann, Chris and Fiona Stewart (2000), *Internet Communication and Qualitative Research*, Thousand Oaks, CA: Sage.

May, Tim (2001), *Social Research: Issues, Methods and Process*, 3rd edn, Buckingham: Open University Press.

Minichiello, Victor, Rosalie Aroni, Eric Timewell, and Loris Alexander (1990), *In-depth Interviewing: Researching People*, Melbourne: Longman Cheshire.

Patton, Michael Q. (2002), *Qualitative Research and Evaluation Methods*, 3rd edn, Thousand Oaks, CA: Sage.

Punch, Keith F. (2001), *Introduction to Social Research: Quantitative and Qualitative Approaches*, London: Sage.

Reinharz, Shulamit (1992), *Feminist Methods in Social Research*, New York: Oxford University Press.

Russell, Brenda and John Purcell (2009), *Online Research Essentials*, San Francisco, CA: Jossey-Bass.

Shaghaghi, Abdolreza, Raj S. Bhopal, and Aziz Sheikh (2011), 'Approaches to recruiting "hard-to-reach" populations into research: a review of the literature', *Health Promotion Perpsectives*, **1** (2), 86–94.

Sharam, Andrea (2007), 'What the gas and electricity arrears of private low-income tenants can tell us about financial stress', *Journal of Economic and Social Policy*, **11** (2), 23–38.

Singer, Eleanor and Robert M. Bossarte (2006), 'Incentives for survey participation: when are they "coercive"?', *Amercian Journal of Preventive Medicine*, **31** (5), 411–18.

UnitingCare Australia (2010), 'Response to April 2010 AER Issues Paper: Developing national hardship indicators', June, Canberra: UnitingCare Australia.

Wesley Mission (2010), 'Making ends meet: financial stress is not just about money', *Wesley Report*, Number 8, October, Sydney: Wesley Mission.

# APPENDIX 18A.1 FOCUS GROUP AND INTERVIEW TOPICS/ QUESTIONS

**Ability to Pay Energy Bills**

1. Electricity and gas prices have increased markedly, in recent years. Does paying electricity or gas bills ever pose a problem for you?
2. If so, how often is paying energy bills a problem? (For example, occasionally if other unexpected expenses crop up? Or seasonally – for example, only in the colder months or hotter months? Or is paying energy bills always difficult?)

**Assistance to Help Pay Energy Bills**

3. What forms of assistance does your energy company provide if you are having trouble
4. Are you aware of any other forms of assistance for households like yours who are having trouble paying energy bills? Who provides it? What kind of help is offered? Is it enough, in your view? What other forms of assistance do you think that people having trouble paying energy bills need that is not available at present?

**Energy Usage**

5. Has the amount of electricity or gas you use changed in response to rising energy bills? If so, how? Have you cutback on the use of particular appliances, for example?
6. Are there any features of the house or flat in which you live that you think might make it hard to reduce your energy use – for example, built-in appliances in your home, or poor insulation, draughts, or lack of blinds and curtains, etc?
7. Are there any other factors that affect the amount of electricity or gas you use – for example, health issues, or medical appliances? Children and their activities?
8. Do you know of any government or other programs to help you decrease energy use or increase energy efficiency? Have you been able to get help through these programs? Has it made a difference? Is there anything that might help you to reduce the amount of energy you have to use at home, if it was available, or affordable?

**Impact on Household Expenditure, Daily Life and Well-Being**

9. How does difficulty in paying energy bills affect you and your household?
10. Have you cut back on any other items of expenditure in order to pay your energy bills? If so, what kinds of things have you cut back on? What have you cut back on most?
11. If you have cut back on other types of expenditure in order to pay energy bills, does this affect your daily life and activities, or those of other members of your family/ household? In other words, does it affect what you are able to do? If so, how?
12. If you have cut back on other expenses in order to pay energy bills, does this affect your physical and mental well-being, or that of other members of your family/

household? If so, how? In other words, how does it affect how you or your family/household *feel*, health-wise, or emotionally?

13. Have you ever been disconnected from electricity or gas because you were unable to pay your bill? If so, what have you done to get reconnected and how has this affected you or your family/household?

14. Do you think your standard of living has changed because of the need to spend more of your income on higher energy bills?

15. How do you view the affordability of your energy bills compared to your other household expenditures?

## APPENDIX 18A.2    PARTICIPANT INFORMATION STATEMENT AND CONSENT FORM

THE UNIVERSITY OF
SYDNEY

Department of Political Economy
School of Social and Political Sciences
Faculty of Arts and Social Sciences

ABN 15 211 513 464

**Dr Lynne Chester**
*Chief Investigator*

Room 451
Merewether Building (HO4)
The University of Sydney
NSW 2006 AUSTRALIA
Telephone:   +61 2 9351 5044
Facsimile:   +61 2  9351 8596
Email: lynne.chester@sydney.edu.au
Web: http://www.sydney.edu.au/

### THE IMPACTS FOR LOW-INCOME HOUSEHOLDS OF RISING ENERGY PRICES

#### Phase 2: Impacts and consequences of higher energy prices

### PARTICIPANT INFORMATION STATEMENT

**(1)    What is the study about?**

Australian household energy use has increased substantially in the last decade and electricity prices have risen rapidly in recent years. Further sizeable increases in energy prices are forecast. At present, there is a limited understanding of the impacts for low-income households of rising electricity prices. The media and emergency relief providers have reported cases of hardship providing a snapshot of difficulties being experienced. Energy ombudsmen have reported an escalation in household complaints and disconnections. But we do not have a coherent understanding of the consequences of significantly higher energy bills for those households with low incomes. This study is investigating the impacts for low-income households of higher energy bills and is being conducted in two phases. Phase 1, an online survey, investigated the relationship between energy use and housing conditions, and the amount of income needed to pay energy bills. Phase 2, this project, involves interviews and group discussions with low-income households about the impact of energy bills on their well-being, health, and lifestyle.

**(2)    Who is carrying out the study?**

The study is being conducted by Dr Lynne Chester of the University of Sydney with the assistance of Dr Fiona Taylor.

**(3)    What does the study involve?**

This phase of the study involves interviews and group discussions. Participants will be asked about the impact and consequences of higher energy bills on their daily lives, well-being, health, and lifestyles.

The interviews and group discussions will be arranged by the researchers and held at rooms in community organisations located close to public transport. Group discussions will involve nine volunteers and be guided by Dr Fiona Taylor, one of the researchers. The interviews will be one-on-one with Dr Fiona Taylor.

The interviews and group discussions will be recorded on audio (voice) recording equipment so that the information can be analysed by the researchers. To protect the privacy of volunteers, strict participant confidentiality and privacy is assured. Only the researchers will have access to these recordings, and the names of participants or contact details will NOT be made available to anyone else.

**(4)    How much time will the interviews or group discussions take?**

The one-on-one interviews and group discussions will each take about one hour. Volunteers can choose to participate in either the group discussion OR the one-on-one interviews so participation in the study will involve a maximum of one hour of each participant's time.

THE UNIVERSITY OF
**SYDNEY**

**(5)   Can I withdraw from the study?**

Participation in the interviews or in the group discussions is completely voluntary. You are not under any obligation to consent and – if you do consent – you can withdraw at any time without it affecting your relationship with the researchers, the University of Sydney or the agency from which you obtained this information sheet.

If you are being interviewed, you can stop the interview at any time if you do not wish to continue. The audio recording will be erased and the information provided will not be included in the study. If you take part in a group discussion and wish to withdraw after the group session has commenced, it will not be possible to exclude your individual voice from the audio recording.

**(6)   Will anyone else know the results?**

All aspects of the study, including results, will be strictly confidential and only the researchers will have access to the information provided by participants. A report of the study may be submitted for publication, but individual participants will not be identifiable in such a report. All data will be published and presented in aggregate form.

**(7)   Will the study benefit me?**

We cannot and do not guarantee or promise that you will receive any benefits from the study. The study has the strong support of many community, charitable and welfare sector organisations. The findings of the study will be of central value to their work and advocacy. The findings will also be written up for publication and used to make submissions to government.

Each participant will be provided with a $50 voucher redeemable at a major supermarket in recognition of their contribution to the study.

**(8)   Can I tell other people about the study?**

You are welcome to tell other people about the study. You can choose to receive feedback about the study and its findings from the researchers.

**(9)   What if I require further information about the study or my involvement in it?**

When you have read this information, Dr Chester will answer any questions you may have. If you would like to know more at any stage, please feel free to contact Dr Chester at lynne.chester@sydney.edu.au or on 02 9351 5044.

Should you wish to participate in an interview or group discussion, please give your contact details to the front counter where you collected this information statement. Your contact details will be forwarded to the research team, who will then contact you directly by phone to make arrangements for your involvement. Alternatively you may ring the research team on **1800 126 208**.

**(10)   What if I have a complaint or concerns?**

Any person with any concerns or complaints about the conduct of the research study can contact The Manager, Human Ethics Administration, University of Sydney, on +61 2 8626 8176 (Telephone); +61 2 8627 8177 (Facsimile) or ro.humanethics@sydney.edu.au (Email).

*This information sheet is for you to keep*

# 19 Marketization and human services providers: an industry study
*Bob Davidson*

## 19.1 INTRODUCTION

There has been a significant marketization of human services over the last 30 years in most developed nations.[1] Services that historically were largely provided outside the market, either by family or directly funded and delivered by state agencies or charities, are now often provided within the framework of contestable and competitive markets. While the purchasing power for these services continues to come substantially from government, they are now commonly delivered by third parties (both non-profit organizations, NPOs, and for-profit organizations, FPOs), with service users having greater choice over the services they receive and who provides them.

While the process of marketization has been partly driven by governments seeking to reduce the fiscal burden of these services, an actual or stated motive of government has almost always been to improve the services that are provided. It is argued by the proponents of marketization that these improvements will arise from the pressures and opportunities created by greater contestability, competition, and consumer choice. In particular, they argue that greater contestability enables the entry of more innovative and efficient new providers and gives all providers more incentive to improve their services (Bartlett and Le Grand 1993; Le Grand 2007; Sturgess 2012).

Critics of marketization, however, dispute this, claiming that the overall effects of contestability and competition are often negative, leading to the excessive entry and growth of profit-maximizing providers and generating incentives for all providers (including NPOs motivated primarily by social goals) to minimize costs, resulting in poorer services (Brennan 2007; Scourfield 2007). Thus while the polar views in this debate essentially agree on the channels by which markets affect providers and the quality of the services they provide – that is, by enabling the entry of new types of providers and by changing the incentives of all providers – they disagree on how those channels work and the direction of the effects.

The research described in this chapter sought to examine these conflicting contentions, first, at a theoretical level by considering the implications for the concept of contestability and its impact on producers when the 'product' is a human service; and second, through an empirical study of the industry and markets for one type of service in one location, namely home care for older people[2] in the Australian state of New South Wales (NSW) (Davidson 2015b). It is the second phase on which the chapter is primarily focused.

Establishing the reality of how any human service is actually provided and its impact on service users is difficult, especially across a service system that has multiple and diverse users, providers, locations, and service elements. In large part, this difficulty derives from the nature of human services (see section 19.2), which creates issues both for the provision of services, and for researchers in establishing the reality of the delivery and impact of the services. This chapter sets out a methodology and research methods that can help in revealing that reality.

A key aim of the research was to examine marketization on its own terms, as far as possible. The debate over marketization is often presented, rightly, as a conflict between economic and social goals and paradigms, but it is also important to examine the validity of the economic arguments used to justify marketization and increased contestability, especially given the widely held concern that many of the arguments may be 'social philosophy masquerading as economic science' (Nevile 1998, p. 169).[3] As well, the aim was to study a human service market and industry in the same way as one would study any other market or industry. Thus, the research was based on a theoretical framework commonly used in industry studies, but adapted as necessary to ensure it properly took account of when the product is a human service. In this context, heterodox approaches and critical realism, the nature and value of which have been outlined in earlier chapters (Morgan, Chapter 1 in this *Handbook*; Lee, Chapter 2 in this *Handbook*), provide essential perspectives to help establish the reality of marketization and its effects.

The next section discusses the distinctive features of human services and some key issues for researchers of these services. There follows a brief outline of the theoretical basis of the above research, then an account of the methods used in the empirical study, and an outline of some further methods that can extend that research. There are then some concluding comments.

## 19.2   HUMAN SERVICES AND HUMAN SERVICES MARKETS

Human services are characterized by a number of features that distinguish them as 'products' in a market. These features have major implications for the way in which human services are provided, and in the context of a market analysis, represent the source of substantial 'market failure'. The features also have major implications for research about human services. I have elsewhere examined these features and the managed (or quasi) markets through which these services are now largely provided (Davidson 2008, 2012, 2015b).[4] A brief summary of the key points relevant to this chapter follows.

In relation to the product itself, there are major limitations in the observability, measurability, and homogeneity of human services. The production and consumption of human services are simultaneous, so that 'the output tends to disappear at the point of delivery, leaving no lasting physical manifestation' (Saunders 1999, p. 40). Thus in general, the product is not observable after it has been produced. Even when it is observable, it can be very difficult to measure the quantity or quality of a service, since human relationships are integral to the delivery and they are commonly aimed at enhancing the mental and social welfare of the user. They are also very heterogeneous, with the final form dependent on the particular individuals providing and receiving the service on each occasion, and thus observation of a small number of service occasions may not reflect what is happening across a service system.

In relation to the production process, providers are limited in their capacity to increase productive efficiency (productivity), as is the case with any product where 'for all practical purposes the labor is itself the end product' (Baumol 1967, p. 416), but is especially so where human relationships are a central element. Then, on the demand side, many service users have limited 'personal agency' (the capacity to make informed decisions) (Althaus, 1997), and/or are unable to pay for the services they receive, given that there is often the need for regular ongoing services over a number of years. However, there are strong moral and public policy imperatives to ensure at least some minimum level of service for everyone and to avoid poor service to anyone.

Clearly, there are also significant differences between the various human services. These arise primarily from the technology of production, the nature of demand, and the information of actors in the industries (Propper 1993, p.40), but are also apparent in relation to other factors such as whether services are aimed at the maintenance of the current welfare of users or their future development, and the extent to which the distinctive features apply. These differences add to the complexity of the research task.

The criteria most commonly used to assess the 'performance' of a human services industry, market, or provider are how well it facilitates: (1) effective services (which is a function of the quantity, quality, and appropriateness of services in meeting user needs); (2) equity of access to services, at both a geographic and individual level; (3) the efficient use of resources; (4) choice and control for service users; (5) stability; and (6) accountability to both the users and funders of services (Bartlett and Le Grand 1993; Le Grand 2007).

The above features have a number of powerful consequences for both the provision of services and research about them in relation to these objectives. First, governments must substantially pay for these services. Second, there are major asymmetries of information between the providers and buyers of services (Akerlof 1970; Weisbrod and Schlesinger 1986). These asymmetries are also very relevant for researchers.

Third, with the growth of New Public Management (Boston 1991; Kettl 2000; Denhardt and Denhardt 2007) and marketization over the last 30 years, there has been an increasing reliance on formal performance indicators and quantitative data to establish the extent to which the above objectives are being achieved. However, there are many qualifications and uncertainties about quantitative data relating to human services. As intimated above, 'everything that can be counted does not necessarily count [and] everything that counts cannot necessarily be counted' (Cameron 1963), while data purporting to show improvements in services may well be misleading and in fact result from poorer services in important respects. Thus in home care, for example, employing more untrained care-workers will enable a provider to increase the total hours of service for a given cost – and hence achieve a greater measured quantity and efficiency – but it would in effect be a different (and inferior) product. Similarly, a provider may achieve higher measured quality by only working with less complex clients ('cream-skimming').

Finally, the above emphasizes the importance for researchers of understanding in detail the production process (or 'technology of production') for the service being studied, since it underpins the quality of services, the potential for greater efficiencies and the potential for opportunism by profit-maximizing providers. There are two major elements in the production process to examine for most services: the 'service session' (such as the school lesson, or a home visit by a care-worker) and the other functions of a provider that occur outside this session. These other functions include ones that are specific to the service, notably professional support (such as staff development, quality assurance, and research) and the logistics of arranging services; and ones that relate to the broader organization, notably governance and back office services (such as personnel and finance). It is these other functions that offer the major opportunities for improving efficiency in human services. Too often, however, action intended to improve efficiency centres on the service session.

**Human Services Markets**

As a result of the distinctive features of human services, markets for these services generally do not form naturally. Where the services are provided through markets, it is mostly via managed (or quasi) markets, which are essentially defined by the fact that government is the source of much, if not all, of the purchasing power for the services.

The nature of the products, buyers, sellers, and the exchange sites in managed markets all differ from conventional markets (Bartlett and Le Grand 1993; Davidson 2009, 2012, 2015b). In particular, government has a more extensive role in a number of ways; non-profit and government providers are very prominent; rationing is common, with funding usually not sufficient to fully cater for the needs of all people eligible to receive services; prices, output, and the market share of providers are often determined by government agencies; and competition is more likely to be focused on quality and equity rather than price.

There are many possible forms of managed markets (Davidson 2012) and the decision as to the form of market is one of the major threshold questions for governments in determining how to marketize each service. The nature and impact of each human service market is unique, varying according to the type of service, the location (including history and institutions),[5] and the form of managed market used. In turn, the impact of marketization on services will be case-specific in many respects.

The issues arising from the distinctive characteristics of human services are not a function of markets per se and can exist regardless of marketization, including in situations where there is only a government monopoly provider. However the use of markets to provide the services can exacerbate the potential for problems arising from these issues, given the commercial pressures on all providers to survive in a competitive environment and the greater presence of profit-maximizing providers. In addition, markets create additional problems for researchers, generating a diversity of possible market forms, each of which has its own effects, and a diversity of providers. I now turn to considering how the impact of markets on human services may be examined in the light of these distinctive features of human services and managed markets.

## 19.3   THEORETICAL AND ANALYTICAL FRAMEWORKS

A central goal of the research was to examine marketization on its own terms as far as possible, and to study human service markets on the same basis as markets in other industries, while taking into account the reality of human services as a different form of product.

**Industrial Organization Theory**

The study of markets and their impact on the decisions and actions of firms in the broader economy is the domain of industrial organization theory.[6] Carlton and Perloff (2005, pp. 2–6) point to two broad approaches within this field. One uses structure–conduct–performance (SCP) models (Mason 1949; Bain 1959), which are based on the principle that the basic conditions of demand and production for a product generate the distinctive structure of the markets and industry for that product. This then drives the conduct of firms, and in turn determines the overall performance of firms and the industry. Government policy can influence, and be influenced by, all stages of this process. Later models have incorporated the complexity and endogeneity of markets with feedback loops between the various stages (Carlton and Perloff 2005, pp. 268–74). Figure 19.1 is an example of a standard SCP model, which shows the major aspects of an industry for which data needs to be collected in empirical studies.

While SCP models can be used to systematically identify and structure the collection and organization of data about an industry and its markets, they are primarily descriptive and in general do not contain an explanation of the links between the various stages. Hence, a second broad approach emerged that utilizes theories that seek to explain the structure and conduct of an industry and the behavior of suppliers 'as the outcome of individuals maximizing behavior' (Carlton and Perloff 2005). One such theory is 'contestable market analysis' (contestability) (Baumol 1982; Baumol et al. 1982).[7]

The concept of contestability as it has been used to justify the marketization of human services is somewhat different from the formal theory of contestable markets developed by Baumol and colleagues in the 1980s.[8] However, the basic principle remains intact, namely the belief that incumbent service providers (and especially monopolies) have little incentive to improve their products or efficiency unless they are continually subject to the possibility of new entrants that may take over part or all of their business. As well, contestability is a precondition for competition between suppliers, and for consumers to have a choice of providers, both of which are argued to generate further incentives for providers to improve their products and efficiency (Bartlett and Le Grand 1993; Le Grand 2007). An empirical study of contestability essentially involves identifying the barriers to entry and competition that exist, and then tracing through their impact on providers and on the structure, conduct, and performance of markets and the broader industry.

**A Heterodox Approach**

The value and major features of heterodox economics have been outlined in earlier chapters in this *Handbook*. Clearly such an approach is necessary for industry studies in general, given the structural and information 'imperfections' of most markets, the multiplicity of factors driving behaviour and outcomes in markets, the potential significance of history and politics, the importance of the particular circumstances in each situation, and the need for a range of government policies to optimize the outcomes of markets.

While there are many industry studies based on orthodox economic theory (Stigler 1968), a heterodox perspective is substantially incorporated within the theory and practice of industrial organization. Figure 19.1 shows a recognition of the complexity of markets and industries, while historically research in the field has centred on imperfect

**Basic Conditions**

*Consumer Demand*
Elasticity of demand
Substitutes
Seasonality
Rate of growth
Location
Lumpiness of orders
Method of purchase

*Production*
Technology
Raw materials
Unionization
Product durability
Location
Scale economies
Scope economies

**Structure**
Numbers of buyers and sellers
Barriers to entry of new firms
Product differentiation
Vertical integration
Diversification

**Government Policy**
Regulation
Antitrust
Barriers to entry
Taxes and subsidies
Investment incentives
Employment incentives
Macroeconomic policies

**Conduct**
Advertising
Research and development
Pricing behavior
Plant investment
Legal tactics
Product choice
Collusion
Merger and contracts

**Performance**
Price
Production efficiency
Allocative efficiency
Equity
Product quality
Technical progress
Profits

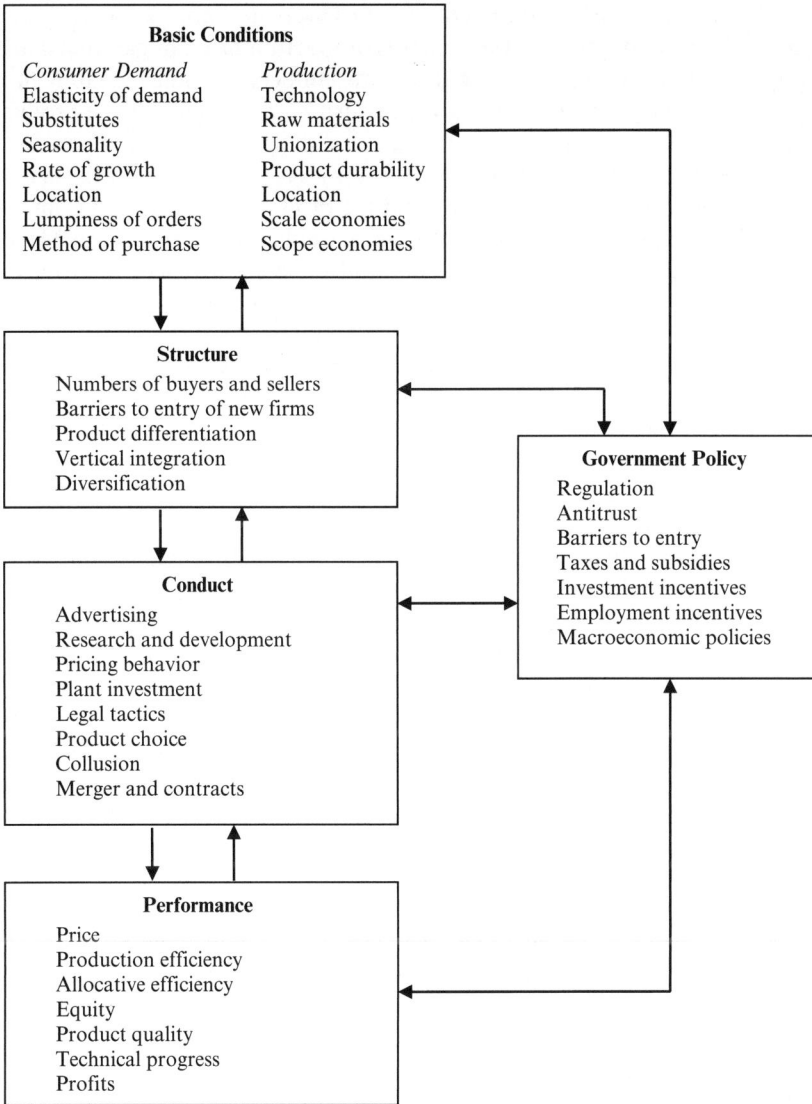

*Source:* Carlton and Perloff (2005, p. 4), with the addition of arrows back to government policy from other boxes.

*Figure 19.1   A standard structure–conduct–performance model*

competition and the behaviour of providers and government policy within that context (Schmalensee 1988). Empirical studies in the field have used a wide range of methodologies and methods (Schmalensee and Willig 1989 [2007], Chs 16–19).

However, it is also the case that empirical studies based on industrial organization theory commonly embody assumptions that are not consistent with the nature of human services and managed markets outlined earlier. These assumptions include a relative homogeneity of the products in a given market, production technologies that can be continually improved to enable greater output at lower unit cost, suppliers mainly motivated by economic gain, and rational well-informed consumers who pay for the products they use. Implicitly, it is also assumed that the inputs and the product are measurable.

With the advent of neoliberalism a new orthodoxy has developed over the last 30 years in relation to public and non-profit bodies and the production of the goods and services that they fund or supply. In the public sector, New Public Management (NPM) has been widely adopted. This is 'a cluster of . . . ideas and practices that seek . . . to use private sector and business approaches in the public sector . . . [not just as] business techniques . . . [but as a] normative model' (Denhardt and Denhardt 2007, pp. 12–13). While NPM is closely linked with marketization, it is also applied in non-market situations across all government functions (Lyons 1998; Denhardt and Denhardt 2007). Alongside this, there has been a similar movement in NPOs, as some, especially larger ones, have increasingly adopted business structures and managerial techniques (Lyons and Chan 1999; Dart 2004).

Both these developments rest on the assumption that the establishment of clearly defined performance indicators, the achievement of which is measurable or at least assessable by experts, will generate the incentives for public and NPO bodies, and the staff within them, to improve their performance in terms of the criteria outlined earlier. In particular, there has been a focus on increasing efficiency and 'value for money' from the resources they receive, while it is also assumed that the indicators and associated benchmarks can be measured or assessed in ways that accurately reflect what they claim to do. However, these approaches commonly focus on narrow objectives, assume a limited range of motivations among actors, and place excessive reliance on quantitative data to assess performance against the objectives. While they may acknowledge the distinctive features of human services, the prevalence and impact of those features is often understated, especially in regard to important, but unmeasured aspects.

Sarantakos (2002, p. 36) points out that 'The interest of critical theorists is to uncover . . . myths and illusions, to expose real structures and present reality as it is.' Reality, however, exists at a number of levels. There is a 'concrete observable' reality that can be agreed by all (such as the number of providers). Then there are the subjective realities that differ between individuals and organizations, depending on their particular circumstances and perceptions. Where incentives are concerned, often 'the perception is the reality', since each provider acts on its view of reality. Then there may also be a commonly accepted, but illusory, 'reality constructed by the powerful to serve their needs' (Sarantakos 2002, p. 36). Finally, critical realism seeks to identify the deeper underlying reality and 'generative mechanisms or structuring processes that cause things to occur as events' (Morgan, Chapter 1 in this *Handbook*).

If research about the marketization of human services is to capture all of these realities, it is necessary to move beyond the neoclassical, NPM, and standard industrial organization approaches and adopt a genuinely heterodox approach. In practice, such an approach in an empirical study of any industry will involve collecting much of the same data and examining many of the same issues as studies using these other approaches. But it involves much more, in particular ensuring that the study does not begin from narrow theoretical assumptions, but takes account of, and captures, the complexity of the drivers and outcomes of these markets and of service providers, as well as recognizing the limitations of quantitative data and the need for qualitative data in assessing the nature and impact of the markets.

**Analytical Framework**

In light of the above considerations, it was necessary to adapt both the basic SCP model and the concept of contestability to take account of the complex reality of human services and managed markets. Table 19.1 shows the analytical framework for studying contestability in human service industries that was subsequently developed. This was intended as a framework that can be used, at least as a starting point, for such studies across human services in general.

The framework enables the development of responses to questions at three levels. First, there are the key research questions for the empirical study which were: (1) What is the form and extent of contestability in the home care industry in NSW? and (2) How does contestability in the industry influence which types of organizations become the major service providers and the incentives for service providers to achieve the major objectives of home care services?[9] Second, there are questions, the responses to which require judgement by the researcher, such as: What are the barriers to entry and competition? What determines which providers and type of providers are most successful in winning funding? How do providers compete and what are the major incentives for providers? Third, to help answer those questions there are a host of specific questions that can be answered by 'concrete' observable 'facts', such as: What is the total cost of services to government? What are the formal rules and procedures within the funding programmes for selecting providers and allocating funds? Who are the major providers? Which providers and types of providers have the largest revenues and market shares, and has that changed over time?

## 19.4   THE EMPIRICAL STUDY

The framework set out in Table 19.1 provides the basis for a range of possible research strategies to study the impact of marketization on human services and service providers. It could, for example, support a study of the extent to which one or more objectives or outcomes were achieved, including examining a range of possible relationships between various determinants and those objectives. It could be used for a study of a particular market at a point of time, a comparison of a market at different times, or a comparison between different markets.

The focus of the study reported here, however, was on the *processes* by which marketization could affect services and service providers in one human service market over an eight-year period. The framework in Table 19.1 was not used in its entirety in the empirical study; the study established the determinants and structure of the market, with a particular focus on the state of contestability, and then sought to identify how these factors influenced the types of providers in the market and the incentives that they faced. It did not systematically examine the motivation and actual behaviour of providers in relation to the services or the outcomes of the services, nor did it formally consult service users.

*Table 19.1   Analytical framework for the study of contestability in human services markets*

| Stage | Factors in each stage |
| --- | --- |
| 1. Determinants of market structure | The service<br>● Service users<br>● Production process<br><br>The location<br>● Demand<br>  – Sources of demand: (a) needs of users; (b) payments by government, users<br>  – Changes in demand<br>● Supply: the providers<br>  – Attractions for entry<br>  – Numbers and types (by structural dimensions)<br>● The broader context<br>  – Government – relevant broader institutions, policy and programs<br>  – History<br>  – Other local factors (e.g., geography and demography) |
| 2. The market structure | Market segments – overview<br>● Structure of segments<br>● Links between segments (users, providers, government)<br><br>Individual market segments<br>● The services<br>● Demand – source, size of the segment<br>● Government – funding programs, regulation<br>● Market forms – managed market, nature of competition<br><br>Profile of providers (by industry and segment)<br>● Needs of users<br>● Market shares, including by type of provider<br>● Change in market shares over time<br>● Extent of entry, exit and growth by providers |
| 3. Contestability<br>  – For each segment and across segments | Contestability – source and extent of limits<br>● Production limits to provider entry and growth<br>● Government limits to provider entry and growth<br>● Extent of user choice of providers |
| 4. Incentives for providers<br>  – Affecting decisions re<br>  (a) entry and growth<br>  (b) capability and behaviour | From (1) to (3), identify incentives<br>● arising from various sources (e.g., production, government programs)<br>● in relation to key objectives of services (see [7] below).<br>● Variation by type of (a) market; (b) provider |
| 5. Behaviour (conduct) of providers | Five major aspects of the activities of an organization<br>● Organizational development<br>● Service development |

*Table 19.1*   (continued)

| Stage | Factors in each stage |
|---|---|
| 5. Behaviour (conduct) of providers | • Service delivery<br>• Other contributions (industry development, social capital)<br>• Business development |
| 6. Competition between providers | • Competitive strategies and actions<br>• Market power |
| 7. Outcomes (performance) of the industry/market<br> – for both clients and the broader public interest. | Objectives of services<br>• effectiveness (quality, responsiveness, diversity)<br>• equity (horizontal, vertical)<br>• efficiency (allocative, productive, dynamic)<br>• stability<br>• choice for service users<br>• accountability (to users and funders) |

Some restrictions were necessary because of time and other resource limits, and it was considered that a study centred on the state of contestability and the resulting incentives cut to the heart of the claim as to how marketization leads to better services.

A further dimension to the heterodox approach was that while an important focus was on contestability, it was not assumed or hypothesized that contestability (or any other theoretical construct) was the major determinant of the structure and conduct of the markets and providers. Rather, data were obtained about the range of relevant factors, and then examined with a critical eye to see how relevant contestability had been in driving the structure of the industry and the conduct of providers, as one of a number of possible explanators. Thus the emphasis was on 'discovery and exploration rather than on hypothesis testing' (Sarantakos 2002, p. 53).

**Home Care in New South Wales**

The specific subject of the empirical study was paid home care for older people in NSW. Home care comprises various types of assistance for people who have some level of physical or mental incapacity, in order that they can continue to live in their own homes.[10] This subject was chosen for a number of reasons, including: the nature of the service as a good exemplar of human services; its social, economic, and policy significance given the ageing population; the variety of providers and market forms in the industry; and the lack of previous research on the sector in Australia from an economic perspective. The study was specific to NSW, although in many respects NSW reflects the situation in other states, while it is also a major part of the overall national picture, being the most populous Australian state with around one-third of the total national population and one-third of national home care funding and clients (SCRGSP 2011).

A popular image of home care is that it is a cottage industry, but with the ageing of the population and an increasing focus by service users and government policy on supporting older people to remain at home as long as possible ('ageing-in-place'), home care has become a substantial industry internationally, projected to have significant growth in future decades (Productivity Commission 2008). The large majority of services in Australia in 2009–10 were funded by two programmes, which were the main focus of the study. In theory, the two programmes formed a continuum of care, with the Home and Community Care programme (HACC) assisting people with low-level needs, and the Department of Health and Ageing (DoHA) Packages assisting people with a higher level of need equivalent to people in nursing homes. Alongside those two programmes, there were also a range of other market segments for home care based on smaller government programmes (for example, for veterans), guardianship and insurance arrangements, subcontracting from funded services, and unsubsidized services. An account of the past, present, and possible future of the industry is in Davidson (2015a).

## Methodology

The methodology for the study was shaped by two core elements: a case study approach, and the use of mixed research methods (see Chapter 15 in this *Handbook*).

### A case study
Yin (2003, p.1) notes that 'in general, case studies are the preferred strategy when "how" or "why" questions are being posed, when the investigator has little control over events and when the focus is on a contemporary phenomenon within some real-life context'. These conditions were very relevant to this study. At the same time, a major limitation of case studies is that the findings may only apply to the specific circumstances of the case study, although as Yin (2003, p. 37) notes, the value of case studies is more in their 'analytical generalizability' to a broader theory rather than the 'statistical generalizability' of specific findings.

This was a case study of human service *markets*, not of providers per se. In effect, it also represents a set of 'nested' case studies (or what I have termed a '*matryoshka*' model).[11] Within the broader case study, the major focus was on the submarkets for care-staff services funded by the two major programmes in two diverse regions.[12] Within those boundaries, there was a sample of providers; and then the people interviewed were restricted to the key decision-makers in those providers and the two funding agencies.

A threshold issue was the number of service providers in the market to include in the sample. An in-depth ethnographic study of only one or two providers would have given rich data on the motivations, perceptions, and actions of those providers, but would have limited the pursuit of an important goal of the study, namely to identify the diversity of the structure, experiences, and responses of providers in human services markets. It was decided to aim for around 20 providers, to allow for some detail about each provider, while enabling inclusion of the range of the types of providers in the industry in terms of five key structural dimensions, namely: ownership, scale, service scope, geographical spread, and longevity.

The actual sample of providers was determined in two major steps. An initial group, chosen on the basis of being the largest providers (by revenue) in the two programmes in the two regions, was then supplemented by purposive sampling (Patton 1990, pp. 182–3) and snowballing sampling techniques (Sarantakos 2002, pp. 153–4). While it was essential to ensure a heterogeneous set of organizations that represented a cross-section of providers with a significant share of the market, it was not an imperative to obtain a rigorously stratified sample across the key structural dimensions.

With regard to the individual interviewees, organizations are complex organisms involving multiple (and often competing) individuals. Given that the aim of the study was to identify strategic factors driving the decisions of buyers and providers in a competitive environment, it was important that the individuals interviewed were the most senior people in each organization or region directly responsible for home care who made or recommended the key strategic decisions concerning this service. Thus, virtually all interviewees were either a principal of the organization (board member, owner of an FPO, chief executive officer) or, in larger organizations, a senior manager.

## Mixed research methods

A key theme of this *Handbook* is the importance of using more than one method for good research. Each method has its own purposes and strengths and can provide a unique perspective on the situation being studied; thus different aspects are revealed that can give a more complete picture of the subject being studied. At the same time, a range of methods enables triangulation to 'corroborate, elaborate and illuminate' (Stake 2004) where there is uncertainty about data.

In this research, quantitative data were able to establish important facts about the development and current structure of the industry, the key market segments, and the providers. However quantitative data were unable to reveal or explain some important factors at the heart of the research questions, many of which are inherently not measurable, such as what represents good services, the historical development of the industry, providers' perceptions of and reaction to incentives, and how decisions are made by both buyers and providers. And they do not begin to explain why providers acted as they did.

Thus qualitative methods, which are 'concerned primarily with *process*' and are 'interested in *meaning*' (Merriam 1988, pp. 19–20) were needed. In addition, there were a range of perspectives and values held by different providers in a situation that is inherently political, and thus the study required qualitative research, which is cross-disciplinary and where '[no] discourse has a privileged place' (Richardson 1991, p. 173).

## Data collection and analysis

Five methods were used to obtain data: document analysis, the analysis of funding data, interviews, two forums of providers, and participant observation. Documents produced by government agencies, providers, and previous research were important in providing data on key aspects of the industry. These included the policy, provisions, and procedures for the funding programmes, which embody the formal rules of the market; 'grey literature' produced by government agencies reporting on the programmes; research on home care; and documents produced by providers.[13]

Detailed funding data for the two programmes that support the large majority of the home care industry in NSW (HACC and the Packages) was obtained in Excel format from the two funding agencies for each year over an eight year period from 2002–03 to 2009–10. Most of these data were not publicly available and were provided on request. The data provided were then used to develop a single database which showed every allocation of funding by the amount, location, type of service, and the name and form of ownership of the provider. In 2009–10, for example, in NSW there were 603 providers receiving 2614 separate allocations of funding. The database gave a unique insight into the structure of the market segments based on the two programmes and their development over nearly a decade. Importantly, it showed – at a level of granularity not available from public data or from the data held by either funding agency – the empirical outcomes of contestability and competition, which providers and which types of providers had been most successful in the marketized environment, and how this had changed over time (for example, in terms of the scale and market share of each one, by type of provider).

Interviews were held with senior representatives of government funding agencies, service providers, and other industry bodies. There were 43 separate interviews attended by 50 people representing a total of 34 organizations, including 22 service providers. A number of the interviewees had also previously held other positions in the industry, each one of which would have made them of interest as a potential interviewee.[14] The interviews were critical in understanding how the markets actually work in practice, why certain providers have been more successful, and how and why providers had developed their services as they did. Moreover, there were issues and data well known in the industry but not recorded elsewhere, data in documents that needed clarification, and a need to probe the reality behind the public relations gloss in some documents. The interviews followed a semi-structured format (Patton 1990, p. 286) based around five core questions, with different planned probes depending on the category of interviewee.[15]

There were a number of issues in relation to these interviews of more general interest for heterodox methodology. First, it was organizations rather than the individual people that were the focus of interest. While the usual principles and techniques for interviewing individuals remain relevant (Patton 1998, pp. 309–34; Blumer 1969; Sarantakos 2002), there are additional complexities. With large providers, each interviewee represents only one part of a complex organism, regardless of their position in the organization. There are almost certainly other experiences and views about the organization. On the other hand, there are generally data already available about an organization, including in writing, and this can enable the interviewer to move onto key issues more quickly, as well as providing a basis for triangulating what is said in interviews. However this public availability of information also imposes constraints in writing up findings, in that if code names or pseudonyms are used, references to some aspects of the organization can inadvertently provide a key to identifying the source of some quotation or idea.

Second, there are significant limits as to what interviews can reveal about the motivations, incentives, and actions of a provider. There are obvious incentives for interviewees to hide this information, to obfuscate, to answer 'strategically', and even to prevaricate, especially where there is a tension between social and commercial objectives. As Arrow (1963, p. 147) noted in relation to medical practitioners, they 'cannot act, or at least appear to act, as if [they are] maximizing [their] income at every moment of time . . . [Each] avoids the obvious stigmata of profit-maximizing [since] . . . [t]he very word, "profit," is a signal that denies the trust relations [essential to their services]'. Patton (1990, p. 278) says that an important purpose of interviews is to enable a researcher 'to enter another's experience' and 'to find out what is in and on someone else's mind'. But what if they actively avoid revealing this?

In such a situation, what can be done to help get closer to the truth? Preparation is important. Prior study of the existing information about an organization and the interviewee enables a richer dialogue to develop, is likely to encourage fuller responses, and means that inconsistencies can, to some extent at least, be dealt with in the interview. However the concept of the reflexivity of the researcher is also important here since one must be conscious that such preparation may condition one to a preconceived view of what the interviewee is saying (Watt 2007).

On the one hand, it is important to establish rapport with an interviewee, to show that you understand their worldview, and to enable them to freely express views without judgement in an unthreatening environment. This will often be more revealing than if a more interrogative style is used, where each problematic and contentious point is challenged along the way. On the other hand, in this research, while many participants were very open about the problems and competing pressures they faced, some saw it as a public relations opportunity and sought to present a 'Pangloss' version of events. The research would lack credibility, let alone validity, if there was no effort to get behind that façade. In general, it is best to begin with a more empathetic approach, changing to the more interrogative style later if needed. Where possible, it is desirable to have at least two interviews with each person. The first one can establish rapport and enable the participant to freely express their views without judgement. The second can then be conducted on the basis of checking understandings from the initial interview, enabling earlier statements and views of the participant to be questioned.

Third, there was an ethical issue that is inevitably present in any interviews regarding competition. In examining the operation of a market and the behaviour of players in the market, it is a reasonable, and indeed essential, element to identify each player's perception of their competitors. In this context, however, it would not have been ethical to interview providers and then be collecting tales about them in other interviews, while it was also likely that some interviewees would not consider it a legitimate line of questioning, and/or be concerned as to how their views were reported and identified. Hence, it was important to emphasize that the aim was to obtain information about generic issues, processes, and actions, not individual providers or people. In truth, however, it must be acknowledged that where names were forthcoming, it often represented very valuable input.

A minor source of data was participant observation arising from my membership of the board of a small community-based provider for most of the period of the research. The provider was one of the 22 sample providers. This enabled first hand-observation of the operation of a small provider, especially in terms of its decision-making processes, its interactions with other bodies, its participation in one of the regular quality reviews of providers by one funding agency, and its management of a merger involving the absorption of another small provider. In addition, a forum with about 20 service providers was held in each of the two sample regions. While somewhat large for a focus group, these forums were conducted along the lines of such a group (Greenbaum 1998; Morgan 1998), with the major themes of the discussion the same as those of the interviews. These provided one of the key benefits of focus groups, namely, 'the explicit use of the group interaction to produce data and insights that would be less accessible without the interaction found in the group' (Morgan 1998, p. 12).

The data were collected in three major stages. First, it was necessary to gain an understanding of the overall structure and major features of the industry, and the key issues for the major stakeholders. To some extent this could be done from documents, but it was also necessary to interview experienced industry figures (for example, from peak bodies).

In part, these initial interviews were similar to a Delphi process (Linstone and Turoff 1975; UNIDO 2005) in that they involved identifying and drawing together the views held by key figures in the industry, but as this was simply an exploratory phase to develop the researcher's knowledge of the industry, the later stages of a formal Delphi process of iteratively moving to an agreed basis for future action were not followed.

The second stage sought to draw together and develop existing evidence about the industry and the sample providers. This largely involved analysis of the documents and funding data. The third stage was a more intensive study of the actual operation of the market and providers, especially through the interviews with senior representatives of the funding agencies and a sample of providers.

In practice, the plan for the three stages was broadly followed, although to some extent the actual process was iterative and not within three clear stages as set out above, given the initial unavailability of some participants and the continual emergence of new data about the industry structure in the later interviews with providers.

**Analysis of Data**

There was little that was exceptional about the methods used to analyse data from the above sources. With the funding data, the techniques available within Excel (such as pivot tables) were able to provide a wealth of data about the entry, growth, and exit of providers, and the various relationships between funding allocations and the five key structural dimensions of providers.

A thematic analysis approach (Bernard and Ryan 2010) was the major technique used for the qualitative data from interviews and documents. Two other aspects of the analysis were particularly important. On the one hand, there was a detailed micro-level analysis of processes which were central to home care. These included the implications of each aspect of the production process for generating barriers to entry, the funding systems and their various potential impacts on providers especially in relation to incentives as to how to deliver its services, and the ways in which incumbents were able to utilize their market power. Alongside this, there was a broader systems perspective in the consideration of all data, in order to identify the various interrelationships and interdependencies that in practice drive the ways in which the industry and its markets operate. Another key element was to identify not just the more common experience and approaches by providers, but also the outliers, which are particularly important in showing the diversity within the system. This was particularly important in relation to those NPOs that had either rejected marketization or moved to a much more commercial approach. The following section further considers the analysis of data in regard to key concepts.

## 19.5   EXAMINING KEY CONCEPTS IN HUMAN SERVICES MARKETS

This section illustrates how various methods are used to examine key concepts in the marketization of human services, using home care as an example, although much of what follows is very relevant across human services. First, there are concepts that were the main focus of the study of home care in NSW (the determinants, structure, and operation of the market, and the incentives faced by providers). Second, there are further concepts that could be investigated by additional methods not used in that study (the motivations of providers and the actual services). Finally, there is a discussion of the potential for ethnographic studies of individual providers that can draw together a number of these methods.

## The Determinants, Structure, and Operation of the Market

A premise of the research was that the distinctive features of human services and managed markets create additional complexities and demands upon methodology when compared with studies of markets for other types of products. In a number of respects, however, this was not the case, and in some ways the task was less complex. In general, using the five methods above, it was no more difficult to establish the determinants, structure, and operation of the markets; the potential drivers of provider behaviour; the profile of the type of providers by each of the key structural dimensions; and the state of contestability.

In large part this derives from the fact that government is the major source of purchasing power. This means that there is usually more data, which is more precise and more easily available than for most conventional markets. For example, there will generally be a statement of the formal 'rules' of the market via policy and procedures for funding programs; as well as funding data, disaggregated by provider, region, type of service, and so on. The 'power of the purse' also gives government agencies the capacity to collect other data (for example, about unmet demand) and publicly report on this.

## Incentives for Service Providers

The incentives for providers in a market essentially derive from the market environment (as a function primarily of the type of service, the location, and the form of market in place), but they also vary by provider depending on the structural dimensions and the motivations of each provider.[16] For example, large and small providers may have different incentives in the same market. Less stringent regulation may be seen by some providers as enabling them to be more flexible and responsive to the needs of each client, but be seen by others as an opportunity to cut costs and reduce the quality of services without being detected. While the market environment and the structural dimensions of each provider are generally observable and measurable to a large extent, determining the motivation(s) of each provider is more complex, as discussed later.

Three major means were used to identify the incentives for providers in the NSW home care market. First, the potential incentives were in part identified through interviews and documents, but it also required a rigorous a priori analysis of the market environment, using systems and process analyses to identify the possible responses of providers to the environment, given the range of possible motivations. Orthodox economic theory may be quite misleading. For example, it would predict that very limited contestability will lead to complacency among incumbents, and hence lower quality and efficiency; but alternatively the greater certainty could encourage some incumbents to invest more in improving their services (Graham and Lawrence 1996). It is important that potential incentives identified are not imputed to any provider without further evidence; at this point, the analysis simply gives a checklist of possible actions of which to be aware.

Second, there were the stated incentives of each provider which were obtained from its public statements and documents, and from interviews with key decision-makers. However, as with motivation, providers may have incentives not to reveal the full range of the actual incentives they face. Third, the behaviour of providers, in relation to both their commercial actions in the market and the services they provide, can both reveal incentives that may not have been evident from an a priori analysis and show what in practice are the most powerful incentives. A further method to identify incentives, not used in this study, would be a full Delphi process with leading industry figures, both to identify incentives and to obtain more robust conclusions.

In seeking to identify the importance of particular incentives there are some further complexities that can confound the interpretation of evidence. It may not be possible to identify the specific impact of one incentive or the particular incentive(s) leading to an action, amongst the many potential ones that can drive the actions of providers; the incentives for any provider may change over time as a result of changes in the industry or the provider; and in some cases, providers may not even be fully aware of the incentives to which they are responding.

**The Motivation of Service Providers**

Orthodox economic theory assumes that all firms are profit-maximizers (or motivated by some other personal gain target such as total sales, revenue, or growth) and that the most effective incentives for providers to improve their products are based on this. However this can paint an overly simplistic picture even for conventional markets (Davidson 2009), and the motivations of providers in a social market are even more complex.

Drawing on Wistow et al. (1996), four broad motivations for providers in human service markets were identified – economic gain, independence, professional fulfillment, and social altruism – all of which may play a role with any given provider, but the mix of which can differ significantly between providers. All providers face tensions and complementarities between their social and commercial objectives. All must have at least one eye to efficiency and financial sustainability, but they all must also ensure at least some minimum quality of services if they are to win funding and clients.

Establishing the motivation of a specific provider is difficult, and ultimately undeterminable in many cases. The methods used to identify incentives can also be applied here, but as noted earlier, human services providers may have strong incentives to conceal their real motivation, especially if they are mainly driven by economic gain. As well, social maximizers may conceal their true motivation if, for example, they disagree with the policy directions of funding agencies. It may also be that the behaviour of a provider under severe commercial pressure may not reflect its main motivation, where it has to sacrifice social benefits in order to survive financially.

Two other methods that have been used to identify motivations in home care in the UK are a questionnaire that directly asks providers about their motivations in various situations (Kendall et al. 2003; Matosevic et al. 2007; Matosevic et al. 2008), and estimation of the extent to which providers have taken advantage of their market power in the prices they set (Forder et al. 2004). The results of the various studies suggest that these methods can be valid to some extent.

## The Services

As outlined earlier, the empirical study did not seek to establish how good the services actually were in terms of the various objectives, but simply to identify the types of providers that were in these markets and the incentives they faced in relation to achieving the objectives. Nevertheless, the study revealed a significant amount of data about the actual services from statements by providers (in both interviews and documents) about the way in which they developed and delivered services, and from independent documented assessments by funding and regulatory agencies of both individual providers and the overall system. These showed a generally positive situation, but (other than informally) they were not confirmed by direct observation of the services.

In order to extend the study to make an assessment of the actual services, additional methods are required. Ethnographic studies of some providers may be possible (see below) but this is not feasible beyond a very small number of providers. Observation of some service sessions of a number of providers can give some useful data, but some of the larger home care providers admitted that the quality of services across the organization was uneven and very dependent on the local managers. Hence, the quality of services across a system generally has to be assessed by a range of less direct means. This could include a survey of the extent to which the various structures and processes for service development and delivery have been put in place, which will help point, for example, to whether measured increases in efficiency are genuine improvements. The collection of detailed cost and price data from each provider is important.

There can also be interviews or surveys of clients, concerning the processes of the services and/or the impact on their lives, although there is evidence that service users and their families tend to overestimate the quality of the services they are receiving or paying for (Press and Woodrow 2005, p. 282). A more controversial approach to capture the perspective of the client – and one being used by some providers for quality assurance – is the use of the 'mystery shopper', essentially an 'undercover' person purporting to require care. Finally, one may try to assess the outcomes of care for users, in terms of whether the services have helped them to maintain or extend their capacities and the activities they can do independently. In home care, this can be by way of an examination by a nurse or other professional; by a review of regular reports by care-workers; and by interviews with the users, their family, associates, and service providers.

## Ethnographic Studies

The study of home care in NSW was essentially a study of a market and service system, rather than of individual service providers. Nevertheless, it relied substantially on evidence from and about providers, but the evidence about the motivation, behaviour, and impact of each provider was necessarily qualified by limits on the capacity to observe the organization and its services in action.

An organizational (or institutional) ethnographic study of a provider can give a more accurate and in-depth knowledge of the motivation and behaviour of a provider. It is essentially a sociological approach involving close and ongoing observation over a period of time of the operation of the organization and its services (Basole and Ramnarain, Chapter 7 in this *Handbook*; Smith 2005; Braithwaite et al. 2007). In the context of this research, an ethnographic study will particularly focus on what happens in the service sessions, on the other support functions of the organization, on the day-to-day decision-making at all levels, and on the relationship of the organization with its service users, their families and other organizations. It can involve 'fly-on-the-wall' techniques, as well as participant observation where the researcher undertakes tasks that contribute to the functioning of the organization and its services.

It will also involve a more intensive use of each of the methods and sources of data used in the study of NSW home care. This would include more extensive and intensive interviews, including ongoing discussions with participants at all levels of the organization and with key external bodies; and access to more documents and data, including material that is confidential to the organization on matters such as directions about and assessments of the production process, data on staff, and data about users. The critical difference with an ethnographic study, however, is the greater access for researchers and their continuing presence, enabling a view of the provider as it actually behaves behind its public façade. This produces new primary data, as well as enabling a more forensic approach with existing data.

However, there are obvious limits to the value of an ethnographic study. First, its value is dependent on the level of access granted to the researcher, and it is likely that the providers representing the greatest potential problems in terms of opportunism or poor practice will be those least likely to grant access. Second, it is very time- and resource-intensive, and hence only possible with a small number of providers. Thus, it is unlikely to reveal the diversity of providers and service practice across a market or service system, although it can reveal issues and demands that a system creates for all providers, even if the response of each provider may differ significantly. Third, the presence of the researcher can affect the behaviour of participants. In turn, overcoming that effect is likely to require a greater commitment of time by a researcher so that they can become 'part of the furniture'.

## 19.6   THE FINDINGS

The key finding of the theoretical part of the research was that some level of contestability and competition in the provision of human services can have positive effects, but that there is an intrinsic and unavoidable need for some limits on these elements in markets for human services, given their distinctive features, and the resulting imperatives on government to protect vulnerable people and to make the best use of public funds. Accordingly, there is likely to be an 'optimum contestability' in these markets, a point beyond which greater contestability will reduce the benefits from the services for both individual users and the wider society.

The picture that emerged from the empirical study indicated that the warnings of both sides in the debate over marketization and contestability had not yet come to pass in the home care industry in NSW. On the one hand, for those concerned about the potential negative effects of marketization, the study revealed an industry where there were very few barriers to initial entry for a new provider via the unsubsidized and subcontracting segments of the market, but very strong limits to contestability in the two government-funded programmes that represented the large majority of the industry, with limits in terms of who could compete, what they could compete for, and how they could compete. Moreover, the processes and criteria used to allocate funding meant that competition was strongly focused on who provided the best services rather than on price and cutting costs. The limits on contestability also meant that there was a major focus on the stability and continuity of services, with incumbents having significant advantages in competition. As a result, there has not been a major influx of for-profit providers, nor the demise of small community-based providers.[17]

On the other hand, for the proponents of marketization, there was evidence of vigorous competition between incumbents, and some entry of new providers despite the tight limits on contestability. Less than 10 per cent of total funding was contestable at any one time, but the competition at the margin generated action by providers to improve all of their services. The system thus had some strong incentives for providers to improve the quality and efficiency of their services.

The complexity of the industry makes it difficult to be conclusive about causal links and the extent to which the limited contestability may have contributed to the broadly positive outlook noted above, but it had not prevented it, and there were clear mechanisms showing how the limits on contestability could contribute to this outcome.

Thus the evidence from the empirical study supported the theoretical analysis, in indicating that contestability implemented in a limited and strategic way can generate a competitive market and have positive effects on services, without destabilizing or unduly compromising the quality of services. In particular, there need to be tight limits on who can be a provider and on the total number of providers, with competition based on quality rather than price.

These findings represent a more nuanced position than commonly emerges from the polarized research and debate about marketization. This reflects the benefits of a heterodox approach that is centred on the economic processes but does not impose a theoretical straightjacket; that seeks to identify and explain actual behaviour of providers and the why and how of processes in the market; and that understands the limits of quantitative data methods and the need for qualitative data and methods. The findings also reinforced the key messages of heterodox economics. This can be seen, for example, in the range and diversity of drivers and outcomes in human services markets; the importance of history and politics; the specificity of each case, with its unique configuration of factors producing unique outcomes; the diversity of providers in terms of structural dimensions, motivations, and their responses to marketization; and the lack of any clear-cut 'correct' policy responses.

## 19.7   CONCLUSION

A major focus of this chapter has been to demonstrate how the distinctive features of human services influence the methodology and methods that need to be used in research about these services. On the one hand, in some respects studying a human services industry is no more complex than studying other industries. On the other hand, it is more complex to establish the reality about a number of other key aspects such as the motivation of providers, how services are actually delivered, and the impact of services on users.

This chapter has shown the importance of a heterodox approach to research in this field. A range of research methods were used in the empirical study of home care in NSW and other methods to extend that study have been outlined. All methods and data sources have their limits and no single method or data source can give a complete picture of human service markets. Thus, mixed research methods drawing on a range of types and sources of data, are essential.

Ultimately, the limitations of measurability and observability, coupled with the other distinctive features of human services, mean that it is unlikely that research in this field can ever be conclusive about whether marketization leads to better or worse home care services, as judged against the objectives of quality, responsiveness, equity, and efficiency. Nevertheless, there are methods, including those used in the study of home care in NSW, that enable researchers to go a long way in obtaining knowledge and insights that can inform the design and management of markets for human services.

The findings from the study show how methodology itself can have important policy implications. From the viewpoint of funding and regulatory agencies, the findings reinforce the point made by Williamson (2000, p. 599) that 'all complex contracts are unavoidably incomplete', given that in such cases, some asymmetries of information inevitably remain. In a large human services system with many providers, there are no methods that can fully establish the reality of how services are delivered or their impact on users, either *ex ante* as to what providers are likely to do with their services, or *ex post* as to what they have done. In light of this, there are strong arguments for limiting the number of funded providers, since this can reduce the likelihood of opportunist or poor providers gaining entry, while giving funding and regulatory agencies a much better chance of monitoring the services of a smaller number of funded providers.

## NOTES

1. 'Human services' encompass a diverse range of activities that contribute to the basic physical, mental, and social welfare and development of people. This includes education, health, child care, aged care, disability care, support for at-risk families, homelessness programmes, and assistance for unemployed people.
2. During the period covered by the research, this service was known in Australia as 'community aged care'. However, since 2012 the more internationally used term, 'home care', has been used by governments.
3. Nevile's comment was actually directed at economic rationalism in general, but it is relevant to this narrower case.
4. For further discussion of the distinctive features of human services, see Arrow (1963), Eriksen (1977), Hasenfeld (1992), and Zins (2001).
5. The term 'location' in this context may refer to groups of nations (Esping-Andersen 1990), individual nations, states and provinces, communities, and even differences within communities.
6. Industrial organization has been defined as 'the broad field within microeconomics that focuses on business behaviour and its implications both for market structures and processes, and for public policies toward them' (Schmalensee and Willig, 1989 [2007], p. xi); or simply, 'the study of the structure of firms and markets and their interactions' (Carlton and Perloff 2005, p. 782).
7. Other major theories used in this way include transaction cost analysis (Coase 1937; Williamson 1998) and game theory (von Neumann and Morgenstern 1944).
8. The theory of contestable markets argues that many sellers are not a necessary condition for competitive efficiency, but that it can be achieved providing there are zero costs of entry and exit for suppliers ('perfect contestability'). In turn, it is argued that potential competition can be as powerful as actual competition. This theory has been subject to extensive criticism on theoretical and empirical grounds, especially because

of the unreality of the notion of 'perfect contestability'. There are almost always some entry or exit costs while incumbents are also able to exercise market power within the market (Shepherd 1984, 1990, 1995; Schwartz 1986). In practice, however, a market is generally considered 'contestable' if there are no insurmountable barriers to prevent at least one competitor from challenging for the business of another, even if there may still be some barriers to entry, exit, or competition. Government industry and competition policies are generally aimed at reducing barriers to entry as far as possible, rather than pretending that they can be eliminated. There is then a further shift in the use of the term in relation to human services, where a major objective has been to use contestability to enhance the quality and responsiveness of services, as well as efficiency.

9. It is important to note that the questions did not imply causality flowing only one way. Providers can both respond to, and shape, contestability in any market.

10. Various forms of assistance can be obtained, depending on the needs of each individual. The large majority of services in NSW in 2009–10 (around 85 per cent of funding) were 'care-staff services' that required a care-worker or nurse, including personal care (such as assistance with bathing), nursing care, domestic assistance, respite care for informal carers, social support, and case management. The other services were allied health services (such as physiotherapy or podiatry) or conventional consumer services provided at little or no cost to users (such as home maintenance, transport, and meals).

11. A *matryoshka* is a Russian nesting doll, consisting of dolls of decreasing size placed one inside another.

12. The two regions were selected because the proportion of older people in both was broadly similar to Australia overall, but they were very distinct in terms of population density and remoteness. One adjoins the Sydney central business district (CBD) and is the most urbanized region in NSW; the other is the least urbanized and most remote region in NSW.

13. One factor not planned for at the beginning, but which proved to be a valuable catalyst for and source of documents and data about the industry and providers, was the (national) Productivity Commission's Inquiry into Caring for Older People (Productivity Commission 2011) which was announced and completed during the course of this study.

14. An audio-recording was made of each interview and a verbatim transcript prepared. The length of the recorded interviews ranged from 35 to 100 minutes, with a mean time of around one hour. Multiple interviews were held with some organizations, including six providers that operated in both sample regions. The total number of 'positions of interest for the study' among the 50 people who were present in the 43 interviews was 65. Thus, for example, one provider chief executive officer (CEO) had also been a senior government official and peak-body CEO, while another had both worked for funding agencies and with a number of providers as a consultant.

15. The five core questions concerned: (a) the factors that make for a good home care service provider; (b) how competition takes place in the industry and how providers compete; (c) the impact of contestability and competition on individual providers; (d) the impact of contestability and competition on the overall industry; and (e) the implications for service providers of future changes to markets in the industry.

16. There is an important distinction between an 'incentive', which is a financial, moral, or coercive inducement or incitement to act, or refrain from acting, in a certain way; and 'motivation', which includes incentives but also includes more deep-seated factors that drive behavior, regardless of specific incentives in a given situation. Incentives may reinforce motivations, create them, reduce them, or be irrelevant in their impact on motivation (Frey 1997; Laffont and Martimort 2002; Kendall et al. 2003).

17. In the final year for which data were obtained (2009–10), 95 per cent of funds in both programmes went to NPO and government providers, with some 25 per cent of total funds going to small community-based NPO providers. There had been relatively little change in either of these measures since 2002–03.

# REFERENCES

Akerlof, George A. (1970), 'The market for "lemons": quality uncertainty and the market mechanism', *Quarterly Journal of Economics*, **84** (3), 488–500.

Althaus, C. (1997), 'The application of agency theory to public sector management', in G. Davis, B. Sullivan, and A. Yeatman (eds), *The New Contractualism?*, South Melbourne: Macmillan Education, pp. 137–54.

Arrow, Kenneth (1963), 'Uncertainty and the welfare economics of medical care', *American Economic Review*, **53** (5), 941–73.

Bain, Joe S. (1959), *Industrial Organization*, New York: John Wiley & Sons.

Bartlett, Will and Julian Le Grand (1993), 'The theory of quasi-markets', in Julian Le Grand and Will Bartlett (eds), *Quasi Markets and Social Policy*, London: Macmillan, pp. 13–34.

Baumol, W.J. (1967), 'Macroeconomics of unbalanced growth: the anatomy of urban crisis', *American Economic Review*, **57** (3), 415–26.
Baumol, W.J. (1982), 'Contestable markets: an uprising in the theory of industrial structure', *American Economic Review*, **72** (1), 1–15.
Baumol, W.J., J.C. Panzar, and R.D. Willig (1982), *Contestable Markets and the Theory of Industry Structure*, San Diego, CA: Harcourt Brace Jovanovich.
Bernard, R. and G. Ryan (2010), *Analyzing Qualitative Data: Systematic Approaches*, Beverly Hills, CA: Sage.
Blumer, H. (1969), *Symbolic Interactionism: Perspectives and Method*, Englewood Cliffs, NJ: Prentice-Hall.
Boston, J. (1991), 'The theoretical underpinnings of public sector restructuring in New Zealand', in J. Boston, J. Martin, J. Pallot, and P. Walsh (eds), *Reshaping the State: New Zealand's Bureaucratic Revolution*, Auckland: Oxford University Press, pp. 1–26.
Braithwaite, J., T. Makkai, and V.A. Braithwaite (2007), *Regulating Aged Care: Ritualism and the New Pyramid*, Cheltenham, UK and Northampton, MA, USA: Edward Elgar.
Brennan, Deborah (2007), 'The ABC of child care politics', *Australian Journal of Social Issues*, **42** (2), 213–25.
Cameron, William Bruce (1963), *Informal Sociology: A Casual Introduction to Sociological Thinking*, New York: Random House.
Carlton, D.W. and J.M. Perloff (2005), *Modern Industrial Organization*, Boston: Pearson-Addison-Wesley.
Coase, R. (1937), 'The nature of the firm', *Economica*, **4** (16), 386–405.
Dart, Raymond (2004), 'Being "business-like" in a nonprofit organisation: a grounded and inductive typology', *Nonprofit and Voluntary Sector Quarterly*, **33**, 290–310.
Davidson, Bob (2008), 'Non-profit organizations in the human services marketplace: the impact of quasi voucher-licensing systems', paper presented at the 37th Annual Conference of the Association for Research on Nonprofit Organizations and Voluntary Action (ARNOVA), Philadelphia, PA, November.
Davidson, Bob (2009), 'For-profit organizations in managed markets for human services', in Gabrielle Meagher and Debra King (eds), *Paid Care in Australia: Profits, Purpose and Practices*, Sydney: Sydney University Press.
Davidson, Bob (2012), 'Contestability in human services markets', *Journal of Australian Political Economy*, **68** (1), 213–39.
Davidson, Bob (2015a), 'Community aged care providers in a competitive environment: past, present and future', in Gabrielle Meagher and Susan Goodwin (eds), *Markets, Rights and Power in Australian Social Policy*, Sydney: Sydney University Press, pp. 191–229.
Davidson, Bob (2015b), 'Contestability in human services – a case study of community aged care', Unpublished PhD thesis, Sydney: University of New South Wales.
Denhardt, J.V. and R.B. Denhardt (2007), *The New Public Service: Serving not Steering*, New York: M.E. Sharpe.
Eriksen, Karen (1977), *Human Services Today*, Reston, VA: Reston Publishing.
Esping-Anderson, Gosta (1990), *The Three Worlds of Welfare Capitalism*, Cambridge: Polity Press.
Forder, J., M. Knapp, B. Hardy, J. Kendall, T. Matosevic, and P. Ware (2004), 'Price, contracts and motivations: institutional arrangements in domiciliary care', *Policy and Politics*, **32** (2), 207–22.
Frey, Bruno S. (1997), *Not Just for the Money: An Economic Theory of Personal Motivation*, Cheltenham, UK and Lyme, NH, USA: Edward Elgar Publishing.
Graham, Edward M. and Robert Z. Lawrence (1996), 'Measuring the international contestability of markets: a conceptual approach', *Journal of World Trade*, **30** (5), 5–20.
Greenbaum, T. (1998), *The Handbook of Focus Group Research*, 2nd edn, Thousand Oaks, CA: Sage.
Hasenfeld, Y. (ed.) (1992), *Human Services as Complex Organizations*, Newbury, CA: Sage.
Kendall, J., T. Matosevic, J. Forder, M. Knapp, B. Hardy, and P. Ware (2003), 'The motivations of domiciliary care providers in England: new concepts, new findings', *Journal of Social Policy*, **32** (4), 489–511.
Kettl, Donald F. (2000), *The Global Public Management Revolution*, Washington, DC: Brookings Institute.
Laffont, Jean-Jacques and David Martimort (2002), *The Theory of Incentives: The Principal-Agent Model*, Princeton, NJ: Princeton University Press.
Le Grand, Julian (2007), *The Other Invisible Hand: Delivering Public Service through Choice and Competition*, Princeton, NJ: Princeton University Press.
Linstone, Harold A. and Murray Turoff (eds) (1975), *The Delphi Method: Techniques and Applications*, Reading, MA: Addison-Wesley, accessed July 1, 2015 at http://is.njit.edu/pubs/delphibook/.
Lyons, Mark (1998), 'The impact of managerialism on social policy: the case of social services', *Public Productivity and Management Review*, **21** (4), 419–32.
Lyons, Mark and V. Chan (1999), 'The effect of competitive markets on nonprofit organizations', paper presented to National Social Policy Conference, Social Policy for the 21st Century: Justice and Responsibility, University of New South Wales, Sydney, July.
Mason, Edward (1949), 'The current state of the monopoly problem in the United States', *Harvard Law Review*, **62** (149), 1265–85.

Matosevic, T., M. Knapp, J. Kendall, C. Henderson, and J. Fernandez (2007), 'Care-home providers as professionals: understanding the motivations of care-home providers in England', *Ageing and Society*, **27** (1), 103–26.

Matosevic, T., M. Knapp, and J. Le Grand (2008), 'Motivation and commissioning: perceived and expressed motivations of care home providers', *Social Policy and Administration*, **42** (3), 228–47.

Merriam, S.B. (1988), *Case Study Research in Education: A Qualitative Approach*, San Francisco, CA: Jossey Bass.

Morgan, D.L. (1998), *Focus Groups as Qualitative Research*, Newbury Park, CA: Sage.

Nevile, John (1998), 'Economic rationalism: social philosophy masquerading as economic science', in Paul Smyth and Bettina Cass (eds), *Contesting the Australian Way: States, Markets, and Civil Society*, Melbourne: Cambridge University Press, pp. 169–79.

Patton, M. (1990), *Qualitative Evaluation and Research Methods*, Newbury Park, CA: Sage.

Press, F. and C. Woodrow (2005), 'Commodification, corporatisation and children's spaces', *Australian Journal of Education*, **49** (3), 278–91.

Productivity Commission (PC) (2008), *Trends in Aged Care Services: Some Implications*, Canberra: Productivity Commission.

Productivity Commission (PC) (2011), *Caring for Older Australians*, Canberra: Productivity Commission.

Propper, C. (1993), 'Quasi-markets, contracts and quality in health and social care: the US experience', in Julian Le Grand and Will Bartlett (eds), *Quasi Markets and Social Policy*, London: Macmillan, pp. 35–67.

Richardson, Laurel (1991), *Writing Strategies: Reaching Diverse Audiences*, Newbury Park, CA: Sage.

Sarantakos, S. (2002), *Social Research*, Melbourne: Macmillan.

Saunders, Peter (1999), 'Changing work patterns and the community services workforce', in Australian Institute of Health and Welfare (AIHW), *Australia's Welfare 1999: Services and Assistance*, Canberra: Australian Institute of Health and Welfare (AIHW), pp. 38–87.

Schmalensee, Richard (1988), 'Industrial economics: an overview,' *Economic Journal*, **98** (392), 643–81.

Schmalensee, Richard and Robert D. Willig (1989 [2007]), *Handbook of Industrial Organization*, reprint, Amsterdam: Elsevier.

Schwartz, Marius (1986), 'The nature and scope of contestability theory', *Oxford Economic Papers*, New Series, **38** (Supplement), 37–57.

Scourfield, P. (2007), 'Are there reasons to be worried about the "caretelization" of residential care?', *Critical Social Policy*, **27** (2), 155–80.

SCRGSP (Steering Committee for the Review of Government Service Provision (2011), *Report on Government Services 2011*, prepared by the Productivity Commission, Canberra, January.

Shepherd, W.G, (1984), 'Contestability vs competition', *American Economic Review*, **74** (4), 572–87.

Shepherd, W.G. (1990), 'Potential competition versus actual competition', *Administrative Law Review*, **42** (5), 5–34.

Shepherd, W.G (1995), 'Contestability vs competition: once more', *Land Economics*, **71** (3), 299–309.

Smith, Dorothy (2005), *Institutional Ethnography: A Sociology for People*, Atlanta, GA: Rowman Altamira.

Stake, R.E. (2004), *Standards Based and Responsive Evaluation*, Thousand Oaks, CA: Sage.

Stigler, George (1968), *The Organization of Industry*, Homewood, IL: Richard D. Irwin,

Sturgess, Gary (2012), *Diversity and Contestability in the Public Service Economy*, Sydney: New South Wales Business Chamber, accessed 1 July 2015 at http://www.nswbusinesschamber.com.au/NSWBC/media/Misc/Policy%20Documents/120615_Contestability-Paper.pdf.

United Nations Industrial Development Organization (UNIDO) (2005), *Technology Foresight Manual: Organization and Methods*, Vol. 1, Vienna: UNIDO.

von Neumann, John and Oskar Morgenstern (1944), *Theory of Games and Economic Behaviour*, Princeton, NJ: Princeton University Press.

Watt, Diane (2007), 'On becoming a qualitative researcher: the value of reflexivity', *Qualitative Report*, **12** (1), 82–101.

Weisbrod, Burton A. and M. Schlesinger (1986), 'Public, private, nonprofit ownership and the response to asymmetric information: the case of nursing homes', in Susan Rose-Ackerman (ed.), *The Economics of Nonprofit Institutions: Studies in Structure and Policy*, New York: Oxford University Press, pp. 133–51.

Williamson, Oliver (1998), 'Transaction cost economics: how it works; where it is headed', *De Economist*, **146** (1), 23–58.

Williamson, Oliver (2000), 'The new institutional economics: taking stock, looking ahead', *Journal of Economic Literature*, **38** (3), 595–613.

Wistow, G., M. Knapp, B. Hardy, J. Forder, J. Kendall, and R. Manning (1996), *Social-Care Markets: Progress and Prospects*, Buckingham, UK: Open University Press.

Yin, R.K. (2003), *Case Study Research: Design and Methods*, 3rd edn, Thousand Oaks, CA: Sage.

Zins, C. (2001), 'Defining human services', *Journal of Sociology and Social Welfare*, **28** (1), 3–21.

# 20 A qualitative case study of the Mexican stock market (BMV) from the perspective of critical realism and grounded theory

*Jesús Muñoz*

Critical realism, as explained in Chapter 1 of this *Handbook*, used for grounding data in theory as explained in Chapter 2, must be based on an appropriate selection of data for the continuing understanding, comparison, and validation of topics, perspectives, assumptions, and methods in any science. This task is relevant for finance since no orthodox explanations are offered for the generation mechanisms, irregularities, or interconnections of the inherently and abruptly volatile financial sector.

Financial events are volatile not only due to economic risks but also because of perceptions, since human behavior patterns are neither eternal nor ubiquitous. The standard explanation of movements in financial markets is related to the dual concepts of efficiency and rationality. But this does not explain the empirical reality of these markets. In this sense the only regularity in finance is uncertainty, which possesses its own rationality and is hence real and susceptible to be researched in qualitative terms.

In addition, since money is an emergent property of developed financial systems, financial interrelationships are complex and are generated by deep mechanisms. Hence analyses of the financial sector must take account of organicism and the existence of permanent and apparently unexplainable fluxes and the implications of these.

Therefore financial investigations must involve a qualitative interpretation of real and dynamically compared data, along with data triangulation, a technique explained in Chapter 15 in this *Handbook*. The qualitative methods of interviews and document analysis are particularly useful for this task. This chapter presents a case study using these methods to obtain and interpret qualitative information for explaining both volatility and irrationality in financial practices. In addition, the research by-product of appropriate historical investigation helps to capture the gist of the development of finance.

The aim is to do justice to heterodox economics and finance by appropriately explaining the causes, interrelations, and consequences of such issues as money, uncertainty, financial stability, and the role of financial institutions. This case study thus examines the Mexican stock market or Bolsa Mexicana de Valores (BMV), an emerging market, which is highly susceptible to permanent volatility and foreign dependence.

Section 20.1 is a theoretical introduction, outlining the usefulness of the methodologies of critical realism, grounded theory, data triangulation, case studies, and other qualitative methods in the face of uncertainty in finance. Section 20.2 provides the context for a case study of the Mexican financial system and specifically of the BMV. Section 20.3 is a qualitative empirical study, by means of interviews and an analysis of documents, of the normal research processes of data collection and data processing undertaken in the BMV, examining whether they have problems with incomplete or faulty data collection and processing. Section 20.4 concludes on the basis of the preceding section that qualitative realistic analyses are required for understanding real phenomena given that normal orthodox research may be insufficient for depicting reality. The implication is that no financial market can be studied in isolation or in a certainty or non-realistic context.

## 20.1 THE CRITICAL PERSPECTIVE IN SCIENCE AND QUALITATIVE METHODS

Realism is an ontology that transcends errors of a priori theories by uncovering the internally related aspects giving rise to phenomena. Reality is always structured and exists at different ontological levels, wherein regularities and laws may be discovered for the sake of explanation. The implication is that critical realism is related to organic interdependence or unity in the explanation of phenomena in terms of causes, interrelations, and consequences.

In other words, in the search of meaning and epistemological values realism is focused on unification, as unity is a concept that may be related to laws and regularities. However, no eternal laws exist in social reality. Everything must be inferred from social dynamics and adapted to particular cases that can be extended to similar cases under special circumstances.

Social concepts lie not only in the subject but also in the reality of the object itself as perceptions and facts are relevant. Human relations are a concrete object of study. Hence motives for conducting research in economics and finance must be realistic, meaning that the essence of phenomena can always be known.

A consequence of these insights is that there is no room in the understanding of social phenomena for excessive formalism and irrelevant – unreal – assumptions,[1] which means that the methodological revision of scientific theories and practices must be continuous, ruling out the use of fictitious techniques and data. Finance is not an exception. An example of a fictitious technique producing unreal data is the consideration that all stock market indices must behave in the same fashion.

**Critical Realism, Grounded Theory, and Data Triangulation as a Methodological Route for this Study**

In this case study I use the method of critical realism, grounded theory, and data triangulation. This methodological route for this study was selected on the basis that money and stock markets are socio-economic phenomena based on perceptions but also grounded on real data, wherein geographic and historical information is also relevant. By contrast, aprioristic (certainty), metaphysical (rationality in profit search) or idealistic concerns, the existence of which has been testified on the basis of experience, may hinder the quest for truth in the study of financial phenomena.

The main aim of science is explanation. Thus it is necessary to find an inner structure and hence a pattern in financial developments as captured by the pricing systems in these markets, since volatility and key insights and methods in financial systems have proved inadequate in the face of the 2007 financial crisis, while the use of deeper methods has been under-researched. In the face of a highly volatile global scenario, and due to the fact that special conditions are required for studying emerging financial systems, it is not realistic to follow models based on certainty schemes, especially in turbulent recessionary periods.

Obtaining and processing of data in financial systems based on the paradigm related to efficiency, rationality, free markets, free trade, certainty, individualism, and democracy have to be examined in both methodological and empirical terms. The rationale for this examination is that such financial indicators as indices and rates do not necessarily capture real happenings. Therefore qualitative and documental information may be jointly used for capturing the essence of financial volatility.

Theory construction must be based on the analysis of collected data. In both economics and finance, cases in point are certainty and equilibrium, which are actually either a fiction or a construct that lead to distorted results. Many investigators agree on this issue: '[r]egarding equilibrium, an important point is Joan Robinson's argument regarding historical versus logical time, the view being that equilibrium is a construct of the latter' (Rosser 2005, p. 12). In this issue of criticizing fictions, heterodoxy and realism go hand in hand.

Since both study objects and theories are real, critical realism is a philosophy of perception (Lawson 1997). This is highly useful for social sciences as social events are inherently volatile[2] in terms of time and space, unlike natural phenomena, thus the critical investigator is able to capture basic strata of reality.

In the studied case the quality of information must be contingent upon the economic and life conditions of both the researcher and the object of study. Non-written data must not be neglected in this case (and probably in others). Qualitative information must be related to normative procedures but also to informal rules, the relevance of symbols or suspected power hierarchies. Hence informational insufficiencies – including that on uncertainty – can be corrected by reviewing observational information. Thus financial developments must be analysed along with economic events, which must be their main casual mechanisms, as well as with complex psychological and sociological attitudes, especially in terms of globalization.

## Case Studies and Other Qualitative Methods for the Case of the BMV

Grounded theory can be informed by quantitative analysis but it is a process based on finding meanings in specific contexts rather than assuming general validity. Therefore case studies are perfectly valid in methodological terms. The relevance of a case study lies in its design, but especially in its method, since casuistic methodology may be highly informative provided that the reach and objectives of the study are relevant and especially appropriate – in terms of space and time – for solving the problem in hand. For instance, Marx does not elaborate a theory of revolution which is good for any occasion, but rather for specific places and historical stages in terms of mode of production.

While such investigations have to be internally consistent they have to go deeper, thus being consistent with evidence and complete, giving an account of the case situation. The point is that data have to be decoded. For that purpose case studies develop categories, structures, and causal mechanisms for both data collection and interpretation. A case study is thus a special qualitative method that increases depth at the price of reducing extension, but its results can cautiously be generalized. In other words data selection and interpretation skills are highly valued.

One general criterion for case choice is representativeness; another popular criterion is convenience. Hence we selected for our investigation a case study supported by both interviews and documentary analysis. The case of Bolsa Mexicana de Valores (BMV) is paradigmatic because it may represent modern financial markets in the emerging world. Further, the case was convenient in that I encountered no resistance on the part of gate-keepers in conducting this type of analysis in the BMV (see section 20.3). Finally, the adequacy of the case rests on how holistic, real, and conclusive the results are.

Interviews, either with individuals or groups, are intentional, conducted in a few cases, based on attitudes, ideographical rather than generalizable, or arise from experience and memory. Further analysis of documents is highly convenient whenever sources are easy to be obtained, as it can be conducted exhaustively. Finally, content is more relevant than the method chosen.

According to the mainstream argument, quantitative data are more accurate and rigor-ous and less subject to bias in selection and interpretation than qualitative data. They cer-tainly validate evidence. This is true but only a part of the story. Qualitative analysis is less generalizable but deeper and more flexible than quantitative analysis. The benefit is that new data can be analysed, interpreted, and reorganized by breaking conceptual barriers. New generalized concepts and categories are found, but evidence must support emerging categories. New qualitative analysis must resolve this question, yielding new properties by means of new language and comparisons. Finance once again is no exception.

Qualitative methods facilitate objective validation and verification (and perhaps falsifi-cation) and therefore provide credibility by uncovering inner structures and mechanisms for future action. They also allow the avoidance of solecisms, weaknesses, or even biases. Finally, qualitative analyses recognize different basic structures, avoiding categories based on illusion. Even so, roles, illusions, fictions, and fetishes must be understood in their proper context.

The point is explaining the entire mechanism underlying finance and the economies. In this sense antagonisms and processes as well as essences must be understood by investiga-tors. The idea that '[m]ore of reality is expressed proceeds from the problem of constitu-tion' (Adorno 1962, p. 11).

Finally, while quantitative techniques of classical statistics and econometrics are nor-mally and exclusively used in financial investigations, there are also other methods coming from outside economics for understanding financial developments. My case study of the Mexican financial market will point to the actual state-of-the-art and relevance in data collection and processing in financial markets.

## 20.2 CONTEXT FOR THE EXAMINATION OF DATA COLLECTION IN THE MEXICAN STOCK MARKET

The goal of this case study is to investigate whether qualitative information can be drawn not from data but out of data by embedding realistic perspectives in the analysis of the BMV. The objective is thus to examine the significance, relevance, and depth of func-tional finance from a critical epistemological perspective when examining the structure of the BMV in terms of its methods and causal mechanisms, especially on the nature of their human agencies.

Orthodox market analysis is based on the concepts of equilibrium and certainty. Financial data are not normally based on real issues such as imperfect expectations, imperfect competition, speculation, indebtedness, the level of development of financial systems, regulation and supervision, corruption, proliferation of instruments, wealth adjustments, financial crises, actual practices, historical frames, or disparities. However this may be insufficient since the financial system is a complex structure with mutual (multidirectional) interrelationships. Financial investigation methods must entail efficiency in terms of data collection, use, dynamics, and interpretation. For that purpose people in stock markets must be creative. Perhaps for this reason they produce speculation, hedging, diversification, and circumvention in terms of both financial regulation and supervision.

In this context financial operations must be investigated on the basis of the impact of uncertainty and both past and future events on financial developments. Thus stock market indicators (just as in any other market) must be based on people's expectations. Further surveys must be conducted in brokerage houses for measuring speculation (for example, hikes in derivatives prices), and test its relation with the development of financial systems (the behavior of stock market indices, new public offers, and marketability of main shares) by assessing the mutual impact between these main variables. Financial development is defined in orthodoxy in terms of measurable volatility or risk with respect to fixed parameters or intervals.

Finally, financial variables must be measured in spatial and time terms, considering that movements in stock market indices reflect social relations and institutional changes. For instance an analysis of real (cultural) practices in the purchasing and sale of shares must be conducted.

Once the relevant financial data are listed, the relevant question is: Is data collection and processing conducted solely in orthodox terms in the BMV? This question will be solved after outlining the context of the BMV.

**BMV in Context**

The IPC (Índice de la Bolsa Mexicana de Valores) is calculated on a daily basis. The BMV represents about 1 per cent of world capital markets in terms of size (the US percentage is 44.9 and the UK's is 8.4).[3] The BMV is an emergent stock market whose heyday occurred in the early 1990s during huge capital inflows into Mexico. The Mexican derivatives market (MexDer) started in 1998.

According to the BMV, its capitalization value amounted to $0.5 trillion in 2012 (as opposed to $54.6 trillion of the total world market in 2012).[4] The capitalization value of the Mexican stock market as a percentage of the Mexican gross domestic product (GDP) was 44.9 per cent in 2012.

Whereas the Mexican GDP grew 5.2 per cent between 2009 and 2013, the IPC (the Mexican stock market index) increased by 17.3 per cent over the same period, its volatility being less than that those of the São Paolo Stock Index (Bovespa) and Dow Jones in 2012 according to BMV. The Mexican stock market possesses 131 issuers out of which ten firms represent 49.5 per cent of the total market capitalization, outstanding amongst them AMX (a mobile phone company) and Wal-Mart de Mexico.

As an emerging market the BMV lacks financial depth and is subject to both systemic and specific volatility. The BMV is thus valuable as a case study since part of being an emergent market means that its development level has an impact on the accuracy and transparency of its information methods in terms of clarity, accuracy, and opportunity. The IPC has a high correlation index (rho or $\rho$) with the Dow Jones, a high $\rho$ with the index of its sector V, Transport and Communication, and a high $\rho$ with AMX. These relations are drawn only from quantitative data for understanding this phenomenon.

Systematic quantitative information exists in the BMV about procedures and legal terms as well as on operations, trends, and expectations. The quality and nature of these informational methods are examined in the next section.

## 20.3 AN EMPIRICAL QUALITATIVE STUDY OF THE INFORMATIONAL POTENTIAL NEEDS OF THE BMV

The BMV's indicators and approaches are studied from two perspectives, interviews and documents, identifying generalized social practices and investigating what the relevant social context must be like for these to occur. Interviews with directors of both the BMV and brokerage houses, enquiries, questionnaires, and surveys are used in order to identify the conditions that either allow or hinder social specific progress in the processing of financial data.

The BMV is not an isolated atom. It is a key element of the financial sector with its own values and symbols. If this statement is true then the relevant issue is whether the BMV captures the essence of such issues as money, timing, uncertainty, information, and volatility when its data processing methods operate in an environment of uncertainty. Thus the relevant question is: are the mutually reinforcing notions of equilibrium and certainty realistic in this case?

### Interviews

The interviewer used to work in three Mexican brokerage houses in the 1990s and the 2000s. Hence he has been a participant observer in the Mexican financial markets and knows how to conduct a specialized interview about data collection, processing, and inference in the Mexican stock market. This market is obviously related to uncertainty. Hence it is a natural arena for assessing the impact of either the existence or absence of qualitative analyses.

Academic interviews are deeper than those undertaken by journalists. The former type capture wider information, longer time spectra, and in the case of critical realism and grounded theory attempt to discover generating mechanisms when analysing real indicators. On the other hand the most relevant and interesting parts of an interview are spontaneous and apparently loose comments, which I haved called 'Addendum'. In-depth interviews are conducted in order to gain insight into perspectives in our study.

The interviewees gave express permission to publish interviews about their qualitative information techniques with them as well to name them. My purpose in interviewing them is solely academic and scientific as it is not in my interest to state any deficiency in their activities, informing about these activities with no ideological bias. See Boxes 20.1 and 20.2.

BOX 20.1   INTERVIEW 1. RODOLFO NAVARRETE, DIRECTOR OF
ANALYSIS, VECTOR CASA DE BOLSA, MEXICO CITY,
FEBRUARY 10, 2014

*1Q1) What are your main qualitative indicators for measuring the interrelation between cause and effect in the issue of the developments of the Mexican stock exchange?*

1A1) In general terms we do not use qualitative data. We only evaluate the actions and activities of firms and have information on initial public offerings. We visit the enterprises of key issuers for checking out our forecasts and their expectations. We supervise the quality of responses. Finally, we conduct risk analyses but these are numerical.

*1Q2) What is the informational technology used in your data?*

1A2) We only undertake four types of numerical analyses: economic, fundamental (about firms' accounting), money market and technical. Main data are both stock and money-market indicators as well as macroeconomic data. The main indicators are GDP evolution and profits (mainly pertaining to the former quarter). We verify our projections of interest rates (especially the Mexican T-bills at 28 days), exchange rates, inflation in Mexico. This type of information is originated in Banco de Mexico and Bolsa Mexicana de Valores (BMV).

*1Q3) How can you predict movements in the stock market index?*

1A3) Predictions are undertaken by means of quantitative projections. It is assumed that certainty and equilibrium will prevail in the medium term.

*1Q4) What is the main generating mechanism of volatility in your stock market?*

1A4) GDP evolution is the answer, along with employment, interest rates, exchange rates, IPC (the stock market indicator), Dow Jones and Standard & Poor's 500. These data explain price volatility in the Mexican stock market. No qualitative data are considered as causes of volatility or uncertainty.

*1Q5) Do your quantitative indicators capture all relevant data, both Mexican and foreign?*

1A5) Mexican figures are not relevant in international markets. Mexican markets are regional markets, the main data coming from the United States. Mexican ADRs are traded in Wall Street.

*1 Addendum*
GDP is the indicator *par excellence* along with IPC, but the latter is analysed in conjunction with Dow Jones. Relevant information for investors in BMV comes from the United States.

Another relevant type of information is data related to international capital flows, especially in the US. Perceptions of major investors are related to information from the US. While particular information on enterprises development is monitored, this method is not systematic, except by isolated reports. We produce daily, weekly, monthly and annual reports in Vector.

Mexican American Depositary Receipts in the US market are more relevant than Mexican shares in Mexico. Mexico is a regional market, such as the Philadelphia Board of Trade, we are a part of the US in that sense. Thus the Mexican market is reproduced in the US, unlike those of Brazil and Chile. Both of them are national markets, although the latter is small. This is only a narrative. The Brazilian stock market is highly developed, especially in terms of futures. It started in 1977, whereas the Mexican market for derivatives started in 1998. We only sell in there warrants, futures, forwards and swaps but not options.

BOX 20.2    INTERVIEW 2. JORGE ALEGRÍA, DIRECTOR OF MEXDER OF BMV (MEXDER IS THE DERIVATIVES ORGANIZED EXCHANGE IN MEXICO CITY), FEBRUARY 10, 2014

*2Q1) Which are your main qualitative indicators for measuring the interrelation between cause and effect in the issue of the developments of the Mexican stock exchange?*

2A1) MexDer sets the operational rules for the Mexican derivatives market in a context of transparency. We measure implicit volatility in options, shares and the Mexican stock market index (IPC). We have a monthly publication about price changes. Our index is called Bimex and it follows suit of Bics (United States). Main data are about shares, futures and options prices. Our information is provided in real time with a lag of 20 minutes at the end of the day. Information is provided at the maturity of each instrument. We have an institute providing information for vendors.

*2Q2) What is the informational technology used in your data?*

2A2) We chiefly process quantitative information about market developments in a context of measurable uncertainty. Hence we provide information to academicians and investors about risk, scenarios and provide technical inputs. We also provide information on volatility for asset managers. Our methodology comes from Stanford University. It is called *Tail Risk Parity*. We also produce data for portfolio managers and academics about hedging strategies along with data about options.

*2Q3) How can you predict movements in the stock market index?*

2A3) We prepare the already mentioned informational inputs. It has to be mentioned that MexDer is only an arena for investors. MexDer is a price taker in a more ample international market. Therefore, we are technology importers in terms of information. You can take a glance of our indicators in our website.

*2Q4) What is the main generating mechanism of volatility in your stock market?*

2A4) We measure the reflex of impact volatility by conducting parametric analysis, so that our information is chiefly financial, accounting and legal. We believe in the existence of black swans, but consider them as an exception. We use risk scenarios, catastrophic scenarios in terms of losses probabilities. In that way we cope with uncertainty.

    BMV is only a filter for the issuance of instruments. We do no design indicators. We only provide information about developments in our markets. Thus MexDer is only an information provider. The Mexican market is a short-term market. Finally we pay special attention to the evolution of the exchange rate Peso/Dollar.

*2Q5) Do your quantitative indicators capture all relevant data, both Mexican and foreign?*

2A5) We attempt to capture uncertainty (remember that volatility is everything in derivatives) with the mentioned tools. Our main variable is related to the divergence between the developments of the Mexican market and those of the American market, by using a sophisticated version of the indicator *rho* (normally our dependence amounts to 90 percent). We use this correlation indicator as an alarm. We also use complex statistical indicators such as Monte Carlo and Value at Risk (VaR). Our main technique is regression to the mean, which assumes rational and efficient markets.

*2 Addendum*
BMV and MexDer are neutral players. BMV administers procedures and requirements, being only a legal filter. We do not rate new issuances. Issuers set their prices and we certificate issuances. This insight tells that the Mexican stock and money markets are not free or that they do not participate in a free market as they do not set prices.

    Our operation provides certainty about small valuations. However most investors in Mexico do not undertake fundamental analyses, they only speculate and hedge. MexDer only settles accounts obviously requesting for margins as guarantees, 'closing' risks after measuring them. Asigna is our clearinghouse which sends information about how these numerical processes are managed.

**Analysis of Documents Related to Developments in BMV**

The purpose of this section is to complement the information provided by the former interviews by conducting a non-exhaustive but representative analysis of documents dealing with the availability of profound and realistic information on the part of the BMV and other financial agencies on the Mexican stock market development and dynamics as well as about its qualitative strategy for coping with volatility.

Such documents as: BMV (annual report), MexDer (its website), Banco Nacional de México or Banamex (*La Semana Bursátil*), Vector Casa de Bolsa (annual report), Banco de México (statistical information and working papers), Comisión Nacional Bancaria y de Valores or CNBV (statistical information) and Instituto Nacional de Geografía e Informática or INEGI (its website) were analysed for the purpose in hand.

Banamex is the main commercial bank in Mexico belonging to CitiGroup. Vector is a leading brokerage house in Mexico. Banco de México is the Mexican central bank, mainly producing macroeconomic data. CNBV is the equivalent to the Securities Exchange Commission in the US, but supervising both banking and stock market related activities. Finally INEGI is a public data producer on demography as well as on economic and financial activities.

In the BMV annual report a myriad of numerical analyses and reports were found, mainly created for generalizing both current and historical development patterns in the Mexican financial system. However, hidden generating mechanisms in the developments of the Mexican stock market were not identified in the periodical reports of the BMV. In addition MexDer is concerned about risk management rather than uncertainty. This insight about quality of methods for searching relevant data was verified after examining documents from INEGI, which produces only numerical reports on the Mexican economy with isolated qualitative reports on the Mexican financial system.

No consideration for the future, no concern for uncertainty or perfect information, and no systematic qualitative analyses prevail in these informational sources. They use the same socio-economic symbols as any stock market, namely those related to winners, losers, bulls, and bears. The analysed documents thus mainly comprise quantitative information, mentioning some objectives and achievements in isolation. Explanations of past events are presented mainly in terms of quantitative indicators, for example, market capitalization as a GDP percentage.

Typical data produced by BMV, and analysed by Banamex and Vector, concern excessive share concentration in terms of marketability; for instance, AMX *L* (its ticker symbol) has a marketability index of 17.5 per cent. Another example of information is registered issuances solely in numerical terms. No information is provided about links between the IPC and the Financial Times Index or the Nikkei indexes.

The BMV daily reports only capture risks, with no mention of causal mechanisms or generating factors. The analysis of the role of BMV in the world is neglected. Finally, the electronic securities daily bulletin is not of any help if one is searching for qualitative systematic studies. Documents by Banco de México and CNBV are similar to those of the BMV with no qualitative forward indicators. It is thus confirmed that Mexican financial institutions are embedded in the international certainty–mathematical paradigm, which requires only generalizations and numerical predictions without investigating patterns.

## 20.4   OPEN CONCLUSIONS

Uncertainty is at the core of modern economics and it is reflected in volatility in modern financial systems. Data from Mexican brokerage houses and the Mexican stock exchange do not fully explain the inner causes of financial volatility to the public. They predict events in quantitative terms and their qualitative information is not provided in a systematic manner. Hence Mexican financial institutions provide only a playground platform for financial players. They do not lead or have an influence on international financial developments. Correspondingly, information is scarce or modest due to a high dependence on foreign external developments.

The Mexican stock market data are real but their twin 'normal' assumptions of certainty and equilibrium used in data collection and processing are not realistic. This is not surprising, as the most relevant information about uncertainty and dependence on foreign markets on the part of stock markets is hardly captured in quantitative data.

Indeed, I found, as an outcome of the study, the 'tyranny' of Wall Street and Dow Jones (and not surprisingly of quantitative foreign techniques) in Mexico after examining real data grounded on facts but also on historical and sociological 'invisible' (transfactual) data. As is normal in the BMV, statistics and mathematics are not part of data collection for the sake of grounding theoretical insights and transfactual outcomes. Nevertheless information is more than processing data via statistics and econometrics and conducting risk analysis. On the other hand the excessive use of mathematics seems to be a saturated method suitable for a simple economic theory. From an abstract perspective, deep social problems are not solved with mechanical models related to certainty. This was the case for this study, which is based on establishing or discovering new categories based on the building of analytical narratives and the inspection of documents.

Tony Lawson has been the inspirational source for economists in terms of critical realism. Roy Bhaskar is the father of critical realism, actually a new way for understanding social phenomena, as Dean (2008) states:

> [B]haskar's Realist Theory of Science opened the path towards understanding causality conventionally rather than naturally, or, it implied a political theory of causality understood as a specific historico-cultural ordering of human and nonhuman life . . . . His Dialectics . . . can be read as a means of theorising the mode of causality . . . which has been emerging from neoliberalism. (Dean 2008, abstract)

This theoretical statement is relevant here since neoliberalism and its core concept, certainty, are related to the methods, workings, and practices prevailing in modern financial systems.

These are the results after attempting to give unity to the problem of method for the identification of real situations and the creation of a realistic investigation, by using the example of qualitative information in the BMV, coming from both interviews and documentary analyses, which showed that the Mexican financial system is helpless in the face of financial crises. This task was done by reconsidering core assumptions and uniting apparently isolated qualitative methods and theories based on similar causal (social) mechanisms.

Uncertainty is the key insight for understanding the relevance of qualitative analyses in economics. Uncertainty, especially when it is persistent and dynamic, is not an isolated phenomenon. Black swans are part of life. Further, no invariant laws or methods exist, even less in finance. Then, the BMV's informational methodology is incomplete, requiring more realistic investigation techniques for explaining phenomena which appear unexplainable. Nonetheless, this is not a problem which is peculiar to Mexico. It is just an example of the need to attain plurality and realism in methods, as the interviews with Mexican directors and Mexican documents demonstrate being stuck in the certainty paradigm.

This is not to say that using modern 'accurate' quantitative techniques is wrong. The use of quantitative techniques in the BMV follows the state of the art, and indicators provide quality and timely information, as we learn in our interviews. In fact quantitative techniques contribute accuracy, but not always scientific rigor. They are not sufficient for grasping reality, especially when times are turbulent and phenomena cannot be generalized or predetermined. Further, not everything is quantifiable, as we may infer from the documentary analyses undertaken in the former section. Hence technical reports must be accurate and systematic but also creative, fresh, pluralistic, interdisciplinary, and deep, including the behavior of non-financial markets. Indeed, qualitative analyses are richer in terms of interrelations widening the explanatory power of information.

An unexplored avenue is the investigation of whether the dynamism of phenomena can be captured in a quantitative formalistic – non-creative – formula. In other words, is the science of finance saturated by the limitation of its methods? Any critical analysis in finance must engage in criticism of organizational, institutional, and exclusionary issues by means of mixed methods, analyses, and proposals.

Another possible unexplored avenue for the study of meaning in finance would be the analysis and interpretation of abstract symbols in the financial system for discovering generating mechanisms. For instance, a symbol might be the (fast) winner in both the stock market and life. For Marx, abstractions have a strong component of realism (see King 2002), although they must be transformed into concrete insights in order to solve practical problems (see Cohen 2008). Thus normal practices in institutions and markets must be thoroughly studied rather than idealized. Marx taught us to look through history. Freud taught us to look through human personality. We have to look through data rather than look at data.

## NOTES

1.  It is not always easy to distinguish irrelevant from relevant assumptions; however, perfect information is an obvious example of an irrelevant assumption because it is unreal.
2.  Most social situations are less volatile than financial markets, as the latter overreact.
3.  According to http://Qvmgroup.com/invest/2012.
4.  According to http://Aei-ideas.org/2013/01/world-stock-markets-capitalization-at54.6 trillion/.

## REFERENCES

Adorno, T. (1962), 'Seminar on Marx', accessed 21 March 2014 at http://reificationofpersonsandpersonificationofthings.wordpress.com/2012/06/25/adorno-1962-seminar-on-marx/.

Cohen, R.S. (2008), 'Karl Marx', *Complete Dictionary of Scientific Biography*, Encyclopedia Com, accessed 5 June 2014 at http://www.encyclopedia.com/topic/Karl_Marx.aspx.

Dean, K. (2008), 'Dangerous liaisons: new objects, new knowledges, or, the problems of theorising contemporary capitalism', *Against the Flow: Critical Realism and Critiques of Contemporary Social Thought*, accessed 3 February 2014 at http://criticalrealism.edublogs.org/.

King, J.E. (2002), *A History of Post Keynesian Economics Since 1936*, Cheltenham, UK and Northampton, MA, USA: Edward Elgar Publishing.

Lawson, T. (1997), *Economics and Reality*, London: Routledge.

Rosser, J.B. (2005), 'Complex dynamics and post Keynesian economics', in M. Setterfield (ed.), *Complexity, Endogenous Money and Macroeconomics: Essays in Honour of Basil J. Moore*, London: Routledge, pp. 74–98.

# 21 Looking into the black box: policy as a contested process

*Jamee K. Moudud*

> ... the reform of capitalist economy by socialist parties is difficult even when they are determined not to interfere with the property system. For the mere possibility that they might decide to do so undermines that type of confidence which in liberal economy is vital, namely, absolute confidence in the continuity of the titles to property. (Karl Polanyi, *The Great Transformation*, 1944, p. 234)

## 21.1 INTRODUCTION

It is perhaps ironic that Alice Amsden's *Asia's Next Giant* (Amsden 1989), Robert Wade's *Governing the Market* (Wade 1990), and Peter Evans's *Embedded Autonomy* (Evans 1995) rose to fame in the 1990s when the free market paradigm reigned supreme. Defying the conventional wisdom at the time, these three important books discussed the central role that the state had played in East Asian industrialization. Subsequently, scholarly work that was historically informed with regard to the role of the state in industrialization multiplied. For example, Ha-Joon Chang in his 'Kicking away the ladder' (Chang 2002a) pointed to the central and varying roles that the state played in the Organisation for Economic Co-operation and Development (OECD) countries as they were developing. As Chang argued persuasively, contrary to the popular view, the state in early American and British development history did not pursue a 'hands-off' policy but used a wide range of industrial policies to promote industrialization. In the same vein, the explosive growth of the national systems of innovation (NSI) literature has analyzed the intricate and important ways in which the state in OECD countries has shaped business productivity growth and innovation (Block 2008; Block and Keller 2011; Fagerberg et al. 2005), in effect acting like a developmental state. For authors in this growing developmental state (DS) literature, the analysis of real-world economic transformation cannot be explained via the static allocation of scarce resources but can only be understand as a dynamic process in which new resources are created within the context of suitable institutions, many in the public sector, that promote industrialization. Authors in this tradition emphasize the need for an institutionally grounded political economy as the *sine qua non* of any realistic economic analysis (Chang 2002b).

While the above authors and others focused on industrial development, the other major literature that came into prominence in the 1990s was the Human Development project of the United Nations Development Programme (UNDP) and the closely related capabilities approach pioneered by Nobel Prize winning economist Amartya Sen (Sen 1999). Although this literature did not directly support the traditional Keynesian welfare state framework, its focus on redistributive policies, social justice, and thus the role of the state certainly made it consistent with this framework and thus an important component of heterodox policy proposals. In recent years, a number of authors have combined the analysis of industrial policy with measures to strengthen the social safety net under increased global integration (Sandbrook et al. 2007; Riesco 2007).

Finally, over the last three decades the policy proposals of the late Hyman Minsky have become popular in heterodox circles and his insights, following Keynes, regarding full employment policies are central to the employer-of-last-resort (ELR) proposals made by many post-Keynesian economists (Wray 1998; Forstater 2001), some of whom have also drawn on other authors such as Abba Lerner and Adolph Lowe (Forstater 2003). In this ELR literature the focus is on the use of budget deficits to attain the full employment that does not prevail under laissez-faire. As with the above literature, post-Keynesian authors have also emphasized the centrality of institutionally grounded economic and policy analysis, suggesting the necessity of combining Keynes with the great institutionalists such as John R. Commons and others; in short, a post-Keynesian institutionalism (Forstater 2001; Whalen 2012).

Thus it can be seen that a common theme running through this broad literature is its twin focus on the centrality of institutions in capitalist economies and the need for activist state policies to bolster or create those institutions that will achieve desirable socioeconomic outcomes, which laissez faire cannot deliver. However, while the state looms large in this literature, no attempt is made in this literature to explicitly discuss opposition by business groups to social democratic policies,[1] and states' responses to such policies.

Heterodox economists would generally be in agreement about two propositions: (1) business and social priorities do not mesh automatically; that is, what is good for business is not necessarily good for society; and (2) capitalist societies are characterized by class relations in which capitalists, by virtue of their ownership of and control over the means of production, wield a disproportionate amount of structural and instrumental power. However, in their policy proposals heterodox economists tend either to ignore capitalist power and the perception of such policies or to assume implicitly the opposite of proposition (1), that is: 'what is good for society is good for business'; state involvement in social sectors would be beneficial to businesses. If this latter claim is correct, then it of course follows that capitalists would never see the need to push back against social democratic policies, and the unequal power relations in capitalist societies would not be relevant to the formulation of such policies. One may wonder why in the United States industry associations such as the National Restaurant Association and the National Retail Federation recently deployed enormous financial resources to kill current government initiatives to raise the minimum wage (Lipton 2014),[2] or why a number of US local government initiatives to raise the minimum wage have had to contend with the threat of capital flight from their jurisdictions.[3]

More broadly there is ample historical evidence, both inside and outside the OECD, to show that businesses are hardly passive policy-takers and, in fact, that they play a very active role in molding, reshaping, or even blocking when necessary, socially desirable policies when these are deemed antithetical to business interests (Phillips-Fein 2009; Rose 2009; Evans 1995; Ferguson 1995; Paster 2012; Streeck 2009; Moudud and Martinez Hernandez 2014; Farnsworth 2004). Not surprisingly, as authors in the above literature have pointed out, business opposition to such policies arises when the latter tend to raise business costs and/or lower expected profits. These higher costs tend to be opposed most vigorously in economic crises when individual firms seek greater labor market flexibility, and push for tax cuts and other pro-business policies (Akard 1992). Writing about expansionary fiscal policies to promote full employment, Kalecki (1943) argued that such measures would be opposed by capitalists to the extent that the lower rate of unemployment emboldens workers politically. Further, quite aside from labor market issues, Kalecki also discussed capitalist opposition to public investments if these competed with private investment.[4]

In short, following Kalecki's insight, social democratic social, labor, and taxation policies are likely to be opposed by capitalists if they are seen as threats to business prerogatives. This became palpably clear in the global economic crisis of the 1970s and 1980s when capitalists in countries as diverse as Mexico (Schneider 2004), Jamaica (Stephens and Stephens 1986), France (Gourevitch 1986), Germany (Paster 2012; Streeck 2009), the UK (Farnsworth 2004), and the US (Phillips-Fein 2009) increased their opposition to such policies with varying degrees of success. As a number of international organizations such as Corporate Europe Observatory (CEO)[5] and the Transnational Institute (TNI)[6] document, powerful business groups continue to play their role in attempting to mold policies to their advantage in the current crisis.

The operative phrase in the previous paragraph is 'with varying degrees of success'. It does not follow that capitalist preferences and pressures can mechanically shape state policies, since capitalist states, while needing to ensure the viability of private capital accumulation, also seek to get legitimation from the larger society, as Claus Offe, David Held, and others have discussed (Held 1989). The state can clearly 'push back' as in the above local-level minimum wage initiative (Gabriel 2013). For example, the Pinochet administration institutionalized the political power of one of Chile's most powerful business groups, the multisectoral business peak organization Confederación de la Producción (CPC), with deep ties to the political establishment and state-level policy-making apparatus (Silva 1997; Fairfield 2010; Roberts 2011; Moudud et al. 2014). This has made the implementation of pro-labor policies under democratic governments fairly difficult, even though important achievements in the health care and pensions sectors have been achieved in recent years (Huber et al. 2010). On the other hand, the historical legacy of street protests in France led to the expansion of social protection in the 1980s despite large-scale privatizations (Levy 2005).

Clearly, such examples show that there is a need to reconceptualize policy by explicitly accounting for politics and power as they have historically evolved in capitalist societies. As Gourevitch succinctly puts it in his *Politics in Hard Times* (1986):

> Policy requires politics. Ideas for solving economic problems are plentiful, but if an idea is to prevail as the actual policy of a particular government, it must obtain support from those who have political power. Economic theory can tell us a lot about policy alternatives, *but unless our economics contains an understanding of power*, it will not tell us enough to understand the choices actually made.
> In prosperous times it is easy to forget the importance of power in the making of policy . . . In difficult times this comfortable illusion disintegrates. (Gourevitch 1986, p. 17, emphasis added)

The centrality of a power-based analysis of economic policy has several implications. To begin with, it implies that both political factors, as well as the standard economic ones, need to be taken into account in understanding business motivations since it is the larger political economy context that shapes the state of business confidence and thus invest-ment decisions.[7]

Further, if in reality the state is not an omniscient and omnipotent institution but exists in a contested terrain, pulled in one direction by business priorities and in the other by social ones, how would one go about investigating the nature of this terrain? In this chapter, my point of departure is the stylized fact that social democratic taxation, social, and labor (TSL) policies are in general likely to face opposition from capitalists whenever such policies threaten profitability. In particular in crisis periods or faced with threaten-ing global competition, capitalists will tend to push for neoliberalism so as to achieve labor market flexibility.[8]

And yet this does not imply that neoliberalism is inevitable, as one strand of the Marxian tradition perhaps implies (Barrow, 1993). On the one hand I take the position, emphasized by several authors (Farnsworth 2004; Hacker and Pierson 2002), that a politically viable state has to reckon with the profitability of the business sector, which after all regulates investment. Thus the structural and instrumental power of capitalists is very important. On the other hand, since the state of business confidence and profit-ability are shaped by a number of interlinked economic and political factors, the state may at times be successful in producing a policy and political mix (PPM) that helps promote business capital accumulation and social goals, that is, social democratic poli-cies. Further, the PPM is also shaped by the degree of inter-capitalist rivalries, enabling the state to either exploit the latter to put in progressive policies or be caught 'between a rock and a hard place'. By its nature this PPM is both historically contingent and subject to contestation both by capitalists, seeking flexible labor markets and the reduction of social regulations, and the larger society, itself pushing for the opposite. The implication of this power-based framework is that policy outcomes – whether social democratic or socially neoliberal – are historically contingent. It is not at all obvious that progressive policy outcomes, for example of the ELR type, can be magically attained just because state managers have the political will.

From a methodological standpoint, an investigation of a country's PPM which would be conducive to social democratic policies requires an understanding of: (1) the nature of the structural and institutional power wielded by capitalists; and (2) and the political processes via which capitalists are made to absorb (for example via the state's political pressure) or are able to modify and perhaps even block progressive TSL policies. Both of these two sets of factors require knowledge of the institutional and political structures via which capitalist power is exercised or contained. An investigation of empirical data on TSL policies, including econometric analysis when relevant, would also be important in order to understand how the tug-of-war between capitalists, on the one hand, and the state with the larger society, on the other hand, actually resolves itself in a given historical moment.

Furthermore, (2) requires an understanding of capitalists' preferences. Authors in what one may call the business power literature (Hacker and Pierson 2002; Paster 2012) have argued that a relative level of business acquiescence to social democratic policies in a particular historical moment does not necessarily imply a fundamental support of such policies, but may be a form of *strategic accommodation* to worker pressure and other political realities. Since business preferences change over time because of dif-ferent economic and political contexts, policy proposals have to be context-based and historically informed, given varying macroeconomic and political circumstances (Paster 2012).[9]

The goal of this chapter is to suggest that the contested terrain of social democratic policy-making has to involve the study of state–business relations, as they evolve historically, in order to understand the nature of structural and institutional power wielded by business. This case study approach also has to entail an investigation of the political factors that may endow state managers with more or less agency in curbing business's push for neoliberalism, given that democratic states are also subject to pressure from workers and civil society groups. Finally, it is shown that the outcome of the tug-of-war between states and business over social democratic policies can sometimes only be gleaned via empirical and even econometric analysis.

Section 21.2 discusses the nature of what I call the *contested terrain* perspective. This section concludes with a discussion of the need to incorporate the study of business preferences and the nature of state–business relations over time in policy analysis. Section 21.3 discusses the relevance of empirical and econometric work to also characterize state–business relations. This section illustrates this point by considering Denmark, Norway, and the USA. These three countries were chosen because the aim was to compare a 'welfare laggard' such as the US with two advanced social democracies with their own differences. The purpose is thus to illustrate the nature of diverse PPMs in capitalism.[10] Finally, section 21.4 is the conclusion.

## 21.2   POLICY IN A CONTESTED TERRAIN

Given their roots in Kalecki and authors in the institutionalist tradition such as John Kenneth Galbraith, '[T]he distribution of income and power is a central concern of most Post Keynesians' (Peterson and Estenson 1996, p.682). And yet, as with neoclassical theory, the state is implicitly assumed to be autonomous in pursuing its desired objectives. The difference is that while in neoclassical economics the autonomy of the state is consistent with the promotion of laissez faire, in post-Keynesian economics it is consistent with the maintenance, without any let or hindrance, of social democratic policies that are to everyone's satisfaction. With a focus on macroeconomic policy, the post-Keynesian tradition relies on a wide range of economic identities (Godley and Lavoie 2007) to make policy prescriptions such as ELR initiatives (Wray 1998). No account is taken of possible capitalist opposition to such policies or the ways in which in which state managers negotiate policy conflicts with capitalists, unions, or social movements.[11]

On the other hand, the centrality of business power in the shaping of policies is a key theme in the Institutionalist tradition outside economics (Farnsworth 2004; Hacker and Pierson 2002; Korpi 2006). Authors in this literature distinguish between the structural and instrumental power wielded by business. Structural power is determined by the fact that the engine of the capitalist economy is business investment which is motivated by profitability. The structural power arises from the fact that capitalists can relocate, or threaten to do so, if public policies lower expected profits and thus business confidence. This control over business investment, which determines growth, employment, and tax revenues for the state, gives individual firms enormous leverage over the state. This power exists quite independently of any political mobilization by firms.

Institutionalists argue that instrumental power by business groups, central to their political attempts to shape policy,[12] also constitutes an additional means of pressure. Instrumental power is exercised via business lobbying; campaign contributions; links between business groups, government ministries, and political parties; business funding of influential think-tanks and research; and informal business networks (Farnsworth 2004; Fairfield 2010; Hacker and Pierson 2002). Finally, as emphasized by Ralph Milliband, instrumental power is also exercised in a more insidious fashion by the ideological and educational training of state managers, making their policy ideology vary from 'strong conservatism to weak reformism' (Barrow 1993, p. 29).

Either implicitly or explicitly, one issue that appears to unite many instrumentalists and structuralists is the emphasis that social democratic reforms in capitalism are very limited. In sharp contrast to the essentially benign vision of social democracy in William H. Beveridge's (1944) *Full Employment in a Free Society* (with the same vision in much of the heterodox policy literature) authors emphasizing business power have tended to conceptualize the market as a prison, as Lindblom put it (Hacker and Pierson 2002), within which the state has only very limited margin of maneuver. While structuralists in the Marxist tradition in particular do not see the prison walls of the market as rigidly fixed, and emphasize the relative autonomy of the state, there is nonetheless an emphasis on the word 'relative' in this view of the state with the implicit focus being on the structural constraints faced by the state (Dass 2006). However this characterization of the state raises more questions than it can answer.

First, it leaves little room for the agency of state managers, workers, and social movements to press for policies that hit or even mold the structural constraints, thereby making it difficult for this framework to explain policy variations (Dass 2006; Barrow 1993). And yet the question of political agency is non-trivial. Consider business opposition to social regulatory policies pertaining to the environment in the 1970s and 1980s. At a time when American businesses were under the twin pincers of a major economic crisis and growing competitive threat from Japanese firms, the Clean Air Act was one policy that was 'costing business more money than any other, the one measure which all three major business groups were heavily lobbying against ... ' (Prasad 2006, p. 80). However, as Prasad (2006) argues, these groups were not successful in reforming this important legislation. The main reason was that there was widespread public support for environmental protection policies. After 1983 the Reagan administration became far more cautious about its anti-environmental stance, especially as regards this Act, because it was concerned about the 1984 elections, in case the Democrats were successful in asserting that the Republican Party was kowtowing to big business with regard to pollution. Clearly, then, even for very right-wing pro-business states pressures from non-business groups matter.

Second, the lack of an adequate investigation of state agency implicitly makes the state out to be an epiphenomenon in the structuralist view. Crudely put, in a functionalist way, the state reacts passively to the structural needs of capital, thereby implying the validity of a 'neoconservative or free-market, model of the business climate as an accurate description of what capitalists need from the state (i.e. to be left alone)' (Barrow 1993, p. 75). The problem is that little account is taken of the ways in which businesses react to pressures from the state and society. Provided there is not an erosion of business confidence, businesses will sometimes react to political pressures from the state and society and absorb them by reconfiguring production and organizational processes. One can see this with the decisions of many large US companies which, after years of lobbying successfully against climate change legislation and even funding research whose goal was to debunk climate science, have realized that, given widespread concerns about global warming, polluters will have to pay a price. Thus, as a *New York Times* article recently reported, these companies are adjusting their production, growth, and financial plans in light of such legislation (Davenport 2013). In the same vein the auto industry for long successfully opposed car safety legislation. However, growing demand for auto safety by the public and the car insurance industry made the auto sector eventually restructure its production to install seatbelts, even though these were not installed with airbags in the 1980s (MacLennan 1988).

Third, the margin of maneuver of state authorities is shaped by intersectoral rivalries between capitalists. For example, in the above car safety case, major insurance companies such as Liberty Mutual and State Farm were involved in pushing for legislation. Sectoral differences may further be exploited by other types of policies. For example, in a sharp departure from neoliberal practice the Argentinian state, in the period after the sovereign default of the early 2000s, imposed hefty export taxes on its highly profitable and internationally competitive soy sector (Fairfield 2011). Because part of this tax revenue was used to provide subsidies to a wide range of industrial sectors, the latter clearly became stakeholders in such a policy. Since export taxes did not adversely affect them and, given the state's commitment not to run huge budget deficits after the sovereign debt default, important business associations such as the Asociación Empresaria Argentina and the Unión Industrial Argentina (UIA) were generally supportive of this tax (Fairfield 2011, p. 445) perhaps because of its links to targeted industrial subsidies.

Fourth, the push for market reforms by business may lead to what Levy (2005) has called *institutional redeployment*. The policy U-turn of the French Socialist Party after 1983 involved the abandonment of *dirigisme* and the implementation of large-scale privatizations. There were also pro-business reforms in connection with labor relations, and '[F]rench employers were able to use this new bargaining arena to introduce labor market flexibility largely on their terms . . . [so that] much of capital's gain in the post-1983 period would come at labor's expense' (Levy 2005, p. 107). And yet this swing to the right in terms of economic policy was accompanied by the reinforcement and further extensions of systems of social protection and various progressive labor market initiatives. The commitment to state activism in the social arena was equally true under the Gaullist Jacques Chirac. As Levy (2005, p. 114) points out, the potential for massive popular protest in the face of socially neoliberal policies is seared deep in the French political culture, and even right-wing governments would not dare to pursue social retrenchment policies. By the same token, the commitment to using the state and innovation policies to propel French capitalists into the Internet Age was equally true of left-wing and right-wing governments (Trumbull 2004).

No ideal state of affairs has been reached in France; for one thing its highly regressive tax structure (Prasad 2006) has also contributed to deep income inequalities (Landais et al. 2011). Equally important, the current Socialist government is desperately attempting to promote business investment since its high business taxes and various pro-worker policies have kept business confidence low despite the state's 'charm offensive' to make the country more business friendly (Alderman 2014, p. B1). In short, the French experience over the past 30 years is an excellent case study which challenges conventional and simplistic notions of the state.

I would suggest that the clue to an alternative perspective on policy has to begin with an important qualification of the word 'neoliberalism' as it is commonly used. For example Prasad (2006, pp. 4–5, emphasis added) says: 'By "free market" or "neoliberal" policies, I mean taxation structures that favor capital accumulation over income redistribution, *industrial policies that minimize the presence of the state in private industry*, and retrenchment in welfare spending.'

This definition is problematic, however, as it is not clear what state minimalism vis-à-vis industry actually means. There is in fact plenty of historical and contemporary evidence that shows that the state policies across the capitalist world have in numerous and intricate ways shaped business capital accumulation. Such policies have taken many different forms, from subsidies and protectionist measures to infrastructure provisioning and national systems of innovation (Chang 2002a; Block and Keller 2011; Pérez Caldentey 2012). The reason for such policies is quite simple of course: politicians need viable economies that generate adequate levels of employment and prosperity in order to be elected. Thus a viable business sector is politically crucial.

And yet, the asymmetric nature of power relations in capitalism is such that intimate state–business linkages may be consistent with socially neoliberal policies, that is, that domain of public policies which deals with labor, social, and environmental protection. On the other hand, labor militance and/or pressures from social movements (say with regard to the environment) may in fact enable the state to force through social reform measures by combining capitalist demands for industrial policies with progressive social policies. In fact the existence of industrial policies may potentially give the state a certain degree of political leverage vis-à-vis capitalists. This leverage may increase if the state can exploit the rivalries between different sectors or types of firms (Hacker and Pierson 2002). These conflicts could arise because of the different priorities of domestic and export-oriented sectors, such as: those between agriculture and manufacturing in the nineteenth century in the UK which led to removal of the Corn Laws; Argentina with regard to export taxes and subsidies to domestic-oriented industries (see above); and possibly Sweden in the early twentieth century with respect to export-oriented manufacturing firms and domestically oriented ones such as those in the building and construction industry (Swenson 1991, 2002).[13]

One way to summarize the above discussion is to say that a country's politics, as it has historically evolved, matters with the implication that the push for social neoliberalism by capitalists will not inevitably be successful. At one level, this focus on the political factors to attain progressive policy goals makes my argument consistent with authors in the power resources approach (PRA) approach (Korpi 2006). Authors in this literature have challenged the views made by Peter Swenson (2002) and others such as those in the so-called varieties of capitalism school (Hall and Soskice 2001), who have argued that progressive social and labor policies have often been initiated by rational capitalists seeking more healthy, educated, and productive workers. Instead, PRA authors have argued the exact opposite: pressure by workers and their allies have usually made capitalists begrudgingly accept the demands, usually as a way to deflect more radical ones. In fact, oftentimes elite support for social democracy arises from the threat of political instability, aggravated perhaps by deep socio-economic cleavages which provoke radical popular demands for change. This, in fact, is the historical context which gave rise to the modern Danish welfare state (Campbell and Hall 2006, pp. 22–3 and fn. 14, p. 47; Korsgaard 2006).

Thus, in this left-wing social democratic perspective of the PRA, political power can, as it were, tame capitalists: 'the working class can decrease its disadvantage in relation to capital' (Korpi 1983, p. 14; cited by Korpi 2006, p. 187). While I would agree that the PRA emphasis on the role of left-wing social democratic politics is very important, the question is: what are the limits to such political pressures? The limits do not appear obvious from this literature and yet, following the structuralist tradition, I would argue that left-wing social democratic policies are likely to work as long they do not threaten profitability or capitalists' control over core investment decisions.[14] On the other hand, provided a democratic state faces political pressure from workers and non-capitalists, a social democratic party may be able to push back against capitalists' pressure for social neoliberalism with a suitable PPM that may remain stable for a certain historical period.

Crucially, then, from a methodological standpoint, social democratic TSL policy proposals have to involve the study of state–business power relations and the evolving nature of capitalist preferences. Hacker and Pierson (2002) caution that the correlation of healthy business performance and progressive social and labor policies should not lead one to conclude that capitalists promote or fundamentally support such policies because they are good for business (for example, because of the availability of a healthy and skilled workforce). As they say, correlation does not imply causation. The historically informed analysis of business power and the state in their work and that of Paster (2012, 2013) provides a very important methodological approach to the study of social democratic policies, both their establishment at a given historical period and their evolution over time. The question of slow processes of institutional and policy change (for example, declining corporate tax rates and real value of the minimum wage in the US over several decades) is a core analytical component of historical institutionalists such as Streeck (2009) and Paster (2012), who have emphasized the centrality of macro-processes such as changing economic conditions (for example, booms and slumps or new global competitors) in shaping business preferences and pressures on the state with regard to social democratic TSL policies. The study of formal and informal business networks, business interest organizations, and business history, drawing in particular on available primary and secondary documents pertaining to business positions on policies as well as legislative initiatives by the state, should be at the heart of such a research endeavour.

Finally, it is important to investigate the sources historians have used to come to certain conclusions. In other words, the analysis of employer support of or opposition to landmark social legislations (such as the US Social Security Act or Sweden's Saltsjöbaden Agreement of 1938) depends crucially on whether the historian consults the positions of employers, unions, or public officials on these issues. For example, even if employers in official statements come out in support of progressive legislations, their internal memoranda or minutes of meetings may show otherwise. In conjunction with historical documents from other sources (say, unions), the policy analyst can come to a better understanding of such policies: whether they were established because of or despite employer preferences.[15] In short, for a given country, both the history and historiography of state–business relations should be central to policy debates and the analysis of power relations.

Finally, when possible, the power tussles between state and business may be complemented by empirical and econometric work to the extent that the issues pertaining to power are quantifiable. Such an analysis may provide further insights about the nature of the contested terrain within which the state operates in attempting to pursue social democratic TSL policies. As shown, the econometric analysis of corporate tax rates can provide an index of business power. The next section deals with these issues.

## 21.3   GAUGING RELATIVE POLITICAL POWER: THE USA AND THE SOCIAL DEMOCRATIC WELFARE STATES

At the heart of the contested terrain perspective is the proposition that power struggles of different types shape distinct PPMs. The historical–institutional–political framework thus has to address some important questions: given state–business power struggles over social democratic TSL, how far can each side go in achieving its own goals? Is business push for social neoliberalism inevitable? On the other hand, what are the limits which constrain the state's ability to pursue social democratic policies? These questions fundamentally speak to the issue of relative power relations in capitalist societies. For example, trends in business tax rates and social expenditure rates can provide indications of the power wielded by capitalists, workers, and the state. The answers to the above questions are largely empirical and may even make econometric analysis relevant. These issues are investigated by comparing the US with two advanced social democracies, Denmark and Norway, with their own distinct PPMs, involving somewhat different tax systems as well as labor market institutions.[16]

As shown below, business profit rates and tax rates appear to be positively correlated in the US, Denmark, and Norway. Given their possible non-stationary (and therefore non-ergodic) nature, a simple ordinary least squares (OLS) regression on these time series may yield what is called a 'spurious regression' (Hill et al. 2011). Thus the question is whether there is an underlying stable trend relationship between the two variables, and if so, what the nature of the interaction is which binds their time paths together. For example, the business power perspective would suggest that low and/or falling rates of profit would place pressure on the state to cut business tax rates. Such an argument would imply the existence of a cointegrating relationship with an associated error correction mechanism (ECM). The existence of an ECM would provide information about the Granger causal mechanisms generating the cointegrating relationship.

It should be emphasized that the existence of cointegration between variables does not imply an equilibrium relationship between them.[17] For example, the two variables may cycle perpetually around each other (as in a limit cycle[18]) without being in 'equilibrium'. Such cycles can be due to stochastic perturbations, reflective of the turbulence and uncertainties of market economies.

The dynamical relationship between the variables can be written as an autoregressive dependent lag (ARDL) equation which can equivalently be rewritten in the form of an ECM as well as a cointegrating equation (Hill et al. 2011). Let $lt$ and $lr$ be the natural logarithms of the tax ($t$) and profit rate ($r$),[19] respectively, so that the ECM is given by:

$$\Delta lt_t = a_0 + b.\Delta lr_t + \sum_{i=1}^{n} c_i.\Delta lt_{t-i} + \sum_{i=1}^{n} d_i.\Delta lr_{t-i} + \beta_1.lt_{t-1} + \beta_2.lr_{t-1} + v_t \qquad (21.1)$$

The ECM shows the accelerations and decelerations of $lr$ and $lt$ around their trends with $\beta_1$ being the error correction coefficient (ECC).[20] The ECC is thus the speed of adjustment coefficient that determines the time it takes for the deviations from the trend to become approximately 0. Crucially, the sign and statistical significance of the ECC provides an indication of causality in the Granger sense between $lr$ and $lt$. It must be understood that causality implies precedence, or what Francis Diebold (2001) calls predictive causality:

> the statement '$y_i$ causes $y_j$' is just shorthand for the more precise, but long-winded, statement, '$y_i$ contains useful information for predicting $y_j$ (in the linear least squares sense), over and above the past histories of the other variables in the system.' To save space, we simply say that $y_i$ causes $y_j$. (Diebold 2001, p. 254, cited by Gujarati and Porter 2009, p. 653)

Clearly, theory has to provide an interpretation of Granger causality. An error correction model linking corporate tax rates and profit rates can provide an important insight into business power by revealing the existence of a causal linkage between the two variables. Theoretically, from a business–power perspective one would expect that the state's ability to extract taxes from the business sector will be constrained by the latter's profitability. During boom periods, when profit rates are relatively higher, the state has more leeway in raising corporate tax rates without seriously compromising capital accumulation; this political space is reduced during slumps when profit rates are relatively lower.[21] It should be emphasized here that if the state were largely free to extract whatever corporate tax shares it desired then the two series would be independent of one another and the ECC would be insignificant in a statistical sense. Thus the sign and significance of the ECC can be considered to be an index of state dependence on the business sector in terms of its ability to extract taxes from the latter.

Consider Figure 21.1 which plots the US corporate pre-tax profit rate[22] versus the corporate tax rate (direct taxes/pre-tax profits) and corporate tax shares (taxes/total taxes) for the period 1929–2012.[23] The huge fall in the values of all three variables in the early 1930s masks the relative movements. I have therefore split up the charts into the periods 1929–44 and 1945–2012 to better illustrate the co-movements.

The graphs show that in the 1945–2012 period there is a very strong positive correlation between the trends of the profit rate, tax rate, and tax revenue share, respectively, even though they deviate from each other cyclically for considerable periods.[24] For example, the big jump in the profit rate between 1960 and 1966 involved a fall in the tax revenue share because of the cut in the tax rate. Similarly in the post-2008 period the rising profit rate has been accompanied by a fall in the tax rate even though the tax share has risen modestly.

On the other hand, while the profit rate started to recover after around 1933 the corporate tax rate fell from 28 percent to 21 percent between 1934 and 1938 and then jumped to a peak of around 58 percent by 1943. The tax share moved with the profit rate, although it accelerated relative to the former after 1938 because of the jump in the tax rate.

While the econometric relations between these variables, including a discussion of the

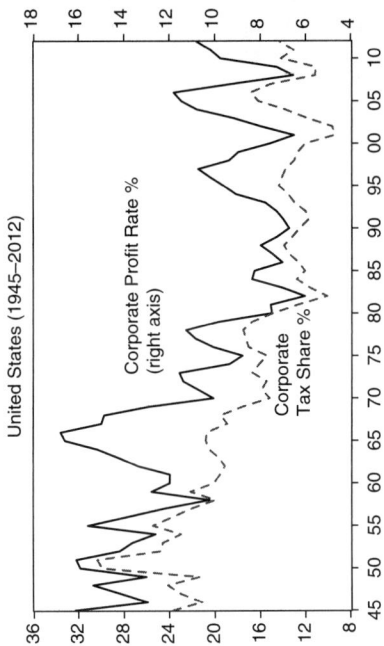

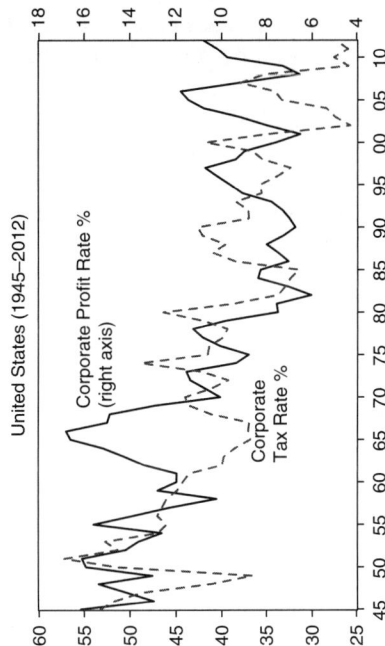

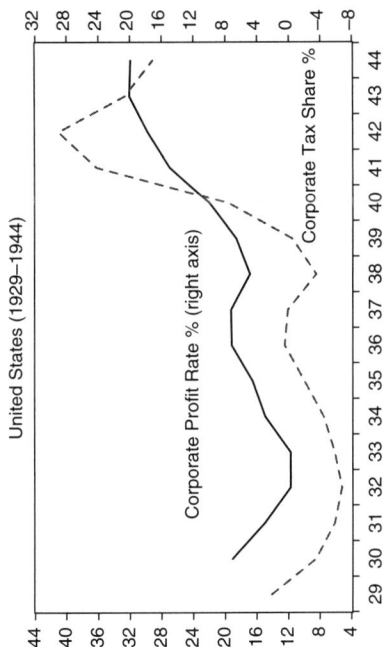

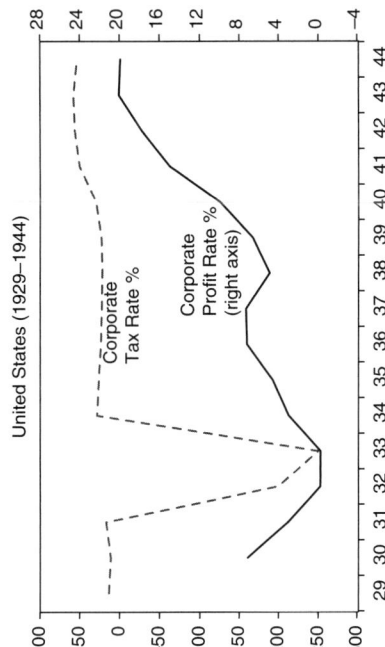

*Source:* BEA, Department of Commerce.

*Figure 21.1 Corporate profit rate, tax rate, and tax shares for the US*

rationale for this type of analysis, will be investigated later on in this section, for now it should be pointed out that the above patterns are consistent with the argument made in the previous section. As Phillips-Fein (2009) argues, throughout the post-war period powerful business groups in the US mobilized in a variety of ways to roll back New Deal policies. This instrumental power was bolstered by the falling rate of profit which placed growing political pressures on the state to reduce tax rates so as to extract progressively lower tax shares from the corporate sector.

The pre-war relationship between these variables is also of theoretical significance. Rising rates of profit during the Great Depression, due to large-scale lay-offs and cutbacks, were accompanied by a modest cut in corporate tax rates between 1934 and 1938. This presumably reflected some sort of a compromise between the politically emboldened Roosevelt administration, with its drive to install social democratic policies, and corporate America. The tax share and the profit rate moved close together because of the small change in the tax rate. What is of equal significance was that the government was not able to raise the corporate tax rate in this period, which I would argue is a reflection of significant business opposition to several New Deal policies, as several authors have also argued (Rose 2009; Hacker and Pierson 2002; Paster 2013).

Figures 21.2 and 21.3 show the relationships between business profit rates and the corporate tax shares in Denmark and Norway, respectively.[25] The tax data were obtained from the OECD Tax Statistics online database.[26] For the business sector this database provides only taxes paid by the corporate sector.[27] Further, the database does not provide corporate tax rates (that is, direct taxes/pre-tax profit) but does provide tax shares (cor-

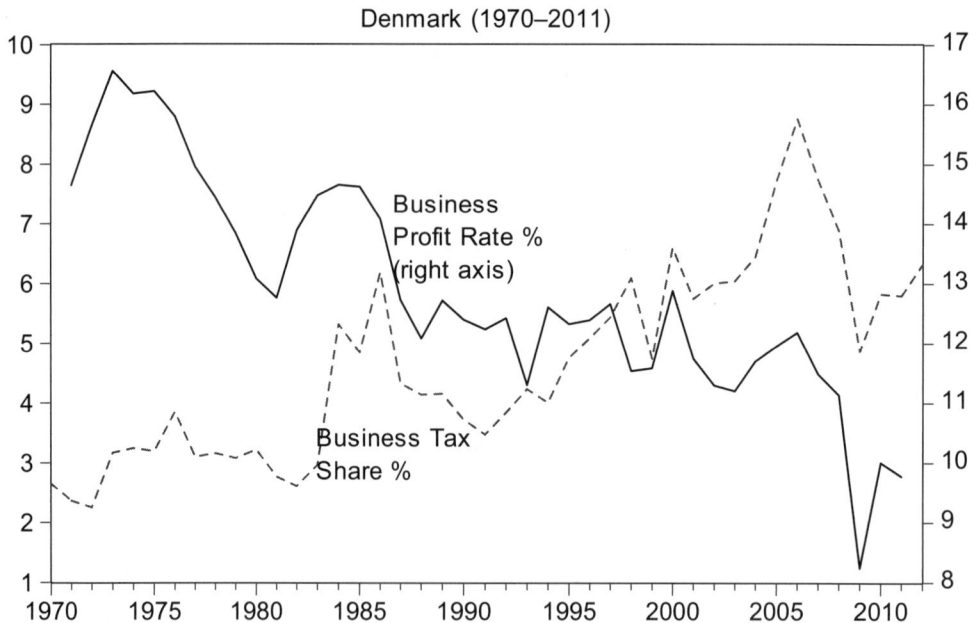

*Sources:*   OECD STAN (Rev. 4) and OECD Tax Statistics databases.

*Figure 21.2   Business profit rate and tax shares for Denmark*

Norway (1970–2011)

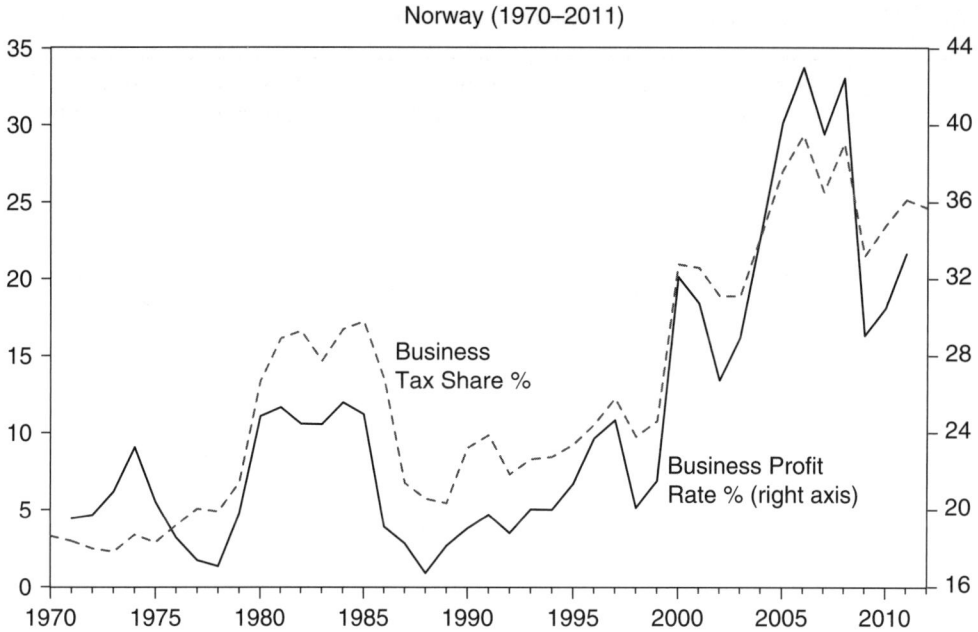

*Sources:* OECD STAN (Rev. 4) and OECD Tax Statistics databases.

*Figure 21.3 Business profit rate and tax shares for Norway*

porate taxes/total taxes). Comparisons of the corporate tax share and the business sector profit rate for Denmark and Norway, respectively, are shown in Figures 21.2 and 21.3. Denmark shows a 'looser' relationship between the two variables compared to the US and Norway. Of course, looks may be deceptive and without any econometric testing it is difficult to conclude what the nature of the underlying relationship is.

Table 21.1 shows the ECCs for the three countries along with the F statistics and the adjusted $R^2$ values. In all cases the F statistics are highly significant. With $\Delta lt_t$ as the dependent variable, all the ECCs are between −1 and 0 and are statistically significant, suggesting that the level of the profit rate drives the variations of the tax share levels in all three countries. The tax share converges to its cointegrating value at the annual rate of 56.7 percent in the case of Denmark, 45.8 percent in the case of Norway, and 43.9 percent in the case of the US (Hill et al. 2011: 503). The F statistic is greater than the upper bound value (in which it is assumed that all variables are $I(1)$) implying the existence of a cointegrating relationship with the profit rate acting as the 'forcing' term. In none of the cases was there any evidence of a positive impact of the tax share on the profit rate.

Tables 21.2, 21.3, and 21.4 show the cointegrating results ($lt$ = natural log of the tax share; $lr$ = natural log of the profit rate). The long-run coefficients imply that for a 1 percent increase in the profit rate the tax share will increase by about 2.4 percent for Denmark, 1.96 percent for Norway, and about 0.5 percent for the US. Appendix 21A.1 shows the various diagnostic tests. Appendix 21A.2 shows the ECM and cointegrating

*Table 21.1   Error correction coefficients and F statistics*

|  | Dependent variable: $\Delta lt_t$ | | Nature of the ARDL | Lower and upper bounds | Adjusted $R^2$ of each ECM |
|---|---|---|---|---|---|
|  | ECC {t} [p value] s.e. | F statistic | | | |
| Denmark | −0.56708 {−6.1048} [0.000] 0.092892 | 8.8514 | ARDL(1, 0) | 7.1046[I(0)]* and 7.9652[I(1)]* | 0.73062 |
| Norway | −0.45813 −5.3067 [0.000] 0.086330 | 14.1162 | ARDL(1, 1) | 5.3277[I(0)]* and 6.1996[I(1)]* | 0.69218 |
| US | −0.43893 {−5.6613} [0.000] 0.077531 | 19.141 | ARDL(2, 1) | 6.8063 [I(0)]* and 7.5710 [I(1)]* | 0.78000 |

*Note:* * 95% level.

*Table 21.2   Estimated long-run coefficients for Denmark from ARDL (1, 0)*

| Regressor | Coefficient | Standard error | t-ratio [p value] |
|---|---|---|---|
| Constant | 0.40603 | 0.91350 | 0.44448 [0.660] |
| Time trend | 0.050399 | 0.0059412 | 8.4830 [0.000] |
| D84 | 0.66860 | 0.23186 | 2.8836 [0.007] |
| D86 | 0.55523 | 0.18290 | 3.0357 [0.005] |
| lr | 2.3797 | 0.50924 | 4.6730 [0.000] |

*Note:* lt is the dependent variable, 1976–2011; D84 and D86 are dummy variables representing shocks in 1984 and 1986, respectively.

relationship between the US corporate profit and tax rates. The results again show the profit rate Granger causing the tax rate.

While these results show the structural dependence of the corporate tax revenue share on profitability it must not be inferred that the state is a passive bystander. Across the capitalist world, state policies, when successful, have historically played a wide variety of roles in promoting business capital accumulation. These policies have ranged from direct subsidies and the funding of research and development to the provisioning of infrastructure, all of which can lower business costs or raise labor productivity.[28] As in the US (Block 2008; Block and Keller 2011), public policies, for example in the development of corporatist arrangements and national systems of innovation (NSI),[29] have played key roles in fostering productivity growth and technological change in Denmark, Norway,

*Table 21.3   Estimated long-run coefficients for Norway, 1976–2011*

| Regressor | Coefficient | Standard error | t-ratio [p value] |
| --- | --- | --- | --- |
| Constant | 0.74192 | 0.29153 | 2.5449 [0.016] |
| lr | 1.9565 | 0.20265 | 9.6548 [0.000] |

*Note:*   *lt* is the dependent variable.

*Table 21.4   Estimated long-run coefficients for the US, 1939–2012*

| Regressor | Coefficient | Standard error | t-ratio [p value] |
| --- | --- | --- | --- |
| Constant | −0.35425 | 0.18193 | −1.9472 [0.056] |
| Time trend | −0.0074871 | 0.0012534 | −5.9736 [0.000] |
| lr | 0.49579 | 0.095496 | 5.1918 [0.000] |

*Note:*   *lt* is the dependent variable.

and elsewhere (Fagerberg et al. 2005). As one author put it: 'Popular folklore notwithstanding, the innovation journey is a collective achievement that requires key roles from numerous entrepreneurs in both the public and private sectors' (Van de Ven et al. 1999, p. 149, cited by Fagerberg et al. 2005, p. 12). Active labor market policies (ALMPs), with their central aim of maintaining labor market flexibility, constitute an excellent example of a policy framework via which states such as Denmark actively promote the competitiveness of firms while maintaining ample social protections for workers and the unemployed (Weller 2009). ALMPs would thus be another example of institutional redeployment.

The above results also show that since profitability itself is time-varying, one would not expect to see convergence in corporate tax shares across countries. Mainstream authors tend to take the view that the pressures of global competition and global capital flows will (or should) force a convergence of taxation and social policies across countries as they seek to become more efficient and competitive in attracting global capital flows. This inevitability-of-neoliberalism view predicts the inexorable growth of social retrenchment policies as well as the erosion of economies' tax bases (Campbell 2005). Yet this thesis has been contested by a number of authors within and outside the broad Marxist tradition (Campbell 2005; Block 1987, Ch. 9). Empirically, we see this claim to be problematic with regard to the corporate tax share in Norway. But one can equally well see that trends in aggregate tax rates and social expenditure shares also contradict this thesis. Despite increased global integration, aggregate tax rates have actually gone up quite dramatically in both Denmark and Norway (see Figure 21.4), both of which are small open economies heavily dependent on trade, and therefore, from the neoliberalism-is-inevitable perspective, most likely to have reduced tax rates. On the other hand, while aggregate tax rates did go up somewhat in the US between 1983 and 2000, since 2001 there has been a general decrease. Overall, though, the US case shows very little variation between 1965 and 2012.

Figure 21.5 shows social expenditures as a percentage of gross domestic product (GDP)[30] for the three countries and the OECD average.[31] Both Denmark's and Norway's

Total Taxes/GDP %

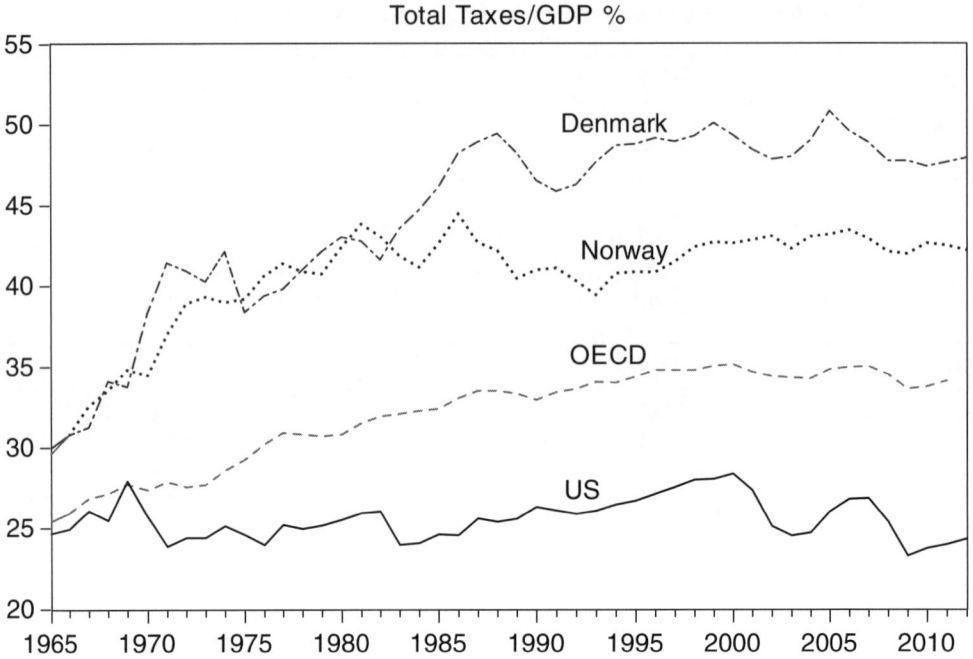

*Source:*    OECD Tax Statistics database.

*Figure 21.4    Aggregate tax/GDP ratios*

social expenditures shares are above the OECD average, although in the 2000s Norway's share has approached the OECD average while Denmark's trend has, on balance, gone up in the same period. The US as a 'welfare laggard' is evident from its average share below the OECD average although it too has experienced an increase in the 2000s,[32] in particular in the wake of the economic crisis of 2008 and the election of Barack Obama who benefited from the overwhelming support of unions and progressive political forces and faced popular pressure to provide social relief. Figure 21.4 is a very good example of the power resources approach of Korpi and others, as it reflects the existence of powerful labor movements in the two Scandinavian countries.

On the other hand, Figure 21.5 should not convey the impression that workers in Scandinavia were able to unilaterally impose a welfare state. In his comparison of various OECD countries, Steinmo observed that social democratic Sweden has historically collected much lower corporate tax shares in comparison to the more regressive forms of indirect taxes, in order to finance its extremely generous welfare state (Steinmo 1993).

Steinmo's observation is borne out when one considers the US and Denmark. Denmark's corporate tax share is less than the OECD average, whereas the US corporate tax share has been at the OECD average since the early 1980s, although it was significantly above the latter before. On the other hand, the US share of the more regressive taxes on goods and services is well below the OECD average, with the Danish share approximately at the latter level (Figure 21.6).

Social Expenditures/GDP %

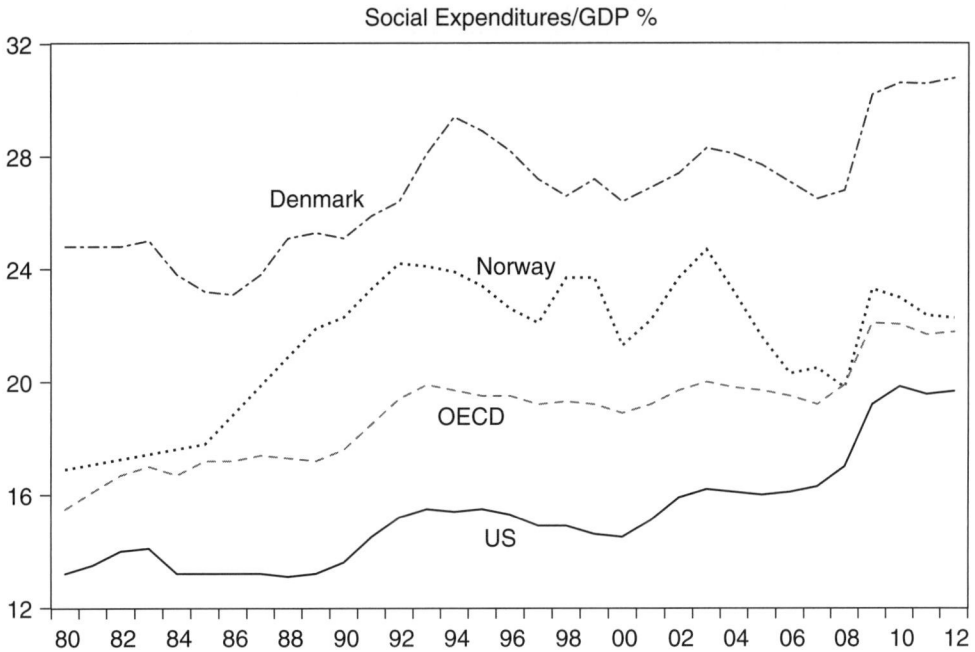

*Source:* OECD Social Protection and Well-being Database.

*Figure 21.5 Social expenditures/GDP*

Meanwhile, the Norwegian corporate tax share has generally trended up because of the variation in profit rate. Furthermore, while Norway's share of taxes on goods and services has been persistently above the OECD average, it has declined significantly since the mid-1990s, around the same time that the corporate tax share rose quite dramatically. All in all, though, Norway's taxes on goods and services share have approached the corporate tax share in the 2000s (see Figure 21.6). In comparison to Denmark, Norway's lower average total tax rate (Figure 21.4) is also consistent with a less generous welfare state (Figure 21.5). And yet, because its rising profit rate has produced a rising corporate tax share, Norway has succeeded in making its tax system less regressive by sharply reducing the share of goods and services taxes. On the other hand, the US's less generous welfare state is consistent with a lower aggregate tax rate (Figure 21.6), even though its share of goods and services taxes is much lower.

Finally, Figure 21.7 plots the difference between capitalists' and workers' contributions to social insurance as a percentage of total taxation. A positive number implies that capitalists' share exceeds that of workers. The significance of Figure 21.7 is that in Denmark, the most generous welfare state, workers' share is larger than that of employers. While in the US case, employers' share exceeds workers' share somewhat, it is still below the OECD average. Finally, Norway has historically been the most 'punitive' with regard to employers (in fact workers' contribution was zero between 1965 and 1972). And yet, the employers' share has declined relative to workers' since the 1970s and now the difference

Corporate Taxes/Total Taxes %

Taxes on Goods and Services/Total Taxes %

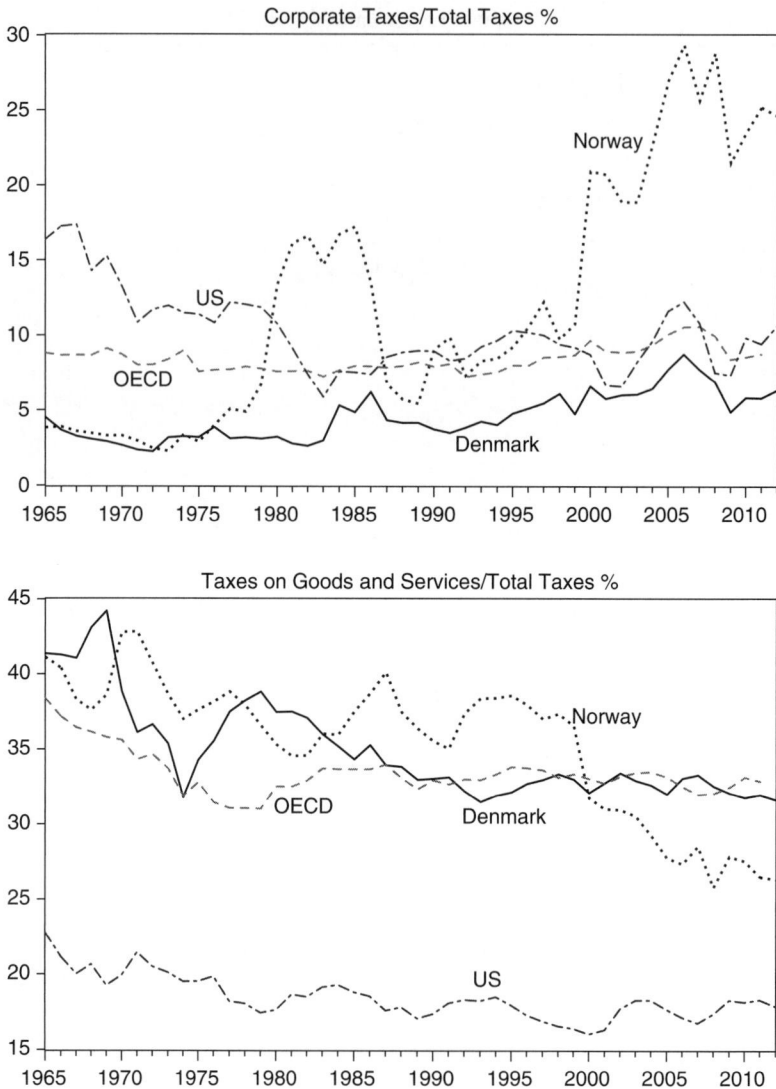

*Source:*    OECD Tax Statistics.

*Figure 21.6    Corporate taxes/total taxes and taxes on goods and services/total taxes*

hovers around the OECD average. Finally, compared to the US, Denmark's far more generous welfare state is also equally generous toward employers as far as social contributions are concerned.

A number of observations can be made. First, the barrier posed by the profit rate as far as the corporate tax rate is concerned is of course a time-varying one, given the historical variations of the former. Furthermore, the state can influence business profitability via

(Employer–Employee Contributions to Social Insurance)/Total Taxes

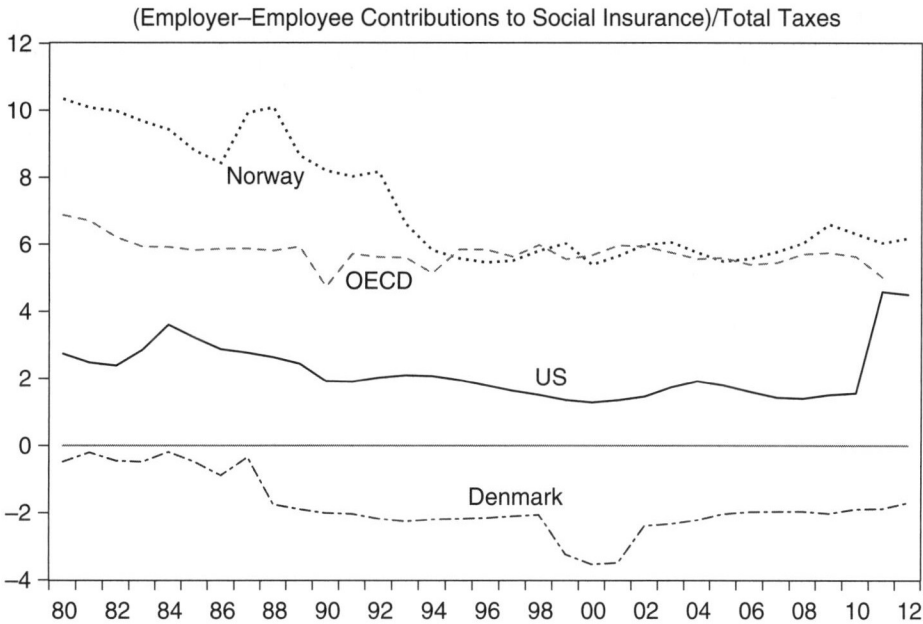

*Source:*  OECD Tax Statistics database.

*Figure 21.7*   *Difference between capitalists' and workers' contributions to social
insurance as percentage of total taxation*

the policy and political environment, the entire gamut of which shapes costs, sales, and
productivity. For example, active labor market policies highlight both the political agency
of the state as well as its need to promote profitability if it is to remain a viable institution. Finally, there is an asymmetry here since the state cannot, obviously, determine the
profit rate: labor struggles within the firm, technological change with its effect on the
capital–output ratio (Shaikh 1992), global competition and macroeconomic conditions,
the various factors that determine business mark-ups on costs,[33] and of course policy and
political factors, all work together to determine profit rates.

Second, this asymmetric relationship between the business sector and the state does
not necessarily make the latter out to be an ancillary institution. Politics does matter,
for better or worse, for social democratic policies, as the power resources approach has
emphasized. The presence of a relatively strong social democratic labor movement has
allowed for both higher aggregate tax rates and social expenditure rates in both of the
Scandinavian countries. On the other hand, while social expenditures have also grown in
the US, their far more modest level (persistently below the OECD average) is a reflection
of domestic political realities including, very importantly, the absence of national-level
left-wing parties and the presence of a federalist political structure with the potential for
great regional political and policy diversity (Swank and Martin 2012). A federalist system
thus has greater potential to nullify or tamp down progressive policies at the national
level.

Third, if one considers taxes on goods and services to be regressive, then the two Scandinavian countries turn out to have more regressive tax systems compared to the US. And yet here too one must bear in mind the Norwegian case: rising corporate tax shares after the mid-1990s have been accompanied by falling shares of taxes on goods and services.

Fourth, despite or perhaps because of their very generous welfare states, employer's relative contributions to social insurance have fallen in the case of Norway or been persistently below workers' contributions as in Denmark. As Paster (2012) argues with regard to Germany, this would presumably be a policy to contain non-wage labor costs so as to boost international competitiveness. Coupled with active labor market policies, industrial and innovation policies (Campbell and Pedersen 2007), we see here again the relevance of a particular type of PPM. On the other hand, its level below the OECD average in the US case has been accompanied by labor market flexibility of the traditional kind (with a poorly developed social safety net) along with generous state industrial policies vis-à-vis business (Block and Keller 2011).

Fifth, and finally, the above analysis shows that if a country is committed to maintaining a viable social democratic economy (that is, a generous welfare state and health capital accumulation), it has to maintain an appropriate 'tax mix' that does not reduce business profitability while maintaining adequate financial resources for the state. This tax composition is shaped by complex political economy factors, as authors in the fiscal sociology literature have argued. In a way that Kaldor would later discuss, for both Schumpeter and Goldscheid (Musgrave 1992, p. 99), taxing the business sector was a particular challenge. This is because its taxable capacity was intimately related to the incentive to accumulate capital: 'The tax must not demand from the people so much that they lose financial interest in production' (Schumpeter 1918 [1991], p. 112, cited by Musgrave 1992, p. 92). Of course, as this chapter has shown, this taxable capacity of the business sector is historically variable and is influenced by state policies, although these issues were not dealt with by the Schumpeter or Goldscheid.[34]

Together, these empirical findings and arguments confirm a kind of 'diversity-in-unity' policy framework: policies in capitalist states that try to remain viable are all united by the common goal of attempting to promote business profitability, and yet the policy mix varies because of different political realities and pressures on the state. The state is not necessarily a prisoner of capitalist interests, nor does it have the type of agency (as is implicit in post-Keynesian analyses) to unilaterally set the policy agenda in the way that it desires in order to satisfy social democratic objectives.

## 21.4   CONCLUSION

Progressive policy proposals by heterodox economists generally tend to be statements of what the state should do. Rather like *Hamlet* without the prince, the analysis of the state and the unequal power relations in capitalist societies that shape policies is missing in this state-centered literature. No attempt is made to analyze the turbulent environment within which state policy-makers exist as they attempt to grapple with the, oftentimes, rival demands of business capital accumulation and social justice. Right-wing assaults against the welfare state and labor protection are generally presented without any grounded analysis of the reasons why business groups across the world generally push back against progressive policies; or, crucially, their varying degrees of success. Equally important, heterodox economists generally tend to be silent about how business power is exercised. The diversity-in-unity perspective alluded to in the previous section suggests the need for the study of both the history[35] and the historiography of business–state power relations in a particular country. For example, I would argue that the use of a variety of different types of sources (primary, secondary, government, and business) to investigate whether or not business supported the establishment of the welfare state in Sweden and the US in the 1930s (Swenson 2002; Hacker and Pierson 2002; Korpi 2006; Paster 2013) is exactly the methodology that should underpin policy analysis. Where relevant, this type of work should be complemented via empirical or econometric analysis.

While the broad Marxist tradition has, on the other hand, dealt with questions of power and the state, the problem is that it tends to underemphasize the state's political agency. The theoretical focus in this tradition is on the relative autonomy of the state, with an implicit emphasis on the adjective of this phrase, that is, the limits to state autonomy in the policy realm. While I would agree with the Marxist focus on the power of capitalists, my main concern is with this literature's highly abstract nature, which leaves little room for an analysis of the concrete ways in which states have sometimes intervened quite successfully into what Marx called the 'hidden abode of production' because of some social needs, and why at other times it has failed. Marx was very aware of the significance of the English Factory Acts, in terms of not only their enormous positive impact on the British working class, but also the fact that they were the culmination of political pressures from the working class and other social groups such as churches, spread over many decades (Booth 1978). As with other social policies in the face of entrenched business opposition, such as the Clean Air Act or car safety legislation in the US, or equitable public health-care and pension reform initiatives in Chile (Huber et al. 2010),[36] it has to be recognized that while business profitability plays a crucial role in capitalist economies, the state's margin of maneuver is not rigidly fixed but itself subject to different types of PPMs.

The purpose of this chapter is to suggest that both qualitative and quantitative methods need to be used to gauge the nature of the contested space within which the state operates when attempting to implement social democratic policies. I have deliberately chosen to use the term 'contested autonomy' to highlight the importance of business pressure on policy and the ways in which the state may, or may not, be able to reconcile business demands with social needs. A key insight of the contested autonomy view is that since the state of business confidence is determined by the PPM the state may be able to include in the mix social policy measures that satisfy both business and social needs. As Streeck (2009) argues, such a compromise is an uneasy one and changed economic conditions may redouble business efforts to unshackle regulations that it deems a threat to its autonomy. In short, in contrast to the implicit view of post-Keynesian authors, capitalists are not passive policy-takers. On the other hand, the state is not a passive policy-maker either, obediently following capitalist diktats.

Methodologically, such an approach to policy does not just require an integration of politics and power, but also necessitates a historically informed or diachronic analysis, for two reasons. First, as mentioned above, changed economic circumstances may in turn change the nature of the business contestation. Second, a diachronic analysis enables a deeper understanding of the processes via which a progressive policy initiative either succeeded or failed. For example, even if businesses eventually come to accept a certain type of progressive policy, their acquiescence may be due to a form of strategic accommodation to political pressure as opposed to a primary preference for such policies. This central point is emphasized by a number of authors who study the history of state–business relations (Paster 2012; Hacker and Pierson 2002; Vogel 1983). As David Vogel (1978, p. 53, emphasis added) notes:

> it is important not to confuse regulations supported by executives *because the alternatives appeared more disadvantageous* – state workman's compensation and federal environmental protection are examples a half-century apart – with corporate support for government intervention. On balance, the preponderance of corporate opinion has been opposed to the overwhelming majority of governmental regulations that attempt to interfere with business.

The potential lack of congruence between business executives' preferences and the social democratic policy proposals is significant as far as the latter are concerned. Faced with business resistance and counter-pressure from society, the initial version of the policy may be modified to reach some sort of a 'compromise' in which the policy proposal is 'toned down' and accompanied by various pro-business policies. For example, in her book *Put to Work*, Nancy Rose (2009) discusses the powerful business opposition in the United States to the New Deal jobs programs, several of whose more 'radical' initiatives were discarded even though others pertaining to nation-building public investment projects were maintained (Leighninger 2007). However, matters did not rest there. Although the New Deal made a landmark policy framework, it came under continuous attack from powerful and well-organized business groups (such as the Business Roundtable) especially from the 1970s. This business mobilization accelerated when government regulatory policies increased, social programs grew, and there was open discussion in 'respectable' circles about the need for a national planning agency and full employment policies (Phillips-Fein 2009; Akard 1992). The fact that the business lobby was highly successfully in eliminating such progressive policy proposals from the national policy discourse is of enormous theoretical significance for post-Keynesian authors who propose policies without taking into account power or politics.

The benefit of this type of historically informed work is that it will allow for a deeper understanding of the tug-of-war between states and capitalists which, given progressive mobilization for social reforms, will be shaped not only by the state's own internal political capacities but also by the degree of cohesiveness or fragmentation of business groups. For example, such a methodological framework will provide a better insight into the very different policy trajectories in two democratic countries such as Argentina and Chile over the past 30 years, with their very different levels of business cohesion (Schneider 2004; Moudud et al. 2014) combined with similar levels of progressive popular mobilization and levels of economic development.

## NOTES

1.  Throughout this chapter 'social democratic policies' refer to universalistic and solidaristic progressive taxation, social, and labor (TSL) policies in the context of a capitalist economy, that is, policies that are in the tradition of the Universal Declaration of Human Rights. I am not referring to the market-

friendly 'third way' approaches of the US Democrats and the UK's Labour Party. There is no assumption that social democratic policies can resolve the structural contradictions or problems of capitalist economies.

2. Lipton discusses the role of a very important conservative think-tank called the Employment Policies Institute, with close ties to industry that has opposed the minimum wage bill. My point in bringing up business opposition to minimum wage increases does not imply that economic analyses of the type carried out by these kinds of institutes are correct. The central point of my chapter is that businesses do oppose certain socially progressive legislations, and so the question becomes: how do proponents of such policies attempt to override the opposition? It should also be observed that an increase in the minimum wage could have effective demand effects or may be absorbed by certain firms such as Costco with no major deleterious impacts on their costs or profitability. This is quite simply because, contra perfect competition, firms within industries are highly heterogeneous with different cost structures.

3. See Gabriel's (2013) article 'Fleeing to next town, bosses may find minimum wage is rising there, too'. This article is also significant from my standpoint because of its mention of the joint policy implemented by several neighboring towns to raise the minimum wage as an attempt to curtail the capital flight.

4. The conundrum, as Kalecki (1943) argued, is that society has no assurance that these pro-business policies will produce higher levels of investment and employment.

5. http://corporateeurope.org/.

6. See TNI's *State of Power* 2014 report.

7. See for example Le (2004) who models private investment in developing countries in terms of socio-political factors and the state of uncertainty which would impact the state of business confidence.

8. See Moudud and Martinez Hernandez (2014) for references to the extensive literature on this topic.

9. For example high profitability and international competitive dominance coupled with a strong labor movement in one historical period may make firms support free trade and – perhaps begrudgingly – social democratic policies. On the other hand, the push for social retrenchment and protectionism or outsourcing to low-wage countries by businesses is likely to increase in an economic crisis with a weakened labor movement.

10. Sweden was not included because of insufficient business sector capital stock data.

11. It is not surprising that Godley entitled one of his publications 'Fiscal policy to the rescue' (Godley 2001), an apolitical and mechanical approach to policy-making that is characteristic of much of the macroeconomics literature.

12. Among modern authors, Ralph Milliband is associated with the instrumental power perspective, and Nicos Poulantzas and Fred Block with the structural power perspective. These authors are generally placed in the broad Marxist tradition although it must be pointed out that the powerful role of business groups in capitalist societies has also been recognized by non-Marxist authors such as C. Wright Mills, G. William Domhoff, and Charles Lindblom (Hacker and Pierson 2002; Held 1989, p. 146).

13. Swenson's argument is that in both Sweden and Denmark intra-class conflicts between capitalists and cross-alliances between certain capitalists and workers combined with certain dominant capitalists' support for social democratic policies – because they benefitted from them – enabled such policies to be consolidated. This view has been contested by other authors (Hacker and Pierson 2002; Korpi 2006; Paster 2013) who have argued that capitalist support for such policies was never a primary preference but rather a form of strategic accommodation to growing working class militancy. One could argue that this strategic accommodation was, in part, due to the relative political weakness of capitalists because of intraclass rivalries.

14. For example, Jonas Pontusson in his book *The Limits of Social Democracy: Investment Politics in Sweden* (Pontusson 1994) discusses Swedish employers' successful opposition to the main trade union's attempts to control investment decisions via wage-earner funds.

15. To see the significance of this point see the debates between Swenson (2002), Hacker and Pierson (2002), Korpi (2006), and Paster (2012).

16. For a comparison of Nordic countries' labor markets see TeamaNord (2010).

17. See Paul Downward's Chapter 10 in this *Handbook*.

18. A good example of a limit cycle is Richard Goodwin's predator–prey model linking the unemployment rate and the wage share.

19. It should be recalled that the regression estimators are slopes, that is, each estimator equals the first difference of the dependent variable divided by the first difference of the corresponding independent variable. Since the first difference of a variable in natural log form gives its percentage change it follows that each regression estimator is in fact a ratio of the percentage changes of the dependent and independent variables, that is, it is an elasticity.

20. The framework tests the null hypothesis $H_0$: $\beta 1 = \beta 2 = 0$ (the 'non-existence of a long-run or trend relationship' between the variables), against the alternative hypothesis $H_A$: $\beta 1 \neq \beta 2 \neq 0$. If this yields an F statistic which is significant then the existence of a levels (or trend) relationship is confirmed (Pesaran et

al. 2001). On the other hand, acceptance of the null (an insignificant F) would allow us to conclude the non-existence of a long-run or trend relationship.

21. Of course when profit rates are relatively high pro-business policies may entail tax cuts (such as the Kennedy–Johnson tax cut).

22. I follow the broad Marxian tradition (Bowles et al. 1986; Duménil and Lévy 1993; Foley 1986; Shaikh 1992) in making use of the profit rate in my analysis.

23. In order to calculate the corporate profit rate, I obtained data for pre-tax corporate profits with inventory valuation adjustment (IVA) and capital consumption adjustment (CCAdj) from Federal Reserve Economic Data standard series Table 1.14. The current-cost net capital stock data are from Table 4.1. The components of the corporate tax share (current taxes on corporate income/current receipts) are from Table 3.1. All these data were downloaded from the Bureau of Economic Analysis (http://www.bea.gov/national/index.htm).

24. The correlation between the corporate profit rate and corporate tax revenue share is 0.89 with a t statistic of 17.23 while the correlation between the corporate profit and tax rates is 0.54 with a t statistic of 5.8.

25. The nominal gross operating surplus and nominal capital stock data were obtained from the OECD STAN (Rev. 4 version) online database which spans the period 1970–2011. The OECD publishes data series for the output and capital stock of the non-agricultural business sector, which excludes: (a) agriculture, forestry and fishery; (b) community, social and personal services; and (c) real estate activities. The rationale for this OECD measure is that in many countries the item (a) contains a certain amount of residential investment; item (b) contains non-market outputs, partly provided by the state; and item (c) contains the category 'owner-occupied dwelling' with its fictitious imputed output. Thus the non-agricultural business sector is an estimate of the core capitalist (that is, profit-making) sector of the economy. Given the corporate sector's dominant role in advanced capitalist economies, I will use the non-agricultural business sector as a proxy for the corporate sector, thereby enabling a comparison of the two time series. I calculated the profit rate by dividing the nominal gross operating surplus by the previous period's nominal capital stock (both variables belong to the D05T82X series: non-agriculture business sector excluding real estate).

26. http://www.oecd-ilibrary.org/taxation/data/oecd-tax-statistics_tax-data-en.

27. I used the 1200 series.

28. A recent *New York Times* article reports that tax-funded investment in extremely high-speed fiberoptic infrastructure in Chattanooga, Tennessee, lowered business costs and made this city a magnet for business investment. See Moudud and Martinez-Hernandez (2014) who discuss the ways in which infrastructure investment of certain types would raise the turnover rate and the profit rate in Marx's theoretical framework (Wyatt 2014).

29. See *The Oxford Handbook of Innovation* (Fagerberg et al. 2005) for an extensive analysis of the NSI approach, including the role of the public sector.

30. Social expenditures include social policy arenas such as old age, survivors, disability benefits, health, family, active labor market policies, housing, unemployment, and so on.

31. The database provided only two data points for the pre-1988 period for Norway. The software used (Eviews 7.0) to make the graphs allowed for the possibility of extrapolating missing values, thereby enabling an approximation to the social expenditure share for the 1980–87 period.

32. On a per capita basis, the US social expenditures (in USD) at constant (2000) prices and constant purchasing power parity (2000) have shown the most dramatic increase between 2000 and 2010, rising from $5704.2 to $8316.7 during the decade.

33. See *Alternative Theories of Competition: Challenges to the Orthodoxy* (Moudud et al. 2012) for a wide range of perspectives that challenge neoclassical theories of the firm and propose various alternatives theories of business price-setting behavior.

34. It is noteworthy, though, that Schumpeter figures prominently in the contemporary national systems of innovation literature (see, e.g., Fagerberg et al. 2005) with its emphasis on, among other things, the ways in which public policies influence business performance. Thus, at least implicitly, one can trace in Schumpeter's broader intellectual framework the state's ability to shape business profitability and thus the taxable capacity.

35. Historical analysis should involve a study of business history and, when possible, the examination of archival work on business–state relations. Case studies of specific state–business relations, the nature of formal business organizations, and the ways in which informal business networks work (Haddad 2012) would be central aspects of such a research agenda. Excellent examples of historically informed studies of state–business relations would be the type of work done by Schneider or Silva on Latin American business groups (Schneider 2004; Silva 1997).

36. Huber et al. (2010, p. 95) observe that the reformed healthcare policy (the AUGE program) under the Lagos government and pension reform under the Bachelet one have 'constituted major departures from the neoliberal model of narrowly targeted and market-driven social policy'. It may be recalled that the Chilean privatized social security model was once hailed as an exemplar for other countries to follow.

The PPM framework is consistent with the Critical Legal Studies (CLS) tradition. CLS authors have rejected the narrowly functionalist view of law (that it is a functional reflection of the economy or an 'epiphenomenon') and have argued instead that, by determining the structure of property relations in capitalism, the law plays a constitutive role in determining the nature of power struggles, including those between capitalists and workers. For a classic article in the CLS tradition see Robert W. Gordon's 'Critical Legal Histories' (Gordon 1984).

# REFERENCES

Akard, Patrick J. (1992), 'Corporate mobilization and political power: the transformation of US economic policy in the 1970s', *American Sociological Review*, **57** (5), 597–615.

Alderman, Liz (2014), 'France tries to tempt in more foreign investment', *New York Times*, B1, B4.

Amsden, Alice H. (1989), *Asia's Next Giant: South Korea and Late Industrialization*, New York, USA and Oxford, UK: Oxford University Press.

Barrow, Clyde W. (1993), *Critical Theories of the State: Marxist, Neo-Marxist, Post-Marxist*, Madison, WI: University of Wisconsin Press.

Beveridge, William H. (1944), *Report on Full Employment in a Free Society*, London: Allen & Unwin.

Block, Fred L. (1987), *Revising State Theory: Essays in Politics and Postindustrialism*, Philadelphia, PA: Temple University Press.

Block, Fred L. (2008), 'Swimming against the current: the rise of a hidden developmental state in the United States', *Politics and Society*, **36** (2), 169–206.

Block, Fred L. and Matthew R. Keller (2011), *State of Innovation: The US Government's Role in Technology Development*, Boulder, CO, USA and London, UK: Paradigm Publishers.

Booth, Douglas E. (1978), 'Karl Marx on state regulation of the labor process: the English factory acts', *Review of Social Economy*, **36** (2), 137–57.

Bowles, Samuel, David M. Gordon, and Thomas E. Weisskopf (1986), 'Power and profits: the social structure of accumulation and the profitability of the postwar US economy', *Review of Radical Political Economics*, **18** (1–2), 132–67.

Campbell, John L. (2005), 'Fiscal sociology in an age of globalization: comparing tax regimes in advanced capitalist countries', in Victor Nee and Richard Swedberg (eds), *The Economic Sociology of Capitalism*, Princeton, NJ: Princeton University Press, pp. 319–418.

Campbell, John L. and John A. Hall (2006), 'The state of Denmark', in John L. Campbell, John A. Hall and Ove K. Pedersen (eds), *National Identity and the Varieties of Capitalism: The Danish Experience*, Montreal and Kingston, Canada and Ithaca, NY, USA: McGill-Queen's University Press, pp. 1–49.

Campbell, John L. and Ove K. Pedersen (2007), 'The varieties of capitalism and hybrid success', *Comparative Political Studies*, **40** (3), 307–32.

Chang, Ha-Joon (2002a), 'Kicking away the ladder: an unofficial history of capitalism, especially in Britain and the United States', *Challenge*, **45** (5), 63–97.

Chang, Ha-Joon (2002b), 'Breaking the mould: an institutionalist political economy alternative to the neo-liberal theory of the market and the state', *Cambridge Journal of Economics*, **26** (5), 539–59.

Dass, Raju J. (2006), 'Marxist theories of the state', in Steven Pressman (ed.), *Alternative Theories of the State*, Basingstoke, UK and New York, USA: Palgrave Macmillan, pp. 64–112.

Davenport, Coral (2013), 'Large companies prepared to pay price on carbon', *New York Times*, December 5, accessed July 31, 2014 at http://www.nytimes.com/2013/12/05/business/energy-environment/large-companies-prepared-to-pay-price-on-carbon.html?_r=0

Diebold, Francis X. (2001), *Elements of Forecasting*, 2nd edn, Mason, OH: South Western Publishing.

Duménil, Gérard and Dominique Lévy (1993), *The Economics of the Profit Rate: Competition, Crisis, and Historical Tendencies in Capitalism*, Aldershot: Edward Elgar.

Evans, Peter (1995), *Embedded Autonomy: States and Industrial Transformation*, Princeton, NJ: Princeton University Press.

Fagerberg, Jan, David C. Mowery, and Richard R. Nelson (eds) (2005), *The Oxford Handbook of Innovation*, New York: Oxford University Press.

Fairfield, Tasha (2010), 'Business power and tax reform: taxing income and profits in Chile and Argentina', *Latin American Politics and Society*, **52** (2), 37–71.

Fairfield, Tasha (2011), 'Business power and protest: Argentina's agricultural producers protest in comparative context', *Studies in Comparative International Development*, **46** (4), 424–53.

Farnsworth, Kevin (2004), *Corporate Power and Social Policy in a Global Economy: British Welfare under the Influence*, Bristol: Policy Press.

Ferguson, Thomas (1995), *Golden Rule: The Investment Theory of Party Competition and the Logic of Money-Driven Political Systems*, Chicago, IL: University of Chicago Press.

Foley, D.K. (1986), *Understanding Capital: Marx's Economic Theory*, Cambridge, MA, USA and London, UK: Harvard University Press.

Forstater, Mathew (2001), 'An institutionalist post Keynesian methodology of economic policy with an application to full employment', Center for Full Employment and Price Stability (CFEPS) Working Paper Series No. 18, Kansas City, MI: University of Missouri–Kansas City.

Forstater, Mathew (2003), 'Toward a new instrumental macroeconomics: Abba Lerner and Adolph Lowe on economic method, theory, history, and policy', in Edward J. Nell and Mathew Forstater (eds), *Reinventing Functional Finance: Transformational Growth and Full Employment*, Cheltenham, UK and Northampton, MA, USA: Edward Elgar, pp. 52–65.

Gabriel, Trip (2013), 'Fleeing to next town, bosses may find minimum wage is rising there, too', *New York Times*, December 6, accessed July 31, 2014 at http://www.nytimes.com/2013/12/07/us/as-employers-grouse-cluster-of-governments-seeks-to-raise-minimum-wage.html.

Godley, W. (2001), 'Fiscal policy to the rescue', Policy Note 2001/1, Annandale-on-Hudson, NY: Jerome Levy Economics Institute of Bard College.

Godley, W. and M. Lavoie (2007), *Monetary Economics: An Integrated Approach to Credit, Money, Income, Production and Wealth*, Basingstoke: Palgrave Macmillan.

Gordon, R.W. (1984), 'Critical legal histories', *Stanford Law Review*, **36** (1), 57–125.

Gourevitch, Peter (1986), *Politics in Hard Times: Comparative Responses to International Economic Crises*, Ithaca, NY: Cornell University Press.

Gujarati, Damodar N. and Dawn C. Porter (2009), *Basic Econometrics*, 5th edn, New York: McGraw-Hill Irwin.

Hacker, Jacob S. and Paul Pierson (2002), 'Business power and social policy: employers and the formation of the American welfare state', *Politics and Society*, **30** (2), 277–325.

Haddad, Bassam (2012), 'Syria, the Arab uprisings, and the political economy of authoritarian resilience', *Interface*, **4** (1), 113–30.

Hall, P.A. and D. Soskice (eds) (2001), *Varieties of Capitalism: The Institutional Foundations of Comparative Advantage*, Oxford: Oxford University Press.

Held, David (1989), *Political Theory and the Modern State*, Stanford, CA: Stanford University Press.

Hill, R. Carter, William E. Griffiths, and Guay C. Lim (2011), *Principles of Econometrics*, 4th edn, New York: John Wiley & Sons.

Huber, Evelyne, Jennifer Pribble, and John D. Stephens (2010), 'The Chilean left in power: achievements, failures, and omissions', in Kurt Weyland, Raúl Madrid and Wendy Hunter (eds), *Leftist Governments in Latin America: Successes and Shortcomings*, New York: Cambridge University Press, pp. 77–97.

Kalecki, M. (1943), 'Political aspects of full employment', *Political Quarterly*, **14** (4), 322–31.

Korpi, Walter (1983), *The Democratic Class Struggle*, London: Routledge and Kegan Paul.

Korpi, Walter (2006), 'Power resources and employer-centered approaches in explanations of welfare states and varieties of capitalism: protagonists, consenters, and antagonists', *World Politics*, **58** (2), 167–206.

Korsgaard, Ove (2006), 'The Danish way to establish the nation in the hearts of the people', in John L. Campbell, John A. Hall, and Ove K. Pedersen (eds), *National Identity and the Varieties of Capitalism: The Danish Experience*, Montreal and Kingston, Canada and Ithaca, NY, USA: McGill-Queen's University Press, pp. 133–58.

Landais, Camille, Thomas Piketty, and Emmanuel Saez (2011), *Pour Une Revolution Fiscale*, Paris: Seuil.

Le, Q.V. (2004), 'Political and economic determinants of private investment', *Journal of International Development*, **16** (4), 589–604.

Leighninger, Robert D. Jr (2007), *Long-Range Public Investment: The Forgotten Legacy of the New Deal*, Columbia, SC: University of South Carolina Press.

Levy, Jonah D. (2005), 'Redeploying the state: liberalization and social policy in France', in Wolfgang Streeck and Kathleen Thelen (eds), *Beyond Continuity: Institutional Change in Advanced Political Economies*, Oxford, UK and New York, USA: Oxford University Press, pp. 103–26.

Lipton, Eric (2014), 'Fight over wage illustrates web of industry ties', *New York Times*, February 10, accessed July 31, 2014 at http://www.nytimes.com/2014/02/10/us/politics/fight-over-minimum-wage-illustrates-web-of-industry-ties.html?_r=0.

MacLennan, Carol A. (1988), 'From accident to crash: the auto industry and the politics of injury', *Medical Anthropology Quarterly*, **2** (3), 233–50.

Moudud, Jamee K., Cyrus Bina, and Patrick L. Mason (eds) (2012), *Alternative Theories of Competition: Challenges to the Orthodoxy*, New York: Routledge.

Moudud, Jamee K., Esteban Perez Caldentey, and Enrique Delamonica (2014), 'State–business relations and the financing of the welfare state in Argentina and Chile', *United Nations Research Institute for Social Development (UNRISD) Working Papers* (2014-23), 1–31.

Moudud, Jamee K. and Francisco Martinez Hernandez (2014), 'The political economy of public investment and public finance: challenges for social democratic policies', *Review of Keynesian Economics*, **2** (3), 333–64.

Musgrave, R.A. (1992), 'Schumpeter's crisis of the tax state: an essay in fiscal sociology', *Journal of Evolutionary Economics*, **2** (2), 89–113.

Paster, Thomas (2012), *The Role of Business in the Development of the Welfare State and Labor Markets in Germany: Containing Social Reforms*, London, UK and New York, USA: Routledge.

Paster, Thomas (2013), 'Business and welfare state development: why did employers accept social reforms?', *World Politics*, **65** (3), 416–51.

Pérez Caldentey, Esteban (2012), 'Income convergence, capability divergence, and the middle income trap: an analysis of the case of Chile', *Studies in Comparative International Development*, **47** (2), 185–207.

Pesaran, M. Hashem, Yongcheol Shin, and Richard J. Smith (2001), 'Bounds testing approaches to the analysis of level relationships', **16** (3), 289–326.

Peterson, Wallace C. and Paul S. Estenson (1996), *Income, Employment, and Economic Growth*, 8th edn, New York: W.W. Norton.

Phillips-Fein, Kim (2009), *Invisible Hands: The Businessmen's Crusade Against the New Deal*, New York: W.W. Norton.

Polanyi, Karl (1944), *The Great Transformation: The Political and Economic Origins of Our Time*, New York: Rinehart & Company.

Pontusson, Jonas (1994), *The Limits of Social Democracy: Investment Politics in Sweden*, Ithaca, NY: Cornell University Press.

Prasad, Monica (2006), *The Politics of Free Markets: The Rise of Neoliberal Economic Policies in Britain, France, Germany, and the United States*, Chicago, IL, USA and London, UK: University of Chicago Press.

Riesco, Manuel (ed.) (2007), *Latin America: A New Developmental Welfare State Model in the Making?*, New York: Palgrave MacMillan and UNRISD.

Roberts, Kenneth (2011), 'Chile: The left after neoliberalism', in Steven Levitsky and Kenneth M. Roberts (eds), *The Resurgence of the Latin American Left*, Baltimore, MD: Johns Hopkins University Press, pp. 325–47.

Rose, Nancy E. (2009), *Put to Work: The WPA and Public Employment in the Great Depression*, 2nd edn, New York: Monthly Review Press.

Sandbrook, R., M. Edelman, P. Heller, and J. Teichman (2007), *Social Democracy in the Global Periphery: Origins, Challenges, Prospects*, Cambridge: Cambridge University Press.

Schneider, Ben Ross (2004), *Business Politics and the State in Twentieth-Century Latin America*, Cambridge, UK and New York, USA: Cambridge University Press.

Schumpeter, Joseph (1918 [1991]), 'The crisis of the tax state', in R. Swedberg (ed.) (1991), *The Economics and Sociology of Capitalism*, Princeton, NJ: Princeton University Press, pp. 99–140.

Sen, Amartya (1999), *Development as Freedom*, New York: Anchor Books.

Shaikh, Anwar M. (1992), 'The falling rate of profit and long waves in accumulation: theory and evidence', in A. Kleinknecht, E. Mandel, and I. Wallerstein (eds), *New Findings in Long Wave Research*, London: Macmillan, pp. 174–95.

Silva, Eduardo (1997), 'Business elites and the state in Chile', in Sylvia Maxfield and Ben Ross Schneider (eds), *Business and the State in Developing Countries*, Ithaca, NY, USA and London, UK: Cornell University Press, pp. 152–88.

Steinmo, Sven (1993), *Taxation and Democracy*, New Haven, CT, USA and London, UK: Yale University Press.

Stephens, Evelyne Huber and John D. Stephens (1986), *Democratic Socialism in Jamaica: The Political Movement and Social Transformation in Dependent Capitalism*, London: Palgrave Macmillan.

Streeck, Wolfgang (2009), *Re-Forming Capitalism: Institutional Change in the German Political Economy*, Oxford, UK and New York, USA: Oxford University Press.

Swank, Duane and Cathie Jo Martin (2012), *The Political Construction of Business Interests: Coordination, Growth, and Equality*, New York: Cambridge University Press.

Swenson, Peter A. (1991), 'Bringing capital back in, or social democracy reconsidered: employer power, cross-class alliances, and centralization of industrial relations in Denmark and Sweden', *World Politics*, **43** (4), 513–44.

Swenson, Peter A. (2002), *Capitalists Against Markets: The Making of Labor Markets and Welfare States in the United States and Sweden*, New York: Oxford University Press.

TeamaNord (2020), 'Labour market mobility in Nordic welfare states', Copenhagen: Nordic Council of Ministers, Copenhagen, accessed February 8, 2010 at http://norden.diva-portal.org/smash/get/diva2:701612/FULLTEXT01.pdf.

Transnational Institute (TNI) in collaboration with Occupy.com (2014), *The State of Power 2014: Exposing the Davos Class*, Amsterdam: Transnational Institute, accessed January 23, 2014 at https://www.tni.org/files/download/state_of_power-6feb14.pdf.

Trumbull, Gunnar (2004), *Silicon and the State: French Innovation Policy in the Internet Age*, Washington, DC: Brookings Institution Press.

Van de Ven, A., D.E. Polley, R. Garud, and S. Venkataraman (1999), *The Innovation Journey*, New York: Oxford University Press.

Vogel, David (1978), 'Why businessmen distrust their state: the political consciousness of American corporate executives', *British Journal of Political Science*, **8** (1), 47–78.

Vogel, David (1983), 'The power of business in America: a re-appraisal', *British Journal of Political Science*, **13** (1), 19–43.

Wade, Robert (1990), *Governing the Market: Economic Theory and the Role of Government in East Asian Industrialization*, Princeton, NJ: Princeton University Press.

Weller, Jurgen (2009), *Regulation, Worker Protection, and Active Labour-Market Policies in Latin America*, Santiago: Economic Commission for Latin America and the Caribbean.

Whalen, Charles J. (2012), 'Post-Keynesian institutionalism after the great recession', Levy Institute Working Paper 721, New York: Levy Institute.

Wray, L. Randall (1998), *Understanding Modern Money*, Cheltenham, UK and Lyme, NH, USA: Edward Elgar.

Wyatt, Edward (2014), 'A city wired for growth: superfast internet attracts business to Chattanooga', *New York Times*, February 4, B1 and B4.

# APPENDIX 21A.1

*Table 21A.1   Diagnostic test statistics*

|  | Test statistics | LM Test | F Test |
|---|---|---|---|
| Denmark | Serial correlation | $X^2_{sc}(1) = 2.9740$ [0.085] | $F(1, 29) = 2.6115$ [0.117] |
|  | Functional form | $X^2_{FF}(1) = 0.039494$ [0.842] | $F(1, 29) = 0.031850$ [0.860] |
|  | Normality | $X^2_{N}(2) = 0.57015$ [0.752] | NA |
|  | Heteroskedasticity | $X^2_{H}(1) = 2.1584$ [0.142] | $F(1, 34) = 2.1685$ [0.150] |
| Norway | Serial correlation | $X^2_{sc}(1) = 0.42340$ [0.515] | $F(1, 31) = 0.36893$ [0.548] |
|  | Functional form | $X^2_{FF}(1) = 12.5135$ [0.000] | $F(1, 31) = 16.5166$ [0.000] |
|  | Normality | $X^2_{N}(2) = 1.4613$ [0.482] | NA |
|  | Heteroskedasticity | $X^2_{H}(1) = 0.70950$ [0.400] | $F(1, 34) = 0.68356$ [0.414] |
| US | Serial correlation | $X^2_{sc}(1) = 0.036917$ [0.848] | $F(1, 67) = 0.033441$ [0.855] |
|  | Functional form | $X^2_{FF}(1) = 0.42620$ [0.514] | $F(1, 67) = 0.38812$ [0.535] |
|  | Normality | $X^2_{N}(2) = 5.1646$ [0.076] | NA |
|  | Heteroskedasticity | $X^2_{H}(1) = 1.5274$ [0.217] | $F(1, 72) = 1.5175$ [0.222] |

*Notes:*
Serial correlation test: based on Lagrange multiplier.
Functional form test: based on Ramsey's RESET test.
Normality test: based the skewness and kurtosis of residuals.
Heteroskedasticity test: based on regressing squared residuals on the squared fitted values.
All the diagnostic test results are satisfactory although Norway does not pass the functional form misspecification test suggesting the possible existence of nonlinearities or asymmetric adjustment processes that this econometric method is not equipped to handle (Pesaran et al. 2001).

# APPENDIX 21A.2

The following tables show the error correction mechanism linking the US corporate tax (*t*) and profit rates (*r*) along with the associated cointegrating relationship and diagnostic test statistics.

*Table 21A.2   Error correction mechanism model statistics*

|  | Dependent Variable: $\Delta t_t$ | | Nature of the ARDL | Lower and upper bounds | Adjusted $R^2$ of the ECM |
|---|---|---|---|---|---|
|  | ECC {t} [p value] s.e. | F statistic |  |  |  |
| US | −0.20511 {−3.5867} [0.001] 0.057187 | 10.1024 | ARDL(1, 0) | 5.1083 [I(0)]* & 5.9698 [I(1)]* | 0.35657 |

*Note:*   * 95% level.

*Table 21A.3   Cointegrating relationship*

| Regressor | Coefficient | Standard error | t-ratio [p value] |
|---|---|---|---|
| Constant | 0.51359 | 0.42144 | 1.2186 [0.227] |
| *D41* | 2.1118 | 0.85476 | 2.4706 [0.016] |
| *lr* | 0.66403 | 0.18553 | 3.5791 [0.001] |

*Note:*   *D41* is a dummy variable representing a shock in 1941.

*Table 21A.4   Diagnostic test statistics*

| | Test statistics | LM Test | F Test |
|---|---|---|---|
| US | Serial correlation | $X^2_{sc}(1) = 2.0395$ [0.153] | $F(1, 73) = 1.9600$ [0.166] |
| | Functional form | $X^2_{FF}(1) = 0.76001$ [0.383] | $F(1, 73) = 0.71829$ [0.399] |
| | Normality | $X^2_{N}(2) = 4.8177$ [0.090] | NA |
| | Heteroskedasticity | $X^2_{H}(1) = 0.77837$ [0.378] | $F(1, 76) = 0.76605$ [0.384] |

*Notes:*
Serial Correlation test: based on Lagrange multiplier.
Functional Form test: based on Ramsey's RESET test.
Normality test: based the skewness and kurtosis of residuals.
Heteroskedasticity test: based on regressing squared residuals on the squared fitted values.
All the diagnostic test results are satisfactory.

# 22 Modeling the economy as a whole: stock-flow models*

*Gennaro Zezza*

The stock-flow-consistent modeling approach, pioneered by Wynne Godley in Cambridge and James Tobin in Yale in the 1970s, is being adopted by a growing number of young (and not-so-young) researchers in the post-Keynesian and other heterodox traditions, especially after the publication of Godley and Lavoie (2007a), which provided a general framework for the analysis of whole economic systems, and after the recognition that macroeconomic models integrating 'real' markets with flow-of-fund analysis had been particularly successful in predicting the Great Recession of 2007 (Bezemer 2010).

In this chapter I first introduce the general features of the stock-flow-consistent (SFC) approach, discussing its standard post-Keynesian closures, and discuss next the most promising new lines of research adopting this approach from a heterodox perspective.

## 22.1 STOCK-FLOW-CONSISTENT MODELS: GENERAL FEATURES

The current post-Keynesian stock-flow-consistent (SFC) literature has been developing quickly in recent years, adopting the methodology described in Godley and Lavoie (2007a). Its main features, however, were already present in Godley and Cripps (1983), a book which tried – without great success at the time – to convey the insights of the New Cambridge approach[1] developed in the previous decade, and successfully adopted for policy analysis of the UK economy.

The consistency requirement of the SFC approach should be respected by any coherent macroeconomic model for the economy as a whole.[2] It is useful to analyze separately the accounting principles, which are not specific to a given theoretical approach, and model closures, which are derived instead from a given theory of macroeconomic behavior.

**Accounting Consistency**

Looking at any economy where sectors are consolidated,[3] stock-flow accounting consistency requires that:

1. Every payment from one sector is a receipt for another sector (there are no 'black holes' where monetary payments disappear, and there is no monetary payment coming from nowhere).
2. Every transaction implies a quadruple entry in the accounting: when a US firm imports goods from Japan, say, the accounting registers an increase in income in Japan, an increase in expenditure in the US, as well as an increase in Japanese

bank deposits and a corresponding decrease in US bank deposits. Current account payments and receipts imply a change in at least one stock of real financial assets/ liabilities.

3.  From (2), and from logic, it follows that every financial asset for a sector is a liability for a different sector: net financial wealth for the system as a whole is zero.

4.  End-of-period stocks are obtained by cumulating the relevant flows, eventually taking capital gains into account. In general, $S_t = S_{t-1} + F_t + CG_t$, where $S$ is the end-period monetary value of a stock, $F$ the corresponding flow during the period, and $CG$ net capital gains given by the change in the market value of $S$ over the period.[4]

These simple rules are the same which guide the construction of national accounts: 'quadruple-entry bookkeeping ... is the accounting system underlying the recording in the System of National Accounts (SNA)' (European Commission et al. 2009, p. 50), where quadruple-entry bookkeeping is an accounting methodology introduced by Copeland (1947, 1949), which merges what the SNA calls the vertical double-entry bookkeeping where 'each transaction leads to at least two entries, traditionally referred to as a credit entry and a debit entry, in the books of the transactor. This principle ensures that the total of all credit entries and that of all debit entries for all transactions are equal', with the 'horizontal double-entry bookkeeping [which] ensures the consistency of recording for each transaction category by counterparties' (European Commission et al. 2009, p. 50).

National accounts are the results of a method for measuring economic activity using internationally agreed standards, and provide a sequence of accounts for each aggregate sector in the economy, going from flow accounting (production, distribution of income, use of income) to flow of funds, which give details of changes in real and financial assets for each sector; to the revaluation account, which measures changes in the value of stocks due to fluctuation in market prices; to balance sheets, which measure end-of-period net real and financial wealth for each sector. National accounts can therefore be viewed as a simplified set of measures of economic stocks and flows, where the assumptions on how to go from reality to accounting have been agreed upon among international institutions.

The accounting parts of SFC models rely on the same sequence of matrices for describing an economy, although their level of detail – in empirical models – is usually extremely simplified relative to national accounts, and where the choice of how to simplify the economy, while keeping consistency, is based on a specific research question.

To provide a simple illustration, assume we are interested in modeling alternative sources of funding for investment, in a closed economy without a public sector. A simple transactions-flow matrix could be presented as in Table 22.1. The first two rows in Table 22.1 record the value of production of consumption goods and investment goods, with a distinction between values recorded in the current account and in the capital account. Payments which imply a change in the end-of-period stock of real or financial wealth are recorded in the capital account; other payments are recorded in the current account. A negative sign implies that the sector in the column is making a payment, while a positive sign implies that the sector is receiving the payment. In such a way, the sum of each element in any row must be zero.

The economy described by Table 22.1 is not relying on specific theoretical assump-

*Table 22.1* *Transactions-flows matrix for a simple SFC model*

| | Households | | Production firms | | Banks | | Total |
|---|---|---|---|---|---|---|---|
| | Current | Capital | Current | Capital | Current | Capital | |
| Consumption | −C | | +C | | | | 0 |
| Investment | | | +I | −I | | | 0 |
| Wages | +W | | −W | | | | 0 |
| Firms dividends | +DIV | | −DIV | | | | 0 |
| Banks distributed profits | +FB | | | | −FB | | 0 |
| Int.on bonds | +IB | | −IB | | | | 0 |
| Int.on loans | | | −IL | | +IL | | 0 |
| Int.on deposits | +ID | | | | −ID | | 0 |
| Net lending | −NLh | +NLh | −NLf | +NLf | −NLb | +NLb | 0 |
| [Total] | 0 | | 0 | | 0 | | 0 |
| Δ in loans | | | | +Δ L | | − Δ L | 0 |
| Δ in deposits | | −Δ D | | | | + Δ D | 0 |
| Δ in bonds | | −Δ B | | + Δ B | | | 0 |
| Δ in equities | | −pe* Δ Eh | | +pe* Δ E | | −pe* Δ Eb | 0 |
| Total | | 0 | | 0 | | 0 | |

tions, but uses a number of simplifying hypotheses, namely that there is no government, no central bank, and no foreign sector, so that financial assets are given only by bank deposits and bank loans. It is additionally assumed that banks do not issue either equities or bonds. Such assumptions can easily be dropped, at the cost of an increase in model complexity which, however, should not be relevant for the problem at hand.

It must also be noted that the degree of realism of the model can be increased by further splitting each sector into its components, using a top-down approach. For instance, we could study separately commercial banks and other financial institutions, or split production firms by sector, or separate workers and rentiers (or capitalists) within the household sector, provided that we keep the same logic in recording each monetary payment/receipt.[5]

The next set of rows in Table 22.1 record transfers among sectors. This is where many textbook models become inconsistent, omitting a formal representation of interest payments from one sector to the other which is implied by the existence of a stock of debt. The 'net lending' row in the first part of Table 22.1 is given by the difference between current receipts and current payments for each sector, and implies an increase in net financial assets when receipts are larger than payments, and the sector is a net lender; or a decrease in net financial assets in the opposite case. For the household sector, for instance, the identity implied by the accounting is:

$$NLh = (W + DIV + FB + IB + ID) - C \qquad (22.1)$$

where the sum in parenthesis defines household disposable income, and *NLh* in this simplified model is synonymous with saving.

The second, bottom part of Table 22.1 is the flow-of-funds matrix, which shows, by column, the possible destination of saving for a sector which is a net lender, or the possible sources of credit for a sector which is a net borrower. For households, saving must take the form of an increase in the end-of-period stock of bank deposits, newly issued bonds or equities, where the latter are assumed to be purchased at the current market price.

The identity from the capital account of the firms' sector implies the budget constraint for investment:

$$I = NLf + \Delta L + \Delta B + ph^*\Delta E \tag{22.2}$$

Investment must be financed either by undistributed profits $NLf$, an increase in bank loans $\Delta L$, or by issuing additional bonds $\Delta B$ or equities $\Delta E$. A proper integration of flow transactions and flow-of-funds payments thus lays the ground for models which provide a realistic description of the linkages between the financial sector and the real sector of the economy.[6]

The columns for the banking sector in Table 22.1 have been constructed without the simplifying assumptions usually adopted, that is, that banks distribute all of their profits so that, at the end of each accounting period, their net lender position is 0. On the contrary, undistributed banks' profits given by banks' receipts less payments, including distributed profits:

$$NLb = iL - iD - FB \tag{22.3}$$

must be equal to the net increase in assets less the net increase in liabilities:

$$NLb = \Delta L + ph^*\Delta Eb - \Delta D \tag{22.4}$$

so that banks could in principle be having a positive,[7] or negative, net financial position.[8]

The rows in the flow-of-funds matrix show that for each increase in liabilities issued by a sector, say firms' equities, there must be a corresponding increase in assets held by other sectors. The balance sheet matrix corresponding to flow transactions in Table 22.1 is represented in Table 22.2. The links between flows in Table 22.1 and end-of-period stocks in Table 22.2 are given by stock-flow identities, that is, for the stock of capital:[9]

$$K_t = (1 - \delta)^*K_{t-1} + I_t \tag{22.5}$$

where $\delta$ is the depreciation rate. For the stock of bank deposits:

$$D_t = D_{t-1} + \Delta D_t \tag{22.6}$$

and similarly for any financial stock which is not traded at a market price which can fluctuate. For equities, on which capital gains can arise, the identity would be:

$$pe_t^*E_t = pe_{t-1}^*E_{t-1} + pe_t^*\Delta E_t + \Delta pe_t^*E_{t-1} \tag{22.7}$$

where the last term in (22.7) measures capital gains, given by the change in the market price of existing equities.

*Table 22.2   Balance sheet matrix for a simple SFC model*

|  | Households | Prod. firms | Banks | Total |
|---|---|---|---|---|
| Fixed capital |  | +K |  | +K |
| Deposits | +D |  | −D | 0 |
| Loans |  | −L | +L | 0 |
| Bonds | +B | −B |  | 0 |
| Equities | +pe*Eh | −pe*E | +pe*Eb | 0 |
| Balance (net worth) | −Vh | −Vf | −Vb | −K |
| Sum | 0 | 0 | 0 | 0 |

Note that the end-of-period value of the stock of wealth for each sector increases/decreases with their net lending/borrowing position, plus net capital gains/losses, that is, for households:

$$Vh_t = Vh_{t-1} + NLh_t + \Delta pe_t * Eh_{t-1} \tag{22.8}$$

Note that for each stock of financial assets/liabilities in Table 22.2 there must be an entry in Table 22.1 identifying the corresponding return on such assets.

Note that – following accounting practices – all stocks are measured at the end of period. This feature is relevant in some models which distinguish between *ex ante*, or target, values for stocks and the *ex post*, realized value of stocks at the end of the period. The distinction is particularly relevant in the approaches linked to the monetary theory of production, which discuss 'initial finance' demanded at the beginning of a production period, and debt outstanding at the end of the period.[10]

Finally, note that accounting identities derived from the accounting in Table 22.1 or Table 22.2 imply that one row, or column, can be uniquely determined from the others. This implies that one of the identities can – and should – be dropped from the model, since it is implied by the others.[11]

## Model Consistency

The previous section has considered the accounting requirement related to the presentation of the variables in any given SFC macromodel. I now add additional requirements that must be present for logical consistency, namely:

1.  Interest and dividend payments must be endogenously determined from the accumulated stock of assets/liabilities. In theoretical models, the flow of interest payments on debt $S$ at time $t$ is given by an interest rate $r$ over the opening stock of debt outstanding, and the determination of the interest rate will depend on the theory adopted by the researcher.[12] These quasi-identities introduce another dynamic dimension to SFC models, on top of the stock-flow identities as (22.8), with an important impact on the trajectories of the model, and the analysis of debt sustainability. Last, but not least, these identities usually introduce non-linearities in the model;

2.  When financial assets/liabilities are included in a model, they must feed back on the

behavior of at least one sector. For instance, if we assume in a model that banks do not distribute all profits and therefore accumulate real or financial wealth, there must be some behavioral rule which shows the implications of the increase in wealth for banking behavior. If such a rule is omitted, the model may easily generate an ever-increasing (or decreasing) level of banking wealth relative to income, which may be stock-flow consistent but is entirely implausible.

## Model Closures

The description of SFC models so far has concentrated on model accounting and logical consistency. In any given model, accounting identities are used to identify a first set of $K$ variables that are necessarily given by the values of a remaining set of $M$ variables.

The next step in model building usually follows a more conventional methodology. Economic theory is used to identify a subset $L$ of the yet-to-be-modeled $M$ variables, and to specify a relationship among them and the initial K variables, conditional on a set of parameters.

In a linear model, for each time period $t$, this implies a specification such as:

$$B \cdot Y_t = C \cdot X_t + D \cdot Y_{t-1} \{+u_t\} \tag{22.9}$$

where, with $N = K + L$ variables explained in the model, Y is a $(N*1)$ vector of endogenous variables, determined either through accounting identities or through 'behavioral' functions; X is a $(P*1)$ vector of exogenous variables (with $P = M - L$); and B, C, D are matrices of model parameters of appropriate dimensions. In empirical models adopting an econometric estimation of model parameters, a vector $u$ is also added to represent random shocks.

In any SFC model, the initial values of the stocks will exert their influence on the solution for the current time period, so that the $D$ matrix is never empty, and comparative static analysis between two different time periods makes little sense.

As a simple example, expanded from Godley and Cripps (1974), we can model a closed economy where the value of production, and thus income, is given by private expenditure plus government expenditure (22.10); government deficit – given by the difference between government outlays and an income tax – is financed by issuing bonds (22.11); and, since bonds are the only financial asset,[13] the demand for new bonds is equal to saving (22.12):

$$Y_t = PE_t + G_t \tag{22.10}$$

$$\Delta B_t^s = G_t + r_t \cdot B_{t-1} - t \cdot (Y_t + r_t \cdot B_{t-1}) \tag{22.11}$$

$$\Delta B_t^d = (1 - t) \cdot (Y_t + r_t \cdot B_{t-1}) - PE_t \tag{22.12}$$

Equations (22.10)–(22.12) form the accounting of the model, determining $Y$, $B^s$, and $B^d$, given $PE$, $G$, $r$, and $t$. Using (22.10) in (22.12) it is straightforward to show that the supply of new bonds, from (22.11), will always be equal to demand in (12), so that an 'equilibrium' condition $B = B^d = B^s$ is not needed.

A simple 'behavioral' rule can be added from economic theory: assume for instance that private expenditure is a function of disposable income and the opening stock of wealth (22.13):

$$PE_t = \alpha_1 \cdot (1 - t) \cdot (Y_t + r_t \cdot B_{t-1}) + \alpha_2 \cdot B_{t-1} \qquad (22.13)$$

The model is now complete, in the sense that the remaining exogenous variables ($G$, $r$, $t$) and parameters ($\alpha_1$, $\alpha_2$) may be expected to be given; that is, not influenced by the values of the endogenous variables. Alternative theories of the determination of private expenditure may replace (22.13) while keeping the stock-flow accounting consistency.

The determination of parameter values in the model – $\alpha_1$, $\alpha_2$ in our simple example – may be challenging. The standard practice in theoretical models is: (1) to adopt parameter values which arise from stylized facts in real economies; and (2) to start from parameter values which should avoid explosive behavior.[14] In empirical models, parameter values are usually obtained through econometric estimation or calibration.

One of the most frequent critiques of theoretical SFC models is the arbitrary choice of parameter values. It is therefore standard practice to verify the robustness of model results under alternative parameter specification, which is usually feasible using computer programs. Another standard practice is to publish the full list of parameter values adopted in the model, so that results can be reproduced.

## Stock-Flow Norms and the Steady State

One of the interesting features of SFC models is the analysis of stock-flow and flow-flow ratios obtained from model solutions, usually obtained by numerical simulations, as well as the properties of steady-state solutions, when they exist. In our simple model, for instance, a steady-state solution is easily obtained by computing the values which correspond to a stable stock of wealth: $B = B_t = B_{t-1}$. It turns out that steady-state income is given by a multiplier over government expenditure,[15] and in the steady state the ratio of wealth to income depends only on model parameters and the interest rate.[16] For models this simple, out-of-equilibrium dynamics can be obtained analytically, and explored through phase diagrams: see Godley and Lavoie (2007a, Ch. 3) or Zezza and Dos Santos (2008). The adjustment to a new steady state after a shock to government expenditure is reported in Figure 22.1.

This figure illustrates the method for analyzing the properties of more complex models: shocking one exogenous variable or one parameter at a time, numerical simulation allows verifying the dynamics and the stability of the model. In this simple case, income converges monotonically to its new steady-state level. In empirical models, Godley placed some emphasis on the mean lag of the adjustment to the new steady state, which is given, for a shock to $Y$ in $t$, by:

$$ML = \frac{\sum_{i=0}^{\infty} i \cdot \Delta Y_{t+i}}{\sum_{i=0}^{\infty} \Delta Y_{t+i}} \qquad (22.14)$$

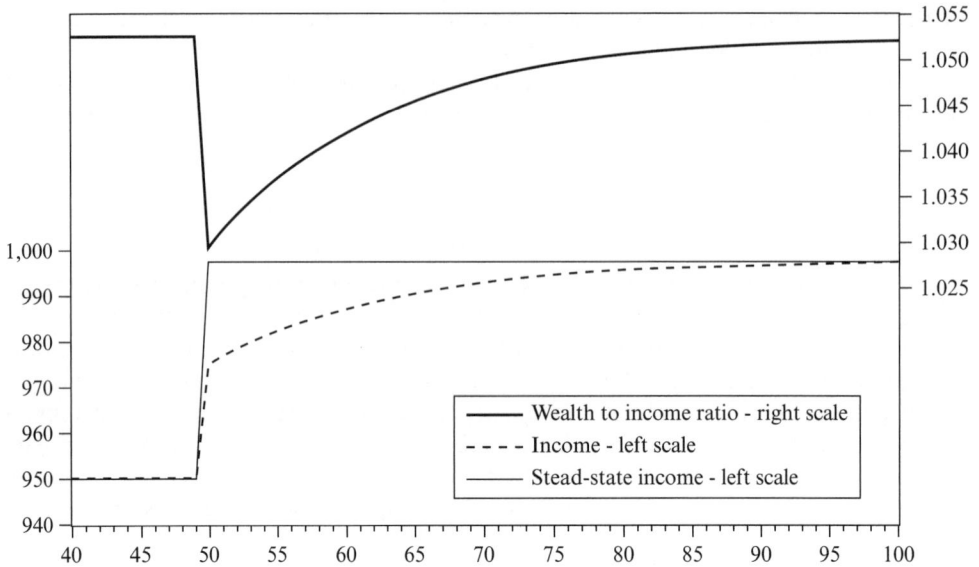

*Figure 22.1    Adjustment to a shock in a simple SFC model*

As shown in Figure 22.1, the adjustment to the new steady state can take a considerable amount of 'time' (simulation periods), and the mean lag is the number of periods it takes for a shock to exert half of its total effect. Estimating the mean lag in an empirical model is relevant: for instance, a government wishing to provide a fiscal stimulus to reduce unemployment will want to know if it takes months, or years, to achieve its target.

More generally, the SFC literature usually places greater attention on time than other modeling approaches. Godley's theoretical models are often built around the notion of a 'production period'. Similarly, some SFC models adopt the concept of a 'financing period', which starts when credit is granted as initial finance for the production process, and ends when credit is reimbursed.[17]

Empirical SFC models are usually loosely grounded in theoretical models, but adopt the time frequency which is compatible with data availability; usually quarters or years. Note that some authors prefer to develop their theoretical models using continuous time, but either need to adapt the model to discrete time when testing it against the data, or simply verify model results with some stylized facts from a real economy.

A very relevant feature of SFC models, as illustrated in Figure 22.1, is the analysis of stock-flow and flow-flow ratios. In our simple model, for instance, the ratio of the stock of wealth to income depends on the parameters in (22.13) and the interest rate. A shock to government expenditure will therefore not change this ratio, to which the economy returns in steady state.

The analysis of stock-flow norms in SFC models has been controversial, especially when it was first introduced as a feature of the 'New Cambridge' approach, which assumed – as in our simple model – the empirical stability of the stock of private sector net financial wealth relative to income (see Godley and Cripps 1983): 'the stock-flow norms which are crucial to determining how actual economic systems work do, as a matter of fact, exhibit a fair degree of stability' (ibid., p. 43). Since the private sector includes both family and households, this assumption could not be tracked back to microeconomic behavior, and therefore led to criticism from mainstream approaches which derive macroeconomic models from the optimizing behavior of representative agents. The answer to such criticism from Godley and Cripps (1983) was based on the simple mechanics of stocks and flows: 'If the flow of a river into a lake increases, the volume of water in the lake will not rise for ever. At some point a new water level will become established; then (and only then) the outflow will equal the inflow' (Godley and Cripps 1983, p. 42).

In Godley and Lavoie (2007a), on the other hand, as in most of the more recent theoretical literature, household and business are modeled separately, and the stability of household wealth to income, or inventories to sales, can be rationalized as 'behavior' of the aggregate sector, following the standard Keynesian and post-Keynesian methodology. More specifically, 'The Godley & Lavoie models rely on procedural rationality, with agents reacting to past disequilibria relative to norms' (Godley and Lavoie 2007a, p. 494).

Note also that, in any model which reaches steady growth (or a steady state), stocks and flows rise at the same rate, and therefore both stock-flow and flow-flow norms converge to a given value. When important stock-flow norms are changing in an economy, this is a signal of adjustment processes out of equilibrium. For instance, Godley's predictions of the 2001 and 2007 recessions were based on the analysis of the systematic increases in the stock of private sector debt relative to income in the US (Godley 1999), as well as of other flow-flow norms such as the US current account relative to GDP.

In post-Keynesian SFC models, adjustment towards a steady state does not occur through prices instantaneously adjusting to clear any gap between supply and demand. Rather, adjustment usually operates through error correction mechanisms, with agents reacting to the distance between the target and the actual level of the variables of interest. It follows that one or more variables in the model act as a buffer. For instance, a Tobinesque approach to portfolio decisions often incorporated into SFC models implies that one of the assets – such as bank deposits – will be off target, as a result of agents' inability to have accurate expectations on their end-of-period stock of wealth, and so on. Price adjustments are introduced in SFC models only for financial markets, but without forcing instantaneous equilibrium. In our experience, attempts to model instantaneous market clearing in SFC models yields instability, and/or unrealistic price volatility.

## 22.2 POST-KEYNESIAN SFC MODELS: STATE OF THE ART

I will not attempt to provide a survey of the literature on post-Keynesian stock-flow-consistent models here. An early assessment, covering the work of Tobin and Godley, can be found in Dos Santos (2006) and Godley and Lavoie (2007a, Ch. 1). Godley and Lavoie (2007a, pp. 21–2) also provide an excellent reconstruction of the relevance of stocks and stock-flow consistency among post-Keynesian authors.

An excellent survey of more recent literature is in Caverzasi and Godin (2014). It seems that the literature is evolving along different, but intersected, lines of research: (1) models of the 'modern' financial sector; (2) the integration of agent-based models at the micro level with stock-flow consistency at the macro level; (3) models of open economies; (4) models including personal income distribution; (5) models for developing countries;

(6) models including environmental externalities; (7) development of simple SFC models for teaching; and (8) empirical models for whole countries.

### Modeling the Financial Sector

One of the main strengths of the SFC approach is the consistent integration of the real and financial sectors, which is lacking in mainstream theoretical models, and their empirical counterparts (dynamic stochastic general equilibrium, DSGE, models). However, some criticism[18] of the SFC approach has focused on its simplistic presentation of the financial system, in the face of the rapid development of a 'shadow' banking sector, the increasing processes of securitization, the widespread use of derivatives, and so on. Some authors are extending the Godley–Lavoie approach to incorporate financial innovation and a Minskian approach, while keeping the analysis at the macro level: see Le Heron (2013), Passarella (2014), and Sawyer and Passarella (2014), among many others.

### Agent-Based Models

Agent-based modeling is developing quickly as an alternative to the microeconomics of rational representative agents. Many authors working in this tradition have recognized the need to adopt the SFC approach for obtaining macroeconomic consistency in their microeconomic simulations. On the other hand, the possibility of complementing a SFC macroeconomic model with micro behavior in the agent-based approach may allow to model speculative behavior in financial markets, which is difficult to present in a realistic way at the macro level. See Seppecher (2012), Kinsella et al. (2011), and Carvalho and Di Guilmi (2014), among others. A research group coordinated by Kinsella, Gallegati, and Stiglitz is producing interesting results, as well as new freely available software code; see Caiani et al. (2014).

### Models of Open Economies

The integrated analysis of real and financial markets make the SFC approach particularly suitable for addressing international imbalances. Recent work in this line, based on the seminal work of Godley and Lavoie (2007b), includes the analysis of the eurozone imbalances (Mazier and Valdecantos 2014), the analysis of the role of the dollar as a reserve currency (Lavoie and Zhao 2010), and the proposal for reforms of the international monetary system (Valdecantos and Zezza 2015).

### The Role of the Personal Distribution of Income

Most SFC models separate household from business, and have a role for the functional distribution of income between wages and profits. More recently, some theoretical models have started to split the household sector into subsectors, such as 'workers' and 'capitalists' or 'rentiers', to explore the role of the personal distribution of income on growth and financial stability. Since a growing number of researchers believe that the concentration of income and wealth is detrimental to growth, this line of research is also promising. See Zezza (2008), Dallery and van Treeck (2011), and Sawyer and Passarella (2014), among many others.

**Models for Developing Countries**

Most post-Keynesian SFC models developed so far are based on the Keynesian assumption that output is demand driven, since firms have spare capacity. This assumption may not be realistic for developing countries with a small industrial base, where the impact of a positive shock to demand may be constrained by the availability of factors of production and, when these have to be imported, by the availability of international reserves. Incorporating supply-side constraints in the SFC methodology, possibly by the use of input–output tables, is an interesting and promising line of research, closely linked to the structuralist approach (see Valdecantos 2015).

**The Environment**

The SFC approach is well suited to study the impact of economic growth on the environment, since some aspects of the quality of the environment, as well as the treatment of natural resources, can be modeled as stocks which are affected, say, by flows of pollution, while at the same time checking the feedback effect from the quality of the environment to growth and well-being. See Naqvi (2014) and Berg et al. (2015).

**Teaching SFC Models**

One drawback of the SFC approach is in its complexity when compared against simple mainstream textbook models, and the fact it relies on numerical simulations, usually obtained through Eviews, which is a licensed software that may not be easily accessible to researchers with a tight budget constraint. Efforts in the direction of simple SFC models to be used for pedagogical purposes include Godley and Lavoie (2007a), who present models of increasing complexity; Zezza and Dos Santos (2008), who present analytical solutions and diagrams for a simple model; and Dos Santos and Macedo e Silva (2009). The development of software code for solving SFC models with an open-source software, R (r-project.org), has recently become available[19] thanks to Antoine Godin and Hamid Raza, and this should enable further research.

**Empirical Models for Whole Countries**

Although the SFC approach is particularly well suited for the empirical analysis of whole economic systems, only a few research teams are working on such models. Researchers at the Levy Economics Institute of Bard College have expanded the work of Godley (1999) on a model for the United States (see Zezza 2009; Papadimitriou et al. 2014b, among others), and a model for Greece (Papadimitriou et al. 2013; Papadimitriou et al. 2014a). A second research group in Limerick is developing a model for Ireland (Kinsella and Tiou-Tagba Aliti 2012). Other empirical work in the context of the SFC literature is being produced at Université Paris XIII, France (see Clevenot et al. 2009, 2010). The Levy Institute models are being developed to produce projections of a whole economic system, conditional on alternative assumptions on the future path of exogenous variables (usually, fiscal policy parameters). Their relative success in predicting the trajectories of these economies is attracting a growing interest in this methodology.

## 22.3    CONCLUDING REMARKS

The stock-flow-consistent approach which originated in the work of Godley, Tobin, and Lavoie is perceived by a growing number of heterodox researchers as the new frontier of macroeconomic theorizing. I endorse the position of Lavoie and, in the words of Caverzasi and Godin (2014), believe that: 'SFC models can provide a useful tool in the consensus-making attempt within the post-Keynesian tradition, since the theoretical discussion and the comparisons are based on a coherent, structured, and at the same time adaptable framework.'

## NOTES

\*    I gratefully acknowledge helpful comments on a previous draft from Marc Lavoie and Antoine Godin. Any remaining errors are my own responsibility.
1.   On the 'New Cambridge' approach see Godley and Cripps (1974, 1983) and McCallum and Vines (1981).
2.   Some mainstream models achieve stock-flow consistency by assuming forward-looking behavior of rational optimizing agents in perfect markets, so that both stocks and flows in any instant are at their optimal level. I will not analyze this literature further here.
3.   Sectors are consolidated when payments within each sector are netted out. For instance, when a household purchases an existing house from another household, the distribution of real assets and liquidity among households changes, but the real value of aggregate household wealth is unaffected. In some cases, national accounts are published without consolidating, say, the government sector, so that – for instance – payments from the central government to local governments appear on both sides of the general government account.
4.   In national accounting, capital gains are presented in the 'revaluation account', which also includes the write-off of debt, when the debtor defaults. See European Commission et al. (2009, p. 218).
5.   In empirical models the ability to increase the level of detail is constrained by the availability of data.
6.   'The Holy Grail of Post-Keynesian economics has always been the full integration of monetary and real macroeconomic analysis'(Lavoie 2011, p. 54).
7.   Equation (22.3) implies that banks could have a loss if firms default on their loans, so that $iL$ and $DIVb$ are both zero. In this case, banks would have to sell previously accumulated financial assets to pay interest on banks deposits, or increase their net debt with households (or the model should be made more complex by introducing additional financial instruments).
8.   Instead of simply acting as intermediaries, as in most mainstream models, or providers of credit and liquidity, as in most heterodox models.
9.   Assuming that firms cannot resell installed physical capital, which therefore does not have a market price.
10.  See Graziani (2003) and Zezza (2011).
11.  Godley named the dropped identity the 'missing' or 'hidden' equation, and used it to check the consistency of the accounting structure of the model.
12.  Note that the opening stock is given by the end-of-period stock, as in (22.6) or (22.8). The interest rate may be determined at time $t$, or time $t-1$, depending on the adopted theory on expectations, the type of contract etc.
13.  See Godley and Lavoie (2007a, Ch. 3) for a similar model where government money is the only financial asset. I chose to have bonds in our example to stress the relevance of tracking interest payments, although a model with no explicit representation of money creation/destruction may be logically inconsistent. Introducing money would greatly increase the complexity of our example. See Godley and Lavoie (2007a) for further examples of increasing complexity. On the other hand, setting the interest rate to 0 transforms bonds in this model into 'money'.

14. For instance, in a model where $Y_t = \sigma \cdot Y_{t-1} + \cdots$, values of $\sigma > 1$ imply an explosive path for $Y$. For a recent proposal of parameters selection see Ciuffo and Rosenbaum (2013).
15. Namely, $Y = \frac{\alpha_2 - \beta}{\alpha_2 \cdot t - \beta} \cdot G$, where $\beta = (1 - \alpha_1)(1 - t)r$. For r = 0, this reduces to $Y = \frac{G}{t}$.
16. Namely, $\frac{\beta}{Y} = \frac{(1 - \alpha_1)(1 - t)}{\alpha_2 - (1 - \alpha_1)r}$.
17. See Zezza (2011) for a discussion of Godley's approach in relation to the theory of the monetary circuit.
18. See Taylor (2008).
19. See sfc-models.net, a website which holds a repository of program codes for SFC models using different software platforms.

# REFERENCES

Berg, M., R. Hartley, and O. Richters (2015), 'A stock-flow consistent input–output model with applications to energy price shocks, interest rates, and heat emissions', *New Journal of Physics*, **17**, 015011.
Bezemer, D.J. (2010), 'Understanding financial crisis through accounting models', *Accounting, Organizations and Society*, **35** (7), 676–88.
Caiani, A., E. Caverzasi, A. Godin, L. Riccetti, A. Russo, M. Gallegati, S. Kinsella, and J. Stiglitz (2014), 'Innovation, demand, and finance in an agent based-stock flow consistent model', paper presented at the Workshop on Agent-based and Stock-Flow Consistent Models, Monte Conero, September 19–20.
Carvalho, L. and C. Di Guilmi (2014), 'Income inequality and macroeconomic instability: a stock-flow consistent approach with heterogeneous agents', CAMA Working Paper No. 60.
Caverzasi, E. and A. Godin (2014), 'Post-Keynesian stock-flow-consistent modelling: a survey', *Cambridge Journal of Economics*, **39** (1), 157–87.
Ciuffo, B. and E. Rosenbaum (2013), 'Comparative numerical analysis of two stock-flow consistent post-Keynesian growth models', paper presented at the Jobs Crisis: Causes, Cures, Constraints Conference, Berlin, 24–26 October.
Clévenot, Mickaël, Yann Guy, and Jacques Mazier (2009), 'Debt and equity financing in France: a macro-economic approach', paper presented to the International Colloquium on recent developments in Post-Keynesian modelling, Centre d'Économie de l'université Paris Nord (CEPN), Paris, November 20–21.
Clévenot, Mickaël, Yann Guy, and Jacques Mazier (2010), 'Investment and the rate of profit in a financial context: the French case', *International Review of Applied Economics*, **24** (6), 693–714.
Copeland, M.A. (1947), 'Tracing money flows through the United States economy', *American Economic Review*, **37** (2), 31–49.
Copeland, M.A. (1949), 'Social accounting for money flows', *Accounting Review*, **24** (3), 254–64.
Dallery, T. and T. van Treeck (2011), 'Conflicting claims and equilibrium adjustment processes in a stock-flow consistent macroeconomic model', *Review of Political Economy*, **23** (2), 189–211.
Dos Santos, C.H. (2006), 'Keynesian theorizing during hard times: stock-flow consistent models as an unexplored "frontier" of Keynesian macroeconomics', *Cambridge Journal of Economics*, **30** (4), 541–65.
Dos Santos, C.H. and A.C. Macedo e Silva (2009), 'Revisiting (and connecting) Marglin-Bhaduri and Minsky: an SFC look at financialization and profit-led growth', Working Paper No. 567, Annandale-on-Hudson, MA: Levy Economics Institute.
Dos Santos, C.H. and A.C. Macedo e Silva (2010), 'Revisiting "New Cambridge": the three financial balances in a general stock-flow consistent applied modeling strategy', Working Paper No. 594, Annandale-on-Hudson, MA Levy Economics Institute.
European Commission, International Monetary Fund, Organisation for Economic Co-operation and Development, United Nations, and World Bank (2009), *System of National Accounts, 2008*, New York: European Commission, International Monetary Fund, Organisation for Economic Co-operation and Development, United Nations and World Bank, accessed December 1, 2009 at http://unstats.un.org/unsd/nationalaccount/docs/SNA2008.pdf.
Godley, W. (1999), 'Seven unsustainable processes: medium-term prospects and policies for the United States and the world', Special Report, Annandale-on-Hudson, MA: Levy Economics Institute.
Godley, W. and F. Cripps (1974), 'Demand, inflation and economic policy', *London and Cambridge Economic Bulletin*, **84** (1); reprinted from *The Times*, January 22–23.
Godley, W. and F. Cripps (1983), *Macroeconomics*, Oxford: Oxford University Press.
Godley, W. and M. Lavoie (2007a), *Monetary Economics: An Integrated Approach to Credit, Money, Income, Production and Wealth*, Basingstoke: Palgrave Macmillan.
Godley, W. and M. Lavoie (2007b), 'A simple model of three economies with two currencies: the eurozone and the USA', *Cambridge Journal of Economics*, **31** (1), 1–23.
Graziani, A. (2003), *The Monetary Theory of Production*, Cambridge: Cambridge University Press.

Kinsella, S., M. Greiff, and E.J. Nell (2011), 'Income distribution in a stock-flow consistent model with education and technological change', *Eastern Economic Journal*, **37** (1), 134–49.
Kinsella, Stephen and Gnanonobodom Tiou-Tagba Aliti (2012), 'Towards a stock flow consistent model for Ireland', *Social Science Research Network*, Abstract 2011462, accessed February 28, 2012 at http://dx.doi.org/10.2139/ssrn.2011462.
Lavoie, M. (2011), 'Money, credit and central banks in post-Keynesian economics', in E. Hein and E. Stockhammer (eds), *A Modern Guide to Keynesian Macroeconomics and Economic Policies*, Cheltenham, UK and Northampton, MA, USA: Edward Elgar, pp. 34–60.
Lavoie, M. and J. Zhao (2010), 'A study of the diversification of China's foreign reserves within a three-country stock-flow consistent model', *Metroeconomica*, **61** (3), 558–92.
Le Heron, E. (2013), 'Confidence, increasing risk and crisis in a post-Kaleckian stock–flow consistent model', in R. Bellofiore. E. Karwowski, and J. Toporowski (eds), *Economic Crisis and Political Economy, Volume 2 of Essays in Honour of Tadeusz Kowalik*, London: Palgrave Macmillan, pp. 118–47.
Mazier, J. and S. Valdecantos (2014), 'Gathering the pieces of three decades of monetary coordination to build a way out of the European crisis', Document de travail du CEPN, n.2014/10.
McCallum, J. and D. Vines (1981), 'Cambridge and Chicago on the balance of payments', *Economic Journal*, **91** (362), 439–53.
Naqvi, A. (2014), 'Climate change and economic growth: an integrated approach to production, energy, emissions, distributions and unemployment', accessed January 30, 2015 at http://media.arbeiterkammer.at/PDF/Paper_Asjad_Naqvi.pdf.
Papadimitriou, D.B., G. Zezza, and M. Nikiforos (2013), 'A Levy Institute model for Greece', Technical Paper, Annandale on Hudson, MA: Levy Economics Institute.
Papadimitriou, D.B., M. Nikiforos, and G. Zezza (2014a), 'Is Greece heading for a recovery?', *Strategic Analysis*, Annandale on Hudson, MA: Levy Economics Institute.
Papadimitriou, D.B., G. Zezza, M. Nikiforos, and G. Hannsgen (2014b), 'Is rising inequality a hindrance to the US economic recovery?', *Strategic Analysis*, Annandale on Hudson, MA: Levy Economics Institute.
Passarella, M. (2014), 'Financialization and the monetary circuit: a macro-accounting approach', *Review of Political Economy*, **26** (1), 128–48.
Sawyer, M. and M. Passarella (2014), 'The monetary circuit in the age of financialisation: a stock-flow consistent take', paper presented at the workshop A Day in Honour of Augusto Graziani, Université Paris Sud, January 20.
Seppecher, P. (2012), 'Flexibility of wages and macroeconomic instability in an agent-based computational model with endogenous money', *Macroeconomic Dynamics*, **16** (Supplement 2), 284–97.
Taylor, L. (2008), 'A foxy hedgehog: Wynne Godley and macroeconomic modelling', *Cambridge Journal of Economics*, **32** (4), 639–63.
Valdecantos, S. (2015), 'Economic structure and external vulnerability', unpublished PhD thesis, Université de Paris XIII, Paris-Nord.
Valdecantos, S. and G. Zezza (2015), 'Reforming the international monetary system: a stock-flow-consistent approach', *Journal of Post-Keynesian Economics*, **38** (2), 167–91.
Zezza, G. (2008), 'US growth, the housing market, and the distribution of income', *Journal of Post Keynesian Economics*, **30** (3), 379–407.
Zezza, G. (2009), 'Fiscal policy and the economics of financial balances', *Intervention: European Journal of Economics and Economic Policies*, **6** (2), 289–310.
Zezza, G. (2011), 'Godley and Graziani: stock-flow-consistent monetary circuits', in D.B. Papadimitriou and G. Zezza (eds), *Contributions to Stock-Flow Modeling*, Basingstoke: Palgrave Macmillan, pp. 154–72.
Zezza, G. and C. Dos Santos (2008), 'A simplified, "benchmark", stock-flow consistent post-Keynesian growth model', *Metroeconomica*, **59** (3), 441–78.

# 23 A mixed methods approach to investigating the employment decisions of aged care workers in Australia

*Therese Jefferson, Siobhan Austen, Rhonda Sharp, Rachel Ong, Valerie Adams and Gill Lewin*

## 23.1 INTRODUCTION

Published research articles generally commence by providing some background on previous research, identifying gaps in existing literature, and defining specific research questions. While these elements are essential for designing a research project, they provide limited insights into some of the institutional and practical issues that inform researchers' motivations for identifying specific research questions and the subsequent design and implementation of their projects. There are strong arguments for locating researchers' motivations and experiences within the 'same critical plane' as the subject matter of their research (Harding 1987, p. 8). Adopting this approach provides critical insights into the relative social power and agenda of the researchers and assists with ensuring the entire research process is open to scrutiny. These are particularly important issues for researchers who wish to identify their research as relevant to the broad objectives of feminist research agendas.

One purpose of this chapter is to provide insights into key factors that informed the choice and design of our mixed methods approach to investigating the employment decisions of aged care workers. These factors might be loosely grouped into two categories. The first category includes relatively traditional issues often included in research articles such as connections with important contemporary policy issues or addressing gaps in existing research literature. However, we also consider a second group of factors relevant to the motivations of research team members. These factors are important because they closely link with some of the key methodological questions relevant to the research project and constraints within the institutional environment in which the research team was working. The latter issues are included to acknowledge explicitly the role of researchers' strategic choices and decisions in defining research agendas. These issues also emphasize the importance of institutional context for determining which projects receive funding and resources within a highly competitive research environment.

Following discussion of the relatively broad context informing the research design, this chapter also summarizes the way in which data collection and analysis were implemented in an integrated manner to gain insights into the employment decisions made by mature-age women working in aged care. This part of the discussion illustrates the advantages of mixed methods research to draw on the strengths of varied, specific research methods to gain a holistic account of the possible causal links relevant to specific labor market outcomes in Australia's aged care sector.

## 23.2   BACKGROUND AND POLICY CONTEXT

The early stages of the design and implementation of this project coincided with national policy discussions aimed at increasing the workforce participation and retention of mature-age workers, particularly women, in Australia's labor markets. In the years preceding the design of this research project, the national Australian government's research and advisory body, the Productivity Commission (2005), had estimated that per capita economic growth could slump by 50 percent by 2025. This was linked with projections of slow labor force growth coupled with imbalances between growth in the tax base and demands on public expenditure associated with health and pension costs. In 2010, the year in which the research team designed the primary data collection process for this project, an Intergenerational Report produced by the Australian Treasury argued that removing the barriers to the participation of mature-age people in the workforce must be a key part of the policy response to Australia's ageing demographic profile. It was further argued that this would require 'a sound understanding of the complex nature of mature-age participation' (Treasury 2010: xiv). Removing barriers to the employment of mature-age women was viewed as particularly important to achieving labor supply growth. Compared to men and younger women, Australian women aged over 45 were much less likely to be classified as participating in the formal labor market. Internationally, it had been recognized that mature-age women were a rapidly growing demographic group with potential for higher rates of workforce participation and improved retention (OECD 2006).

The research team in this project considered that the importance of understanding mature-age women's labor supply was particularly high in the aged care sector. At the time of designing the project, women comprised more than 90 percent of the aged care workforce and the median age of workers in this sector was already more than 45 years. The sector was also characterized by a strong growth in labor demand and ongoing problems with the retention of workers. It had been projected that the number of full-time equivalent direct care workers needed for aged care accommodation alone would rise by 325 percent between 2003 and 2031 (Hugo 2007).

Despite the perceived advantages of greater workforce participation among older women, the factors affecting mature-age women's retention in paid work were, and continue to be, poorly understood. United States research suggested that a glaring limitation of the existing literature on older workers was 'the intense focus on elderly white men, to the virtual exclusion of most other groups' (Currie and Madrian 1999, p. 353). European research also concluded that little was known about the work and retirement patterns of women in their later years (Hanks 2004). These observations were, and remain, relevant to Australian research (Austen and Jefferson 2012a). The current invisibility of women aged 45 and over in analyses of mature-age workers' employment undermines the capacity of Australia and similar countries to ensure the provisioning of critical community needs as the population ages.

An analysis of previous research demonstrates the significant gaps in empirical studies of mature-age women's employment. Discussions of mature-age women's experiences can be found in some studies of the labor-market experiences of women of all ages (e.g., Birch 2005a), and in studies of older men's and women's employment (e.g., Cai and Kalb 2004, 2006; Berger and Messer Pelkowski 2004; Campolieti 2001; Chan and Huff

Stevens 2001; Clark et al. 1999; Peracchi and Welch 1994). Such studies lack specificity of the employment decision contexts of older women, including the potential importance of household and caring roles for their employment decisions. Only a few empirical studies have made the specific employment circumstances of mature-age women the focus of modeling or analysis. Cross-sectional studies specifically examining the decisions of mature-age women have been undertaken by Evans and Kelley (2002), Hill (2002), Evandrou and Glaser (2003), and Austen and Giles (2003). A key finding of these studies is that mature-age women not in paid work are commonly engaged in relatively high levels of unpaid care work. However, these studies have had limited success in establishing a causal relationships between unpaid and paid work roles.

There have been a small number of longitudinal studies of links between paid and unpaid work roles, with only four studies identified as directly relevant to the focus of our project. Employment transitions of women in late mid-life were investigated in the United States using data from the 1970s (Pavalko and Artis 1997). In the UK a study of the effects of informal care obligations on workforce participation among mid-life women was undertaken using data from the 1990s (Henz 2004). In addition, there were two European studies, the first exploring links between German women's reproductive histories and their late-life labor market behavior (Hanks 2004), and the second investigating the effects of care roles on hours of paid work among mid-life women (Spiess and Schneider 2003). These international studies demonstrated that, in their particular contexts, unpaid work demands significantly increased the likelihood of mature-age women leaving paid work. Importantly, however, reductions in care roles were not identified as increasing the chances that a mature-age woman would return to paid work.

The attraction, employment, and retention of care workers were the focus of Australian research that was completed in the years immediately preceding the design of our project (Adams and Nelson 2009; Meagher 2007; Martin and King 2008; King et al. 2012). However, these studies provided limited insights on the types of issues identified as potentially important in international studies that have focused specifically on mature-age women workers. Further, policy initiatives introduced at around the time of designing our project, such as a $6000 cash bonus aimed at enticing nurses into aged care, apparently had very little success in addressing the labor shortages in the aged care sector (Franklin 2010).

## 23.3   THEORY, INSTITUTIONAL RESEARCH CONTEXT, AND RESEARCH TEAM

Most economic theorizing and empirical research on the determinants of Australian mature-age employment patterns has been dominated by mainstream economic analyses of labor supply, which typically do not identify mature-age women as a distinct group. In mainstream analytical frameworks employment decisions are usually modeled as the product of an attempt by autonomous individuals to maximize their own utility and, thus, largely subject only to factors directly affecting financial rewards and individual utility considerations. The influence of social structures, norms relating to paid and unpaid roles, emotional connections with others, and how these vary with age and gender through time, are typically not explored in research based in mainstream economic traditions (Sharp and Broomhill 1988; Jefferson and King 2001; England and Folbre 2003; Austen et al. 2013). Similarly, previous mainstream economic theorizing and empirical studies have provided little insight into the employment decisions of women carers and have notably produced such findings as that a badly paid nurse is a good nurse (Heyes 2005).

Outside of mainstream economic theory, the largest body of theory to focus on gender and care can be characterized broadly as situated within feminist economics. The employment decision-making context identified in feminist economics is one where the decision-maker is 'embodied and in relation to the world, as well as constrained by physical and social circumstances' (Nelson 1993, p. 32). Decisions about employment are not made simply on the basis of expected financial rewards and contractual requirements (England and Folbre 1999). The rewards and contractual obligations associated with different jobs do affect the decisions individuals make about their continued employment. However, personal aspects of the work environment (including relationships with others) and the respect and the legitimacy associated with different types of work interact with these rewards and obligations and, thus, also affect the employment decisions that are made (Broomhill and Sharp 2007; Meagher and Healy 2006; Austen et al. 2013). This decision context reflects non-commodified elements of paid work. Work is viewed in feminist economics as central to a person's concept of herself and her relationships with others (Himmelweit 1999; Adams and Sharp 2011, 2013). The research team members were relatively familiar with feminist economics' theoretical contributions to the analysis of care work and highly motivated to utilize their insights and methods in an Australian study of the aged care workforce.

The researchers who designed and implemented this project were working within an institutional context that gives a high priority to the achievement of nationally competitive grants to fund research projects. Grants which are formally classified as 'nationally competitive' within Australia's university system are frequently used as a key indicator of researcher performance and are often included as a key selection criterion in recruitment and promotion processes. At the same time, the national government in Australia was implementing new and extensive processes for measuring the quality of research outputs produced by Australian universities. Nationally competitive grant funds were included in this process as a measure of research quality. Individual universities were therefore motivated to encourage staff to achieve success in this arena.

One highly prestigious type of nationally competitive research in Australia is the Discovery Project Grant, administered by the Australian Research Council (ARC). There is a success rate of approximately 15–20 percent for research proposals submitted in the ARC's annual call for Discovery Project applications. The research team members had strong reasons to be individually motivated to achieve success with an ARC grant application. This goal was supported by their institutions and firmly embedded within the group's research strategies.

Among the criteria determining success in the Discovery Project process are the requirements to demonstrate the research track record of team members and, preferably, the coherence of the research team in terms of previous collaborations and successful working relationships. In this context it was important to develop a project design which enabled previous research outputs such as journal publications and conference presentations to be included within a large application for Discovery Project funding.

A further characteristic of the Discovery Project applications process is a peer review process undertaken by ARC assessors. Assessors are recognized experts in their particular disciplines and have generally had previous success in obtaining ARC grants themselves. Institutional processes in Australia, as elsewhere, have been less than kind to economists who publish and research outside of mainstream economics (Lee and Elsner 2008) and it is reasonable to expect that relatively few heterodox economists have the status of ARC assessor. This made it likely that most assessors would be relatively familiar with the use of standard national data sets and regression analysis favoured in mainstream economic analyses. A capacity to engage with standard data sets and analytical approaches in addition to a capacity to provide informed critiques of existing data and analyses were perceived by the research team as potentially important factors in achieving grant success.

We turn, firstly, to lessons about securing research funding and proposal development. As part of the application process we were required to provide key words and 'field of research' codes, which are used by the ARC, in part, to assist with selecting assessors to review the proposal. Words and codes were selected to emphasize the social policy implications of the project and, we hoped, to maximize the chances of assessors having a social research background and experience in mixed methods research. As the review process is confidential we do not know the extent to which this strategy played a part in the success of our funding application. We are inclined to believe that our proposal was reviewed by assessors who were familiar with research methods that are used largely outside the confines of mainstream economic modeling. Another strategy that may have contributed to the successful funding application was that our proposed collection of survey data was designed to ensure some limited capacity to make international comparisons of data analysis.

The research project design evolved during discussions between the six team members held over a period of about 12–15 months prior to the submission of the grant application. Prior to this period, each of the team members had worked with some of the other team members at some stage in their career, but the entire team had not previously worked together. Some of the team members had long-standing and strong interests in feminist and institutional approaches to economics. For example, four of the team members had previously published research articles in *Feminist Economics*. Those who had not published specifically in areas generally recognized as feminist research had established backgrounds in applied research that focused on utilizing appropriate methods to address pressing issues of social policy or health and care service provision. In terms of methodological issues, therefore, the team had a low a priori commitment to embedding the study in mainstream economic theory and gave a high priority to selecting methods appropriate to answering the specific issues of social and economic importance that were framed in their research questions.

The team members also had diverse research skills. Three of the team members had research backgrounds and training that focused mostly on quantitative research techniques, and three had research backgrounds that emphasized qualitative data collection and analysis. This range of skills enabled the team to consider a wide range of data sources and types of analysis as feasible options. This was an important consideration during the stages of defining research questions and identifying appropriate research methods.

In summary, the context for this project contained five important elements. Firstly, it was focused on a recognized, pressing policy question. Secondly, it addressed important gaps in previous empirical research. Thirdly, it was an issue where mainstream theoretical approaches appeared to generate little insight but where there was an apparent fit with theoretical contributions from feminist economists. Fourthly, the team had explicit goals of achieving a nationally competitive grant and were aware that this required that the researchers demonstrate publication and collaboration track records. Finally, as a team, we had backgrounds in feminist economics, applied social research, and a combination of quantitative and qualitative research skills.

## 23.4   CONCEPTUAL FRAMEWORK: METHODOLOGICAL DEBATES AND CRITIQUES

In addition to the above contextual issues, the design for this project was closely informed by some important methodological debates about the data and analyses used in many mainstream economic studies of employment. The key methodological critiques considered in most detail by the research team were those relating to feminist insights on employment choices and critical realists' critiques of mainstream economists' use of regression analysis to provide insights into causal relationships in labor markets. Critiques of the use of statistical significance as a proxy for economic significance or importance were also influential in the design of our project (Austen et al. 2014).

The conceptual framework that guides most economic analysis of employment decisions can be linked to mainstream models which characterize employers and workers as being involved in contract negotiations over labor services. These models usually make a set of simplifying behavioral assumptions about employment decision-making by these participants. Very briefly, employers are characterized as being motivated to demand labor services only by the prospect of individual gain. With such gains in mind, the price (wage) they offer will reflect the expected extra monetary value achieved from the worker's contribution to production, usually referred to as the 'marginal revenue product'. Thus, on the 'demand side', wage differences between sectors are predicted to be positively related to both the market value of the commodities being produced by the worker and her productiveness.

Workers are characterized in this approach as the sellers of labor who are motivated by a desire to maximize their self-interest. As such, they are assumed to require a price (wage) that at least matches the value of alternative uses of their labor time and will reflect the relative disamenity involved with the work. Thus, it is predicted that the 'reservation wage'[1] of workers will rise with the value of alternative uses of their time (increasing, for example, when young children are present in the household). In addition, jobs that involve occupational hazards or unsocial work hours are predicted to be associated with higher wage rates, *ceteris paribus*.

Outside of the mainstream approach, a range of different conceptual frameworks for understanding the exchange of labor services and the determination of wage rates exist. To varying degrees, approaches within the alternative 'institutional' and 'feminist' frameworks reject the notion of complete contracts for labor services and emphasize instead that the interactions between employers and workers take place within given cultural, relational and historical contexts. The institutional context of the labor exchange critically affects how different types of work are evaluated by participants in the exchange, their motivations, the rules governing the determination of wage rates, the bargaining power of the participants, and their 'outside' options.

These alternative approaches to the economic analysis of labor exchange typically discount the notion that wage rates will reflect objective notions of the monetary value of the worker's contribution to production. Wage outcomes are viewed as reflecting employers' notions of what they should pay, in addition to what might be financially viable or attractive or both. They also reflect workers' notions of what they can or should legitimately demand as remuneration for their labor. Notions of fair or legitimate wages are formed largely with reference to prevailing (and historical) wage relativities and are heavily influenced by social norms relating to work roles, including gender norms. These insights add to a large and complex literature that emphasizes how wages might diverge from marginal product for reasons of bargaining power (linked, for example, to the presence of monopolies and monopsonies in particular labor markets) and information asymmetry (see Kaufman and Hotchkiss 2006 for an overview).

The themes of specific areas of institutional labor economics are important to feminist economic perspectives on gender and employment. A large and diverse literature in feminist economics discusses the way in which apparently gender-neutral market institutions fail to adequately value the care work performed by women (Waring 1988; Himmelweit 1995; Ironmonger 1996; Hewitson 1999); how the motivations of participants to labor and other exchanges are shaped by social structures and relationships and are not universally based on self-interest (Sharp and Broomhill 1988; Pujol 1997; Strassman 1997); and how social norms associated with providing care, the distribution of unpaid household work, and the nature and configuration of work can become reflected in gendered outcomes from labor exchange (Deacon 1985; Folbre 1994; Rosewarne 2001; Broomhill and Sharp 2007; Austen et al. 2013). Feminist economists have also argued that the construction of mainstream economic theory has excluded significant aspects of women's lives (Hewitson 1999; Strassman 1994; Strober 1994; Nelson 1996, 2003; Jefferson and King 2001). These analyses have identified gender bias in mainstream economic theory as contributing to the relative lack of data about social and economic issues that are particularly relevant to women, including care work, the working conditions of outworkers, and the distribution of resources within households (Folbre 1994). Critiques have been made of the social constructions of the categories used in survey data with statistical classifications such as occupation, sex, and race capturing certain collectivities but obscuring others (Barker 2005). A response has been to promote the use of a range of research methods in the analysis of women's status and role in paid and unpaid work.

While feminist literature provides insights into some key areas of neglect in mainstream analyses of labor market issues, critical realist critiques of deductive modeling provide insights into another set of limitations associated with mainstream analyses. These insights have some areas of commonality with feminist critiques, although they are largely informed by concerns based in ontological theory rather than the epistemological foundations of many feminist critiques (Austen and Jefferson 2006, 2010).

Discussions among critical realist scholars emphasize the need for analyses that recognize the complexities of social ontology and consider the interrelationship of human agency and institutions or structures (Lawson 1997, 2003). Researchers are charged with the tasks of elaborating on the motivational dimension of agency, analyzing the mechanisms that facilitate action or behavior, and accounting for the relational context of behavior. This requires that they adopt methods that extend well beyond regression models and identify mixed methods techniques as particularly appropriate to some projects (e.g., Downward and Mearman 2007). In this context, qualitative methods are viewed as especially relevant because they can enable phenomena to be empirically elucidated in greater detail and, as such, help to reveal aspects of the constituency of phenomena and support theory development. Qualitative data analysis is also seen of particular value in helping to reveal the importance of countervailing influences because the focus is on the unit of analysis and contextual relations are explored. Downward and Mearman (2007) posit that while quantitative data may be used to reveal some patterns of general sets of occurrences, interpretative research using qualitative methods is given the key role of exploring the processes associated with behavior that produce particular empirical patterns.

The identification of some advantages from employing qualitative techniques does not deny a role for regression analysis and some critical realist scholars define a substantial role for quantitative methods within a mixed methods framework. Finch and McMaster (2002) emphasize the importance of 'demi-regularities', or partial event regularities which prima facie indicate the actualization of a causal mechanism or tendency over a defined region of time and space. They focus on the potential for non-parametric techniques (especially measures of association between samples) to assist in the identification and analysis of demi-regularities from quantitative data. Qualitative data and analyses also play a role in the type of approach recommended by Finch and McMaster. They acknowledge that the process of generating claims about causal explanation needs to draw on much broader sets of information than the results of regression techniques. Consistent with critical realist arguments, they give specific mention to retroductive reasoning, which involves the use of analogy and metaphor to explore the mechanisms, structures, or conditions that, at least in part, may be responsible for a particular phenomenon.

The rationale for undertaking quantitative analysis within a critical realist framework therefore differs markedly from mainstream approaches because demi-regularities are identified as an observation warranting further investigation in order to draw conclusions about possible causal factors. The demi-regularities are not assumed to provide evidence of causal relations between two particular variables. Measures of statistical significance or the 'fit' between a deductively derived mathematical model and specific data therefore have a minimal role to play in this type of analysis.

In addition to literature situated within discussions of critical realism, McCloskey's long-standing critiques of statistical significance also informed the research team's approach to the project design. The limitations of standard regression analyses are serious but appear to be poorly understood. As Ziliak and McCloskey (2004, p. 666) highlight, these problems include the emphasis given to statistical significance, which they describe as a 'bone-headedly misguided' way of assessing the nature of economic phenomena. They point out that statistical significance simply indicates the likelihood that, given limitations in the sample size, a statistical proposition about a relationship between two particular variables is reasonable. However, statistical significance does not imply economic significance, which is about the practical consequences of particular relationships between economic variables. They emphasize that economists should be concerned with economic significance (what they term the 'oomph', or likely magnitude of a relationship), rather than statistical significance (which refers to the 'precision' of a particular, even if negligible, measured effect).

A further problem with economic analyses based on regression models is the tendency to focus on the measures of fit, such as the likelihood ratios, of alternative regression models. These tests only compare how well alternative models 'explain' observed patterns in the available (sample) data. The tests do not address the possibility that the available quantitative data might have only limited relevance to the phenomena of interest or concern. As Ziliak and McCloskey (2004, p. 667) note:

> 'Fit' in a wider scientific sense . . . cannot be brought solely and conveniently under the lamp-post of sampling theory . . . How well for example does the model (or parameter estimate) fit phenomena elsewhere? Are there entirely different sorts of evidence – experimental, historical, anecdotal, narrative, and formal – that tend to confirm it? Does it accord with careful introspections about ourselves?

This critique of standard economic analysis does not deny a role for regression analysis. Rather, it suggests improvements in the way regression results are interpreted and reported, and an increased use of other types of data and analysis, where appropriate. This also suggests a role for a mixed methods approach.

Support for mixed methods approaches to social research is not, however, unanimous. Debates exist about the appropriate roles of quantitative and qualitative data in a mixed methods approach in economic research. Lawson (1997), for example, has questioned the value of qualitative data derived from interviews or focus groups:

> The usefulness of agents' understandings articulated as explanations is tempered for critical realists by the limited extent of that knowledge, and by difficulties in articulating its inevitable tacit and unreflective content, often summarized as agents' opaque understandings of the physical and social structural properties of their situations. (Lawson 1997, pp. 192–3)

Against this, many other heterodox scholars, including feminist economists, place a high value on individuals' own understanding of phenomena and causal processes affecting them. Feminist scholars have given extensive attention to the potential biases that arise by conducting research without the inclusion of the knowledge of those who are 'the subjects' of the research. Qualitative data provide an opportunity to gain insights into how agents make sense and meaning of the situations in which they live. They also provide insights into the discourses which are available and used by agents faced with particular choices or situations, such as decisions to remain in a particular area of employment (Mills et al. 2014). This is particularly important when the research community itself draws from particular sectors of society which underrepresent women.

More recently, feminist scholars have also engaged with literature examining the use of mixed methods investigation. This has partly been necessitated by institutional concerns associated with the funding and authority given to traditional quantitative techniques, and partly motivated by the insights that can be gained by using mixed methods to explore women's economic and social experiences. Particular attention has been given to the need for the use of multiple types of data and analysis to gain insights into 'complex and multi-dimensional issues' (Hesse-Biber 2008, p. 360). This has been coupled with awareness that specific types of data collection provide a particular lens on people's perceptions of the issues under investigation. Further, different accounts of social phenomena are generated by different media of data collection (Irwin 2008, pp. 415–16).

Given their understanding of the above range of methodological debates, the research team considered that it was important for the project to include the following elements: (1) key data and issues for analysis (including variables in quantitative analysis) should relate directly with women's experiences and perceptions within the contemporary Australian aged care sector; (2) regression analysis should be used for identifying patterns of mature-age women's workforce participation, not primarily for hypothesis testing within a framework of deductive modeling; (3) qualitative data collection and analysis of mature-age women aged carers' experiences and perceptions should inform discussion of possible causal processes and identify emergent issues; and (4) economic significance rather than statistical significance should inform discussions of the findings and implications of the project's quantitative analysis.

## 23.5   FAMILIARIZATION STUDY, DEVELOPMENT OF RESEARCH QUESTIONS, AND PROJECT DESIGN

The research program commenced with an exploratory study of face-to-face interviews with 14 aged care workers from one large aged care service organization. This study was undertaken for a number of reasons. Firstly, only two of the team's six members had direct experience with aged care provision and an exploratory study was considered an important step with familiarizing other team members with the issues that some aged care workers consider important to their employment experiences and decisions. This provided an opportunity for emergent issues to be included in the design of later parts of the project. Secondly, the small program of interviews provided an opportunity to learn about the language that aged care workers use to describe their work experiences. This was important for the later design of survey and qualitative interview questions. Thirdly, the design and implementation of a small-scale qualitative project provided an opportunity for researchers with backgrounds in quantitative analysis techniques to develop greater familiarity with semi-structured interview data and their analysis. A further benefit of the familiarization study was the opportunity to strengthen research ties with a key researcher who worked within the aged care service organization that facilitated the recruitment of interview participants. The strengthening of these ties was an important part of the project and in later stages of the project this research team member would play a major role in gaining support and participation from other aged care organizations in national, large-scale data collection exercises.

While important for addressing the aims outlined above, 'research findings' from the familiarization study were limited. Despite this, one emergent issue identified in this part of the study became increasingly important in later data collections and analyses. The key emergent issue involved the concept of 'recognition' of aged care work by the carers' families and community. Analysis of the interview transcripts revealed that some aged care workers were prepared to accept relatively low levels of pay in return for various perceived 'benefits' such as flexible working or re-entry to the workforce. At the same time, some of the workers expressed a level of strong indignation about the lack of respect or social status that they perceived was attached to low wages. By reference to existing literature we identified similarities between the aged care workers' perceptions and discussions of 'recognition' in previous research (Fraser and Honneth 2003; Austen and Jefferson 2011, 2012b). Our investigations into recognition in subsequent stages of the project provide a key illustration of the insights that can be gained from mixed methods approaches to research, and we discuss it further below.

Following our familiarization study, the project was designed specifically to address three research questions:

1. What are the key economic, social, and demographic characteristics associated with mature-age women who decide to maintain or leave employment in Australia's aged care sector?
2. How do mature-age women workers describe their experiences and perceptions of work, and reasons for staying employed in or considering exit from Australia's aged care sector?
3. What do findings relevant to questions 1 and 2 suggest for economic theory and policy relevant to the attraction and retention of mature-age women workers in Australia's aged care sector?

These questions formed the basis of a Discovery Project grant application to the ARC. The research proposal was based on the collection and analysis of four main sources of data within an integrated mixed methods framework: (1) a large national survey of Australian households which contains some data on occupation and employment status; (2) staff records of a large aged care service provider; (3) two rounds of survey data to generate panel, or longitudinal, data of current and past employees in the aged care sector and gain insights into work retention intentions and behaviors over a 12-month period; and (4) qualitative data collected from women aged 45 and over working in paid aged care roles.

Each of the data sets required analytical methods implemented in an appropriate way to ensure complementarity across the project. Drawing on the terminology used by Creswell and Plano Clark (2009), the project was conceptualized as 'explanatory'. That is, the purpose of the project was to identify and investigate possible causal relations that might assist with explaining the decisions of mature-age women to remain in or leave their work in the aged care sector. In broad terms, women's intention to stay or leave their employment might be described as the key 'dependent variable' or issue of interest that was at the heart of the project. Despite this, the exploratory nature of the project meant that we did not, a priori, define 'independent variables' or preclude the possibility that intention to stay or leave employment was not the only factor that might inform actual actions of leaving employment. The goal was to retain an exploratory approach to data and analysis. The project was also planned to be 'sequential', meaning that specific forms of earlier data collection and analysis would inform later stages of the project. A diagram outlining the key steps and data in the project is provided in Figure 23.1 and each step is discussed more fully in the remainder of this chapter.

The research design captured the potential of quantitative data to identify national patterns of mature-age women's employment, the employment decisions made by aged care workers at an organizational level, and patterns of employment exit and retention

**QUAL**
Objective: Familiarization with issues and language relevant to mature-age women working in aged care
Data: 14 semi-structured interviews
Analysis: Exploratory, open coding
Outcome: Context for future analysis and design of survey and interview schedules

**QUANT**
Objective: Utilize existing data sources and establish collaborative research track record
Data: HILDA national panel survey
Analysis: Hazard analysis, patterns of retention/exit women 45+
Outcome: National context showing patterns of mature-age women's workforce participation, retention and exit in Australia

**QUANT**
Objective: Utilize existing data sources and establish collaborative research track record
Data: Employment records of aged care service provider
Analysis: Hazard analysis, patterns of retention/exit women 45+
Outcome: Organizational context showing patterns of mature-age women's workforce participation, retention and exit within the aged care sector

**QUANT**
Objective: Primary data collection and analysis relevant to employment intentions, experiences of mature-age women working in aged care
Data: National survey of aged care workers
Analysis: Characteristics of planned leavers and stayers
Outcome: Analysis of key issues for investigation in interviews and T2 surveys

**QUANT**
Objective: Primary data collection and analysis relevant to employment behavior (stay or exit) and experiences of mature-age women working in aged care
Data: Follow-up surveys with previous survey respondents – leavers and stayers
Analysis: Longitudinal, characteristics of leavers and stayers

**QUAL**
Objective: Rich data describing experiences and perceptions of working in aged care and decisions to stay or leave work in the sector
Data: Semi-structured interviews
Analysis: Deductive and open coding
Outcome: Interpretation of quant and emergent issues.

**FINDINGS AND IMPLICATIONS**
Compare/contrast and integrate outcomes from each separate data set
Consistent findings and contradiction from different forms of data and analysis

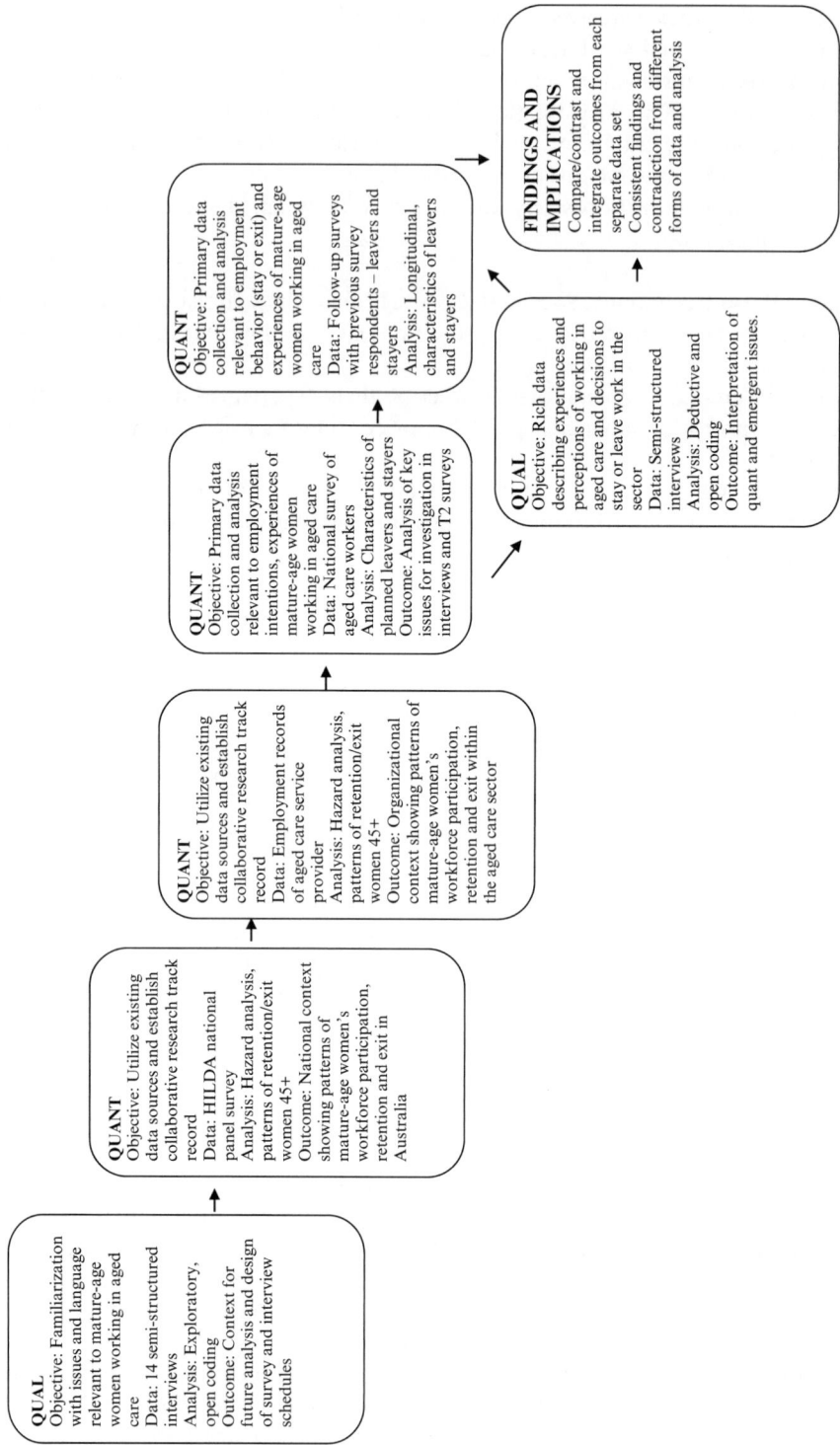

*Figure 23.1    Planned study design: explanatory, sequential mixed methods framework*

by aged care workers at an industry level. This was complemented by qualitative data collection and analysis which provided insight into the perceptions and experiences of mature-age women working in the Australian aged care sector. The qualitative data assisted in the interpretation of the causal relationships suggested by quantitative data analysis. The combination of data and analytical approaches afforded a robust framework to identify possible causal relationships and drew on aged care workers' discussions of their social context and experience to explain the identified patterns of employment decision-making.

**Project Stage 1: Analyses of Existing National and Organizational Data Sets**

Our understanding of national patterns of exit and entry from the labor market by mature-age women was informed through analysis of quantitative data from an annual panel study of Australian households. The Household Income and Labor Dynamics Australia (HILDA) Survey began in 2001 and five waves of data were used in our initial analysis. The HILDA survey collects data about economic and subjective well-being, labor market dynamics, and family dynamics from more than 7000 households and 19 000 individual members of those households. Data are collected through annual interviews conducted with adult members of each household.

The HILDA data were analyzed for economy-wide patterns of mature-age women's employment and employment transitions into and out of paid employment. Logit regression models were calibrated to measure the impact of measured personal, social, and economic characteristics of mature-age women on the probability of leaving paid employment within the survey period. While the standard approach to regression modeling is the ordinary least squares estimation technique, the outcome we were seeking to explain was not linear but dichotomous (a woman will either leave paid employment, or not). Hence, the ordinary least squares approach was inappropriate for our study and we applied a technically more robust maximum likelihood estimation method in the form of logit regression models. The purpose of this analysis was to identify patterns of 'early' departure from paid work by mature-age Australian women, and establish the context and priorities for the other data collection exercises planned for the study.

The key findings from this study were that poor health and care roles were associated with reduced chances of employment among mature-age Australian women. However, reductions in time spent caring or improvements in health were not associated with an increased chance of returning to work by members of this group. Thus many mid-life women who experience poor health and/or undertake major care roles face substantial long-term negative consequences for their employment chances and, thus, their retirement and pre-retirement incomes (Austen and Ong 2010, 2013). The analysis was undertaken with the purpose of gaining insights into apparent, partial regularities or patterns in the data relevant to mature-age Australian women. As expected, this part of the project confirmed a need for closer investigation of the aged care sector with further appropriate data and methods.

Purposeful analysis of the aged care sector using existing data was facilitated through the analysis of staff employment records of a large aged care organization. The organization had a workforce of close to 2500 in 2007 and provided care to almost 40 000 people. The objective of this part of the study was to undertake an analysis of the patterns of employment and employment transitions of mature-age women working specifically within aged and community care services. Hazard models were used to measure the impact of key occupational characteristics of mature-age women (such as their specific care roles and completed tenure) on the probability of employment cessation. This analysis provided important contextual details missing from the HILDA data and assisted with the identification of patterns of 'early' departure from paid work by mature-age women in the aged care sector. There were two key findings from this part of the study. Firstly, carers and domestic assistants recorded the shortest job tenures among the various occupational groups within the organization. The median length of time that carers remained in the organization (at 15.1 months) was almost 32 percent lower than the median job duration of administrators, and 24 percent lower than the median job duration of nurses. Domestic assistants recorded a median job duration that was marginally higher than that of carers (15.4 as compared to 15.1 months). In addition, employees who started with the organization aged between 55 and 64 years recorded a median job duration 41 percent higher than that recorded by workers who commenced employment when aged 25 to 34 years. The small group of workers (25 in total) who started with the organization when they were aged over 65 years recorded the highest median job duration of 21.6 months. 'Early departure' or exit from the organization therefore appeared more closely related with issues relevant to occupation rather than age.

**Project Stage 2: Primary Data Collections and Analysis**

Stage 2 of the project was more closely aligned with methodological debates and discussions by heterodox economists seeking to expand the range of data and methods employed by economists to explore institutions, behaviors, and decisions. The conceptual approach for stage 2 of the project was also more purposeful in terms of its focus on mature-age women and aged care.

As noted above, our framework recognized that carers' decision-making context was one in which employment decisions are the product of the person's physical, economic, and social circumstances and the institutional environment in which these are situated. Physical and economic aspects of the working environment (such as the financial rewards associated with paid work) comprise one set of factors influencing workers' evaluation of their continued employment. These aspects interact with personal concerns (including health, relationships in the workplace, and unpaid care commitments) to determine workers' ability and willingness to remain in paid work. Through our familiarization study we had also become more closely aware of carers' perceptions of the respect and legitimacy associated with their particular work roles. Our awareness suggested that carers' institutional environment, comprising social norms relating to paid and unpaid work roles, together with the provision of support for unpaid care roles, also play a critical role in determining the decisions that are made about continued employment.

The research team members were aware of an existing survey instrument used to study nurses' patterns of employment in Europe. We secured permission to use the survey instruments for the European longitudinal Nurses' Early Exit Study (NEXT), which had been used to collect data from 56 400 participants in 11 countries. Its aims are to investigate the reasons, circumstances, and consequences surrounding premature departure of nurses from paid work, with a particular focus on nurses aged over 45 (Hasselhorn et al. 2005, p. 2).

While the NEXT survey provided a helpful basis for considering our survey design, a first step was to modify the survey instruments to reflect the context of aged care workers in Australia and to include questions relevant to the issue of recognition that emerged in the initial familiarization study of interview data. Modifications to the survey were also suggested by two of the research team members who had experience working with aged care organizations in Australia. The modified survey instruments were labelled the Mature-Age Women in Aged Care (MAWAC) Survey.

There were two waves of the MAWAC Survey, designed to reflect the collection of longitudinal data to address issues of potential endogeneity. An initial survey was distributed in late 2011 via aged care service providers to 6867 women aged 45 or over, working in aged care. Nineteen aged care providers identified appropriate study participants from their personnel data and mailed survey documents to their employees on behalf of the research team. Electronic versions of the survey were also available via the Australian Nursing Federation website. In total 3945 aged care workers responded to this survey (2850 paper and 1095 electronic responses). In the second wave of the MAWAC Survey (in late 2012), each of the original survey participants was sent a 'leavers' and a 'stayers' questionnaire and asked to complete the relevant document. We received responses from 2138 'stayers' (who were still working in the aged care sector) and 211 'leavers'.

Two regression models were used to analyze the data from the questionnaires to investigate patterns between factors that affect mature-age women's chances of leaving employment in the aged care sector, and to measure the magnitude and significance of these factors. The first regression analysis modeled mature-age women's intention to leave aged care employment. This involved the use of a cross-section logit model to explore the links between ageing, perceived work ability, and the intention to leave aged care, while controlling for other socio-demographic and economic factors such as occupational position and type of institution. The second regression analysis used the longitudinal nature of the questionnaires to model the probability of older women actually exiting the aged care sector. The analysis of survey data is ongoing and this reflects the complexity of the analysis and the potential range of issues that have emerged for future analysis during the life of this project.

A program of qualitative data collection was designed to address the second research question (listed above, in section 23.5). Between late 2011 and 2012, 43 semi-structured interviews were conducted to collect detailed case descriptions of how and why elements of a mature-age woman's personal life and/or work circumstances affect her chances of remaining in paid work. We explicitly adopted an 'embedded' qualitative study, recognizing that the design and purpose of the interviews would be strongly informed by the MAWAC surveys. This was reflected in the nature of the questions included in the interview schedule and supporting documentation such as participant information sheets and consent forms. While the interview schedule was designed to allow considerable scope for participants to raise issues of importance to their particular context, it was expected that the data would have at least some relevance to the key research question of experiences and perceptions of working in aged care and that this would, in turn, relate to decisions about remaining or leaving work in aged care.

Recruitment of interview participants was achieved by asking participants in the initial

MAWAC survey whether they were prepared to participate in an interview to further discuss their experiences of working in aged care. In response, 1568 survey participants indicated their willingness to participate in this part of the project. Potential interview participants were selected to ensure a diversity of carers in terms of occupation, residential and community care roles, intentions to stay or leave aged care, and geographic location. The interviews were held between the two waves of survey data collection.

The analytical approach applied to interview transcripts was twofold. Firstly, all transcripts were analyzed using a constant comparison approach to open coding. This allowed key concepts and constructs relevant to mature-age women's employment decisions to emerge from the experiences of interview participants. Key areas of commonality and uniqueness among participants' experiences were identified during this process. Secondly, the transcripts were analyzed for key developments and changes during the study period. This allows for the development of insights into the dynamics of employment decision-making and for the identification of key variables that may be important over time.

## 23.6   PRELIMINARY FINDINGS, TRIANGULATION, AND EMERGENCE

Preliminary findings suggest that the combination of data and analysis have generated insights that are rarely considered in mainstream economic analysis. As discussed, one key example relates to the important role played by wages as a 'signal' to workers of the value that society places on their work. While some aged care workers acknowledged that they had accepted work in a low-paid sector and were prepared to accept low wages, they expressed a strong dissatisfaction with the lack of respect and recognition that these wages indicated. The link between low wages and 'misrecognition', which was initially identified as an emergent theme in our first, small-scale program of exploratory interviews, is being reinforced through the range of data and analytical methods that have been utilized in our project.

The national data have given the team a capacity to explore perceptions of recognition by family, management, and the community with carers' stated employment intentions. Preliminary results suggest that intentions to leave the aged care sector are linked with perceptions that work in the sector is poorly recognized within the community. The perceptions of poor recognition and links with intentions to leave (or stay) in the sector are being more fully explored through analysis of the interview data. Themes of recognition have emerged strongly in the data both as a result of purposeful questions included in the interview schedule and in comments and discussions throughout other parts of the interviews in which participants took the opportunity to raise issues of importance to their situation.

By comparing insights from the various data collections (particularly the interviews and surveys) it is likely that we will be able to contribute convincing analyses that will allow the outcomes from our project to be integrated with important areas of debate and critique from other areas of social science (Fraser and Honneth 2003). This will, we expect, be an important theme in the findings published from our project.

The issue of recognition is one example of the way in which the rich body of data collected through interviews has allowed for a finely grained appreciation of the institutional and social factors relevant to carers' perceptions of recognition for their work, and its potential influence on a woman's decision to stay or leave aged care work. The interview data therefore both 'triangulated' findings from earlier data sets and analyses, and added to our understanding of potential causal links between wages, recognition, and employment decisions. As our data analyses continue we expect that there will be other examples of triangulation where the findings from one form of data and analysis reinforce the findings from another.

There were, however, important differences in some of the outcomes from analysis of the survey and interview data. One example is the identification of further emergent issues from the interview data. Although there were no specific questions that related to carers from culturally and linguistically diverse (CaLD) backgrounds, many participants commented on the importance of this during the semi-structured interviews. Of 43 interviews conducted, 28 interviewees spoke about this issue in their interview. An increase in the employment of staff from CaLD backgrounds was mentioned by interview participants in all Australian states and in both metropolitan and regional areas. Among the carers we interviewed, it seemed to be a more immediate issue among those working in residential aged care facilities.

This was an unexpected finding because neither the data from our familiarization study nor our search of previous literature had alerted us to this potential issue. In addition, our first MAWAC survey showed that the majority of aged care workers were born in Australia, and the issue was not prominent in 'open text' responses in the survey forms. This may, however, reflect a bias towards English speakers in the data collection method, as participants were required to independently answer the survey questionnaire in English. This may have meant that aged care workers with English as a second language declined to answer the survey questionnaire. There was therefore a lack of comparability or complementarity across these two forms of data.

However, the importance of CaLD background workers again emerged during analysis of data from MACAW survey 2 when participants responded in free text to questions about the issues that they most liked or disliked about their work. Various comments about the participation of CaLD background workers in the aged care workforce again emerged during analysis of these data. Comparison of the two different data analyses provides few conclusive findings. However the identification of this broad issue in two different data collections suggests an important area for future research through more purposeful investigation.

## 23.7 LESSONS AND FUTURE STEPS

It is now approximately five years since the inception of the mixed method research project outlined above. During that time we have been aware that, as researchers, we have been participating in a study where we have a degree of power to set a research agenda and define specific research questions. As a group we have attempted to be aware of the way in which specific forms of data collection and analysis privilege some forms of knowledge and insights over others. As discussed at the start of this chapter, we view these as particularly important epistemological issues for researchers who wish to identify their research as relevant to the broad objectives of feminist research agendas.

One result of this awareness is that we have integrated detailed interviews with care workers into the design of our data collection, and analysis of these interviews into the design of the survey instruments. The outcome is richer data and the capacity to produce a nuanced understanding of the factors that contribute observed patters of employment among mature-age women working in Australia's aged care sector. This approach has not been without challenges and we believe there are some key lessons that are likely to be of interest to other heterodox researchers. Some of these lessons are quite instrumental in terms of achieving research funding for heterodox economic research. Nonetheless, we consider these to be important, pragmatic lessons that may be useful for others in similar contexts. Other lessons are more closely aligned with issues of methodology and theory development within a mixed method framework.

We turn, firstly to some lessons about research funding applications. When designing the project, we gave considerable thought to the selection of key words and 'field of research' codes which are required by the ARC, in part, to assist with selecting assessors to review the proposal. Words and codes were selected to emphasize the social policy implications of the project and, we hoped, to maximize the chances of assessors having a social research background and experience in mixed methods research. As the review process is confidential we do not know the extent to which this strategy played a part in the success of our funding application. We are inclined to believe that our proposal was reviewed by assessors who were familiar with research methods that are used largely outside the confines of mainstream economic modeling, and this is a strategy we would consider in future applications. A second strategy that may have contributed to the successful funding application was that our proposed collection of survey data was designed to ensure some limited capacity to make international comparisons of data analysis.

The other lessons we have learned are more closely aligned with issues of methods, methodology, and theory. A first key lesson was the opportunity for project development that arises from working in a team of diverse researchers with different analytical skills and experience. This has been an important aspect allowing us to develop and effectively utilize a range of different data sources throughout the project. It also gave us considerable flexibility to define research questions we considered important for policy-makers, care workers, and theorists.

A second lesson was that the use of both quantitative and qualitative analyses facilitated a research approach aimed at identifying patterns of data rather than hypothesis testing. This has considerably expanded the types of causal patterns that we have been able to explore. Perhaps most importantly, it has extended the analysis beyond issues that have traditionally been included in research based on deductive modeling and which, to date, has produced limited insights.

Thirdly, we have found that the multiple forms and stages of data collection and analysis have provided rich opportunities for interplay between the design of different data collection instruments. For example, our survey design was informed by exploratory interviews with aged care workers. Our semi-structured interview schedule was able to accommodate questions aimed at more fully exploring preliminary survey data analysis. As a result, the data analysis and interview design, and qualitative data analysis, were richer and are generating a greater number of insights than anticipated. As discussed above, some of the findings are 'surprises' that were not considered in the research design but appear to be important emergent findings for further investigation.

Finally, the diversity of data and researcher skills appears to provide considerable scope for contributions to theory development. This is a part of the project that is yet to be more fully explored but one which the research team members are looking forward to. We believe that the rich data and their analysis will raise important issues of method, theory, and collaboration that we hope to contribute and discuss with the heterodox economics community as our project continues.

# NOTE

1.  The reservation wage is the minimum wage rate required by the worker to supply labor.

# REFERENCES

Adams, Valerie and Julie A. Nelson (2009), 'The economics of nursing: articulating care', *Feminist Economics*, **15** (4), 3–29.
Adams, Valerie and Rhonda Sharp (2011), 'Reciprocity: the case of aged care nurses' work', in Lynne Chester, Michael Johnson, and Peter Kriesler (eds), *Heterodox Economics: Ten Years and Growing Stronger! Proceedings of the 10th Annual Society for Heterodox Economics Conference*, December 5–6, Sydney, pp. 1–14.
Adams, Valerie and Rhonda Sharp (2013), 'Reciprocity in caring labor: nurses work in residential aged care in Australia', *Feminist Economics*, **19** (2), 100–121.
Austen, Siobhan and Margaret Giles (2003), 'The likely effects of ageing on women's involvement in the paid workforce', *Australian Bulletin of Labour*, **29** (3), 253–73.
Austen, Siobhan and Therese Jefferson (2006), 'Comparing responses to critical realism', *Journal of Economic Methodology*, **13** (2), 257–82.
Austen, Siobhan and Therese Jefferson (2010), 'Feminist and post Keynesian economics: challenges and opportunities', *Cambridge Journal of Economics*, **34** (6), 1109–22.
Austen, Siobhan and Therese Jefferson (2011), 'Plain old disrespect: explorations of recognition and intrinsic motivation in care work', in Lynne Chester, Michael Johnson, and Peter Kriesler (eds), *Heterodox Economics: Ten Years and Growing Stronger! Proceedings of the 10th Annual Society for Heterodox Economics Conference*, December 5–6, Sydney, pp. 36–45.
Austen, Siobhan and Therese Jefferson (2012a), 'Intersections in Australian research: older workers, women's labour supply and paid work in aged care', *Refereed Proceedings of the 26th Annual Conference Association for Industrial Relations Academics of Australian and New Zealand*, Hotel Grand Chancellor, Gold Coast, Australia, February 8–10, accessed October 25, 2012 at http://www.airaanz.org/2012-conference-main.html.
Austen, Siobhan and Therese Jefferson (2012b), 'Recognition and aged care work', paper presented to the International Association for Feminist Economics Annual Conference, Barcelona, Spain, July.
Austen, Siobhan, Therese Jefferson, and Alison Preston (2013), 'Contrasting economic analyses of gender, work and pay: lessons from an equal remuneration case', *Journal of Industrial Relations*, **55** (1), 60–79.
Austen, Siobhan, Therese Jefferson, Rhonda Sharp, Valerie Adams, Rachel Ong, and Gill Lewin (2014), 'Mixed methods research: what's in it for economists?', *Economics and Labour Relations Review*, **25** (2), 290–305.
Austen, Siobhan and Rachel Ong (2010), 'The employment transitions of mid-life women: health and care effects', *Ageing and Society*, **30** (2), 207–27.
Austen, Siobhan and Rachel Ong (2013), 'The effects of ill-health and informal care roles on the employment retention of mid-life women: does the workplace matter?', *Journal of Industrial Relations*, **55** (5), 663–80.
Australian Government, Productivity Commission (2005), *Economic Implications of an Ageing Australia, Research Report*, Canberra: Productivity Commission.
Australian Government, The Treasury (2010), *Intergenerational Report 2010*, Canberra: Australian Government, accessed October 17, 2013 at http://archive.treasury.gov.au/igr/igr2010/report/pdf/IGR_2010.pdf.
Barker, Drusilla (2005), 'Beyond women and economics: rereading "women's work"', *Signs: Journal of Women in Culture and Society*, **30** (4), 2189–209.

Berger, M., and J. Messer Pelkowski (2004), 'Health and family labor force transitions', *Quarterly Journal of Business and Economics*, **43** (3/4), 113–28.

Birch, Elisa R. (2005a), 'The determinants of labour supply and fertility behaviour: a study of Australian women', PhD Thesis, Business School, University of Western Australia, Perth. accessed July 24, 2009 at http://theses.library.uwa.edu.au/adt-WU2005.0061/.

Birch, Elisa R. (2005b), 'Studies of the labour supply of Australian women: what have we learned?', *Economic Record*, **81** (252), 65–84.

Broomhill, Ray and Rhonda Sharp (2007), 'Gender and restructuring in Australia', in Marjorie Griffin-Cohen and Janine Brodie (eds), *Remapping Gender in the New Global Order*, London: Routledge, pp. 85–108.

Cai, Lixin and Guyonne Kalb (2004), 'Health status and labor-force participation: evidence from the HILDA data', Working Paper 4/04, Institute of Applied Economic and Social Research, Melbourne: University of Melbourne, accessed July 21, 2011 at http://www.melbourneinstitute.com/wp/wp2004n04.pdf.

Cai, Lixin and Guyonne Kalb (2006), 'Health status and labour force participation: evidence from Australia', *Health Economics*, **15** (3), 241–61.

Campolieti, Michelle (2001), 'Disability insurance and the labour force participation of older men and women in Canada', *Canadian Public Policy*, **27** (2), 179–94.

Chan, Sewin and Ann Huff Stevens (2001), 'Job loss and employment patterns of older workers', *Journal of Labor Economics*, **19** (2), 484–521.

Clark, Robert L., E. Anne York, and Richard Anker (1999), 'Economic development and labor participation of older persons', *Population Research and Policy Review*, **18** (5), 411–32.

Creswell, John W. and Vicki L. Plano Clark (2009), *Designing and Conducting Mixed Methods Research*, Thousand Oaks, CA, USA and London, UK: Sage.

Currie, Jan and Brigitte Madrian (1999), 'Health, health insurance and the labor market', in O. Ashenfelter and D. Card (eds), *Handbook of Labor Economics*, Vol. 3, Amsterdam: Elsevier Science, pp. 310–415.

Deacon, D. (1985), 'Political arithmetic: the nineteenth century Australian census and the construction of the dependent woman', *Signs: Journal of Women in Culture and Society*, **11** (1), 27–47.

Downward, P.M. and A. Mearman (2007), 'Retroduction as mixed-methods triangulation in economic research: reorienting economics into social science', *Cambridge Journal of Economics*, **31** (1), 77–99.

England, Paula and Nancy Folbre (2003), 'Contracting for care', in Marianne A. Ferber and Julie A. Nelson (eds), *Feminist Economics Today: Beyond Economic Man*, Chicago, IL: University of Chicago Press, pp. 61–79.

England, Paula and Nancy Folbre (1999), 'The cost of caring', *Annals of the American Academy of Political and Social Science*, **561**, 39–51.

Evandrou, Maria and Karen Glaser (2003), 'Combining work and family life: the pension penalty of caring', *Ageing and Society*, **23** (5), 583–601.

Evans, M.D.R. and Jonathan Kelley (2002), 'Women's employment in middle and old age', *Australian Social Monitor*, **5** (2), 39–51.

Finch, J.H. and R. McMaster (2002), 'On categorical variables and non-parametrics statistical inference in the pursuit of causal explanations', *Cambridge Journal of Economics*, **26** (6), 753–72.

Folbre, Nancy (1994), *Who Pays for the Kids? Gender and the Structures of Constraint*, London: Routledge.

Franklin, Matthew (2010), 'Cash fails to lure aged care nurses', *Australian*, January 1, p. 2.

Fraser, Nancy and Axel Honneth (eds) (2003), *Redistribution or Recognition? A Political-Philosophical Exchange*, London: Verso.

Hanks, K. (2004), 'Effects of early life family events on women's late life labour market behaviour', *European Sociological Review*, **20** (3), 189–98.

Harding, Sandra (1987), 'Introduction: is there a feminist method?', in Sandra Harding (ed.), *Feminism and Methodology*, Bloomington, IN: Indiana University Press, pp. 1–14.

Hasselhorn, Hans-Martin, Peter Tackenberg, Andreas Buescher, Michael Simon, Angelika Kuemmerling, and Bernd Hans Mueller (2005), 'Work and health of nurses in Europe – results from the NEXT-Study', accessed February 7, 2012 at http://www.next.uni-wuppertal.de/EN/index.php?articles-and-reports.

Henz, U. (2004), 'The effects of informal care on paid-work participation in Great Britain: a life course perspective', *Ageing and Society*, **24** (6), 851–80.

Hesse-Biber, Sharlene Nagy (2008), 'Part 2: Innovation in research methods design and analysis', in S.N. Hesse-Biber and P. Leavy (eds), *Handbook of Emergent Methods*, New York: Guilford, pp. 359–62.

Hewitson, Gillian J. (1999), *Feminist Economics: Interrogating the Masculinity of Rational Economic Man*, Cheltenham, UK and Northampton, MA, USA: Edward Elgar.

Heyes, Anthony (2005), 'The economics of vocation or "Why is a badly paid nurse a good nurse"?', *Journal of Health Economics*, **24** (3), 561–69.

Hill, Elizabeth (2002), 'The labor force participation of older women: retired? working? both?', *Monthly Labor Review*, **125** (9), 39–48.

Himmelweit, Susan (1995), 'The discovery of "unpaid work": the social consequences of the expansion of "work"', *Feminist Economics*, **1** (2), 1–19.
Himmelweit, Susan (1999), 'Caring labor', *Annals of the American Academy*, **56**, 27–38.
Hugo, Graeme (2007), 'Contextualising the "crisis in aged care" in Australia: a demographic perspective', *Australian Journal of Social Issues*, **42** (2), 169–82.
Ironmonger, Duncan (1996), 'Counting outputs, capital inputs and caring labour: estimating gross household product', *Feminist Economics*, **2** (3), 37–64.
Irwin, Sarah (2008), 'Data analysis and interpretation: emerging issues in linking qualitative and quantitative evidence', in Sharlene Nagy Hesse-Biber and Patricia Leavy (eds), *Handbook of Emergent Methods*, New York: Guilford, pp. 415–35.
Jefferson, Therese and John King (2001), 'Never meant to be a theory of everything: domestic labour in neo-classical and Marxian economic theory', *Feminist Economics*, **7** (3), 71–101.
Kaufman, Bruce E. and Julie L. Hotchkiss (2006), *The Economics of Labor Markets*, 7th edn, Fort Worth, TX: Dryden Press.
King, Debra, Kostas Mavromaras, Zhang Wei, Bryan He, Joshua Healy, Kirsten Macaitis, Megan Moskos, and Llainey Smith (2012), *The Aged Care Workforce*, Canberra: Department of Health and Ageing, Australian Government.
Lawson, T. (1997), *Economics and Reality*, London: Routledge.
Lawson, T. (2003), 'Ontology and feminist theorizing', *Feminist Economics*, **9** (1), 119–50.
Lee, Frederic S. and Wolfram Elsner (2008), 'Publishing, ranking and the future of heterodox economics', *On the Horizon*, **16** (4), 148–76.
Martin, Bill and Debra King (2008), *Who Cares for Older Australians? A Picture of the Residential and Community Based Aged Care Workforce, 2007*, Adelaide: National Institute of Labour Studies.
Meagher, Gabrielle (2007), 'The challenge of the care workforce: recent trends and emerging problems', *Australian Journal of Social Issues*, **42** (2), 151–67.
Meagher, Gabrielle and Karen Healy (2006), *Who Cares? Employment Structure and Incomes in the Australian Care Workforce*, Volume 2, Strawberry Hills, Australia: Australian Council of Social Service, accessed October 17, 2013 at http://acoss.org.au/images/uploads/389__Paper_141_care_workers_vol2_for_website.pdf.
Mills, Julie E, Suzanne Franzway, Judith Gill, and Rhonda Sharp (2014), *Challenging Knowledge, Sex and Power: Gender, Work and Engineering*, New York: Routledge.
Nelson, Julie A. (1993), 'The study of choice or the study of provisioning? Gender and the definition of economics', in Marianne Ferber and Julie A. Nelson (eds), *Beyond Economic Man*, Chicago, IL: University of Chicago Press, pp. 23–36.
Nelson, Julie A. (1996), *Feminism, Objectivity and Economics*, London: Routledge.
Nelson, Julie A. (2003), 'Confronting the science/value split: notes on feminist economics, institutionalism, pragmatism and process thought', *Cambridge Journal of Economics*, **27** (1), 49–64.
Organisation for Economic Co-operation and Development (OECD) (2006), *Live Longer, Work Longer*, Paris: OECD.
Pavalko, Eliza K and Julie E. Artis (1997), 'Women's caregiving and paid work: causal relationships in late mid-life', *Journal of Gerontology: Social Sciences*, **52B** (4), S170–S179.
Peracchi, Franco and Finis Welch (1994), 'Trends in labor force transitions of older men and women', *Journal of Labor Economics*, **12** (2), 210–42.
Pujol, M. (1997), 'Broadening economic data and methods', *Feminist Economics*, **3** (2), 119–20.
Rosewarne, Stuart (2001), 'Women, work and inequality' [Review of *Women, Work and Inequality: The Challenge of Equal Pay in a Deregulated Labour Market*, Jeanne Gregory, Rosemary Sales, and Ariane Hegewisch (eds) (1999)], *Journal of Australian Political Economy*, **47** (1), 123–37.
Sharp, Rhonda and Ray Broomhill (1988), *Short-Changed: Women and Economic Policies*, Sydney: Allen & Unwin.
Spiess, C. Katharina and A. Ulrike Schneider (2003), 'Interactions between caregiving and paid work hours among European midlife women, 1994 to 1999', *Ageing and Society*, **23** (1), 41–68.
Strassman, Diana (1994), 'Feminist thought and economics: or, what do the Visigoths know?', *American Economic Review Papers and Proceedings*, **84** (2), 153–58.
Strassman, Diana (1997), 'Expanding the methodological boundaries of economics', *Feminist Economics*, **3** (2), vii–ix.
Strober, Myra H. (1994), 'Can feminist thought improve economics? Rethinking economics through a feminist lens', *American Economic Review Papers and Proceedings*, **84** (2), 143–47.
Waring, Marilyn (1988), *If Women Counted*, North Sydney: Allen & Unwin.
Ziliak, Stephen and Deidre McCloskey (2004), 'Significance redux', *Journal of Socio-Economics*, **33** (5), 665–75.

# 24 Combining qualitative and quantitative methods in fieldwork: an application to research on gender, migration, and remittances in Ghana
*Lynda Pickbourn*

## 24.1 INTRODUCTION

As a result of the rise in migration and remittance flows around the world, economists are increasingly becoming interested in understanding the motivations for migration and remittances and the impacts of both on poverty and development. In recent work on the impact of remittances on development, researchers have attempted to identity differences in patterns of resource allocation between households that receive remittances and those that do not (see, for example, Adams and Cuecuecha, 2010). Underlying these studies are important, but often unstated, assumptions about the way households make decisions about migration and remittances. For example, the majority of models used to analyze migration and remittance behavior are based on household models that typically characterize the sending household as a harmonious unit in which all members are united in a common objective of maximizing household income. Bargaining models that entertain the possibility of conflict within the household retain the assumption that non-migrant household members act as a unit in making decisions about migration of other members. Likewise, analyses of the impact of remittances on receiving households, like models of migration decision-making, assume that households act as a unit in receiving remittances and making decisions about their use. These assumptions also shape the way data about migration and remittances are collected: for example, most surveys of migration and remittances simply ask the head of the household about remittances received by the household and the uses to which these remittances are put. Implicit in this question is an assumption that the household head is fully aware of all remittances received by the household and how those remittances are used.

This approach has many limitations. To begin with, it overlooks the fact that migration takes place within a specific social and institutional context. This social context may play a role in determining who migrates and who participates in the migration decision. The social context may also play a role in determining who sends remittances, to whom, and why, as well as the uses to which remittances are put. More importantly, this approach also overlooks the abundance of evidence from anthropology and from other disciplines that indicate that the workings of real households may differ from the assumptions made in these models about how households work.

The objective of this chapter is to show how the use of qualitative and quantitative methods in field research can enrich economic analyses of migration and remittance behavior and of the impact of migrants' remittances on receiving households. Field research by economists is generally understood to mean the application of a survey to a randomly selected sample of individuals, households, or firms and the statistical analysis of the quantitative data that are gathered through this means. The design and content of the survey questionnaire are typically informed by a model based on a theoretical framework developed outside the context of the area under study, and the data analysis constitutes an empirical test of the conclusion and predictions of this model (see Chapter 6 in this *Handbook*). Qualitative field research, in contrast, involves the use of unstructured interviews, participant observation and focus groups to generate data (see Chapter 7 in this *Handbook*). These methods may be used on their own or in conjunction with quantitative methods. For researchers interested in migration and remittance behavior, qualitative methods can enrich a quantitative analysis by expanding the questions that are asked, and by facilitating the generation and interpretation of quantitative data about migration and remittances that more closely reflect the actual workings of households. They also provide information about processes underlying migration and remittances decisions, which, although they may not be readily quantifiable, are still important for understanding the impacts of migration and remittances on households. Most importantly, by broadening our understanding of the motivations of migrants and remitters and their origin households, they can contribute to the development of more relevant and empirically grounded theories about the migration, remittance and development nexus.

In this chapter, I draw on my own research on the impact of remittances from rural–urban migrants on the education expenditures of receiving households in northern Ghana to discuss the contributions of combining qualitative and quantitative fieldwork methods to the study of migration and remittances in economics. The decision to focus on internal migration in an African country was motivated by the relative neglect of internal migration in the literature on migration and remittances, despite its importance as a livelihood strategy for the majority of poor people in the developing world generally and in Africa in particular. One of the most important changes in population movements within sub-Saharan Africa has been the rise in the participation of women in migration streams that were previously dominated by men. According to the International Organization for Migration (IOM), the number of female migrants in the region increased from 3.369 million in 1965 to 7.237 million in 1990 (IOM 2000).[1] In South Africa, for example, female migration has accounted for most of the increase in the internal migratory movements of the country's African population, with the percentage of women in the migrant population rising from approximately 30 per cent in 1993 to about 34 per cent in 1999 (Posel 2003). In Ghana, available data from the Fifth Round of the Ghana Living Standards Survey (GLSS 5) and the 2010 Population Census suggest that internal migrants account for more than 50 per cent of the population and that about half of these migrants are women (Ackah and Medvedev 2010; Litchfield and Waddington 2003; Ghana Statistical Services 2010). One might expect this so-called 'feminization' of migration flows in sub-Saharan Africa to have implications for the impacts of migration and remittances on households in the region. However, with few exceptions, most analyses of migration and remittances have either focused solely on male migration, or have assumed that female migration can be subsumed under existing models of male migration. My research in Ghana was an attempt to fill this lacuna in the literature.

## 24.2  MIGRATION, REMITTANCES, AND ECONOMIC DEVELOPMENT: A REVIEW OF THE LITERATURE

In this section I review a selection of the vast literature on migration and remittances. This literature can be classified into three categories: the literature on household migration decision-making, the literature on the determinants of remittances, and the literature on the impact of remittances on households in developing countries. What all three categories have in common are their assumptions regarding how households and migrants make decisions about migration and remittances.

### Household Models of Migration Decision-Making

Until relatively recently, migration was assumed to be the result of individual optimizing behavior (Todaro 1969; Harris and Todaro 1970). Increasingly, this assumption has been challenged by household models of migration decision-making that seek to better approximate the realities of migration decision-making in developing countries where family farming systems predominate in rural areas. One version of these household models of migration is essentially an application of the 'new household economics' (NHE) to migration decision-making.[2] In these models, the migration of an individual from a household is undertaken to maximize household utility obtained from the consumption of goods, subject to time and income constraints. A household that needs extra income either for consumption or investment, or that needs to insure itself against risk, decides that this can be achieved through the migration of a family member (see, e.g., Bhattacharyya 1985; Low 1986; Bigsten 1996; Agesa and Kim 2001).

An important shortcoming of the NHE conception of migration as a household strategy or 'family decision' is its presumption that there is consensus among household members over the decision of who in the household should migrate.[3] As many feminist economists have noted, decisions about the allocation of household labor and other resources are often subject to competing interests, conflict, and negotiation (see, e.g., Agarwal 1997; Katz 1991; Posel 1999; Dodson 2000).

An alternative body of work that has provided perhaps the most systematic theoretical treatment of the role played by labor migration in household economic strategies is the 'new economics of labor migration' (NELM). Like the NHE approach, its central premise is that migration decisions are made not by isolated individual actors but by families or households. In the presence of fragmented capital markets that are unable to supply adequate credit or insurance coverage for rural households, the risk-averse household can reduce risk and accumulate financial surpluses by diversifying its sources of income; one such income diversification strategy would involve the migration of a household member, usually the eldest son, to find work in the city and remit part of his urban income. In this way, migration serves as a means of mitigating risk, or as a means of financing investments for households that are credit-constrained (Stark 1978, 1984, 1999; Stark and Levhari 1982; Stark and Bloom 1985; Lucas and Stark 1985; Katz and Stark 1986).

**The Motives for Remittances**

The NELM literature is dominated by models of the determinants of remittances that treat remittances as the outcome of intra-family bargaining and strategic behavior by family members. These models begin with the premise that the decision to migrate is a joint decision made by two agents: the migrant and the non-migrant members of the household. The two parties enter into an implicit contractual arrangement in which the household funds the cost of migration and requisite education for the migrant to find employment in the urban destination, and the migrant in return agrees to make remittances to the household. The migrant adheres to this contract so long as they expect to gain from doing so. Important gains to the migrant include support from the family to hedge against unemployment at the destination, or the expectation of a bequest from the family when the migrant returns.

Within this framework, the magnitude of remittances that the migrant makes depends on the relative bargaining power of both parties. Variables that enhance the bargaining power of the family relative to the migrant, such as highly valued family property that can be inherited by the migrant, or unstable urban labor markets, will increase the magnitude of migrant-to-family remittances; variables that enhance the bargaining power of the migrant relative to the family, such as worsening economic conditions in the origin community, or stable urban labor markets, will reduce the magnitude of these remittances (Stark 1984; Hoddinott 1994; Lucas and Stark 1985; Stark and Lucas 1988). While some of these studies simply ignore female migration altogether (e.g., Hoddinott 1994), others have noted the presence of systematic gender differences in the motivations of migrants who make remittances, although they do not explore the reasons for these gender differences in migrants' motivations (e.g., Lucas and Stark 1985; Stark and Lucas 1988; de la Brière et al. 2002; Vanwey 2004).

The focus on instrumentalist motives alone as an explanation of migrants' remittance behavior overlooks the role that social norms may play in determining who sends remittances, how much is sent, and to whom remittances are sent. In an attempt to explore this dimension of the determinants of remittances behavior, Clark and Drinkwater (2001) find that large and significant inter-ethnic differences in remittance probabilities remain even after controlling for other influences on the incidence and magnitude of remittances sent by immigrants living in the United Kingdom. Alba and Sugui (2011) also find that overseas Filipino workers typically remit small amounts on a regular basis; they suggest that this behavior may be consistent with Filipino giving norms, in which individuals are socially obliged to give gifts, but to do so only in small amounts. However, because of the limitations of their data which do not capture the institutional contexts within which migrants make decisions, the authors of both papers are unable to go beyond merely pointing to social norms as a possible explanation for the patterns they observe, or to explore whether there are differences in the ways in which social norms impact the remittance behavior of different migrants from the same country.

**The Impact of Remittances on Development**

A significant segment of the literature on migration and remittances has focused on the impact of remittances on the origin household. This literature has revolved primarily around an ongoing debate over how remittances are used and whether they are used primarily for consumption or whether they are used to finance investments in human and physical capital by origin households.

Probably the most widespread view is that remittances are perfectly fungible with other sources of income, so that the impact of a marginal increase in household income from remittances has exactly the same impact as a marginal increase in income from any other source. A second perspective is that the receipt of remittances induces recipients to act in ways that reduce economic activity, and increases their preference for status-oriented consumer goods. As a result, remittances are spent on consumption rather than on investments in physical capital, and hence they have little impact on economic growth and development (Chami et al. 2003). This is in contrast to a third line of argument, which holds that marginal increases in remittance income are more likely to be reflected in increased investment in human and physical capital than in increased consumption (Adams 1998; Yang 2006; Adams and Cuecuecha 2010).

The bulk of this literature devotes little attention to the impact of remittances on intra-household resource allocation.[4] The studies upon which this literature has been based have generally proceeded as though the household members who remain in the area of origin act as a unit in receiving remittances and deciding how those remittances are used. At its most basic level, the assumption that the impact of migrant remittances on origin households can be analyzed as though remittances flow to unified households is reflected in the collection of remittance data at the level of the household: most migration surveys, for example, ask only the household head or primary respondent whether 'the household' has received any remittances from the migrant. This assumption overlooks the substantial evidence from the intra-household bargaining literature that shows that the identity (and in particular, the gender) of income recipients matters for intra-household resource allocation.

In the handful of studies that do consider the role of women's control of resources in shaping the impact of remittances on households, the gender of the household head is the key variable: women are assumed to have greater control over the allocation of remittances in female-headed households than in male-headed households. For example, Guzman et al. (2008), using data from the fourth round of the Ghana Living Standards Survey (GLSS 4), find that households receiving remittances from the head's (migrant) wife allocate much less of their budgets to education than households receiving remittances from the head's (migrant) husband. They interpret this as being the result of the wife's inability to control and monitor expenditures while she is away. This interpretation, however, stands in sharp contrast to their other finding: households receiving remittances from the head's daughter allocate a higher share to food and education than other households. The authors offer no explanation for why migrant daughters might be better able to control and monitor household expenditures while they are away and to ensure that their remittances are used for food and education, while migrant wives are less able to ensure that their remittances are used for education.

The key to understanding this inconsistency lies in the fact that the gender of the household head may be far less important in determining how remittances are used than the gender of the person who actually receives the remittances. Due to the lack of survey data on the identity of the actual recipients of remittances, Guzman et al., like De and Ratha (2005) in their study of the impact of remittances on household welfare in Sri Lanka, and Malone (2007) in her study of the uses of remittances in Mexican households, implicitly assume that all migrant remittances are received and controlled by household heads. But women may, and often do, receive and exercise control over remittance income even if they are not household heads, and this may be reflected in household expenditure patterns. If female migrants in Ghana are more likely to send remittances to other women in the household, this would explain Guzman et al.'s findings that households that receive remittances from daughters allocate a greater budget share to food and education, since these remittances might be directed towards their mothers, even in male-headed households. Furthermore, if household members maintain separate budgets and manage these independently of each other, as is the case in many countries in sub-Saharan Africa, then the receipt of remittances by female household members, by increasing the income that women have to spend, could have important implications for household expenditure patterns, regardless of the gender of the household head. An important question worth exploring, therefore, is how the likelihood of women receiving remittances in the household is affected by female out-migration.

In this review of the literature, I have highlighted some of the central assumptions of the literature on migration and remittances. These include the fundamental assumption that households (or at least the non-migrant members) act as a unit in making decisions about migration. The other assumption that closely follows from this is that non-migrant household members act as a unit in receiving remittances and in making decisions about their use, so that the identity of the remitter and the recipient of the remittances do not matter for how remittances are used. Even when this latter assumption is relaxed, it is simply replaced by the assumption that household heads receive and make decisions about the use of remittances on behalf of the rest of the household. In the rest of this chapter, I draw on my research in Ghana to question these assumptions and to highlight the contributions of field research and qualitative methods to enhancing our understanding of remittance behavior and the impact of remittances on receiving households.

## 24.3   MIGRATION FROM NORTHERN GHANA TO THE SOUTH

Ghana, like many other countries in sub-Saharan Africa, has a long history of labor migration. One important migration stream that dates back to the early years of colonial rule is the migration of labor from the northern regions of the country to the south. This migration stream was dominated by men migrating during the off-farm season, either to work as casual laborers on cocoa farms in the south, or to take advantage of the different rainfall patterns in the south by working as tenant farmers. More recently, increasing numbers of young men and boys travel to the south after the harvest is over to work in the informal sector of the scrap metal industry, gathering copper, brass, and other semi-precious metals from discarded electronic waste for resale to middlemen. They return to their villages just before the planting season to begin preparing their land.

In the 1980s, however, the number of women moving from rural agricultural communities in the north to urban centers in the south began to increase.[5] The capital, Accra, is a major destination for many of these women; in 2010, women made up 52 per cent of migrants from the Northern Region of Ghana living in the city (GSS 2010). This migration may be characterized as short-term circular or seasonal migration, with women leaving their origin communities for five to six months at a stretch to work in the south, often right after the harvest is over in November to December, and returning home either in April or May to help with planting or gathering shea nuts when they are in season, or in September to October to help with the harvest, and then leaving again.[6] In contrast to the usual perception of female migrants as simply following their male relatives, the majority of these women migrate independently of their families. In the south, where they work primarily as porters in the markets, they are known as *kayayei*, a word that loosely translates as 'women who carry loads on their heads'.[7] Their clients are mainly traders and shoppers who hire them to carry their goods between storage points and market centers, or between market centers and transport terminals. The demand for their services as porters is determined by congestion in the markets which makes vehicular transport difficult, as well as by the expansion of petty trading activities in the informal sector that require the rapid movement of goods from one part of the market to another. Many women migrants also work as domestic servants or do other jobs in the informal economy. While male out-migration is considered part of the normal cycle of economic activity, particularly for younger men, the migration of these women is widely considered to be an undesirable phenomenon, both within their own communities as well as within the wider national discourse. Existing studies have focused on the challenges faced by the migrant women at their destinations and on the ways in which they cope with these challenges (Awumbila and Ardayfio-Schandorf 2008; Yeboah 2008; Bemah 2010), and policy has mostly focused on discouraging northern women from migrating to the south and encouraging female migrants from the north to return home.[8] Little is known about the impacts of their migration and remittances on the households left behind.

In 2007–08, I travelled to Ghana to conduct fieldwork for my doctoral dissertation. My research was initially an attempt to locate the rising migration of women from rural communities in northern Ghana within the political economy of persistent poverty and deteriorating agricultural livelihoods in this part of the country, and to learn more about the impacts of the growing migration of women on their households. I decided to carry out field research because the questions I was asking could not be answered with secondary data. For one thing, there is very limited data on internal migration in Ghana. The only sources of information are the population census, which provides information on the magnitude of internal migration but little else besides, and the different rounds of the Ghana Living Standards Survey (GLSS) which hold more detailed information on migration and remittances. However, the GLSS contains no information on the details of migration decision-making, nor does it provide information on the actual recipients of remittances within the household. Moreover, the definition of migration in both of these sources excludes short-term, seasonal, or circular migration. For example, the population census asks for the place of birth and usual residence of each person enumerated, as well as the usual place of residence five years prior to the census. The place of usual residence is defined as the place in which the person has lived for at least six months. Migrants who move for short periods of time are likely to consider their origin communities as their usual place of residence; if they are enumerated in their origin communities, this will result in them being considered as non-migrants. Likewise, the GLSS defines a migrant as a person who has lived or intends to live in a different district for a continuous period of at least 12 months. Again, short-term moves are likely to be overlooked when migration is defined in this way. The fact that short-term moves constitute the bulk of migration between northern and southern Ghana meant that if I wanted to study this particular group of migrants, I would have to collect my own data. Informed by the extant literature on migration, as well as by prior research on these migrants, I had initially assumed that their migration was part of a household strategy, in which households decided upon the migration of these women as a way to mitigate risk or income vulnerability. However, within a few days of starting my field research, it became clear to me that this was not necessarily the case.

## 24.4   FIELD STUDY IN GHANA

My fieldwork took place in two parts. The first part took place between August and December of 2007 in Accra, the capital of Ghana and the most popular destination for both male and female migrants from the north of Ghana. With the help of a male field assistant who also acted as an interpreter, I interviewed a total of 253 female migrants in five separate locations in the city, all chosen for their proximity to market centers where the majority of female migrants from northern Ghana live and work. A migrant was defined as any female aged 15 or older who had moved from the north of Ghana to live in the south for at least three months prior to the interview, or who intended to stay in the south for at least three months following the interview. Because of the difficulties of generating a sampling frame for a transient population such as this one, we used a snowball sampling technique to select the respondents. After spending a few days at the market centers observing the women at work, and occasionally falling into conversation with them, I began the process of selecting respondents by walking up to women whom we identified as possible migrants from the north, explaining the details of the project and asking if they would be willing to talk to us. The women who worked as market porters were easiest to identify, since they all carried a metal basin in which they placed the loads they were hired to carry. Once an individual had agreed to be interviewed, I asked her if she would be willing to recommend others to interview. In this way, I was able to generate a sample based on the networks of the initial respondents. As a result, although the majority of the women in the initial sample were market porters, a number of the migrants in later rounds of the sample worked as domestics or as dish washers for food vendors. Since the migrants tended to form networks based on age and origin community, there was the possibility that each migrant would only recommend other migrants who were similar to her in important ways. Thus, I purposely selected the initial sample to ensure diversity in age, marital status, and origin community. This component of my research involved the administration of a survey as well as in-depth interviews with all survey respondents who were willing to spend more time talking to us. The survey included a combination of pre-coded and open-ended questions and was designed to elicit general demographic information about the women, while the in-depth interviews were designed to gain deeper insights into the decision-making processes that had led to their migration, the women's motivations for migrating and sending remittances, and their experiences of life in the origin and destination areas.

The second part of my fieldwork took place between February and July 2008 in the Savelugu-Nanton district, one of the 18 administrative districts of the Northern Region of Ghana, where I administered household surveys to a randomly selected sample of

181 households in 24 rural communities. My original intention had been to generate a sample in which the migrants I interviewed in Accra would be matched to their households in the Northern Region. However, given my limited resources, the logistics of this proved difficult once I arrived in the region and I decided to limit my household surveys to the Savelugu-Nanton district, which has been identified by government and nongovernmental organization (NGO) sources as having one of the highest rates of female out-migration in the Northern Region. It was also the third most frequently cited district of origin of the migrants I interviewed in Accra, and most of the communities in the district were relatively easy to access by motorbike. This meant that Dagomba households constituted the majority of households in my sample.[9]

Each household survey consisted of four separate parts. The first part was designed to gather information on household membership and migration history, asset ownership, and experience of livelihood shocks over the previous ten years. The second part was a migration survey, which was applied only to households from which at least one person had moved to live in a village, town, or city outside the district for at least three months in the previous five years. In these migrant households, I conducted in-depth interviews with the closest relatives of the migrants, both male and female, as well as with returned migrants if they were present. I collected data on the individual migrants' migration history, reasons for migrating, the migration decisions, remittances sent in the previous 12 months, and the uses to which these remittances were put. The third part of the survey was an expenditure survey, in which I collected detailed expenditure data on food, household durables, and other miscellaneous items. Finally, I collected data on women's status and roles in decision-making in the household. Because of the large household sizes and the number of women in the household, this survey was administered only to women migrants who had returned – or if the migrant was still away, her closest female relative – as well as the most senior woman in the household (usually the household head's oldest wife). In non-migrant households, this meant that I spoke only to the latter. The decision to include the senior wife was initially based on the advice of my field assistants that it would be unwise to offend the senior woman in the household. However, as I discuss below, these interviews ultimately turned out to be useful in providing information about differences between the rights and responsibilities of older women and younger women in the rural households.

I also held focus group discussions with women and men separately in six communities to get a better understanding of the norms and perceptions regarding female migration from the district, and on the responsibilities of men and women within the household. Each of these focus groups was purposely constituted differently. For example, in one village, I spoke with a group of older women, none of whom had ever migrated to the south, but a few of whom had daughters who were migrants. In another village, the majority of women in the group were young women who had returned from the south. In yet another village, I spoke with a group of men, some of whom had wives or daughters who had migrated, or who had migrated themselves. In each village I visited, I also interviewed chiefs, village elders, and religious elders because of their role in shaping perceptions about which forms of behavior are acceptable and which are not. The purpose of these focus groups was to understand the social context within which migration and remittance decisions were being made and to explore the ways in which this social context might have shaped migration and remittance decisions.

Finally, while in the district, I also held in-depth interviews with 21 male migrants and 50 female migrants who had recently returned home for the farming season, about the motivations underlying their remittance decisions; the purpose of this was to determine whether and how motivations for making remittances differed between men and women and if so, why. The decision to do so was informed by findings from the first part of my field research, which are discussed below.

## 24.5   THE CONTRIBUTIONS OF COMBINED FIELDWORK METHODS TO ANALYSES OF MIGRATION AND REMITTANCES: FINDINGS FROM RESEARCH IN GHANA

In this section, I draw on my research findings to identify the contributions of qualitative fieldwork methods to economic analyses of migration and remittances in developing countries. One of the most important benefits of using qualitative methods at the beginning of a research project is that they permit the researcher to identify patterns of behavior that do not fit easily into, or are not satisfactorily explained by, existing theoretical frameworks. Not only is this helpful in refining one's research questions, but it may also have the added benefit of expanding the range of questions that the researcher may ask.

I found that the use of qualitative methods at the beginning of my research project was helpful in shaping the direction of my research, in generating broad hypotheses, and in designing my household surveys. For example, the combination of survey and unstructured interviews that I used during the first part of my fieldwork in Accra yielded two important findings that led to me to revise my initial hypothesis that the migration of women from the north of Ghana to the south was part of a simple household strategy. Fifty-three per cent of the women I interviewed had either experienced opposition from family members when they first broached the idea of migrating to the south, or simply decided not to tell any family members that they were leaving (Table 24.1). In a number of other cases, family members had been split over their migration, often along gender lines, with mothers or older female relatives supporting a daughter's migration and fathers, husbands, and other male relatives opposed to it. Often, women had been able to migrate only after wearing down such opposition by making repeated requests for permission to leave, or by running away. It was clear from my in-depth interviews with many of these women that female migration in this context could not always be assumed to be a household strategy. This is not to suggest that it could be ascribed to a simple individual utility-maximizing strategy either; even when women had migrated against the wishes of parents and spouses, they had often done so with family considerations in mind, identifying a desire to work and send money home to 'help out' as one of their primary reasons for leaving.[10]

The second finding that emerged from my initial interviews with migrant women in Accra was that women who sent remittances had very specific purposes for which these remittances were intended. Often, the money they sent home was intended to pay for food or to pay for children's clothing and educational expenses. At other times, they sent money home to invest in non-farm enterprises operated by female members of the household. Even more interestingly, female remitters were especially likely to send their

*Table 24.1    Intra-household conflict and consensus in women's migration decisions*

| Degree of consensus in migration decision | Married (%) | Unmarried (%) | Widowed/ divorced (%) |
|---|---|---|---|
| No opposition from any family member | 36.3 | 50.9 | 100 |
|     Received financial support from spouse | 45.5 | n/a | |
|     Received financial support from both parents/guardians | 12.12 | 11.25 | |
|     Received financial support from mother/ female relative only* | 27.3 | 46.25 | |
|     Received financial support from father/male relative only** | 0 | 2.5 | |
| Opposition from at least one family member | 47.3 | 34.5 | 0 |
| Did not tell anyone in anticipation of opposition | 16.4 | 14.6 | 0 |
| Total | 91 | 157 | 5 |

*Notes:*
* Father was household member.
** Mother was household member.

*Source:*    Author's interviews with female migrants in Accra (from Pickbourn 2011).

*Table 24.2    Gender and the intra-household flow of remittances*

| Gender of primary recipient* | Gender of remitter | | | |
|---|---|---|---|---|
| | Female | | Male | |
| | Freq. | % | Freq. | % |
| Male | 18 | 14.8 | 30 | 65.2 |
| Female | 104 | 85.2 | 16 | 34.8 |
| Total | 122 | 100 | 46 | 100 |

*Note:*    * The primary recipient was defined as the individual who received the largest share of total remittances made by the migrant. All the households that received remittances only from female migrants were male-headed households. One of the three female-headed households in the sample received remittances from a male migrant and the other received remittances from both male and female migrants; the third had no migrants.

*Source:*    Author's household survey.

remittances directly to other female household members – their mothers, aunts, co-wives, and sisters-in-law – an observation that was confirmed by the quantitative data on remittances obtained from my household surveys (Table 24.2). In only a very small handful of cases did female migrants send money home to their fathers to finance investments in the farms of the latter. As a reason for sending money to female relatives, many women cited a desire to ensure that the money they sent be used to pay for food or to benefit children. Later interviews with male migrants who had returned to the Savelugu-Nanton district indicated that male migrants were more likely to send remittances to male relatives and to direct that this money be used to purchase farming inputs, furniture, and consumer electronics, or to pay for marriage ceremonies.

These early insights were helpful in constructing my household surveys. Instead of asking only the household head about remittances, as is done in a typical household survey on remittances, I directed questions about remittances to the household head as well as to the closest female and male relatives of the migrant. This approach indicated that male household heads often had no knowledge of the remittances that had been sent by female migrants to their female relatives. In the majority of households, the list of remittance receipts presented by the male household head was very different from the list of remittance receipts presented by female household members, not only in amounts received, but even in the identities of the remitters, suggesting that men and women were recipients of different flows of remittances. Likewise, the majority of male household heads claimed to have had little knowledge of how the remittances from female migrants had been used. A probit regression to identify the factors that determine the gender of the recipient of remittances confirmed the findings obtained from the qualitative work: the gender of the remitter was an important determinant of the gender of the recipient in these households and female remitters were more likely than male remitters to target their remittances to other women in the household (Pickbourn 2011, 2015).[11] Clearly, the common assumption that remittances flow to a 'unified household' is wrong, certainly in northern Ghana and probably in many other rural contexts in sub-Saharan Africa.

Why were women migrants more likely to contribute to female-centered networks of remittance flows and why were there such gendered differences in the preferences of migrants for how their remittances are used? Through individual interviews with migrants and focus group discussions, I was able to gain insights into the specific cultural and institutional structures within which both women and men made decisions about migration and remittances. An important finding that emerged from these discussions is that the gendered norms of household provisioning that prevail in northern Ghana play an important role in shaping the preferences of migrants for how remittances are used and in their decisions regarding to whom their remittances are directed.

The typical rural household in the northern half of Ghana is an extended family unit built around a small group of closely related men and their families. The core livelihood strategy is based on the collective farming of staple crops (maize, sorghum, and yams) together with arrangements for individual economic activity. Each household has a designated head, usually the oldest male in the senior generation of the compound, who is responsible for managing the household farm and ensuring the provision of the food staple and shelter for the entire household. Although the largest part of the household's land is used to cultivate the staple crop, male household members, once they reach puberty, are allocated individual parcels of farmland by the household head. On these private farms, they cultivate cash crops such as groundnuts and soybeans. Each individual plot holder is responsible for acquiring the inputs for his private farm and controls the income generated from the sale of his crops. In contrast, women are not entitled to own or inherit land, on the grounds that they do not have a normatively defined responsibility for farming within the household division of labor. Occasionally, in land-rich households, married women who have had one or more children and who have attained the status of senior women in the household may be allocated small parcels of land by their husbands, usually less than 1 acre, on which they may cultivate vegetables including legumes for household consumption and occasional sale. However, women's control over any land allocated to them is tenuous; their husbands retain the right to claim this land from them at any time.[12]

This distinction between household and individual farms has important implications for household budgeting arrangements. As is common in other parts of Africa, husbands and wives in Dagomba households do not pool their incomes, and apart from the shared output from the household farm, there is no such thing as a common housekeeping budget. Their respective responsibilities are defined by gendered social norms of household provisioning and by their position within the household hierarchy. Married women who have attained senior status (that is, have had one or two children and undergone certain rites of passage) are responsible for supplementing the food staples with vegetables including legumes, and other protein sources. When food stocks run low, as tends to happen over the course of the year, women may even become the main providers of food for the household. Women are also responsible for various other items of expenditure, such as children's clothing and other needs. Although both parents are expected to jointly contribute to children's education, with men responsible for paying school fees and women for other expenditures such as uniforms and supplies, in the majority of households surveyed, women indicated that they were responsible for the bulk of education expenditure, including the payment of school fees. Young unmarried men and women are expected to contribute labor to the household farm; in addition, young unmarried women are expected to assist more senior women with their income-generating activities and to contribute to the household any in-kind payments they receive in exchange for providing labor on neighboring farms.

The obligation to make up for household food shortfalls and to ensure that children are fed, clothed, and healthy constitutes an important motivation for married women to engage in various productive activities independently of the household and results in women using almost all the income earned from these activities for these purposes (Warner et al. 1997). Because of their limited access to land, credit, and agricultural extension services, the only option available to most women who wish to generate an independent income is through non-agricultural self-employment, usually in activities such as petty trading, the processing of agricultural products, and food preparation. In the context of deteriorating agricultural livelihoods in this part of the country, migration presents an opportunity for women to generate start-up capital for these economic activities, to supplement their income from these activities or, in the case of younger unmarried women, to assist their older female relatives in meeting these obligations.

Because of the disproportionate responsibility that they bear for child rearing, family care, and household provisioning in general, women migrants often prefer that their remittances be used on expenses that are in line with these norms of household provisioning, such as food, education, and health care. This is true even for single women, who, in line with the expectation for unmarried women to contribute to household provisioning, indicated that the money they sent home was intended to be used for these purposes. In contrast, male migrants, the majority of whom are young and single, and who are therefore not subject to the same expectations, prefer their remittances to be used to acquire assets for their personal benefit, such as bicycles and radios, or invested in their personal farms on their return. In other words, gendered norms of household provisioning contribute at least in part to the differences in the preferences of male and female migrants for how their remittances are used that have been observed in other contexts (e.g., de la Cruz 1995; de la Briere et al. 2002; IOM 2005).

However, the ability of individual migrants to ensure that their remittances are used as intended depends on a number of factors: the frequency of their visits home, their proximity to the community of origin, as well as other factors related to household and family structure such as their age and gender and position in the intra-household hierarchy. For example, younger women who migrate from subordinate positions in patriarchal families are unlikely to be able to exert much control over the allocation of the remittances they make to the household. But this does not mean that migrants have no influence over the allocation of their remittances: if migrants realize that their ability to influence how their remittances are used is limited, then they are likely to direct their remittances to those in the household who are most likely to ensure their preferences are met, that is, those who are subject to similar norms and whose decisions over the use of remittances are most likely to be in line with their own preferences.

Female migrants who want to ensure that their remittances are used to purchase food, or to pay for children's educational needs, may thus be more likely to direct their remittances to other women in the household because gendered norms of household provisioning ensure the latter will use the remittances in ways that are in line with their own normatively shaped preferences. Most importantly, they may do so even if the head of the household is male. Likewise, male migrants who want to ensure that the money they send is used in ways that they intend – for example to purchase inputs for their personal farms or, less frequently, to contribute to purchases of inputs for the household farm – may be more likely to send remittances to those in the household most likely to have similar preferences, that is, other men in the household. In this way, gendered norms of household provisioning can give rise to gendered networks of remittance flows among household members in migrant households based on perceptions of common interests regarding the use of the remittances. This is consistent with evidence from the Philippines and the Dominican Republic indicating that female migrants from these countries prefer to send remittances to other women within their households (UN-INSTRAW 2006, 2008; Parreñas 2005).

Why do these findings matter, and why are they relevant for economists' analyses of the impacts of remittances on origin households? The literature on intra-household expenditure patterns has consistently shown that household expenditure on children's education, health, and nutrition increases with the extent of resources controlled by women (Quisumbing and Maluccio 2000; Quisumbing 2003; Hallman 2000; Thomas 1990, 1994). Extrapolating from this literature suggests that whether remittances are received or controlled by men or women should have important implications for how remittances are used. Yet, beyond merely controlling for the gender of the household head, this possibility has not been explored in regression analyses of the impact of remittances on receiving households.

Based on the insights obtained from my qualitative research that household heads were not necessarily the primary recipient of migrants' remittances, I thought it would be informative to examine how the gender of the remitter and recipient of remittances impacts household expenditures. I therefore collected extensive data on household expenditures on food, education, health, and other items. A regression analysis of household expenditure data on education revealed that households that received remittances from only female migrants spent almost one and a half times as much on education per child of school-going age, compared to households that received remittances from only male migrants.[13] Likewise, households in which the primary recipient of remittances was female spent twice as much on education per child of school-going age than households in which the primary recipient of remittances is male (Pickbourn, 2015).

What would have been the results if I had simply assumed that the identity of the remitter and recipient did not matter for the outcome, or that all remittances were received by the household head? A quantitative analysis that controlled only for whether or not households had received remittances showed that households that received remittances spent less on education per child of school-going age than households that did not receive remittances, although the variable was not statistically significant. The conclusion following from this would have been that it was not possible to reject the hypothesis that migration and remittances do not lead to an increase in household investment in education. Collecting remittance data from the predominantly male household heads, under the assumption that they received or knew about all remittances received by household members, would have led to the erroneous conclusion that very few of the households in my sample even received remittances from women who had migrated to the south, simply because their remittances were not included in the list of remittances presented by the household heads.[14] However, by making a set of assumptions about household and individual behavior grounded in empirical evidence obtained through the use of qualitative fieldwork methods, and as a result, asking a different set of questions from those asked by the majority of studies of migration and remittances, this study has demonstrated that social norms are important in shaping decisions about remittances and that the gender of the recipient, and by implication that of the remitter, does matter for the impact of migrant remittances on household expenditures.

## 24.6   CONCLUSIONS

The choice of research methods can present a major conundrum for economists who wish to expand their research toolkit in a discipline in which quantitative methods are practically *sine qua non*. This chapter argues that the use of qualitative fieldwork methods, in conjunction with quantitative techniques, can be useful for economists trying to understand migration and remittance behavior.

More generally, however, the use of qualitative techniques in field research has much to offer researchers in other areas of economics. They can facilitate the conceptualization of economic processes and provide insights into how institutional and cultural factors shape individual choices and encourage or discourage particular economic outcomes. Although these factors are frequently difficult to quantify, they are still important for understanding economic outcomes. Qualitative techniques also permit insights into the perspectives of agents on the choices they make, and help the analyst to construct interpretations of this behavior that are derived from the meaning that agents ascribe to their actions. In this way, they can help in the development of theory. When used in conjunction with quantitative methods, these techniques help to enrich our quantitative analyses and to expand the questions that researchers can ask beyond the limits imposed by large secondary data sets. Not only do they help to generate more reliable quantitative data, but they may also be helpful in interpreting quantitative outcomes and in determining which quantitative results are the most useful for policy.

These contributions are especially valuable for those economists whose research centers on marginalized groups, such as the women who were the focus of this study. The actions, motivations, and decisions of the marginalized are often overlooked in the formulation of economic theory which assumes a narrowly defined rationality, and ignores the constraints and institutional contexts that shape and influence their choices and decision-making. These conceptualizations of human behavior that have little to do with reality lead to questionable research findings which are then used to inform policies that are intended to benefit these marginalized populations. However, the research is never blamed when these policies fail to work. The use of qualitative techniques as an integral part of field research provides a way for conscientious economists to avoid some of these pitfalls. Rather than impugning these methods as 'unscientific', economists have much to gain from going beyond their self-imposed methodological boundaries to explore the ways in which their work can be enhanced by the use of qualitative fieldwork methods either alone, or in conjunction with quantitative methods.

# NOTES

1.  This number includes both internal migrants as well as women who have migrated across national borders within the region.
2.  The NHE approach to household decision-making assumes that the preferences of household members can be aggregated in a common utility function and that household income is fully pooled. Altruism is assumed to be a basic feature of the household; each individual conceives of their own utility in terms of the collective welfare of the household, and household members subordinate their individual inclinations to the pursuit of common household goals (Katz 1991). In particular, the head of the household is conceptualized as a 'benevolent dictator' who makes decisions that maximize the welfare of the entire household.
3.  There is an extensive literature in feminist economics that critiques the NHE approach to household decision-making more broadly (see Katz 1991). Here, I focus only the application of this approach to migration decision-making.
4.  Only a few studies of migrant remittances have even considered the possibility that remittances may flow towards specific individuals or groups within the household. Posel (2001) finds that the magnitude of migrant remittances to households in South Africa is more strongly influenced by the presence of some household members (for example, older children and spouses) than others, suggesting that migrants might be making remittances not so much to households as to individuals within households. In a recent unpublished study of remittances in multi-family households in Senegal, De Vreyer et al. (2009) show that not only do remittances accrue to members of subgroups within the household, but they also alter the expenditure patterns of that group alone, while having no impact on the expenditure patterns of other subgroups within the household.
5.  Unfortunately, I was unable to obtain raw census data from the 1970 and 1984 population censuses from the Ghana Statistical Service. This made it impossible to identify long-term trends in female migration in Ghana. However, there is quite a substantial literature across different disciplines and in the policy world that points to this increase in female migration between the north and south of Ghana.
6.  A distinction has been drawn between migration that occurs on a seasonal basis (for example, farmers migrating during the dry season to look for work in other parts of the country) and migration that is circular, in which migrants return to the place of origin after a defined period – for example, a day, month, weeks, and so on. The main distinction is that circular migration need not occur on a seasonal basis (see Bilsborrow et al. 1984 for a distinction between the different types of migration).
7.  The word is actually a combination of the Hausa word for load (*kaya*) and the Ga word for women (*yei*).
8.  For example, in 2009, the Ministry of Women's and Children's Affairs, with funding from the United Nations Children's Fund (UNICEF), began registering female porters in Accra. This initiative was part

of a program code-named 'Operation Let's Send Them Home', the goal of which was to repatriate female migrants under the age of 16 to the north for 'rehabilitation and vocational school enrolment' (Tufuor 2010).

9. This is the dominant ethnic group in the Northern Region of Ghana.
10. Interestingly, my later interviews in the Savelugu-Nanton district with male migrants who had returned home for the farming season did not reveal the same extent of family opposition to male migration. Nevertheless, for reasons that I explain later, it was not clear that male migration was necessarily the result of a family strategy.
11. The dependent variable in this regression is the probability that the primary recipient of migrant remittances to the household is female.
12. It is more often the case that women are permitted to plant their vegetables, including legumes, along the borders of their husbands' farms.
13. The study focused on education expenditures for a number of reasons. Education expenditures, being large and fairly infrequent, are less likely to be subject to recall errors of the type that affect other categories of expenditure. Collecting education expenditures at the level of the individual student also allows for greater accuracy. Finally, it is possible to independently verify the accuracy of education expenditures such as school fees and to identify gross outliers.
14. Only three out of 181 households had female heads.

# REFERENCES

Ackah, C. and D. Medvedev (2010), 'Internal migration in Ghana: determinants and welfare impacts', World Bank Policy Research Working Paper Series No. 5273, Washington, DC: World Bank.
Adams, Jr, R. (1998), 'Remittances, investment and rural asset accumulation in Pakistan', *Economic Development and Cultural Change*, **47** (1), 155–73.
Adams, Jr, R. and A. Cuecuecha (2010), 'Remittances, household expenditure and investment in Guatemala', *World Development*, **38** (11), 1626–41.
Agarwal, B. (1997), 'Bargaining and gender relations: within and beyond the household', *Feminist Economics*, **3** (1), 1–51.
Agesa, R.U. and S. Kim (2001), 'Rural to urban migration as a household decision: evidence from Kenya', *Review of Development Economics*, **5** (1), 60–75.
Alba, M. and J. Sugui (2011), 'Motives and giving norms behind remittances: the case of Filipino overseas workers and their recipient households', PEP PMMA Working Paper No. 2011-06, Manila: Philippine Institute for Development Studies.
Awumbila, M. and E. Ardayfio-Schandorf (2008), 'Gendered poverty, migration and livelihood strategies of female porters in Accra, Ghana', *Norwegian Journal of Geography*, **62** (3), 171–79.
Bemah, A. (2010), 'Social protection for informal migration workers: the case of Kayayei in Kumasi, Ghana', Masters thesis, Institute of Social Studies, The Hague, Netherlands.
Bhattacharyya, B. (1985), 'The role of family decision-making in internal migration: the case of India', *Journal of Development Economics*, **18** (1), 51–66.
Bigsten, A. (1996), 'The circular migration of smallholders in Kenya', *Journal of African Economies*, **5** (1), 1–20.
Bilsborrow, R., A. Oberai, and G. Standing (1984), *Migration Surveys in Low-income Countries: Guidelines for Survey and Questionnaire Design*, London, UK and Sydney, Australia: Croom Helm.
Chami, R., C. Fullenkamp, and S. Jahjah (2003), 'Are immigrant remittance flows a source of capital for development?', International Monetary Fund Working Paper 03/189, Washington, DC: International Monetary Fund.
Clark, K. and S. Drinkwater (2001), 'An investigation of household remittance behavior', University of Manchester School of Economics Discussion Paper Series No. 0114, accessed August 19, 2014 at http://www.nottingham.ac.uk/shared/shared_levevents/Seminars/ken.pdf.
De, P. and D. Ratha (2005), 'Remittance income and household welfare: evidence from Sri Lanka integrated household survey', unpublished manuscript, Washington, DC: World Bank.
de la Briere, B., Elisabeth Sadoulet, Alain de Janvry, and Sylvie Lambert (2002), 'The roles of destination, gender and household composition in explaining remittances: an analysis for the Dominican Sierra', *Journal of Development Economics*, **68** (2), 309–28.
de la Cruz, B.E. (1995), 'The socioeconomic dimensions of remittances: a case study of five Mexican families', *Berkeley McNair Journal*, **3** (1), 1–10.
De Vreyer, P., S. Lambert, and A. Safir (2009), 'Remittances and poverty: who benefits in the household?',

accessed August 18, 2014 at http://gdri.dreem.free.fr/wp-content/d5-2de_vreyer_lambert_safir-remittances_and_poverty.pdf.

Dodson, B. (2000), 'Women on the move: gender and cross-border migration to South Africa from Lesotho, Mozambique and Zimbabwe', in D. A. McDonald (ed.), *On Borders: Perspectives on International Migration in Southern Africa*, New York: St Martin's Press, pp. 119–150.

Ghana Statistical Services (GSS) (2010), *2010 Population Census*, Accra, Ghana: Ghana Statistical Services.

Guzman, J. C., Andrew R. Morrison, and Mirja Sjoblom (2008), 'The impact of remittances and gender on household expenditure patterns: evidence from Ghana', in Andrew R. Morrison, Maurice W. Schiff, and Mirja Sjöblom (eds), *The International Migration of Women*, New York: Palgrave Macmillan and Washington, DC: World Bank, pp. 125–52.

Hallman, K. (2000), 'Mother–father resource control, marriage payments, and girl–boy health in rural Bangladesh', FCND Discussion Paper 93, Washington, DC: International Food Policy Research Institute.

Harris, J. and M. Todaro (1970), 'Migration, unemployment and development: a two-sector analysis', *American Economic Review*, **60** (1), 126–42.

Hoddinott, J. (1994), 'A model of migration and remittances applied to Western Kenya', *Oxford Economic Papers*, **46** (3), 459–76.

International Organization for Migration (IOM) (2000), *IOM Migration Policy for Sub-Saharan Africa*, International Organization for Migration, Eightieth Session, Geneva: International Organization for Migration, accessed December 10 2010 at Http://www.iom.int/jahia/webdav/shared/shared/mainsite/about_iom/en/council/80/MC_INF_244.pdf.

International Organization for Migration (IOM) (2005), *Migration and Remittances in Moldova*, Geneva: International Organization for Migration.

Katz, E. (1991), 'Breaking the myth of harmony: theoretical and methodological guidelines to the study of rural third world households', *Review of Radical Political Economics*, **23** (3–4), 37–56.

Katz, E. and O. Stark (1986), 'Labor migration and risk aversion in less developed countries', *Journal of Labor Economics*, **4** (1), 134–49.

Litchfield, J. and H. Waddington (2003), 'Migration and poverty in Ghana: evidence from the Ghana living standards survey', Sussex Migration Working Paper No.10, Brighton: Sussex Centre for Migration Research.

Low, A. (1986), *Agricultural Development in Southern Africa: Farm-Household Economics and the Food Crisis*, London: James Currey.

Lucas, R.E.B. and O. Stark (1985), 'Motivations to remit: evidence from Botswana', *Journal of Political Economy*, **93** (5), 901–18.

Malone, L. (2007), 'Migrants remittances and investments in children's human capital: the role of asymmetric preferences in Mexico', unpublished paper, accessed May 5, 2011 at http://ideas.repec.org/p/cdl/glinre/402953.html.

Parreñas, R. (2005), 'Long-distance intimacy: class, gender and inter-generational relations between mothers and children in Filipino transnational families', *Global Networks*, **5** (4) 317–36.

Pickbourn, L. (2011), 'Migration, remittances and intra-household allocation in northern Ghana: does gender matter?', PhD dissertation, University of Massachusetts, Amherst.

Pickbourn, L. (2015), 'Remittances and household expenditures on education in Ghana's Northern Region: why gender matters', *Feminist Economics*, available at http://dx.doi.org/10.1080/13545701.2015.1107681.

Posel, D. (1999), 'Intra-family transfers and the household division of labor: a case-study of migration and remittance behavior in South Africa', PhD dissertation, University of Massachusetts, Amherst.

Posel, D. (2001), 'Women wait, men migrate: gender inequality and migration decisions in South Africa', in P. Webb, and K. Weinberger (eds), *Women Farmers. Enhancing Rights, Recognition and Productivity*, Frankfurt: Peter Lang, pp. 91–117.

Posel, D. (2003), 'Have migration patterns in post-apartheid South Africa changed?', paper prepared for Conference on African Migration in Comparative Perspective, Johannesburg, South Africa, June 4–7, accessed January 11, 2011 at http://pum.princeton.edu/pumconference/papers/1-posel.pdf.

Quisumbing, A. (2003), *Household Decisions, Gender and Development: A Synthesis of Recent Research*, Baltimore, MD: Johns Hopkins University Press for International Food Policy Research Institute (IFPRI).

Quisumbing, A. and J. Maluccio (2000), 'Intra-household allocation and gender relations: new empirical evidence from four developing countries', FCND Discussion Paper 84, Washington, DC: International Food Policy Research Institute.

Stark, O. (1978), *Economic-Demographic Interaction in Agricultural Development: The Case of Rural to Urban Migration*, Rome: United Nations Food and Agriculture Organization.

Stark, O. (1984), 'Bargaining, altruism and demographic phenomena', *Population and Development Review*, **10** (4), 679–92.

Stark, O. (1999), *Altruism and Beyond: An Economic Analysis of Transfers and Exchanges within Families and Groups*, Cambridge: Cambridge University Press.

Stark, O. and D. Bloom (1985), 'The new economics of labor migration', *American Economic Review*, **75** (2), 173–8.
Stark, O. and D. Levhari (1982), 'On migration and risk in LDCs', *Economic Development and Cultural Change*, **31** (1), 191–6.
Stark, O. and R.E.B. Lucas (1988), 'Migration, remittances and the family', *Economic Development and Cultural Change*, **36** (3), 465–81.
Thomas, D. (1990), 'Intra-household resource allocation: an inferential approach', *Journal of Human Resources*, **25** (4), 653–4.
Thomas, D. (1994), 'Like father, like son; like mother, like daughter: parental resources and child height', *Journal of Human Resources*, **29** (4), 950–88.
Todaro, M.P. (1969), 'A model of labor migration and urban unemployment in less developed countries', *American Economic Review*, **59** (1), 138–48.
Tufuor, T. (2010), 'Gender and women's housing problems in Accra: the case of old Fadama, ministry of water resources', Accra, Ghana: Works and Housing, Republic of Ghana, accessed January 15, 2011 at http://www. hdm.lth.se/fileadmin/hdm/alumni/papers/SDD_2009_242a/Theresa_Tufuor_-_Ghana.pdf.
UN-INSTRAW (2006), *Gender, Remittances and Development: The Case of Women Migrants from Vicente Noble, Dominican Republic*, Santo Domingo, Dominican Republic: United Nations International Research and Training Institute for the Advancement of Women (UN-INSTRAW).
UN-INSTRAW (2008), *Gender, Remittances and Development: The Case of Filipino Migration to Italy*, Santo Domingo, Dominican Republic: United Nations International Research and Training Institute for the Advancement of Women (UN-INSTRAW).
Vanwey, L. (2004), 'Altruistic and contractual remittances between male and female migrants and households in rural Thailand', *Demography*, **41** (4), 739–56.
Warner, M., R. Alhassan and J. Kydd (1997), 'Beyond gender roles? Conceptualizing the social and economic lives of rural peoples in sub-Saharan Africa', *Development and Change*, **28** (1), 143–68.
Yang, D. (2006), 'International migration, remittances and household investment: evidence from Philippine migrants exchange rate shocks', *Economic Journal*, **118** (528), 591–630.
Yeboah, M.A. (2008), 'Gender and livelihoods: mapping the economic strategies of porters in Accra, Ghana', unpublished PhD dissertation, Morgantown, WV: West Virginia University.

# 25 A data triangulation approach to understanding the behavior of small landholders in Bulgaria
## Mieke Meurs

## 25.1 UNDERSTANDING SMALLHOLDER BEHAVIOR IN POST-SOCIALISM

In economics, much of the research on smallholder behavior takes the form of regression analysis, based on large, multipurpose data sets. Behaviors as diverse as credit use, innovation, and response to property rights are studied in this way (Hertz 2009; Conley and Udry 2010; Goldstein and Udry 2008). Economists rely on standard economic models, grounded in basic assumptions about maximizing behavior and revealed preferences, to interpret the patterns found in the data. This approach has become more dominant and much more sophisticated with the ever-increasing supply and quality of data sets.

Standard statistical data and analytical techniques often do not permit us to verify whether the assumed reasoning is that which actually underlies the outcome. The omission of preferences, goals, and perceptions from the analysis, because data on these variables are not collected in standard surveys, may result in biased or incomplete conclusions. Misdirected policy may result.

In this chapter, I apply a data triangulation approach to explaining one important aspect of smallholder behavior in post-socialism – the decision of landholders to produce agricultural goods for sale (or not) – using data from one post-socialist country, Bulgaria. In post-socialist economies, limited smallholder movement into commercial production has been a topic of significant debate (Wegren 2008). I use statistical analysis to examine patterns of smallholder engagement in commercial production and their relationship to variables that standard models of utility maximizing households suggest would be relevant to such decisions (available resources, alternative uses of time, market development). I then supplement this analysis with in-depth interviews, in which smallholders are given an opportunity to explain their motivation and decisions in their own words. The interviews suggest alternative explanations for smallholder behavior. They also suggest that some standard policy responses to improving rural outcomes may be ineffective. This case study thus illustrates the benefits of a data triangulation approach, which may enrich the set of models economists use to explain patterns in statistical data.

## 25.2 THE PUZZLE

After 1989, private property rights in land were restored in post-socialist countries. Many economists predicted that new owners of agricultural land would remove it from collectivized farms, adjust holdings to optimize returns given their skills and resources, and in turn, boost agricultural efficiency and incomes (Deininger 1995; Wegren 2008). The term 'farmers' came into common use to describe the expected new breed of commercially oriented owner-producers. However, in many places these small commercial farmers have not emerged (Kilic et al. 2009; Gogodze et al. 2005; Wegren 2008). In Bulgaria, for example, about half of privatized, smallholder land has remained in large production units, often with unclear governance structures, returning little revenue to landowners. Even more puzzling is that large amounts of smallholder land and labor are idle, while smallholders produce little for sale and report low standards of living.

Economists studying this phenomenon initially focused on the difficulties faced by relatively poor households organizing private production in a context of weakly developed markets and legal systems (Wegren 2004) and thus facing high transaction (or political) costs (Mathijs and Swinnen 1998; Meurs 2001). Households may not have the mix of land, labor, and capital needed to farm their land efficiently, and poorly developed markets and legal systems may make it difficult to adjust inputs. Researchers studying post-socialist smallholders in the early 1990s found evidence that transaction costs, proxied by market structure, were related to limited expansion of small-scale production (Mathijs and Swinnen 1998; Meurs 2001). Policy recommendations that follow from this analysis include improving clarity and enforcement of property rights, and development of land markets, in order to facilitate the expansion of private production and 'farming'.

During the last 20 years, markets and related institutions have developed significantly. The majority of the households interviewed in 2008 (interviews discussed below) used land markets to adjust landholding size. Many households reported borrowing to finance consumption and agricultural production, and many households with successful commercial production reported having developed their enterprise without access to credit. These developments suggest a decline in the size and importance of transaction costs, but production for sale among smallholders remains very limited (only 10 percent of smallholding farming households, according to a very broad definition explained below). Perhaps other factors also play an important role in production orientation.

Some more behavioral explanations appear promising. Studying smallholder behavior in Russia, for example, Stephen Wegren (2004) argues that differences in entrepreneurial attitudes play a role in differing household productive behavior. In the 1980s, George Patrick (1981) found that even in a context of well-developed and long-standing markets (the USA), households expressed multiple, and differing, goals[1] for their farms, and that these differences affected production orientation. Looking at differences in production goals among small Swedish non-farm enterprises in the 1980s, Davidsson (1989) hypothesized that differences were related to an entrepreneur's perception of their need, abilities, and opportunities.

These findings that goals are central to producer behavior, and differ among producers, appear related to the literature on satisficing. Herbert Simon (1988) suggested that rather than searching a complete set of possible production strategies to find the optimal plan, agents would evaluate only a subset of strategies, searching to satisfy (possibly modest) goals. Once a plan is found which will satisfy the goal, no further options are considered. However, goals may be updated in light of outcomes. Households may drop goals that they come to see as unachievable or add new goals, previously excluded because they were

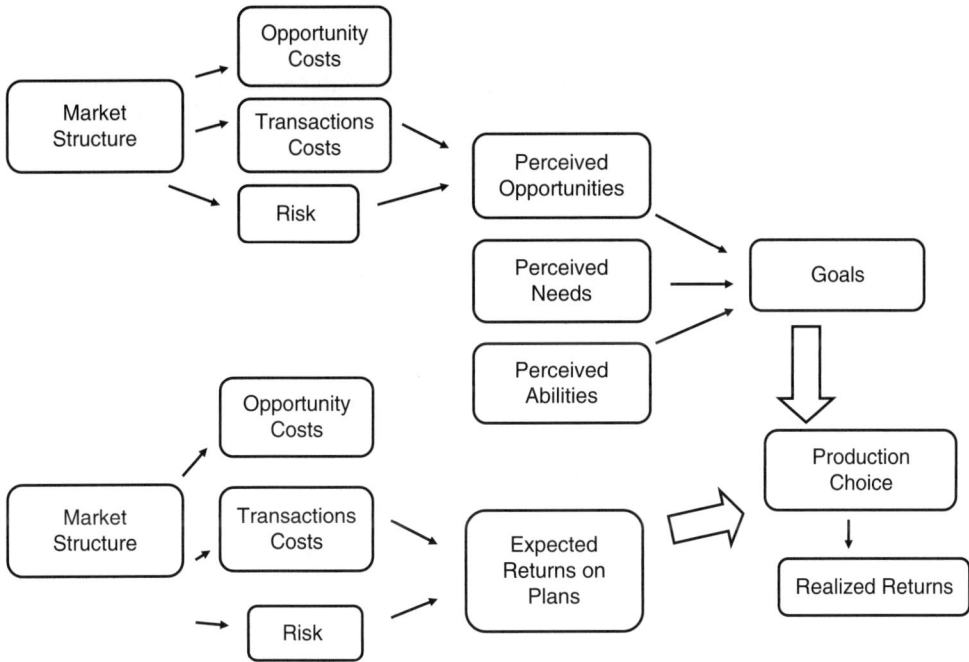

*Figure 25.1   Theoretical approaches to formation of goals and expected returns, production decision*

not seen as feasible. Not all producers will update at the same rate; some might update very slowly.

These studies suggest an explanation for why, even as transaction costs decline, some households might fail to increase commercial production; and for why households with similar institutional contexts and available resources might choose different production orientations. A more complete model of smallholder behavior, combining these insights with existing work on in post-socialist contexts, might be a decision-making process like that summarized in Figure 25.1. The figure illustrates a framework in which market structure plays a role in production choice, but farmer goals, and perceptions contributing to goal formation, also play an independent role.

However, information about households' goals and reasoning about productive decisions cannot be found in, or deduced from, current statistical data sets. Including these behavioral characteristics in the analysis requires recourse to an alternative data and methodology; in this case, the use of in-depth interviews. To understand more fully the factors underlying to weak development of commercial farming among Bulgarian smallholders, I therefore use a data triangulation approach. I use statistical data to examine patterns of resources and production behavior among smallholding households and combine this with in-depth interviews with smallholders (and aggregate data about their production context).

## 25.3    STATISTICAL INVESTIGATION

In the first, statistical part of this analysis, I examine differences between commercial farming households and the general population of farming households, using the 2003 Bulgarian Integrated Household Survey (BIHS) conducted by BBSS Gallup International under the supervision of the World Bank.[2] For this survey, a nationally representative sample of 3023 households was drawn from the pre-census listing of the 2001 Population Census. The questionnaire contains information on land use, agricultural production and consumption, and employment. This analysis uses only the 1218 households that reported farming at least some of their land themselves. I define a commercial farming household very broadly, as one that sells at least 50 percent of any one product that it produces, to capture the intent to produce for sale. Sales of a smaller share of production seem more likely to be sales of a surplus of goods produced mainly for own consumption. (In the regression analysis, I also include a definition that includes households that report selling any agricultural production.)

As can be seen in Table 25.1, farming households owned an average of 1.3 ha, of which they farmed an average of 0.6 ha themselves. They put most of the remaining land in a co-operative or corporate farm, left some idle, and rented a small amount to others. Farming households owned few machines. Only 2.6 percent owned a tractor. About a third of households purchased some machine services. Farming households had an average of 2.4 working-age household members, but the majority of households (61 percent) did not have any member who considered farming either their full- or part-time job. Instead, the average household earned the majority of their income off-farm or from pensions. The smallholding sector is not made up primarily of 'farmers'.

Land-owning households spent limited amounts on purchased inputs, such as seeds or fertilizer; 27 percent reported spending no money at all on agricultural inputs. Few households reported spending on hired labor, machines, or land.

Finally, most households (63 percent) reported no sales of any agricultural product. The most commonly sold product was milk (30 percent of households). This appears to be a continuation of a practice from the socialist period, when rural households were

*Table 25.1    Characteristics of landholding households*

|  | All farming households<br>n = 1218, 100% | of which: | Commercial farm<br>n = 139, 11.4% |
| --- | --- | --- | --- |
| Owned land (ha) | 1.3 | | 1.5 |
| Farmed land (ha) | 0.6 | | 1.3 |
| Working-age members | 2.4 | | 3.2 |
| % owning tractor | 2.6 | | 8.0 |
| % w/ag expenses | 73 | | 92 |
| Ag. sales income | 163 | | 1345 |
| Job income | 2037 | | 3217 |
| Pension income | 1145 | | 1154 |
| Total cash income | 3345 | | 5696 |

*Source:*   BIHS 2003.

encouraged to produce small amounts of milk beyond their own needs, for delivery to state-run collection stations.

Using the broad definition of commercial farming, 139 households (10 percent of the smallholding households) engage in commercial production. Comparing them to the general population of farming households, they look generally similar. Commercial farming households owned only slightly more land than the average household (an average of 1.5 ha), and farmed more, just over 1 ha. Some put their unused land in a co-operative or corporate farm (19 percent of these households) or left it idle (9 percent). Only 11 percent of these farms were larger than 2 ha. Commercial farming households also owned more machinery than the average household, but the level of investment remained low. Eight percent of these households owned a tractor, 7 percent owned a truck, and 4 percent a planting machine. An important difference is that nearly all commercial farming households (92 percent) purchased inputs.

Commercial farming households have a larger number of members between the ages of 15 and 65 (3.2) compared to all farming households, and more had members (40 percent) who considered the farm to be their full-time job. Another 33 percent had a member who considered the farm a part-time job.

Not surprisingly, given this description of the farms, the most common commercial products were garden vegetables and tobacco (15–19 percent of households). The most commonly marketed livestock were pigs and sheep (3 percent of households). Sixty-five percent of these households produced milk for sale. Commercial farming households do quite well compared to farming households in general, earning monthly monetary incomes of 5696 leva, presumably supplemented by agricultural products in-kind, compared with cash income of 3345 leva on average in farming households.

To better understand factors related to households' engagement in commercial farming, I use a simple regression model. This model looks for statistically significant relationships between smallholder engagement in commercial production and factors that standard economic theory suggests would be relevant to such decisions (available resources, alternative uses of time, market development). A significant relationship identifies only a pattern that exists. It establishes that, holding other factors in the regression constant, a change in the significant variable is, on average, associated with a change in the outcome. The regression cannot help us to understand why that relationship exists, or even whether the relationship would still exist if we included some other variables in the regression. Economists may use standard theoretical models to deduce likely causes of the relationship. Alternatively we may, as below, use interview data to ask producers to explain any relationship they see and to suggest other factors that may affect the relationship.

I use a simple probit model to examine the relationship. The outcome variable is bivariate – yes, no – and measures whether the smallholder reported sales of more than 50 percent of any one product. Because of the necessarily subjective nature of my definition of commercial farming, I include a second measure, the choice to sell any production at all.

Owned land and labor are key inputs into smallholder farming and are less likely than some other inputs to be subject to reverse causality (resulting from the decision to farm commercially rather than preceding it). Households' owned land is still mainly a product of the post-socialist land reform, as adjustment of land through rental markets is much more common than adjustment through sale. I include owned land (in hectares) in the regression. Household labor is measured by the number of working-age members, as well as the number of pensioners (included separately). Machine holdings and credit seem more likely to be endogenous to the decision to farm commercially and are thus not included in the regression. However, using credit card borrowing as a (less endogenous) proxy for access to agricultural credit, Hertz (2009) found little evidence that credit constraints limited agricultural production by households in Bulgaria.

Location can impact production decisions in a variety of ways. Location affects transportation costs and production costs through distance to markets and the availability of infrastructure. Location can affect transaction costs, as information and markets develop unevenly across the regions. Finally, location may affect production decisions through more behavioral impacts, as agricultural traditions, norms, and knowledge vary significantly across regions of Bulgaria, in part due to the history of specialization under socialist planning. Grain production has traditionally dominated certain regions (in the plains, often farther from urban centers), while other areas (more mountainous and/or closer to urban markets) have strong traditions of vegetable growing or livestock grazing. I examine the impact of location using two measures. As a control for local conditions, including market development and infrastructure, I include a region dummy. The regions are constructions of my own, agglomerations of 2–6 districts[3] designed to capture broad patterns of inherited developmental levels and locational (dis)advantages (level and type of economic development, proximity to growth centers, and physical geography – plains versus mountains; see Figure 25.2, bold

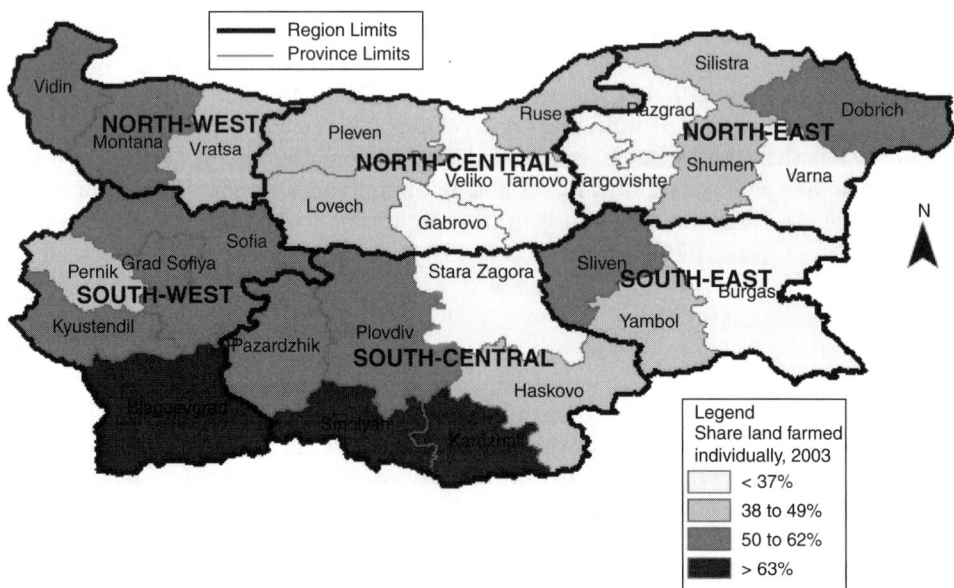

*Figure 25.2   Bulgarian regions and provinces, share of land farmed by private individuals*

*Table 25.2*　*Factors associated with farm type, landholding households, Bulgaria, 2003*

| Dependent variable | Commercial farms | | Farms with any sales | |
|---|---|---|---|---|
| *n* | 1218 | | 1218 | |
| *Pseudo R²* | 0.09 | | 0.07 | |
| Independent variables | Marginal effect | Z | Marginal effect | Z |
| *Land Owned (ha)* | 0.000 | 0.61 | 0.000 | 0.98 |
| *Working-Age Members* | 0.023 | 5.11** | 0.025 | 4.65** |
| *Pensioners* | 0.001 | 0.10 | 0.002 | 0.34 |
| *% district land in grain* | 0.002 | 2.48** | 0.001 | 0.56 |
| *North-West Region* | −0.057 | −1.66 | −0.044 | −1.13 |
| *North-Central Region* | −0.025 | −0.80 | −0.063 | −1.88 |
| *North-East Region* | −0.053 | −1.81* | −0.091 | −2.82** |
| *South-Central Region* | 0.105 | 2.88** | 0.069 | 1.81* |
| *South-West Region*** | 0.156 | 2.96** | 0.550 | 1.14 |

*Notes:*
* $p < 0.10$.
** $p < .05$.
*** The omitted region is the south-east region.

outlines). Finally, I include the share of land in the district that was under grain in 1988, as a measure of agricultural traditions and knowledge. Share of land in grain might also be related to transaction costs. If grain is the traditional crop and requires larger farms for efficiency, smallholders might need to assemble a large number of plots to engage in production.

I run the regressions as d-probit using the STATA program.[4] The d-probit allows me to report the, more intuitive, marginal effects of changes in the household and local characteristics on the outcome variable in place of the basic coefficients. Because the data were collected using a cluster method (sampling by population point), I run the regression using the robust cluster option,[5] in order to correct for possible correlation in the error terms within the population point. Results are presented in Table 25.2.

Household members between the ages of 15 and 65 were significantly positively associated with commercial farming (the number of pensioners was not). Owned land was not, despite the limited amount of land owned by most households. Location in the south-west and south-central regions of Bulgaria, which are proximate to consumers in the capital city of Sofia and are traditional vegetable-producing areas, was positively related to engaging in commercial farming, compared to location in the south-east region. Location in the more distant north-east region had a negative impact. Location in a grain-growing region had a positive relationship to agricultural production, perhaps because such regions had more highly developed agricultural infrastructure. Factors related to a household reporting any sales of agricultural products (compared to households which sell nothing) were the same, with the exception that location in a grain-growing region was not a significant factor and that location in the south-west region is no longer significant.

Overall, there is no evidence that inability to form larger landholdings limits engagement in commercial production. The correlation between location in a traditional grain-growing region and commercial farming further supports this conclusion that the need to achieve scale efficiency is not a factor in the decision. The significance of the number of working-age members may indicate that farm labor markets are not working well. The importance of location in the south-central and south-west regions suggests that transportation costs may play a role, but this relationship between location and commercial farming may also be capturing an impact of access to market information or diverse agricultural traditions. Finally, low $R^2$ suggests that a number of other factors may play a role in the decision to produce for sale.

Households producing agricultural products for sale earn significantly more than households that do not, and many households report low standards of living. At the same time, further expansion of agricultural production seems possible, but is not undertaken. On average, households own more land than they farm and, while the availability of working-age household members is significantly related to commercial production, many households (38 percent) appear to have inactive working-age members available for expanded production. Even households that are commercially oriented farm less land than they own. Additional information is needed to establish whether factors not captured in this analysis are keeping costs of smallholder resource adjustment high, or whether some of the other, more behavioral explanations (outlined earlier) might be involved in the continued low level of smallholder production.

## 25.4   AN INTERVIEW APPROACH

To understand the reasoning behind the limited expansion of commercial farming, even in the presence of unused resources, I organized in-depth interviews with 68 Bulgarian smallholding households, recruiting a local interview team. These interviews allowed smallholders to explain their decision-making process, the goals that affect these decisions, and their process of adjusting goals and production. This provides an alternative to the more deductive method of understanding the production patterns that is common in quantitative work.

Drawing on a grounded theory approach, our interview team used the theoretical literature discussed earlier as a point of departure for the interviews and a base for comparison of the results. Interviewers used a guide (Appendix 25A.1) to structure the discussions about how smallholders made decisions about land use and commercial production, but farmers explained decisions in their own words.

Unfortunately, no list of all farming households is available from which to draw an interview sample. The team used a snowballing method to locate households which farmed some land of their own and had working-age members.[6] The snowballing sampling method has a long track record in qualitative research, where the researcher needs to reach a population that is 'hidden' in official records (Atkinson and Flint 2004; Bryant 1999). Researchers identify one respondent who meets the criteria for inclusion,[7] and then ask this informant to recommend an additional contact. This is repeated with the new contact. The snowballing method allowed us to locate relevant households in the absence of a population list.

The resulting sample is not statistically representative (as the survey used in the

*Table 25.3    Characteristics of municipalities in sample, by district*

| Location | Total area[a] (dk) | Total land per producer (dk) | Arable land per producer (dk) | Arable land (% total) | Grain land (% total) | Fruit, veg. (% total) |
|---|---|---|---|---|---|---|
| Bulgaria | 290447960 | 443.56 | 501.62 | 0.92 | 0.06 | 0.00 |
| *Vratsa* | 1383557 | 52.58 | 63.53 | 0.95 | 0.69 | 0.01 |
| Munic. 1 | 311000 | 50.00 | 69.00 | 0.91 | 0.70 | 0.01 |
| Munic. 2 | 339000 | 74.00 | 87.00 | 0.99 | 0.70 | 0.00 |
| Munic. 3 | 37000 | 13.00 | 12.00 | 0.65 | 0.70 | 0.02 |
| *Pazardjik* | 461983 | 14.24 | 13.69 | 0.79 | 0.64 | 0.11 |
| Munic. 1 | 19000 | 4.00 | 2.00 | 0.49 | 0.09 | 0.75 |
| Munic. 2 | 210000 | 23.00 | 23.00 | 0.94 | 0.64 | 0.10 |
| Munic. 3 | 32000 | 26.00 | 27.00 | 0.87 | 0.56 | 0.02 |
| *Yambol* | 1429278 | 82.03 | 98.71 | 0.96 | 0.60 | 0.01 |
| Munic. 1 | 104000 | 72.00 | 93.00 | 0.95 | 0.63 | 0.00 |
| Munic. 2 | 229000 | 83.00 | 130.00 | 0.95 | 0.56 | 0.09 |
| Munic. 3 | 277000 | 73.00 | 87.00 | 0.94 | 0.60 | 0.01 |

*Note:*    [a] To ensure the confidentiality of the respondents, figures are rounded and municipalities are identified by number only.

*Source:*    Ministry of Agriculture and Forestry (2005).

statistical analysis was) and our conclusions cannot be generalized to the broader population. Instead, we used the in-depth interviews to bring to light aspects of behavior which were not captured in the large sample surveys including the attitudes and intentions of households and their reasoning. Through a process of comparison (Chapter 2 in this *Handbook*; Dey 2007) of the smallholders' comments, we identified patterns of goals and behaviors.

We sampled households in three provinces (Vratsa, Yambol, and Pazardjik), drawing approximately seven households from each of three municipalities in each province. We sought to interview a broadly representative range of types of household farms. In selecting the provinces and municipalities, we sought different types of agriculture (grain-oriented plains regions, more garden-oriented areas, and mountainous areas with less arable land), and context (varied access to urban areas and infrastructure). These characteristics are summarized in Table 25.3. The number of households successfully interviewed per municipality ranges from five to nine. We used all completed interviews in our analysis. A complete list of the 68 interviewed households and their characteristics is provided in the table in Appendix 25A.1.[8]

The purpose of the interviews was to understand households' underlying objectives in using the land, as a way of understanding why so few households pursued commercial production. Therefore, interviews focused on the issues of household objectives, how households arrived at these objectives, and the process by which objectives might change.

As found by Patrick (1981) for US farmers, I found that the goals of Bulgarian smallholders varied widely. After reviewing and comparing the transcripts from all 68

*Table 25.4    Goals and production orientation*

| Goal | Importance of goal | | | |
|---|---|---|---|---|
| | Cluster 1 | Cluster 2 | Cluster 3 | Cluster 4 |
| Survival as commercial enterprise | Not a goal | Not a goal | Important | Important |
| Family consumption | Predominant weight (in-kind only, not via cash) | Predominant weight (mainly in-kind, occasionally via cash) | Important (mainly cash, occasionally in-kind) | Important (cash only) |
| Growth | Not a goal | Not a goal | Not a goal | Important |
| Farming as leisure activity | Not a goal | Occasional Importance | Occasional Importance | Not a goal |
| Overall orientation | Food security | Supplemental income | Viable commercial enterprise | Growth-oriented competitor |

interviews, I identified four clusters of goals. These are described in Table 25.4 along with the resulting production orientation. One group, which I call 'food security households', expressed only goals of family (in-kind) consumption. A second group, 'viable commercial enterprise households', described success as a viable commercial enterprise as a goal, while often also expressing a goal of meeting family consumption needs. Respondents in this group did not have a goal of farm growth. A third group, 'growth-oriented competitor households', expressed a goal of ongoing enterprise growth in addition to other goals. A fourth group of households was distinguished by the fact that they earned the majority of their incomes off-farm. In these households, the farming goal was limited to household consumption, and only to the extent needed to supplement off-farm income. Table 25A.1 in Appendix 25A.2 organizes households by the production orientation associated with their goals.

In some cases (18 of the 68), the household appears borderline between two of the identified clusters: in terms of its goals the household is most like those in one cluster, but it also shows some interest in a goal of another cluster. For example, a household may currently mainly aspire to meet consumption needs, but express a plan to move into more commercial production should certain conditions change, or a household currently oriented toward commercial viability may express plans to scale back to meeting only household needs.

In Table 25A.1, households which appear borderline between two clusters are noted, with a plus sign indicating that they express some interest in a goal of the following category, and a minus sign indicating that they express interest in goals similar to the previous category. These households may be transitioning between goal clusters. Some other households, which fall clearly into one goal cluster, describe a process of adjustment by which they arrived at these goals. For example, some commercially oriented households described how they adopted these goals after initially aspiring only to meeting household food needs; while other households focused only on food security described the process of scaling back their goals after finding that commercial production did not provide the expected returns.

As can be seen from Table 25A.1, households with different goals and production orientations are fairly similar in landholding, household size, age, and education. One exception to this is that landholdings of growth-oriented farms are significantly larger, but this is likely a result, rather than a cause, of their orientation.

## 25.5  EXAMPLES

Below, I describe the goals and production orientation in each cluster and provide examples of such households. I also document examples of adjustment of production orientation, as households updated their goals in response to farming outcomes and changing needs, opportunities, and abilities.

**Food Security**

Farmers in this group were focused on assuring food for the household. They did not aspire to farming as a commercial enterprise, although some households sold a little surplus production. They did not expect farming to help them accumulate capital. Obtaining personal satisfaction from production was rarely mentioned. Landholding size was not a determinant of this orientation: households in this cluster ranged from very small operations to operations of some significant size. Often, these households produced less than they were capable of producing, stating explicitly that this level of production was 'enough' (3.1.1.4, 3.1.2.3). Among small operations, examples are:

- In Vratsa, Municipality 3, a couple live with their two small children and the woman's handicapped mother, farming less than 2 of her 30 dk; 4 dk are rented out, and the rest of the household's land is idle. The family is paid in grain for the use of their 4 dk and uses the grain to feed their chickens. They also raise nine sheep and have two gardens, selling a little surplus. The man does occasional work in forestry, and they receive some money from the woman's sister who works in Italy, but mainly they live off their smallholding (1.3.4.2).
- In Yambol, Municipality 3, a 72-year-old woman lives with two grown-up sons, one of whom was laid off years ago. Together the mother and the unemployed son cut 8 dk of hay for their three sheep, and keep a garden and vineyard. The rest of their land (92 dk) is rented out. They say that they could raise more sheep with their 8 dk, but that three 'are enough for us'. They own a small tractor, which they use for their garden and vineyard. The employed brother does not participate in farming and mainly uses his income for his own needs. The other son and mother supplement the food they produce with the rent they receive from their land (2.3.6.1).

An example of a more significant operation is:

- In Yambol, Municipality 2, a couple, previously employed in non-farm jobs, work about 200 dk, of which about 50 dk is their own. They also own 16 dk elsewhere which is idle. They grow grain, which they feed to cows that their son raises. They also have ten sheep, four pigs, calves, and chickens. They produce almost all of the food needed for their family (two generations in three households), as well as the food needed for their livestock. They exchange part of their grain for bread coupons.[9] They sell a little production to cover expenses like electricity. They have not applied for any government or international support for improvements of their agricultural production. They consider that it is 'better to sit outside and drink a beer' than expand 'uncertain ventures' (2.2.7.2).

A number of these households had adjusted their goals and production orientation as they gained new information about expected returns. In the Pazardjik case (3.1.2.2), the household farming 2 dk had previously farmed 15 dk of potatoes and raised four cows with calves for sale, but had given up commercial production after income did not meet expectations. Similarly, the Yambol family working 200 dk (2.2.7.2) had farmed double the grain the previous year, for sale, but gave up when returns were lower than expected. None of the households expected to exit farming altogether as a response to disappointing returns, however.

In other cases, households adjusted their goals in response to a change in abilities. One Yambol multigenerational household (2.3.6.5) stopped small-scale commercial production of livestock after the death of the grandfather, who had previously worked in livestock farming. Similarly, two households in Vratsa gave up their small commercially oriented operations due to declining physical abilities, but continue production to meet household needs (1.2.2.4, 1.2.3.7).

The interviews also showed, however, that many of the households oriented toward food security were poorly informed about commercial opportunities and subsidy programs which might have made small-scale production more lucrative (and did not seek information about these opportunities). In one Yambol household (2.3.6.5), there are two young farmers, possibly eligible to apply for the Young Farmer subsidy program.[10] But they had only second-hand, incomplete information about the program and did not investigate the program further. Pazardjik household 3.1.2.2, headed by a former village official, also had only second-hand information about unsuccessful experiences with subsidy programs, although many similarly situated respondents benefited from such programs. Uncertainty and risk aversion also appear to play a role in these households' evaluation of the returns to various plans. Yambol household 2.2.7.2 noted that while they might be able to qualify for European Union- and government-subsidized loans to expand production for sale, they did not want to assume the risk: 'We are not used to handling (such large sums).'

**Supplementing Labor Market Income**

A second commonly expressed goal for production was to supplement labor market incomes. Households in this group did not mention commercial viability or capital accumulation as goals for their farm activity. Like households with a food security orientation, this second group of households focused mainly on meeting their own food needs (Table 25.3). Labor market income is their main source of support, but many explained that their pay was insufficient to fully support their family. The small farming operations were an important source of in-kind or supplemental cash income. But the off-farm employment provided apparently preferred alternatives to farming. Households in this group often mentioned the personal satisfaction they got from farming as an additional reason to continue the activity. Some examples of these households include:

- In Vratsa, Municipality 2, a couple, 47 and 39 years old, farm 80 dk with the help of their 17-year-old son and mother (in-law). The son helps significantly. They keep two pigs, five cows, a few sheep and chickens, grow oats, corn, and hay for the livestock, and keep a garden. They sell some milk and surplus livestock, collecting the state subsidy for such production. The agricultural income and their combined salaries as a pre-school teacher and food industry worker contribute approximately equally to the household income. They are not considering expanding production, but they would continue at least some of this production even if they did not need the income: the cows are central to their family traditions (1.2.3.8).
- A household in Yambol, Municipality 3, composed of four working-age adults (a couple and two grown-up sons), all employed off-farm, farm 70 dk plus a 3 dk garden, all in vegetables. They also keep eight sheep, a cow, a few pigs and chickens. They produce most of their own food, and sell about half of their production, benefiting from the easy access to markets in Municipality 3. They collect a state subsidy for their production. They taught themselves about farming after the decollectivization of land in the early 1990s, and they enjoy farming, but there are plenty of jobs nearby. They are not interested in expanding production (2.3.6.4).
- In Pazardjik, Municipality 1, a couple in their fifties grow 2 dk of potatoes for sale in shops owned by their two grown-up sons. The parents both lost their jobs after the collapse of socialism, but the sons' shop, with the potatoes, produces what the family sees as adequate income for the household (which also includes a wife and small child). They also keep a cow for their own use (3.1.1.2).

The households with a supplemental income orientation were better informed about prices, subsidies, and production opportunities than the households with a food security orientation. A number of farmers commented on relative returns to their particular farming operation and off-farm options: 'If you do the math, it's just not worth farming more land. It doesn't pay!' (1.2.3.5). Their limited farming goals were not only the result of having other employment options, however. At least one household had a member with no alternative employment, available to expand production, but did not expand as household needs were adequately met (1.1.1.4). In the Pazardjik potato-growing household (3.1.1.2), one son had purchased 6 dk of land to expand into commercial dairying. But his parents had vetoed this, as agricultural production was too risky compared to the shops.

Some households in this cluster had adjusted their goals from a more commercial orientation when profits fell short of expectations (1.2.3.6). As with households with a food security orientation, changes in the household conditions could also lead to adjustment. The household in Vratsa, Municipality 2 (1.2.3.8), for example, may expand production when the 17-year-old son finishes school.

## Maintaining a Viable Commercial Enterprise

The last two groups of households are distinguished from the first two by their efforts to maintain their farm as a viable commercial enterprise. Households in the third group differ from the final group in their disinterest in further expansion. Like the first two groups, households in the third group support family consumption, mainly by earning income, although most also planted a garden for their own use. Farming was rarely described as a hobby or leisure activity, although a number of these farmers mentioned that they enjoyed farming as an occupation. Examples of such households include:

- In Vratsa, Municipality 1, a couple are employed full-time on their vegetable farm, where two teenage sons and the man's father also work. They farm 40 dk with only a horse and a gravity irrigation system. They have applied to the Young Farmer program, hoping to support some technological improvements. They watch the market, and adjust their production in response. But they do not aspire to expansion, because their family labor is fully utilized (1.1.1.3).
- In Yambol, Municipality 2, a couple in their late thirties farm 10 dk, 6 dk in greenhouses, producing vegetables for sale. They own the land and all their own machinery and collect a state subsidy for production. They hire four employees, but do not expect to expand further (3.2.1.7).
- In Pazardjik, Municipality 2, a couple in their fifties farm about 14 dk: 10 dk in grain and 4 dk in vegetables, mainly for sale. They take the vegetables to a nearby exchange, but sell the grain as livestock feed to villagers. The couple has no children, and during the grain harvest they hire a couple of local women. They both work full-time on the farm, after losing their off-farm jobs. They supplement their farm income by using their tractor to clear snow from roads in winter. They might expand, if they can get more grain land and a safe place to keep machinery, but this would be limited to what they could farm themselves (3.3.3.1).

These farmers clearly see themselves as running commercial enterprises, and all these farms provided the sole employment for at least one household member – in many cases, someone who had become unemployed in the post-socialist restructuring. The farmers spoke knowledgably about prices, and they have all adjusted their production in response to commercial considerations. However, their goal is generally to provide employment to family members and adequate financial support for the family, and this often limited their interest in expanding their business. Several households in this category also mentioned other benefits to this type of employment, including being your own boss, being outside in the (relatively) clean environment, and reduced stress compared to a desk job. A number of these households, like the vegetable-producing household 1.1.1.3, maintain the commercial enterprise with very limited resources.

In some cases, this orientation is an adjustment from a more growth-oriented approach. One farmer now working 100 dk in Yambol, Municipality 2, had previously grown his farm to 650 dk, but 'failed' and no longer expected to expand beyond his current, smaller size (2.2.2.3). Several households shifted to this commercial orientation from one of supplementing off-farm income when a household member lost their job (2.2.1.3) (3.3.1.3) or after receiving new information about opportunities.

Households with a goal of commercial viability rarely adjusted to this after an orientation toward food security. But some households that were oriented toward food security after failing in commercial production did hope that, in the future, they might again aspire to commercial production. Other households oriented toward commercial viability, while having no current goal of expansion, were monitoring the situation for indications that their agricultural enterprise could be expanded (3.3.5.1, 2.1.8.1, 2.1.5.2).

**Becoming a Growth-Oriented Competitor**

A significant number of farmers expressed a goal of enterprise growth. We found such farmers in all three provinces, and in a number of different agricultural sectors. Examples include:

- Two brothers in Vratsa, Municipality 2, who inherited 80 dk, then purchased 450 dk more and now rent around 2000 dk, which they farm in grain. They have used the Young Farmer program and other programs for agricultural modernization to access credit for machinery upgrades. They expect to continue expanding (1.2.3.3).
- In Yambol, Municipality 2, a couple and their adult children farm their 100 dk and rent in another 2300 dk (2.2.1.2). They have been buying more land over time (50 dk last year). The son and daughter are registered as Young Farmers and receive subsidies. They grow coriander for sale, but they use their grain mostly as feed for the dairy operation, which has a total of 40 cows. The Young Farmer program supported the purchase of a new tractor and assistance in making the business plan. They adjusted production away from vegetables, which were too labor-intensive.
- A household in Pazardjik, Municipality 2 (3.2.2.1) farms 10 dk of cucumbers and tomatoes, all in greenhouses. This provides employment for a couple, both in their fifties, and their grown son. They expanded from 3 dk of greenhouses, renting land, and plan to expand their vegetable production to an additional 9 dk of land that they own, once they have paid down their loans and can qualify for new ones. They do not keep any livestock and have only a small garden for themselves; they are too busy with their commercial operation to produce food.

These farming households have strong growth aspirations, are well informed about markets and government programs, and they have updated their goals in response to success. As they grow, they rent land from households less able to use it. As represented by a potato-growing family in Vratsa (1.2.3.9), many are families of fairly modest means, but have goals of growth.

## 25.6   DISCUSSION

The interviews revealed that Bulgarian households, like Russian (Wegren 2004) and US farming households (Patrick 1981), have varying goals for their farms. These cluster as shown in Table 25.4. As suggested by Davidsson's (1991) interviews with Swedish entrepreneurs, producers' goals vary with their perceptions of their needs, abilities, and opportunities (as suggested in Figure 25.1). Households with a food security orientation noted their need for the food they produced, but also often the minimal level of their needs, as in a Yambol household that noted that three sheep 'are enough for us' (2.3.6.1). Households supplementing off-farm incomes noted both the need for additional income (3.3.9.1, 2.2.1.1, 1.1.1.4) and the fact that their off-farm incomes made additional agricultural production unnecessary ('We aren't hungry') (1.2.3.8). When someone lost a job, changing needs could shift goals from supplementing off-farm income to maintaining a viable commercial enterprise (3.3.1.3) or food security (3.1.1.4).

Abilities were also often noted as affecting farm goals, especially by households oriented toward food security. In particular, some such households noted health and age (3.3.2.3, 1.2.3.2), as well as poor land quality (1.3.2.2), in explaining why they did not aspire to greater agricultural output. In explaining a decision to try commercial farming, farmers often pointed to skills learned in school (2.2.1.1, 3.2.1.8) or previous jobs (1.2.3.5, 2.2.2.1).

Opportunities, too, were mentioned frequently. Food security households mentioned a perceived lack of opportunities in explaining their limited aspirations: poor access to markets (3.1.2.3, 2.2.3.2) or credit (2.3.6.1), for example. (Note that these are perceived opportunities. Neighbors who appeared similar in terms of access to resources often perceived opportunities quite differently from each other.) Many households noted that they were watching for information about opportunities, and that their goals might change if new opportunities were perceived (1.1.2.2, 1.2.3.8, 2.1.3.6).

As noted in the statistical analysis, households' opportunities and skills may be spatially correlated, leading to spatial clustering of goal orientations. Appendix Table 25A.1 indicates that households interviewed in the Yambol region (part of the south-east region identified as the reference group in the statistical analysis) were heavily represented in the categories of viable commercial enterprise and large-scale competitor. Yambol is a province with a high share of arable land and, at the same time, Yambol municipalities where we interviewed were among the least urban in our sample, resulting in fewer alternatives to farm employment (Table 25.3).

Households in Vratsa province (located in the north-west region) were heavily represented among those oriented toward food security and supplemental income. Agricultural land in use fell significantly in Vratsa post-socialism due to its poor quality. Much of the land is suitable only for pasture or hay. At the same time, the relatively urban Vratsa region has particularly high unemployment (Malamova 2009). Many households depend on their land for food.

In Pazardjik (part of the south-east region identified as correlated with commercial orientation in the statistical analysis), smallholders we encountered were likely to have goals in the middle two categories: supplemental income and maintaining a viable commercial enterprise. Pazardjik, which is mountainous, experienced the largest post-socialist fall in agricultural land in use (much non-arable land is no longer used), and one of our interview municipalities had only 2 dk of arable land per producer (Table 25.3). Many households explained that the arable land was suitable for only a limited number of uses (potatoes). At the same time, Pazardjik is relatively urban, allowing more households to combine off-farm employment with farming. Other areas of Pazardjik are fertile valleys with a history of intensive vegetable and flower production.

These differences in context and opportunities do not fully explain goal differences among producers, however. We found diverse goal types and production orientations in every municipality, including smallholders pursuing commercial production, often with few resources.

Households reported evaluating only a few production plans, in a process suggestive of satisficing (Simon 1988). Family history was the most frequently mentioned source of plans that households evaluated. A grandfather's love of cows led to a focus on milk in one case; no other option was considered (2.2.1.1). In a growth-oriented farm, a family history in grain production determined the kind of plan the sons evaluated (1.2.3.3). Family knowledge from pre-socialist times (a grandfather who had worked as a migrant gardener in pre-war Hungary) (1.2.3.8), the socialist 'accord' system (1.1.1.3) (3.1.6.2) which encouraged households to produce on a small scale under contract to the socialist state, and experience on socialist collective (and post-socialist large) farms (1.2.3.5) (1.2.3.9) (2.1.5.1), also affected the plans considered. Other plans came from knowledge of locally common production (1.1.1.1) (2.2.2.1) (2.1.3.1). Few farmers reported searching more widely for information about possible production options, although some did report getting input from agronomists once they had chosen a general plan (2.3.6.2).

While goals play an important role in smallholder decisions about production, the interviews show that many households update their goals, shifting, for example, into commercial production. Many farmers who responded that they were not interested in certain goals (commercial production, growth) admitted that they would reconsider in light of new information about opportunities (3.3.2.2, 1.2.3.1, 1.2.3.8). Likewise, if no plan was found with which the household could meet its targets, households reported switching to a new production orientation. A farmer gave up the goal of being a growth-oriented enterprise, for example, and focused on surviving as a viable commercial enterprise (2.2.2.3). Others gave up the goal of being a viable commercial enterprise, focusing instead on the family food supply (1.2.3.1) (2.2.3.2).

We saw little willingness to abandon farming (or land ownership) altogether, however. Decisions about small-scale agricultural production involved not just economic costs and benefits but also goals for leisure, fulfillment of social norms, and maintenance of traditions. Compared to decisions about farm size and production orientation, the decision of whether to farm at all appeared to weight the non-economic factors more heavily. Households oriented toward food security, unwilling to abandon farming in response to poor results, commented: 'The land feeds us!' but also, 'If we give up the cows, we'll still grow a little something. It's the village!' (2.1.3.1), and 'Even if we find jobs, we'll work (the land). The land came from my father, who got it from his father' (2.2.2.2). And while many households were willing to rent out land they could not productively use (if a renter could be found), many also expressed a strong belief that land should not be sold (2.2.2.2). Land held by such smallholders is unlikely to move into commercial use.

## 25.7   CONCLUSIONS

While the research into limited expansion of smallholder production in post-socialist agriculture has emphasized limitations on smallholder access to land and other productive resources (Wegren 2004; Allina-Pisano 2008), statistical analysis of data from the 2003 BIHS provides only mixed support for this explanation. Further, the statistical approach relies on using standard economic models to deduce the relationship between variables in the analysis. Households are assumed to want to expand production, and the analysis focuses on searching for constraints on this expansion.

Using this approach, as in the statistical analysis above, we may conclude that access to land is not a limitation to engaging in commercial production, but that access to labor may be. Agricultural labor markets are not well developed and hired agricultural labor is notoriously hard to monitor. Location is also significantly related to engagement in commercial farming, which might be explained by higher transportation costs or weaker market infrastructure and development. This suggests that commercial production might be promoted through policies to promote labor exchanges and access to markets in the regions more distant from the capitol city.

More behavioral approaches suggest that other factors may play a role. In particular, smallholders may have different goals for their agricultural production, and these may play a role in production choices. Interviews allow smallholders to explain their goals and production decisions in their own words, and these explanations suggest that many households do not seek to maximize returns on farm activities, or on the combination of farm and off-farm activities. Some households reject commercial production as a goal, and some commercially oriented households do not aspire to expand beyond a modest level of production. Goals appear influenced by local conditions, but we found a range of goals and production orientations in all regions.

The production plans smallholders used to fulfill their goals were heavily influenced by family history or local production norms and traditions; no one reported doing a broad investigation of options or consulting with experts. As suggested by a theory of satisficing, some smallholders adjust their goals and production toward more income-generating activities as they understand their potential for higher returns (Odhnoff 1965), but others reported less inclination to adjust. Smallholders did adjust goals downward in response to disappointing results, but few farmers were willing to exit farming. As a result, the specific production plan smallholders started with had an important independent impact on outcomes, as the starting point influenced whether initial goals would be fulfilled, and thus whether adjustment to new goals was likely. These historically determined starting points and uneven adjustment of goals in response to performance limit the movement of smallholders into commercial production.

Our data triangulation approach suggests that, in addition to the previously considered factors of uneven market development and resource inequality, smallholder attitudes and farming goals play a role in explaining the uneven impact of land privatization on smallholder productivity and incomes. While policies to promote the expansion of property rights, a fuller development of markets and improving market infrastructure may facilitate movement for some, they are unlikely to provide a quick solution to raising rural productivity and incomes. As one successful Bulgarian commercial farmer noted: 'The process . . . is costly and slow.'

## NOTES

1. See Payne et al. (1993) for a broader discussion of such multi-attribute choices.
2. I thank the Bulgarian National Statistical Institute for permission to use these data. This analysis was

carried out jointly with Angel Bogushev and a longer version of this was published jointly with him (Meurs and Bogushev 2009).
3. Bulgaria was divided into 28 administrative districts in 1988 and significant amounts of data were published at this level of disaggregation. The district-level data provide a convenient way to control for local agricultural traditions.
4. http://www.ats.ucla.edu/stat/stata/dae/probit.htm.
5. http://www.stata.com/support/faqs/statistics/standard-errors-and-vce-cluster-option/.
6. We define working age as between 18 and 65, considering those under 18 as school age. Bulgarian children rarely work in agriculture, although our sample did identify a few older teenagers who took an active part in family farming. Age 65 is the retirement age for Bulgarian men, although women may retire a bit earlier. In practice, only three of the households we interviewed had no adult member under 60. In the 2003 nationally representative Bulgarian Integrated Household Survey, approximately 26 percent of households which owned and farmed land contained no working-age members. Such households seem unlikely to be able to engage in significant commercial farming activities under any circumstances, and for this reason we exclude them from this study.
7. Also excluded from our sample were very large producers farming mainly rented land in corporate-type farms. A small number of our growth-oriented producers (defined below) approached this barrier, but we included them because they had started as smaller-scale farmers and illustrated a commericializing path farmers might take.
8. The interviewees are identified using a numerical system. The first number identifies the province (Vratsa, 1; Yambol, 2; Pazardjik, 3), the second number identifies the municipality, the third number identifies the village, and the fourth identifies the household.
9. This is a common arrangement, whereby farmers provide grain to bread producers. Rather than being paid in cash, they receive coupons that they can use later to purchase bread.
10. A European Union program which offers support for young people entering farming.

# REFERENCES

Allina-Pisano, Jessica (2008), *The Post-Soviet Potemkin Village: Politics and Property Rights in the Black Earth*, New York: Cambridge University Press.
Atkinson, Rowland and John Flint (2004), 'Snowball sampling', in Michael Lewis-Beck, Alan Bryman and Tim Futinglao (eds), *The SAGE Encyclopedia of Social Science Research Methods*, London, Sage, pp. 1044–5.
Bryant, L. (1999), 'The detraditionalization of occupational identities in farming in South Australia', *Sociologia Ruralis*, **39** (2), 236–61.
Conley, Timothy G. and Christopher R. Udry (2010), 'Learning about a new technology: pineapple in Ghana', *American Economic Review*, **100** (1), 35–69.
Davidsson, P. (1989), 'Entrepreneurship and after? A study of growth willingness in small firms', *Journal of Business Venturing*, **4** (3), 211–26.
Davidsson, P. (1991), 'Continued entrepreneurship: ability, need, and opportunity as determinants of small firm growth', *Journal of Business Venturing*, **6** (6), 405–29.
Deininger, K. (1995), 'Collective agricultural production: a solution for transition economies?', *World Development*, **23** (8), 1317–34.
Dey, Ian (2007), 'Grounding categories', in Antony Bryant and Kathy Charmaz (eds), *The Sage Handbook of Grounded Theory*, Beverly Hills, CA: Sage, pp. 167–90.
Gogodze, J., I. Kan, and A. Kimhi (2005), 'Development of individual farming in Georgia: descriptive analysis and comparisons', paper presented to the Privatization, Liberalization, and the Emergence of Private Farms in Former Soviet Countries conference, Tiblisi, Georgia.
Goldstein, M. and C. Udry (2008), 'The profits of power: land rights and agricultural investment in Ghana', *Journal of Political Economy*, **116** (6), 981–1022.
Hertz, T. (2009), 'The effect of non-farm income on investment in Bulgarian family farming', *Agricultural Economics*, **40** (2), 161–76.
Kilic, T., C. Carletto, J. Miluka, and S. Savastano (2009), 'Rural non-farm income and its impact on agriculture: evidence from Albania', *Agricultural Economics*, **40** (2), 119–23.
Malamova, N. (2009), 'Divergence of labor market in the rural zones of the planning regions', in M. Draganova, L. Granberg and J. Nikula (eds), *Reinventing the Rural: Between Social and Natural. The Bulgarian Case*, Sofia: Bulgaria Rusticana, pp. 13–19.
Mathijs, E. and J. Swinnen (1998), 'The economics of agricultural decollectivization in East Central Europe and the Former Soviet Union', *Economic Development and Cultural Change*, **47** (1), 1–26.

Meurs, Mieke (2001), *The Evolution of Agrarian Institutions: A Comparative Study of Post-Socialist Hungary and Bulgaria*, Ann Arbor, MI: University of Michigan Press.

Meurs, M. and A. Bogushev (2009), 'Forward to the past? Agricultural restructuring in Bulgaria', *Mediterrannee*, 110, 93–104.

Odhnoff, J. (1965), 'On the techniques of optimizing and satisficing', *Swedish Journal of Economics*, **67** (1), 24–39.

Patrick, G. (1981), 'Effects of alternative goal orientations on farm firm growth and survival', *North Central Journal of Agricultural Economics*, **3** (1), 29–39.

Payne, J.W., J.R. Bettman, and E.J. Johnson (1993), *The Adaptive Decision-Maker*, Cambridge: Cambridge University Press.

Simon, Herbert (1988), 'Rationality as a process and product of thought', in David E. Bell, Howard Raiffa, and Amos Tversky (eds), *Decision Making: Descriptive, Normative, and Prescriptive Interactions*, Cambridge: Cambridge University Press, pp. 58–77.

Wegren, S. (2004), 'Rural adaptation in Russia: who responds and how do we measure it?', *Journal of Agrarian Change*, **4** (4), 553–78.

Wegren, S. (2008), 'The limits of land reform in Russia', *Problems of Post-Communism*, **56** (2), 14–24.

# APPENDIX 25A.1   INTERVIEW GUIDE

## I. Basic information about the household:

**How much land does the household own?**
Total . . . . . . dka
Of these: In the village boundaries . . . . . . dka
            In another village:
                Where . . . . . . . . . . . . . . . . . . . . . . . . . dka
                . . . . . . . . . . . . . . . . . . . . . . . . . . . dka
                . . . . . . . . . . . . . . . . . . . . . . . . . . . dka

**Which household members own this land, by parcel?** (List)

**Has the household bought or sold land in the last 10 years?**

**Members of the household** (List)
Include sex, household position, age, education, employment.

**How does the household use the land?**

- Amount farmed by the household . . . . . . dka
- Amount placed in a cooperative – in this village . . . . . . dka, elsewhere . . . . . . dka
- Rented out – in this village . . . . . . dka, elsewhere . . . . . . dka
- Given out another way – in this village . . . . . . dka, elsewhere . . . . . . dka
- Abandoned – in this village . . . . . . dka, elsewhere . . . . . . dka

**Does the household have plans to sell any of this?** Seek explanation.

**What does the household produce on land it farms?** (List by plot)

**II. The following questions seek to understand the household's decision-making process regarding land use. Direct the questions to the household member most involved in such decisions. Note which household member this is.**

**Which household member(s) decides how the land should be used?**

**What factors are important to the decision about how much land to farm yourselves, versus how much to put in a cooperative, rent out, and so on?**
*Probes:* Financial resources, physical resources, returns, markets.

**Do you know about any programs for support and development of agriculture/small farmers?**
*Follow up:* Does the household participate in these? What information do they have? Why participate or not? Importance of support to decisions about land use?

**How do you decide which products to produce?**
*Focus on:* Goals of the household. Is the household focused on achieving the highest possible financial returns? Maintaining a certain standard of living? Is land a source of income? Security?

*Probes:* Do any factors limit how household can use the land? Credit, access to machinery, labor needs. How else might household use the land? Are there potential renters for this land? What are rental conditions like in this area? Have you used the land differently in the past 5–10 years?

*Follow up:* Do you have information about new options/crops?

**Tell us more about how the land that you work influences your household?** (Note discussion of income, security, habits and norms, building assets/economic base)
*Probes:* Is your land a source of food? Income? Would you say farming is a hobby? Is farming part of your family tradition?

**What share of household food do you supply from your land? Which products are for your own consumption? Are some products for family or friends?**
**Do you use some of the products to feed livestock?**
*Follow up:* Are the livestock for own use or sale? Are you able to supply all your feed needs? Could you produce more feed? Under what circumstances?

**Do you sell part of your production?**
*Follow up:* What share, which products? Discuss prices received? What is role/share of these sales in household income? To whom do you sell – where, how (city market, traveling buyers, in the street, to neighbors)?

**Do you give away or exchange informally part of your production? How often, with whom? What factors influence which share of your production you sell?**
*Probes:* Quantity produced; market conditions, crop type. Are regular, dependable sales possible?

What are marketing possibilities in this region?
If the household sells nothing, has it had any experience with sales? Tell us about that experience. Why did you give it up?

**How many household members work only in household agricultural production and have that as their only income?**

**How many household members have another source of income?**

**Are there unemployed household members who do not participate in farming the household land?**

**Would it be possible for the household to produce more on the household land (not including land that you have rented out or in a cooperative)? Under what conditions?**
*Note:* Discussion of any abandoned land.

**Are there conditions under which the household would itself use land currently rented out or in a cooperative?**
*Note:* Discussion of market conditions, resource constraints, norms/traditions, information, technology.

**Are there conditions under which the household would focus more on production for sale?**
*Note:* Discussion of market conditions, resource constraints, norms/traditions, information, technology.

# APPENDIX 25A.2 CHARACTERISTICS OF INTERVIEWED HOUSEHOLDS, BY PRODUCTION ORIENTATION

*Table 25A.1 Characteristics of interviewed households, by production orientation*

Production Orientation: Food Security

| | Land owned | Land farmed | Idle land | Working-age members | Main farmer* education | Main farmer gender | Main farmer age |
|---|---|---|---|---|---|---|---|
| **Vratsa** | | | | | | | |
| 1.1.1.2 | 72.5 | 1.5 | 0 | 3 | High school | Male | 50 |
| 1.2.3.1 (+) | 100 | 100 | 0 | 4 | High school | Male | 27 |
| 1.2.3.2 | 11 | 1 | 0 | 3 | High school | Female | 50 |
| 1.2.3.7 | 51 | 1.1 | 0 | 1 | Missing | Male | 60 |
| 1.3.3.1 | 24 | 1 | 24 | 2 | Primary school | Male | 63 |
| 1.3.3.2 | 20 | 18 | 2 | 2 | High school | Male | 24 |
| 1.3.4.2 | 30 | 3 | 22 | 2 | High school | Female | 25 |
| Average Vratsa | 44.07 | 17.94 | 6.86 | 3.40 | | 0.71 | 43 |
| **Yambol** | | | | | | | |
| 2.2.2.2 | 12.5 | 12.5 | 0 | 1 | Primary school | Male | 55 |
| 2.2.3.2 | 60 | 200 | 16 | 2 | Missing | M, M | 35 |
| 2.3.6.1 | 100 | 8 | 0 | 2 | High school | Male | 53 |
| Average Yambol | 57.50 | 73.50 | 5.33 | 1.67 | | 1.00 | 48 |
| **Pazardjik** | | | | | | | |
| 3.1.1.4 | 4.3 | 4.3 | 0 | 5 | Missing | Female | 47 |
| 3.1.2.2 | 25 | 2 | 13 | 2 | Missing | M, M | 72, 50 |
| 3.1.2.3 (+) | 2 | 2 | 0 | 4 | Primary school | Female | 67 |
| 3.3.1.1 (+) | 18.8 | 8.8 | 5 | 3 | High school | Male | 56 |
| 3.3.2.3 | 1.5 | 1.5 | 0 | 3 | Primary school | Female | 51 |
| Average Pazardjik | 6.26 | 1.66 | 2.60 | 2.20 | | 0.50 | 56 |
| Average all regions | 36.96 | 31.72 | 5.26 | 2.82 | | 0.71 | 49 |

*Table 25A.1* (continued)

Production Orientation: Supplemental Income

| | Land owned | Land farmed | Idle land | Working-age members | Main farmer* education | Main farmer gender | Main farmer age |
|---|---|---|---|---|---|---|---|
| **Vratsa** | | | | | | | |
| 1.1.1.4 | 22 | 0.5 | 0 | 3 | High school | Male | 57 |
| 1.2.3.4 | 47 | 47 | 0 | 3 | High school | M, F | 34, 32 |
| 1.2.3.5 | 31 | 12 | 0 | 7 | Primary school | Male | 70 |
| 1.2.3.6 | 30 | 4 | 0 | 3 | Some college | Female | 52 |
| 1.2.3.8 (+) | 80 | 80 | 0 | 3 | High school | Male | 47 |
| 1.3.2.2 | 10 | 10 | 0 | 4 | High school | Male | 47 |
| 1.3.2.3 | 10 | 100 | 0 | 4 | High school | Male | 42 |
| 1.3.4.1 | 15 | 1.5 | 8 | 2 | High school | Male | 59 |
| Average Vratsa | 30.63 | 31.88 | 1.00 | 3.63 | | | 51 |
| **Yambol** | | | | | | | |
| 2.2.1.1 | 10 | 218 | 0 | 3 | High school | M, F | 44, 39 |
| 2.3.6.4 | 133 | 73 | 0 | 5 | High school | Male | 50 |
| 2.3.9.1 | 200 | 200 | 0 | 2 | College | Male | 57 |
| Average Yambol | 114.33 | 163.67 | 0.00 | 3.33 | | | 50 |
| **Pazardjik** | | | | | | | |
| 3.1.1.1 | 4 | 2 | 2 | 6 | High school | Female | 46 |
| 3.1.1.2 | 8 | 2 | 6 | 5 | Primary school | Female | 52 |
| 3.1.1.3 | 6 | 6 | 0 | 4 | Primary, High | F, M | 42, 46 |
| 3.2.1.3 | 3 | 1.5 | 1.5 | 3 | Missing | F, M | 50, 50 |
| 3.2.1.5 (+) | 24 | 20 | 0 | 3 | High school | Male | 29 |
| 3.3.1.2 (+) | 37 | 7 | 0 | 2 | High school | Male | 25 |

| | Land owned | Land farmed | Idle land | Working-age members | Main farmer* education | Main farmer gender | Age main farmer |
|---|---|---|---|---|---|---|---|
| 3.3.2.1 (+) | 5 | 33 | 0 | 4 | High school | Male | 49 |
| 3.3.2.2 | 20 | 20 | 0 | 3 | High school | Female | 55 |
| Average Pazardjik | 13.38 | 11.44 | 1.19 | 3.75 | | | 44 |
| Average all regions | 52.78 | 69.00 | 0.73 | 3.57 | | | 48 |

*Production Orientation: Viable Commercial Farm*

| | Land owned | Land farmed | Idle land | Working-age members | Main farmer* education | Main farmer gender | Age main farmer |
|---|---|---|---|---|---|---|---|
| Vratsa | | | | | | | |
| 1.1.1.3 | 42 | 42 | 0 | 4 | High school | Male | 47 |
| 1.1.2.2 (+) | 70 | 200 | 0 | 4 | High school | Male | 47 |
| 1.3.2.1 (−) | 37 | 57 | 0 | 3 | High school | Male | 43 |
| Average Vratsa | 49.67 | 99.67 | 0.00 | 3.67 | | | 46 |
| Yambol | | | | | | | |
| 2.1.3.1 | 10 | 10 | 0 | 3 | High school | Male | 53 |
| 2.1.4.2 | 180 | 200 | 180 | 2 | High school | Male | 60 |
| 2.1.5.1 | 28 | 950 | 20 | 2 | High school | Male | 52 |
| 2.1.5.2 (+) | 10.5 | 0.5 | 0 | 3 | High school | Male | 49 |
| 2.1.6.1 (+) | 7 | 572 | 0 | 2 | High school | Male | 34 |
| 2.1.8.1 (+) | 60 | 150 | 0 | 2 | High school | M, F | 54, 54 |
| 2.1.8.2 (+) | 20 | 200 | 0 | 2 | High school | Female | 34 |
| 2.2.1.3 | 6 | 300 | 0 | 2 | High school | Female | 61 |
| 2.2.2.1 | 16 | 6 | | 3 | Missing | M, F | 58, 48 |
| 2.2.2.3 | 70 | 100 | 0 | 1 | High school | Male | 58 |
| 2.2.3.1 | 23 | 100 | 0 | 2 | High school | Male | 57 |
| 2.3.6.2 | 230 | 200 | 0 | 4 | High school | Male | 51 |
| 2.3.6.3 (+) | 21 | 41 | 0 | 4 | High school | M, F | 40, 42 |
| 2.3.6.5 (−) | 82 | 82 | 0 | 4 | Primary school | Male | 52 |
| 2.3.9.2 | 17 | 17 | 0 | 3 | High school | Male | 60 |
| Average Yambol | 52.03 | 195.23 | 13.33 | 2.60 | | | 51 |

*Table 25.4.1* (continued)

*Production Orientation: Viable Commercial Farm (continued)*

| | Land owned | Land farmed | Idle land | Working-age members | Main farmer* education | Main farmer gender | Main farmer age |
|---|---|---|---|---|---|---|---|
| Pazardjik | | | | | | | |
| 3.2.1.2 (+) | 52 | 2 | 5 | 5 | High school | M, F | 30, 55 |
| 3.2.1.4 (+) | 3 | 1.5 | 1.5 | 3 | High school | Male | 53 |
| 3.2.1.6 | 4.5 | 25 | 0 | 1 | High school | Male | 40 |
| 3.2.1.7 | 10 | 10 | 0 | 2 | High school | Male | 37 |
| 3.2.1.8 | 22 | 6 | 11 | 3 | High school | Male | 33 |
| 3.3.1.3 | 12 | 2 | 0 | 2 | High school | Male | 32 |
| 3.3.3.1 (+) | 60 | 10 | 0 | 2 | High school | Male | 44 |
| Average Pazardjik | 20.44 | 7.06 | 2.19 | 2.25 | | | |
| Average All Regions | 44.25 | 101.28 | 7.26 | 2.98 | | | 46 |

*Production Orientation: Growth-Oriented Enterprise*

| | Land Owned | Land Farmed | Idle Land | Working Age Members | Main Farmer* Education | Main Farmer Gender | Age Main Farmer |
|---|---|---|---|---|---|---|---|
| Vratsa | | | | | | | |
| 1.1.1.1 | 1230 | 4230 | 0 | 2 | High school | Male | 60 |
| 1.2.4.1 | 20 | 22.5 | 0 | 4 | Missing | Female | 52 |
| 1.3.3.3 | 450 | 2650 | 0 | 3 | College | Male | 26 |
| Average Vratsa | 416.67 | 1417.50 | 0.00 | 3.00 | | | 37 |

| | | | | | | | |
|---|---|---|---|---|---|---|---|
| **Yambol** | | | | | | | |
| 2.1.4.3 | 30 | 1600 | 30 | 4 | High school | Male | 53 |
| 2.2.1.2 | 100 | 2300 | 0 | 4 | High school | Male | 21 |
| 2.3.6.6 | 520 | 320 | 0 | 3 | High school | Male | 30 |
| Average Yambol | 206.67 | 873.33 | 10.00 | 2.33 | | | 35 |
| **Pazardjik** | | | | | | | |
| 3.1.2.1 | 30 | 100 | 10 | 3 | High school | Male | 53 |
| 3.2.1.1 | 16 | 12 | 4 | 3 | High school | M, F | 54, 52 |
| 3.3.3.2 | 85 | 15 | 50 | 4 | High school | M, F | 50 |
| Average Pazardjik | 43.67 | 42.33 | 21.33 | 3.33 | | | 52 |
| Average all regions | 275.67 | 1249.94 | 10.44 | 3.33 | | | 44 |

*Notes:*

* If two parties reported that they farmed jointly, both are included.

(+) Household has at least one goal similar to the next, more commercial, orientation.

(−) Household has at least one goal similar to the previous, less commercial, orientation.

# 26 Measuring the intra-household distribution of wealth in Ecuador: qualitative insights and quantitative outcomes*

*Carmen Diana Deere and Zachary B. Catanzarite*

## 26.1 INTRODUCTION

Among the concerns in the study of gender inequality is the role played by unequal access to resources within households. According to the bargaining power hypothesis, outcomes for women are often conditioned by the resources they command relative to others in the household, specifically their partners. Thus, women who own and control assets are expected to have a larger say in household decision-making than those who do not, and to use their bargaining power to secure outcomes more favorable to them and their children. For example, women's relatively greater bargaining power within the household might be expected to result in consumption patterns that de-emphasize male-only (vice) goods or be associated with a lower incidence of intimate partner violence, among other outcomes (Doss 2013).

Most studies following a bargaining approach have utilized women's level of education or income (either absolute or relative to their spouse), their ownership of a particular asset (such as land or housing) or access to credit as proxies for women's bargaining power.[1] This chapter reports on a study that measured the intra-household distribution of wealth directly for such a purpose, and in a manner that contributes to the development of a feminist economics methodology.[2]

In developed countries, government statistical agencies routinely carry out household wealth surveys where one respondent is asked about all the assets owned by members of the household. Rarely is the question posed of who in the household owns each asset, since it is assumed that ownership of major assets, such as housing, cannot be attributed to specific individuals.[3] This means that the only kind of (partial) gender analysis that can be carried out is with respect to household structure or composition (that is, comparing sole-female-headed versus sole-male-headed households with households consisting of a couple) (Deere and Doss 2006). Thus the very manner in which data is collected precludes an analysis of the intra-household distribution of wealth, and hence, of gender inequality and potential power differences between husbands and wives.

Similarly, in developing countries the Living Standard Measurement Study (LSMS) surveys, sponsored by the World Bank, increasingly contain questions regarding the assets owned by the household; relatively few of these gather information on to whom, specifically, these assets belong (Doss et al. 2008).[4] The review of these existing surveys served as one of the motivations for the Gender Asset Gap project, a comparative study of Ecuador, Ghana, and the state of Karnataka in India, upon which this chapter – on the Ecuadorian experience – is based.

As a team of feminist economists with considerable research experience in developing countries, we anticipated that developing the appropriate methods to estimate the intra-household distribution of wealth would be a complicated undertaking. First, we expected that the notion of ownership might depend on context and, potentially, gendered notions of property. Second, we expected that who was reported to be an asset owner might differ depending on who in the household was asked. Third, we knew that the existence of markets for all physical and financial assets could not always be assumed, complicating any attempt to value assets and hence to estimate wealth. Finally, we could not discard the fact that the very valuation of assets could also be gendered.

On the first point, in the context of developing countries, Western private property rights cannot be assumed to be the general case (Meinzen-Dick et al. 1997). This issue could be even more complex in countries where men and women do not enjoy similar property rights. Moreover, social norms could systematically discourage women from even thinking of themselves as property owners.

There is now an emerging literature around the second issue, related to the question of how many people should be interviewed in a household survey. Interviewing only one person assumes that there is perfect information within the household and that there will be one person (usually the head) who knows about all of the economic activities of other household members. Studies have shown that this assumption is often incorrect and that self-reporting provides better information than when data on an individual's economic activities are collected by proxy (Bardasi et al. 2010). For example, husbands may not know their wives' incomes and thus if only the male household head is interviewed, he may underestimate his wife's income and thus total household income (Fisher et al. 2010). Moreover, studies that have interviewed husbands and wives separately on household economic activities and outcomes have shown that spouses often disagree, since, given gender roles, they may have different perceptions of these issues (Valentine 1999; Becker et al. 2006; Cloke 2007).

With regard to valuation, a number of factors influence whether respondents are able to value their assets at market prices. To begin with, there is the issue of whether a market even exists for the assets in question. In addition, a range of personal characteristics may influence an individual's ability to estimate the value of the assets that they own, such as their level of literacy and schooling, occupation, mobility, ability to participate in markets, and access to information. Complicating the issue further, the value of an asset to an individual may include more than its exchange value (the potential market or sales price) and be influenced by a series of other factors, such as its use value or how difficult it would be to ever garner the income to replace the asset.

These concerns informed our decision to pursue a mixed methods approach to the study of the intra-household distribution of wealth; an approach that has now become practically the standard among feminist economists intending to carry out quantitative survey research in developing countries. As Berik (1997, p. 122) explains, 'qualitative methods not only help generate more reliable quantitative data by delineating the meaning of concepts which are to be measured, but also provide non-meaningfully-quantifiable, detailed information about the processes underlying economic outcomes without which our understanding would be incomplete'.

All three country studies in the Gender Asset Gap project relied on a mixed methods approach, with the first phase of the study dedicated to qualitative field research, followed by a second phase where a representative household asset survey was carried out in order to collect information on individual-level asset ownership (Doss et al. 2011; Doss et al. 2012). It was expected that the qualitative fieldwork would inform the design of the survey protocols and instruments in such a way that we would be able to minimize systematic measurement error in estimating household wealth. This phase was also expected to assist in generating hypotheses regarding the intra-household distribution of wealth and, subsequently, in the interpretation of the results.

One of the main ways in which the three household asset surveys differed in their implementation was with respect to who in the household provided the initial information regarding the household's stock of assets, to whom they belonged, and their value. While all three surveys intended to interview the person or persons in the household who were the most knowledgeable about the assets owned, the protocols for selecting this person differed. Based on the results of the qualitative fieldwork, in Ecuador it was determined that the survey protocol should be to carry out the household inventory with both members of the couple together whenever possible. In contrast, in India and Ghana only one person, the most knowledgeable, provided the initial inventory. In all three countries an individual questionnaire was then separately administered to up to two household members of the opposite sex and gathered further information on asset ownership, among other questions.

The main purpose of this chapter is to present the qualitative data for Ecuador regarding the existence of asset markets and men's and women's participation in these that informed the decision to interview couples together. We then triangulate the qualitative and quantitative data to explore whether interviewing couples together in this case may have contributed to reducing measurement error in the estimates of gross household wealth and the intra-household distribution of wealth.

## 26.2   QUALITATIVE RESEARCH METHODS

The first phase of the Ecuador research, conducted between August and December 2009, began with the selection of the provinces and municipalities (*cantones*) where qualitative fieldwork was to be carried out. This required the development of hypotheses specific to Ecuador regarding the processes that might facilitate the accumulation of assets by women.

Theoretically, asset accumulation by individuals depends on two major factors: what people are able save out of their income or acquire through credit, and what they might receive through inheritance or public or other private transfers. The first point required a prior analysis of the labor and credit markets to identify the different ways in which women were inserted in these and their spatial distribution. The second required the selection of provinces in different regions of the country to also capture differences in inheritance practices as well as in rates of international migration, another potentially important factor in Ecuador due to the volume of remittances.

Based on a reading of the secondary literature and informal interviews with experts, three provinces were selected: one in the northern highlands (Pichincha), another in the southern highlands (Azuay) and one on the coast (Manabí), representing the major geographical divisions of the country. The aim was to carry out fieldwork in at least three municipalities within each, including that of the provincial capital, and a minimum of one rural municipality. In urban areas women's income-generating activities are quite diverse yet fairly similar across the country, including a broad range of activities in both the formal and informal sectors. They differ most across rural municipalities, thus it was these that were chosen to represent different modes of insertion of rural women to the broader economy. In Pichincha, the rural municipalities chosen are located in the heart of the cut-flower industry, the main source of stable wage employment for rural women in Ecuador, which exists alongside a relatively vibrant peasant economy. In Azuay, remittances from international migration along with craft production constitute the main sources of women's incomes, and fieldwork was carried out in three rural municipalities of declining peasant agriculture. Manabí has a diverse agricultural economy and three rural municipalities were selected to highlight this diversity, along with two urban centers, to capture women's employment in the fisheries and tourism sectors.[5]

The main methods employed in the fieldwork included focus groups, interviews with key informants, and participant observation of asset markets, complemented by the collection of additional secondary data. In total, 40 focus groups were conducted with the logistical support of 23 different organizations. The facilitating organizations were primarily women's organizations, farmer co-operatives and peasant associations, and microfinance non-governmental organizations (NGOs). Most of the focus groups, which averaged 15 persons in size, were composed of all women, although at least one all-male group discussion was also held in each province. On several occasions, only mixed-sex groups could be organized. In addition, in each provincial capital focus groups consisting of women from the middle and upper-middle classes, primarily business and professional women, were held.

The focus groups addressed four themes, following a semi-structured guide:[6] (1) income-generating activities and the role of assets when facing economic shocks; (2) the meaning of owning assets and knowledge of asset markets; (3) the accumulation of assets over the life cycle; and (4) household decision-making over the acquisition and use of assets. The focus groups lasted from one and a half to two hours and usually covered one to two themes; the themes were rotated in such a manner that all were covered in at least one of the urban and rural groups in each province. The discussions were led by the project's four researchers (three economists and an anthropologist), working in teams of two, and were tape-recorded with the contents subsequently transcribed for analysis.

A total of 58 semi-structured interviews were carried out with key informants, including lawyers, judges, public notaries, real estate agents, leaders of grassroots movements, academics, and representatives of NGOs, local government, and financial institutions. In addition, to better understand asset prices and the working of markets, we carried out participant observation in certain asset markets, including livestock markets; appliance, hardware, and equipment stores; and pawnbroker and second-hand stores.

The preparatory phase for the national survey ran from the end of the first phase of fieldwork to March 2010, and included further testing and revisions of the survey instrument[7] during the training of the enumerators and the execution of a pilot survey of 165 households in Quito, Guayaquil and a rural area of Manabí.[8] The researchers were directly involved in the training and pilot survey and this facilitated early testing of many of the insights gained from the qualitative work, influencing the final survey design and content of the survey instrument. The representative national survey was carried out between April and June 2010.

## 26.3   THE FUNCTIONING AND KNOWLEDGE OF ASSETS MARKETS

Ecuador, with a 2010 population of around 14.5 million, is categorized as a high-medium human development country. It has a fairly extensive transportation system that supports a relatively well-integrated market economy.[9] The vibrancy of markets tends to correspond to the size of urban centers and political divisions. The two major cities, Quito (highlands) and Guayaquil (coast), are major industrial centers and the capitals of their respective provinces (Pichincha and Guayas). The other provincial capitals, as well as some of those of the municipalities, serve as dynamic poles that concentrate economic activity and non-farm employment within their respective areas.

In this section we summarize some of the salient information gained during the qualitative phase of research on the functioning of asset markets, and men's and women's knowledge of these markets as well as of asset values. Each of the main asset markets is described in turn.[10]

### The Housing Market

All of the cities have well-developed housing markets characterized by the presence of multiple real estate agencies and agents; considerable ongoing construction of new housing stock; and houses, apartments, and lots being advertised for sale or rent. It is common to see 'For sale' or 'For rent' signs posted on windows or fencing, sometimes including the price. All the major national and provincial newspapers carry real estate listings, usually on a weekly basis, and often with price information. They also carry advertisements placed by developers for new housing developments, usually aimed at the middle class, with information on the price range.

Real estate agents, who are found even in some of the small municipal towns, have a very good notion of the potential market value of housing lots and dwellings, based on locale, size, and the quality of construction materials. They readily provide estimates of the going price per square meter. However, there is no organized source of information (such as a website) of properties for rent or sale, and their price, available either to real estate agents or the public at large. Thus agents primarily rely on their own experience and networks, as well as newspapers, for price information.[11]

According to focus groups, among the 'popular classes' (the bottom 60 percent of the income distribution), it is much more common to build a dwelling than to purchase it, whether in urban or rural areas. Housing lots are obtained through inheritance (particularly in rural areas), purchase, or sometimes squatting. Information on the availability of housing lots is often acquired by walking through a neighborhood looking for postings, or passed by word of mouth. Homes tend to be built bit by bit, as savings allow. Many urban popular neighborhoods seem to be in perpetual construction, since once the basic one-story house is finished, a second story is frequently begun, either to accommodate an expanding family (particularly, as children marry) or to serve as a rental unit. Some microfinance institutions provide mortgages to low-income groups for housing construction, but it appeared more frequent for people to access credit for home improvements, such as building a second story and using the main dwelling as collateral.[12] Among the middle class it is much more common to purchase a home outright and to rely more on private bank mortgages and direct financing by developers.

While the urban housing sales and rental markets can be characterized as well developed, this is not the case in rural areas outside of the municipal capitals. In focus groups in all three provinces, it was reported that very few houses, if any, were for sale and that it was also unusual to rent homes. Sales of dwellings generally only come about in the case of migration of whole families and are often tied to the sale of agricultural land. The occasional housing rental is also linked to the migration dynamic, with homes built by absent migrants sometimes available for rent, such as in rural Azuay, where migrant remittances fed a construction boom in the late 1990s. Migrant investments in real estate have notably increased the supply of housing available for rent in some of the municipal and provincial capitals.

In the focus groups it was evident that the women most likely to have a sense of housing prices were those who had recently purchased or built a home, or had a neighbor who had recently sold one or was trying to do so. Similarly, those who currently rented out a room or a second dwelling were the most confident in discussing rental values. Another factor that seemed to increase the likelihood of women having a good notion of the potential value of their home was whether the dwelling was being purchased on credit, or whether they had taken out a loan for an expansion or remodeling project, since the dwelling might be serving as collateral.

Also, being involved in litigation or a member of a neighborhood organization appeared to be associated with women's awareness of the potential sales value of their home. For example, in the informal settlement of Pisulí on the outskirts of Quito, that had begun as a land takeover in the 1980s and where residents were still trying to formally title their lots and homes, focus group participants were nearly unanimous that the average price of a 300 square meter home built of concrete walls and good flooring was in the order of US$25000, with the lot representing almost half of that value. Each time that they filled out the paperwork related to obtaining titles, or when they demanded services from the city, they had to declare the value of their property. In this and in other popular sector neighborhoods that were well organized, focus group participants were well aware of any homes that were currently for sale or rent as well as the price.

Those most likely not to have any idea at all about the potential sale or rental values of their homes were rural women residing in areas where real estate markets are thin or nonexistent. Nonetheless, we also found some urban women who did not have any notion of the potential market value of their home, although sometimes they were savvy about the cost of building materials given that home improvements are such a constant activity.

One of the issues that came up in the pretesting of the survey questionnaire and in the pilot survey was that sometimes women would respond to the question of how much they thought their dwelling, in its current condition, would sell for today with the answer to a different question: for how much they would be willing to sell their home. The response that they would be unwilling to sell their home at any price (or to mention an unreasonably high price) was not infrequent, given the sweat and tears that had gone into obtaining the lot and/or constructing the dwelling. This was consistent with focus group discussions regarding the intrinsic value placed on owning one's own home, which was the aspiration of most who did not already own one. For most women homeowners, the dwelling was their most valued asset, one that provided them with a sense of security in raising their family in addition to being the most valuable asset they owned. This could be a factor that would lead women to overestimate the value of their homes. At the same time, in the pretesting and pilot survey, it seemed that women respondents were more hesitant than men to provide an estimate of the potential sales value of their home when they had no objective basis to draw upon.

According to real estate agents, owners who come to them to list their dwellings for sale generally tend to overestimate the value of their home – whether men or women – related to the intrinsic value of homeownership. Our general sense, then, upon completing the fieldwork was that in the case of Ecuador, we could reasonably expect survey respondents to be able to estimate at least one among the potential sales, replacement, or rental value of their homes, if we paid proper attention to wording and follow-up questions. At the same time we were cognizant that there might be a tendency to overestimate home values, but perhaps not a systemic gender bias. How this qualitative data informed our final survey instrument is discussed in a subsequent section.

**The Market for Agricultural Land**

The main offer of land for rent or sale in many rural communities is by migrants or from older peasants who no longer have family labor available to work the land. Migrants generally prefer to rent rather than sell their land, since they often intend to eventually return to their communities. Rentals are usually short term, for the duration of the crop season; among peasants, sharecropping seems more common than cash rentals, with the latter characterizing larger holdings and capitalist farming. In some locales, hacienda land (from large landholdings) would occasionally be placed on the market when it was undergoing a process of subdivision, often linked with a succession (inheritance) process. Besides supply constraints, another reason why it seemed easier for peasants to access the rental market compared to the sales market is the lack of access to credit for purchasing land.

Awareness of land prices was best in locales where the land market was more dynamic and had experienced recent increases in price, such as in Cayambe in Pichincha. In this and the neighboring municipality of Pedro Moncayo, land prices were rising until recently due to the expansion of flower plantations, and land purchases by international migrants and the urban upper middle class from Quito for weekend homes and, in some cases, hobby farms. The 2008 international financial crisis dampened demand and in 2010 land prices appeared to be stabilizing, given the consistent figures often reported for valley-bottom land. While peasants have been priced out of valley-bottom land, some sales of hacienda lands at higher elevations were taking place in which groups of peasants were participating. In certain regions of rural Azuay in the southern highlands, it was reported that international migrants had bid up the price of agricultural land, although they tended not to farm it, and this facilitated a more dynamic rental market for smallholders.

In the rural focus groups there was general recognition by both men and women of the factors that influence land prices, such as the locale (particularly, the elevation), access to transportation and markets, irrigation, and soil quality. While there tended to be more interest in discussing land values in the men's focus groups, rural women were often cognizant of land values and it was not unusual for some rural women to be more aware of land values than they were of housing values. This is partly because those who wish to sell land will frequently post a notice on the property or a by-way, sometimes including the price. Otherwise, land prices are shared by word of mouth, information readily available to those who belong to peasant associations who are primarily, although not exclusively, men.

**Livestock Markets**

All of the provincial and most of the municipal capitals have weekly markets where large and small farm animals are bought and sold. Cattle and work animals (horses, donkeys, mules, and so on) tend to be bought and sold at the most dynamic regional markets, whereas sheep, goats, pigs, poultry, and other small animals are more likely to be bought and sold at local markets.

Of all the different assets that make up household wealth, potential animal sales prices were probably the most readily known, and not just by those residing in rural areas. Animal-raising activities are often carried out by women in semi-peripheral urban areas and both urban and rural women participate in these markets as consumers. Knowledge of livestock prices tends to follow the gender division of labor in animal raising and marketing, with men more confident of the going prices for large livestock and women more confident of those of smaller animals.

Animals were also considered to be the most liquid of all physical assets owned since these could be readily sold if faced with an emergency, with the animal that might be sold (a pig versus poultry, for example) depending on the magnitude of the economic shock. In the rural focus groups, ownership of animals was also discussed as an important means of accumulating savings, with hogs in particular being the 'piggy bank'.

**The Market for Consumer Durables**

One of the main differentiating factors between the middle class and the popular sector is the ownership of an automobile. Ownership of a vehicle is also an important means of upward mobility, often tied to specific (and generally male) occupations, such as taxi drivers, truck drivers, and delivery services. Automobile dealerships (and those for trucks and motorcycles) for both new and used vehicles are located in all the provincial capitals and other large urban centers. The most well-developed second-hand market of all consumer durables is for vehicles. There is a website that lists the inventory of used vehicles at all the major dealerships nationally, by type, make, price, and so on. Dealerships provide credit for both new and used vehicles. Those being sold privately are listed in weekly sections of most newspapers and include the price.

Those most confident about the potential market value of their vehicles were the individuals who owned them and had purchased them relatively recently, as was the case for other consumer durables. In the focus groups it was widely reported that men were more likely than women to own a vehicle of some sort. For women who did not own a vehicle, if their partner did, they were most likely to know its value if it was purchased on credit, for it was likely that the loan was in both of their names.

Ecuador has several chain stores that specialize in kitchen appliances and electronic goods (La Ganga and Comandato), and these are located in every provincial and municipal capital. While prices and credit terms appear to be fairly standard, in some focus groups it was reported that better prices were available in provincial capitals, indicating awareness of prices. Prices are advertised widely in newspapers and through other media, such as television ads, and store credit is readily available for their purchase.

The most standard consumer durable owned by most households is a gas stove, purchased by most couples upon setting up a home. Ecuador engaged in a major rural electrification push in the 1980s (as a result of new petroleum wealth), and this also opened up the possibility for households in rural areas to purchase a variety of consumer goods (most commonly, television sets and sound systems and, to lesser extent, refrigerators – the latter being more common on the coast than in the highlands). Washing machines are still considered a luxury item.

We were particularly interested in the potential liquidity of appliances since these were the main assets owned by the majority of popular sector women. We learned that these are generally purchased with the idea that they would last a lifetime and are rarely purchased second-hand. One of the factors discouraging the purchase of used appliances is the relative ease of obtaining store credit with a minimum down payment, even among lower-income groups. There was general awareness that consumer durables could be sold or pawned in an emergency. Yet, second-hand markets are generally thin and these, as well as pawn shops, are limited to urban areas. Some women noted that, in a crisis, you could always sell a television set or small appliance to a neighbor, but it was preferable to get a loan. The concern was that if you tried to sell a consumer durable you would not get a price close to its replacement value, and moreover that if you did sell it, it would be difficult to replace later. Several focus group participants who had pawned items in the past noted that they had never been able to reclaim them.

In focus group discussions, some women were adamant that they would never sell their gas stove, for how would they cook for their families? In an emergency, women were more likely to consider selling or pawning a television, a sewing machine, or small kitchen items such as a blender. Men mentioned a television set or sound system, or perhaps a bicycle, as the items they would be most likely to sell or pawn if need be. Gold jewelry seems to be a fairly liquid asset and women from both the popular and middle classes reported having sold or pawned jewelry. Besides pawn shops, some co-operatives and NGOs offer jewelry pawning facilities as sources of emergency loans. We now turn to how these insights from the qualitative fieldwork informed the design of the survey and questionnaires.

## 26.4   QUALITATIVE INSIGHTS AND SURVEY DESIGN

Among the main conclusions from the qualitative filed work in Ecuador was that, with the exception of some rural areas, asset markets are generally well developed and private property rights over assets are relatively well defined, so that men and women within households can usually differentiate between what belongs to each of them separately or jointly together.[13] Another is that men and women often have very different links to and experience with asset markets, which in turn is related to the gender division of labor both inside and outside the household. Moreover, men and women often have different access to information based on their own gendered networks. In the case of the housing market, for example, the focus group discussions suggested that in urban neighborhoods women are more likely than men to learn through their networks about dwellings that are for sale or rent, and the prices for which these are being sold or rented. Thus, if they themselves had no idea about the potential sales value of their home, they could draw upon their knowledge of what similar dwellings in their neighborhood have sold for to provide an estimate. In contrast, in the case of the land market, land prices seem to be a focus of greatest interest in the male-dominated peasant associations where information on any land transaction is quickly socialized among the members.

Another insight was that, within a given household, owners of a particular asset have a better understanding of that particular asset market, including of prices, than non-owners. Thus, since men tend to be the owners of the majority of vehicles, they are more likely to be aware of vehicle prices than their wives; the exception being the cases where the vehicle was purchased on credit and constitutes a joint liability of the couple. In terms of major kitchen appliances, women tend to be the owners of these and seem more likely to be aware of market prices compared with men.

The implication of these insights is that it matters who is interviewed in an assets or wealth survey. In the case of Ecuador we came to the conclusion that to enhance the likelihood of capturing reasonable estimates of the potential sales value of the assets owned by members of a household, it would be important to interview both the principal man and woman of the household. However, should they be interviewed together or separately? There are arguments pro and con.

An advantage of interviewing a couple together is that if one of them does not have knowledge of the market for a particular asset that is owned, the other person might, thus reducing the rate of potential missing observations. In our pretesting of the instrument with couples we observed that it was not uncommon for a man to defer to his wife on the value of certain assets, and for a wife to defer to her husband on others.

Another potential benefit of interviewing a couple together is that they can discuss their potential answer to a question, coming to a consensus on their response. Such a process might lead to more accurate responses if, for example, men tend provide a valuation estimate whether or not they actually have a clue about the potential market value of their asset, or if women on their own are more likely not to provide an estimate at all if they are not certain about the potential value.

Consider the following scenario that took place in one of our first practice interviews with a couple together, in Portoviejo, Manabí. After establishing that the couple had constructed their home together some 20 years ago in what had then been the outskirts of the city, when asked how much this two-story house could be sold for today, the husband immediately gave an estimate of US$50 000. The wife then interjected that a home down the street that was newer and larger had recently sold for US$50 000, so his estimate was probably optimistic. After some back-and-forth they settled on an estimate of US$45 000.

Whether a process of providing a consensual response to valuation questions is even feasible, however, very much depends upon gender relations and the extent of female subordination. If women always defer to their husbands, or at the extreme do not speak to outsiders in the presence of their spouse, a joint interview will not yield the desired results. Generating a consensual response thus depends upon social norms and women having the right as well as the confidence to disagree with their spouse. Another disadvantage of interviewing a couple together is the potential time and cost of being able to arrange an interview where both are present.

The advantage of interviewing a man and woman in a couple separately is that in the intimacy of a one-on-one interview they may be more forthcoming in discussing what assets they own and their potential value. This would be particularly the case if there are 'hidden' assets, such as financial assets or other property that a spouse might not know about and that they would not divulge in the other's presence. Another issue favoring separate interviews is whether the enumerator and respondent need to be paired by sex to ensure the development of greater rapport and trust. The main disadvantages of interviewing a man and woman separately in a survey is that it could also involve greater costs (since it involves more time and/or more enumerators), and could result in conflicting information regarding the ownership and valuation of an asset which then complicates the analysis of wealth.

As noted above, the pretesting of the survey instrument during the qualitative fieldwork and the period of training of the enumerators provided us with the opportunity to experiment with different interview protocols and observe first-hand the pros and cons of interviewing a couple together versus separately. We finally came to the conclusion that in the case of Ecuador, where gender relations within the household are relatively equitable and women seem to have little problem speaking their minds, interviewing a couple together would enhance the quality of the information gathered, particularly the valuation measures. We also did not find that sex pairing of enumerators and respondents was crucial to establishing rapport for the interview.

With respect to the valuation questions, one of the important insights from the qualitative fieldwork was that, in effect, in many locales there were no markets for certain assets, and if we wanted to be true to the lived experience of our respondents, we would have to provide the option in the questionnaire for respondents to indicate that alternative ('missing markets'), along with an honest 'don't know'. Such purposely missing observations could, of course, potentially result in an underestimation of household and individual wealth unless such values were subsequently imputed. Our primary concern was whether such a practice would introduce a gender bias in our results, for example if women were more likely than men to report 'missing markets' or 'don't know', a possibility we test in the subsequent section of the chapter.

On the basis of the qualitative fieldwork and field testing of the instrument, it seemed that sometimes it was easier for people to provide information on the potential sales price of owned assets than on their replacement cost, and at other times, the reverse. In the case of housing, since home construction and improvements seems to be a never-ending process in popular sector neighborhoods, the price of building materials was relatively well known and thus what it would cost to build the same home today could be estimated without much difficulty. However, for those who had finished constructing their homes years ago or had purchased a home, it was easier to provide a potential sales price as opposed to replacement cost. In addition, in the case of houses, the latter would need to take into account the price of purchasing the housing lot today, requiring an additional piece of information. Another problem is that to the replacement cost question people would sometimes respond with the estimated cost of the home that they wished they could build, made of materials of much higher quality than those in their current house. Given the variation in the measure with which people were more familiar, we finally decided to include all three measures of valuation (sales, replacement, and rental) for dwellings and two for agricultural land (sales and rental) in the questionnaire, to allow us to analyze the responses for their statistical properties at a later date, and the results are discussed below.

While people might not be certain of the price they could sell their home for in its current condition, they could draw upon knowledge of recent sales in their neighborhood to provide a reasonable estimate. In case respondents were not sure of the potential sales price, we made the important decision to include such a prompt. This prompt was also useful in case respondents insisted that they would not sell their home (or any other valued asset) at any price because it was too important to them.

In the case of consumer durables we decided that it made little sense to ask for the replacement cost, since responses to such questions inevitably referred to what it would cost to purchase a new appliance, rather than a used one, which would overstate the value of the asset that was owned. Thus, in this case we only asked about the potential sales price, cognizant that markets for used appliances were thin. On the other hand, given the generally dynamic market for used vehicles, estimating the potential sales price was relatively straightforward for most owners.

Valuing businesses presented its own special difficulties. Given the heterogeneity of the businesses owned, particularly in the informal sector, we did not dedicate much time exploring market and valuation issues relating to these in the focus group discussions. The main insight we garnered was with respect to the importance of access to and use of credit, both formal and informal, for the acquisition of business assets as well as working capital. This gave us some degree of confidence that people would be able to estimate the value of their business assets. In the pretesting of the instrument and pilot survey, we experimented with asking about the value of businesses in two ways – the estimated price for which a business could be sold today, and by taking a detailed inventory of existing assets of the business and their potential value – and included both questions in the final instrument.

## 26.5  QUANTITATIVE RESEARCH AND TRIANGULATION

The 2010 Ecuador Household Assets Survey (EAFF, by its Spanish initials) is a nationally representative sample of 2892 households.[14] Most households surveyed, 68.5 percent, were composed of a principal couple, with the remaining 31.5 percent consisting of a sole female (24.8 percent) or male (6.7 percent) head. In half of what we term 'couple-headed' households, we achieved our aim of interviewing both members of the principal couple together, a group representing 34.4 percent of the total household sample. In another 27.5 percent of the total sample the household assets inventory was completed by only one member of the couple, but both spouses completed the individual questionnaire separately.[15] Only in 4.6 percent of the total sample were we not able to interview the second person of a couple, either because they were temporarily absent from the home or because they refused to be interviewed.[16] In this case (as in the case of non-partnered respondents, the sole heads) only one person completed both the household and individual questionnaires. This distribution of interviews provides us with an unusual opportunity to compare the results of interviewing men and women in a couple together and

*Table 26.1    Share of missing values by form of valuation and type of respondent (%)*

| Principal residence | n | Sales value | Replacement value | Rental value |
|---|---|---|---|---|
| Male | 273 | 1.8 | 2.2 | 2.2 |
| Female | 832 | 2.9 | 4.0 | 4.1 |
| Couple | 622 | 3.9 | 4.0 | 6.9 |
| Total | 1727 | 3.1 | 3.7 | 4.8 |
| Chi-squared test | | $p = 0.248$ | $p = 0.355$ | $p = 0.004$ |

| Agricultural parcels | n | Sales value | $n^a$ | Rental value |
|---|---|---|---|---|
| Male | 66 | 1.5 | 58 | 6.9 |
| Female | 201 | 3.5 | 189 | 14.3 |
| Couple | 245 | 4.9 | 230 | 17.4 |
| Total | 512 | 3.9 | 477 | 14.9 |
| Chi-squared test | | $p = 0.418$ | $p = 0.128$ | $p = 0.128$ |

*Notes:*
* $p < 0.10$, ** $p < 0.05$, *** $p < 0.01$.
[a] The number of observations for land parcels differs, since the potential sales value includes all parcels while potential rental value includes only those parcels which are not currently rented.

*Source:*    Doss et al. (2013), based on authors' calculations from EAFF 2010.

separately, and we do so below to triangulate the results on missing observations and the valuation of two of the major assets, the principal residence and agricultural parcels.

**Missing Observations**

First consider valuation responses regarding the principal residence. As Table 26.1 shows, we had a higher share of missing values overall for rental values (5 percent), compared with potential sales (3 percent) or replacement values (4 percent). Moreover, in each case there is a greater share of missing values for couples than for women or men interviewed separately, with men always reporting the lowest share of missing values. The differences by type of respondent are only statistically significant, however, in the case of rental values, with a greater share of values missing for couples than for those interviewed separately, particularly men.

With respect to agricultural parcels, there was also a much higher share of missing values with regard to potential rental values (15 percent) than for estimates of the sales price (4 percent). A similar trend in the case of housing is apparent in terms of the type of respondent, there being a higher share of missing values for couples than for female and, particularly, male respondents, although the differences are not statistically significant.

These data suggest that for Ecuador, taken as a whole, respondents were more likely to be able to provide valuation estimates for the potential sales price than for other value measures.[17] When they did not provide a response, in all cases this was principally because they reported that there was not a market for the asset in their locale, rather than because they did not know or refused to provide an answer.[18]

Based on our qualitative fieldwork we had expected that interviewing a couple together was more likely to result in fewer cases of missing variables, since perhaps at least one spouse could provide the information, given gender-differentiated relations to markets and access to information. The data nonetheless suggest that both male and female respondents may be more likely to provide an answer to a valuation question when interviewed separately than when interviewed together as a couple, perhaps because the presence of the other spouse makes them less likely to guess in the face of missing markets or when they do not know the potential value of the asset. Thus, rather than reducing the percentage of missing observations, this suggests that one of the advantages of interviewing a couple together may be to improve the reliability of the estimates at the cost of more missing values.

**Estimates of Value**

Table 26.2 compares the mean estimates for residences and agricultural parcels by the form of valuation and type of respondent. With respect to housing values, it shows that men on average report higher values than women or couples, and that these differences are statistically significant. In terms of land values, however, this trend only holds for annual rental values, and only these differences are significant.

With respect to the other statistical properties of these estimates, for housing values, estimates of the potential sales price have a lower coefficient of variation, skewness, and kurtosis than either the estimated replacement value or rental value, and similarly for agricultural land, comparing the potential market value with the annual rental value (Doss et al. 2013, Tables 5 and 6). This suggests that, for Ecuador, valuation by potential sales prices provides the most reliable estimates, based both on statistical properties and the share of missing values.

*Table 26.2   Mean value of asset by form of valuation and type of respondent (USD)*

| Principal Residence | $n^a$ | Sales value | Replacement value | Monthly rental value |
| --- | --- | --- | --- | --- |
| Male | 259 | 37 734 | 43 975 | 156 |
| Female | 768 | 28 264 | 33 747 | 123 |
| Couple | 559 | 21 309 | 24 412 | 97 |
| Total | 1586 | 27 359 | 32 127 | 119 |
| F-test | | $p < 0.000^{***}$ | $p < 0.000^{***}$ | $p < 0.000^{***}$ |

| Agricultural parcels | $n^a$ | Sales value | | Annual rental value |
| --- | --- | --- | --- | --- |
| Male | 54 | 11 454 | – | 1067 |
| Female | 161 | 9688 | – | 366 |
| Couple | 190 | 14 029 | – | 395 |
| Total | 405 | 11 960 | – | 473 |
| F-test | | $p = 0.215$ | – | $p = 0.006^{***}$ |

*Notes:*
\*\*\* $p < 0.01$.
[a] Based on those observations where respondents provided valuation estimates for all measures of value.

*Source:*   Doss et al. (2013), based on authors' calculations from EAFF 2010.

*Table 26.3   Comparison of mean sales values reported by husbands and wives interviewed separately (USD)*

|  | Principal residence | Agricultural parcels |
|---|---|---|
| Male | 32 435 | 13 683 |
| Female | 31 040 | 11 002 |
| N | 338 | 79 |
| T-test | $p = 0.230$ | $p = 0.064*$ |

*Note:*   $*p < 0.10$.

*Source:*   Doss et al. (2013), based on authors' calculations from EAFF 2010.

Thus far we have not taken into account housing and land quality and other characteristics of the asset. In Table 26.3 we adjust for these factors by comparing the estimates of potential sales prices for housing and land provided by husbands and wives for the same asset, but who were interviewed separately. It shows that while the trend is for husbands to report higher mean values than their wives, the difference is only statistically significant in the case of agricultural parcels. Nevertheless, via this test we cannot discount the fact that the spouse that was first interviewed may have shared the questions that were posed and their answer, so that the second spouse provided a similar figure (in the case of housing), or corrected the estimate of the first (in the case of land).

**Modeling by Type of Respondent**

Another way to investigate whether there are systematic differences in valuation due to who was interviewed is by constructing a model based upon 'objective' measures of value and comparing this model among the different types of respondents. In this way, we are able to examine potential differences among more types of respondents, since we are not restricted to only those where two respondents report separately on the same asset. For instance, we can pose the question whether men and women, responding individually, differ from when both a man and a woman are interviewed together. Here we conduct this analysis only for the principal residence.

The first step is to construct a relatively simple model of objective characteristics that adequately accounts for the variance in housing values. We collected information on whether the dwelling was in an urban or rural locale and whether it was titled (there was a registered or unregistered property document), as well as on the number of rooms,[19] and square meters. In addition, information was collected on housing quality such as the building material for the walls, floor, and roof as well as on the source of the water supply (for example, public network, public well, river, and so on), where it was located (inside the house, outside the house but on the lot, and so on), and on the type of sewage system employed. We ordered these six housing quality variables and combined them to form a housing quality index that demonstrated good overall internal consistency ($\alpha = 0.80$). Table 26.4 presents the overall basic descriptive statistics for these variables and the market value of the principal residence. For modeling purposes, we then centered the number of rooms, square meters, and housing quality on the overall averages such that

*Table 26.4   Descriptive statistics*

| Variable[a] | Minimum | Maximum | Mean | Std deviation |
|---|---|---|---|---|
| Market value principal residence | 100.00 | 400 000.00 | 27 399.99 | 32 941.043 |
| Urban | 0.00 | 1.00 | 62.5% | 0.484 |
| Title | 0.00 | 1.00 | 68.9% | 0.463 |
| Number of rooms | 1.00 | 14.00 | 3.11 | 1.284 |
| Square meters | 6.00 | 696.00 | 88.16 | 60.392 |
| Housing quality | 0.00 | 18.00 | 12.68 | 3.816 |

*Note:*   [a] n = 1561 for each variable.

*Source:*   EAFF 2010.

the intercepts represent undocumented rural residences with three rooms, average square meters, and average housing quality.

Next, in Table 26.5, we compare the regression results for a reduced (nested) model that does not incorporate the type of respondent ($R^2 = 0.36$) to a model that is fully interacted with type of respondent ($R^2 = 0.38$). This analysis reveals that the complete model, with unique coefficients for each type of respondent, results in a significant improvement in model fit, $F (12, 1542) = 3.20$, $p < 0.001$. This is a primary indication that it may not be appropriate to ignore the type of respondent when analyzing the valuation of residences.

Even were we to find that the fully interacted model was not a significant improvement we would still want to address the question of whether the model coefficients are equal across respondents. There may be structural differences in the model according to the type of respondent. In other words, the model could account for a similar amount of variance in potential sales value across respondents but may be accounting for this variance in different ways within the different groups. Shown in Table 26.6, these tests reveal that there are significant differences in the resulting intercepts for male respondents (b = 30798.93) when compared to females (b = 18052.98) or couples (b = 17327.07) but not between females and couples. That is to say, the predicted value of rural undocumented residences with average characteristics is significantly greater for male respondents than females or couples.[20] There are significant differences in the coefficient for square meters between male respondents (b = 205.06), female respondents (b = 128.85), and couple respondents (b = 107.57), but not between female and couple respondents. Likewise, there are significant differences in the coefficient for the housing quality index, with male respondents (b = 3829.80) greater than females (b = 2619.47) and couples (b = 2108.27). Again, with housing quality, there is no significant difference between females and couples and coefficients for female and couple respondents are very similar.[21] Finally, there appears to be a significant difference in the coefficient for urban between males (b = −769.54) and females (b = 7428.93) and a similar, though not significant, difference between males and couples (b = 7066.26).

Now that we have evidence that we should incorporate the type of respondent in the analysis of housing valuation, we want to pose the question whether this model differs among the type of respondents. Similar to above, we want to know whether this model fits one type of respondent significantly better than others.[22] To do so, we perform a Fisher's

*Table 26.5   Comparison of the reduced model with the complete model*

| Variable | b | SE | β | |
|---|---|---|---|---|
| Reduced model | | | | |
| *Intercept* | 19400.43 | 1565.55 | | |
| *Urban* | 6899.28 | 1526.15 | 0.10 | *** |
| *Titled* | 4858.92 | 1572.01 | 0.07 | *** |
| *Number of rooms* | 3165.21 | 629.45 | 0.12 | *** |
| *Square meters* | 140.89 | 13.26 | 0.26 | *** |
| *Housing quality* | 2529.64 | 220.48 | 0.29 | *** |
| Complete model | | | | |
| *Intercept* | 30798.93 | 4655.09 | | *** |
| *Urban* | −769.54 | 4466.35 | −0.01 | |
| *Titled* | 900.02 | 4377.56 | 0.01 | |
| *Number of rooms* | 3728.23 | 1438.32 | 0.15 | *** |
| *Square meters* | 205.06 | 28.43 | 0.38 | *** |
| *Housing quality* | 3829.80 | 630.71 | 0.44 | *** |
| *Female x Intercept* | −12745.95 | 5242.03 | −0.19 | ** |
| *Female x Urban* | 8198.47 | 4959.03 | 0.12 | * |
| *Female x Titled* | 4539.79 | 4950.99 | 0.07 | |
| *Female x Number of rooms* | −754.32 | 1693.96 | −0.02 | |
| *Female x Square meters* | −76.21 | 34.39 | −0.10 | ** |
| *Female x Housing quality* | −1210.33 | 707.62 | −0.09 | * |
| *Couple x Intercept* | −13471.86 | 5196.42 | −0.20 | *** |
| *Couple x Urban* | 7835.80 | 5115.84 | 0.09 | |
| *Couple x Titled* | 3949.99 | 5018.26 | 0.05 | |
| *Couple x Number of rooms* | −1155.56 | 1814.13 | −0.03 | |
| *Couple x Square meter* | −97.49 | 36.74 | −0.10 | *** |
| *Couple x Housing quality* | −1721.53 | 719.20 | −0.13 | ** |

*Notes:*
n = 258 for males; n = 747 for females; n = 556 for couples.
$R^2 = 0.36$ for Reduced model; $R^2 = 0.38$ for Complete model, $F (12, 1542) = 3.20$, $p < 0.001$.
* $p < 0.10$, ** $p < 0.05$, *** $p < 0.01$.

*Source:*   EAFF 2010.

Z transformation on the resulting R values for each type of respondent separately using this same model.[23] These tests reveal that there are no significant differences in overall model fit between male respondents (R = 0.589) and female respondents (R = 0.575) or couple respondents (R = 0.780). There is, however, a significant difference in overall model fit between female respondents and couple respondents (p = 0.03). Therefore, there is some, albeit weak, evidence that the model may fit somewhat better for couples than males or females, as the p values for these comparisons (0.17 and 0.03, respectively) are far smaller than that between males and females (0.78). This is also in line with the qualitative research where it was noted that providing men and women with the ability to deliberate and form a consensus on the potential sales value of their residence may result in greater precision.

*Table 26.6   Comparison of the complete model coefficients among types of respondent*

| Variable | Comparison | | | | | |
|---|---|---|---|---|---|---|
| | Male–Female | | Male–Couple | | Female–Couple | |
| | $b_1 - b_2$ | p | $b_1 - b_2$ | p | $b_1 - b_2$ | p |
| *Intercept* | 12 745.95 | ** | 13 471.86 | *** | 725.91 | |
| *Urban* | −8198.47 | * | −7835.80 | | 362.67 | |
| *Titled* | −4539.79 | | −3949.99 | | 589.80 | |
| *Number of rooms* | 754.32 | | 1155.56 | | 401.24 | |
| *Square meters* | 76.21 | ** | 97.49 | *** | 21.27 | |
| *Housing quality* | 1210.33 | * | 1721.53 | ** | 511.20 | |

*Note:*   $* p < 0.10$, $** p < 0.05$, $*** p < 0.01$.

*Source:*   EAFF 2010.

Taken together, these results show that there are structural differences in this model according to the type of respondent such that males differ from females and couples. First, there is evidence that male respondents provide significantly higher values than females or couples for rural undocumented homes but not urban documented homes. Second, there is evidence that the value of the residence provided by male respondents is significantly more sensitive to the size of the residence, in square meters, than values provided by females or couples, such that a similar change in square meters results in a significantly greater change in value for male respondent values than female or couple respondent values. Finally, there is evidence that the value of the residence provided by male respondents is significantly more sensitive to the quality of the residence than couple respondents, such that a similar change in quality results in a significantly greater change in value for male respondent values than couple respondent values. Overall, this conforms to the insight from the qualitative research that men and women may differ in how they value residences. Moreover, our results suggest that couples may incorporate the woman's perspective of values in that there appear to be no significant structural differences in the model between female and couple respondents. There is also some weak evidence to suggest that couples weigh the man's perspective as well, given that the couple coefficients for urban and titling are between those of males and females, suggesting that the presence of a partner may, in some cases, result in an attenuation effect.

## 26.6   CONCLUSIONS

In this chapter we aimed to contribute to a feminist economics methodology in several ways. First, we posed a question not usually considered by mainstream economists: the intra-household distribution of wealth – a potentially important source of gender inequality and a variable that may be crucial in supporting broader structures of gender inequality. Second, we utilized a mixed methods approach to establish the feasibility of conducting research on this topic. The study of personal wealth requires that markets exist and that people be familiar enough with them to be able to estimate the value of what they own. Further, to analyze the intra-household distribution of wealth, individual ownership of assets must be sufficiently defined so that people can differentiate what belongs to them individually versus jointly with someone else. Third, we have demonstrated that it matters how you go about collecting quantitative data on wealth, and the importance of doing so in a gender-sensitive manner.

Valuing assets in a household survey is a complicated undertaking. Missing markets are a real phenomenon in developing countries that must be taken into account in designing a survey instrument to measure wealth. Our qualitative research suggested a range of situations where people might be more or less likely to be able to report on the value of the assets that they owned, but yielded no consistent insight on which measure of value might be captured most reliably. Triangulating the qualitative with quantitative data and statistical analysis leads us to conclude that, in the case of Ecuador, the potential sales price provides the most reliable estimates, but whether this result can be generalized to other countries requires further research.[24]

Our qualitative research strongly reinforced our initial intention to interview both men and women, and led us to experiment with interviewing both members of a couple together and separately. While we had expected that interviewing both members of a couple together would lead to fewer missing responses, data triangulation showed that this was generally not the case for housing and land values, but rather, it perhaps improved the reliability of our estimates by reducing the tendency to guess when there were in fact missing markets, or the person really did not know the answer.

We had also expected that interviewing a couple together would improve the estimates by allowing them to reach a consensus on the potential asset value. The focus groups with women had highlighted the factors that might lead women to overvalue their assets. We did not carry out sufficient focus groups with men or mixed groups to develop strong expectations regarding men's perception of values, although testing of the questionnaire in the various types of interviews suggested that men were often more confident than women in reporting asset values, and perhaps more prone to exaggeration. The quantitative findings of a tendency toward men overvaluing and/or women undervaluing their dwelling thus conforms to this insight.

Overall, this series of quantitative analyses suggests that it makes a difference who you interview, not only in terms of their sex, but also the form of the interview: whether couples are interviewed separately or together. We found that our model fit was greatest among respondents who are couples interviewed together, and that there are structural differences according to the type of respondent; these differences are such that only male respondents tended to differ from female and couple respondents. We also found that predicted values for male respondents were greater than those for female respondents and couples, particularly in rural areas with regards to undocumented residences. Though relatively simple, this model adjusts for 'objective' measures of the residence and as such these differences in predicted values are likely to be partially reflecting a perceptual bias, where rural male respondents may be overvaluing or female and couple respondents may be undervaluing the residence, or perhaps both. In short, we find evidence that valuation of potential sales prices is likely to depend on the gender of the respondent, whether a couple are interviewed separately or together, and whether they are located in an urban or rural locale.

One aspect that we did not investigate is whether the marital status of the respondent makes a difference. In the analysis presented the category of male respondents includes those who are non-partnered (single, separated, divorced, or widowed) and those who are partnered (married or in a consensual union) but who were interviewed separately from their spouse. Studies in developed countries suggest that the mean wealth of married couples is substantially greater than that of sole household heads (whether male or female), and much greater than explained by the fact that the former generally consist of two adults compared to one (Schmidt and Sevak 2006; Deere and Doss 2006). Since housing wealth makes up such a large share of personal wealth, it may be the case that couples own more valuable homes, due to economies of scale of various types, greater access to credit, and so on. If this were to be the case, then we might expect partnered spouses to report higher values whether they were interviewed alone or together with their spouse.

In the case of Ecuador, those who are partnered – whether responding as a couple or individually – report lower average home values than those reported by non-partnered individuals. Nonetheless, it would be worth investigating whether non-partnered male and female respondents are responsible for the structural differences noted above, expecting there to be fewer differences among partnered male respondents, partnered female respondents, and couple respondents. This would be the case if men and women who are married tend to share other personal characteristics and are more similar (that is, 'marriage sorting') than the pool of non-partnered individuals. Also, we cannot totally discount the fact that some degree of information sharing may take place among husbands and wives, such that when interviewed alone about housing values they provide values more similar to those of couples when interviewed together as compared to non-related individuals.

# NOTES

\*  The field research study reported on here was hosted by the Latin American Faculty of Social Sciences (FLACSO-Ecuador) and led by Carmen Diana Deere, principal investigator, and Jackeline Contreras, co-coordinator. Jennifer Twyman also participated in all of the field research. The field research was funded by the Dutch Foreign Ministry's MDG3 Fund for Gender Equality as part of the Gender Asset Gap project, a comparative study of Ecuador, Ghana, and India. The authors are grateful to the co-PIs of the comparative study, Cheryl Doss, Caren Grown, Abena D. Oduro, and Hema Swaminatham, and other team members for permission to draw upon our joint work, and to the Vanguard Foundation and United Nations Women for financing the analytical work presented herein. An earlier version of this chapter was presented at the Union for Radical Political Economics (URPE) Session on Research Methods and Applications in Heterodox Economics, Allied Social Science Associations (ASSA) meetings, Philadelphia, PA, January 3–5, 2014.

1.  See Vyas and Watts (2009), for example, for a review of a large number of studies focusing on the relationship of different measures of women's empowerment and the incidence of intimate partner violence.

2.  We draw upon the distinction in the literature that 'methods' refer to particular research tools or techniques, while 'a methodology is a combination of techniques, the practices we conform to when we apply them, and our interpretation of what we are doing when we do so' (Olsen and Morgan 2005, p. 257). A feminist methodology is one based on feminist principles and vision of social change; that is, doing research to advance an agenda of social justice for women (see Miner-Rubino et al. 2007, and other essays in Hesse-Biber 2007). A feminist economics methodology is still in the process of construction, but includes an emphasis on what Robeyns (2000, p. 4) terms a 'thick' definition of gender, 'the power differences between men and women in society, and the structures and constraints that make these power-differences occur and persist'.

3.  For example, in the US, the Panel Study of Income Dynamics of non-pension wealth – which is frequently

utilized to study household wealth trends – does not ask who in the couple owns the major assets (Schmidt and Sevak 2006). In the UK, the Family Resource Survey does collect information on pension wealth by individuals and their sex, but for couples, housing and financial assets are reported only at the household level (Warren 2006). The exception thus far seems to be the German Socio-Economic Panel, which collected wealth information on all adult household members (Sierminska et al. 2010).

4.  Deere et al. (2012) in a detailed review of 167 household survey instruments utilized by 23 Latin American and Caribbean countries since the 1990s found that only 11 countries had collected some asset ownership data at the individual level in one of their household surveys. The most frequent asset for which individual-level information was available was for housing, for nine countries. Only one survey collected information on a large number of assets (housing, land, livestock, businesses, consumer durables) at the individual level, but the inconsistent manner in which value information was collected precluded a rigorous analysis of the intra-household distribution of wealth.

5.  Fieldwork was carried out in the following municipalities: in the province of Pichincha, in Quito, Cayambe, and Pedro Moncayo; in Azuay, in Cuenca, Gualaceo, Paute, and Sig Sig; in Manabí, in Portoviejo, Manta, Montecristi, 24 de Mayo, and Olmedo.

6.  The focus group themes were developed collectively by the Gender Asset Gap project team, and modified appropriately by each country team.

7.  The template for the Gender Asset Gap project surveys was derived from the previous review of survey instruments reported in Doss et al. (2008). The generic template was then adapted to each country situation, informed by the qualitative fieldwork.

8.  The national survey was executed by the consulting firm HABITUS Inc., and included more than 50 enumerators and supervisors.

9.  The exception to this description is the Amazon region of Ecuador, which actually covers more then half of the country's geographic extension but holds only 5 percent of the nation's population. This region, as well as the Galapagos Islands, was excluded from our study.

10. For lack of space, we exclude a description of the market in agricultural equipment and tools, the market for existing businesses, or the financial market.

11. Other sources of information on real estate values that we pursued in order to educate ourselves about dwelling and land prices were the municipal-level cadaster offices and property registries. The cadaster offices are charged with valuing real estate for tax purposes and do so based on fixed rates according to location and square footage. These tables are updated approximately every ten years, and we found that in many cases they were considerably out of date, severely undervaluing property compared to current market values. Each real estate transaction must be recorded in the local property registry, so this is another potential source of information on current values. However, the records of neither of these offices is systematically computerized, thus it proved impossible to gather administrative data from these sources to incorporate into our study.

12. There is also a government housing program, the Bono de Vivienda, which provides a housing subsidy for low-income groups of up to US\$5000 (in 2009–10) for housing construction for those who already own a titled lot, and of up to US\$1500 for home improvements.

13. For lack of space, this information is not presented herein; however, among the topics discussed in the focus groups was the bundle of rights that ownership confers. In Ecuador it became quickly apparent that most people consider ownership of an asset, including land, to entail the right to sell and rent it, use it as collateral, and to bequeath it. There was greater confusion over the property rights entailed in marriage, and these results of the qualitative research are reported in Deere et al. (2014).

14. It was a stratified random sample, based on socio-economic status as determined from the 2001 Ecuadorian National Population and Housing Census and two-stage random sampling. For the sampling method, see Deere and Contreras (2011).

15. The protocol was to make three attempts to interview the couple together. Due to time and budget constraints, if after the third try this was impossible to arrange, whoever was present (the husband or wife) completed the household inventory and the other spouse was interviewed separately at a later moment.

16. There were 15 households where the household inventory was completed by the couple together, but where for various reasons it proved impossible to complete the individual questionnaire with one of the spouses.

17. See Doss et al. (2013) for a comparative analysis of this issue across the three country sites.

18. With respect to rural–urban differences, for the principal residence, the only measure that was statistically significant was for the rental value, with 10 percent of rural respondents compared to only 1 percent of urban respondents reporting this variable as missing, as expected, principally because of missing markets. In terms of agricultural parcels, there was a significant difference by locale with respect to the potential sales price, with 5 percent of rural and less than 1 percent of urban respondents not reporting this measure, again primarily because of missing markets (see Doss et al. 2013).

19. The number of rooms excludes the kitchen, bathrooms, garage, or rooms dedicated exclusively to business purposes.

20. A similar test for the predicted value of the average residence that is urban and documented does not reveal significant differences among male (b = 30875.84), female (b = 30844.03), and couple (b = 28970.91) respondents.
21. Similar overall results are obtained from the log transformed potential sales values such that model fit is improved by modeling values separately by type of respondent (male, female, and couple) and that there exist structural differences in the coefficient for housing quality for male respondents when compared to female or couple respondents.
22. Note that beta coefficients will not differ between the fully interacted model and the separate models for type of respondent.
23. Here we report R rather than $R^2$ values, because this is the coefficient utilized in the Fisher Z transformation.
24. See Doss et al. (2013) for a comparative analysis with Ghana and India on this question.

# REFERENCES

Bardasi, Elena, Kathryn Beegle, Andrew Dillon, and Pieter Serneels (2010), 'Do labor statistics depend on how and to whom the questions are asked? Results from a survey experiment in Tanzania', Policy Research Working Paper 5192, Washington, DC: World Bank.
Becker, Stan, Fannie Fonseca-Becker, and Catherine Schenck-Yglesias (2006), 'Husbands' and wives' reports of women's decision-making power in western Guatemala and their effects on preventive health behaviors', *Social Science and Medicine*, **62**, 2313–26.
Berik, Günseli (1997), 'The need for crossing the method boundaries in economics research', *Feminist Economics*, **3** (2), 121–5.
Cloke, Jonathan (2007), 'Gender, taboo and deceit: the alternative truths of household research', *GeoJournal*, **70** (1), 33–45.
Deere, Carmen Diana, Gina Alvarado, and Jennifer Twyman (2012), 'Gender inequality in asset ownership in Latin America: female owners versus household heads', *Development and Change*, **43** (2), 505–30.
Deere, Carmen Diana and Jackeline Contreras (2011), *Acumulación de Activos: Una Apuesta por la Equidad* (*Asset Accumulation: The Challenge for Equity*), Quito, Ecuador: FLACSO-Ecuador, accessed August 21, 2014 at http://www.genderassetgap.org.
Deere, Carmen Diana, Jackeline Contreras, and Jennifer Twyman (2014), 'Patrimonial violence: a study of women's property rights in Ecuador', *Latin American Perspectives*, **41** (1), 143–65.
Deere, Carmen Diana and Cheryl Doss (2006), 'The gender asset gap: what do we know and why does it matter?', *Feminist Economics*, **12** (1–2), 1–50.
Doss, Cheryl (2013), 'Intrahousehold bargaining and resource allocation in developing countries', *World Bank Research Observer*, **28** (1), 52–78.
Doss, Cheryl, William Baah-Boatang, Louis Boakye-Yiadom, Zachary Catanzarite, Carmen Diana Deere, Hema Swaminathan, Rahul Lahoti, and J.Y. Suchitra (2013), 'Measuring personal wealth in developing countries: interviewing men and women about asset values', Gender Asset Gap Project Working Paper No. 15, accessed August 24, 2014 at http://www.genderassetgap.org.
Doss, Cheryl, Carmen Diana Deere, Abena Oduro, Hema Swaminathan, Suchitra J.Y., Rahul Lahoti, W. Baah-Boateng, L. Boakye-Yiadom, Jackeline Contreras, Jennifer Twyman, Zachary Catanzarite, Caren Grown, and Marya Hillesland (2011), 'The gender asset and gender wealth gaps: evidence from Ecuador, Ghana and Karnataka, India', Bangalore: Indian Institute of Management Bangalore, accessed August 24, 2014 at http://www.genderassetgap.org.
Doss, Cheryl, Carmen Diana Deere, Suchitra J.Y., Abena Oduro, and Marya Hillesband (2012), 'Lessons from the field: implementing individual asset surveys in Ecuador, Ghana, India and Uganda', The Gender Asset Gap Project, Bangalore: Indian Institute of Management Bangalore, accessed August 24, 2014 at http://www.genderassetgap.org.
Doss, Cheryl R., Caren Grown, and Carmen Diana Deere (2008), 'Gender and asset ownership: a guide to collecting individual-level data', World Bank Policy Research Working Paper No. WPS4704, Washington, DC: World Bank, accessed August, 24 2014 at http://econ.worldbank.org/docsearch.
Fisher, Monica, Jeffrey J. Reimer, and Edward R. Carr (2010), 'Who should be interviewed in surveys of household income?', *World Development*, **38** (7), 966–73.
Hesse-Biber, Sharlene Nagy (ed.), *Handbook of Feminist Research: Theory and Praxis*, Thousand Oaks, CA: Sage.
Meinzen-Dick, Ruth S., Lynn R. Brown, Hilary Sims Feldstein, and Agnes Quisumbing (1997), 'Gender, property rights and natural resources', *World Development*, **25** (8), 1303–15.
Miner-Rubino, Kathi, Toby Epstein Jayaratne, and Julie Konik (2007), 'Using survey research as a quantitative

method for feminist social change', in S.N. Hesse-Biber (ed.), *Handbook of Feminist Research: Theory and Praxis*, Thousand Oaks, CA: Sage, pp. 199–222.

Olsen, Wendy K. and Jamie Morgan (2005), 'A critical epistemology of analytical statistics: addressing the skeptical realist', *Journal for the Theory of Social Behavior*, **35** (3), 255–84.

Robeyns, Ingrid (2000), 'Is there a feminist economic methodology?', translation of 'Esiste una metodologia economica feminista?', in P. Di Cori and D. Barazetti (eds), *Gli Studi della Donne in Italia: Una Guida Critica*, Rome: Carocci, pp. 119–45.

Schmidt, Lucie and Purvi Sevak (2006), 'Gender, marriage and asset accumulation in the United States', *Feminist Economics*, **12** (1–2), 139–66.

Sierminska, Eva, Joachim R. Frick, and Markus Grabka (2010), 'Examining the gender wage gap', *Oxford Economic Papers*, **62** (4), 669–90.

Valentine, Gill (1999), 'Doing household research: interviewing couples together and apart', *Area*, **31** (1), 67–74.

Vyas, Seema and Charlotte Watts (2009), 'How does economic empowerment affect women's risk of intimate partner violence in low and middle income countries? A systematic review of published evidence', *Journal of International Development*, **21**, 577–602.

Warren, Tracey (2006), 'Moving beyond the gender wealth gap: on gender, class, ethnicity and wealth in the United Kingdom', *Feminist Economics*, **12** (1–2), 195–219.

# 27 The use of quasi-experimental design in urban and regional policy research and political economy
*Thomas E. Lambert and Michael Bewley*

## 27.1 INTRODUCTION

Often in the name of economic development or local economic revitalization, tax incentives and/or regulatory relief are granted to existing business firms within a region so as to spur business expansion, investment, and hiring, or at the least to keep an existing business from removing its capital, laying off its workers, and relocating to another jurisdiction. Likewise, such incentives and/or relief can be offered to potential new firms thinking about locating to a jurisdiction (or to a specific, targeted part of a jurisdiction) in order to entice these firms to locate within the region. Again, the goal of the local government(s) is to generate local economic growth through direct job creation and investment by current or new firms.

Economic development incentives and/or regulatory relief (hereafter, 'incentives') offered by municipal or state governments or both are some form of tax expenditures or cost, the burden of which is shifted to other taxpayers. Therefore, good public policy requires or warrants some type of accountability for the effectiveness of the incentives (Rivlin 1971; Kettl 2011). Some common tools used in public policy to assess policy programs and their financial effectiveness are benefit–cost analysis and cost-effectiveness analysis (Weimer and Vining 2011; Dunn 2012; Kraft and Furlong 2013) as well as various statistical techniques such as regression, testing differences of means, and so on. Some authors believe that program evaluation is a low priority for most policy-makers for various reasons: a lack of research funding; the difficulty of getting programs approved, much less implemented and later assessed; as well as various other reasons (Kettl 2011; Kraft and Furlong 2013). This is one big obstacle that makes program evaluation difficult, in addition to other factors.

Experimental methods similar to those in the natural sciences are often used when the random assignment of subject or target populations or regions into experimental and control groups is possible and would be useful in evaluating the efficacy of public policy programs (that is, 'treatments', or 'X' such as economic development incentives offered to firms) in a way that allows for comparisons between the two groups (please see Chapter 8 in this *Handbook* for more details).

Many different examples of experimental design exist. In farming, new pesticides or growing techniques could be tested with crops in one area of a farm, whereas the traditional or usual method could be used in another area. In education and the military, experimental design could be employed when pilot tests of new curriculum or other school or training innovations are tried. Students or trainees with the same backgrounds and capabilities could be randomly assigned into experimental (new curriculum) or control (placebo or old curriculum) groups to see if a new training or teaching technique is more efficacious than the one currently being used (Cook and Campbell 1979). In experimental economics, human subjects are often randomly assigned to experimental and control groups in order to gauge the impact of some type of stimulus on participants' decision-making or a group's decision-making when it comes to markets, competitive games, or cooperation, among other situations (Smith 2008). For example, to mimic decision-making under uncertainty in market situations, one group of participants may be asked to bid on a certain item (stock, real estate) while being told certain basic information about the item, whereas another group may be told the same information but with one additional piece of information which is hypothesized to possibly sway or influence purchase decisions, such as that a piece of property was once owned by a famous person or has certain sentimental value, even though this should connote no additional value in a competitive, fully rational market. In economic research that involves public policy evaluation, experimental design has been claimed to test the effects of changes in unemployment compensation, workmen's compensation benefits, changes in different social insurance programs, the impact of negative income taxes, of taxation on alcohol and drinking behavior, and changes in earnings of immigrants (Meyer 1995; Institute for Research on Poverty 2013).

When it comes to human subjects, experimental design is not without controversy. Access denied to pilot testing of an innovative training program or curriculum due to one being assigned to a placebo or control group can have harmful educational or career effects to control group members. Even if warned of such adverse consequences, and even if participants grant informed consent, ethical and moral issues abound in the use of experimental methods with human subjects. For this reason, they are often avoided when the stakes are relatively high in human subject research (Babbie 2013).

Also, random assignment is often not possible or practical when it comes to human subjects or other entities such as geographic regions, not only because of ethical considerations, but also because the need for program evaluation is not well conceived or thought out prior to program implementation. Often in the case of urban and regional economic development, political considerations and priorities play a role in which certain regions are targeted for economic development incentives because they may have a disproportionate number of unemployed, poor, or people living in blighted neighborhoods with high crime rates (Blair 1995). Because of the urgency or need to solve such problems, a similar region or locale which does not receive such incentives is not considered a priori as a control group for program evaluation later; or, for example, if all regions below a certain per capita income level are eligible and all receive incentives, it may be difficult if not impossible to find a similar region or locale which does not receive such incentives for purposes of comparison later. It would also not be just for policy-makers to create a program and then deny it to certain regions for purposes of an experiment. However, the lack of random assignment and exact control groups cause a potential threat to validity in later studies since any regions receiving tax incentives or stimulus may not exactly match any control groups chosen later for purposes of assessment.

In a study of enterprise zones in New Jersey, USA, Boarnet and Bogart (1996) had a somewhat quasi-experimental situation in which around 28 different cities within the state had applied for or were eligible for enterprise zone (EZ) status. Some applied for and were accepted for program incentives and EZ designation and chose to participate (seven zones), some were not accepted by state officials for program participation despite applying (14 areas), and some were eligible to participate but chose not to participate (seven areas). Whether a region participated seemed somewhat akin to a random process, and after performing econometric analyses, the authors did not find that EZ programs had much impact. Similarly, and using zip code level data, Bondonio and Greenbaum (2007) did a sample of EZ programs from ten US states and the District of Columbia over a ten-year period and compared various economic trends and outcomes to comparable non-EZ zip codes. Pre-test and post-test measurements and regression were used in a study which tried to come as close to an experimental design as possible, although the authors admit that randomized experiments are impossible in EZ evaluations.

In research that mimics to a certain degree quasi-experimental design, the federal government allows airports in the US to 'opt-out' of having US Homeland Security Transportation Security (TSA) Administration personnel perform screening of luggage and passengers as long as such private security companies meet TSA security and performance requirements. There are 25 approved airports for participation, and as of 2012, 16 were actively participating (GAO 2012). The comparisons and differences between the private and government security screening efforts have sparked much debate, not only about airport security privatization but also about the accuracy of the methods used for the comparisons (Frances Kernodle Associates 2006).

Another series of papers using quasi-experimental design to evaluate local urban and regional economic policy involved studies on the Louisville-Jefferson County, Kentucky EZ by Lambert (1997), Cummings and Lambert (1997), Lambert and Coomes (2001), and Lambert and Nelson (2002). These research efforts and papers were made possible by grants from the Louisville Board of Aldermen and were instrumental in policy debate and influencing decisions in the state of Kentucky with regard to EZ policies and their continuance (Office of the State Budget Director 2002; Richards-Hill 2001). In section 27.3, they are summarized in order to illustrate quasi-experimental design implementation. However, first, in section 27.2, a discussion of external and internal validity is needed.

## 27.2   VALIDITY: EXTERNAL AND INTERNAL

The validity of an experiment or quasi-experiment refers to events or occurrences that could undermine valid conclusions from the experiment. One wants to know if what is being tested is also being measured accurately before, during, and after the experiment. There are two types of validity: internal and external. Internal validity refers to whether the experiment is set up appropriately and has appropriate controls to prevent outside interference that could confound experimental results and their interpretation (Babbie 2013). Threats to internal validity from outside events include the following:

- Maturation. These are the developments within subjects which act as a function of the passage of time. For example, if an experiment lasts a few years, such as a new curriculum innovation in a school, most participants may improve their performance regardless of treatment or exposure to the new curriculum.
- Selection. These are the biases which may come about in the selection of control or

comparison groups. Random assignment of group membership is a counter-attack against this threat.

- Sample mortality or subject(s) attrition. Loss of experimental or test subjects as time passes.
- Testing. The effects of taking a test on the outcomes of taking a subsequent test. Improvements in test scores may come about not so much to treatment effects but because participants become better at taking the same test repeatedly.
- Instrumentation. A change in the assessment instrument. For example, giving a pre-test, and then a completely different post-test which may be easier or more difficult than the pre-test.
- History. Between the introduction of the treatment and the measurement of outcomes, other events can intervene. For example, in local and regional policy, new governmental programs (new job training programs for residents, grants for small businesses in the area) can be introduced as other incentives are under way.
- Regression toward the mean. If during the random selection, worse or extreme subjects are chosen for either group, any improvement by the experimental group will look good and tend toward any average.

External validity is also known as the concept of 'reliability'. That is, research findings can be replicated in other experiments, perhaps by other experimenters, in other tests with different subjects or with different regions. The biggest threat to external validity would therefore be the inability to replicate findings anywhere else, and this is often because of the fact that experiments using human participants often use small samples obtained from a single geographic location or with idiosyncratic features (for example, volunteers). These samples are often not representative of a larger population about which inferences are desired. Because of this, one cannot be sure that the conclusions drawn about cause–effect relationships do actually apply to people in other geographic locations or to people without these features. With regard to regional policy, it is hard or impossible to replicate treatments or incentives and make inferences about local and state government policies to other jurisdictions in the US, and so any inferences about causality have to be limited to only certain similar jurisdictions. For this reason, studies of EZ policies and incentives were mostly limited to one state (for example, California – Dowall 1996; or New Jersey) or one city–county area (for example, Louisville-Jefferson County, Kentucky).

For quasi-experiments, selection is the greatest threat to internal validity. Therefore, great care has to be exercised in choosing control or comparison groups in trying to get as close a match as possible to the treatment group. Also, external validity or reliability is obviously a concern, although careful consideration of the results would warrant that limitations to study outcomes are necessary. This perhaps limits the inferences of quasi-experimentation and its usefulness, but in the absence of the possibility of using a regular experiment, it is a viable alternative.

## 27.3 APPLYING QUASI-EXPERIMENTATION

The primary research design used by Lambert (1997), Cummings and Lambert (1997), Lambert and Coomes (2001), and Lambert and Nelson (2002) for the Louisville EZ studies was a quasi-experiment using two groups and before and after testing or data as discussed by Cook and Campbell in *Quasi-Experimentation* (1979) and Caporaso and Roos (1973). Quasi-experimentation played a role in these studies because it was essential to compare and contrast similar areas within Louisville-Jefferson County, Kentucky. Since local county incentives (for example, the waiver of certain planning and zoning fees) were mixed in with state incentives, it would not have been accurate to compare the Louisville EZ to other EZs that existed in the state. Areas within the county that received the economic development stimulus of EZ incentives (such as state capital gains tax, sales tax exemptions and motor vehicle use tax exemptions) were compared to counterpart areas in the county that did not receive the benefits of EZ incentives. These counterpart or comparison or control areas were chosen because of their similarity either to the entire EZ or its sub-areas.

The EZ incentives were designed to stimulate economic activity and entrepreneurial and/or existing business activity within targeted areas and thereby help to alleviate problems of high unemployment, blight, and poverty (Kentucky Revised Statutes 1994, 154.45). In general, those census tracts in the county that had fallen below a certain poverty level and had had higher than normal unemployment rates for a given period of time were eligible for EZ status and participation. Also, many tracts contiguous to those census tracts meeting eligibility requirements were allowed to participate in the EZ so long as the averages of all the tracts participating in the program fell below the thresholds established for program participation.[1]

If the economic incentives accomplished their mission, then one would expect to see changes occurring within the EZ or its component areas that were not occurring in the control areas over a given time period. For example, if EZ incentives were successful, then one would expect that unemployment and blight would decrease in the EZ at rates higher than comparable areas not eligible for incentives. Also, according to the logic of the legislation, one should see substantial job and business growth as well as new construction in the EZ over time, but not in the control or comparison communities. Such incentives would be expected to reverse the decline previously experienced in an EZ designated area. Perhaps the EZ area could even be expected to overtake those portions of the county not included in the EZ in terms of growth rates of job and business creation as well as growth rates of residential and commercial investment. Finally, one would expect to see a stop to the outward migration from an EZ designated area over time. On the other hand, if incentives did not work, one would expect to see continued economic decline and outward migration from EZ neighborhoods at a rate greater than or equal to that experienced by control or comparison areas. Similarly, one would expect to see job and business growth within the EZ to continue to at least remain flat, if not continue to decline, when compared to other areas of the county which did not receive EZ incentives. In order to implement the quasi-experiment, it was necessary to have a pre-test and a series of post-tests, and control communities that are as close to being identical as possible in all respects save for the presence of the EZ incentives. In the Louisville EZ studies, several outcome measures spanning the years 1980 to 1997 or 2000 were used to evaluate the EZ program. Next follows a brief outline of the outcome measures and data sources used in the studies, an overview of some tabular results, and then a comparison of the results of the different studies to other assessment results performed for this chapter.

Jefferson County census tract data for 1980 were listed in descending order according to levels of poverty, household income, unemployment, and outward population migration.[2] Those census tracts which came closest to EZ census tracts with regard to these variables, yet were not in the EZ area, were chosen as control groups. Using data from the Census Bureau's 1980 *County Business Patterns*, the number of jobs in census tracts that corresponded to EZ areas were estimated and compared to other Jefferson County tracts that corresponded to the EZ control group tracts.[3] Since the EZ was started in mid-1983 and allowed to end in mid-2003, the 1980 census data and the 1980 County Business Patterns data serve as 'pre-test' or baseline data to be compared to 1990 data (short-run 'post-test' results) and 1997 or 2000 data (long-run post-test results).[4]

Because the EZ was expanded several times beyond its original 1983 boundaries, comparisons over the decades were made between: (1) the original EZ and a similar census tract or neighborhood in another part of Jefferson County where both areas only encompassed only a few square miles; (2) an area taken in by the 1984 expansion (a 3 square mile area containing the Louisville airport with a United Parcel Service, hub and its complementary enterprises and a few adjacent tracts) to the rest of Jefferson County outside of the EZ which included several major local industrial parks; (3) its 1986 expansion area (around 38 square miles) with the rest of Jefferson County outside of the EZ area, because the 1986 expansion area along with the first two versions of the EZ now encompassed around 46 square miles; and (4) the entire EZ with all of Jefferson County.[5] For the purposes of assessing job creation, a similar approach was taken except that the 1984 EZ expansion area, which included major United Parcel Service (UPS) shipping operations and other establishments, was compared to a major industrial park in a part of the county that was not in the EZ. The maps in Figures 27.1–27.4 show the growth of the EZ program from the original EZ area through subsequent

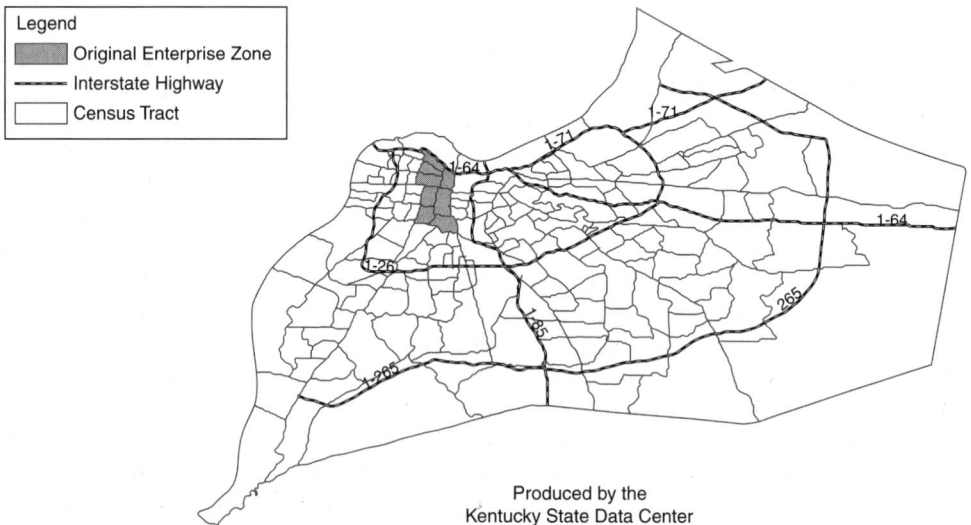

*Figure 27.1   Jefferson County: original enterprise zone*

expansions which continued until the late 1990s. As one can see, the program's geographic focus changed radically over time, as it grew from a program targeted toward a small economically distressed area to one that encompassed roughly one-third of the county's size.

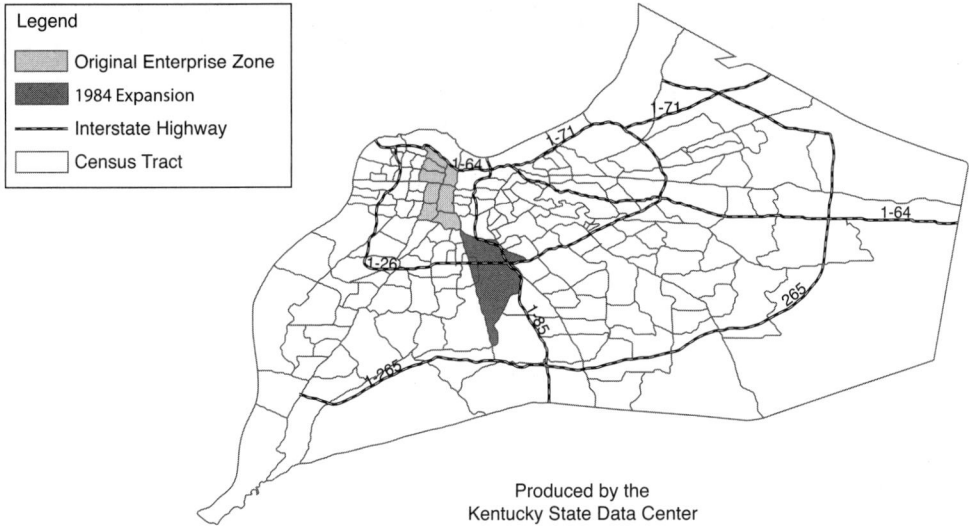

*Figure 27.2   Jefferson County: 1984 expansion of the enterprise zone*

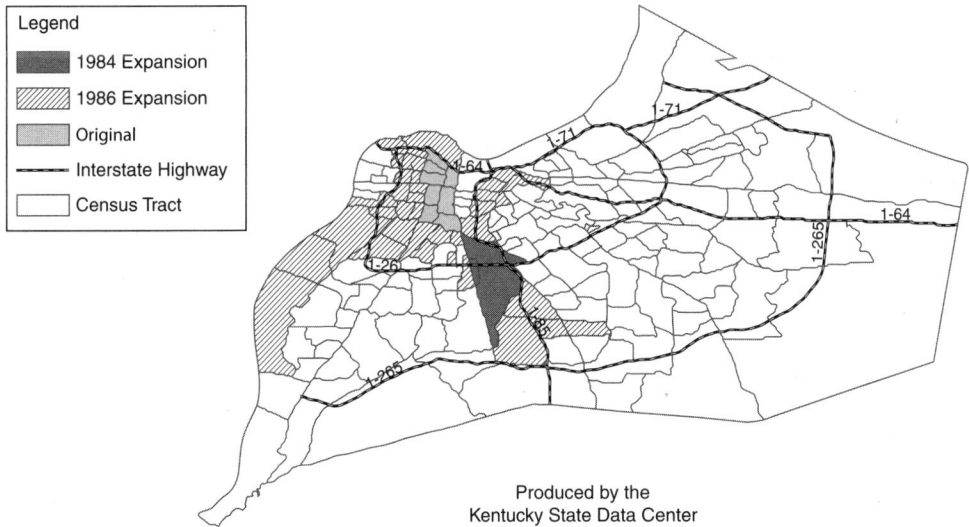

*Figure 27.3   Jefferson County: 1986 expansion of the enterprise zone*

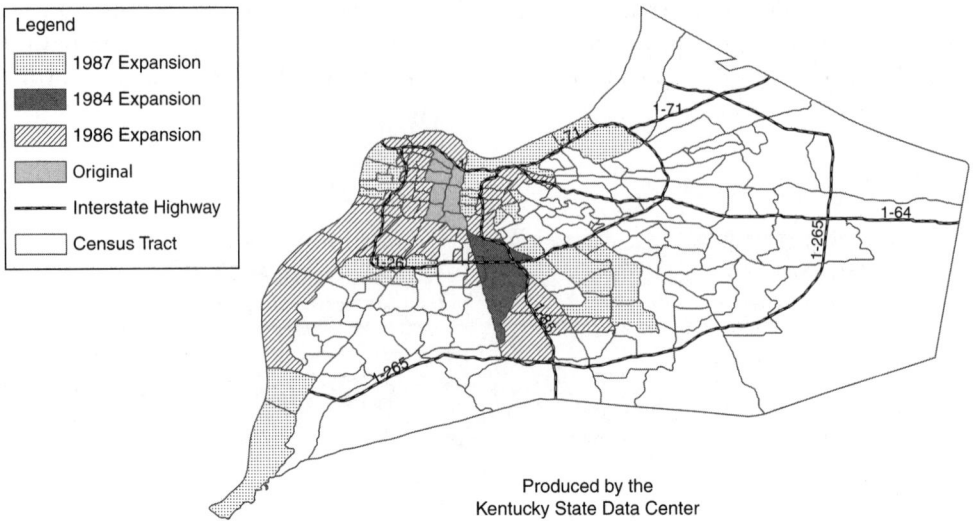

*Figure 27.4   Jefferson County: 1997 and later expansions*

**1980 to 1990**

In looking at Table 27.1, all the regions examined lost population during the decade, with the EZ areas showing the worse performance, although during this time the 1984 EZ addition had most of its population loss due to the expansion of the Louisville airport in which homes were bought and neighborhoods razed by the state and local governments with financial assistance from the Federal Aviation Administration (Lambert 1997; Cummings and Lambert 1997; Lambert and Coomes 2001). Therefore, EZ incentives do not appear to have had much if any impact with regard to outward migration, all else held constant.

Table 27.2 shows improvement in the unemployment rates in all areas except for the 1984 EZ addition. The other EZ areas showed greater drops in unemployment than their counterparts, although by 1990, their rates of unemployment were still around 1.5 to three times higher than their counterparts. If most of the people leaving these areas in the 1980s were unemployed, then that could explain why the EZ areas had greater drops in unemployment rates than the comparison areas, although this is not entirely possible to pinpoint from the census data.[6] Nonetheless, to give the incentives the benefit of the doubt, the unemployment rate improvements in the EZ are attributed to the incentives, and we assume that the incentives have made a difference here.

In looking at the income level changes from 1980 to 1990 (Table 27.3), the EZ areas showed gains, but not as great as those of the control or comparison areas. Holding all else constant, one cannot conclude that EZ incentives made a contribution to income increases in the EZ areas.

With regard to poverty alleviation, Table 27.4 shows that families in poverty became worse in all portions of Jefferson County, EZ or otherwise. This reflects US national trends of increasing poverty rates during the 1980s after poverty rates reached historical

Table 27.1 *Population changes, 1980–90*

| | Original EZ | | | 1984 EZ addition | | | 1986 EZ addition | | | Total EZ | | |
|---|---|---|---|---|---|---|---|---|---|---|---|---|
| | 1980 | 1990 | % Chg. | 1980 | 1990 | % Chg. | 1980 | 1990 | % Chg. | 1980 | 1990 | % Chg. |
| Population | 13241 | 10811 | −11.9 | 3990 | 2303 | −42.3 | 101265 | 86844 | −14.2 | 118502 | 100024 | −15.6 |

| | Comparison area for original EZ | | | Jefferson Co. outside EZ | | | Jefferson County | | |
|---|---|---|---|---|---|---|---|---|---|
| | 1980 | 1990 | % Chg. | 1980 | 1990 | % Chg. | 1980 | 1990 | % Chg. |
| Population | 26119 | 26439 | −1 | 566502 | 564913 | −0.3 | 685004 | 664931 | −2.9 |

Table 27.2 *Unemployment rates, 1980–90*

| | Original EZ | | | 1984 EZ addition | | | 1986 EZ addition | | | Total EZ | | |
|---|---|---|---|---|---|---|---|---|---|---|---|---|
| | 1980 | 1990 | % Chg. | 1980 | 1990 | % Chg. | 1980 | 1990 | % Chg. | 1980 | 1990 | % Chg. |
| Unemployment | 26.1 | 22.9 | −3.2 | 7.6 | 8.3 | 0.7 | 15.2 | 13 | −2.2 | 16.3 | 13.7 | −2.6 |

| | Comparison area for original EZ | | | Jefferson Co. outside EZ | | | Jefferson County | | |
|---|---|---|---|---|---|---|---|---|---|
| | 1980 | 1990 | % Chg. | 1980 | 1990 | % Chg. | 1980 | 1990 | % Chg. |
| Unemployment | 8.7 | 8.4 | −0.3 | 6.6 | 5.1 | −1.5 | 7.9 | 6.1 | −1.8 |

Table 27.3  Income levels, 1980–90

| | Original EZ | | | 1984 EZ addition | | | 1986 EZ addition | | | Total EZ | | |
|---|---|---|---|---|---|---|---|---|---|---|---|---|
| | 1980 | 1990 | % Chg. | 1980 | 1990 | % Chg. | 1980 | 1990 | % Chg. | 1980 | 1990 | % Chg. |
| Avg. hh. inc. | $8296 | $11132 | 34.2 | $14710 | $21605 | 46.9 | $12290 | $19849 | 61.8 | $11897 | $18913 | 59 |

| | Comparison area for original EZ | | | Jefferson Co. outside EZ | | | Jefferson County | | |
|---|---|---|---|---|---|---|---|---|---|
| | 1980 | 1990 | % Chg. | 1980 | 1990 | % Chg. | 1980 | 1990 | % Chg. |
| Avg. hh. inc. | $16935 | $23987 | 41.6 | $21491 | $37715 | 75.4 | $19879 | $35079 | 76.5 |

Table 27.4  Poverty levels, 1980–90

| | Original EZ | | | 1984 EZ addition | | | 1986 EZ addition | | | Total EZ | | |
|---|---|---|---|---|---|---|---|---|---|---|---|---|
| | 1980 | 1990 | % Chg. | 1980 | 1990 | % Chg. | 1980 | 1990 | % Chg. | 1980 | 1990 | % Chg. |
| % below poverty | 48.80 | 64.40 | 15.60 | 17.00 | 26.30 | 9.30 | 28.90 | 34.30 | 5.40 | 27.80 | 37.40 | 6.6 |

| | Comparison area for original EZ | | | Jefferson Co. outside EZ | | | Jefferson County | | |
|---|---|---|---|---|---|---|---|---|---|
| | 1980 | 1990 | % Chg. | 1980 | 1990 | % Chg. | 1980 | 1990 | % Chg. |
| % below poverty | 14.9 | 23.4 | 8.5 | 8.3 | 9.9 | 1.6 | 12.2 | 14 | 1.8 |

lows in the 1970s (US Bureau of the Census 2013). However, the EZ areas had greater increases in poverty than their counterparts. Therefore, EZ incentives do not seem to have had much of an impact with regard to EZ program goals of reducing poverty, *ceteris paribus*.

Finally, during the 1980s, most of the EZ regions showed slight or large job losses with the exception of the 1984 EZ addition. Table 27.5 shows a big gain in jobs for the industrial park area, even greater than that for the 1984 EZ addition, its counterpart for comparison purposes. The comparison area to the original EZ has small job losses, whereas job growth in Jefferson County as a whole was a modest 12.78 percent. One could claim that EZ incentives were successful in the 1984 addition, although not in the other locales that received incentives, especially in the original EZ area. The 1984 addition also received more than $0.5 billion in local, state, and federal government assistance in order to expand the Louisville airport, which in turn helped increase the level of employment at UPS from 1000 in 1981 to more than 14 000 by 1996, although most of the jobs were part-time (Lambert and Coomes 2001; Lambert and Nelson 2002). In an interview, UPS confirmed that EZ incentives made a difference with respect to its expansion decisions, although in a survey of around two-thirds of the 1200 or so firms in the EZ that also signed up and were allowed to participate in the EZ program, around 26.5 percent of the survey's respondents said that the EZ incentives had helped to save or retain existing jobs, and a little less than half of the respondents (48.5 percent) said that EZ incentives had helped to create new jobs (Lambert 1997; Cummings and Lambert 1997; Lambert and Coomes 2001).

In the early 1990s, local and state officials claimed that around 24 000 new jobs had been created and/or saved in the entire EZ thanks to the incentives, although later this estimate was trimmed to 18 000 jobs created and 'thousands of more jobs saved'. The survey results of EZ participating firms estimated around 6333 jobs created and/or saved. This number would only be around one-third of the Office of Economic Development (OED) claim of 18 000 jobs created, although admittedly, not all EZ firms were interviewed in the survey.

The fact that success could be measured by jobs created and/or saved made evaluating the EZ areas through census jobs data difficult because the jobs data shown in Table 27.5 only show net gains or losses. The data cannot show something like the specific number of 'jobs retained'. On the one hand, the fact that the 1984 addition grew dramatically, and that job losses could have been worse in other EZ areas than would have been the case otherwise had the EZ not existed, could support claims of EZ job creation and retention success. On the other hand, given that the EZ areas came up short with respect to their non-EZ counterparts in total job creation during the decade, there can be some doubt created with regard to these claims, especially since the control or comparison areas received no other incentives besides those offered to all firms, EZ or otherwise, throughout the county by state and local governments, although most of these incentives were given to large EZ participating firms such as UPS and Ford Motor Company (Lambert and Coomes 2001). In fact, the only other 'location'-specific program that offered incentives was the Louisville Foreign Trade Zone (FTZ),[7] a federal customs and fees deferment and waiver program, of which all of its participating firms were located in the EZ with the exception of one, General Electric's Appliance Park, which was located in the comparison area juxtaposed to the original EZ in the studies. Yet, this comparison area also suffered slight job losses from 1980 to 1990 (Lambert and Coomes 2001; Lambert and Nelson 2002).[8]

In summary, the results from the 1980s for the EZ program are mixed at best. In general, the EZ regions came up short when compared to their control counterparts. There were some improvements in all or some areas for some of the variables (unemployment in general, and jobs in the 1984 addition, for example), but not to the same degree as counterpart regions.

**1980 to 2000**

In examining longer-term results in Table 27.6, the EZ areas still did not perform as well as their control group counterparts. All EZ regions continued to lose population as their counterparts gained population. There were improvements in the unemployment rate for all EZ areas, and at greater rates of improvement than the control areas. Yet the 2000 unemployment rates were still much higher than in the comparison areas, and the improvements in the EZ area unemployment rates could mostly be due to population losses, since the civilian labor force continued to shrink in the EZ areas. Table 27.6 also shows that only the 1986 EZ addition showed gains in income comparable to control group areas, whereas other EZ regions, although the income gains were good, failed to keep up with their counterparts. Finally, over the 20-year time period, there were improvements in poverty rates in three of the four EZ areas, although the poverty rates remained very high in each one compared to the control groups. In fact, poverty increased in the original EZ as well as the comparison area, although the overall poverty rate in the original EZ was the highest of all regions at over 50 percent.

Table 27.7 shows continued job losses in the original EZ and the total EZ, although there were big improvements in the 1984 EZ addition and in the 1986 EZ addition to a lesser degree. Overall, however, the EZ areas did worse in job creation, with the exception of the 1984 EZ addition in comparison to the counterpart or control groups.

Long-run results therefore show mixed results at best, which was the case with short-run outcomes. There were improvements in the EZ regions in the variables examined, but these were not to the same degree in terms of improvement as in the control groups.

## 27.4   COMPARING QUASI-EXPERIMENT RESULTS TO BEFORE AND AFTER T-TEST RESULTS

If adequate control groups cannot be found for a quasi-experimental design, and yet a researcher wants to try to draw some conclusions about the efficacy of an intervention, then one option is a simple before-and-after test wherein only pre- and post-tests are conducted on the target groups:

Before and after:         $O_1$        X        $O_2$

This method is subject to greater threats to validity (for example, regression toward the mean) than a regular or quasi-experimental group, but absent random assignment for a regular experiment or roughly comparable control groups for a quasi-experiment,

Table 27.5  Jobs, 1980–90

| | Original EZ | | | 1984 EZ addition | | | 1986 EZ addition | | | Total EZ | | |
|---|---|---|---|---|---|---|---|---|---|---|---|---|
| | 1980 | 1990 | % Chg. | 1980 | 1990 | % Chg. | 1980 | 1990 | % Chg. | 1980 | 1990 | % Chg. |
| Jobs | 26383 | 19493 | –26.12 | 13829 | 20221 | 46.22 | 63279 | 62651 | –0.99 | 103491 | 102365 | –1.09 |

| | Comparison area for original EZ | | | Industrial park | | | Jefferson County | | |
|---|---|---|---|---|---|---|---|---|---|
| | 1980 | 1990 | % Chg. | 1980 | 1990 | % Chg. | 1980 | 1990 | % Chg. |
| Jobs | 34167 | 34061 | –0.31 | 8116 | 15751 | 94.07 | 296677 | 334590 | 12.78 |

Table 27.6  Population, unemployment, income, and poverty, 1980–2000

| | Original EZ | | | 1984 EZ addition | | | 1986 EZ expansion | | | Total EZ | | |
|---|---|---|---|---|---|---|---|---|---|---|---|---|
| | 1980 | 2000 | % Chg. | 1980 | 2000 | % Chg. | 1980 | 2000 | % Chg. | 1980 | 2000 | % Chg. |
| Population | 13247 | 7132 | –46.2% | 3990 | 1653 | –58.6% | 101265 | 84580 | –16.5% | 118502 | 82009 | –30.8% |
| Unemployment | 26.10% | 19.30% | –6.8% | 7.60% | 4.90% | –2.7% | 15.20% | 9.90% | –5.3% | 16.30% | 10.70% | –5.6% |
| Avg. household inc. | $8296 | $14829 | 78.7% | $14710 | $24950 | 69.6% | $12290 | $33184 | 170.0% | $11897 | $30217 | 154.0% |
| % below poverty | 48.80% | 52.50% | 3.7% | 17.00% | 14.70% | –2.3% | 28.90% | 22.00% | –6.9% | 30.80% | 25.50% | –5.3% |

| | Comparison area for original EZ | | | Jefferson Co. outside of EZ | | | Jefferson County | | |
|---|---|---|---|---|---|---|---|---|---|
| | 1980 | 2000 | % Chg. | 1980 | 2000 | % Chg. | 1980 | 2000 | % Chg. |
| Population | 26719 | 28890 | 8.1% | 566502 | 611595 | 8.0% | 685004 | 693604 | 1.3% |
| Unemployment | 8.70% | 8.50% | –0.2% | 6.60% | 4.10% | –2.5% | 7.90% | 5.00% | –2.9% |
| Avg. household inc. | $16935 | $34895 | 106.1% | $21497 | $53967 | 151.0% | $19879 | $52893 | 166.1% |
| % below poverty | 14.90% | 16.70% | 1.8% | 8.30% | 7.40% | –0.9% | 12.20% | 9.50% | –2.7% |

Table 27.7  *Jobs, 1980–1997*

|  | Original EZ | | | 1984 EZ addtion | | | 1986 EZ addition | | | Total EZ | | |
|---|---|---|---|---|---|---|---|---|---|---|---|---|
|  | 1980 | 1997 | % Chg. | 1980 | 1997 | % Chg. | 1980 | 1997 | % Chg. | 1980 | 1997 | % Chg. |
| Jobs | 26 383 | 18 224 | −30.9% | 13 829 | 29 566 | 113.8% | 63 279 | 65 723 | 3.9% | 103 491 | 95 289 | −7.9% |

|  | Comparison area for original EZ | | | Industrial park | | | Jefferson County | | |
|---|---|---|---|---|---|---|---|---|---|
|  | 1980 | 1997 | % Chg. | 1980 | 1997 | % Chg. | 1980 | 1997 | % Chg. |
| Jobs | 34 167 | 31 712 | −7.2% | 8116 | 23 256 | 186.5% | 296 677 | 396 534 | 33.7% |

this may be a researcher's best option. To try to bolster one's findings, a t-test for the means for paired groups can be used. This is often referred to a before-and-after t-test in a matched sample design where the same participants or entities are evaluated according to the group's mean performances on pre- and post-tests (Anderson et al. 2011, Ch. 10). The two samples are 'matched' in that they are the same cases or entities tested before and after an intervention occurred, such as a new training program for workers or tax incentives for businesses. The equation is:

$$t = \frac{\bar{d} - \mu_d}{s_d / \sqrt{n}} \qquad (27.1)$$

where $\bar{d}$ is the average of the differences in results or performance between the participants or cases on pre- and post-tests; $\mu_d$ is the hypothesized difference, usually 0; $s_d$ is the sample standard deviation; and $n$ is the sample size. If $t$ is a value outside of the rejection region given by the cut-off value(s) from a t-distribution, the null hypothesis of zero as a value for the average of the differences is rejected and the difference is deemed to be statistically significant.

In doing t-tests where 1980 results are compared to 1990 and then to 1997 or 2000 results for the four EZ areas, it is appropriate to do one-tailed tests for all the variables examined since improvement was the goal of EZ incentives. Table 27.8 shows t-test results. Using an upper tailed test and testing for population gains, the t-test showed no statistically significant difference between 1980 and 1990 EZ population numbers, as well as for 1980 to 2000 population numbers. In fact, the average difference was around a 10000 population loss from 1980 to 1990, and average difference of a 15000 person loss from 1980 to 2000. For unemployment, there was not a statistically significant average difference from 1980 to 1990, but there was from 1980 to 2000 (p-value < 0.05). There were statistically significant gains in household income for both time periods, and the gains of around $7000 per decade average out to be increases of 6.4 percent per year.

*Table 27.8   t-test results*

| Variable | Mean difference 1980–90 | p-value |
|---|---|---|
| *Population* | −9254 | 0.0585 |
| *Unemployment Rate* | −1.83% | 0.062895 |
| *Average Household Income* | $6076.50 | 0.005693 |
| *% Below Poverty* | 9.23% | 0.013529 |
| *Jobs* | −563 | 0.424614 |
| Variable | Mean difference 1980–2000 | p-value |
| *Population* | −15407.50 | 0.068831 |
| *Unemployment Rate* | −5.1% | 0.004841 |
| *Average Household Income* | $13996.75 | 0.012661 |
| *% Below Poverty* | −2.7% | 0.165781 |
| Variable | Mean difference 1980–97 | p-value |
| *Jobs* | 455 | 0.47058 |

According to the US Bureau of Labor Statistics, it took $2.09 to have the same purchasing power as $1.00 in 1980, indicating an overall doubling in prices over the 20-year period (US Bureau of Labor Statistics 2013). Average income for the four EZ areas went from around $12 000 in 1980 to almost $26 000 in 2000, so the average increases in income were just enough to push average household income for all EZ areas a little above what they would have been had they just kept up with inflation alone.

With regard to poverty, the t-test shows statistically significant results from comparing 1980 to 1990 poverty levels, but only because poverty rates increased. On the other hand, there is no statistically significant average difference between 1980 and 2000 poverty results as poverty rates started to decline in these areas in the 1990s. For jobs, whether for 1980 to 1990 comparisons or for 1980 to 1997 comparisons, the average differences are not statistically significant for the EZ areas. The average difference for each time period was a loss of around 600 jobs for 1980 to 1990, and a gain of around 500 from 1980 to 2000.

Based on these t-test results, the overall performance of the EZ seems to appear to be slightly better than was shown in the quasi-experiment results, although one would probably still judge the results mixed at best using the criteria or objectives of the original enabling statute passed in the early 1980s. Of course, the t-test outcomes are on the basis of before-and-after testing and do not involve any comparisons with any type of control groups. The absence of such groups would cause some to argue that the t-test analysis is an oversimplification and has threats to validity that are controlled for in a quasi-experimental design: history, regression toward the mean, maturation, repeated testing, and subject attrition.

## 27.5   CONCLUSION

From the various reports issued from 1997 to 2002, most of them relying upon quasi-experimental design, the Louisville EZ program was judged to be a mixed success at best, with only some original program goals that could be considered accomplished. However, there was some doubt as to whether EZ incentives really made the difference. In fact, the Kentucky Office of the State Budget Director issued a report (2002) that noted that it also found little evidence of strong EZ success, and that 50 percent of EZ tax incentives and benefits went to the eight largest firms in the EZ program; firms such as Ford Motor Company, General Electric, United Parcel Service, and so on. This was contrary to the original enterprise zone concept envisioned by some who thought that the focus should be on small entrepreneurs and small businesses (Hall 1982; Butler 1981, 1991, 1992). Additionally, zones were envisioned to be small geographically, mostly centered on one or a few neighborhoods.

In 2002, the Kentucky Legislative Research Commission found the same results for the other nine EZs in Kentucky. The LRC wrote:

> Comparisons of economic data from the zones provide little indication that the economic well-being of the residents in the zones has improved since the creation of the program. While the decline in the areas may have even been more dramatic without zone designation, the analysis indicates that enterprise zone areas continued to decline economically relative to their counties and the state. (Kentucky Legislative Research Commission 2002)

In fact, in a comprehensive study it was found by Fisher and Peters (2002) that most state EZ programs had low to modest success, with only a few performing quite well. For these reasons and because of the other studies mentioned in this report, the Kentucky General Assembly decided not to extend or renew the EZ program for any of the ten EZ programs in the state beyond their 20-year terms (Richards-Hill 2001). Although perhaps not considered as sound a method as regular experimentation, which has the feature of random selection, the results of quasi-experimental design in several Louisville-Jefferson County EZ studies seemed to be strong enough to influence policy-makers to try other economic development programs instead of continuing the EZ program.

## NOTES

1.  More specifically, under the EZ enabling statute, the average unemployment rate in a proposed zone census tract had to be at least 1.5 times greater than the national average for an 18-month period. Also, 70 percent of the people in the zone were to have incomes below 80 percent of the city's median income, or the area must have lost 10 percent or more of its population between 1970 and 1980.
2.  Other variables such as demographics, occupational status, housing variables, and the educational attainment of residents were examined, but for the purposes of this chapter, the focus will be on the three most important variables addressed in the enabling statue.
3.  At the tract level, the Census Bureau identifies the number of people who report working regardless of whether their job or work is in the tract. Job numbers at the sub-county level can be found at the zip code level using the census's County Business Patterns database. Using a method similar to Dowall (1996), tract-level jobs data were estimated by finding tract boundaries that corresponded to zip code boundaries as closely as possible. Pro-rating the zip code job numbers was necessary when zip code boundaries were greater than tract boundaries. When two or more tracts made up a zip code, zip code employment numbers were allocated to each tract according to each tract's population size.
4.  The year 1997 was the last year that the Standard Industrial Code (SIC) classification was used for zip code-level jobs data. After that year, the North American Industrial Classification System (NAICS) was used by the Census Bureau to classify industries and jobs at the zip code level. Many industries were reclassified in the transition between the two sets of codes, and changes were made in code numbering. Because of the differences between SIC and NAICS codes and the lack of continuity in some of the data from one code to another, comparisons from 1980 to 1997 at the zip code level were used instead of 1980 to 2000.
5.  There was another expansion of the EZ in 1999 which took in a General Electric factory site, but no neighborhoods were included, and since the EZ was slated to end in 2003, this area was not examined in the 2002 study.
6.  However, the census data did show that there were declines in the eligible civilian labor force in each of the EZ areas from around 12–43 percent, whereas the comparison areas had gains from 0.3 to 6.2 percent. Therefore, this may cause one to doubt the impact of EZ incentives with regard to the declines in the unemployment rates.
7.  Although originally meant for firms located at ports – ocean, river, or airports – foreign trade sub-zones were later created to enable firms engaging in foreign trade but not located in or next to a port to participate in the FTZ program (Lambert and Nelson 2002).
8.  A simple arithmetic technique called shift-share or mix-share analysis was employed to see, after controlling for overall trends in a reference region (national, state, or county) and reference region industry-specific trends, if any possible local factors could be used to explain job gains or losses. Although shift-share analysis cannot pinpoint specific factors and is a residual that only shows job growth/loss that cannot be explained by overall reference-region job growth trends and industry-specific trends, it is often used in urban and regional analysis (Blair 1995). For all the EZ regions examined with the exception of the 1984 addition (the Louisville airport area) there were still job losses after controlling for overall county and county-level industry-specific trends within the county. The control areas, other than Jefferson County itself, showed only gains after controlling for other trends. When compared to the nation, Jefferson County showed losses, indicating that its growth was behind that of overall national job growth and industry-specific growth. When the other regions are compared to US trends, all of them except for the industrial park and the 1984 EZ addition showed losses, with the EZ areas faring worse than their control counterparts.

# REFERENCES

Anderson, David R., Dennis J. Sweeney, and Thomas A. Williams (2011), 'Chapter 10: Inference about means and proportions with two populations', in *Statistics for Business and Economics*, 11th edn, Independence, KY: Cengage Learning, pp. 406–47.
Babbie, Earl R. (2013), *The Practice of Social Research*, 13th edn. Independence, KY: Cengage Learning.
Blair, John P. (1995), *Local Economic Development: Analysis and Practice*, Thousand Oaks, CA: Sage Publications.
Boarnet, M.G. and W.T. Bogart (1996), 'Enterprise zones and employment: evidence from New Jersey', *Journal of Urban Economics*, **40** (2), 198–215.
Bondonio, Daniele and Robert T. Greenbaum (2007), 'Do local tax incentives affect economic growth? What mean impacts miss in the analysis of enterprise zone policies', *Regional Science and Urban Economics*, **37** (1), 121–36.
Butler, Stuart (1981), *Enterprise Zones: Greenlining the Inner Cities*, New York: Universe Books.
Butler, Stuart (1991), 'The conceptual evolution of the enterprise zones', in Roy E. Green (ed.), *Enterprise Zones: New Directions in Economic Development*, Newbury Park, CA: Sage Publications, pp. 27–40.
Butler, Stuart (1992), 'Testimony before the Subcommittee on Select Revenue Measures, Committee on Ways and Means, House of Representatives, US Congress', 102nd Congress, 1st Session, June 25 and July 11.
Caporaso, James A. and Leslie L. Roos, Jr (1973), *Quasi-Experimental Approaches: Testing Theory and Evaluating Policy*, Evanston, IL: Northwestern University Press.
Cook, Thomas D. and Donald T. Campbell (1979), *Quasi-Experimentation: Design and Analysis Issues for Field Settings*, Boston, MA: Houghton Mifflin Co.
Cummings, Scott B. and Thomas E. Lambert (1997), *A Performance Evaluation of Louisville's Enterprise Zone*, Louisville, KY: University of Louisville, Urban Studies Institute, Center for Policy Research and Evaluation.
Dowall, David E. (1996), 'An evaluation of California's enterprise zone programs', *Economic Development Quarterly*, **10** (4), 352–68.
Dunn, William F. (2012), *Public Policy Analysis*, 5th edn, New York: Pearson Publishing.
Fisher, Peter S. and Alan H. Peters (2002), *State Enterprise Zone Programs: Have They Worked?*, Kalamazoo, MI: W.E. Upjohn Institute for Employment Research.
Frances Kernodle Associates (2006), *Federal vs. Private-Security Screeners: Where's the buzz?*, accessed December 22, 2013 at http://www.fkassociates.com/Fed%20vs%20Private%20Security%20Screeners.html.
Hall, Peter (1982), 'Enterprise zones: a justification', *International Journal of Urban and Regional Research*, **6** (3), 416–21.
Institute for Research on Poverty, University of Wisconsin (2013), 'Negative income tax', accessed May 27, 2013 at http://www.irp.wisc.edu/research/nit.htm
Kentucky Legislative Research Commission (2002), *The Costs, Benefits, and Monitoring of Kentucky's Enterprise Zones*, Frankfort, KY: Program Review and Investigations Committee Staff Report.
Kentucky Revised Statutes (1994), *Kentucky Revised Statues*, 1994 Edition, Subchapter 45: Enterprise Zone Development, pp. 412–23.
Kettl, Donald F. (2011), *The Politics of the Administrative Process*, 5th edn, Thousand Oaks, CA: CQ Press/Sage.
Kraft, Michael E. and Scott R. Furlong (2013), *Public Policy: Politics, Analysis and Alternatives*, 4th edn, Thousand Oaks, CA: CQ Press/Sage.
Lambert, Thomas E. (1997), 'A program evaluation of the Louisville Enterprise Zone: a study of local planning and economic development', unpublished doctoral dissertation, University of Louisville, Louisville, KY.
Lambert, Thomas E. and Paul A. Coomes (2001), 'An evaluation of the effectiveness of Louisville's enterprise zone', *Economic Development Quarterly*, **15** (2), 168–80.
Lambert, Thomas E. and John P. Nelson III (2002), 'A second look at Louisville's enterprise zone and a review of other local business incentives', Louisville, KY: Spalding University, School of Business.
Meyer, Bruce (1995), 'Quasi and natural experiments in economics', *Journal of Business and Economics*, **13** (2), 151–61.
Office of the State Budget Director (2002), 'The costs of Kentucky's enterprise zones', Policy Paper Series 2, Issue 1, Frankfort, KY: Commonwealth of Kentucky.
Richards-Hill, Toya (2001), 'Enterprise zone program's end means more expenses for participating companies', *Business First*, June 2, accessed January 6, 2014 at http://www.bizjournals.com/louisville/stories/2003/06/02/story2.html.
Rivlin, Alice M. (1971), *Systematic Thinking for Social Action*, Washington, DC: Brookings Institute Press.
Smith, Vernon L. (2008), 'Experimental economics', in L.E. Blume and S. Durlauf (eds), *The New Palgrave Dictionary of Economics Online, 2nd Edition*, New York: Palgrave Macmillan, accessed December 6, 2013 at http://www.dictionaryofeconomics.com.proxy2.ulib.iupui.edu/article?id=pde2008_E000277.

US Bureau of Labor Statistics (2013), CPI Inflation Calculator accessed January 8, 2014 at http://www.bls.gov/data/inflation_calculator.htm.

US Government Accountability Office (GAO) (2012), *Screening Partnership Program: TSA Should Issue More Guidance to Airports and Monitor Private versus Federal Screener Performance*. GAO-13-208, December 6, 2012, accessed December 22, 2013 at http://www.gao.gov/products/GAO-13-208.

Weimer, David and Aidan R. Vining (2011), *Policy Analysis: Concepts and Practice*, 5th edn, New York: Pearson Publishing.

# 28 Detecting business cycles
## Susan K. Schroeder

## 28.1 INTRODUCTION

Business cycles have been and continue to be a notoriously elusive phenomenon for theorists, practitioners, and policy-makers to understand, yet important, as cyclical phenomena manifest as changes in output, inflation, and employment as well other economic and social ills. How one goes about detecting cyclical patterns in data depends, in part, on how one envisions the underlying dynamics of business cycles to unfold. This chapter in the *Handbook* reviews the key paradigms in thinking how business cycles occur and the ways that heterodox economists have tried to detect them empirically, paying particular attention to the methodological challenges that they face and the advantages they hold for unlocking the dynamics behind data.

It is important to be clear by what is meant by 'business cycle'. Business cycles are just one of a multitude of cyclical behaviors that a capitalist market economy exhibits. Cyclical behavior is conventionally thought to have four types: long waves or Kondratieff cycles (50–60 years in duration), cycles in structures or Kuznets cycles (15–25 years), cycles in fixed investment or Juglar cycles (7–10 years), and inventory or Kitchin cycles (3–4 years). Business cycles are typically defined as Juglar cycles or fluctuations in output generated by changes in fixed investment, where fixed investment is comprised of equipment and structures used in production of goods and services. Fixed investment in structures for the Juglar are distinguished from construction which takes place in the Kuznets cycle; Kuznets cycles involve larger capital projects associated with structures which are long-lived (for example, infrastructure investment pertaining to transportation, energy, and housing); patterns of immigration are also thought to be a key dynamic driving Kuznets cycles (Solomou 2008a, 2008b).

The detection of business cycles is integrally related to a vision of the dynamics that generate them, that is, a vision of the channels through which fluctuations in fixed investment influence output. Section 28.2 provides an overview of mainstream and heterodox theories of the business cycle. Detection of business cycles involves the specification of the variables associated with the theory a researcher chooses, and then the selection of time series data which correspond to the variables. The techniques presented in section 28.3 are selected for their intuitive appeal, their ease of use, and appearance within the heterodox research on business cycles. This section focuses on the removal of non-cyclical components from time series data and the application of techniques which tease out information from time series data as to the state of evolution of the underlying process. Section 28.4 discusses the use of mixed methods in heterodox business cycle research. It provides examples of how mixed methods have been used. Section 28.5 draws conclusions. This chapter seeks to provide readers with a good basis from which to delve into the theory of business cycles and nuances of how to detect patterns.

## 28.2   THEORETICAL APPROACHES

A vision of what drives a business cycle involves the specification of the cycle's key dynamics. One can broadly categorize approaches to business cycles in one of two ways: the activity of fixed investment is either a stabilizing influence or a destabilizing influence. On the one hand, mainstream approaches to the business cycle envision fixed investment as a stabilizing influence, requiring something external to upset that influence. Keynes and heterodox economists, on the other hand, view fixed investment as ultimately destabilizing (leads to instability). I first begin with the mainstream approaches to cycle analysis, as their underlying methods are quite similar and set a point of reference with which to compare the heterodox approaches.

Mainstream approaches to cycle theory include the pre-Keynesian or classical macro-economics, early monetary theorists, neo-Keynesians, new classicals, new Keynesians, and the new neoclassical synthesis (a hybrid of new classicals and new Keynesians). These paradigms can be identified by their microeconomic foundations, typically some form of general equilibrium framework. The idea is that there is an equilibrium set of real prices which clear the markets for goods and services, including (non-reproducible) capital goods. So long as prices are flexible, they will adjust to balance supply and demand for both inputs to production and outputs. In a non-monetary economy, Say's law ensures that general gluts will not occur. In a monetary economy, however, Say's law is insufficient to ensure an absence of general gluts. That is, savings can occur and upset the self-adjustment of the system back to a position characterized by fully employed resources (including labor) and markets that have cleared. Fixed investment appears as an injection to counterbalance – through the behavior of the interest rate – any leakage that occurs in the form of saving. So long as the interest rate (a price) is flexible, it will adjust to balance the supply of saving with the demand for saving (investment). The activity of the interest rate and investment's response to it – the classical theory of interest – will help ensure that general gluts or recessions do not occur, that is, any shock to the system is immediately corrected. (Ideally, adjustments are so quick that little, if any, attention needed to be paid to them since they will self-correct.) Business cycles, according to this vision, should not occur. But, they do.

To explain cycles, early monetary cycle theorists focused on problems with the interest rate; either its flexibility or its level. Problems with the interest rate meant that Say's law may not hold, opening up the possibility for a recession. Irving Fisher, for instance, believed that the interest rate is too sluggish to adjust to price changes (after a change in the quantity of money). In a scenario where the interest rate is below that which is warranted, borrowers could take on more debt, leading to the stimulation of investment and production, until the interest rate rises (Fisher 1922, Ch. 4; Schumpeter 1954, p. 1122). Knut Wicksell examined, in the context of what caused inflation, how the difference between the natural and market rates of interest generated a cumulative process which impacted on investment, output, employment, and prices. If the market rate was set, by banks, to be less than the natural rate, investment would increase and, in turn, stimulate output and employment. Eventually prices of consumer and investment goods and inputs would rise (Wicksell 1935) and Schumpeter (1954, p. 1120). The process stops when banks bring the market interest rate back in line with the natural rate. R.G. Hawtrey (1926) placed the problem with the interest rate squarely with the money supply.

In the trough of a cycle, banks become willing to lend and lower the interest rates (as they have built up reserves). This lowers the costs of holding inventories and motivates distributors to expand them. The expansion of inventories stimulates production and employment, which in turn stimulates production further through enhanced consumption. Hawtrey's cumulative process ends when productive capacity is reached and prices start to rise. Deutscher (1990) provides a very good overview of early monetary cycle theory, detailing these issues.

In contrast to the early monetary theorists, Keynes's (1936, Ch. 22) cycle theory was innovative in that he believed the volatility of investment was dependent upon firms' expectations of demand for their output, the marginal efficiency of capital (relative to the interest rate), the marginal propensity to consume, liquidity preference, and business confidence or expectations of demand by firms. These factors include a strong psychological element. The multiplier effect, grounded in the marginal propensity to consume, amplifies the effect on output that changes in investment can generate. Firms' expectations of the strength of demand for output, which are influenced by the profitability of investment, are reflected in the estimated stream of returns from assets. Liquidity preference, a key determinant of the interest rate, captures the speculative nature of the demand for money. Moreover, the propensity to consume can vary over a cycle's phases. Whereas for early cycle theorists changes to the interest rate led to changes in investment and output, for Keynes changes in investment were stimulated by the changing relationship between the marginal efficiency of capital (MEC) and the interest rate. If the MEC is greater than the interest rate, firms are stimulated to invest as the demand price for capital assets (its discounted stream of returns) is greater than the supply price (the cost of producing a comparable capital asset). As investment takes place, output increases via the multiplier effect (with associated changes in consumption). So, at this point, one can see how the differences in vision as to what generates cyclical behavior lead to differences in what to monitor, and how theory can help guide the timing in the relationships between the variables.

Modern economic theory added to the discussion in a number of ways. Neo-Keynesian cycle theory, for instance, built on the multiplier process by incorporating an accelerator (Samuelson's multiplier-accelerator) where changes in output feed back onto investment (Samuelson 1939). However, the neo-Keynesians shifted away from Keynes's Marshallian basis towards a general equilibrium microfoundation meant the return of price flexibility (and the importance of market clearing) to the analysis of cycles. The more flexible prices are, the more likely the system can self-adjust back to a full-employment level of output. By modifying the conception of general equilibrium, new classicals, in turn, managed to re-justify the role of flexible prices in attenuating cyclical behavior, where cyclical behavior involves adjustment of the economy in the aftermath of a shock. Here, one often finds shock-propagation mechanisms. One variant of the new classical paradigm places the key shock-propagation mechanisms in the monetary sphere, monetary business cycles, where changes in the money supply (anticipated or unanticipated) influence investment through the signal extraction problems of agents. Signal extraction problems, such as relative price confusion and confusion between permanent and transitory dynamics, arise in the context of imperfect information. Another variant, the real business cycle (RBC) school, emphasizes the source of shocks via the real sector. The new Keynesian paradigm incorporates a role for the presence of market incompleteness and imperfections.

These elements permit reverberations in the aftermath of a shock to have a cyclical form. Snowden and Vane (2005) provide a succinct overview of the new classical and RBC approaches to the business cycle.

Although the mainstream analyses can, at first blush, seem quite different, what unites them is a fairly restrictive methodological basis associated with a general equilibrium concept. Mainstream analyses begin with an agent-based microeconomic foundation, typically focused on how a shock to the system influences the behavior of households through consumption, non-financial firms through investment and the supply of output (and employment), and/or banks through investment and consumption through their lending decisions. The approach reflects the Euclidean or Cartesian mode of thought in the sense that it relies on closed system 'whose bounds are known and whose constituent variables and relations are known, or at least knowable' (Dow 1996, p. 13). The unit of analysis is the individual, whose behavior is captured by a set of axioms. The implications for the determination of price, output, distribution, and consumption are drawn by the application of deductive logic to the axioms. This foundation requires unknown elements be treated stochastically, that is, 'conform to a known frequency distribution' (ibid.). The general equilibrium microfoundation of neoclassical marginalist economics entails an axiomatic method akin to mathematics.

Unlike mainstream economics, heterodox traditions of cyclical analysis begin with a class or group as the unit of analysis. Heterodox economists have approached the business cycles in a number of ways, with post-Keynesians, institutionalists and Marxists at the forefront of research. What unites them is an emphasis on evolutionary processes, the importance of institutions, distribution of income, and investment instability. At the heart of post-Keynesian cycle analysis one often finds the work of Michał Kalecki. For Kalecki (1971) the difference between the profit rate and the interest rate was key for understanding the investment decisions of firms, where the rates of both profit and interest are, in turn, dependent upon investment; the mark-up over cost (profit), for each firm, is influenced by the degree of monopoly power held by the firm for the price of its products.[1] The idea is that in an upswing of the cycle, the production of investment goods increases as orders for them increase. The production of investment goods leads to accumulation or a positive growth rate in all goods needed for reproduction to take place and the expansion of capital, fixed and inventories. Accumulation leads to additional investment activity. At some point, the volume of capital equipment expands and begins to limit the pace of investment activity. Eventually, orders decline and the cumulative process reverses. Kalecki notes that consumption by workers and capitalists will reinforce the demand for consumer goods and the profit per unit of output rises, stimulating firms to continue to invest. He argues that the profits of capitalists are ultimately determined by the extent to which they invest and consume, because '(t)he aggregate production and profit per unit of output will ultimately rise to such an extent as to assure an increment in real profits equal to that of production of investment goods and capitalists' consumption' (Kalecki 1971, p. 12). The distribution of income, monopoly power, and cumulative processes are important for Kaleckian theories of the business cycle.

The idea of cumulative causation perhaps finds its most developed form in Hyman Minsky's financial instability hypothesis (FIH). Minsky (1975) examines the evolution of firms' liability structures over the cycle. When the economy is in a trough the firms are robust (or 'hedged') in the sense that in the aftermath of the previous recession they were strong enough to survive and are now in a position where their cash inflows generated by their assets more than cover the stream of payment commitments emitted by their liabilities. At some point, they are stimulated to invest, by either a new innovation which stimulates profit or perhaps a softening of the interest rate. As firms invest, the growth of output strengthens as do employment and consumption. These bolster cash inflows and lead firms to become less risk adverse, and more willing to use debt to finance new investment. They do, and for a while the cumulative process continues. With firms' increased use of debt, their debt service payments increase relative to cash flows. Their liability structures take on a different configuration. Their cash flows are not enough to complete new investment in its entirety (though they will be able to service debt payments). The firms have shifted from a hedged position (where cash flows cover payment commitments) to a speculative position (where cash flows cover only part of payment commitments). At some point, cash flows weaken, though it may take time for firm owners to realize that the expected, future rate of return on new investment is falling. Some firms will not be able to complete debt service payments let alone new investment. These are Ponzi firms; they need to borrow to complete payments. Minsky captured this idea by visualizing a distribution of hedged, speculative, and Ponzi firms, evolving with the cycle. During the expansion phase of a boom, the distribution shifts from robust (most firms hedged or speculative) to fragile (most firms speculative or Ponzi). As the economy nears the peak, the strength of demand for funds leads to a rising interest rate. Minsky identified this rise in the rate of interest as a key element in tipping the economy into a contraction. This approach has gained interest among mainstream economists; however, to accommodate the FIH into a general equilibrium framework, the FIH has been interpreted as a theory about irrational behavior (e.g., Bernanke 1983). Skott (2012) provides a succinct overview of post-Keynesian cycle theory.

The institutionalists tend to draw on the work of Thorstein Veblen and Wesley Mitchell, a student of Veblen's. Mitchell's (1941) dual focus on theory of cycles and empirical measures of detection led him also to understand cycles as cumulative processes, the dynamics of which are shaped by the institutional configuration of the period. As such, each cycle has its own unique characteristics. His empirical research informed the theory that he constructed: that theory was centered on profit. At the trough of a cycle, interest rates tend to soften, which stimulates investment and profit. Wages have a tendency to increase more slowly relative to prices during an expansion, which stimulates firms' profit margins. Consumption grows, but not as fast as investment. The costs of raw materials have a tendency to increase faster than the price of output, but the rising prices have a dampening effect on consumption which alleviates some of the pressure on prices of inputs and final goods and services. Eventually, the conditions that permitted the expansion lay the foundation for the contraction. The peak is characterized by slowing demand and rising costs of output. Howard Sherman (2003) extends the work of Mitchell by incorporating elements that Mitchell did not develop, such as government and trade. Epstein (1999) and Sherman (2001) provide comprehensive overviews of Mitchell's method.

Although distributional concerns appear in the traditions discussed above, these are of particular importance to Marxist economists. However, Marx did not leave a clear theory of the business cycle. As a result there appears to be some confusion as to whether Marx's theory of crisis is associated with a long wave or with a business cycle proper. One of the clearest attempts to construct a Marxian analysis of a business cycle is that of Richard Goodwin. Goodwin (1972) was concerned about the dynamics of cyclical growth, and formalized Marx's understanding of the relationship between the cyclical pattern of accumulation, the tension between profit and wage shares, and the employment of workers. (Harvie 2000 aptly notes that Goodwin's model is independent of a labor theory of value.) Provided that output and labor grow in the same proportion, the economy can grow until it reaches the limit of the availability of workers. Workers realize they have the ability to increase their wage rate rises, and do so. As that happens the profit rate falls and accumulation weakens, and the economy begins to reverse. The rate of employment, in a sense, acts as a gauge for workers' ability to request higher wage rates. The power struggle over the wage and profit shares is very much like a predator–prey model.

What makes the heterodox traditions so distinctive is their use of open systems of thought, in contrast to the axiom-deductive approach of mainstream economics. As Dow (1996) notes, the methods employed by heterodox economists are open in the sense that elements such as variables and structural relationships cannot be wholly knowable. As an open system, the historical, social, political, and institutional features and behavior become integral parts of the foundation of the analyses. For instance, whereas the mainstream begins with an analysis of the individual, heterodox economists are much more apt to begin with a class-based analysis that emphasizes historical and institutional contexts and political, sociological, and psychological influences on class or group structures.[2] The conception of equilibrium is not confined to a general equilibrium orientation. There can be a short-period versus long-period distinction but the economy need not gravitate towards a position characterized by market clearing and full utilization of resources. Rather, equilibrium is cast in the context of tendential regulation.

The above sampling of cycle theories ought to provide a sense of the first issue a researcher confronts when attempted to empirically detect cycles: which theory captures the key dynamics they envision? The next choice involves the identification of the variables associated with their dynamics; then, which data series provides adequate representation of those variables. For instance, a heterodox economist interested to apply the Goodwin model could decide that a key dynamic of output fluctuations is the distribution of income, and select indicator(s) which represent that concept. At some point, researchers need to consider whether modifying a time series may help more closely align concepts with data. To understand the quantitative techniques employed in heterodox analyses of the business cycle one needs to have a good understanding the methodological aspects underpinning their theory.

## 28.3  METHODS OF DETECTION

Business cycle detection inherently involves the analysis of time series data, which are series of data observations taken at repeated intervals. After selecting the data indicators, as guided by theory, one needs to consider data series as having four components: trend, cycle, seasonal, and noise. Time series techniques which detect cycles are effectively isolating the cyclical component of a data time series. The functional form of a time series hinges on whether the series exhibits exponential growth and the value around which the seasonal component varies. If a time series does not exhibit an exponential growth pattern and seasonal variation does not increase over time, then the series' components can be expressed additively (notation after Daniel and Terrell 1992):

$$Y_t = T_t + C_t + S_t + R_t \qquad (28.1)$$

where $Y_t$ is the observation of the series at time $t$, $T_t$ is the trend component at $t$, $C_t$ is the cyclical component at $t$, $S_t$ is the seasonal component at $t$, and $R_t$ is random or irregular variation. If the series exhibits exponential growth and the seasonal variation increases over time, the series components should be expressed multiplicatively:

$$Y_t = T_t \times C_t \times S_t \times R_t \qquad (28.2)$$

Multiplicative forms can be transformed to linear expression by converting the data into rates of change or a logged series:

$$Log\ Y_t = log\ T_t + log\ C_t + log\ S_t + log\ R_t \qquad (28.3)$$

Data series, such as gross domestic product, fixed investment, and trade series, which are measured in terms of levels, can exhibit strong trends and obscure volatility and information about the cycle. An advantage of transforming the original data series into differences or rates of change of the observations is that the transformed data can bring out that volatility. (See more below on stationary and non-stationary series.)

Seasonality pertains to the predictable patterns in time series that are related to the seasons of the year (for example, battery sales spike at Christmas time, or suntan product sales increase in the late spring). If one uses annual time series data, seasonality is not a concern. However, most economists use data series with are quarterly or monthly, and financial market data is more frequent still (weekly, daily). With higher-frequency data, seasonality needs to be addressed. Deseasonalizing data involves the creation of a seasonality index with which to adjust the time series. Assuming a monthly time series, the first step in the creation of a seasonal index is to form an estimate of the trend from the original series. The trend is typically estimated with a moving average, exponential smoothing, or a linear regression. The moving average is just that: an average of a set of designated, consecutive observations, centered around the middle observation, which shifts over time.[3] Exponential smoothing is another averaging technique, where the more recent observations are weighted more heavily than past observations. And, one could also remove the trend component by creating a linear estimate of the trend (linear regression or parametric trend estimation). (See Koop (2013) for more detail on these techniques.)

To calculate a seasonal index, the moving average calculation is typically based upon a 12-month period. The original series is then divided by the trend in order to create a ratio called the ratio-to-trend ('ratio-to-moving average' if the trend is estimated with a moving average). The ratio-to-trend is an estimate of the combined variation of seasonal and irregular variation. One then calculates the mean value for a particular month by averaging all observations of the ratio, across years, for that month. If the monthly means do not sum to 12, then the means needs to be adjusted so they do so by creating an adjustment factor defined as 12 divided by the average of the means. The means are multiplied by the adjustment factor to yield a seasonal index. Deseasonalizing the original data series involves dividing each observation by its corresponding index. Please note, however, that software packages (for instance, SPSS, Eviews) often have deseasonalization features in order to avoid adjusting a time series for seasonal variation by hand. Daniel and Terrell (1992) and Sherman and Meerpol (2013) provide detailed examples of deseasonalization.

Isolating cyclical variations involves removing the trend component from a time series. For annual series, this means creating an estimate of the trend (again, a moving average, exponentially smoothed series, a linear trend, or something comparable) and, for a multiplicative structure, dividing each observation of the original series by the corresponding observation of the trend. If the time series has an additive structure, one can subtract the trend from the original series. The resulting series is often referred to as the cyclical relative. (For simplicity, it has been assumed that the noise component has little influence on the annual data series; bear in mind, it may not.) Creating a cyclical relative for a monthly or quarterly series is a bit trickier. If the series has a multiplicative structure, one de-trends the original by dividing each observation by both the corresponding observation for the estimated trend and seasonal adjustment (where components are multiplicative); if the time series has an additive structure, one subtracts from each observation the corresponding observation for the trend, adjusted for seasonality. The result, however, contains the noise component.

More sophisticated methods of detection include the correlation of the current period observation of a time series with its past (lagged) observations (the autocorrelation function) and establishing whether a phase or regime change has taken place (the Markov switch, transition models, and threshold analysis). The autocorrelation function employs a variation of the correlation statistic ($r$). $r$ gauges the correlation in the movements between two time series of the same periodicity and length; a correlation matrix is used when there are three or more data series. $r$ varies between $-1$ and $1$, where $1$ indicates perfect positive correlation, $-1$ is perfect negative correlation, and $0$ indicates that the two series are uncorrelated. The autocorrelation gauges the degree of similarity in the movement between the data series and lagged version(s) of itself to ascertain whether there are movements in the time series that repeat (fluctuations). For instance, $r_2$ gauges the degree of correlation between a times series and that time series lagged two periods. An autocorrelation function contains correlations of the times series with various lagged versions of itself.

Autoregression or autoregressive model (AR) probes a bit deeper into an analysis of time series data by attempting to gauge the strength of explanatory power which variables may have upon the dependent variable (the time series). With the shift from autocorrelation to autogression one to gravitates towards a statement of causality. However, the results of autogressive models stop short of providing that definitiveness. The AR(1) is an autoregressive model where the one-period lag of the explanatory variable is used as the dependent variable; AR(p) is a model with p lags of the dependent variable as explanatory variables:

$$AR(1): y_y = \mu + \Phi_1 y_{t-1} + \varepsilon_t \qquad (28.4)$$

$$AR(p): y_t = \mu + \Phi_1 y_{t-1} + \Phi_2 y_{t-2} + \ldots + \Phi_p y_{t-p} + \varepsilon_t. \qquad (28.5)$$

If (the absolute value of) the coefficient on the lagged variable has the value of 1, the series is not stationary or has a unit root (that is, there is a strong trend component to it). If the coefficient is less than 1, the series is stationary and it does not have a unit root. It is important to establish this, as a series with a strong trend needs to be transformed (by differencing or applying a natural log) into a series which is stationary before further econometric techniques can be applied. The application of regression techniques requires that the error terms be random (or not correlated). One can determine whether a time series has a unit root by using the Dickey–Fuller test, a common test which most statistical software packages will have. It is necessary to add a deterministic trend (add time as an explanatory variable) and verify that the estimated coefficient on the highest lagged variable is significant. Koop (2013) and Mills (2003) provide examples of specific AR models.

The structure of the AR appears in a variety of models. For instance, the autoregressive distributed lag model (ADL) regresses the independent variable on lags of itself ($p$) and lags of the explanatory variable ($q$) for ADL($p$, $q$). It is with this particular model that we can introduce the idea of Granger causality. Granger causality works with the structure of time series – the fact that explanatory variables needs to change prior to the dependent variable – in order to make stronger statements about whether the appearance of correlation suggests causality (Koop 2013). If an estimated coefficient of an explanatory variable is significant, then the variable is said to Granger-cause the independent variable. This idea can also be applied to a system of ADLs, known as vector autoregression or VAR analysis. This would seem really useful; however, for heterodox economists using them there is a concern about the congruence of the assumptions which enable these models to work and the assumptions that heterodox economists use to construct their theories. That has not stopped these models from appearing in heterodox empirical work (more on this below).

Regime switch models attempt to detect changes in time series which could signal a phase change in the cycle. The typical techniques include threshold models, smooth transition models and Markov switches. The basic idea behind threshold analysis is that thresholds are constructed for a set of indicators (represented with time series) and if enough of the indicators cross the threshold – or signal – about the same time, a phase change may have occurred in the economy. This style of analysis is attributed to the work of Goldstein et al. (2000) and its appeal is its relative simplicity with non-parametric data. A disadvantage is its reliance on subjective decisions for creating windows for signals, selection of indicators and rejection regions. The Markov switch and smooth transition models are related to the autoregression in that states or phases of a cycle (for example, crisis and non-crisis) are directly incorporated into the models. The dependent variable is regressed on lagged observations of itself where each of the coefficients of the lagged variables is defined for the possible states in addition to the associated lag. For smooth transition models, all parameters are dependent on the state.[4]

As alluded to above, a key drawback to the use of these econometric techniques is that the assumptions underlying the techniques often conflict with the method underlying heterodox theory. Methodological differences carry implications as to how to detect cycles and to infer causality. For instance, the use of statistics and econometrics involves a deterministic treatment of time which is generally unrealistic from the viewpoint of heterodox economists (see Chapter 10 in this *Handbook*). A deterministic treatment of time suggest that, 'the passage of time unfolds in a lawful progression of causally connected events' (Foley 2001, p. 49). It suggests that as the past and future are definitive, the economic processes being modeled or captured empirically are reversible. This allows uncertainty to be defined as probabilistic risk (quantifiable) and represented by probability distributions; hence, the use of econometric techniques is well supported.[5]

The heterodox community, on the other hand, has generally emphasized the need to treat time dialectically or historically. Time progresses in such a way that the past is definite but the future is indefinite. This is due to qualitatively new phenomena emerging in response to the contradictions created by existing structures. As economic processes are not reversible, uncertainty cannot be captured well by probabilistic risk (it is not quantifiable). This makes the application of econometric techniques problematic, that is, the results are not likely to be robust as the techniques invoke assumptions which run counter to what the heterodox community generally envisions. Heterodox economists have approached business cycles by clearly articulating a theory and supporting this as best they can with empirical evidence, using techniques which do not involve the restrictive conditions entailed with econometrics.

That said, recent work by heterodox economists suggests there is an interest to experiment with the Markov switch, filters (band pass, BP; the high pass, HP; and the Hodrick Prescott and penalized splines), wavelets and spectral analysis (see, e.g., Korotyev and Tsirel 2010; Cruz 2005; Schroeder 2009; Gallegati et al. 2013).

## 28.4 MIXED METHODS IN HETERODOX BUSINESS CYCLE RESEARCH

In the previous section the emphasis was on detecting patterns in data. This section examines how mixed methods can enhance one's understanding of the dynamics generating those patterns. Mixed methods involve aspects of both quantitative research and qualitative research. Quantitative research is generally believed to be better suited for testing propositions, whereas qualitative research is better for extending theory. Both methods entail a data component, but the types of data and manner of analyses are different. The quantitative approach tends to apply statistical or econometric techniques to numerical secondary data (for instance, Bureau of Economic Analysis national income accounts; financial market data – Datastream; US Department of Labor labor market data) which measure or represent characteristics of the object of analysis. This approach involves establishing a vision of some aspect or process of reality, and creating concepts and frameworks or theories of analysis within which concepts help to organize and define the key features of that vision. Numerical data represent those concepts empirically and facilitate tests of propositions about the concepts and the relationships which may exist between them. It is important to be mindful to not use data which have been constructed for one purpose to evaluate another. Moreover, economic and social processes, which are complex, cannot be fully reduced to single dimensions.

The qualitative approach, on the other hand, tends to employ primary data (for example, surveys and interviews) and the techniques used to analyze them are more open (figures, tables, and charts). The idea here is that a researcher is interested to explain some aspect of social experience. The approach often yields more in-depth insights about social phenomena, carrying the potential to reveal multiple dimensions involved in explaining 'why'. An advantage of the qualitative approach is the flexibility it affords a researcher in terms of ability to adapt a research design to different contexts. A disadvantage is the inability to quickly cross-compare the results of analyses cast in different contexts.

The use of data within the quantitative and qualitative approaches illustrates the emphasis within the social sciences on comparing theory with reality through the senses, where data help to capture and validate what people sense and express through theory. Features of one's reality that lie outside the social realm entail methods of exploration associated with religion, morality, and philosophy (Neuman 2006). It is interesting to note that the late Robert Heilbroner's application of the term 'worldly philosophers' to economists suggests the inadequacy of qualitative and quantitative approaches to social research for understanding our social contexts. That is, methods associated with philosophy and history, for instance, are just as relevant, from a heterodox perspective, for understanding our social – and economic – experiences.

The use of mixed methods typically involves the combination of a quantitative research project with support from qualitative research in order to corroborate or triangulate the evidence and analysis yielded by the quantitative research. This is not the only rationale for employing mixed methods. Other justifications include the ability of qualitative analysis to support quantitative analysis with more detail, or to provide a broader analysis of an issue, and helping to establish relationships between concepts, or establishing links between the micro (behavioral) and macro (structural or aggregate) levels of a piece of research. It is also possible that a quantitative approach can support a qualitative approach to a research project. Quantitative techniques can assist the identification of important structural aspects, helping to sharpen the focus of the (main) qualitative component. Punch (2001, p. 247) discusses the justification of mixed methods in more detail.

As noted above, the heterodox community often provides deeper analyses of social and economic issues by incorporating insights and methods traditionally associated with philosophy and history. Often one will see reference to Marx's historical materialism, which suggests that concepts are historically defined, or discussions of the philosophical implications of the selection of particular methods of analysis. What are some of the ways in which post-Keynesians have employed mixed methods in business cycle analysis? As seen the previous section, post-Keynesian cycle analysis emphasizes the role of aggregate demand (investment, particularly), income distribution, monopoly power, historical periods, the monetary production, and endogenously generated instability. Institutionalists are similar to post-Keynesians in their emphasis on cumulative, endogenous processes and historical specificity of concepts and the non-deterministic treatment of time. Institutionalists have also emphasized the role that inductive reasoning has in guiding the selection of objects of analysis, which in deductive and Babylonian-style analyses create the chains of reasoning underpinning theory. Moreover, the work of Mitchell (1941) and later generations of institutional economists have emphasized the need to support various aspects of theory with empirical evidence, data analysis in particular.

Box 28.1 provides examples of heterodox business cycle research which employed mixed methods in their analyses. They suggest that mixed methods can support a wide range of research on various aspects of a cycle and phenomena related to it. As such,

BOX 28.1   EXAMPLES OF MIXED METHODS USED IN HETERODOX
ANALYSES OF THE BUSINESS CYCLE

'Why is this cycle different from all other cycles?' (Sherman and Sherman 2008) presents 26 adjusted, quarterly national income accounting data for the United States, and calculates averages of particular phases of successive cycles to visually verify that the patterns which Mitchell discovered held through the recent financial crises. The authors then examine more closely how the struggle between the classes over the distribution of income became reflected in the patterns of consumption, savings, debt and the impact of government spending.

'Mitchell's grand design and its critics: the theory and measurement of business cycles' (Epstein 1999) analyzes data series drawn from national income accounts using criteria established by Mitchell, and definition of the cycle relative, to identify turning points. He compares turning points in gross domestic product (GDP) time series with National Bureau of Economic Research (NBER) reference dates, and then proceeds to analyze why it is that the turning points of the components of GDP do not seem to correspond as well with the reference dates.

'Defining and detecting financial fragility: New Zealand's experience' (Schroeder 2009) develops a cash flow accounting framework styled after Minsky in order to detect, and graphically illustrate, the evolution of the New Zealand and Australian economies. The times series are smoothed using a Hodrick–Prescott filter. She proceeds to set the analysis within a historical discussion which sheds light on the underlying dynamics of the New Zealand economy and its financial sector.

'Distributive and demand cycles in the US economy: a structuralist Goodwin model' (Barbosa-Filho and Taylor 2006) uses national income account data for the United States to demonstrate the presence of cyclical fluctuations between labor's share of income and capacity utilization, where a filter has been used to smooth the data. They develop a Goodwin-style model with which they analyze the relationship between effective demand and income distribution, using a VAR econometric estimation. The results appear to capture effects noted by Kalecki and Steindl.

'Cyclical growth in a Goodwin–Kalecki–Marx model' (Sasaki 2013) examines Kaleckian growth cycles in Japan by first analyzing time-connected scatterplots of capacity utilization, employment rate, and profit share (to proxy income distribution). He delves deeper by examining the effects of labor-saving technological progress, a Marxian 'reserve army' effect, and the Goodwin relationship between the employment rate and profit share. The extension is performed with the help of comparative statics and numerical simulations.

'A three-regime business cycle for an emerging economy' (Cruz 2005) uses a Markov switch to detect regime changes along the lines of Minsky's three stages in the upswing of a cycle: hedged, speculative, and Ponzi. It extends Minsky's analysis of dynamics for a developed economies to emerging economies.

'Testing Goodwin: growth cycles in 10 OECD countries' (Harvie 2000) examines the Goodwin model for ten countries using national income accounting data. He defines the center of each cycle with econometric (ordinary least squares, OLS) estimates for productivity growth, growth in the labor force, capital–output ratio, and the Phillips curve. Although he found the estimated centers did not perform well historically, Harvie did find that the actually trajectories of the workers' share of income and employment rates more accurately depict Goodwin's ideas.

mixed methods are potentially more effective than the mainstream's limited approach for getting at the social context of business cycles. They provide venues for exploring various aspects of complex processes and how they could shape cyclical behaviors.

## 28.5   CONCLUSION

This chapter has sought to convey three things to heterodox economists who are interested in conducting business cycle research. Firstly, vision matters: differences in vision are reflected in differences in theories of business cycles. Secondly, method matters: the broad differences between mainstream and heterodox methods carry implications for the selection and application of quantitative techniques used to detect business cycles. And, thirdly, this chapter provided an overview of the basic techniques used to detect cycles, with a discussion of the challenges that heterodox economists face, because of method, when selecting techniques. The open system of thought which characterizes heterodox economics provides a more holistic approach for incorporating social, political, historical, and institutional influences on cyclical fluctuations. This is a crucial advantage that heterodox economists have over those using mainstream approaches. Open systems provide venues for exploring the interconnectedness of social, political, and institutional aspects of cyclical behavior.

The distinction between qualitative and quantitative research can be somewhat disconcerting. At first glance, textbooks on research methods in the social sciences appear to advocate the use of statistics and econometric techniques which facilitate the incorporation of mainstream economics, grounded in some form of neoclassical theory of value and distribution. While empirical support is important to establish or validate one's ideas, within the heterodox traditions the use of data and quantitative techniques of analysis should be more judiciously applied in order not to compromise the evolutionary nature of the processes being studied. Quantitative techniques which emphasize a deterministic treatment of time, for instance, may not be suitable for a heterodox framework which favors a historical or dialectical treatment of time. The use of mainstream quantitative techniques may be suitable, but needs considered justification; otherwise, the analyst runs the risk of obtaining results which undermine rather than support the framework they seek to extend and support.

## NOTES

1.  The idea of Kalecki's theory of price is that the price of a good or service depends not on the amount of direct and indirect labor entailed in its production, but simply some degree of mark-up above the cost of producing it. A key issue for the Kaleckian price theories are the lack of explanation as to how, exactly, the mark-up is determined. It is simply understood that the stronger a firm's power over price in the marketplace, the greater is the mark-up. This approach is very much grounded in the sphere of production, emphasizing the role of profitability of investment.
2.  By doing so, they can avoid the aggregation problem and proceed to analyze aggregates, providing, when needed, an analysis at the level of the individual (worker or firm).
3.  It is quite possible, if there is little trend in the data, that a cyclical pattern emerges; however, care needs to be taken that this pattern is not due to residual noise or the moving calculation itself.
4.  For further readings on regime switch models, see http://www.eviews.com/EViews8/ev8ecswitch_n.html.

5.  Mirjiam-Sent (1998) carefully documents Thomas Sargent's recasting of economic concepts, within the new classical macroeconomic paradigm, in order to create models of a capitalist economy which are amenable to the application of quantitative techniques, with the hope of drawing out new insights about this form of social organization.

# REFERENCES

Barbosa-Filho, N.H. and L. Taylor (2006), 'Distributive and demand cycles in the US economy: a structuralist Goodwin model', *Metroeconomica*, **57** (3), 389–411.

Bernanke, B. (1983), 'Nonmonetary effects of the financial crisis in the propagation of the Great Depression', *American Economic Review*, **73** (3), 257–76.

Cruz, M. (2005), 'A three-regime business cycle for an emerging economy', *Applied Economic Letters*, **12**, 399–402.

Daniel, W. and J. Terrell (1992), *Business Statistics for Management and Economics*, 6th edn, Boston, MA: Houghton Mifflin Co.

Deutscher, P. (1990), *R.G. Hawtrey and the Development of Macroeconomics*, London: Macmillan Press.

Dow, S. (1996), *The Methodology of Macroeconomic Thought*, Cheltenham, UK and Northampton, MA, USA: Edward Elgar Publishing.

Epstein, P. (1999), 'Mitchell's grand design and its critics: the theory and measurement of business cycles', *Journal of Economic Issues*, **33** (3), 525–53.

Fisher, I. (1922), *The Purchasing Power of Money: Its Determination and Relation to Credit, Interest and Crises*, New York: Macmillan Company.

Foley, D.K. (2001), 'Hyman Minsky and the dilemmas of contemporary economic method', in R. Bellofiore and P. Ferri (eds), *Financial Keynesianism and Market Instability: The economic legacy of Hyman Minsky*, Vol. 1, Cheltenham, UK and Northampton, MA, USA: Edward Elgar, pp. 47–59.

Gallegati, M., J. Ramsey, and W. Semmler (2013), 'Time scale analysis of interest rate spreads and output using wavelets', *Axioms*, **2** (1), 182–207.

Goldstein, M., G. Kaminsky, and C. Reinhart (2000), *Assessing Financial Vulnerability, An Early Warning System for Emerging Markets*, Washington, DC: Institute for International Economics.

Goodwin, R. (1972), 'A growth cycle', in E.K. Hunt and J. Schwartz (eds), *A Critique of Economic Theory*, Harmonsworth: Penguin, pp. 442–9.

Harvie, D. (2000), 'Testing Goodwin: growth cycles in 10 OECD countries', *Cambridge Journal of Economics*, **24** (3), 349–76.

Hawtrey, A. (1926), 'The trade cycle', *The Economist*, **75**, 169–85.

Kalecki, M. (1971), *Selected Essays on the Dynamics of the Capitalist Economy, 1933–1970*, Cambridge: Cambridge University Press.

Keynes, J.M. (1936), *The General Theory of Employment, Interest and Money*, London: Macmillan.

Koop, G. (2013), *Analysis of Economic Data*, 4th edn, Chichester: John Wiley.

Korotyev, A. and S. Tsirel (2010), 'A spectral analysis of world GDP dynamics: Kondratieff waves, Kuznets swings and Juglar and Kitchin cycles in global and economic development, and the 2008–2009 economic crisis', *Structure and Dynamics*, **4** (1), accessed August 8, 2014 at http://www.escholarship.org/uc/item/9jv108xp.

Mills, T. (2003), *Modeling Trends and Cycles in Economic Theory*, Basingstoke, UK and New York, USA: Palgrave Macmillan.

Minsky, H. (1975), *John Maynard Keynes*, New York: Columbia University Press.

Mirjiam-Sent, S. (1998), 'Sargent and the unbearable lightness of symmetry', *Journal of Economic Methodology*, **5** (1), 93–114.

Mitchell, W. (1941), *Business Cycles and their Causes*, Berkeley, CA: University of California Press.

Neuman, W. (2006), *Social Research Methods: Qualitative and Quantitative Approaches*, 6th edn, New York: Pearson Education/Allyn & Bacon.

Punch, Keith F. (2001), *Introduction to Social Research: Quantitative and Qualitative Approaches*, London: Sage.

Samuelson, P. (1939), 'Interactions between the multiplier analysis and the principle of acceleration', *Review of Economics and Statistics*, **21** (2), 75–8.

Sasaki, H. (2013), 'Cyclical growth in a Goodwin–Kalecki–Marx model', *Journal of Economics*, **108** (2), 145–71.

Schroeder, S. (2009), 'Defining and detecting financial fragility: New Zealand's experience', *International Journal of Social Economics*, **36** (3), 287–307.

Schumpeter, J. (1954), *History of Economic Analysis*, New York: Oxford University Press.

Sherman, H. (2001), 'The business cycle theory of Wesley Mitchell', *Journal of Economic Issues*, **35** (1), 85–97.

Sherman, H. (2003), 'Institutions and the business cycle', *Journal of Economic Issues*, **37** (3), 621–42.
Sherman, H. and M. Meerpol (2013), *Principles of Macroeconomics: Activist vs. Austerity Policies*, Armonk, NY: M.E. Sharpe.
Sherman, H. and P. Sherman (2008), 'Why is this cycle different from all other cycles?', *Journal of Economic Issues*, **42** (1), 255–68.
Skott, P. (2012), 'Post Keynesian theories of business cycles', in J.E. King (ed.), *The Elgar Companion to Post Keynesian Economics*, Cheltenham, UK and Northampton, MA, USA: Edward Elgar, pp. 55–60.
Snowden, B. and H. Vane (2005), *Modern Macroeconomics: Its Origins, Development and Current State*, Cheltenham, UK and Northampton, MA, USA: Edward Elgar.
Solomou, S.N. (2008a), 'Kitchin, Joseph (1861–1932)', in Steven N. Durlauf and Lawrence E. Blume (eds), *The New Palgrave Dictionary of Economics*, 2nd edn, New York: Palgrave Macmillan, accessed August 17, 2014 at http://www.dictionaryofeconomics.com/article?id=pde2008_K000028.
Solomou, S.N. (2008b), 'Kondratieff cycles', in Steven N. Durlauf and Lawrence E. Blume (eds), *The New Palgrave Dictionary of Economics* 2nd edn, New York: Palgrave Macmillan, accessed August 17, 2014 at http://www.dictionaryofeconomics.com/article?id=pde2008_K000037.
Wicksell, K. (1935), *Lectures on Political Economy*, Vol. 2: *Money*, London: George Routledge & Sons.

# 29 A *Régulationist* analysis of an industry sector using mixed research methods
## Lynne Chester

## 29.1  INTRODUCTION

This chapter discusses the analysis of an industry sector using the example of the Australian electricity sector (Chester 2007). The research problem was to determine the outcomes and beneficiaries from this sector's radical structural change which commenced in the early 1990s. The task required an analytical framework able to explain the process of change over time and at the level of an industry sector, to consider the outcomes of structural change beyond the dimensions of employment, investment, and industry composition, and to consider the distributional consequences. *Régulation* theory fully satisfies these criteria for a dynamic, historical, and multidimensional analysis which is not limited to economic factors and incorporates quantitative and qualitative dimensions.

A *Régulationist* sector analysis requires two levels of analysis: first, the five institutional forms of the macro mode of *régulation*; and second, the sector's reflection of these macro institutional forms. A four-point method defines the parameters of the sector-based analysis which was used for the Australian study. The research design was guided by this method and the study's theoretical framework. This required the collection of both qualitative and quantitative data from the 1980s onwards.

Document analysis and secondary analysis were the two data collection methods used by the study. Documentary sources provided a rich source of qualitative and quantitative empirical material. Annual reports, budget papers, legislation, policy papers, reports from official inquiries and regulatory determinations, inquiry submissions, prospectuses, media statements, and statistical collections were some of the wide range of documents sourced. A critical content analysis was conducted to make an overall judgment about each document's meaning and significance. A protocol of ten core questions was developed to interrogate all documents in order to identify conceptualizations, the definitions of problems presented, explanations given for problems, preferred solutions advocated to overcome problems, what was not considered problematic, as well as to determine the explanations and solutions not included and for whom the documents 'spoke'. A similar protocol was developed for the quantitative data sets and used to ascertain whether any were deliberately or unintentionally biased.

The following sections in this chapter discuss the purpose of the Australian study sector, and briefly outline a *Régulationist* analytical framework before explaining the study's research design to move the chosen theoretical framework to an empirical representation, the mixed methods research design, and the approaches considered to undertake document and secondary analyses, the data sources used, and the key findings of the study. The chapter concludes with some observations about the study's analytical framework, triangulation, and a mixed methods research design.

## 29.2   PURPOSE OF THE STUDY

The 1990s delivered a decade of structural change, with astonishing rapidity, to electricity sectors around the world. This transformation occurred as part of a far-reaching restructuring of the economic, social, and political conditions for capital accumulation following the global recession of the 1970s and was driven by the ideology of neoliberalism's metamorphosis into the 'central guiding principle of economic thought and management' (Harvey 1989, p. 2). Australia was at the forefront with its electricity sector restructuring hailed by the Organisation for Economic Co-operation and Development's (OECD) International Energy Agency (IEA 2005) as a role model against which other countries should benchmark their own progress.

The common conceptualization of this global sectoral restructuring has been narrowly based around sector-specific regulatory changes and the creation of wholesale trading markets. This led to a narrow focus of research about this sector limited to aspects such as wholesale market prices or the operation of wholesale trading arrangements. There was no substantive examination of the overall change process, the outcomes arising, or the primary beneficiaries of this structural change.

There was discussion of attendant aspects such as the introduction of retail competition, the privatization of electricity assets, industrial relations issues, retail price caps, wholesale price volatility, the role of the state, industry structure, and more. Nevertheless these aspects were discussed as single issues or sets of issues concerning the operation of a wholesale electricity market such as Australia's National Electricity Market (NEM). All discussion, however, was consistently framed within a context of regulatory change and wholesale trading being the driving forces behind this industrial sector's restructuring (see, e.g., Abbot 2002; Bardak Ventures 2005; COAG 2002; Fairbrother and MacDonald 2000; Quiggin 2002; Roarty 2003; Willett 2005).

A focus on regulatory change and wholesale trading presents a partial and misleading picture. For example, the Australian electricity sector's transformation has been shaped not only by these electricity-centric elements but also by the shift to workplace bargaining over wages and working conditions, the rapid growth of financial markets and new money forms, Australia's increasing global integration, and a range of public sector policies including market provision of infrastructure and privatization. The structure, characteristics, and operation of today's electricity sector can only be explained by considering all these drivers of change, progressively introduced over more than a decade, and all of which are underpinned by the political and economic ideology of neoliberalism.

The limited discussion of the drivers of change led to a similarly narrow discourse about the outcomes arising from the sector's transformation. The most commonly discussed outcome has been the movement of wholesale electricity prices followed by changes to end-use electricity prices (see, e.g., Australian Government 2004; Booth 2004; Productivity Commission 2005; Sayers and Shields 2001). Annual performance reports for government-owned electricity companies provide some information about financial and operating outcomes (e.g., NSW Treasury 2005). The sector's peak organization, the Energy Supply Association of Australia (ESAA), publishes each year a statistical profile of the sector's operation. There is annual reporting by public agencies of consumer complaints, pricing regulators issue details of determinations, and there is occasional media reporting of consumer issues and service interruptions following blackouts. Yet the information about outcomes is reported more on an issue or interest group basis, thus providing a piecemeal picture even in terms of a narrow conceptualization of the sector's restructuring.

These lacunae – the drivers of the electricity sector's restructuring and the outcomes arising – formed the core research focus of this study which sought to answer the fundamental question: what are the outcomes and who benefits from the restructuring of the Australian electricity sector? Such an analysis raises the question of what is meant by the terms 'outcomes' and 'beneficiaries'. The outcomes discussed in the literature, as already pointed out, were predominantly within the context of regulatory change and the NEM. Notable exceptions are three labor market studies (Fairbrother and Testi 2002; Gryst 2000; MacDonald and Bray 2002). Structural change is assessed usually in terms of industry composition, employment, and investment (see, e.g., Productivity Commission 1998). However, I was of the view that using this framework overlooked important dimensions arising from the restructuring, and that a much broader spectrum of outcomes should be considered, a spectrum not determined by a narrow conceptualization of structural change or the unusual characteristics of electricity (that is, its non-storability, a derived demand, and a demand which must be met with instantaneous supply). At the same time, I did not wish to prejudge what those outcomes may be or set boundaries as to the type of outcomes that may have occurred.

With respect to beneficiaries, the literature shows some discussion of pricing outcomes for business and residential consumers, employment losses, and the proceeds from privatizations (see, e.g., Fairbrother and Testi 2002; Walker and Con Walker 2002). The range of industry sector stakeholders which may be impacted by structural change is much wider and in the case of the Australian electricity sector includes the federal and state governments (as policy-makers, owners, and regulators), Australian and offshore private owners, financial institutions which may provide debt or other forms of financing to electricity companies, and labor as workers and also collectively as unions.

Hence, the scope of the research task required an analytical framework with the capacity to explain structural change emanating from multiple factors, not just regulatory change, over a period of time and to show a wide range of outcomes spanning but not limited to ownership, company and market operations, finance, employment, and pricing, and the stakeholder interests upon which these outcomes impact. This is precisely what this study sought to do: to explain the outcomes arising from the restructuring of an electricity sector which occurred over a period of more than ten years as the drivers of the restructuring impacted progressively during this period.

## 29.3   A *RÉGULATIONIST* ANALYTICAL FRAMEWORK

Five core institutional forms, comprising the mode of *régulation*, shape the capitalist economy because their conjunction governs, guides, supports, and secures the accumulation regime. Each is the codification of capitalism's fundamental social relations through laws, rules, regulations, compromises, negotiated outcomes, or common value systems. These institutional forms are the financial regime, the form of competition, the wage–labor nexus, the form of the state, and the nature of a national economy's international integration (Boyer 1990).

A dominance of particular institutional forms has been found to characterize different modes of *régulation* (Boyer and Saillard 2002). The mode, evident from the end of World War II until the 1970s and commonly referred to as Fordism, is dominated by the wage–labor nexus (collective wage negotiations) and, to a lesser extent, the monetary regime (strong growth of credit money). Since the late 1970s, post-Fordism has become the nomenclature for the current period, the monetary regime (depicted by financialization) and 'the internationalisation of competition' have replaced the dominance of the wage–labor nexus (Boyer and Saillard 2002, p. 39).

A framework to analyze change at the macro level is immediately apparent given that the mode can be explained by considering the nature of its five institutional forms and their conjunction over time. Given the extensive range of factors which define each of the mode's institutional forms, this means that the outcomes of change are not limited in type (for example, to output, investment, or employment) and a far more holistic picture of the change process and its short-term outcomes and long-term consequences is provided.

Although generally regarded as a macroeconomic theory, *Régulation* theory has also been applied to meso-economic analysis focusing upon large sectors of productive activity.[1] A sector's dynamic will be determined by its own sector-based aspects (institutional arrangements) in conjunction with its place in the accumulation regime. This means that the sectoral mode of *régulation* can only be understood in terms of the macro mode. It cannot be understood purely through analysis of a five-dimensional grid.

The *Régulationist* method of sector analysis, crafted by Boyer from Bartoli and Boulet's study of the French wine sector (Saillard 2002), requires the identification of the following four elements:

1. a sector's social and historical origins, and its collective actors and spatial implications;
2. the institutional arrangements that both define the sector and enable it to function;
3. the sector's place in the accumulation regime and macroeconomic interdependences; and
4. the drivers or points which cause transformations of the sector and the overall economic system.

This method has been used in the majority of *Régulationist* sector-based studies and was that adopted for the study of the Australian electricity sector.

## 29.4   THE STUDY'S RESEARCH DESIGN

The social research literature attributes a number of different meanings to the term 'research design'. At one level, the term is used broadly to include all aspects of a research project from problem identification to publication of results (Ackoff 1953; Miller 1983). Alternatively, it may refer to 'the way a researcher guards against, and tries to rule out, alternative interpretations of results' (Punch 2001, p. 66). A third meaning, and that which underpinned the Australian study, is how theoretical paradigms are connected 'to strategies of inquiry and . . . to methods for collecting empirical material' (Denzin and Lincoln 2000, p. 22). In other words, the research design moves a theoretical framework to an empirical representation by providing a connection between the research questions and data. A research design:

> *ensure[s] that the evidence obtained enables us to answer the initial question as unambiguously as possible.* Obtaining relevant evidence entails specifying the type of evidence needed to answer the research question . . . In other words, when designing research we need to ask: given this research question . . . what type of evidence is needed to answer the question . . . *in a convincing way?'* (de Vaus 2001, p. 9)

Five core issues shaped the design of this study, namely: the connection between the chosen theoretical framework and empirical material; the strategy or reasoning by which the study proceeded to answer the research question; the capability of empirical material to illuminate change and praxis; who or what will be studied; and the tools and procedures to collect and analyze empirical materials (Denzin and Lincoln 2000, p. 368).

## 29.5 THE RESEARCH STRATEGY AND THEORETICAL FRAMEWORK

Using the analytical framework provided by *Régulation* theory, the following steps were undertaken to determine the outcomes (and beneficiaries) arising from the electricity sector's restructuring:

1. The nature of each institutional form was determined.
2. An assessment was made of the key characteristics for each institutional form at the macro (nation-state) level for post-Fordist Australia and the most salient changes that have occurred from the 1980s to late 2006.
3. The representation of each institutional form at the level of the electricity sector was determined and compared to its macro Australian post-Fordist manifestation.
4. The outcomes defining each institutional form's representation within the electricity sector were ascertained as well as the most appropriate form of measurement. Only those outcomes most indicative of the institutional form were considered.
5. Outcomes were classified as beneficial if positive results were evident or a gain was measured over time, and the recipient(s) of each identified benefit (or loss) was identified.

This five-point research strategy is summarized in Figure 29.1.

**Change and Praxis**

The empirical material collected was selected for its ability to demonstrate the fundamental characteristics of each institutional form, over time, at the level of the Australian nation-state and within the electricity sector. Therefore, the empirical material was not collected for one single point in time but from the 1980s through to late 2006, because the time period needed to cover the electricity sector's restructuring as well as prior years in order to enable comparisons to be made. Not all data collected were available for this

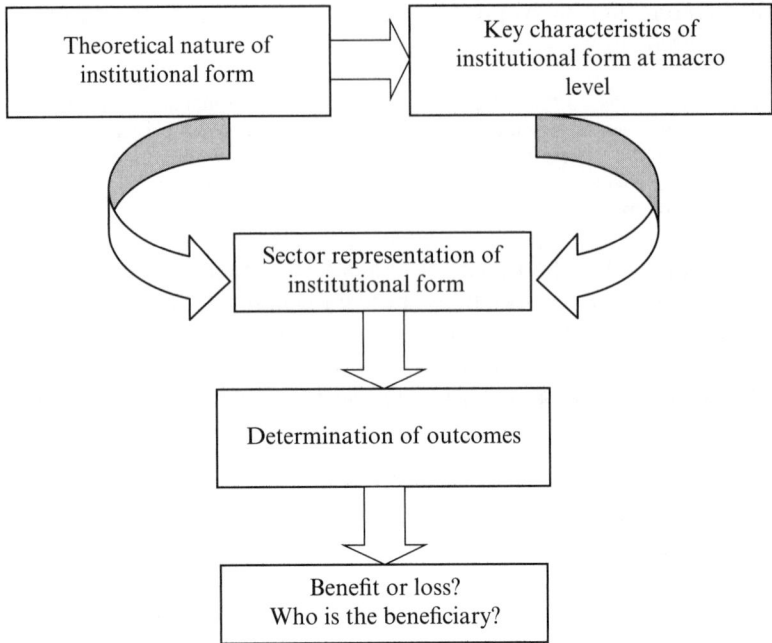

*Figure 29.1   Summary of research strategy steps*

entire period but there were sufficient data to allow comparisons and conclusions to be drawn.

**Who and What Was Studied**

Each of the analytical framework's five institutional forms was analyzed to determine the outcomes that have occurred from the sector's restructuring. Although there is considerable interaction between the institutional forms, it was possible to delineate the most significant outcomes for each institutional form during the period of the restructuring. Each outcome was assessed to determine whether a benefit or loss was conferred and the recipient.

A benefit was defined as an outcome which yields something advantageous, not deleterious, to an identifiable recipient either relative to the recipient's previous position or relative to another recipient. The nature of a benefit may change over time. Benefits available for some recipients may not be available at a subsequent point in time or the recipient may change over time. Similarly, future benefits or gains may be different from those previously available. Hence, the research considered whether there had been any change over time in benefits and/or recipients.

Beneficiaries were determined by assessing which interest group category was the primary target of the measured benefit or loss. The study's analytical framework determined the interest group categories: the state (nation or local), the owners of capital (industrial, financial, and fictitious), and labor (consumers, electricity sector workers, and unions).

**Tools and Procedures**

Multiple collection methods and data sources were used to collect the empirical data used, that is, multiple triangulation (Denzin 1997). Document analysis and secondary analysis were the methods used to collect information and data. Official records – public and private – were the primary sources accessed for data.

Denzin observes that different views of reality are provided by each research method. 'Consequently, [we] must learn to employ multiple methods in the analysis of the same empirical events' (Denzin 1989, p. 13) which will partially ameliorate the inherent bias in using a single method or data source. Using both quantitative (secondary analysis) and qualitative (document analysis) methods, and a variety of data sources, deepened the study's interpretative base as well as reduced the limitations of using a single method or data source, and increased the validity of the findings. This is not to suggest that the findings from the use of different research methods all fell into a coherent picture or pattern, which is not possible given that each method provides a different 'slice' of reality (Denzin 1997).

**Data Sources**

Documentary sources are a very rich source about post-Fordist Australia and its electricity sector, and provided all empirical material used for this study. In some cases, such as pricing and financial data, it would not have been possible, practical, or feasible to attempt data collection. Timing and cost would have been prohibitive. Moreover, it is highly unlikely that sufficient data would have been made available from the electricity sector's companies, owners, and regulators to allow a credible and reliable analysis.

The documents used were materials capable of being read, had been produced for another purpose other than this research, were available for analysis, and were relevant to the primary focus of this research (Bryman 2001, p. 370). Scott's typology classifying documents by access and authorship is shown in Table 29.1. All documents used for this research could be classified as public (state and private) and open-published, that is, generally available and the most accessible of all document types. These represent types 8 and 12 in Scott's classification.

The range of official documents used included the following: legislation; parliamentary

*Table 29.1   Classification of documents by access and authorship*

| Access | Authorship | | |
|---|---|---|---|
| | Personal | Official | |
| | | Private | State |
| Closed | 1 | 5 | 9 |
| Restricted | 2 | 6 | 10 |
| Open-archival | 3 | 7 | 11 |
| Open-published | 4 | 8 | 12 |

*Source:*   Scott (1990, p. 14).

debates; reports from official inquiries; annual budget papers of governments; registered industrial awards and agreements; policy papers and reports issued by government departments and agencies; reports prepared by public and private sector research agencies; issues and discussion papers issued by regulators; determinations and reports from regulators; submissions to regulatory inquiries by electricity companies; annual reports of electricity companies; and media statements by government ministers, regulators, and electricity companies. These documents provided both qualitative and quantitative data.

In addition, a range of documentary evidence was accessed from statistical collections published by the Australian Bureau of Statistics (ABS); the Australian Bureau of Agricultural and Resource Economics (ABARE); the Productivity Commission (and its predecessor, the Industry Commission); the ESAA; the National Electricity Market Management Company (NEMMCO); and the National Electricity Code Administrator (NECA).

The nature and content of official – public and private – documents are determined by the structure and activities of the state (Scott 1990). Public documents are invariably the outcome of a policy or administrative process and, as such, will naturally reflect the interests and priorities of the originating agency of the state. Many of the most important public documents form part of the systems of surveillance and social control that have become an integral part of bureaucratic nation-states.

While private official records (for example, company annual reports) are structured by the legal and organizational forms of the bodies producing them, they too are indirectly shaped by systems of regulation and monitoring established by nation-states and, increasingly, by international agencies. Many private administrative documents simply would not be produced – certainly not in their existing form – if it were not for the need to meet legally imposed requirements (Scott 1990, p. 59).

Consequently, public documents are not neutral reports of events because their production is shaped by a context, or 'there is always some element of production and shaping, some process by which the source came into being' (Finnegan 1996, p. 145). Careful and deliberate account was taken of this factor when analyzing the data contained in each documentary source and the approach taken is set out below. Knowledge of the processes of and influences upon the production of a document provided a better appreciation of the uses and limitations of the documentary sources used, their internal validity, and their adequacy in relation to the analytical framework.

## 29.6   RESEARCH METHODS

The research methods employed for this study were document analysis and secondary analysis. The relationship between the key steps of the research strategy and each research method is shown in Figure 29.2. The analysis of documents provided the substantive basis for the study and was used to develop an overall picture of the research topic, its theoretical and empirical representations, and the outcomes arising. Secondary analysis – of wages, employment, pricing, financial and operating performance data – facilitated the measurement of outcomes, determination of whether these outcomes provided benefits, and the recipients.

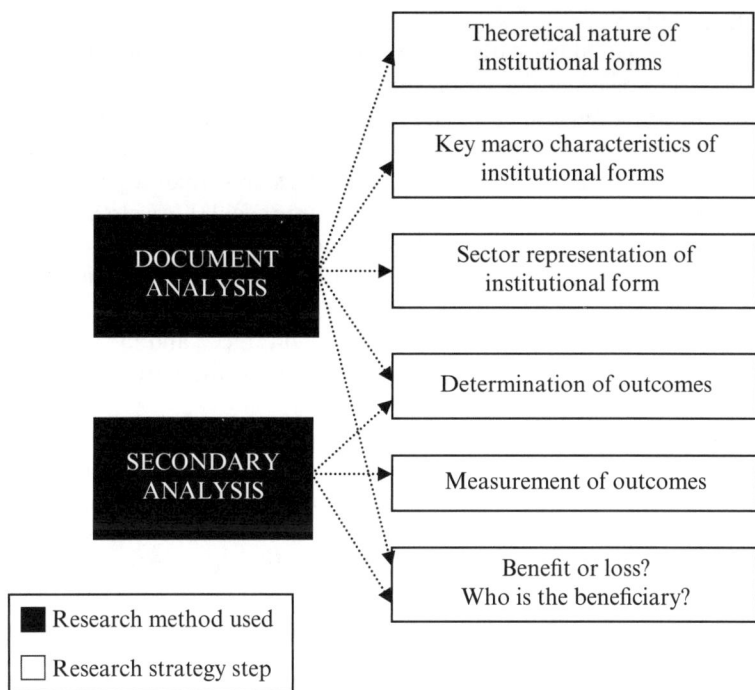

*Figure 29.2    Relationship of research methods to research strategy*

## Document Analysis

Much of the research methods literature pays scant attention to document analysis. Consequently it was necessary to develop a specific approach for this study's analysis of documents. Scott's (1990) typology to classify documents was used as a starting point to evaluate and interpret the documents collected because:

> it poses four key questions pertaining to the validity of particular documentary sources. Who has and has not authored a document, and the degree to which a document is accessible or with-held, influences its *authenticity* (whether it is original and genuine); its *credibility* (whether it is accurate); its *representativeness* (whether it is representative of the totality of documents of its class); and its *meaning* (what it is intended to say). (Jupp 1996, p. 303)

Each document was assessed against these four criteria of authenticity, credibility, representativeness, and meaning.

Authenticity refers to whether a document is genuine, complete, and reliable as well as being of unquestioned authorship. Bryman (2001) suggests that official documents deriving from the state can unquestioningly be seen as authentic, although others have proposed a series of questions against which all documents, notwithstanding their origin, should be judged (Platt 1981). These questions include: Are obvious errors apparent? Does the document make sense? Are there different versions of the document? Does the document contain internal inconsistencies? Has the available version been derived from

578 *Handbook of research methods and applications in heterodox economics*

an unreliable secondary source? Is the style and content consistent with documents of the same class? The study used these questions to test authenticity, although no public documents were found to be other than what they purported to be.

Credibility concerns the issue of bias, that is, whether the evidence presented in the document is free from error or distortion. The possibility of bias requires the researcher to determine who produced the document, why it was produced, when, for whom was it produced, and in what context (Macdonald and Tipton 1993). As already noted, official documents – public and private – contain an inherent bias because their very existence is directly linked to the structure and activities of the state, most notably regulation and monitoring (Scott 1990). Consequently, when assessing the credibility of a document, the approach adopted was to determine why it was produced and in what context, these being considered the primary determinants to illustrate the nature of bias in official documents.

Representativeness refers to the problem of the evidence being typical of its kind, and if not, the extent of 'untypicality'. The immediate relevance of this criterion is apparent when considering the availability of documents. If it is determined that something is missing, 'the questions of what is missing, how much, and why it is missing become important' (Macdonald and Tipton 1993, p. 196). In addition, it is useful to assess whether gaps in available documents demonstrate a pattern and whether anyone could have a vested interest in certain documents not being available. For example, Cabinet documents of a government are generally not publicly available until 30 years after their creation. Governments may decide that certain documents should not be available for commercial, security, defense, or political reasons. In some respects, the issue of availability – and hence, representativeness – of private official documents is more problematic. Those documents which are available are usually required to be so by virtue of a government or legislative requirement such as company annual reports. Otherwise there is little to compel a company to maintain or make available any other records.

It was not possible to determine for this study the total number and type of relevant official documents that might have been produced in the first place, as this information is impossible to obtain. Thus, the primary consideration was to determine whether there were any known missing documents (for example, reports made by regulators, annual reports of electricity companies) and make a judgment as to whether the data and information derived from available documents was inherently biased because of any known gaps.

The final criterion, meaning, is the fundamental reason for examining documents. Two meanings can be derived for a document: a literal, surface meaning, and a deeper meaning based on some form of analysis or interpretative understanding (Macdonald and Tipton 1993). A literal understanding is the first step towards an interpretative understanding of a document but provides little more than a meaning at face value. Interpretation requires a hermeneutic process, an understanding of concepts, the context by which concepts are related in a document, and an overall judgment about the document's meaning and significance (Scott 1990). In other words, there needs to be a content analysis of the document to determine its meaning and significance. This required the study to determine the most appropriate form of content analysis to use: quantitative content analysis, which seeks to demonstrate content regularities or patterns through repetition; or qualitative content analysis, which seeks to show the context of the document's content.

Quantitative content analysis rests on the assumption that the most valuable indicator of significance is repetition. The importance of an issue or subject is measured by the number of times it is mentioned in a document. Basically, the words of a text or particular phrases are classified into content categories and counted (Weber 1985). It is limited to only that which can be quantified, leading to:

> a concentration on aspects that are simple, measurable, and subject to standardization. Important dimensions are likely to be overlooked. Instead of searching for the anomaly and focusing upon its significance, the researcher looks no further than what his or her predefined categories have told him or her to see. (Ericson et al. 1991, p. 51)

Consequently, this approach is not systematic and arbitrary when dealing with anything more complex than newspapers, and can only deal with what has been produced, not the process of the document's creation. It also uncritically reproduces all the meanings used by authors and fails to recognize that all texts are open to multiple interpretations (May 2001). It is for these reasons that quantitative content analysis was not used.

Hammersley and Atkinson (1991) posit that documents should be read with regard to the context of their production, their intended audience, and the author's intent, which is akin to Scott's (1990, p. 34) notion that 'texts must be studied as socially situated products'. In other words, the meaning and significance of a document can be found by looking at the intentions of the author and the social context of the document's production. This can be done with a number of different types of qualitative content analysis and the study proceeded to consider the suitability of semiotics, the critical hermeneutic approach, ethnographic content analysis, discourse analysis, and critical analysis for the document analysis.

Semiotics was found to be an extremely complex method and not able to easily analyze the study's wide range of documents of different origin and authorship, having traditionally been used to examine single documents (Altheide 1996). A similar weakness was found in the critical hermeneutic approach – developed to interpret company documents (Forster 1994; Phillips and Brown 1993) – which analyses the documents of a single organization, not multiple organizations with disparate objectives and interests in an industry sector. It was also found that ethnographic content analysis (ECA) suffers from similar problems as quantitative content analysis in that only that which is measurable is included, and important dimensions are lost. However, ECA does construct protocols 'to ask questions of a document . . . [it] is a list of questions, items, categories, or variables that guide data collection' (Altheide 1996, pp. 26–7) which was considered to warrant further consideration because a systematic approach would enhance the validity of interpretations drawn. On the other hand, the precise procedures used in discourse analysis – which focuses attention on the way language is used, what it is used for, and the social context of its use – were found to be not easily described or detailed (Potter and Wetherell 1994).[2] This posed a fundamental problem in determining its suitability for the document analysis required for this study. The final approach considered was critical analysis, which does not take for granted what is being stated and involves uncovering the assumptions upon which an account may rest, and a consideration of what other aspects are hidden or excluded. Jupp (1996, p. 311) characterizes the key features of a critical analysis of documents as:

1.  identification of the conceptualizations put forward at the macro level by the data contained in official texts;
2.  a critical reading to determine the definitions of problems, explanations for the cause of problems, preferred solutions, what is not seen as problematic, explanations not included, and solutions not advocated;
3.  seeking to challenge the definitions, explanations, and solutions put forward; and
4.  identification of the section of society for whom the document speaks, and potential consequences.

These features provide a far deeper understanding of a document's meaning and significance than the other qualitative content analysis approaches considered. Consequently it was decided to adopt this approach for the study's document analysis. However, there are no formal protocols to conduct a critical analysis as there are, for example, for a survey, an experiment or for an ECA. Yet the documents used for this study required some form of systematic method to ensure consistency with which each was interrogated, and hence validity in the interpretations and conclusions drawn. This problem was overcome by the use of a protocol, an '"agenda", organised around a series of questions to be asked of data . . . based on a distillation of ideas from discourse analysis' (Jupp and Norris 1993, p. 50). Drawing on Jupp and Norris's 'agenda' as a template, a protocol of ten core questions was adopted for the study's critical analysis of documents (Box 29.1).

The progressive steps taken to develop the document analysis approach utilized by this study are summarized in Figure 29.3.

**Secondary Analysis**

Secondary analysis, the second research method applied in this study, is 'simply a further analysis of information that has already been obtained. Such an analysis . . . may address an issue quite different from that which prompted the original data gathering effort. It may involve the integration of information from several sources' (Stewart 1984, p. 11).

Secondary analysis provides conclusions, interpretations, or knowledge that are additional to, or different from, previous results presented from an existing data set (Hakim 1982). Procter (1993, p. 262), however, reminds the researcher that 'the real challenge in

---

BOX 29.1   PROTOCOL OF QUESTIONS USED TO INTERROGATE ALL DOCUMENTS

(i)     What is the general framework or perspective presented?
(ii)    What is defined as 'right', 'wrong', and problematic?
(iii)   What explanation is given for defined problems?
(iv)    What are advocated as solutions?
(v)     What is not seen as problematic?
(vi)    What explanations are excluded?
(vii)   Which solutions are not preferred?
(viii)  Who does the author represent or purport to represent?
(ix)    What is the intended audience?
(x)     What is the type or kind of document?

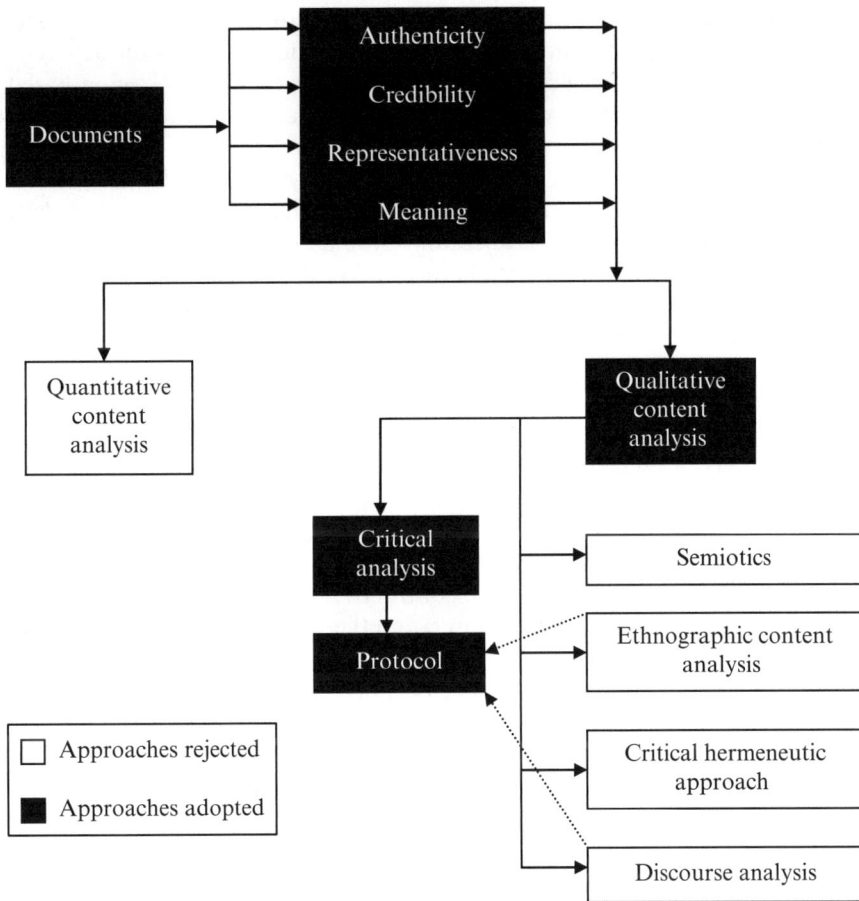

*Figure 29.3   Steps to develop the document analysis approach for this research*

secondary analysis lies in finding ways of forcing the data, collected by someone else, quite often with entirely different theoretical and analytical intentions to answer your questions'.

The choice of secondary analysis was driven by the advantages that it offered in terms of time, cost, data quality, the opportunity for longitudinal analysis, and access to otherwise inaccessible data. Considerable time was saved because data suitable to the research problem already existed. In addition, the cost to collect the data would have been prohibitive given the amount of data needed and the time span over which the data were required. The quality of the data obtained was in all probability higher than that which could be obtained independently by the researcher given that much of the data would not have been accessible to the researcher.

One example of the data used for secondary analysis – NEM bidding prices – illustrates these advantages. The NEM aims to balance electricity supply and demand requirements by scheduling generators to produce sufficient electricity to meet demand. Generators submit bids for every half-hour of the day, specifying how many megawatts they can provide and at what prices. The NEM operator forecasts demand for every half-hour, schedules and dispatches generating units into production at five-minute intervals, and determines the half-hourly spot price for each NEM region based on a time-weighted average of the six dispatch prices for each half-hour. At least 130000 spot prices were set during the eight-year period to December 2006. It was decided that the spot prices paid to generation companies should be analyzed when determining the outcomes of one of the five institutional forms: competition. To collect these spot prices – independently of the NEM operator – would have taken considerable time and cost, even should the access to the data have been granted, which was considered highly unlikely.

These advantages considerably outweighed the limitations of secondary analysis, particularly given the researcher's lack of familiarity with the data, the data's complexity, and no control over the data quality. Primary data collection means that the researcher becomes very familiar with the structure and contours of their data. However, with data collected by others, a familiarization period is necessary to understand each variable, any coding, and how the data are organized. Much of the pricing data for the NEM and the pricing determinations of each state government regulator are particularly complex and required a substantial period of familiarization, notwithstanding the sheer volume of pricing data. In addition, there was no control over the quality of the data and, in the majority of cases, it was not possible to ascertain the validity and reliability of the original data collection procedures.

Data are generally collected for a specific purpose and this itself may produce a deliberate or unintentional bias (Stewart 1984). Consequently all secondary sources used for this were carefully evaluated. A protocol, similar to the document analysis protocol, was developed and used to evaluate each source of quantitative data prior to any statistical analysis. The six questions forming the protocol, based on those suggested by Stewart (1984) and Procter (1993), are shown in Box 29.2. This protocol proved useful to ascertain whether the original data were misleading in any way. In addition, the protocol established the context of the data's original collection in much the same way as the document protocol established the context of a document's production.

---

BOX 29.2   PROTOCOL OF QUESTIONS USED TO INTERROGATE QUANTITATIVE DATA

(i)    Why was the data collected?
(ii)   Who collected the data? Are any potential biases represented?
(iii)  What data was collected? What were the units of measurement and how were these defined? How reliable and valid is the data?
(iv)   When was the data collected? Are the results obsolete in any way? Are all evident relationships relatively invariant over time?
(v)    How was the data collected? What methodology was used?
(vi)   Is the data consistent with that available from other sources?

## 29.7 DATA SETS USED

The data sets used were both official statistics and data collected by non-government organizations such as the ESAA, all of which are publicly available, that is, there were no restrictions on access. Much of the data sourced from the ABS collections are based on surveys or samples. This raises potential problems such as the sample being too small for statistically reliable results, insufficient cases to conduct the desired statistical analysis, or it not being possible to detect errors made in the original survey (Kiecolt and Nathan 1985).

Both micro data and aggregate data were used. The micro data contained information relating to individual electricity companies and, on occasion, were used to create aggregate data to compare outcomes between subsectors within the electricity sector and between Australian states.

There are six types of data source for secondary analysis, namely: censuses; continuous and regular surveys; ad hoc surveys; cohort (longitudinal) studies; data sets derived for administrative and public records; and multi-source data sets (Hakim 1982). Administrative and public records provided the data sets used for the secondary analysis in this study. Administrative records are:

> collections of documents containing mainly factual information compiled in a variety of ways . . . and used by organizations to record the development and implementation of decisions and activities that are central to their functions. They are typically large in number; are unusually high in content rigidity and narrow in content scope; and are often available for considerable stretches of time. (Hakim 1993, p. 131)

The administrative records used for secondary analysis were primarily the annual reports of all electricity companies and the annual budget papers of the federal and state governments. A range of quantitative evidence was also accessed from statistical collections published by the ABS, ABARE, the Productivity Commission (and its predecessor), ESAA, and the NEM operator.[3]

## 29.8 FINDINGS AND OBSERVATIONS

A central argument of the study was that the common conceptualization of the sector's restructuring has been narrowly based around sector-specific changes, namely the creation of a national electricity market and its regulatory regime. The study demonstrated that three closely interrelated layers of policies and actions implemented, either concurrently or progressively, by the nation-state and local state have driven the sector's transformation. These policies and actions transcend electricity-centric policies and encompass policies which have become systemic to the Australian public sector, as well as a third layer which has transformed the prevailing industrial paradigm across all sectors. Neoliberalism's virtues of the market, competition, and less government intervention are imbued in the policy framework that has propelled the electricity sector's restructuring, although a disjuncture between rhetoric and praxis is very evident, and increasingly so. All Australian governments have been actively and willingly involved in the sector's transformation, championing the changes as integral to Australia's structural competitiveness and prospects for sustained economic growth.

The analysis revealed that the electricity sector has been Australia's second-largest contributor of privatization proceeds, and remains dominated by government ownership and fluctuating levels of foreign ownership. Higher relative wage levels and union membership are also evident as have been job losses and substantial real price increases for households, whereas those for business have generally fallen. The purported 'reform' centerpiece, the National Electricity Market, was found to be increasingly uncompetitive due to its own regulatory regime and market manipulation by government-owned companies.

But the analysis yielded far more than these structural descriptors of the sector, its change process, and outcomes that can be quantitatively measured. The analysis yielded insights into something far less tangible about the sector, namely the precipice upon which it was poised after at least a decade of structural change. The analysis exposed a financial vulnerability given the high use of debt to fund privatizations, ongoing acquisitions, as well as special financial distributions to state government owners. This vulnerability had been compounded by a high use of derivative contracts to manage risk; the reported exposure exceeds, for many companies, the value of current debt and/or equity levels. The long-term sustainability of such a financial position is questionable if there is an adverse movement in domestic and overseas interest rates and these liabilities have not been used to fund income-generating assets. Moreover, this vulnerability has been further increased by the practice of government-owned electricity companies maintaining annual dividend payout ratios close to or greater than 100 per cent of after-tax profits.

Another aspect which the analysis highlighted about the sector's heightened precariousness flows from the global integration following the privatizations, ongoing ownership changes, and enmeshing of privately owned electricity companies into global business strategies. Should decisions by offshore owners lead to ramifications such as significant job losses, blackouts, or a complete loss of service, an Australian government may be politically impelled to provide redress or restore supply. Thus part of the electricity sector's structural change has also created a potential exposure of the local state to a range of financial and political risks, which deepens with foreign ownership and the more that ownership changes occur.

A further analytical insight was evidence of the winners and losers from the sector's transformation. There has been a definite unevenness in the distribution of the 'gains' arising from the restructuring. The clear winners from the restructuring were found to have been capital, although the interests of some fractions of capital have benefited more than others.

Financial capital – the owners of interest-bearing credit such as banks and other financial institutions – benefited through much higher levels of debt exposure and the increased use of offshore financial markets to access debt finance. These benefits have been bolstered by the Australian monetary regime's low interest rate policy. Fictitious capital – financial speculation – benefited from the explosion in the electricity's sector's use of derivatives to manage interest rate, foreign exchange, and trading risks, and the creation of the Australian electricity derivatives market. Benefits for industrial capital – the owners of investment in production – commenced with the privatization of electricity assets and have progressed with the unhindered consolidation in market structure, and the reintegration of generation with retail activities. These gains have been bolstered by the opportunity for larger generation companies to 'game' the market for considerable financial gain, and productivity gains outstripping real wage growth. For industrial capital outside the electricity sector, real reduction in end-use prices has been delivered.

The state and the neoliberal agenda were also winners. The state's 'restructuring model' has received international endorsement and provided a blueprint for structural change. The state's regulatory role has been considerably strengthened and the local state has tapped into a substantial source of funds despite the rhetoric of a less interventionist and a benign state. The neoliberal agenda has been reinforced by the concepts of market discipline and competition underpinning all policies and actions of the state that have driven the sector's restructuring. Moreover, the state's strong interventions through policies impacting on the industrial paradigm, such as through the wage–labor nexus, are based on shifting the balance of power between capital and labor, further entrenching the neoliberal agenda.

Labor, as electricity workers and consumers of electricity, has been the loser and faces the bleakest prospects. Residential consumers have experienced substantive real price increases and more are expected. The real wage growth of electricity sector workers has lagged changes in productivity and is now on a downward slide. Without capital deepening or technology spin-offs, productivity is expected to decline. Giving the tying of wage increases to productivity since the mid-1990s, the likelihood of real wage increases is severely diminished. The ability of labor to maintain the sector's higher relative wage levels, payment for actual hours worked, real wage falls being less than that for productivity, workers covered by enterprise agreements instead of individual contracts, and marginal use of casual and non-standard work forms, will depend on its bargaining strength. Decentralized bargaining, from workplace to workplace, strongly increases the prospect of inequality in working conditions and rates of pay across the sector, the spread of individual contracts, and the growth of non-standard employment.

In addition the analysis clearly found an electricity sector mode of *régulation*. Unique institutional arrangements were evident within this Australian industry sector for all five, not just three, institutional forms of the macro mode. These unique sector institutional arrangements are either derived from the sector's own specificity or are a result of the macro institutional form acting on the sector. With respect to money and finance, form of competition and form of the state, the institutional arrangements are very sector-specific in their origin. On the other hand, the sector dimensions of the wage–labor nexus and international position are just as unique but derive from their respective macro institutional form which has also been strongly shaped by the Australian state.

These analytical insights into the electricity sector's vulnerabilities, exposures, and potential risks enrich our understanding of the outcomes of the sector's structural change. They move beyond quantifiable results, adding a complexity but providing a more perceptive understanding of the impact of the restructuring process on this industry sector and the issues it faces in the short and long term. This richness of the analysis attests to the strengths of the analytical framework of *Régulation* theory to explain real (not hypothesized) structural change.

The analysis also generated a number of propositions about the application of *régulation* theory to sector-based research. Will the institutional arrangements comprising a sectoral mode of *régulation* reflect the heterogeneity of sectors? Will the sectoral mode for an input sector (like electricity) differ from those for output sectors, the focus of other *Régulationist* sector studies? Does a hierarchy of sector institutional arrangements mirror those of the macro mode or does this only apply for particular, say leading, sectors? Is a sectoral mode reflected through both those institutional arrangements derived from its own specificity and those arising from a macro institutional form directly acting on the sector? Can a macro institutional form act on sector institutional arrangements which relate to other macro forms, as well as be reflected in specifically designed sector arrangements? Do different interactive relationships between macro institutional forms and sector institutional arrangements explain the conjunction of institutional arrangements comprising a sector mode of *régulation*? Should a sector analysis presuppose the existence of all or only some reflections of the macro institutional forms?

This study found clear evidence of a sectoral mode reflecting all five institutional forms of the macro mode of *régulation*, a hierarchy of institutional arrangements derived from its own specificity and from the macro institutional forms acting in the sector, as well as two-way interrelationships between the macro and sector. The analysis also illustrated the very strong role played by the nation-state in shaping all macro institutional forms during the post-Fordist era, and the omnipresent role of the state in the electricity sector's mode of *régulation*. Actions by the state at macro and sector levels have been critical to the sector's radical transformation and provide evidence of the strategic importance accorded to this sector by the state. These findings suggest the analytical framework of *Régulationist* sector studies should not preclude any of the five macro institutional forms. To do otherwise would have led to a very partial and inaccurate view of the sector's dynamic, process of change, outcomes, and beneficiaries. This is not an issue of the four-point method of *Régulationist* sector analysis. It is an issue of how that method is applied.

These propositions and questions do not weaken the strengths of *Régulation* theory to explain change. The mode of *régulation* provides a very powerful framework to analyze the outcomes of structural change – at the macro and sector levels – through a wide lens of contributory factors which go well beyond the economic and the quantitative. The narrow focus of the vast majority of research on structural change results in an analysis which is devoid of context and thus has limited explanatory value. This study avoided this much easier path and provides new insights into the structural change of an industry sector.

Finally, the study's use of triangulation – of methods and data sources – as a heuristic tool, and its mixed methods design, yielded a number of beneficial outcomes. First, triangulation of data sources meant that much more comprehensive data were obtained to give greater depth and breadth of insight into the structural change process, the outcomes, and the distributional consequences. It also permitted easier identification of inconsistencies between data sets such as that for employment, price changes, or the volume of trading in financial derivatives. Moreover, data and information from multiple sources reinforces the legitimacy, validity, and reliability of the conclusions drawn.

Second, a much more thorough understanding of the research problem and the study's findings was 'accomplished by utilizing both quantitative and qualitative data and not just the numerical or narrative explanation alone' (Hesse-Biber 2010, p. 4). In many respects, the qualitative data added a narrative understanding in which to situate the quantitative data collected. This helped considerably to explore the process of change and outcomes over time and thus provide a dynamic historically grounded analysis.

Third, quantitative and qualitative data were equally weighted and collected concurrently throughout the study. This meant that the 'strengths of the qualitative data (for example data about the context) offset the weaknesses of the quantitative data (for example, ecological validity), and the strengths of the quantitative data (for example generalizability) offset the weaknesses of the qualitative data (for example context dependence)' (Gay et al. 2009, p. 463). Thus the explanation of the sectoral process and outcomes of structural change were not limited to quantitative data about economic factors.

In sum, the richness of the analysis of the Australian electricity sector lies not only in the strengths of the analytical framework of *Régulation* theory to explain real (not hypothesized) structural change, but also in the strengths of triangulation and a mixed methods research design.

## NOTES

1.  Sectors have included wine, agriculture, computers and communications, telecommunications, building and public works, and the services sector (see Chester 2007, p. 64). The geographic focus of these sector studies has been primarily France and Europe although US agriculture is one exception. Chester (2007) is the first known *Régulationist* study of an electricity sector and an Australian industry sector.
2.  Two types of discourse analysis are distinguishable. The first type is the study of discourse structure for its own sake using linguistic analytical techniques and tools. The second type concerns discourse as it relates to social, political, and cultural processes and outcomes, that is, 'discourse as evidence' (Punch 2001). The latter type was considered to be of more direct relevance to this study.
3.  Initially the market operator was the National Electricity Market Management Company (NEMMCO) which was replaced by the Australian Energy Market Operator (AEMO).

## REFERENCES

Abbot, Malcolm (2002), 'Completing the introduction of competition into the Australian electricity industry', *Economic Papers*, **21** (2), 1–13.
Ackoff, Russell L. (1953), *The Design of Social Research*, Chicago, IL: University of Chicago Press.
Altheide, David L. (1996), *Qualitative Media Analysis*, Thousand Oaks, CA: Sage.
Australian Government (2004), *Securing Australia's Energy Future*, Canberra: Department of Prime Minister and Cabinet.
Bardak Ventures Pty Ltd (2005), *The Effect of Industry Structure on Generation Competition and End-user Prices in the National Electricity Market*, Report prepared for the Energy Users Association of Australia, Bowman, Australia: Bardak Ventures.
Booth, Robert (2004), *Too Much Volatility is Bad for You*, Bowman, Australia: Bardak Ventures.
Boyer, Robert (1990), *The Regulation School: A Critical Introduction*, New York: Columbia University Press.
Boyer, Robert and Yves Saillard (2002), 'A summary of Régulation theory', in Robert Boyer and Yves Saillard (eds), *Régulation Theory: The State of the Art*, London: Routledge, pp. 36–44.
Bryman, Alan (2001), *Social Research Methods*, Oxford: Oxford University Press.
Chester, Lynne (2007), 'What are the outcomes and who benefits from the restructuring of the Australian electricity sector?', unpublished PhD thesis, University of New South Wales, accessed August 9, 2014 at http://www.library.unsw.edu.au/~thesis/adt-NUN/public/adt-NUN20071017.113919/.
Council of Australian Governments Energy Market Review (COAG) (2002), *Towards a Truly National and Efficient Energy Market*, Final report, Canberra, Australia: AusInfo.
Denzin, Norman K. (1989), *The Research Act: A Theoretical Introduction to Sociological Methods*, 3rd edn, Englewood Cliffs, NJ: Prentice Hall.
Denzin, Norman K. (1997), 'Triangulation in educational research', in Jonathan P. Keeves (ed.), *Educational Research, Methodology, and Measurement: An International Handbook*, 2nd edn, New York: Pergamon, pp. 318–22.

Denzin, Norman K. and Yvonna S. Lincoln (2000), *Handbook of Qualitative Research*, 2nd edn, Thousand Oaks, CA: Sage.
de Vaus, David A. (2001), *Research Design in Social Research*, London: Sage.
Ericson, Richard V., Patricia M. Baranek, and Janet B.L. Chan (1991), *Representing Order: Crime, Law, and Justice in the News Media*, Milton Keynes: Open University Press.
Fairbrother, Peter and Duncan MacDonald (2000), 'Multinational versus state ownership: labour–management relations in the electricity industry', *Journal of Industrial Relations*, **42** (2), 314–33.
Fairbrother, Peter and Jonathan Testi (2002), 'The advent of multinational ownership of the Victorian electricity generating plants: questions for labour', in Peter Fairbrother, Michael Paddon, and Julian Teicher (eds), *Privatisation, Globalisation and Labour: Studies from Australia*, Sydney: Federation Press, pp. 102–30.
Finnegan, Ruth (1996), 'Using documents', in Roger Sapsford and Victor Jupp (eds), *Data Collection and Analysis*, London: Sage, pp. 138–51.
Forster, Nick (1994), 'The analysis of company documentation', in Catherine Cassell and Gillian Symon (eds), *Qualitative Methods in Organizational Research: A Practical Guide*, London: Sage: pp. 146–66.
Gay, Lorraine R., Geoffrey E. Mills, and Peter W. Airasian (2009), *Educational Research: Integrating Qualitative and Quantitative Methods*, 9th edn, London: Allyn & Bacon.
Gryst, Roma (2000), 'Contracting employment: a case study of how the use of agency workers in the SA power industry is reshaping the employment relationship', ACCIRT Working Paper 59, Sydney: Australian Centre for Industrial Relations Research and Training.
Hammersley, Martyn and Paul Atkinson (1991), *Ethnography: Principles in Practice*, London: Routledge.
Hakim, Catherine (1982), *Secondary Analysis in Social Research: A Guide to Data Sources and Methods with Examples*, London: George Allen & Unwin.
Hakim, Catherine (1993), 'Research analysis of administrative records', in Martyn Hammersley (ed.), *Social Research: Philosophy, Politics and Practice*, London: Sage, pp. 131–45.
Harvey, David (1989), *The Condition of Postmodernity: An Enquiry into the Origins of Cultural Change*, Oxford: Basil Blackwell.
Hesse-Biber, Sharlene Nagy (2010), *Mixed Methods Research: Merging Theory with Practice*, New York: Guildford Press.
International Energy Agency (IEA) (2005), *Energy Policies of IEA Countries: Australia 2005 Review*, Paris: OECD/IEA.
Jupp, Victor (1996), 'Documents and critical research', in Roger Sapsford and Victor Jupp (eds), *Data Collection and Analysis*, London: Sage, pp. 298–316.
Jupp, Victor and Live Norris (1993), 'Traditions in documentary analysis', in Martyn Hammersley (ed.), *Social Research: Philosophy, Politics and Practice*, London: Sage.
Kiecolt, K. Jill and Laura E. Nathan (1985), *Secondary Analysis of Survey Data*, Beverly Hills, CA: Sage.
MacDonald, Duncan and Mark Bray (2002), 'Preparing for the national electricity market: the NSW electricity industry', in Peter Fairbrother, Michael Paddon, and Julian Teicher (eds), *Privatisation, Globalisation and Labour: Studies from Australia*, Sydney: Federation Press, pp. 78–101.
Macdonald, Keith and Colin Tipton (1993), 'Using documents', in Nigel Gilbert (ed.), *Researching Social Life*, London: Sage, pp. 187–200.
May, Tim (2001), *Social Research: Issues, Methods and Process*, 3rd edn, Buckingham: Open University Press.
Miller, Delbert C. (1983), *Handbook of Research Design and Social Measurement*, 4th edn, New York: Longman.
NSW Treasury (2005), 'Performance of NSW government businesses 2003–04', Research and information paper TRP 05-1, Sydney: NSW Treasury.
Phillips, Nelson and John L. Brown (1993), 'Analyzing communication in and around organizations: a critical hermeneutic approach', *Academy of Management Journal*, **36** (6), 1547–76.
Platt, Jennifer (1981), 'Evidence and proof in documentary research: 1. Some specific problems of documentary research', *Sociological Review*, **29** (1), 31–52.
Potter, Jonathan and Margaret Wetherell (1994), 'Analyzing discourse', in Alan Bryman and Robert G. Burgess (eds), *Analyzing Qualitative Data*, London: Routledge, pp. 47–66.
Procter, Mike (1993), 'Analysing other researchers' data', in Nigel Gilbert (ed.), *Researching Social Life*, London: Sage, pp. 255–69.
Productivity Commission (1998), 'Aspects of structural change in Australia', Research Report, Canberra: Ausinfo.
Productivity Commission (2005), 'Modelling impacts of infrastructure industry change over the 1990s: Supplement to review of national competition policy reforms', Inquiry Report No. 33, Canberra: Productivity Commission.
Punch, Keith F. (2001), *Introduction to Social Research: Quantitative and Qualitative Approaches*, London: Sage.
Quiggin, John (2002), *Looking Back on Microeconomic Reform*, School of Economics, Canberra: Australian National University.

Roarty, Michael (2003), 'Electricity deregulation outside the New South Wales and Victorian markets', Research Note No. 40 2002–03, Canberra: Parliamentary Library.

Saillard, Yves (2002), 'Globalisation, localisation and sector-based specialisation: what is the future of national *régulation*?', in Robert Boyer and Yves Saillard (eds), *Régulation Theory: The State of the Art*, London: Routledge, pp. 183–9.

Sayers, Chris and Diane Shields (2001), 'Electricity prices and cost factors', Productivity Commission, Staff Research Paper, Canberra: AusInfo.

Scott, John C. (1990), *A Matter of Record: Documentary Sources in Social Research*, Cambridge: Polity Press.

Stewart, David W. (1984), *Secondary Research: Information, Sources and Methods*, Beverly Hills, CA: Sage.

Walker, Bob and Betty Con Walker (2002), *Privatisation: Sell off or Sell Out? The Australian Experience*, Sydney: ABC Books.

Weber, Robert P. (1985), *Basic Content Analysis*, Beverly Hills, CA: Sage.

Willett, Ed (2005), 'Where the Australian energy sector is heading', ACCC Commissioner, Speech to 2005 Energy Summit, Sydney, March 17.

# Index

Miner-Rubino, K. 531
Minichiello, V. 353
Minsky, H. 320, 401, 557–8, 565
Mirjiam-Sent, S. 567
Mirowski, P. 81
Mitchell, W. 558, 564, 565
mixed method research
  business cycle detection 563–6
  care workers, employment decisions, *see*
    employment decisions of aged care
    workers
  and critical realism 286–8, 297
  data triangulation, *see* data triangulation;
    mixed method research, triangulation;
    triangulation
  diagramming 293–3
  ethical considerations 297
  experimental methods and data 178
  gender, migration, and remittance flows
    in Ghana, *see* gender, migration, and
    remittance flows in Ghana
  integration of methods 293–6
  interdisciplinary perspective 56, 57–61, 64–5
  intra-household wealth distribution, *see*
    intra-household wealth distribution in
    Ecuador
  investment behavior, *see* investment behavior
  low-income households study and electricity
    prices 347–8
  marketization of human services providers
    study 375
  policy as contested process, *see* policy as
    contested process
  purposes 290–91
  *Régulationist* analysis of industry sector, *see*
    *Régulationist* analysis of industry sector
  research design 290–92
  retroduction 287
  transformatory potential 287–8
  triangulation 286–7, 289–91, 294, 297–8
  validity 296
  *see also* qualitative and quantitative analysis
    headings
Mizruchi, M. 250
modeling as research method in heterodox
  economics 272–85
  abstract, direct representation (ADR) model
    274, 279–80, 281
  critical realist–grounded theory (CR–GT)
    approach 273, 274–6, 278–81
  heterodox versus mainstream modeling
    274–6
  Marx's simple reproduction schema of the
    circuit of commodity capital 272, 277–8
  model as theorizing tool 278–9

pricing model of economy example 281–2
real world structures and causal mechanisms
  274–6, 279–81
representing and modeling distinctions
  277–8
Moher, D. 296
Mohun, S. 27, 28
Mojon, B. 327
Molina, J. 242
Moran-Ellis, J. 294
Morgan, D. 377
Morgan, J. 15–34, 42, 89, 156–7, 531
Morgan, M. 28, 232, 273, 275, 276, 278, 284
Morgan, S. 213
Morrison, K. 168, 171
Morse, J.M. 39, 288, 290, 292, 295
Morton, R. 167
Moser, C. 77
Moudud, J. 400–430
Mullainathan, S. 167
multiple method research 286–300
  and critical realism 286–8, 297
  ethical considerations 297
  transformatory potential 287–8
  triangulation 286–7, 289–90
  validity 296
Mumtaz, H. 328
Muñoz, J. 388–99
Murphy, E. 289
Murray, M. 123–4, 132, 190–209
Mutari, E. 159
Mutch, C. 289
'mystery shopper' use 381

Naqvi, A. 441
Nathan, L. 583
Neihaus, L. 295
Nell, E. 190, 193–4, 196
Nelson, J. 447, 448, 451, 537, 538–9, 545, 546,
  551
Nelson, R. 195
neo-Keynesianism and price flexibility 556–7
neoclassical economics 223–6, 327, 335; *see*
  *also* mainstream economics
network analysis, social, *see* social network
  analysis
Neuman, W. 564
New, C. 15
New Cambridge modeling approach 431,
  438–9
new economics of labor migration (NELM)
  468–9
New Public Management (NPM) 366, 370
Newman, A. 135, 160
Newman, M. 247, 248